HOLT SCIENCE & TECHNOLOGY

TEXAS EDITION

6

GRADE 6

HOLT, RINEHART AND WINSTON

A Harcourt Classroom Education Company

Austin · New York · Orlando · Atlanta · San Francisco · Boston · Dallas · Toronto · London

Staff Credits

Editorial

Robert W. Todd, Executive Editor
Maureen Kilpatrick, Managing Editor
Anne C. Earvolino, Senior Editor
Leigh Ann García, Senior Editor
Laura Zapanta, Senior Editor
Karin Akre, Bill Burnside, Chris Colby, Molly Frohlich, Shari Husain, Michael Mazza, Kristen McCardel, Kharissia Pettus, Ben Pickle, Sabelyn Pussman, Bill Rader, Jim Ratcliffe, Kelly Rizk, Erin Roberson, Kenneth Shepardson, Clay Walton, David Westerberg

ANCILLARIES

Jennifer Childers, Senior Editor
Jen Driscoll, Niamh Gray-Wilson, Betsy Roll, Douglas P. Rutley

COPYEDITORS

Dawn Marie Spinozza, Copyediting Supervisor
Brooke Fugitt, Jane A. Kirschman, Kira Watkins

EDITORIAL SUPPORT STAFF

Benny Carmona, III, Jeanne Graham, Mary Helbling, Stephanie Sanchez, Tanu'e White

EDITORIAL PERMISSIONS

Cathy Paré, Permissions Manager
Jan Harrington, Permissions Editor

Art, Design, and Photo

BOOK DESIGN

Richard Metzger, Design Director
Marc Cooper, Senior Designer
Ron Bowdoin, Designer
Andrew Lankes, Rina May Ouellette, Design Associates
Alicia Sullivan, Designer (ATE)
Ruth Limon, Design Associate (ATE)
Eric Rupprath, Designer (Ancillaries)

IMAGE ACQUISITIONS

Joe London, Director
Elaine Tate, Art Buyer Supervisor
Julie Kelly, David Knowles, Angela Parisi, Art Buyers
Tim Taylor, Photo Research Supervisor
Stephanie Friedman, Photo Researcher
David Saldaña, Assistant Photo Researcher

PHOTO STUDIO

Sam Dudgeon, Senior Staff Photographer
Victoria Smith, Staff Photographer
Lauren Eischen, Photo Specialist

DESIGN NEW MEDIA

Susan Michael, Design Director
Amy Shank, Design Manager
Czeslaw Sornat, Designer

MEDIA DESIGN

Curtis Riker, Design Director
Chris Smith, Designer

GRAPHIC SERVICES

Kristen Darby, Manager
Jane Dixon, Dean Hsieh, Cathy Murphy, Linda Wilbourn, Image Designers
Holly Whittaker, Senior Traffic Coordinator
Joyce Gonzalez, Sarah Hudgens, Traffic Coordinators

COVER DESIGN

Marc Cooper, Senior Designer

COMPOSITION

Umlaut, LLC

Production

Mimi Stockdell, Senior Production Manager
Adriana Bardin-Prescott, Senior Production Coordinator
Beth Sample, Senior Production Coordinator
Kim Anderson-Scott, Senior Production Manager
Suzanne Brooks, Production Assistant

Manufacturing and Production

Jevara Jackson, Manufacturing Coordinator
Ivania Lee, Inventory Planning Analyst

Research and Curriculum

Mike Tracy, Joyce Herbert, Jennifer Swift, Patty Kolar, Guadalupe Solis, Anji Garcia, Pam Jaeger
Jan Bond, Product Correlation

New Media

Armin Gutzmer, Director of Product Development
Rainy Day, Project Manager
Melanie Baccus, Nina Degollado, Cathy Kuhles

Printed in the United States of America
ISBN 0-03-064361-9

3 4 5 6 7 048 05 04 03 02

Acknowledgments

Chapter Writers

Linda Ruth Berg, Ph.D.
Adjunct Professor—Natural Sciences
St. Petersburg Junior College
St. Petersburg, Florida

Kathleen Meehan Berry
Science Chairman
Canon-McMillan School District
Canonsburg, Pennsylvania

Andrew Champagne
Former Physics Teacher
Ashland High School
Ashland, Massachusetts

Mapi Cuevas, Ph.D.
Professor of Chemistry
Sante Fe Community College
Gainesville, Florida

Jennie Dusheck
Science Writer
Santa Cruz, California

Robert H. Fronk, Ph.D.
Chair of Science and Mathematics Education Department
Florida Institute of Technology
West Melbourne, Florida

William G. Lamb, Ph.D.
Science Teacher and Dept. Chair
Oregon Episcopal School
Portland, Oregon

Karen J. Meech, Ph.D.
Associate Astronomer
Institute for Astronomy
University of Hawaii
Honolulu, Hawaii

Robert J. Sager
Chair and Professor of Earth Sciences
Pierce College
Lakewood, Washington

Mark F. Taylor, Ph.D.
Associate Professor of Biology
Baylor University
Waco, Texas

Lab Writers

Diana Scheidle Bartos
Science Consultant and Educator
Diana Scheidle Bartos, L.L.C.
Lakewood, Colorado

Angela Berenstein
Science Writer and Consultant
Urbana, Illinois

Charlotte Blassingame
Technology Coordinator
White Station Middle School
Memphis, Tennessee

Phillip G. Bunce
Former Physics Teacher
Bowie High School
Austin, Texas

Kenneth E. Creese
Science Teacher
White Mountain Junior High School
Rock Springs, Wyoming

Linda Culp
Science Teacher and Dept. Chair
Thorndale High School
Thorndale, Texas

James Deaver
Science Teacher and Dept. Chair
West Point High School
West Point, Nebraska

Denise Garza
Science Writer
Austin, Texas

Bruce M. Jones
Science Teacher and Dept. Chair
The Blake School
Minneapolis, Minnesota

William G. Lamb, Ph.D.
Science Teacher and Dept. Chair
Oregon Episcopal School
Portland, Oregon

Alyson Mike
Science Teacher
East Valley Middle School
East Helena, Montana

C. Ford Morishita
Biology Teacher
Clackamas High School
Milwaukie, Oregon

Joseph W. Price
Science Teacher and Dept. Chair
H.M. Browne Junior High School
Washington, D.C.

Denice Lee Sandefur
Science Chairperson
Nucla High School
Nucla, Colorado

Patti Soderberg
Science Writer
The BioQUEST Curriculum Consortium
Beloit College
Beloit, Wisconsin

Phillip Vavala
Science Teacher and Dept. Chair
Salesianum School
Wilmington, Delaware

Albert C. Wartski
Biology Teacher
Chapel Hill High School
Chapel Hill, North Carolina

Lynn Marie Wartski
Science Writer and Former Science Teacher
Hillsborough, North Carolina

Academic Reviewers

Mead Allison, Ph.D.
Assistant Professor
Department of Geology
Tulane University
New Orleans, Louisiana

Sonal Blumenthal, Ph.D.
Lecturer, Biological Sciences
Department of Biology
The University of Texas
Austin, Texas

John A. Brockhaus, Ph.D.
Director—Mapping, Charting, and Geodesy Program
Department of Geography and Environmental Engineering
United States Military Academy
West Point, New York

Dan Bruton, Ph.D.
Professor, Physics and Astronomy
Department of Physics and Astronomy
Stephen F. Austin State University
Nacogdoches, Texas

Wesley N. Colley, Ph.D.
Postdoctoral Fellow
Harvard-Smithsonian Center for Astrophysics
Cambridge, Massachusetts

Scott A. Ericsson, Ph.D.
Assistant Professor
Department of Animal Sciences
Sul Ross University
Alpine, Texas

Arthur Few, Ph.D.
Professor
Space Physics and Environmental Science
Rice University
Houston, Texas

Frank Guziec, Ph.D.
Dishman Professor of Science
Department of Chemistry
Southwestern University
Georgetown, Texas

Roy W. Hann, Jr., Ph.D.
Professor of Civil Engineering
Department of Civil Engineering
Texas A & M University
College Station, Texas

Kenneth Johnson, Ph.D.
Assistant Professor of Geochemistry
Department of Geology
Texas Tech University
Lubbock, Texas

Gloria Langer, Ph.D.
Professor of Physics
University of Colorado
Boulder, Colorado

Philip LaRoe
Professor
Helena College of Technology
Helena, Montana

M.A.K. Lodhi, Ph.D.
Course Coordinator and Lecturer, Astronomy
Department of Physics and Astronomy
Texas Tech University
Lubbock, Texas

Paul Manzo, Ph.D.
Lecturer
Department of Biological Sciences
Boston University
Beverly, Massachusetts

Donald Olson, Ph.D.
Professor of Physics and Astronomy
Department of Physics
Southwest Texas State University
San Marcos, Texas

Barron Rector, Ph.D.
Assistant Professor and Extension Range Specialist
Texas Agricultural Extension Service
Texas A&M University
College Station, Texas

Ernest O. Reesing, D.V.M.
Professor and Director, Vet Tech Program
Department of Animal Sciences
Sul Ross University
Alpine, Texas

Acknowledgments (cont.)

David Rohr, Ph.D.
Professor and Chair
Department of Earth and
    Physical Sciences
Sul Ross University
Alpine, Texas

Kevin Urbanczyk, Ph.D.
Associate Professor of Geology
Department of Earth and
    Physical Sciences
Sul Ross University
Alpine, Texas

Jim Whitford-Stark, Ph.D.
Assistant Professor
Department of Earth and
    Physical Sciences
Sul Ross University
Alpine, Texas

Mary K. Wicksten, Ph.D.
Professor of Biology
Department of Biology
Texas A&M University
College Station, Texas

Safety Reviewer

Jack Gerlovich, Ph.D.
Associate Professor
School of Education
Drake University
Des Moines, Iowa

Teacher Reviewers

Barry L. Bishop
Science Teacher
San Rafael Junior High
Ferron, Utah

Gladys Cherniak
Science Teacher
St. Paul's Episcopal School
Mobile, Alabama

Connie Cook–Fontenot
Science Teacher
Wilson Intermediate School
Houston, Texas

Jack Cooper
Science Teacher
Ennis Middle and High
    School
Ennis, Texas

Georgiann Delgadillo
East Valley School District
Continuous Curriculum
    School
Spokane, Washington

Alonda Droege
Science Teacher
Pioneer Middle School
Steilacom, Washington

Vicky Farland
Science Teacher and Dept. Chair
Centennial Middle School
Yuma, Arizona

Rebecca Ferguson
Science Teacher
Northridge Middle School
North Richland Hills, Texas

Laura Fleet
Science Teacher
Alice B. Landrum Middle
    School
Ponte Vedra Beach, Florida

Jennifer Ford
Science Teacher and Dept. Chair
Northridge Middle School
North Richland Hills, Texas

Dennette Gibson
Science Teacher
Mitchell Intermediate School
Conroe, Texas

Woody Golden
Science Teacher
Moorhead Junior High School
Conroe, Texas

Susan Gorman
Science Teacher
Northridge Middle School
North Richland Hills, Texas

Norman E. Holcomb
Science Teacher
Marion Local Schools
Maria Stein, Ohio

Ken Horn
*Science Teacher and Dept.
    Chair*
Fallston Middle School
Fallston, Maryland

Karma Houston-Hughes
Science Teacher
Kyrene Middle School
Tempe, Arizona

Kerry A. Johnson
Science Teacher
Isbell Middle School
Santa Paula, California

David Jones
Science Teacher
Andrew Jackson Middle
    School
Cross Lanes, West Virginia

Meredith Keelan
Science Teacher
O. H. Herman Middle School
Van Vleck, Texas

Meredith Kisiah
Science Teacher
Fairview Middle School
Tallahassee, Florida

Michael E. Kral
Science Teacher
West Hardin Middle School
Cecilia, Kentucky

Kathy LaRoe
Science Teacher
East Valley Middle School
East Helena, Montana

Edith C. McAlanis
Science Teacher
Socorro Middle School
El Paso, Texas

Alyson Mike
Science Teacher
East Valley Middle School
East Helena, Montana

Mike Minium
*Vice President of Program
    Development*
United States Orienteering
    Federation
Forest Park, Georgia

Annette Moran
Science Teacher
Richardson North Junior
    High School
Richardson, Texas

Bernadette Ochoa
Science Teacher
Montwood Middle School
El Paso, Texas

Joseph W. Price
Science Teacher
H.M. Browne Junior High
    School
Washington, D.C.

Terry Rakes
Science Teacher
Elmwood Junior High School
Rogers, Arkansas

Bert J. Sherwood
Science Specialist
Socorro Independent School
    District
El Paso, Texas

David Sparks
Science Teacher
Redwater Junior High School
Redwater, Texas

Elsie Waynes
Science Teacher
Terrell Junior High
Washington, D.C.

Walter Woolbaugh
Science Teacher
Manhattan School System
Manhattan, Montana

Sharon L. Woolf
Science Teacher
Langston Hughes Middle
    School
Reston, Virginia

Lee Yassinski
Science Teacher
Sun Valley Middle School
Sun Valley, California

John Zambo
Science Teacher
E. Ustach Middle School
Modesto, California

Gordon Zibelman
Science Teacher
Drexel Hill Middle School
Drexel Hill, Pennsylvania

Texas Teacher Consultants

Connie Cook–Fontenot
Science Teacher
Wilson Intermediate School
Houston, Texas

Sandra Geisbush
Science Coordinator
San Antonio Independent
    School District
San Antonio, Texas

Sue L. Harris
Science Teacher
Harry S. Truman Middle
    School
San Antonio, Texas

Barbara ten Brink
Science Coordinator
Round Rock Independent
    School District
Round Rock, Texas

Contents in Brief

Contents

Matter and Motion 34
Science Across Texas

A World of Energy 114
Science Across Texas

UNIT 3

Living Things 180
Science Across Texas

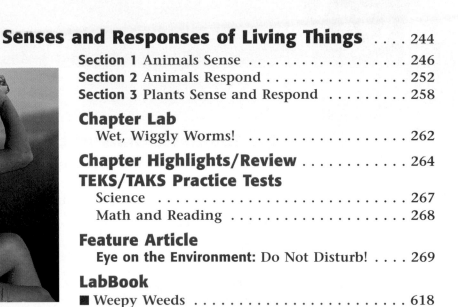

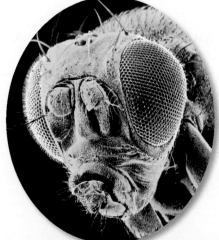

UNIT 5

Exploring the Earth's Surface **404**

Science Across Texas

UNIT 6

Earth Systems and Structure 452
Science Across Texas

Heat

Wear safety goggles when using a heating device or a flame. Whenever possible, use an electric hot plate as a heat source instead of an open flame. When heating materials in a test tube, always angle the test tube away from yourself and others. To avoid burns, wear heat-resistant gloves whenever instructed to do so.

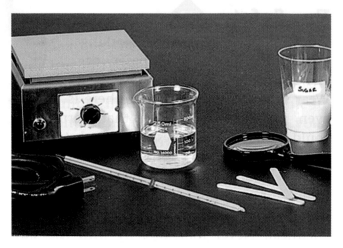

Electricity

Be careful with electrical cords. When using a microscope with a lamp, do not place the cord where it could trip someone. Do not let cords hang over a table edge in a way that could cause equipment to fall if the cord is accidentally pulled. Do not use equipment with damaged cords. Be sure your hands are dry and that the electrical equipment is in the "off" position before plugging it in. Turn off and unplug electrical equipment when you are finished.

Chemicals

Wear safety goggles when handling any potentially dangerous chemicals, acids, or bases. If a chemical is unknown, handle it as you would a dangerous chemical. Wear an apron and protective gloves when working with acids or bases or whenever you are told to do so. If a spill gets on your skin or clothing, rinse it off immediately with water for at least 5 minutes while calling to your teacher.

Never mix chemicals unless your teacher tells you to do so. Never taste, touch, or smell chemicals unless you are specifically directed to do so. Before working with a flammable liquid or gas, check for the presence of any source of flame, spark, or heat.

Animal Safety

Always obtain your teacher's permission before bringing any animal into the school building. Handle animals only as your teacher directs. Always treat animals carefully and respectfully. Wash your hands thoroughly after handling any animal.

Plant Safety

Do not eat any part of a plant or plant seed used in the laboratory. Wash your hands thoroughly after handling any part of a plant. When in nature, do not pick any wild plants unless your teacher instructs you to do so.

Glassware

Examine all glassware before use. Be sure that glassware is clean and free of chips and cracks. Report damaged glassware to your teacher. Glass containers used for heating should be made of heat-resistant glass.

Science in Our World

Pre-Reading
Questions

1. What are scientific methods?
2. What is a model, and what are the limitations of models? ⊛TEKS
3. What tools are used to measure mass and volume?

WHAT IS THAT?

Did you ask this question when you first saw the image on this page? This image shows what scientists think some living things on Earth looked like over 540 million years ago! Remains of living things found in rocks, such as the one shown at right, help scientists find answers to their questions about what an organism might have looked like. In this chapter, you will learn about science. You will also learn about the process used to help answer questions such as, What IS that?

These are thought to be the remains of one of the first large multicellular living things on Earth!

MISSION IMPOSSIBLE? ⭐TEKS

In this activity, you will do some creative thinking to solve what might seem like an impossible problem.

Procedure

1. Examine an **index card.** Take note of its size and shape. Your mission is to fit yourself through the card.

2. Brainstorm with a partner about ways to complete your mission. Keep the following rules in mind: You can only tear and fold the card. You cannot use tape, glue, or anything else to hold the card together.

3. When you and your partner have a plan, write your procedure in your ScienceLog.

4. Test your plan. Did it work? If necessary, get another index card and try again. Record your new plan and results in your ScienceLog.

5. Share your plans and results with other groups in your class.

Analysis

6. Why was it helpful to come up with a plan in advance?

7. How did testing your plan help you complete your mission?

8. How did sharing your ideas with your classmates help you complete your mission? What did your classmates do differently?

SECTION 1

READING WARM-UP

Terms to Learn

science

What You'll Do

- Describe three methods of investigation.
- Identify benefits of science in the world around you.
- Describe jobs that use science.

Science and Scientists

You are on a hike in the mountains when you see something strange. You pick it up. It looks like a shell. You wonder, How could a shell be up on this mountain?

Congratulations! You just completed the first steps of being a scientist. How did you do it? You observed the world around you. Then you asked a question about your observations. And that's part of what science is all about.

Science Starts with a Question

Science is a process of gathering knowledge about the natural world. Asking a question can help you gather knowledge. The world around you is full of amazing things that can lead you to ask questions, such as those in **Figure 1.**

Figure 1 *Part of science is asking questions about the world around you.*

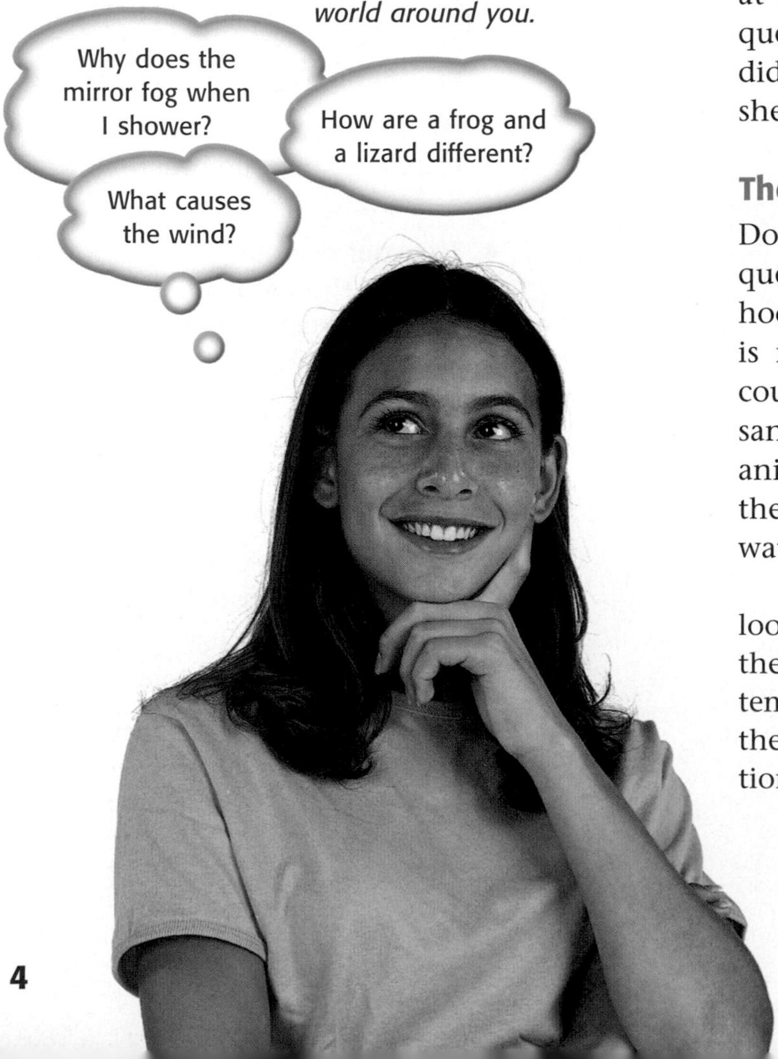
Why does the mirror fog when I shower?
How are a frog and a lizard different?
What causes the wind?

In Your Own Neighborhood

Take a look around your school and around your neighborhood. Most of the time, you take things that you use or see every day for granted. However, one day you might look at something in a new way. That's when a question hits you! The student in Figure 1 didn't have to look very far to realize that she had some questions to ask.

The World and Beyond

Do you think you might get tired asking questions about things in your neighborhood? Then just remember that the world is made up of many different places. You could ask questions about deserts, forests, or sandy beaches. Many different plants and animals live in each of these places. And then there are the rocks, soil, and flowing water in the environment.

But the Earth is not the final place to look for questions. You can look outward to the moon, sun, and planets in our solar system. And beyond that, you have the rest of the universe! There seem to be enough questions to keep scientists busy for a long time.

READING WARM-UP

Terms to Learn

scientific methods
observation
hypothesis
data

What You'll Do

- Identify the steps used in scientific methods.
- Formulate testable hypotheses. ⭐TEKS
- Explain how scientific methods are used to answer questions and solve problems.

Scientific Methods

Imagine that you are standing in a thick forest on the bank of a river. The sun is shining through the needles of the trees. Insects are buzzing. It is the Jurassic period, 150 million years ago.

Standing beside the water, several long-necked dinosaurs quietly chew on plants. As you look through the trees, you spot a different kind of dinosaur on the hunt for food. It is an allosaurus (AL oh SAWR uhs), the most common meat-eating creature of this time.

You Feel the Earth Move

Suddenly, you hear a booming noise, and you feel the ground begin to shake. The allosaurus stops and looks in the direction of the sound as the booming gets louder. You notice a creature's head rising over the tops of the trees. The neck of the creature must be 20 m (about 60 ft) long! Then the whole animal comes into view, and you understand why the ground is shaking. The animal is *Seismosaurus hallorum* (SIEZ moh SAWR uhs hah LOHR uhm), the "earth shaker." You are looking at one of the largest known dinosaurs.

Seismosaurus hallorum

Not Just Imagination

What you just read about is not based on imagination alone. Scientists have been studying dinosaurs for years—even though no one has ever seen one! How can that be? Scientists gather bits and pieces of information about dinosaurs and their environment. Then they re-create what the Earth might have been like 150 million years ago from their information. How do they put it all together? They use a little imagination and scientific methods.

What Are Scientific Methods?

When scientists observe the natural world, they often think of a question or problem. But scientists don't just guess at answers. **Scientific methods** are the ways in which scientists answer questions and solve problems.

As scientists look for answers, they often use the same steps. But there is more than one way to use the steps. Look at **Figure 9.** Scientists may use all of the steps or just some of the steps during an investigation. They may even repeat some of the steps or do them in a different order. It all depends on what works best to answer their question.

Figure 9   **Steps of Scientific Methods**

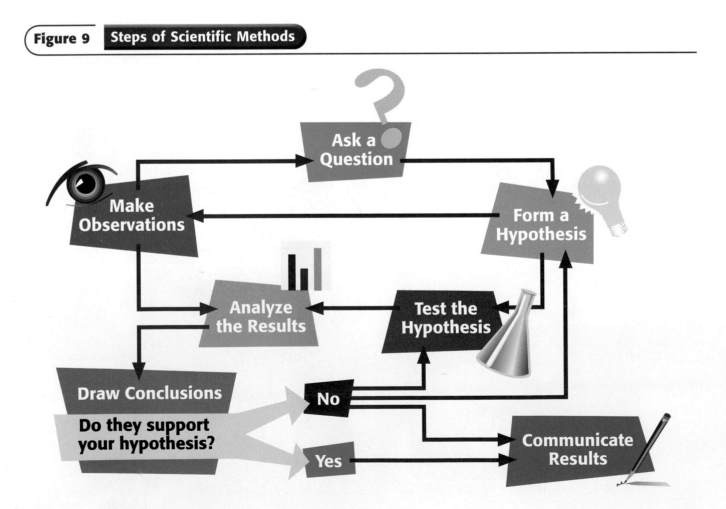

Ask a Question

Asking a question helps focus the purpose of an investigation. Scientists often ask a question they want to answer after making many observations. An **observation** is any use of the senses to gather information. Keep in mind that observations can be made at any point during an investigation.

There are many different kinds of observations. Observations may describe the hardness or softness of a rock. They may describe the color of a substance. Even the patterns in behavior of an animal can be described by observations. Measurements are observations that are made with tools, such as metersticks, stopwatches, and thermometers. But even if you have asked a great question, your observations will help you find an answer only if they are accurate and carefully recorded.

A Dinosaur-Sized Question

In 1979, two people on a hike came across dinosaur bones in the area of northwestern New Mexico shown in **Figure 10.** Soon after, David D. Gillette, a scientist who studies fossils, went to see the bones.

After observing the bones, Gillette may have asked, What kind of dinosaur did these bones come from? Gillette knew that to answer this question, he would have to use scientific methods to come up with an answer he could trust.

Figure 10 *Bones were found in this part of New Mexico.*

Form a Hypothesis

When scientists want to investigate a question, they form a hypothesis. A **hypothesis** is a possible explanation or answer to a question. It is sometimes called an educated guess. The hypothesis is a scientist's best answer to the question. But it can't be just any answer. Someone must be able to test it.

Based on his observations and on what he already knew about dinosaurs, Gillette formed a hypothesis. He said that the bones, seen in **Figure 11,** came from a kind of dinosaur not yet known to scientists. This was Gillette's best testable explanation for what kind of dinosaur the bones came from. To test his hypothesis, Gillette would have to do a lot of research.

Figure 11 *Gillette and his team had to carefully dig out the bones before studying them.*

MID-SECTION REVIEW

❶ What are scientific methods?

❷ **Comparing Concepts** Compare an observation and a hypothesis.

❸ **Developing Hypotheses** The following statements could have been made during Gillette's field investigation. Which statement is a testable hypothesis? Explain your reasoning. ⭐TEKS

  a. Dinosaur bones were found in New Mexico.

  b. The bones are from a known dinosaur.

  c. One of the ribs is 2 m long.

Making Hypotheses ⊛TEKS

Scientists exploring the Texas Gulf Coast have discovered American Indian artifacts that are thousands of years old. What is odd about these artifacts is that they were buried in the sea floor several meters below sea level. These artifacts had not been moved since they were first buried.

The *observation* is that there are American Indian artifacts several meters below sea level. The *question* is, Why are the artifacts there? Your job is to *form a hypothesis* that answers this question. (Remember, you must write the hypothesis so that you can find evidence that supports it or shows it to be wrong.)

Test the Hypothesis

Once a hypothesis is formed, it must be tested. Scientists test hypotheses by gathering data. **Data** are any pieces of information gathered through experimentation. The data can help scientists tell if the hypotheses are valid or not.

To test a hypothesis, a scientist may do a *controlled experiment.* A controlled experiment is an experiment that tests only one factor at a time. By changing only one factor, the *variable,* scientists can see the results of just that one change. Some scientists, however, often depend more on observations than experiments to test their hypotheses. Scientists can often observe nature and collect large amounts of data to test their hypotheses.

To test his hypothesis, Gillette took hundreds of measurements of the bones, as shown in **Figure 12.** He compared his measurements with those of bones from known dinosaurs. He visited museums and talked with other scientists. After gathering all of these data, Gillette was ready for the next step in answering his question.

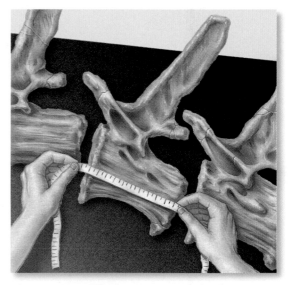

Figure 12 *Gillette measured the bones to test his hypothesis.*

Analyze the Results

Once scientists finish their tests, they must analyze the results. Analyzing results helps scientists construct reasonable explanations based on the evidence they've collected. Scientists often make tables and graphs to arrange their data. When Gillette analyzed his results, he found that the bones of the mystery dinosaur did not match the bones of any known dinosaur. The bones were either too large or too different in shape.

Draw Conclusions

After carefully analyzing the results of their tests, scientists must conclude if the results support the hypothesis. If the hypothesis is not supported, scientists may repeat the investigation to check for mistakes. Or they may ask new questions and form new hypotheses.

Based on all his work, Gillette concluded that the bones found in New Mexico, shown in the model in **Figure 13,** were indeed from a yet unknown dinosaur. The dinosaur was about 45 m (148 ft) long and had a mass of almost 100 metric tons. The creature certainly fit the name Gillette gave it—*Seismosaurus hallorum,* the "earth shaker."

Communicate Results

After finishing an investigation, scientists communicate their results. In this way, scientists share what they have learned with others. People may want to repeat the investigation to see if they get the same results. Science depends on the sharing of information. Scientists share information by writing reports for scientific journals and giving talks on their results. They can also put their results on the Internet.

Gillette shared his discovery of *Seismosaurus* at a press conference at the New Mexico Museum of Natural History and Science. He later sent a report that described his investigation to the *Journal of Vertebrate Paleontology.*

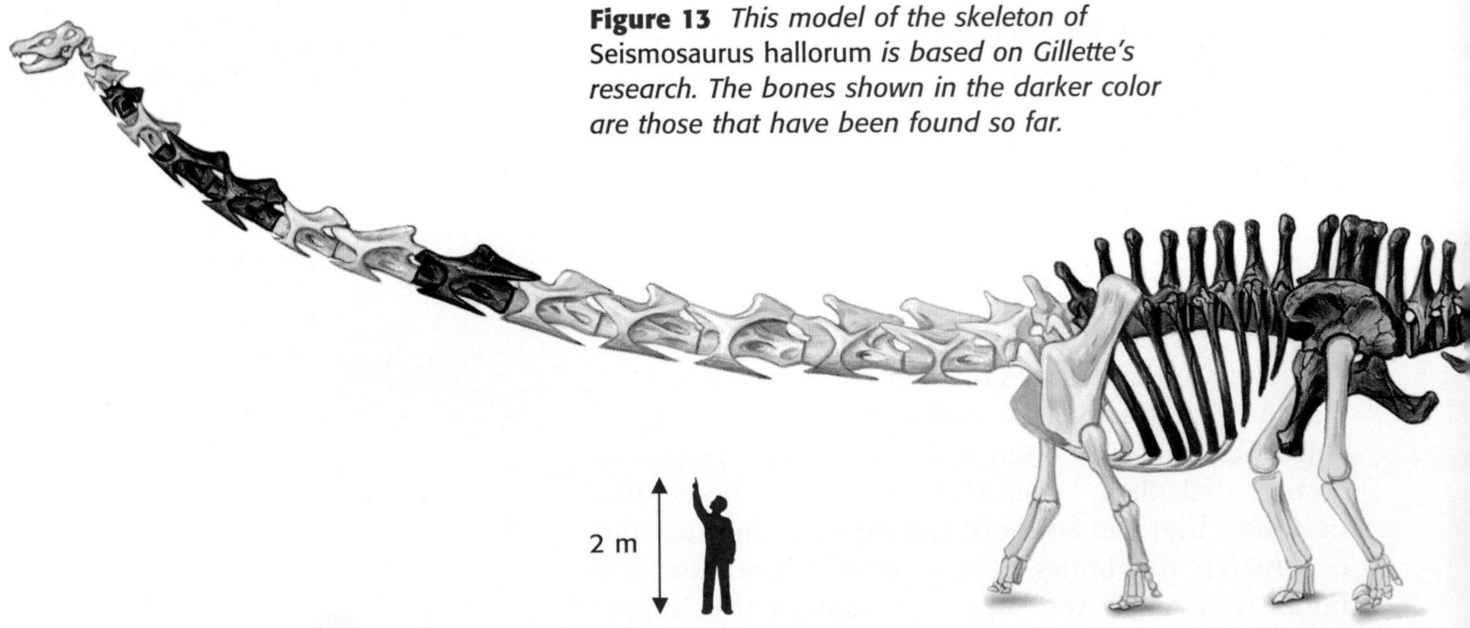

Figure 13 *This model of the skeleton of* Seismosaurus hallorum *is based on Gillette's research. The bones shown in the darker color are those that have been found so far.*

2 m

Case Closed?

All of the *Seismosaurus* bones that Gillette found have been dug up. But as shown in **Figure 14,** the fun is not over yet! The work on *Seismosaurus* continues. The remains of one of the largest dinosaurs ever discovered are still being studied. Like so many other investigations, Gillette's work led to new questions to be answered using scientific methods.

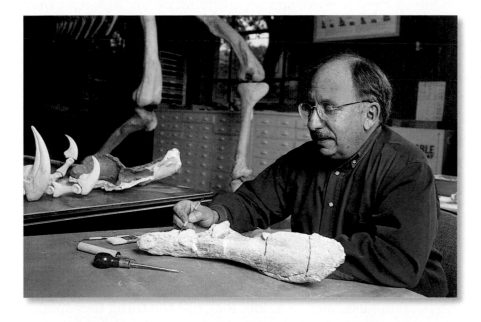

Figure 14 *David Gillette continues to study the bones of* Seismosaurus *for new views into the past.*

SECTION REVIEW

① What are the six basic steps of scientific methods?

② Why do scientists communicate the results of their investigations?

③ **Analyzing Hypotheses** Review Gillette's hypothesis as to its strengths and weaknesses using scientific evidence and information. ⭐TEKS

④ **Applying Concepts** Why might two scientists have different hypotheses based on the same observations?

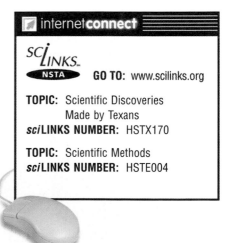

internet**connect**

SCI*LINKS*

NSTA   **GO TO:** www.scilinks.org

TOPIC: Scientific Discoveries
Made by Texans
*sci***LINKS NUMBER:** HSTX170

TOPIC: Scientific Methods
*sci***LINKS NUMBER:** HSTE004

READING WARM-UP

Terms to Learn

model
theory
law

What You'll Do

- Use models to represent the natural world. ★TEKS
- Identify the limitations of models. ★TEKS
- Describe theories and laws.

Scientific Models

Imagine you are studying volcanoes. How do you think baking soda, vinegar, and some clay could help you?

You might not think these things alone could help you. But you could use them to build a model of a volcano. Then they might help you understand volcanoes a little better!

Types of Scientific Models

A **model** is a representation of an object or system. Models often use familiar objects or ideas that stand for other things. That's how a model can be a tool for understanding the natural world. A model uses something familiar to help you understand something that is not familiar. Models can be used to explain the past and the present. They can even be used to predict future events. However, keep in mind that models have limitations. Three major kinds of scientific models are physical, mathematical, and conceptual models.

Physical Models

Model airplanes, maps, and dolls are physical models. Some physical models, such as a doll, look like the thing they model. However, a limitation of a doll as the model of a baby is that the doll doesn't act like a baby. Other models, such as the one shown in **Figure 15,** look and act at least somewhat like the real thing.

Figure 15 *The model volcano looks a little bit like the real volcano, but it has its limitations. The model cannot destroy acres of forests with hot lava like a real volcano can!*

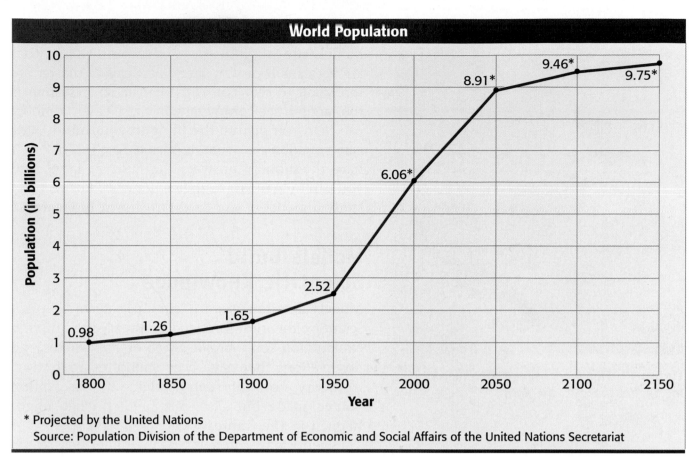

World Population

* Projected by the United Nations
Source: Population Division of the Department of Economic and Social Affairs of the United Nations Secretariat

Figure 16 *This graph shows human population growth predicted by a mathematical model run on a computer.*

Mathematical Models

A mathematical model is made up of mathematical equations and data. Some mathematical models are simple. These models allow you to calculate things such as how far a car will go in an hour or how much you would weigh on the moon. Others are so complex that only computers can handle them. Look at **Figure 16.** Scientists use a mathematical model to help predict how fast the number of people on Earth will grow and how many resources they will use. Some of these very complex models have many variables. Using the most correct data does not make the prediction correct. A change in a variable that was not thought of could cause the model to fail.

Conceptual Models

The third kind of model is a conceptual model. Some conceptual models are systems of ideas. Others are based on making comparisons with familiar things to help illustrate or explain an idea. One example of a conceptual model is the system scientists use to classify living things. By using a system of ideas, scientists can group living things by what they have in common. This model allows scientists to better understand each group of living things.

Self-Check

What are some of the limitations of the model used to make the graph in Figure 16? (Hint: What are some events that could change the information that was used in the model?)
(See page 640 to check your answer.) ⊛TEKS

Figure 17 *This model shows the different layers that make up the Earth.*

Models Are Just the Right Size

Models are often used to represent things that are very small or very large. Particles of matter are too small to see. The Earth or the solar system is too large to see completely. In these cases, a model can help you picture the thing in your mind. How can you observe what is inside Earth? That is a hard question to answer. The Earth is large, and you can't dig down to the center of it. But you can study a model of the Earth, as shown in **Figure 17.**

Models Build Scientific Knowledge

Models are often used to help illustrate and explain scientific theories. In science, a **theory** is a unifying explanation for a broad range of hypotheses and observations that have been supported by testing. A theory not only can explain an observation you've made but also can predict what might happen in the future.

Scientists use models to help guide their search for new information. This information can help support a theory or show it to be wrong. Keep in mind that models can be changed or replaced. These changes happen because new observations that cause scientists to change their theories are made. You can compare an old model with a current one in **Figure 18.**

Figure 18 *Scientists' model of Earth changed as new information was gathered.*

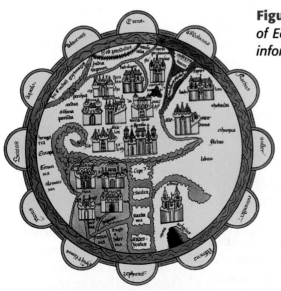

Model of Earth: 1000 CE

Model of Earth: Current

Scientific Laws

What happens when a theory and its models correctly predict the results of many different experiments? A scientific law could be formed. In science, a **law** is a summary of many experimental results and observations. A law tells you how things work. Laws are not the same as theories. Laws tell you only what happens, not why it happens.

A law tells you to expect the same thing to happen every time. Look at **Figure 19.** Every object in the universe is attracted to every other object. This fact is summed up by the *law of universal gravitation.* This law says that you can always expect two objects to be attracted to one another. It also helps you calculate the size of the attraction. The size of the attraction depends on the masses of the objects and the distance between them. However, the law does not explain why there is an attraction.

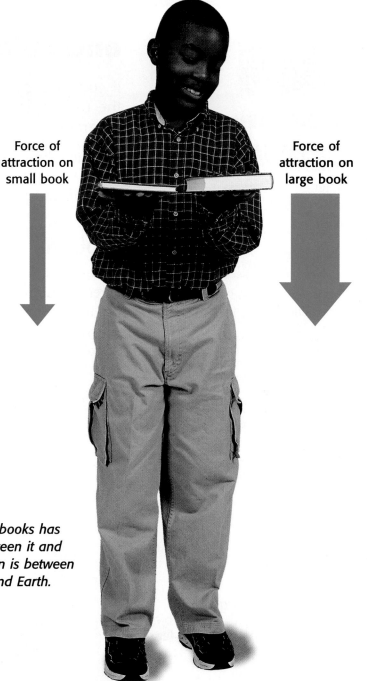

Force of attraction on small book

Force of attraction on large book

Figure 19 *Each of these books has a different attraction between it and Earth. The larger attraction is between the more massive book and Earth.*

SECTION REVIEW

1. How are models used to represent the natural world?

2. Identify two limitations of models. ⊛TEKS

3. **Applying Concepts** Draw a map showing the way from your school to your home. What type of model have you made? Identify any symbols you used to represent things on your map. What are some limitations of your model? ⊛TEKS

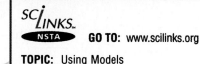

internet**connect**

*sci*LINKS.
NSTA   GO TO: www.scilinks.org

TOPIC: Using Models
***sci*LINKS NUMBER:** HSTP015

READING WARM-UP

Terms to Learn

meter   mass
area   temperature
volume

What You'll Do

● Collect, record, and analyze information using various tools. ⭐TEKS

● Explain the importance of the International System of Units.

● Calculate area.

● Identify lab safety symbols, and demonstrate safe practices during lab investigations. ⭐TEKS

Tools, Measurement, and Safety

If you were building a birdhouse, would you pound in the nails with a screwdriver? You wouldn't if you had a hammer!

For each stage of building a birdhouse, you need the correct tools. Scientists use many different tools to help them in their experiments. A tool is anything that helps you do a task.

Tools for Seeing

If you look at a jar of pond water, you may see a few creatures swimming around. But if you use a microscope, you can see many more creatures that you couldn't see before. And all of the creatures will appear much larger. Microscopes help you make careful observations of things that are too small to see with just your eyes.

Compound Light Microscope

Look at the compound light microscope in **Figure 20.** It is made up of three main parts—a tube with lenses at each end, a stage, and a light. Place what you want to see on the stage. This lets light pass through it. The lenses magnify the image. Sometimes dyes are used to allow you to see the image more clearly.

Figure 20 *A compound light microscope can make an image that is up to 1,000 times (1,000×) larger than the actual object.*

Ocular lens

Objective lenses

Stage

Light

Paramecium (200×)

Figure 21 Measurement Tools

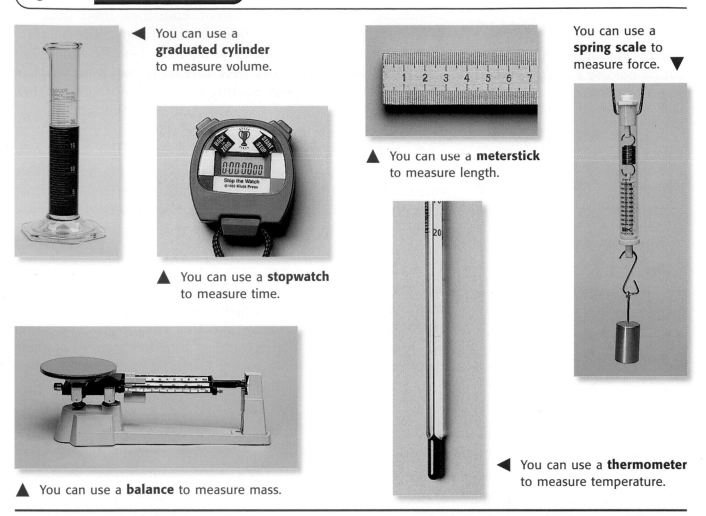

◄ You can use a **graduated cylinder** to measure volume.

▲ You can use a **stopwatch** to measure time.

▲ You can use a **meterstick** to measure length.

You can use a **spring scale** to measure force. ▼

▲ You can use a **balance** to measure mass.

◄ You can use a **thermometer** to measure temperature.

Tools for Measuring

You might remember that one way to collect data during an experiment is to take measurements. To have the best measurements possible, you need to use the proper tools. Stopwatches, metersticks, and balances are some of the tools you can use to make measurements. Thermometers, spring scales, and graduated cylinders are also helpful tools. Some of the uses of these tools are shown in **Figure 21.**

Tools for Analyzing

After you collect data, you need to analyze them. Perhaps you need to find the average of your data. Calculators are handy tools to help you do calculations quickly. Or you might show your data in a graph or a figure. A computer with the correct software can help you make neat, colorful figures. Of course, even a pencil and graph paper are tools that you can use to graph your data.

QuickLab

See for Yourself

1. Use a **metric ruler** to measure the length and width of one of your fingernails. In your ScienceLog, draw and describe what you see.

2. Look at the same fingernail through a **magnifying lens.** In your ScienceLog, draw how your nail looks when it is magnified.

3. How does using a magnifying lens change what you can see?

 TEKS

Measure the width of your desk, but do not use a ruler. Pick an object to use as your unit of measurement. It could be a pencil, your hand, or anything else. Find how many units wide your desk is. Compare your measurement with those of your classmates. In your ScienceLog, explain why using standard units of measurement is important.

•• ⭐TEKS •••••••••••••••••

Measurement

Hundreds of years ago, different countries used different systems of measurement. At one time in England, the standard for an inch was three grains of barley placed end to end. Other modern standardized units were originally based on parts of the body, such as the foot. Such systems were not very reliable. Their units were based on objects that had different sizes.

The International System of Units

In time, people saw that they needed a simple and reliable measurement system. In the late 1700s, the French Academy of Sciences set out to make that system. Over the next 200 years, the metric system was formed. This system is now called the International System of Units (SI).

Today, most scientists and almost all countries use the International System of Units. One advantage of using SI measurements is that they help all scientists share and compare their observations and results. Another advantage of SI is that all units are based on the number 10. This makes changing from one unit to another easier. The table in **Figure 22** shows SI units for length, volume, mass, and temperature.

Figure 22 *Prefixes are used with SI units to change them to larger or smaller units.*

Common SI Units and Conversions		
Length	**meter (m)**	
	kilometer (km)	1 km = 1,000 m
	decimeter (dm)	1 dm = 0.1 m
	centimeter (cm)	1 cm = 0.01 m
	millimeter (mm)	1 mm = 0.001 m
	micrometer (μm)	1 μm = 0.000 001 m
	nanometer (nm)	1 nm = 0.000 000 001 m
Volume	**cubic meter (m^3)**	
	cubic centimeter (cm^3)	1 cm^3 = 0.000 001 m^3
	liter (L)	1 L = 1 dm^3 = 0.001 m^3
	milliliter (mL)	1 mL = 0.001 L = 1 cm^3
Mass	**kilogram (kg)**	
	gram (g)	1 g = 0.001 kg
	milligram (mg)	1 mg = 0.000 001 kg
Temperature	**Kelvin (K)**	
	Celsius (°C)	0°C = 273 K
		100°C = 373 K

Length

How long is your arm? The student in **Figure 23** could describe the length of her arm using the **meter** (m), the basic SI unit of length. You may remember that SI units are based on the number 10. If you divide 1 m into 100 parts, for example, each part equals 1 cm. In other words, 1 cm is one-hundredth of a meter. To describe the length of microscopic objects, micrometers (μm) or nanometers (nm) are used. To describe the length of larger objects, kilometers are used. One kilometer is equal to 1,000 m.

Area

How much carpet would it take to cover the floor of your classroom? To answer this question, you must find the area of the floor. **Area** is a measure of how much surface an object has. Area is based on two measurements. To calculate the area of a square or rectangle, first measure the length and width, and then use the following equation:

$$area = length \times width$$

The units for area are called square units, such as m^2, cm^2, and km^2. The MathFocus below will help you understand square units.

Figure 23 *This student's arm is 0.65 m long.*

MathFocus ·····························

Finding Area

What is the *area* of a rectangle that has a *length* of 4 cm and a *width* of 5 cm?

Step 1: Write the equation for area.

$$area = length \times width$$

Step 2: Replace the length and width with the measurements given in the problem, and solve.

$$area = 4 \text{ cm} \times 5 \text{ cm} = 20 \text{ cm}^2$$

The equation for area can also be rearranged to find the length and width, as shown.

$$length = \frac{area}{width} \quad \text{(Rearrange by dividing by width.)}$$

$$width = \frac{area}{length} \quad \text{(Rearrange by dividing by length.)}$$

Now It's Your Turn

1. What is the area of a square whose sides measure 5 m?

2. What is the area of a photograph that is 10 cm long and 15 cm wide?

3. A rectangle has an area of 36 cm^2 and a length of 9 cm. What is its width?

Figure 24 *The volume of the liquid in this beaker is about 250 mL.*

Volume

Suppose that some hippos born in a zoo are being moved to Africa. How many hippos will fit into a cage? The answer depends on the volume of the cage and the volume of the hippos. **Volume** is the amount of space that something occupies or, as in the case of the cage, the amount of space that something contains.

The volume of a liquid is often given in liters (L). Liters are based on the meter. A cubic meter (1 m^3) is equal to 1,000 L. So 1,000 L will fit into a box measuring 1 m on each side. A milliliter (mL) will fit into a box measuring 1 cm on each side. So $1 \text{ mL} = 1 \text{ cm}^3$. Beakers, such as the one in **Figure 24,** and graduated cylinders are used to measure liquid volume.

The volume of a large, solid object is given in cubic meters (m^3). The volumes of smaller objects can be given in cubic centimeters (cm^3) or cubic millimeters (mm^3). To calculate the volume of a box-shaped object, multiply the object's length by its width and then by its height. To find the volume of an irregularly shaped object, measure the volume of liquid the object displaces. This process is shown in **Figure 25.**

Mass

How many sacks of grain can a mule carry? The answer depends on the strength of the mule and the mass of the sacks of grain. **Mass** is the amount of matter that something is made of. The kilogram (kg) is the basic unit for mass. The kilogram is used to describe the mass of things such as sacks of grain. Many common objects are not so large, however. The mass of smaller objects, such as an apple, can be described using grams. One thousand grams equals 1 kg. The mass of large objects, such as an elephant, is given in metric tons. A metric ton equals 1,000 kg.

Figure 25 *Adding the rock changes the water level from 70 mL to 80 mL. So the rock displaces 10 mL of water. Because $1 \text{ mL} = 1 \text{ cm}^3$, the volume of the rock is 10 cm^3.*

70 mL

80 mL

Temperature

How hot is a lava flow? To answer this question, a scientist would need to measure the temperature of the lava. **Temperature** is a measure of how hot (or cold) something is. You are probably used to describing temperature with degrees Fahrenheit (°F). Scientists often use degrees Celsius (°C). However, kelvins (K), the SI base unit for temperature, is also used. The thermometer in **Figure 26** shows how two of these units are related. Degrees Celsius is the unit you will see most often in this book.

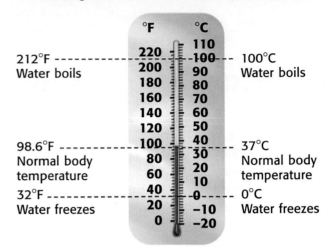

Figure 26 *This thermometer shows the relationship between degrees Fahrenheit and degrees Celsius.*

Safety Rules!

Science is exciting and fun. However, it can also be dangerous. So don't take any chances! Always follow your teacher's instructions. Don't take shortcuts—even when you think there is no danger.

Before starting any science investigation, get your teacher's permission. Read the lab procedures carefully. Pay special attention to safety information and caution statements. The table to the right shows the safety symbols used in this book. Be sure you know these symbols and their meanings. If you haven't already done so, read the safety information starting on page xxiv. **This is important!** If you are still not sure about what a safety symbol means, ask your teacher.

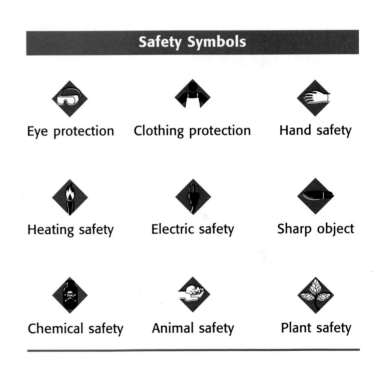

Safety Symbols

Eye protection   Clothing protection   Hand safety

Heating safety   Electric safety   Sharp object

Chemical safety   Animal safety   Plant safety

SECTION REVIEW

1 During an experiment, you must mix chemicals in a glass beaker. What should you wear to protect yourself during this experiment? **TEKS**

2 Which measuring tools would you select in order to find the time it takes for a bug to crawl 1 m? **TEKS**

3 **Math Practice** What is the area of a garden that is 12 m long and 8 m wide?

internet connect

*sci*LINKS
NSTA   GO TO: www.scilinks.org

TOPIC: SI Units
*sci*LINKS NUMBER: HSTE020

Discovery Lab

Exploring the Unseen ⭐TEKS

Your teacher will give you a box that has a special divider. Your task is to describe this divider as much as possible—without opening the box! Your only aid is a marble inside the box. This task will allow you to show your understanding of scientific methods. Good luck!

MATERIALS

• sealed mystery box

Ask a Question

1 In your ScienceLog, record the question that you are trying to answer by doing this experiment.

Form a Hypothesis

2 In your ScienceLog, write a hypothesis that states how much you think you will be able to determine about the divider.

Test the Hypothesis

3 Using all the methods you can think of (except opening the box), test your hypothesis. Record your methods and observations in your ScienceLog.

Analyze the Results

4 What characteristics of the divider were you able to identify? Draw or write your best description of the interior of the box.

5 Do your observations support your hypothesis? Explain. If your results do not support your hypothesis, write a new hypothesis, and test it.

6 With your teacher's permission, open the box and look inside. Record your observations.

Communicate Results

7 Write a paragraph summarizing your experiment. Be sure to include what methods you used and whether your results supported your hypothesis. Also include how you could improve your methods.

Skill Builder Lab

Measuring Liquid Volume ⭐TEKS

In this lab, you will use a graduated cylinder to measure and transfer precise amounts of liquids. Remember, to accurately measure liquids in a graduated cylinder, you should read the level at the bottom of the meniscus, the curved surface of the liquid.

MATERIALS

- masking tape
- marker
- 6 large test tubes
- test-tube rack
- 10 mL graduated cylinder
- 3 beakers filled with colored liquid
- small funnel

Procedure

1. Using the masking tape and marker, label the test tubes "Tube A" through "Tube F." Place them in the test-tube rack.

2. Using the graduated cylinder and the funnel, pour 14 mL of the red liquid into Tube A. Rinse the graduated cylinder and funnel between uses.

3. Measure 13 mL of the yellow liquid. Pour it into Tube C. Measure 13 mL of the blue liquid. Pour it into Tube E.

4. Transfer 4 mL of liquid from Tube C into Tube D. Transfer 7 mL of liquid from Tube E into Tube D.

5. Measure 4 mL of blue liquid from the beaker. Pour it into Tube F. Measure 7 mL of red liquid from the beaker. Pour it into Tube F.

6. Transfer 8 mL of liquid from Tube A into Tube B. Transfer 3 mL of liquid from Tube C into Tube B.

Collect Data

7. Make a data table in your ScienceLog. Record the color of the liquid in each test tube. Record your color observations in a table of class data. Copy the completed table into your ScienceLog.

8. Measure the volume of liquid in each test tube. Record the volumes in your data table.

Analysis

9. Did each group report the same colors? Explain why the colors were the same or different.

10. Why should you not fill the graduated cylinder to the very top?

Section 1

Vocabulary
science (p. 4)

Section Notes

- Science is a process of gathering knowledge about the natural world.

- Science involves making observations and asking questions about those observations.

- Doing research, making observations, and doing experiments are ways to search for answers to questions.

- Many different careers use science, including environmental science, cartography, and engineering.

Section 2

Vocabulary
scientific methods (p. 10)
observation (p. 11)
hypothesis (p. 12)
data (p. 13)

Section Notes

- Scientific methods are the ways in which scientists answer questions and solve problems.

- Any information you gather through your senses is an observation. Observations often lead to questions or problems.

- A hypothesis is a possible explanation or answer to a question. A good hypothesis is testable. **★TEKS**

- After you test a hypothesis, you should analyze your results and draw conclusions about whether your hypothesis is supported.

- Communicating your results allows others to check them or to continue to investigate your problem.

Section 3

Vocabulary
model (p. 16)
theory (p. 18)
law (p. 19)

Section Notes

- A model is a representation of an object or system. Models often use familiar things to help describe unfamiliar things. Models have limitations and can be changed because of new evidence. **★TEKS**

- A scientific theory is a unifying explanation for a broad range of hypotheses and observations that have been supported by testing.

- A scientific law is a summary of many experimental results and observations. A law can describe what happens but does not explain why it happens.

Section 4

Vocabulary
meter (p. 23)
area (p. 23)
volume (p. 24)
mass (p. 24)
temperature (p. 25)

Section Notes

- Tools such as microscopes, metersticks, balances, thermometers, and calculators are used to make observations, take measurements, and analyze data. **★TEKS**

- The International System of Units is the standard system of measurement used by scientists around the world.

- Length, volume, mass, and temperature are quantities of measurement. Each quantity of measurement is expressed with a particular SI unit.

- Area is a measure of how much surface an object has.

- Safety rules are important and must be followed at all times during scientific investigations. **★TEKS**

LabBook **★TEKS**
Graphing Data (p. 602)

For each pair of terms, explain how the meanings of the terms differ.

1. science/scientific methods

2. hypothesis/observation

3. theory/law

4. model/theory

5. volume/mass

UNDERSTANDING CONCEPTS

Multiple Choice

6. To search for answers to questions, you can
   a. do research.
   b. make observations.
   c. do an experiment.
   d. All of the above

7. Which of the following is NOT an SI unit?
   a. meter
   b. foot
   c. liter
   d. degree Celsius

8. A lab has the safety icons shown below. These icons mean that you should wear

   a. only safety goggles.
   b. only a lab apron.
   c. safety goggles and a lab apron.
   d. safety goggles, a lab apron, and gloves.

9. Which of the following is a limitation of models? ⭐TEKS
   a. They are large enough to see.
   b. They do not act exactly like the things they model.
   c. They are smaller than the things they model.
   d. They use familiar things to model unfamiliar things.

10. Gillette's hypothesis was
    a. supported by his results.
    b. not supported by his results.
    c. based only on observations.
    d. based only on what he already knew.

11. A pencil is 14 cm long. How many millimeters long is it?
    a. 1.4 mm   c. 1,400 mm
    b. 140 mm   d. 1,400,000 mm

Short Answer

12. How did Gillette determine that the dinosaur he found was new to scientists?

13. How and why do scientists use models?

14. What are three types of models? Give an example of each type.

15. Explain what each of the following tools is used to measure: balance, thermometer, stopwatch, spring scale, and graduated cylinder.

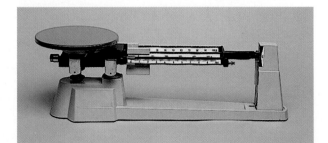

CONCEPT MAPPING

16. Use the following terms to create a concept map: *science, scientific methods, hypothesis, problems, questions, experiments,* and *observations.*

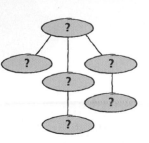

CRITICAL THINKING AND PROBLEM SOLVING

Write one or two sentences to answer the following questions:

17. Why are there many ways to follow the steps of scientific methods?

18. Why might two scientists working on the same problem draw different conclusions?

19. Investigations often begin with observation. How does observation limit what scientists can study?

20. Why should scientists be careful about making predictions from models? ⭐TEKS

MATH IN SCIENCE

21. A mirror is 20 cm wide and 30 cm long. What is the area of the mirror?

22. A roll of wrapping paper is 0.8 m wide and contains 10 m² of paper. How long is the paper?

23. A graduated cylinder contains 22 mL of water. When a piece of lead is added, the water level rises to 27 mL. What is the volume of the lead in cm³?

24. A sample of a liquid has a mass of 125 g and a volume of 127.5 mL.
    a. What is the mass of the liquid in centigrams?
    b. What is the volume of the liquid in liters?

INTERPRETING GRAPHICS

Examine the illustration below of an experiment set up to test the following prediction: *If bees are more attracted to yellow flowers than to red flowers, **then** bees will visit yellow flowers more often than they will visit red flowers.*

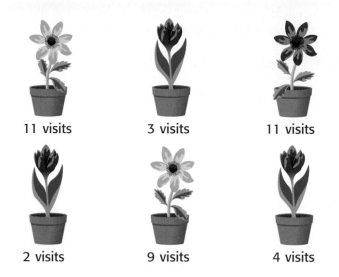

11 visits   3 visits   11 visits

2 visits   9 visits   4 visits

25. What percentage of the total visits occurred at yellow flowers? at red flowers? ⭐TEKS

26. What is the average number of visits for a yellow flower? What is the average number of visits for a red flower? ⭐TEKS

27. The above data were collected over 2 hours. Based on the average number of visits per flower, what is the frequency with which bees visited a yellow flower? a red flower? ⭐TEKS

28. In what ways could the experiment be improved based on the prediction?

Reading Check-up

⭐TEKS

Take a minute to review your answers to the Pre-Reading Questions found at the bottom of page 2. Have your answers changed? If necessary, revise your answers based on what you have learned since you began this chapter.

Chapter 1

1 Abby heats a test tube containing 5.0 grams of green powder. After heating, 3.2 grams of black powder remain in the test tube. Analyze the explanations below as to their strengths and weaknesses based on this evidence. Which is the most reasonable explanation of what happened?

A The balance is broken.

B Some of the green powder spilled out.

C Heating the green powder caused a gas in the air to join with the green powder.

D Heating the green powder caused a gas to leave the powder.

2 Rae Lynn wants to measure the temperature of a glass of warm water every 30 seconds. She will need to use a

F thermometer.

G stopwatch.

H graduated cylinder.

J thermometer and a stopwatch.

3 Uyen measured the time 5 sugar cubes took to dissolve in 5 glasses of water. The times she recorded were 2.3 minutes, 3.1 minutes, 1.9 minutes, 2.6 minutes, and 2.1 minutes. What was the average time it took for a sugar cube to dissolve?

A 1.2 min

B 12 min

C 2.3 min

D 2.4 min

4 Santos needs to measure the mass of a bowl of water. He should use a

F spring scale.

G graduated cylinder.

H balance.

J meterstick.

5 The temperature of water was taken during a laboratory experiment. What is the temperature according to the thermometer above?

A 12°C

B 22°C

C 27°C

D 32°C

Chapter 1

Math

1 A jar contains only red beans and white beans. The probability of selecting a red bean is $\frac{1}{2}$. What is most likely to be the number of red and white beans in the jar?

  A 20 red, 10 white

  B 30 red, 10 white

  C 20 red, 20 white

  D 10 red, 35 white

2 Using exponents, write the prime factorization of 16,875.

  F $3^4 \times 5^3$

  G $3^3 \times 5^4$

  H $3^7 \times 5^7$

  J 15^7

3 There are 16 girls and 14 boys in Tamara's science class. The name of each student is written on a piece of paper and placed in a box. If 1 name is chosen at random, what is the probability that Tamara's name will be chosen?

  A $\frac{1}{16}$

  B $\frac{7}{8}$

  C $\frac{8}{15}$

  D $\frac{1}{30}$

Reading

Read the passage. Then read each question that follows the passage. Decide which is the best answer to each question.

In 1979, two people were hiking over a hot, windswept mesa in northwestern New Mexico. They were on their way to see some 1,000-year-old American Indian rock carvings on a sandstone cliff. Just before reaching the site, however, the hikers came across a row of several huge half-buried tailbones. They weren't sure what kind of animal the bones had come from. But based on the size, the hikers guessed that the bones belonged to some kind of dinosaur.

1 What were the hikers going to see?

  A A large mesa

  B Dinosaur bones

  C Some American Indian rock carvings

  D A national park in New Mexico

2 Which sentence best summarizes the paragraph?

  F Two hikers were out looking for dinosaur bones and found some.

  G While they were out hiking, two people discovered some large bones.

  H Two people went hiking in New Mexico.

  J While looking for dinosaur bones, two people discovered some rock carvings.

Science Fiction

Once upon... who had a ...tic ship ...in a faraway... of silver ...land... ...a great ...there... haircut that ...lived a... was the gala... ...space

"The Homesick Chicken"

by Edward D. Hoch

OK, OK why *did* the chicken cross the road? Oh sure, you know the answer to this old riddle, don't you? Or maybe you just think you do! But "The Homesick Chicken," by Edward D. Hoch, may surprise you. That old chicken may not be exactly what it seems...

You see, one of the chickens at Tangaway Research Farms has escaped—not just flown the coop, mind you, but really escaped. It pecked a hole in a super-strength security fence and then crossed the eight-lane highway to get away. But after all that effort, it just stopped! It was found in a vacant lot across the highway from Tangaway, pecking away contentedly.

Barnabus Rex, a specialist in solving scientific riddles, is called in to work on the mystery. He is intrigued by this escaping chicken. Why would it go to all the trouble to peck through the tough security fence, risk being flattened on the superhighway, and then just stop when it got to the other side?

There are a few clues in the story. As you read it, maybe you can see what Mr. Rex sees. If you know anything about chickens, you might be able to solve the mystery. Escape to the *Holt Anthology of Science Fiction* and read "The Homesick Chicken."

UNIT 1

Matter and Motion

SCIENCE

Place to Visit

The Hill Country Flyer is a steam-powered train based in Cedar Park, just northwest of Austin, Texas. The locomotive used for the trains is the Southern Pacific Number 786. Built in 1916, the locomotive operated on the Southern Pacific's Texas and Louisiana lines until 1956. Since 1992, however, the 786 has powered an excursion train on Saturdays and Sundays. The train covers a 53 km route between Cedar Park and Burnet. The ride from one town to the other takes about 2 hours, which means that the train travels at an average speed of 7.4 m/s.

Cedar Park

All aboard! Tickets, please, for the Hill Country Flyer!

Science Fact

Amarillo ★

Ninety percent of the world's helium comes from the Amarillo area in the Texas panhandle. The Helium Centennial Time Columns Monument celebrates Amarillo's claim to fame as the "Helium Capital of the World." The monument has four columns to model the structure of a helium atom. Each column is a time capsule that contains everyday items, such as plant seeds, movies, a projector, and even a dehydrated apple pie! The capsules are also filled with helium, which is unreactive. The helium will help preserve the items in the capsules until the capsules are opened at specific times in the future.

Science Career

Austin ★

Sara McElroy is Conservator at the Blanton Museum of Art, in Austin, Texas. Her career combines art and science. She finds the best way to care for the museum's art objects, and she looks for ways to preserve and exhibit the objects. McElroy uses several scientific tools, including X-ray machines, in her work. Sometimes, she must determine whether a painting is genuine. McElroy looks at X-ray images of a painting to discover the kinds of paint that an artist used, or she uses X-ray images to study the artist's technique.

internet**connect**

go.hrw.com

go to: go.hrw.com
KEYWORD: HTXU61

The Properties of Matter

Pre-Reading Questions

1. What is matter? ★TEKS
2. What is made when two or more substances are chemically combined? ★TEKS
3. How would you classify water, salt, and sugar according to their physical and chemical properties? ★TEKS

NICE ICE

You've seen water in many forms: steam rising from a kettle, dew collecting on grass, and tiny crystals of frost forming on the windows in winter. But no matter what its form, water is still water. In this chapter, you'll learn more about the many different properties of matter such as the property of state. You'll also learn about changes in matter that take place all around you.

SACK SECRETS ⭐TEKS

All objects have certain properties. In this activity, you will test your skills in determining the identity of an object based on some of its properties.

Procedure

1. You and two or three of your classmates will receive a **sealed paper sack** containing a **mystery object**. Do not open the sack!

2. For 5 minutes, make as many observations as you can about the object. You may shake the sack and touch, smell, or listen to the object through the sack. Be sure to write down your observations.

Analysis

3. At the end of 5 minutes, discuss your findings with your partners.

4. In your ScienceLog, list the object's properties. Make a conclusion about the object's identity.

5. Share your observations, list of properties, and conclusion with the class. Now you are ready to open the sack.

6. Did you properly identify the object? If so, how? If not, why not? Write your answers in your ScienceLog. Share them with the class.

READING WARM-UP

Terms to Learn

matter   mass
volume   weight
meniscus   inertia

What You'll Do

- Define matter. ⭐TEKS
- Describe how volume and mass are measured.
- Compare mass and weight.
- Explain the relationship between mass and inertia.

What Is Matter?

What do you have in common with a toaster, a steaming bowl of soup, or a bright neon sign?

You are probably thinking this is a trick question. After all, it is hard to imagine that a human—you—has anything in common with a kitchen appliance, some hot soup, or a glowing neon sign.

Everything Is Made of Matter

From a scientific point of view, you have at least one characteristic in common with these things. You, the toaster, the bowl, the soup, the steam, the glass tubing, and the glowing neon gas are all made of matter. But what exactly is matter? If so many different kinds of things are made of matter, you might expect the definition of the word *matter* to be complicated. But it is really quite simple. **Matter** is anything that has volume and mass.

Matter Has Volume

One characteristic of all matter is that it takes up space. The amount of space taken up, or occupied, by an object is known as the object's **volume.** The Statue of Liberty, the Atlantic Ocean, and a cloud all have volume. Because these things have volume, they cannot share the same space at the same time. Even the tiniest speck of dust takes up space. There's no way another speck of dust can fit into that space without somehow bumping the first speck out of the way. **Figure 1** shows another example of how two things cannot share the same space at the same time. Try the QuickLab on the next page to see for yourself how matter takes up space—even if you can't see it.

Figure 1 *Because CDs are made of matter, they have volume. Once your CD storage rack is filled with CDs, you cannot fit another CD in the rack.*

Liquid Volume

Lake Erie, the smallest of the Great Lakes, has a volume of about 483 trillion (that's 483,000,000,000,000) liters of water. Can you imagine that much liquid? Think of a 2-liter bottle of soda. The water in Lake Erie could fill more than 241 trillion 2-liter soda bottles. On a smaller scale, a can of soda has a volume of 355 milliliters. This is about one-third of a liter. You can check the volume of a soda can using a measuring cup from your kitchen.

Liters (L) and milliliters (mL) are the units used most often to express the volume of liquids. The volume of any amount of liquid, from one raindrop to a can of soda to an entire ocean, can be expressed in these units.

Measuring the Volume of Liquids

In your science class, you'll use a graduated cylinder instead of a measuring cup to measure the volume of liquids. Keep in mind that the surface of a liquid in a graduated cylinder is curved. This curve is called the **meniscus** (muh NIS kuhs). To measure liquid volume, you must look at the bottom of the meniscus, as shown in **Figure 2.** In fact, liquid in any container, even a measuring cup or a large beaker, has a meniscus. The meniscus is just too flat to see in a wide container.

BRAIN FOOD

The volume of a typical raindrop is about 0.09 mL. It would take almost 4,000 raindrops to fill a soda can.

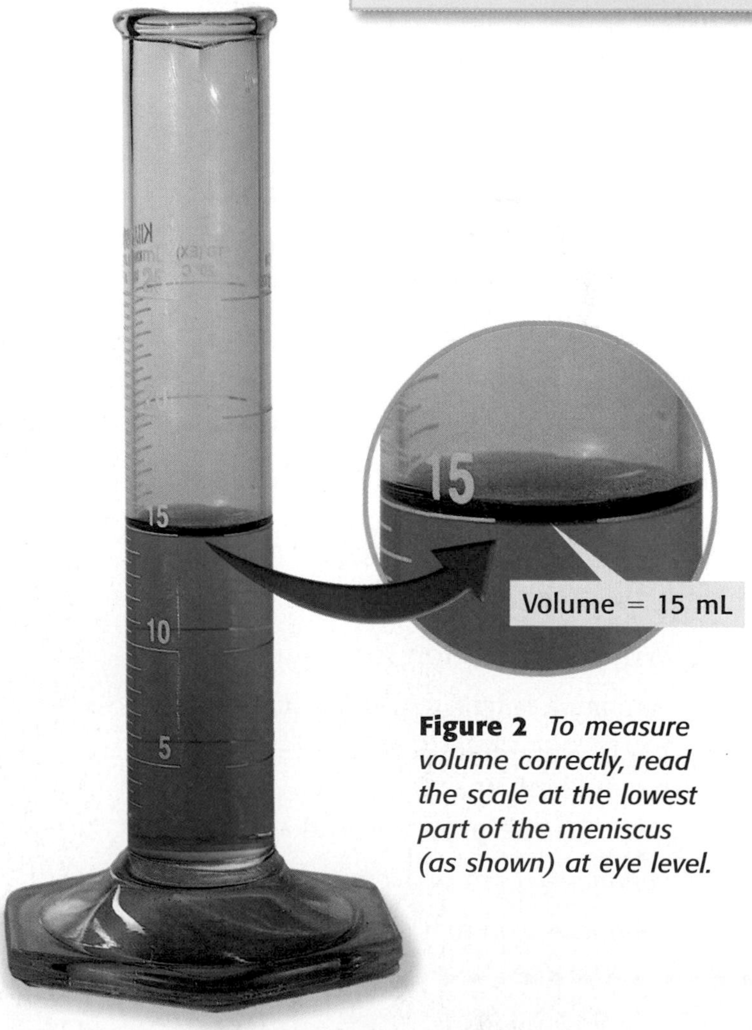

Volume = 15 mL

Figure 2 *To measure volume correctly, read the scale at the lowest part of the meniscus (as shown) at eye level.*

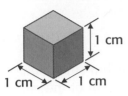

Figure 3 *A cubic centimeter (1 cm³) can be pictured as a cube that has a length, width, and height of 1 cm.*

Solid Volume

The volume of any solid object is expressed in cubic units. The word *cubic* means "having three dimensions." In science, cubic meters (m^3) and cubic centimeters (cm^3) are the units used most often to express the volume of solid things. The 3 in these unit abbreviations shows that three quantities, or dimensions, were multiplied to get the result. You can see the three dimensions of a cubic centimeter in **Figure 3.** Volume can be found using the following equation:

$$volume = length \times width \times height$$

Measuring the Volume of Solids

How do you find the volume of a solid that isn't rectangular? For example, to find the volume of a 12-sided die, you cannot use the equation given above. You can measure the volume of any solid object by measuring the volume of water that it displaces. In **Figure 4,** when the die is added to the water in a graduated cylinder, the water level rises. Because 1 mL is equal to 1 cm^3, you can express the volume of the water displaced by the die in cubic centimeters. The volume of water displaced is equal to the volume of the die. (Although volumes of liquids can be expressed in cubic units, volumes of solids should not be expressed in liters or milliliters.)

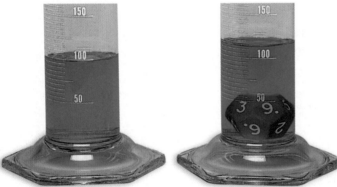

Figure 4 *The die displaced 15 mL of water, so the die's volume is 15 cm³.*

MathFocus ....

Finding the Volume of Rectangular Solids

What is the *volume* of a rectangular box with a *length* of 5 cm, a *width* of 1 cm, and a *height* of 2 cm?

Step 1: Write the equation for volume.

$$volume = length \times width \times height$$

Step 2: Replace the length, width, and height with the measurements given in the problem, and solve.

$$volume = 5 \text{ cm} \times 1 \text{ cm} \times 2 \text{ cm}$$

$$volume = 10 \text{ cm}^3$$

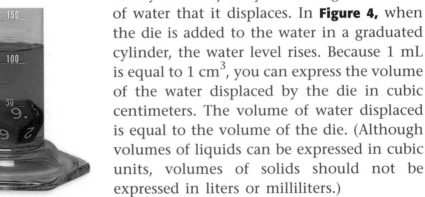

Now It's Your Turn

1 A CD case has a length of 14.2 cm, a width of 12.4 cm, and a height of 1.0 cm. What is its volume?

2 What is the volume of a suitcase with a length of 95 cm, a width of 50 cm, and a height of 20 cm?

Matter Has Mass

Another characteristic of all matter is mass. **Mass** is the amount of matter that something is made of. You are made of matter. A peanut is also made of matter. You are made of more matter than a peanut, so you have more mass. The basic SI unit of mass is the kilogram (kg). Mass is often expressed in grams (g) and milligrams (mg) as well.

The mass of an object is the same no matter where the object is in the universe. The only way to change something's mass is to change the amount of matter it is made of.

Self-Check

What are the two characteristics of all matter? *(See page 640 to check your answer.)* ✪TEKS

The Difference Between Mass and Weight

The terms *mass* and *weight* are often used as though they mean the same thing. But they don't. **Weight** is a measure of the gravitational force exerted on an object. Gravitational force is what keeps objects on Earth from floating into space. Also, the gravitational force between an object and the Earth depends partly on the object's mass. The more massive an object is, the greater the gravitational force on it and the greater the object's weight. An object's weight can also change depending on where it is in the universe. For example, an object would weigh less on the moon than it does on Earth. **Figure 5** will help you understand more about the differences between mass and weight.

Figure 5	Differences Between Mass and Weight
Mass	**Weight**
◆ Mass is a measure of the amount of matter in an object.	◆ Weight is a measure of the gravitational force on an object.
◆ Mass is always constant for an object no matter where the object is in the universe.	◆ Weight varies depending on where the object is in relation to the Earth (or any large body in the universe).
◆ Mass is expressed in kilograms (kg), grams (g), and milligrams (mg).	◆ Weight is expressed in newtons (N).
◆ Mass is measured with a balance (shown below).	◆ Weight is measured with a spring scale (shown at right).

Mass, Weight, and Bathroom Scales

Ordinary bathroom scales are spring scales. Many scales used today show readings in both pounds and kilograms. (Pounds are an ordinary, though not SI, unit of weight.) How do such readings add to the confusion between mass and weight?

Figure 6 *Why is a car hard to push? It's hard to push because of inertia.*

Mass Is a Measure of Inertia

Imagine trying to kick a soccer ball that has the mass of a bowling ball. It would be painful! The reason has to do with inertia (in UHR shuh). **Inertia** is the tendency of all objects to resist any change in motion. Because of inertia, an object at rest will remain at rest until something causes it to move. Also, a moving object continues to move at the same speed and in the same direction unless something acts on it to change its speed or direction.

Mass is a measure of inertia. Something with a large mass is harder to get moving and harder to stop than something with a smaller mass. The reason is that the object with the larger mass has greater inertia. Imagine that you are going to push a grocery cart. It's easy, right? But suppose you are pushing a car instead, as in **Figure 6.** The total mass—and the inertia—of the car is much greater than the mass and inertia of the grocery cart. It is harder to get the car moving, but it is also harder to stop the car once it is moving. You might step in front of a moving grocery cart to stop it, but you would never step in front of a moving car.

internetconnect

SCiLINKS.
NSTA GO TO: www.scilinks.org

TOPIC: What Is Matter?
sciLINKS NUMBER: HSTP030

SECTION REVIEW

❶ Define matter. ⭐TEKS

❷ How is volume measured? How is mass measured?

❸ Which has more inertia, a motorcycle or a truck?

❹ **Math Practice** A suitcase has a length of 60 cm, a width of 40 cm, and a height of 20 cm. What is the volume of clothes that it can hold?

Terms to Learn

physical property
density
chemical property
physical change
chemical change

What You'll Do

- Give examples of different properties of matter.
- Classify substances by their physical and chemical properties. ⭐TEKS
- Explain what happens to matter during physical and chemical changes.
- Compare the properties of new substances with those of the original substances after a chemical change has taken place. ⭐TEKS

Describing Matter

Have you ever played the game 20 Questions? If you can figure out what object another person is thinking of by asking 20 yes/no questions or less, you win!

What if you can't figure out the object's identity after asking 20 questions? You may not be asking the right kinds of questions. What kinds of questions should you ask? You might ask questions about the properties of the object. Knowing the properties of an object can help you find out what it is.

Physical Properties

The questions shown below help the person asking them gather information. He asks about *color* (Is it orange?), *odor* (Does it have an odor?), and *mass* and *volume* (Could I hold it in my hand?). Each piece of information is a physical property of matter. A **physical property** can be observed or measured without changing the identity of the matter. For example, you don't have to change the identity of an apple to see that it is red or to measure its volume.

Could I hold it in my hand?   Yes.
Does it have an odor? Yes.
Is it safe to eat?   Yes.
Is it orange? No.
Is it yellow? No.
Is it red? Yes.

Is it an apple?

YES!

·····Activity····

With a partner, play a game of 20 Questions. One person will think of an object. The other person will ask yes/no questions about it. When the object is identified or when the 20 questions are up, switch roles. Good luck!

TRY at HOME

Figure 7 Examples of Physical Properties

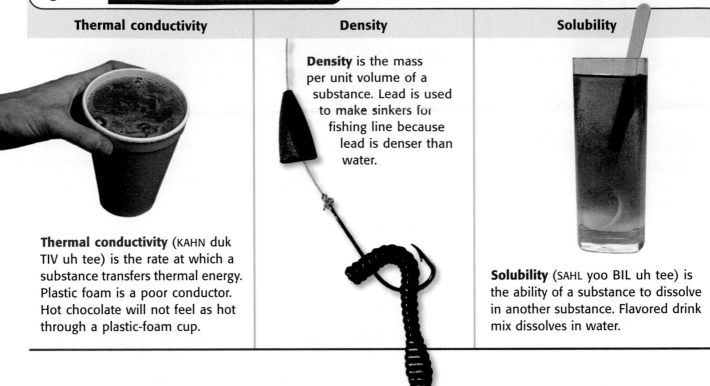

| Thermal conductivity | Density | Solubility |

Thermal conductivity (KAHN duk TIV uh tee) is the rate at which a substance transfers thermal energy. Plastic foam is a poor conductor. Hot chocolate will not feel as hot through a plastic-foam cup.

Density is the mass per unit volume of a substance. Lead is used to make sinkers for fishing line because lead is denser than water.

Solubility (SAHL yoo BIL uh tee) is the ability of a substance to dissolve in another substance. Flavored drink mix dissolves in water.

Physical Properties Identify Matter

You use physical properties all the time. For example, physical properties help you determine if your socks are clean (odor), if you can fit all your books into your backpack (volume), or if your shirt matches your pants (color). **Figure 7** shows some more examples of physical properties that are useful in describing or identifying matter.

mass = 46 g

mass = 2 g

Figure 8 *A golf ball is denser than a table-tennis ball. That's because the golf ball contains more matter in a similar volume.*

Spotlight on Density

The definition of *density* given in the chart above is mass per unit volume. If you think back to what you learned in Section 1, you can define *density* in other terms. **Density** is the amount of matter in a given space, or volume. Look at the golf ball and the table-tennis ball in **Figure 8.** The balls have similar volumes, but the golf ball has more mass. So, the golf ball is denser.

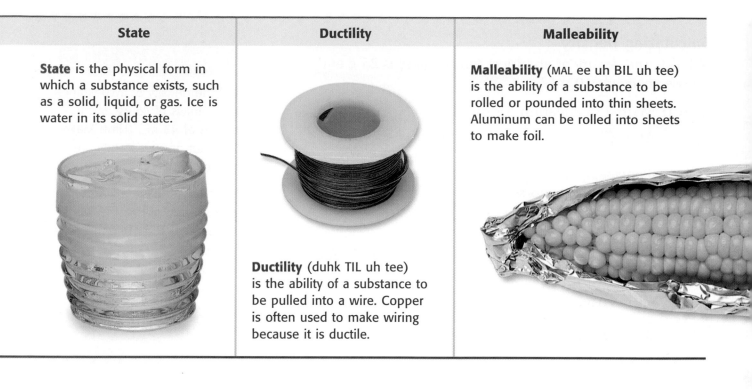

State	Ductility	Malleability
State is the physical form in which a substance exists, such as a solid, liquid, or gas. Ice is water in its solid state.	**Ductility** (duhk TIL uh tee) is the ability of a substance to be pulled into a wire. Copper is often used to make wiring because it is ductile.	**Malleability** (MAL ee uh BIL uh tee) is the ability of a substance to be rolled or pounded into thin sheets. Aluminum can be rolled into sheets to make foil.

Liquid Layers

What do you think causes the liquid in **Figure 9** to look the way it does? Is it magic? No, it's differences in density! In fact, there are six different liquids in the graduated cylinder. Each liquid has a different density. Because of these differences in density, the liquids separate into layers. The densest layer settles on the bottom, and the least dense layer settles on top. The order in which the layers separate shows you their order by increasing density: yellow, then colorless, then pink, then blue, then green, then brown.

When you mix oil and vinegar to make salad dressing, the liquids separate. The oil rises to the top. What would happen if you added more oil? What would happen if you added so much oil that there was several times as much oil as there was vinegar? Would the oil sink below the vinegar? No! No matter how much oil you have, it will always be less dense than the vinegar. The oil will always rise to the top. Density does not depend on the quantity of a substance.

Figure 9 *This graduated cylinder contains six different liquids. From top to bottom they are corn oil, water, shampoo, dish detergent, anti-freeze, and maple syrup.*

Finding Density

To find an object's density (D), first measure its mass (m) and volume (V). Then use the equation below. Units for density are expressed using a mass unit divided by a volume unit, such as g/cm^3, g/mL, kg/m^3, and kg/L.

$$density = \frac{mass}{volume} \quad \text{or} \quad D = \frac{m}{V}$$

MathFocus

Calculating Density

What is the *density* of an object whose *mass* is 25 g and whose *volume* is 10 mL?

Step 1: Write the equation for density.

$$D = \frac{m}{V}$$

Step 2: Replace *m* and *V* with the measurements given in the problem, and solve.

$$D = \frac{25 \text{ g}}{10 \text{ mL}} = 2.5 \text{ g/mL}$$

The equation for density can also be rearranged to find mass and volume, as shown.

$$m = DV \text{ (rearrange by multiplying by } V\text{)}$$

$$V = \frac{m}{D} \text{ (rearrange by dividing by } D\text{)}$$

Now It's Your Turn

1. Find the density of a substance with a mass of 15 kg and a volume of 43 m^3. (Hint: Make sure your answer's units are units of density.)

2. Suppose you have a lead ball with a mass of 454 g. What is its volume? (Hint: Use the table below.)

Comparing Densities of Different Substances

The density of a substance changes with changes in pressure and temperature. When the densities of different substances are being compared, the substances must be at the same temperature and pressure. The standard conditions under which density is measured are 20°C and normal atmospheric pressure. Look at the table below to compare densities of several substances.

Densities of Common Substances*			
Substance	Density (g/cm^3)	Substance	Density (g/cm^3)
Helium (gas)	0.0001663	Oxygen (gas)	0.001331
Water (liquid)	1.000	Lead (solid)	11.35
Gold (solid)	19.32	Mercury (liquid)	13.55

* at 20°C and normal atmospheric pressure

MID-SECTION REVIEW

1. List three physical properties of water.

2. How can you determine the densities of liquids?

3. **Interpreting Graphics** The grease separator shown at left is used to collect meat juices for making gravies. Describe how this device works in terms of density.

Chemical Properties

Other properties that describe matter are chemical properties. A **chemical property** describes matter based on its ability to change into new matter with different properties. For example, a piece of wood can be burned to create new matter (ash and smoke). The new matter has very different properties than the original piece of wood. Wood has the chemical property of *flammability*—the ability to burn. Gold, which does not burn, has the chemical property of nonflammability. Some everyday chemical properties are shown in **Figure 10.** (Note: The word *reactivity* refers to the ability of two or more substances to combine and form a new substance or substances.)

Chemical properties aren't as easy to observe as physical properties. For example, you observe the flammability of wood only while the wood is burning. Similarly, you observe the nonflammability of gold only when you try to burn it and it won't burn. But a substance always has its chemical properties. A piece of wood is flammable even when it's not burning.

Figure 10   Examples of Chemical Properties

Reactivity with oxygen	Nonreactivity with oxygen	Flammability	Nonflammability
The iron used in this old car has the chemical property of **reactivity with oxygen.** When iron is exposed to oxygen, it rusts.	The bumper on this car is rust-free because it is coated with chromium. Chromium has the chemical property of **nonreactivity with oxygen.**	The propane gas used as fuel in this camping stove has the property of **flammability.**	The aluminum mixture used to make cooking pots for camping has the chemical property of **nonflammability.**

Figure 11 Physical Vs. Chemical Properties

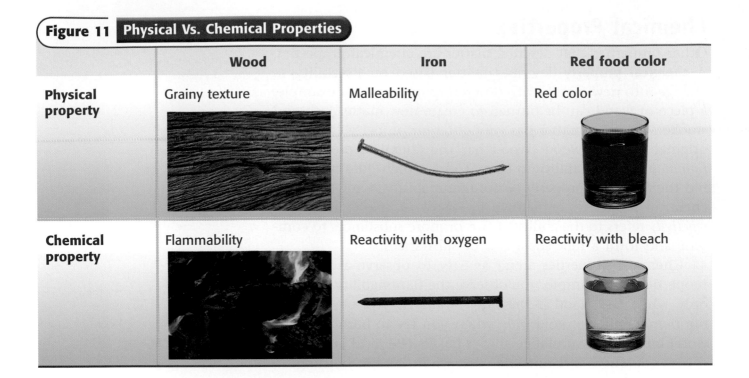

	Wood	Iron	Red food color
Physical property	Grainy texture	Malleability	Red color
Chemical property	Flammability	Reactivity with oxygen	Reactivity with bleach

Comparing Physical and Chemical Properties

It is important to remember the differences between physical and chemical properties. For example, you can observe physical properties without changing the identity of the substance. You can observe chemical properties only when the identity of the substance can change. **Figure 11** shows the distinction between physical and chemical properties for some substances.

Characteristic Properties

You can describe matter by both physical and chemical properties. The properties that are most useful in identifying a substance are its characteristic properties. Density, solubility, and reactivity with acids are characteristic properties. The *characteristic properties* of a substance are always the same no matter what size the sample is. Scientists rely on characteristic properties to identify and classify substances.

Physical Changes Don't Form New Substances

A **physical change** is a change that affects one or more physical properties of a substance. Imagine that you break a piece of chalk in two or more pieces. You are changing its physical properties of size and shape. But no matter how many times you break it, chalk is still chalk. The chemical properties of the chalk remain the same. Each piece of chalk would still give off bubbles if you placed it in vinegar.

BRAIN FOOD

Bending a bar of tin produces a squealing sound known as a tin cry.

Examples of Physical Changes

The butter in **Figure 12** has gone through the physical change of melting. Another physical change happens when a substance dissolves in another substance. Imagine dissolving sugar in water. The sugar seems to disappear into the water. But the identity of the sugar does not change. If you taste the water, you will taste that the sugar is still there. The sugar has gone through a physical change. The list below shows more examples of physical changes.

◆ Freezing water for ice cubes
◆ Sanding a piece of wood
◆ Cutting your hair
◆ Crushing an aluminum can
◆ Bending a paper clip
◆ Mixing oil and vinegar

Figure 12 *A physical change turned a stick of butter into the liquid butter that makes popcorn so tasty, but the identity of the butter did not change.*

Matter and Physical Changes

Physical changes do not change the identity of the matter involved. If you leave butter out on a warm counter, it will undergo a physical change—it will melt. Putting it back in the refrigerator will reverse this change. In the same way, if you make a figure from a lump of clay, you change the clay's shape and cause a physical change. The identity of the clay does not change. The clay has the same properties as a figure that it had when it was just a lump.

Chemical Changes Form New Substances

A **chemical change** happens when two or more substances are changed into one or more new substances with different properties. The chemical properties of substances describe which chemical changes will or will not happen. Keep in mind that chemical changes and chemical properties are not the same thing. A chemical property describes a substance's ability to go through a chemical change. A chemical change is the process in which two or more substances change into one or more new substances. You can observe chemical properties only when a chemical change might occur.

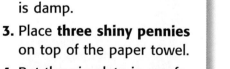

QuickLab

Changing Change

1. Place a **folded paper towel** in a **small pie plate.**
2. Pour **vinegar** into the pie plate until the paper towel is damp.
3. Place **three shiny pennies** on top of the paper towel.
4. Put the pie plate in a safe place. Wait 24 hours.
5. Describe the chemical change that took place.
6. Compare the properties of the new substance formed with those of the original substances.

★TEKS

What Happens During a Chemical Change?

A fun (and delicious) way to see what happens during chemical changes is to bake a cake. When you bake a cake, you combine eggs, flour, sugar, oil, and other ingredients, as shown in **Figure 13.** Each ingredient has its own set of properties. But if you mix the ingredients together and bake the batter in the oven, you get something completely different. The heat of the oven and the interaction of the cake ingredients cause a chemical change. In the end, you get a cake that has properties that are different from any of the ingredients. **Figure 14** shows other examples of chemical changes.

Figure 13 *Each of these ingredients has different physical and chemical properties.*

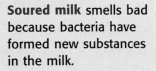 **Examples of Chemical Changes**

Soured milk smells bad because bacteria have formed new substances in the milk.

Effervescent tablets bubble when dropped in water. The citric acid and baking soda in them combine in water to form a gas.

Hot gas forms when hydrogen and oxygen join to make water. This chemical change helps blast the space shuttle into space.

The Statue of Liberty was made of shiny, orange-brown copper. But the metal's interaction with moist air has formed new substances, copper sulfate, copper chloride, and copper carbonate. These chemical changes made the statue green over time.

Get a Clue!

Look back at the bottom of the previous page. In each picture, there is at least one clue that signals a chemical change. Can you find the clues? Below is a list of clues that tell you that a chemical change is taking place.

◆ Changes in color
◆ Heat
◆ Fizzing and foaming
◆ Production of sound or light

In the cake example, you would probably smell the sweetness of the cake as it baked. If you looked into the oven, you would see the batter rise and begin to brown. When you cut the finished cake, you would see the air pockets made by gas bubbles that formed in the batter. All of these clues are signs of chemical changes.

Matter and Chemical Changes

Chemical changes change the identity of the matter involved. So, most of the chemical changes in your daily life, such as a cake baking or milk turning sour, would be hard to reverse. Imagine trying to unbake the cake shown in **Figure 15** by pulling out each ingredient. It would never work! However, some chemical changes can be reversed under the right conditions with more chemical changes. For example, the water formed in the space shuttle's rockets could be split back into hydrogen and oxygen using an electric current.

Figure 15 *Are you looking for the original ingredients? You won't find them. Their identities have changed.*

SECTION REVIEW

1. Classify each of the following properties as either physical or chemical: reacts with water, dissolves in oil, is blue, and does not react with hydrogen.

2. Using one physical property, classify the following substances as a group: water, oil, mercury, and alcohol. **⭐TEKS**

3. Hydrogen gas and oxygen gas can chemically combine to make water. How do the physical and chemical properties of the original substances (hydrogen and oxygen) differ from those of the new substance (water)? **⭐TEKS**

4. **Comparing Concepts** Describe the difference between physical and chemical changes in terms of what happens to the matter involved in each kind of change.

internet**connect**

SCi**LINKS**

NSTA GO TO: www.scilinks.org

TOPIC: Salt in Texas
*sci*LINKS NUMBER: HSTX160

TOPIC: Describing Matter
*sci*LINKS NUMBER: HSTP035

Skill Builder Lab

White Before Your Eyes ⊙TEKS

You have learned how to describe matter based on its physical and chemical properties. You have also learned some clues that can help you determine if a change in matter is a physical change or a chemical change. In this lab, you'll use what you have learned to describe four substances based on their properties and the changes they undergo.

- 4 spatulas
- baking powder
- plastic-foam egg carton
- 3 eyedroppers
- water
- stirring rod
- vinegar
- iodine solution
- baking soda
- cornstarch
- sugar

Procedure

1 Copy Tables 1 and 2, shown on the next page, into your ScienceLog. Be sure to leave plenty of room in each box to write down your observations. Before you start the lab, put on your safety goggles.

2 Use a spatula to place a small amount of baking powder (just enough to cover the bottom of the cup) into three cups of your egg carton. Look closely at the baking powder. Record your observations about its appearance, such as color and texture, in Table 1 in the column titled "Unmixed."

3 Use an eyedropper to add 60 drops of water to the baking powder in the first cup. Stir with the stirring rod. Record your observations in Table 1 in the column titled "Mixed with water." Clean your stirring rod.

4 Use a clean dropper to add 20 drops of vinegar to the second cup of baking powder. Stir. Record your observations in Table 1 in the column titled "Mixed with vinegar." Clean your stirring rod.

5 Use a clean dropper to add five drops of iodine solution to the third cup of baking powder. Stir. Record your observations in Table 1 in the column titled "Mixed with iodine solution." Clean your stirring rod.
Caution: Be careful when using iodine. Iodine will stain your skin and clothes.

6 Repeat steps 2–5 for each of the other substances (baking soda, cornstarch, and sugar). Use a clean spatula for each substance.

Table 1 Observations				
Substance	Unmixed	Mixed with water	Mixed with vinegar	Mixed with iodine solution
Baking powder				
Baking soda				
Cornstarch				
Sugar				

Table 2 Changes and Properties						
	Mixed with water		Mixed with vinegar		Mixed with iodine solution	
Substance	Change	Property	Change	Property	Change	Property
Baking powder						
Baking soda						
Cornstarch						
Sugar						

Analysis

7 What physical properties do all four substances share?

8 In Table 2, write the type of change you observed for each substance, and state the property that the change demonstrates.

9 Classify the four substances by their chemical properties. For example, which substances are reactive with vinegar (acid)?

10 Communicate your results to your classmates.

Section 1

Vocabulary

matter *(p. 38)*
volume *(p. 38)*
meniscus *(p. 39)*
mass *(p. 41)*
weight *(p. 41)*
inertia *(p. 42)*

Section Notes

- Matter is anything that has volume and mass. ⭐TEKS

- Volume is the amount of space taken up by an object.

- The volume of liquids is expressed in liters and milliliters.

- The volume of solid objects is expressed in cubic units, such as cubic meters.

- Mass is the amount of matter in an object.

- Mass and weight are not the same thing. Weight is a measure of the gravitational force on an object, usually in relation to the Earth.

- Mass is usually expressed in milligrams, grams, and kilograms.

- Inertia is the tendency of all objects to resist any change in motion. Mass is a measure of inertia. The more massive an object is, the greater its inertia.

Section 2

Vocabulary

physical property *(p. 43)*
density *(p. 44)*
chemical property *(p. 47)*
physical change *(p. 48)*
chemical change *(p. 49)*

Section Notes

- Physical properties of matter can be observed without changing the identity of the matter.

- Density is the amount of matter in a given space, or mass per unit volume.

- The density of a substance is always the same at a given pressure and temperature, regardless of the size of the sample of the substance.

- Chemical properties describe a substance based on its ability to change into a new substance or new substances with different properties.

- Chemical properties can be observed only when new substances can be made.

- The characteristic properties of a substance are always the same no matter if the sample you're observing is large or small. Physical and chemical properties can be used to classify substances and to distinguish between different substances. ⭐TEKS

- When a substance undergoes a physical change, its identity remains the same.

- A chemical change happens when one or more substances are changed into new substances with different properties. ⭐TEKS

LabBook ⭐TEKS

Layering Liquids *(p. 603)*
Determining Density *(p. 604)*

Review

USING VOCABULARY

For each pair of terms, explain how the meanings of the terms differ.

1. mass/volume

2. mass/weight

3. liter/kilogram

4. physical property/chemical property

5. physical change/chemical change

UNDERSTANDING CONCEPTS

Multiple Choice

6. Which of these is NOT matter? ⭐TEKS
   a. a cloud   c. sunshine
   b. your hair   d. the sun

7. The mass of an elephant on the moon would be
   a. less than its mass on Mars.
   b. more than its mass on Mars.
   c. the same as its weight on the moon.
   d. None of the above

8. Which of the following is NOT a chemical property?
   a. reactivity with oxygen
   b. malleability
   c. flammability
   d. reactivity with acid

9. Your weight could be expressed in which of the following units?
   a. pounds
   b. newtons
   c. grams
   d. both (a) and (b)

10. Breaking your pencil in half is an example of
    a. a physical change.
    b. a chemical change.
    c. density.
    d. volume.

11. Which of the following statements about density is true?
    a. Density is mass per unit volume.
    b. Density is weight per unit volume.
    c. Density is measured in milliliters.
    d. Density is a chemical property.

12. Inertia increases as __?__ increases.
    a. time   c. mass
    b. length   d. volume

Short Answer

13. You, the food you eat, and the air you breathe are all made of matter. Define matter. ⭐TEKS

14. In one or two sentences, explain the different processes in measuring the volume of a liquid and measuring the volume of a solid.

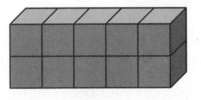

15. Explain the relationship between mass and inertia.

16. Classify gold and wood according to their chemical and physical properties. ⭐TEKS

17. Use the following terms to create a concept map: *matter, chemical properties, mass, physical changes, volume, chemical changes,* and *physical properties.*

CRITICAL THINKING AND PROBLEM SOLVING

Write one or two sentences to answer the following questions:

18. You are making breakfast for your picky friend, Filbert. You scramble the eggs. He asks, "Would you please take these eggs back to the kitchen and poach them?" What scientific reason do you give Filbert for not changing his eggs? ⭐TEKS

Poach these, please!

19. You look out your bedroom window and see your new neighbor moving in. Your neighbor bends over to pick up a small cardboard box, but he cannot lift it. What can you conclude about the item(s) in the box? Use the terms *mass* and *inertia* to explain how you came to this conclusion.

20. David wanted to find out which substance had the chemical property of reactivity with acid. He added a drop of vinegar to the first substance. Then he added a drop of water to the second substance. How could he have improved his experiment?

MATH IN SCIENCE

21. A book has a width of 10 cm, a length that is two times the width, and a height that is half the width. What is the book's volume?

22. A jar contains 30 mL of glycerin (*mass* = 37.8 g) and 60 mL of corn syrup (*mass* = 82.8 g). Which liquid is on top? Show your work, and explain your answer.

INTERPRETING GRAPHICS

Examine the photograph below, and answer the questions that follow.

23. List three physical properties of this can.

24. Did a chemical change or a physical change cause this can to change?

25. Can you tell what the chemical properties of the can are just by looking at the picture? Explain your answer.

Reading Check-up

⭐TEKS Take a minute to review your answers to the Pre-Reading Questions found at the bottom of page 36. Have your answers changed? If necessary, revise your answers based on what you have learned since you began this chapter.

Chapter 2

1 Which of the following best defines matter?

A Matter is all things.

B Matter is anything that has mass and weight.

C Matter is anything that has volume and mass.

D Matter is anything that has volume.

2 In an experiment to compare densities of liquids, you must analyze the jar shown above. Which liquid is the least dense?

F L

G M

H N

J The liquids have the same density.

3 Hydrogen and oxygen chemically combine to form water. Which statement is false?

A This is a chemical change.

B Water has the same properties as hydrogen.

C This is not a physical change.

D Hydrogen and oxygen have different properties.

4 Marcia is studying the chemical properties of the soil in her neighborhood. The tests are most accurate when performed on undisturbed soil. However, the chemicals used in the tests are poisonous to most plants and animals. Marcia decides to collect small samples of soil outside. Then, she takes the soil samples to her lab and performs the tests. Why does Marcia choose to do her study in this way?

F The tests are more accurate in the lab.

G She cannot collect large enough samples outside.

H She wants to reduce the impact of her tests on the environment.

J It costs more money to do the tests in the field.

Properties of Some Substances*		
Substance	State	Density (g/cm³)
Helium	Gas	0.0001663
Iron pyrite	Solid	5.02
Mercury	Liquid	13.55
Gold	Solid	19.32
* at room temperature and pressure		

5 Using the information above, what could you use to tell iron pyrite (fool's gold) and gold apart?

A Color

B Density

C Mass

D State

Chapter 2

Math

1 How is the product $8 \times 8 \times 2 \times 2 \times 2 \times 2 \times 2$ expressed in exponential notation?

A $8^5 \times 2^2$

B $2^8 \times 8^2$

C $8^2 \times 2^5$

D $8^8 \times 2^2$

2 What is the *volume* of the figure below?

F 2 square units

G 4 square units

H 2 cubic units

J 4 cubic units

3 On Saturday, Seresh spent $11.09 at the grocery store, $7.98 at the comic book store, and $1.96 at the newsstand. What is the total cost of Seresh's purchases?

A $19.07

B $20.03

C $21.03

D $21.97

Reading

Read the passage. Then read each question that follows the passage. Decide which is the best answer to each question.

Astronomers noticed something odd while they were studying the motions of galaxies in space. They expected to find a lot of mass in the galaxies. Instead, they discovered that the mass of the galaxies was not great enough to explain the large gravitational force causing the galaxies' rapid rotation. So what was causing the additional gravitational force? Some scientists think that the universe contains matter that we cannot see with our eyes or our telescopes. Astronomers call this invisible matter dark matter.

1 Which of these statements is a FACT in this passage?

A Galaxies rotate rapidly because of a large gravitational force.

B The motions of galaxies in space are odd.

C Dark matter accounts for all of the matter in a rotating galaxy.

D Astronomy is an exciting branch of physical science.

2 Why do you think astronomers use the term dark matter?

F It refers to dark objects.

G It refers to matter we can't see.

H You need a telescope to see it.

J All heavy objects are dark.

Building a Better Body

Have you ever broken an arm or a leg? If so, you probably wore a cast while the bone healed. But what happens when a bone is too badly damaged to heal? In some cases, a false bone made out of a metal called titanium can take the original bone's place. Could using titanium bone implants be the first step in making bionic body parts? Think about it as you read about some of titanium's amazing properties.

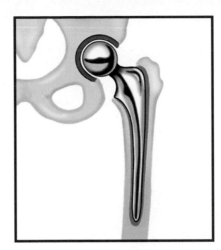

▲ *Are titanium bones even better than the real thing?*

Imitating the Original

Why would a metal like titanium be used in place of real bone? Well, it turns out that a titanium implant passes some key tests for bone replacement. First of all, real bones are incredibly lightweight and strong. Also, healthy bones last for many years. A bone-replacement material has to be lightweight but also long lasting. Titanium passes this test because it is well known for its strength and is also lightweight.

Second, the human body's immune system is always on the lookout for foreign substances. If a doctor puts a false bone in place and the patient's immune system attacks it, damage to the tissue near the false bone can result. Somehow, the false bone must be able to chemically trick the body into thinking that the bone is real. Does titanium pass this test? Keep reading!

Accepting Imitation

By studying the human body's immune system, scientists found that the body accepts certain metals. The body almost always accepts one metal in particular. You guessed it—titanium!

This discovery turned out to be quite important. Doctors could implant pieces of titanium into a person's body without causing an immune reaction. A bond can even form between titanium and existing bone tissue!

Titanium is shaping up to be a great bone-replacement material. It is lightweight and strong, and it is accepted by the body. It can join to existing bone. Also, it resists chemical changes such as corrosion. But scientists have come across a small problem. Friction can wear away titanium bones, especially those used near the hips and elbows.

Real Success

An unexpected surprise from the field of nuclear physics may have fixed the problem. Scientists can add a form of nitrogen to the surface of a piece of metal. This creates a surface layer on the metal that is especially durable. When this form of nitrogen is added to titanium bones, the bones keep all of the properties of pure titanium bones, but they become very long lasting. The new bones should last through years of heavy usage without needing to be replaced.

Think About It

▶ What will the future hold? As time goes by, doctors become better at implanting titanium bones. What do you think would happen if the titanium bones some day became better than real bones? ⭐TEKS

States of Matter

Sections

Pre-Reading Questions

1. What are four states of matter?
2. Compare the motion of particles in a solid, a liquid, and a gas.
3. Name three ways matter changes from one state to another.

IT TAKES METTLE TO MELT METAL

If you wanted to make a frozen juice pop, you would pour juice into a mold and freeze it. You are able to make the juice pop into the desired shape because liquids will take the shape of their container. Metal workers use this important property of liquids when they create metal parts that have complicated shapes. They melt the metal at extremely high temperatures and then pour it into a mold. In this chapter, you will find out more about the properties of liquids and other states of matter.

VANISHING ACT

In this activity, you will use rubbing alcohol to study a change of state.

Procedure

1. Pour **rubbing alcohol** into a **small plastic cup** until the alcohol just covers the bottom of the cup.

2. Moisten the tip of a **cotton swab** by dipping it into the alcohol in the cup.

3. Rub the cotton swab on the palm of your hand.
   Caution: Avoid touching cuts or irritated areas.

4. Record your observations in your ScienceLog.

5. Wash your hands thoroughly.

Analysis

6. Explain what happened to the alcohol.

7. Did you sense hot or cold? If so, how do you explain what you observed?

8. Record your answers in your ScienceLog.

READING WARM-UP

Terms to Learn

states of matter   pressure
solid   Boyle's law
liquid   Charles's law
gas   plasma

What You'll Do

- Describe properties that particles of all matter share.
- Describe how four states of matter differ.
- Classify substances according to their physical property of state. ⭐TEKS
- Predict how a change in pressure or temperature will affect the volume of a gas.

Four States of Matter

You've just walked home on one of the coldest days of the year. A fire is blazing in the fireplace, and there is a pot of water on the stove to make hot chocolate.

When the water begins to bubble and steam is rising from the pot, you know that the water is ready. You stir in your hot chocolate mix, but it's still too hot to drink! Rather than wait for it to cool down, you add an ice cube. You watch the ice melt in the hot liquid until the drink is at just the right temperature. Now you can enjoy your favorite hot beverage while warming yourself by the fire.

The scene described above includes examples of the four most familiar states of matter: solid, liquid, gas, and plasma. The **states of matter** are the physical forms in which a substance can exist. For example, water can exist in three different states of matter: solid (ice), liquid (water), and gas (steam).

Moving Particles Make Up All Matter

Matter is made up of tiny particles. They are too small to see without a very powerful microscope. The particles are always in motion and are always bumping into one another. State is a physical property. The state of matter that a substance takes depends on how fast the particles move. It also depends on how strongly the particles are attracted to one another. **Figure 1** describes three of the states of matter—solid, liquid, and gas—in terms of the speed and attraction of their particles. You'll learn about plasma later on in this section.

Figure 1   **Models of a Solid, a Liquid, and a Gas**

Solid	Liquid	Gas

Particles of a solid do not move fast enough to overcome the strong attraction between them. So, they are close together and vibrate in place.

Particles of a liquid move fast enough to overcome some of the attraction between them. The particles are close together but are able to slide past one another.

Particles of a gas move fast enough to overcome nearly all of the attraction between them. The particles are far apart and move independently of one another.

Solids Have Definite Shape and Volume

Imagine dropping a marble into a bottle. Even in a bottle, a marble keeps its original shape and volume. What if you moved the marble to a larger bottle? The marble's shape and volume still would not change. The state in which matter has a definite shape and volume is **solid.**

The particles of a substance in a solid are very close together. The attraction between them is stronger than the attraction between the particles of the same substance in the liquid or gaseous states. The particles in a solid do move. However, they do not move fast enough to overcome the attraction between them. Each particle vibrates in place. So, it is locked in position by the particles around it.

Two Types of Solids

Solids can be divided into two types—*crystalline* (KRIS tuhl in) and *amorphous* (uh MAWR fuhs). Crystalline solids have a very orderly, three-dimensional arrangement of particles. The particles are arranged in a repeating pattern of rows. Examples of crystalline solids are iron, diamond, and ice. Amorphous solids are made of particles that are in no special order. That is, each particle is in one spot, but the particles are in no pattern. Examples of amorphous solids are glass, rubber, and wax. Look at **Figure 2.** You can see the differences in the arrangement of particles in these two solids.

····· Activity ·····

Sitting in your chair, imagine that you are a particle in a solid. In your ScienceLog, describe the types of motion that are possible. (Remember, you cannot leave your chair.)

TRY at HOME

Figure 2 *The different arrangements of particles in crystalline solids and amorphous solids lead to different properties. Imagine trying to hit a home run with a rubber bat!*

The particles that make up a **crystalline solid** have a very orderly arrangement.

The particles in an **amorphous solid** do not have an orderly arrangement.

Figure 3 *Particles in a liquid can slide past one another. So, the liquid takes the shape of its container.*

Liquids Change Shape but Not Volume

A liquid will take the shape of any container it is put in. You are reminded of this fact every time you pour yourself a glass of juice. The state in which matter takes the shape of its container and has a definite volume is **liquid.** The particles in liquids move fast enough to overcome some of the attractions between them. The particles slide past each other until the liquid takes the shape of its container. **Figure 3** shows a model of the particles in juice.

Even though liquids change shape, they do not easily change volume. A can of soda contains a certain volume of liquid. That volume stays the same if you pour the soda into a large container or a small one. **Figure 4** shows the same volume of liquid in two different containers.

The Squeeze Is On

The particles in liquids are close to one another. So, it is difficult to push them closer together. For this reason, liquids are ideal for use in hydraulic (hie DRAW lik) systems. For example, brake fluid is the liquid used in the brake systems of cars. Stepping on the brake pedal applies a force to the liquid. The particles in the liquid move away rather than squeezing closer together. So, the fluid pushes the brake pads against the wheels. The car then slows down.

BRAIN FOOD

The Boeing 767 Freighter, a type of commercial airplane, has 187 km (116 mi) of hydraulic tubing.

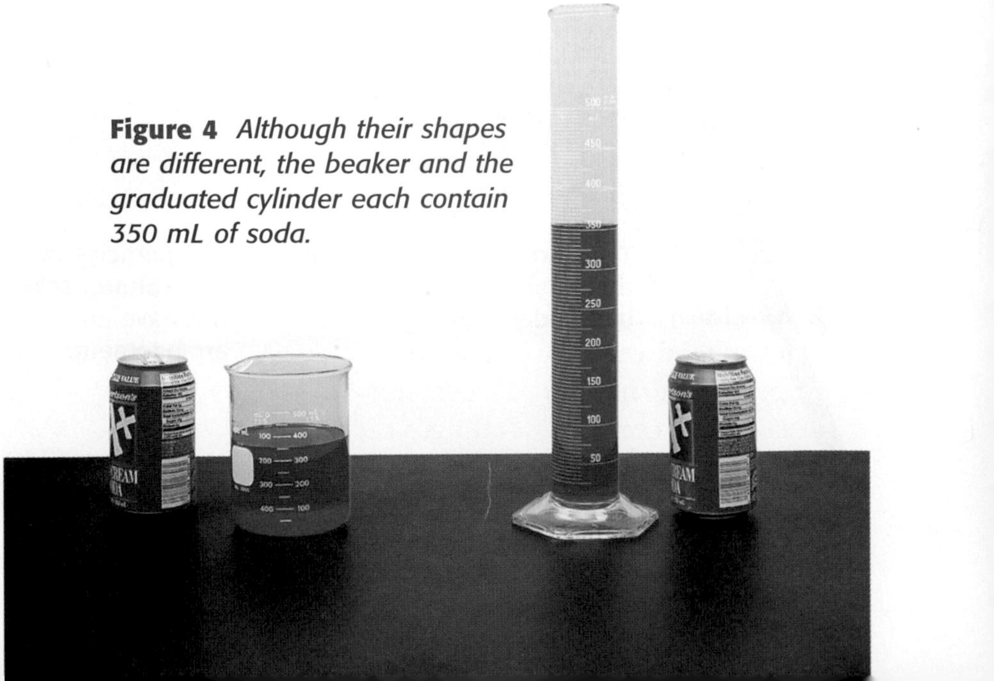

Figure 4 *Although their shapes are different, the beaker and the graduated cylinder each contain 350 mL of soda.*

A Drop in the Bucket

Two other important properties of liquids are *surface tension* and *viscosity* (vis KAHS uh tee). Surface tension is a force that acts on the particles at the surface of a liquid. It causes the liquid to form spherical drops, as shown in **Figure 5.** Different liquids have different surface tensions. For example, rubbing alcohol has a lower surface tension than water. Mercury, however, has a higher surface tension than water.

Viscosity is a liquid's resistance to flow. In general, the stronger the attractions between a liquid's particles, the more viscous the liquid is. Think of the difference between pouring honey and pouring water. Honey flows more slowly than water. So, honey has a higher viscosity than water.

Figure 5 *Liquids form spherical drops because of surface tension.*

Gases Change Both Shape and Volume

How many balloons can be filled from a single metal cylinder of helium? The number may surprise you. One cylinder of helium can fill about 700 balloons. How is this possible? After all, the volume of the metal cylinder is equal to the volume of only about 5 filled balloons. The answer has to do with helium's state.

It's a Gas!

Helium is a gas. **Gas** is the state in which matter changes in both shape and volume. The particles in a gas move very quickly. So, they can break away completely from one another. That is, the particles of a substance in the gaseous state have less attraction between them than particles of the same substance in the solid or liquid state. In a gas, there is empty space between particles.

The amount of empty space between the particles in a gas can change. Look at the example in **Figure 6.** The helium in the metal cylinder is made up of particles that have been forced very close together. As the helium fills the balloon, the particles spread out. So, the amount of empty space in the gas becomes greater. As you continue reading, you will learn how this empty space is related to pressure.

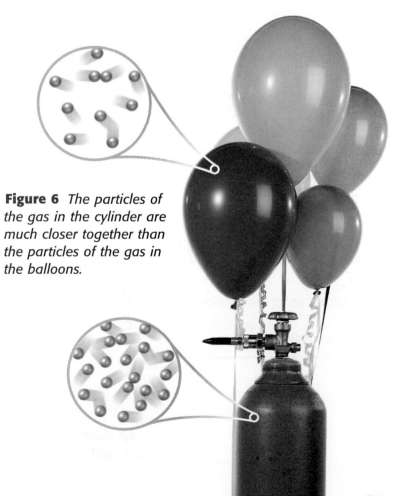

Figure 6 *The particles of the gas in the cylinder are much closer together than the particles of the gas in the balloons.*

Gas Under Pressure

The amount of force exerted on a given area is called **pressure.** You can think of pressure as the number of times the particles of a gas hit the inside of their container. For example, the balls in **Figure 7** have the same volume. They both hold particles of gas (air). These particles are always bumping into each other and into the inside surface of the balls.

Notice, however, that there are more particles in the basketball than in the beach ball. So, more particles hit the inside surface of the basketball. When more particles hit the inside surface of the ball, the force on the inside surface of the ball becomes greater. This greater force leads to greater pressure.

Figure 7   **More Force Means a Greater Pressure**

Higher pressure	Lower pressure
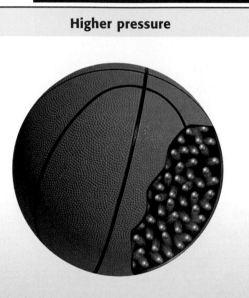	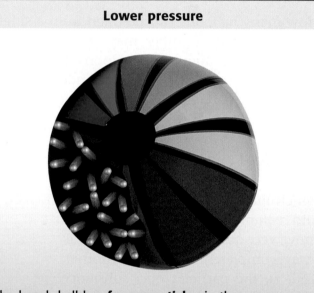
The basketball has **more particles** in the same volume. The particles hit the inside of the ball more often.	The beach ball has **fewer particles** in the same volume. The particles hit the inside of the ball less often.

MID-SECTION REVIEW

❶ Name two properties that particles of all matter share.

❷ Describe solids, liquids, and gases in terms of shape and volume.

❸ Classify each substance according to its state of matter: ice, apple juice, a slice of bread, helium in a balloon, air, water, a textbook, and steam. ⭐TEKS

❹ **Applying Concepts** Explain what happens inside the ball when you pump up a flat basketball.

Laws Describe Gas Behavior

Earlier in this chapter, you learned that the particles of solids and liquids are packed together more closely than particles of gases are. For that reason, solids and liquids do not change volume very much. Gases, on the other hand, act differently. The volume of a gas can change by a large amount.

It is easy to measure the volume of a solid or liquid. But how do you measure the volume of a gas? Isn't the volume of a gas the same as the volume of its container? The answer is yes, but there are other things, such as pressure, to consider.

Boyle's Law

Imagine that a diver 10 m below the surface of a lake is blowing a bubble of air. As the bubble rises, its volume gets larger. When the bubble reaches the surface, its volume will have doubled because of the decrease in pressure. The relationship between the volume and pressure of a gas was first described by Robert Boyle, a seventeenth-century Irish chemist. The relationship is now known as Boyle's law. **Boyle's law** states that for a fixed amount of gas at a constant temperature, the volume of the gas increases as its pressure decreases. Also, the volume of the gas decreases as its pressure increases. Boyle's law is described in **Figure 8.** Each drawing shows the same piston and the same amount of gas at the same temperature.

Figure 8 Boyle's Law

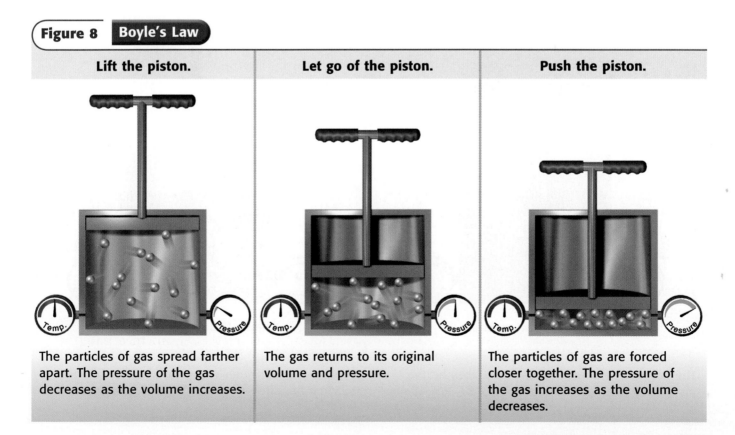

Lift the piston.	Let go of the piston.	Push the piston.
The particles of gas spread farther apart. The pressure of the gas decreases as the volume increases.	The gas returns to its original volume and pressure.	The particles of gas are forced closer together. The pressure of the gas increases as the volume decreases.

MathBreak

Gas Law Graphs

Each graph below illustrates a gas law. However, the variable on one axis of each graph is not labeled. Answer the following questions for each graph:

1. As volume goes up, what happens to the missing variable?
2. Which gas law is shown?
3. What is the missing label?

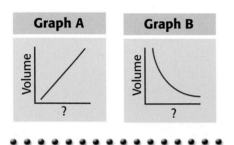

Boyle's Law and Weather Balloons

Weather balloons show a practical use of Boyle's law. A weather balloon carries equipment into the atmosphere to collect information. This information is used to predict the weather. The pressure is lower at higher altitudes. So, the volume of gas inside the balloon becomes greater as the balloon rises. For this reason, weather balloons are filled with only a small amount of gas. If the balloon were filled with too much gas, it would pop as the volume of the gas increased.

Charles's Law

An air-filled balloon will also pop when it gets too hot. This fact shows another gas law—Charles's law. **Charles's law** states that for a fixed amount of gas at a constant pressure, the volume of the gas increases as the temperature of the gas increases. Also, the volume of the gas decreases as the temperature of the gas decreases. Charles's law is shown by the model in **Figure 9.** Each drawing shows the same piston and the same amount of gas at the same pressure. You can see Charles's law in action by putting an air-filled balloon in the freezer. Wait about 10 minutes, and see what happens!

Figure 9 Charles's Law

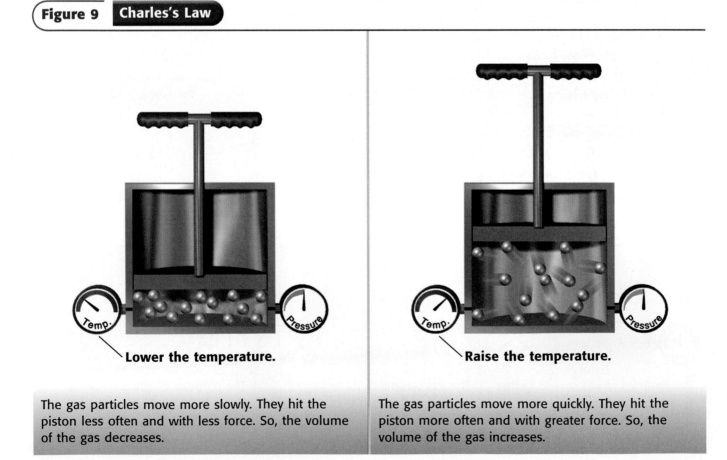

Lower the temperature.

Raise the temperature.

The gas particles move more slowly. They hit the piston less often and with less force. So, the volume of the gas decreases.

The gas particles move more quickly. They hit the piston more often and with greater force. So, the volume of the gas increases.

APPLY

Charles's Law and Bicycle Tires

Your friend put too much air in the tires on her bicycle. Use Charles's law to explain why she should let out some of the air before going for a ride on a hot day.

Plasmas

Scientists think that more than 99 percent of the known matter in the universe is made of a fourth state of matter called plasma. That matter includes the sun and other stars. **Plasma** is the state of matter that does not have a definite shape or volume and whose particles have broken apart.

Plasmas have some properties that are quite different from the properties of gases. Plasmas conduct electric current, while gases do not. Electric and magnetic fields affect plasmas but do not affect gases. In fact, strong magnetic fields are used to hold very hot plasmas that would destroy any other container.

Here on Earth, plasmas are found in lightning and fire. The beautiful light show called the aurora borealis (aw RAWR uh bawr ee AL is) in **Figure 10** also comes from plasma. Artificial plasmas are found in fluorescent lights and plasma balls. They are created by passing electric charges through gases.

Figure 10 *Auroras, like the aurora borealis seen here, form when high-energy plasma hits gas particles in the upper atmosphere.*

SECTION REVIEW

❶ When scientists record the volume of a gas, why do they also record the temperature and the pressure?

❷ List two differences between gases and plasmas.

❸ **Applying Concepts** What happens to the volume of an inflated balloon that is left on a sunny windowsill? Explain your answer.

🖥 internet**connect**

*SCI*LINKS.
NSTA   GO TO: www.scilinks.org

TOPIC: Natural and Artificial Plasma
*sci*LINKS NUMBER: HSTP065

Terms to Learn

change of state   boiling
melting   evaporation
freezing   condensation
vaporization   sublimation

What You'll Do

- Describe how substances change from state to state.
- Explain the difference between an exothermic change and an endothermic change.
- Compare the changes of state.

Changes of State

It can be tricky to eat an ice-cream cone outside on a hot day. In just minutes, the ice cream will start to melt. Soon, the solid ice cream will become a liquid mess!

When solid ice cream melts and becomes liquid, it goes through a change of state. A **change of state** is the change of a substance from one physical form to another. All changes of state are physical changes. In a physical change, the identity of a substance does not change. In **Figure 11,** the ice, liquid water, and steam are all the same substance—water. In this section, you will learn about the four changes of state shown in Figure 11. You will also learn about a fifth change of state called sublimation (SUHB luh MAY shuhn).

Energy and Changes of State

You have learned that the particles of a substance move differently depending on the state of the substance. The particles of a substance also have different amounts of energy when the substance is in different states. For example, particles in liquid water have more energy than particles in ice. Particles in steam have even more energy than the particles in liquid water.

During a change of state, a substance changes from one state to another. When a change of state happens, the energy of the particles of the substance changes. So, to change a substance from one state to another, you must add or remove energy.

Figure 11 *The terms in the arrows are changes of state. Water can go through the changes of state shown here.*

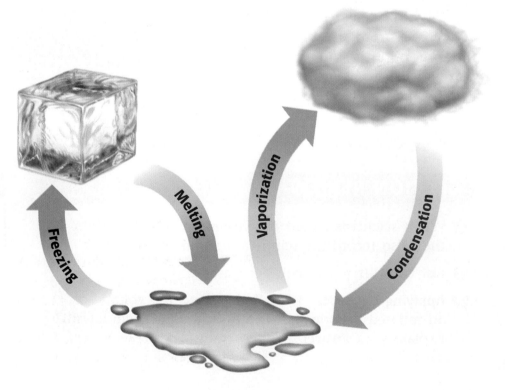

Melting: Solids to Liquids

One change of state that happens when you add energy is melting. **Melting** is the change of state from a solid to a liquid. This change of state is what happens when ice melts. You must add energy to a solid to increase the temperature of the solid. As the temperature increases, the particles of the solid speed up. However, when a certain temperature is reached, the solid will melt.

The temperature at which a substance changes from a solid to a liquid is the *melting point* of the substance. Melting point is a physical property. Different substances have different melting points. **Figure 12** shows the metal gallium melting. The melting point of gallium is 30°C. Because your normal body temperature is about 37°C, gallium will melt right in your hand! Table salt, however, has a melting point of 801°C. Most substances have a unique melting point that can be used with other properties to identify substances. The melting point of a substance is always the same no matter how much of the substance is present. For this reason, melting point is called a *characteristic property* of a substance.

Figure 12 *Even though gallium is a metal, it would not be very useful as jewelry!*

Adding Energy

For a solid to melt, particles must overcome some of their attractions to each other. When a solid is at its melting point, any energy added to it is used to overcome the attractions that hold the particles in place. Melting is an *endothermic* change because energy is gained by the substance as it changes state.

Figure 13 *Liquid water freezes at the same temperature that ice melts—0°C.*

Freezing: Liquids to Solids

The change of state from a liquid to a solid is called **freezing**. The temperature at which a liquid changes into a solid is the *freezing point*. Freezing is melting in reverse. This means that freezing and melting happen at the same temperature, as shown in **Figure 13.**

Removing Energy

For a liquid to freeze, the attractions between the particles must overcome the motion of the particles. Imagine that a liquid is at its freezing point. Removing more energy will cause the particles to begin locking into place. Freezing is an *exothermic* change because energy is removed from, or taken out of, the substance as it changes state.

If energy is added at 0°C, the ice will melt.

If energy is removed at 0°C, the liquid water will freeze.

Self-Check

Is the vaporization of water an endothermic or exothermic change? Explain your answer. *(See page 640 to check your answer.)*

Vaporization: Liquids to Gases

One way to see vaporization (VAY puhr i ZAY shuhn) is to iron a shirt using a steam iron. You will notice steam coming up from the iron as the wrinkles disappear. This steam comes from the vaporization of liquid water by the iron. **Vaporization** is the change of state from a liquid to a gas. **Figure 14** shows two kinds of vaporization.

Vaporization that takes place throughout a liquid is called **boiling.** The temperature at which a liquid boils is called the *boiling point.* Boiling point is a physical property. Like the melting point, the boiling point is also a characteristic property of a substance. The boiling point of water is 100°C. The boiling point of liquid mercury is 357°C.

Evaporation (ee VAP uh RAY shuhn) is vaporization that occurs at the surface of a liquid below the liquid's boiling point. When you sweat, your body is cooled through evaporation. Your sweat is mostly water. Water absorbs energy from your skin as it evaporates. You feel cooler because your body transfers energy to the water. Evaporation also explains why water in a glass on a table disappears after several days.

Figure 14 | **Two Kinds of Vaporization**

Boiling	Evaporation

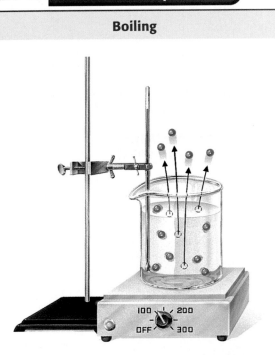

Boiling happens in a **liquid at its boiling point.** As energy is added to the liquid, particles throughout the liquid move faster. When they are fast enough to break away from other particles, they become a gas.

Evaporation happens in a **liquid below its boiling point.** Some particles at the surface of the liquid move fast enough to break away from the particles around them and become a gas.

Pressure Affects Boiling Point

Earlier you learned that water boils at 100°C. In fact, water boils at 100°C only at sea level because of atmospheric pressure. Atmospheric pressure is caused by the weight of the gases that make up the atmosphere.

Atmospheric pressure varies depending on where you are in relation to sea level. Atmospheric pressure is lower at higher elevations. The higher you go above sea level, the less air there is above you and the lower the atmospheric pressure is. Imagine boiling water at the top of a mountain. The boiling point would be lower than 100°C. For example, Denver, Colorado, is 1.6 km (1 mi) above sea level. In Denver, water boils at about 95°C. You can make water boil at an even lower temperature by doing the QuickLab at right.

Condensation: Gases to Liquids

Look at the cool glass of water in **Figure 15**. Notice the beads of water on the outside of the glass. These beads do not come from the water in the glass. They form because of condensation of gaseous water in the air. **Condensation** is the change of state from a gas to a liquid. The *condensation point* of a substance is the temperature at which the gas becomes a liquid. The condensation point of a substance is the same temperature as its boiling point at a given pressure. So, at sea level, steam condenses to form water at 100°C. This temperature is the same temperature at which water boils.

For a gas to become a liquid, large numbers of particles must clump together. Particles will clump together when the attraction between them overcomes their motion. For this to happen, energy must be removed from the gas to slow the particles down. So, condensation is an exothermic change.

Figure 15 *Gaseous water in the air will become liquid when it touches a cool surface.*

Boiling Water Is Cool

1. Remove the cap from a **syringe**.
2. Place the tip of the syringe in the **warm water** provided by your teacher. Pull the plunger out until you have 10 mL of water in the syringe.
3. Tightly cap the syringe.
4. Hold the syringe. Slowly pull the plunger out.
5. Observe any changes you see in the water. Record your observations in your ScienceLog.
6. Why would you not be burned by the boiling water in the syringe?

⭐TEKS

Meteorology
CONNECTION

The amount of gaseous water that air can hold gets smaller as the temperature of the air gets lower. As air cools, some of the gaseous water condenses to form small drops of liquid water. These drops form clouds in the sky and fog near the ground.

Sublimation: Solids to Gases

Look at the solids shown in **Figure 16.** The solid on the left is ice. Notice the drops of liquid collecting as the ice melts. On the right, you see carbon dioxide in the solid state, also called dry ice. It is called dry ice because instead of melting into a liquid, it goes through a change of state called sublimation. **Sublimation** is the change of state from a solid directly to a gas. Dry ice is colder than ice. Unlike ice, dry ice doesn't melt into a puddle of liquid. It is often used to keep food, medicine, and other materials cold without getting them wet.

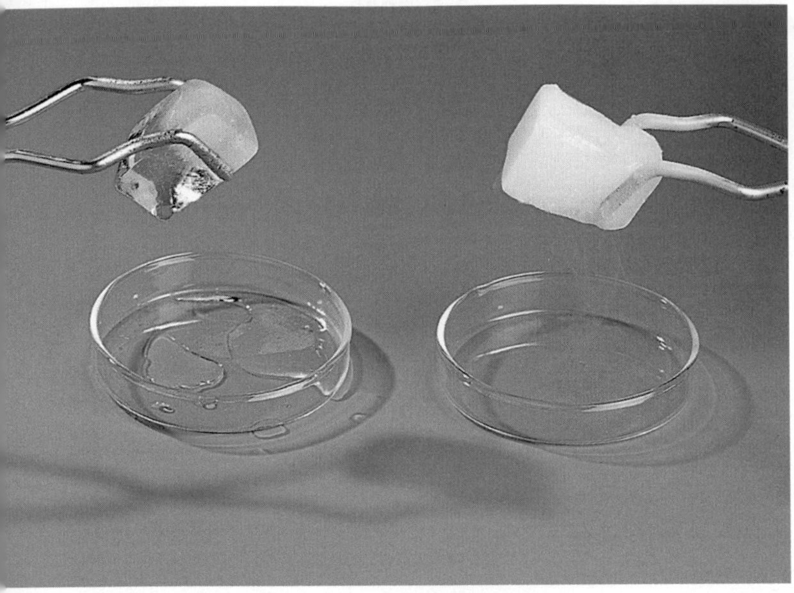

For a solid to change directly into a gas, the particles must move from being very tightly packed to being very spread apart. The attractions between the particles must be completely overcome. The substance must gain energy for the particles to overcome their attractions. So, sublimation is an endothermic change.

Figure 16 *Ice (left) melts, but dry ice (right) turns directly into a gas.*

Comparing Changes of State

As you learned in Section 1, the state of a substance depends on how fast its particles move. It also depends on how strongly the particles are attracted to each other. A substance may change from one state to another by an endothermic change if energy is added. A substance goes through an exothermic change if energy is removed. The table below shows the differences between the changes of state described in this section.

Summarizing the Changes of State			
Change of state	Direction	Endothermic or exothermic	Example
Melting	Solid → liquid	Endothermic	Ice melts into liquid water at 0°C.
Freezing	Liquid → solid	Exothermic	Liquid water freezes into ice at 0°C.
Vaporization	Liquid → gas	Endothermic	Liquid water vaporizes into steam at 100°C.
Condensation	Gas → liquid	Exothermic	Steam condenses into liquid water at 100°C.
Sublimation	Solid → gas	Endothermic	Solid dry ice sublimes into a gas at −78°C.

Change in Temperature Versus Change of State

When most substances lose or gain energy, one of two things happens to the substance: its temperature changes or its state changes. The temperature of a substance is related to the speed of the particles. So, when the temperature of a substance changes, the speed of the particles changes. But while a substance changes state, its temperature does not change until the change of state is complete. In the chart below, you can see what happens to ice as energy is added.

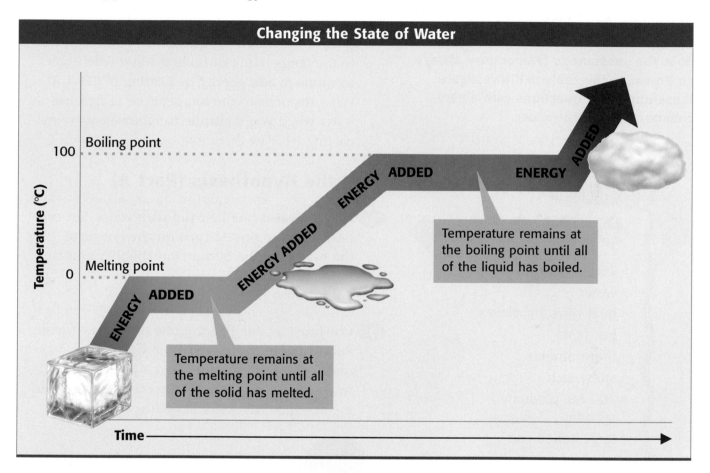

Changing the State of Water

Temperature (°C)

Boiling point — 100

Melting point — 0

Time →

ENERGY ADDED

ENERGY ADDED

ENERGY ADDED

ENERGY ADDED

Temperature remains at the melting point until all of the solid has melted.

Temperature remains at the boiling point until all of the liquid has boiled.

SECTION REVIEW

❶ Compare endothermic and exothermic changes.

❷ Classify each change of state (melting, freezing, vaporization, condensation, and sublimation) as endothermic or exothermic.

❸ Describe how the motion and arrangement of particles change as a substance freezes.

❹ **Comparing Concepts** How are evaporation and boiling similar? How are they different?

internet connect

SC*LINKS*
NSTA   GO TO: www.scilinks.org

TOPIC: Glass Manufacturing and Use in Texas
sci**LINKS NUMBER:** HSTX070

TOPIC: Changes of State
sci**LINKS NUMBER:** HSTP070

A Hot and Cool Lab ⊛TEKS

When you add energy to a substance by heating it, does the substance's temperature always go up? When you remove energy from a substance by cooling it, does the substance's temperature always go down? In this lab you'll investigate these important questions with a very common substance—water.

MATERIALS

- 250 or 400 mL beaker
- water
- heat-resistant gloves
- hot plate
- thermometer
- stopwatch
- 100 mL graduated cylinder
- large coffee can
- crushed ice
- rock salt
- wire-loop stirring device
- graph paper
- computer (optional)

Form a Hypothesis

1. In your ScienceLog, form a hypothesis to answer each of the following questions: What happens to the temperature of boiling water when you continue to add energy by heating it? (Part A) What happens to the temperature of freezing water when you continue to remove energy by cooling it? (Part B)

Test the Hypothesis (Part A)

2. Fill the beaker one-half full with water. Put on heat-resistant gloves. Turn on the hot plate. Put the beaker on the burner. Put the thermometer in the beaker.
   Caution: Do not touch the burner.

3. Construct a table like the one on the next page. Record the temperature of the water every 30 seconds. Take readings until about one-fourth of the water boils away. Note the first temperature reading at which the water is boiling steadily.

4 Turn off the hot plate. While the beaker is cooling, use graph paper or a computer to make a graph of temperature (*y*-axis) versus time (*x*-axis). Add an arrow pointing to the first temperature at which the water was boiling steadily.

5 Follow your teacher's instructions for cleanup and disposal.

Test the Hypothesis (Part B)

6 Put 20 mL of water in the graduated cylinder. Put the graduated cylinder in the coffee can. Fill the can with crushed ice. Pour rock salt on the ice. Place the thermometer and the wire-loop stirring device in the graduated cylinder.

7 In a new table, record the temperature of the water in the graduated cylinder every 30 seconds. Add ice and rock salt to the can as needed. Stir the water with the stirring device.
Caution: Do not stir with the thermometer.

8 Once the water begins to freeze, stop stirring. Do not try to pull the thermometer out of the solid ice in the cylinder.

9 Record the temperature when you first see ice crystals forming in the water. Take readings until the water is completely frozen.

10 Use graph paper or a computer to make a graph of temperature (*y*-axis) versus time (*x*-axis). Add an arrow pointing to the temperature reading at which the first ice crystals formed in the water.

Analyze the Results (Parts A and B)

11 What does the slope of each graph represent?

12 How does the slope when the water is boiling compare with the slope before the water boils? Explain why the slopes differ.

13 How does the slope when the water is freezing compare with the slope before the water freezes? Explain why the slopes differ.

Draw Conclusions (Parts A and B)

14 Adding or removing energy leads to changes in the movement of particles that make up solids, liquids, and gases. Use this idea to explain why the temperature graphs of the two experiments look the way they do.

Time (s)	30	60	90	120	150	180	210	etc.
Temperature (°C)			DO NOT WRITE IN BOOK					

Section 1

Vocabulary

states of matter *(p. 62)*
solid *(p. 63)*
liquid *(p. 64)*
gas *(p. 65)*
pressure *(p. 66)*
Boyle's law *(p. 67)*
Charles's law *(p. 68)*
plasma *(p. 69)*

Section Notes

- The states of matter are the physical forms in which a substance can exist. Four states are solid, liquid, gas, and plasma.

- Substances can be classified according to their physical property of state. ⭐TEKS

- All matter is made of tiny particles that move constantly.

- A solid has a definite shape and volume.

- A liquid has a definite volume but not a definite shape.

- A gas does not have a definite shape or volume. A gas takes the shape and volume of its container.

- Pressure is force per unit area. Gas pressure increases as the number of collisions of gas particles increases.

- Boyle's law states that the volume of a gas increases as the pressure decreases if the temperature does not change.

- Charles's law states that the volume of a gas increases as the temperature increases if the pressure does not change.

- Plasmas are composed of particles that have broken apart. Plasmas do not have a definite shape or volume.

LabBook ⭐TEKS

Full of Hot Air! *(p. 605)*

Section 2

Vocabulary

change of state *(p. 70)*
melting *(p. 71)*
freezing *(p. 71)*
vaporization *(p. 72)*
boiling *(p. 72)*
evaporation *(p. 72)*
condensation *(p. 73)*
sublimation *(p. 74)*

Section Notes

- A change of state is the conversion of a substance from one physical form to another. All changes of state are physical changes.

- Energy is added during endothermic changes. Energy is removed during exothermic changes.

- Melting changes a solid to a liquid. Freezing changes a liquid to a solid. The freezing point and melting point of a substance are the same temperature.

- Vaporization changes a liquid to a gas. There are two kinds of vaporization: boiling and evaporation.

- Boiling occurs throughout a liquid at the boiling point.

- Evaporation occurs at the surface of a liquid at a temperature below the boiling point.

- Condensation changes a gas to a liquid. The condensation point and boiling point of a substance are the same temperature.

- Sublimation changes a solid directly to a gas.

- Temperature does not change during a change of state.

LabBook ⭐TEKS

Can Crusher *(p. 606)*

Review

USING VOCABULARY

For each pair of terms, explain how the meanings of the terms differ.

1. solid/liquid

2. Boyle's law/Charles's law

3. evaporation/boiling

4. melting/freezing

UNDERSTANDING CONCEPTS

Multiple Choice

5. Which of the following best describes the particles of a liquid?
   a. The particles are far apart and are moving fast.
   b. The particles are close together but are moving past each other.
   c. The particles are far apart and are moving slowly.
   d. The particles are closely packed and are vibrating in place.

6. Boiling points and freezing points are examples of
   a. chemical properties.   c. energy.
   b. physical properties.   d. matter.

7. During which change of state do particles become more ordered?
   a. boiling   c. melting
   b. condensation   d. sublimation

8. Which of the following describes what happens as the temperature of a gas in a balloon increases?
   a. The speed of the particles decreases.
   b. The volume of the gas increases.
   c. The volume decreases.
   d. The pressure decreases.

9. Dew collects on a spider web in the early morning. This is an example of
   a. condensation.   c. sublimation.
   b. evaporation.   d. melting.

10. Which of the following changes of state is exothermic?
    a. evaporation   c. freezing
    b. sublimation   d. melting

11. If the temperature does not change but the pressure is reduced, the volume of a gas inside a chamber sealed by a piston
    a. gets larger.   c. gets smaller.
    b. stays the same.   d. equals the temperature.

12. The particles of matter
    a. are very tiny.
    b. are constantly moving.
    c. move faster at higher temperatures.
    d. All of the above

13. Which of the following contains plasma?
    a. a fluorescent light   c. dry ice
    b. steam   d. a hot iron

Short Answer

14. Classify each substance according to its state of matter: a baseball, honey, oxygen in the air, lemonade, lightning, a marble, and the steam from an iron. ⭐TEKS

15. Explain why liquid water takes the shape of its container but an ice cube does not.

16. Rank solids, liquids, and gases in order of decreasing particle speed.

17. Compare the distance between the particles of iron in the solid, liquid, and gaseous states.

CONCEPT MAPPING

18. Use the following terms to create a concept map: *states of matter, solid, liquid, gas, plasma, changes of state, freezing, vaporization, condensation,* and *melting.*

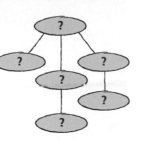

CRITICAL THINKING AND PROBLEM SOLVING

Write one or two sentences to answer the following questions:

19. After taking a shower, you notice that small droplets of water cover the mirror. Explain why this happens. Be sure to describe where the water comes from and what changes it goes through.

20. In the photo below, water is being split to form two new substances, hydrogen and oxygen. Is the water going through a change of state? Explain your answer.

21. To protect their crops during freezing temperatures, orange growers spray water onto the trees and allow it to freeze. In terms of energy lost and energy gained, explain why this practice protects the oranges from damage.

22. At sea level, water boils at 100°C, while methane boils at –161°C. Which of these substances has a stronger force of attraction between its particles? Explain your reasoning.

MATH IN SCIENCE

23. Kate placed 100 mL of water in five different pans, placed the pans on a windowsill for a week, and measured the amount of water that evaporated. Draw a graph of her data, shown below, with surface area on the *x*-axis. Is the graph linear or nonlinear? What does this tell you?

Pan number	1	2	3	4	5
Surface area (cm^2)	44	82	20	30	65
Volume evaporated (mL)	42	79	19	29	62

INTERPRETING GRAPHICS

24. Examine the graph below, and answer the following questions:
  a. What is the boiling point of the substance? What is the melting point?
  b. Which state is present at 30°C?
  c. How will the liquid change if energy is added to it at 20°C?

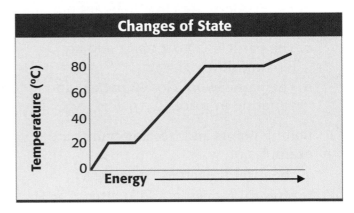

Reading Check-up

Take a minute to review your answers to the Pre-Reading Questions found at the bottom of page 60. Have your answers changed? If necessary, revise your answers based on what you have learned since you began this chapter.

Chapter 3

1 Which of the following safety equipment should you have on hand when using concentrated acids in the laboratory?

A Fire extinguisher

B Carbon monoxide detector

C Apron

D Heat-resistant gloves

2 Classify fire according to its state of matter.

F Solid

G Liquid

H Gas

J Plasma

3 What equipment would you use to measure 10 milliliters of water for an experiment?

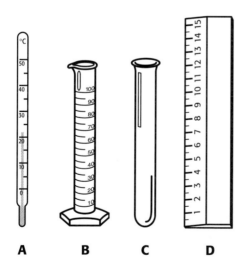

A　　**B**　　**C**　　**D**

Freezing Points of Different Brands of Antifreeze	
Brand	Freezing point (°C)
Ice-B-Gone	−5
Freeze Free	−7
Liqui-Freeze	−9
Auntie Freeze	−11

4 Philip wants to purchase an antifreeze for his car. An antifreeze is added to the water in a car's radiator in order to lower its freezing point. The temperature in his area never falls below –10°C. Given the information in the chart above, which of the following products would be the best for Philip's car?

F Ice-B-Gone

G Freeze Free

H Liqui-Freeze

J Auntie Freeze

5 Jacquelyn conducted an experiment to find out what happens to the temperature of water after it starts boiling. She measured the water's temperature every 30 seconds during the experiment. She wants to graph her data. If she puts temperature on the *y*-axis, what variable belongs on the *x*-axis?

A Water

B State of matter

C Time

D Boiling point of water

Chapter 3

Math

1 Gerard wants to buy a kite. The kite regularly costs $7.95, but it is on sale for $4.50. How much will he save if he buys the kite on sale?

A $0.50

B $1.20

C $3.45

D $12.45

2 Francis bought a 2-liter bottle of juice. How many milliliters of juice does this bottle hold?

F 0.002 mL

G 0.2 mL

H 200 mL

J 2000 mL

3 Which group contains ratios that are all equivalent to $\frac{3}{4}$?

A $\frac{3}{4}, \frac{6}{8}, \frac{15}{22}$

B $\frac{6}{10}, \frac{15}{20}, \frac{20}{25}$

C $\frac{3}{4}, \frac{15}{20}, \frac{20}{25}$

D $\frac{3}{4}, \frac{6}{8}, \frac{15}{20}$

Reading

Read the passage. Then read each question that follows the passage. Decide which is the best answer to each question.

Did you know that lightning can turn sand into glass? If lightning strikes sand, the sand can reach temperatures of up to 33,000°C. That's as hot as the surface of the sun! This intense heat melts the sand into a liquid. The liquid quickly cools and hardens into glass. The result is a rare and beautiful type of natural glass called fulgurite.

The same basic process is used to make light bulbs, windows, and bottles. But instead of lightning, glassmakers use hot ovens to melt solid silica (the main ingredient of sand) and other ingredients into liquid glass. Then, before the glass cools and solidifies, the glassmaker forms the glass into the desired shape.

1 In the glassmaking process, what happens after the glassmaker forms the material into the desired shape?

A Solid silica melts over a hot oven.

B Solid silica is struck by lightning.

C The glass melts and becomes a liquid.

D The glass cools and solidifies.

2 Which statement is an OPINION in this passage?

F Lightning can form fulgurites.

G Fulgurites are beautiful.

H Lightning heats the sand to 33,000°C.

J Glassmakers use very hot ovens.

Eureka!

Full Steam Ahead!

It was huge. It was 40 m long and about 5 m high, and it weighed 245 metric tons. It could pull a 3.28-million-kilogram train at 100 km/h. It was a 4-8-8-4 locomotive, called a Big Boy, delivered in 1941 to the Union Pacific Railroad in Omaha, Nebraska. It was also one of the final steps in a 2,000-year search to harness steam power.

A Simple Observation

For thousands of years, people used wind, water, gravity, dogs, horses, and cattle to do work. But until about 300 years ago, people had little success finding other sources. Then in 1690, Denis Papin, a French mathematician and physicist, noticed that steam expanding in a cylinder pushed a piston up. As the steam then cooled and contracted, the piston fell. Watching the motion of the piston, Papin had an idea. He connected a water-pump handle to the piston. As the pump handle rose and fell with the piston, water was pumped.

More Uplifting Ideas

Eight years later, an English naval captain named Thomas Savery made Papin's machine more efficient. He used water to cool and condense the steam. Savery's improved pump was used in British coal mines. As good as Savery's pump was, steam power kept changing!

In 1712, an English blacksmith named Thomas Newcomen improved Savery's device. He added a second piston and a horizontal beam that acted like a seesaw. One end of the beam was connected to the piston in the steam cylinder. The other end of the beam was connected to the pump piston. As the steam piston moved up and down, it created a vacuum in the pump cylinder and sucked water up from the mine. Newcomen's engine was the most widely used steam engine for more than 50 years.

Watt a Great Idea!

In 1764, James Watt, a Scottish technician, was repairing a Newcomen engine. He realized that heating the cylinder, letting it cool, and then heating it again wasted a huge amount of energy. Watt added a separate chamber where the steam could cool and condense. The two chambers were connected by a valve that let the steam escape from the boiler. This idea improved the engine's efficiency—the boiler could stay hot all the time!

A few years later, Watt turned the whole machine on its side so that the piston was moving horizontally. He added a slide valve that let in steam first to one end of the chamber, which pushed the piston in one direction. Then the valve let in steam to the other end, which pushed the piston back. This idea changed the steam pump into a true steam engine that could drive a locomotive the size of Big Boy!

Explore Other Inventions

▶ Watt's engine helped start the Industrial Revolution. Many new uses for steam power were found. Find out more about the many other inventors who harnessed the power of steam. ⭐TEKS

Matter in Motion

Pre-Reading
Questions

1. How is motion measured?
   ★TEKS

2. What is a force?

3. How does friction affect
   motion? ★TEKS

4. How does gravity affect
   objects? ★TEKS

SLICK SPEED

Imagine yourself in a front-row seat at the Winter Olympics.
Wow! Those speedskaters move really fast! In fact, some
speedskaters can skate as fast as 14 m/s (about 31 mi/h).
Speedskaters have to be strong athletes. They must be able
to exert enough force to move at high speeds. And they
have to be skilled at controlling their movements on the
ice—a surface that has very little friction. In this chapter,
you will learn more about speed, friction, and the many
other aspects of matter in motion.

THE DOMINO DERBY ⭐TEKS

Speed is the rate at which an object moves. In this activity, you will observe how one factor affects the speed of falling dominoes.

Procedure

1. Set up **25 dominoes** in a straight line. Try to keep equal spacing between the dominoes.

2. Using a **meterstick,** measure the total length of your row of dominoes, and write it down.

3. Using a **stopwatch,** time how long the entire row of dominoes takes to fall. Record this measurement.

4. Using distances between the dominoes that are smaller and larger than the distance used in your first setup, repeat steps 2 and 3 several times.

Analysis

5. Calculate the average speed for each trial by dividing the total distance (the length of the domino row) by the time taken to fall.

6. How did the spacing between dominoes affect the average speed? Is this result what you expected? If not, explain your answer.

Terms to Learn

motion   velocity
speed   acceleration

What You'll Do

● Identify motion in relation to a reference point.
● Demonstrate that changes in motion can be measured and graphically represented. ★TEKS
● Determine the difference between speed and velocity.
● Analyze the relationship between velocity and acceleration.

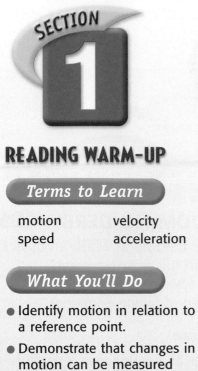

Measuring Motion

Earth circles the sun. Air particles vibrate around you. Blood travels through your veins and arteries. What do these very different things have in common? They all involve motion!

Everywhere you look, you're likely to see something in motion. Your teacher may be walking across the room. Or perhaps a bird is flying outside a window. Even if you don't see anything moving, motion is happening all around you.

Observing Motion

You might think that the motion of an object is easy to see. You just watch the object, right? Actually, you must watch the object in relation to another object that appears to stay in place. The object that appears to stay in place is a *reference point*. When an object changes position in relation to a reference point over a period of time, the object is in **motion.** When an object is in motion, you can describe the direction of its motion using a reference direction. Some familiar reference directions are north, south, east, west, up, and down.

Common Reference Points

The Earth's surface is a common reference point for determining position and motion. Nonmoving objects on Earth's surface, such as buildings, trees, and mountains, are also useful reference points. Look at **Figure 1.** You can tell that the balloon is moving by using the mountain as a reference point.

A moving object can also be used as a reference point. For example, imagine you were on the balloon shown at left. You could watch a bird fly by and see that it was changing position in relation to your moving balloon. Also, Earth itself is a moving reference point—it is moving around the sun.

Figure 1 *Between the times when these pictures were taken, the hot-air balloon changed position relative to a reference point—the mountain.*

Speed Depends on Distance and Time

The rate at which an object moves is **speed.** Speed depends on the distance traveled and the time taken to travel that distance. Look back at Figure 1. Suppose the two pictures were taken 10 seconds apart. Also, suppose the balloon traveled 50 m in that time. Speed is distance divided by time. So, the speed of the balloon is 50 m/10 s, or 5 m/s.

The SI unit for speed is meters per second (m/s). Kilometers per hour (km/h), feet per second (ft/s), and miles per hour (mi/h) are other units used to express speed.

Finding Average Speed

Most of the time, objects do not travel at a constant speed. For example, you probably do not walk at a constant speed from one class to the next. So, calculating average speed using the following equation is very useful:

$$average\ speed = \frac{total\ distance}{total\ time}$$

Representing Speed on a Graph

Suppose a person drives from one city to another. The blue line in the graph below shows the distance traveled every hour. Notice that the distance traveled every hour is different because the speed is not constant. For example, the driver may change speed because of weather, traffic, or varying speed limits. The average speed can be calculated by adding up the total distance and dividing it by the total time:

$$average\ speed = \frac{360\ km}{4\ h} = 90\ km/h$$

The red line shows the average distance traveled each hour. The slope of this line is the average speed. Try the MathFocus on the next page to practice finding average speed.

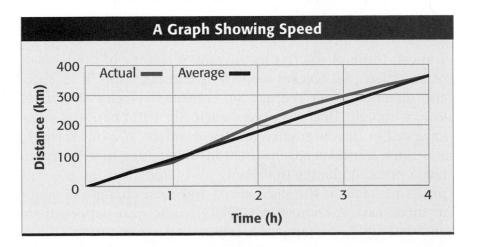

A Graph Showing Speed

Actual ▬ Average ▬

Distance (km) / Time (h)

MathFocus ....

Calculating Average Speed

An athlete swims a *distance* from one end of a 50 m pool to the other in a *time* of 25 seconds. What is the athlete's *average speed*?

Step 1: Write the equation for average speed.

$$average\ speed = \frac{total\ distance}{total\ time}$$

Step 2: Replace the total distance and total time with the values given in the problem, and solve.

$$average\ speed = \frac{50\ m}{25\ s}$$

$$average\ speed = 2\ m/s$$

Now It's Your Turn

❶ If you walk for 1.5 hours and travel 7.5 km, what is your average speed?

❷ A bird flies at a speed of 15 m/s for 10 seconds, 20 m/s for 10 seconds, and 25 m/s for 5 seconds. What is the bird's average speed?

Velocity: Direction Matters

Here's a riddle for you: Two birds leave the same tree at the same time. They both fly at 10 km/h for 1 hour, 15 km/h for 30 minutes, and 5 km/h for 1 hour. But they don't end up at the same place. Why not?

Have you figured out the riddle? The birds went in different directions. Their speeds were the same, but they had different velocities. **Velocity** (vuh LAHS uh tee) is the speed of an object in a particular direction.

Be careful not to confuse the terms *speed* and *velocity*. They do not mean the same thing. Because velocity must include direction, saying that an airplane's velocity is 600 km/h would not be correct. You would need to include a direction. For example, you could say that the plane's velocity is 600 km/h south. Velocity always has a reference direction.

Velocity Changes as Speed or Direction Changes

You can think of velocity as the rate of change of the position of an object. An object's velocity is constant only if its speed and direction don't change. So, constant velocity always follows a straight line. An object's velocity will change if either its speed or direction changes. For example, if a bus traveling at 15 m/s south speeds up to 20 m/s, a change in velocity has taken place. A change in velocity also happens if the bus continues to travel at the same speed and then changes direction to travel east. A change in velocity would also happen if the bus sped up and changed direction at the same time.

Combining Velocities

Imagine that you're riding in a bus traveling east at 15 m/s. You and all the other passengers are also traveling at a velocity of 15 m/s east. But suppose you stand up and walk down the aisle of the bus while the bus is moving. Are you still moving at the same velocity as the bus? No! **Figure 2** shows how you can combine velocities to determine the *resultant velocity*.

But what happens if the person in Figure 2 walks toward the back of the bus? To combine two velocities that are *in opposite directions*, subtract the smaller velocity from the larger velocity to find the resultant velocity. The resultant velocity is in the direction of the larger velocity. So a person walking with a velocity of 1 m/s west on the bus would have a resultant velocity of 15 m/s east − 1 m/s west = 14 m/s east.

Figure 2 *To combine two velocities that are **in the same direction**, add them together to find the resultant velocity.*

Person's resultant velocity:
15 m/s east + 1 m/s east = 16 m/s east

Acceleration: The Rate at Which Velocity Changes

The word *accelerate* is commonly used to mean "speed up." But in science, there's more to the meaning of *accelerate*. **Acceleration** (ak SEL uhr AY shuhn) is the rate at which velocity changes. To accelerate means to change velocity. You just learned that velocity changes if speed changes, if direction changes, or if both change. Suppose you are inline skating. If you slow down and turn to avoid a rock on the sidewalk, you are accelerating.

Often, an increase in speed is called *positive acceleration*. A decrease in speed is called *negative acceleration* or *deceleration*. Acceleration is how much velocity changes over a specific amount of time. The more velocity changes in a given amount of time (or the faster velocity changes), the greater the acceleration.

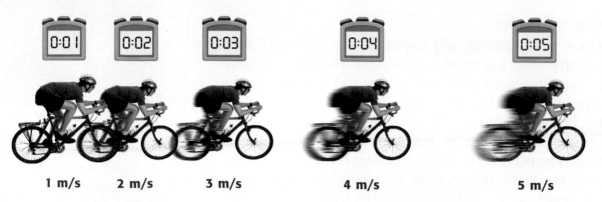

1 m/s   2 m/s   3 m/s   4 m/s   5 m/s

Figure 3 *This cyclist is accelerating at 1 m/s² south.*

Calculating Average Acceleration

You can find average acceleration using the following equation:

$$average\ acceleration = \frac{final\ velocity\ -\ starting\ velocity}{time\ it\ takes\ to\ change\ velocity}$$

Velocity is expressed in meters per second (m/s), and time is expressed in seconds (s). So, acceleration is expressed in meters per second per second, (m/s)/s, or m/s². Look at **Figure 3.** Suppose you get on your bicycle and accelerate southward at a rate of 1 m/s². (Like velocity, acceleration has size and direction.) So, every second, your southward velocity increases by 1 m/s. After 1 second, you have a velocity of 1 m/s south. After 2 seconds, you have a velocity of 2 m/s south, and so on. If your final velocity after 5 seconds is 5 m/s south, your average acceleration can be calculated as follows:

$$average\ acceleration = \frac{5\ m/s\ -\ 0\ m/s}{5\ s} = 1\ m/s^2\ south$$

MathFocus ....

Calculating Average Acceleration

A teenager moves her skateboard south from a *starting velocity* of 0 m/s to a *final velocity* of 6 m/s in a *time* of 3 seconds. What is her *average acceleration*?

Step 1: Write the equation for average acceleration.

$$average\ acceleration = \frac{final\ velocity\ -\ starting\ velocity}{time\ it\ takes\ to\ change\ velocity}$$

Step 2: Replace the final velocity, starting velocity, and time with the measurements given in the problem, and solve.

$$average\ acceleration = \frac{6\ m/s\ -\ 0\ m/s}{3\ s}$$

$$average\ acceleration = 2\ m/s^2\ south$$

Now It's Your Turn

❶ A car traveling with a velocity of 32 m/s comes to a complete stop at a stop sign in 4 seconds. What is the car's average acceleration?

❷ A coconut falls from the top of a tree and reaches a velocity of 19.6 m/s when it hits the ground 2 seconds later. What is the coconut's average acceleration?

Circular Motion: Continuous Acceleration

You may be surprised to know that even when you are completely still, you are experiencing acceleration. You may not seem to be changing speed or direction, but you are! You are traveling in a circle as the Earth rotates. An object traveling in a circular motion is always changing its direction. Therefore, its velocity is always changing, so acceleration takes place. The acceleration that occurs in circular motion is known as *centripetal* (sen TRIP uht'l) *acceleration.* Another example of centripetal acceleration is shown in **Figure 4.**

Representing Acceleration on a Graph

Suppose that you have just gotten on a roller coaster. The roller coaster moves up the first hill slowly until it stops at the top. Then you're off, racing down the hill! The graph below shows your velocity for the 10 seconds that you are coming down the hill. You can tell from this graph that your acceleration is positive because your velocity increases as time passes. Because the graph is not a straight line, you can also tell that your acceleration is not constant for each second.

Figure 4 *The blades of this windmill are constantly changing direction as they travel in a circle. Thus, centripetal acceleration is taking place.*

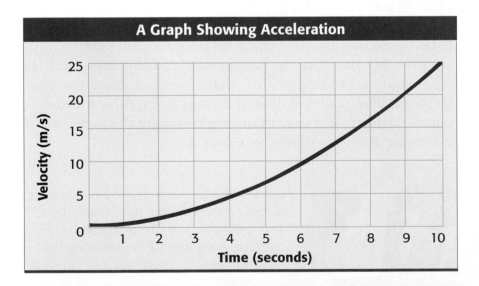

A Graph Showing Acceleration

Velocity (m/s) vs *Time (seconds)*

SECTION REVIEW

1. What is a reference point?

2. What is the difference between speed and velocity?

3. Does a change in direction affect velocity? Explain.

4. **Graphing Data** A wolf decelerates after chasing a rabbit. Graph the wolf's motion using the following data: 15 m/s at 0 seconds, 10 m/s at 1 second, 5 m/s at 2 seconds, 2.5 m/s at 3 seconds, 1 m/s at 4 seconds, and 0 m/s at 5 seconds. **TEKS**

READING WARM-UP

Terms to Learn

force
newton
net force

What You'll Do

- Give examples of different kinds of forces.
- Determine the net force on an object.
- Compare balanced and unbalanced forces.
- Identify and describe the changes in position, direction of motion, and speed of an object when acted upon by a force. ⭐ TEKS

What Is a Force?

You have probably heard the word *force* in everyday conversation. People say things such as, "That storm had a lot of force" or "Our football team is a force to be reckoned with." But what, exactly, is a force?

In science, a **force** is simply a push or a pull. Like velocity and acceleration, all forces have both size and direction. A force can change the position of an object and the speed or direction of a moving object. In fact, any time you see something moving, you can be sure that its motion was created by a force. Scientists express force using a unit called the **newton** (N).

Forces Act on Objects

All forces are exerted by one object on another object. For any push to occur, something has to receive the push. You can't push nothing! The same is true for any pull. When doing schoolwork, you use your fingers to pull open books or to push the buttons on a computer keyboard. In these examples, your fingers are exerting forces on the books and the keys. However, motion does not have to occur just because a force is being exerted by one object on another. For example, you are probably sitting on a chair as you read this book. But the force you are exerting on the chair does not cause the chair to move. The reason is that the chair is exerting a force on you. Sometimes it is easy to determine where the push or pull is coming from, as shown in **Figure 5.**

Figure 5 *It is obvious that the bulldozer is exerting a force on the pile of soil. But did you know that the pile of soil also exerts a force, even when it is just sitting on the ground?*

Look at **Figure 6.** Sometimes it is not so easy to tell what is exerting a force or what is receiving a force. You cannot see the force that pulls magnets to refrigerators. Nor can you see that the air that you breathe is affected by gravity. (You will learn more about gravity later in this chapter.) Often you will find that many forces act together on an object.

Forces in Combination

More than one force can be exerted on an object at the same time. The **net force** is the force that results from combining all the forces exerted on an object. So how do you determine the net force? The following examples can help you answer this question.

Figure 6 *Something unseen exerts a force that makes your socks cling together when they come out of the dryer. You have to exert a force to separate the socks.*

Forces in the Same Direction

Suppose you and a friend are asked to move a piano for your music teacher. To move the piano, you pull on one end, and your friend pushes on the other end. Together, your forces add up to enough force to move the piano. The reason is that your forces are in the same direction. Look at **Figure 7.** The forces can be added together to determine the net force because the forces are in the same direction. In this case, the net force is 45 N. This force is large enough to move a piano—if it is on wheels!

Figure 7 *When the forces are in the same direction, you add the forces together to determine the net force.*

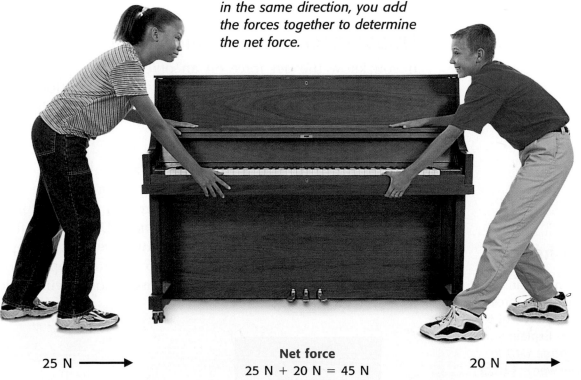

25 N ⟶

Net force
25 N + 20 N = 45 N
to the right

20 N ⟶

Forces in Different Directions

Look at the two dogs playing tug of war in **Figure 8.** Each dog is exerting a force, but the forces are in opposite directions. Notice that the dog on the left is pulling with a force of 10 N and the dog on the right is pulling with a force of 12 N. Which dog do you think will win the tug of war?

Because the forces are in opposite directions, the net force is determined by subtracting the smaller force from the larger one. In this case, the net force is 2 N in the direction of the dog on the right. Give that dog a dog biscuit!

Figure 8 *When the forces are in different directions, you subtract the smaller force from the larger force to determine the net force.*

← 10 N   12 N →

Net force
12 N − 10 N = 2 N
to the right

Unbalanced and Balanced Forces

If you know the net force on an object, you can determine the effect the force will have on the object's motion. Why? The net force tells you whether the forces on the object are balanced or unbalanced.

Unbalanced Forces Produce a Change in Motion

In the examples in Figures 7 and 8, the net force on the object is greater than zero. When the net force on an object is not zero, the forces on the object are *unbalanced*. Unbalanced forces produce a change in motion. In the two previous examples, the receivers of the forces—the piano and the rope—move. Unbalanced forces are necessary to cause a nonmoving object to start moving.

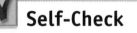

Self-Check

Describe the change in position of an object when a force of 7 N north and a force of 5 N south act on it. Explain your answer. *(See page 640 to check your answer.)* ⊛TEKS

Unbalanced forces are also necessary to change the motion of moving objects. For example, think of a soccer game. The soccer ball is already moving when it is passed from one player to another. When the ball reaches the second player, the player exerts an unbalanced force—a kick—on the ball. After the kick, the ball moves in a new direction and with a new speed.

Keep in mind that an object can continue to move even when the unbalanced forces are removed. A soccer ball, for example, receives an unbalanced force when it is kicked. However, the ball continues to roll along the ground long after the force of the kick has ended.

Balanced Forces Produce No Change in Motion

When the forces applied to an object are *balanced*, the forces produce a net force of zero. Balanced forces do not cause a non-moving object to start moving. Furthermore, balanced forces will not cause a change in the motion of a moving object.

Many objects around you have only balanced forces acting on them. For example, a light hanging from the ceiling does not move because the force of gravity pulling down on the light is balanced by the force of the cord pulling upward. A bird's nest in a tree and a hat resting on your head are other examples of objects that have only balanced forces acting on them. **Figure 9** shows another case in which the forces on an object are balanced. Because all the forces are balanced, the house of cards does not move.

Figure 9 *The forces on this house of cards are balanced. An unbalanced force on one of the cards would cause motion—and probably a mess!*

internet **connect**

SCi LINKS
NSTA   GO TO: www.scilinks.org

TOPIC: Forces
sciLINKS NUMBER: HSTP107

SECTION REVIEW

❶ Give four examples of a force being exerted.

❷ Explain the difference between balanced and unbalanced forces, and explain how each force affects the motion of an object. ⭐TEKS

❸ **Interpreting Graphics** In the picture at right, two bighorn sheep push on each other's horns. The arrow shows the direction in which the two sheep are moving. Describe how the speed, direction of motion, and position of the sheep on the right is changed by the force of the other sheep. ⭐TEKS

Matter in Motion   **95**

READING WARM-UP

Terms to Learn

friction

What You'll Do

● Describe how the force of friction can change the speed of an object. ⭐TEKS

● Explain why friction occurs.

● List the types of friction, and give examples of each type.

● Explain how friction can be both harmful and helpful.

Friction: A Force That Opposes Motion

While playing ball, one of your friends accidentally bounces the ball just out of your reach. Rather than running for the ball, you decide to walk after it because you know that the ball will eventually stop. But do you know why?

You know that the ball is slowing down. You also know that an unbalanced force is needed to change the speed or direction of a moving object. So, what is the force that is stopping the ball? The force is called friction. **Friction** is a force that opposes motion between two surfaces that are touching. Friction can cause a moving object, such as the ball, to slow down and eventually stop.

The Source of Friction

Friction occurs because the surface of any object is rough. Some surfaces look or feel very smooth. However, even smooth surfaces, such as the pages of this textbook, are covered with microscopic hills and valleys. Just look at **Figure 10**! When two surfaces are in contact, the hills and valleys of one surface stick to the hills and valleys of the other surface. This contact causes friction even when the surfaces appear smooth.

The amount of friction between two surfaces depends on many factors. Two factors include the roughness of the surfaces and the force pushing the surfaces together.

Figure 10 *Under magnification, a smooth paper surface has a rough texture.*

Rougher Surfaces Create More Friction

Rougher surfaces have more microscopic hills and valleys. So, the rougher the surface is, the greater the friction. Think back to the example above. The ball slows down because of the friction between the ball and the ground. A large amount of friction is produced because the ground has a rough surface. But imagine that the same situation happened when you were playing ice hockey. If the puck passed out of your reach, it would slide across the ice for a long while instead of slowing down. The reason is that the ice is a smooth surface that has very little friction.

Greater Force Creates More Friction

The amount of friction also depends on the force pushing the surfaces together. If this force is increased, the hills and valleys of the surfaces can come into closer contact. As a result, the friction between the surfaces increases. A less massive object exerts less force on surfaces than a more massive object does. This result is illustrated in **Figure 11.** Notice that even if you change how much of one surface touches the other surface, the amount of friction remains the same.

Types of Friction

The friction you observe when sliding books across a tabletop is called sliding friction. Other types of friction include rolling friction, fluid friction, and static friction. You will learn more about these types of friction in the next few pages.

Figure 11 Force and Friction

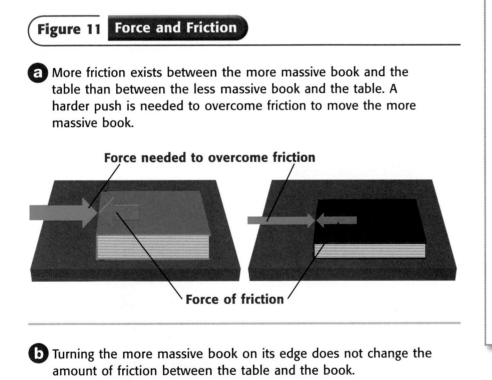

a More friction exists between the more massive book and the table than between the less massive book and the table. A harder push is needed to overcome friction to move the more massive book.

Force needed to overcome friction

Force of friction

b Turning the more massive book on its edge does not change the amount of friction between the table and the book.

Force needed to overcome friction

Force of friction

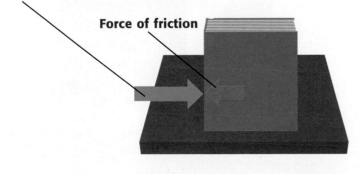

Quick Lab

The Friction 500

1. Make a short ramp out of **a piece of cardboard** and **one or two books** on a table.

2. Put a **toy car** at the top of the ramp, and let go. If necessary, adjust the ramp height so that your car does not roll off the table.

3. Put the car at the top of the ramp again, and let go. Use a **meterstick** to measure the distance the car travels after leaving the ramp. Repeat three times, and calculate the average for your results.

4. Change the surface of the table by covering it with **sandpaper** or **cloth.** Repeat step 3. Change the surface one more time, and repeat step 3 again.

5. Which surface caused the most friction and why? Describe what would happen if the car were heavier.

⭐TEKS

Sliding Friction

If you push an eraser across your desk, the eraser will move for a short distance and then stop. The force that caused the eraser to stop moving is called *sliding friction*. Sliding friction is very effective at opposing the motion of objects. You can feel the effect of sliding friction when you push a heavy dresser across the floor. You must exert a lot of force to overcome the sliding friction, as shown in **Figure 12.** You use the effect of sliding friction when you apply the brakes on a bicycle or when you write with a piece of chalk.

Rolling Friction

Look again at Figure 12. If the same heavy dresser were on wheels, you would have an easier time moving it. The friction between the wheels and the floor is an example of *rolling friction*. The force of rolling friction is usually less than the force of sliding friction. Therefore, moving objects on wheels is generally easier than sliding them along the floor.

Rolling friction is an important part of almost all means of transportation. Anything with wheels—bicycles, in-line skates, cars, and trains—uses rolling friction between the wheels and the ground to move forward.

Figure 12 | Comparing Sliding Friction and Rolling Friction

Sliding friction	Rolling friction

Moving a heavy piece of furniture in your room can be hard work because **the force of sliding friction is large.**

Moving a heavy piece of furniture is easier if you put it on wheels. **The force of rolling friction is smaller** and easier to overcome.

Fluid Friction

Why is walking on a freshly mopped floor harder than walking on a dry floor? On the wet floor, the sliding friction between your feet and the floor is replaced by *fluid friction* between your feet and the water. In this case, fluid friction is less than sliding friction, so the floor is slippery. *Fluids* include liquids, such as water and milk, and gases, such as air and helium.

Fluid friction opposes the motion of objects traveling through a fluid, as illustrated in **Figure 13.** For example, fluid friction between air and a fast-moving car is the largest force opposing the motion of the car. You can observe this friction by holding your hand out the window of a moving car.

Figure 13 *Swimming provides a good workout because you must exert force to overcome fluid friction.*

Static Friction

When a force is applied to an object but does not cause the object to move, *static friction* occurs. The object does not move because the force of static friction balances the force applied. Static friction disappears as soon as an object starts moving, and another type of friction immediately occurs. **Figure 14** shows how static friction affects an object.

Friction Can Be Harmful or Helpful

Friction is both harmful and helpful to you and the world around you. Think about how friction affects a car. Without friction, the tires could not push against the ground to move the car forward. Also, the brakes could not stop the car. Without friction, a car is useless. However, friction can cause problems in a car, too. Friction between moving engine parts increases their temperature and causes the parts to wear down. Oil is added to the engine to reduce friction and to keep the parts from wearing out.

Figure 14 Static Friction

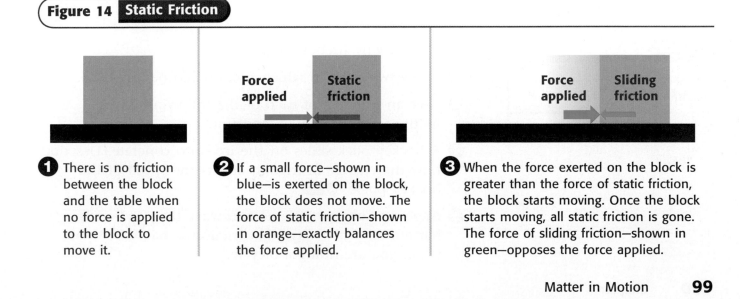

❶ There is no friction between the block and the table when no force is applied to the block to move it.

❷ If a small force—shown in blue—is exerted on the block, the block does not move. The force of static friction—shown in orange—exactly balances the force applied.

❸ When the force exerted on the block is greater than the force of static friction, the block starts moving. Once the block starts moving, all static friction is gone. The force of sliding friction—shown in green—opposes the force applied.

Some Ways to Reduce Friction

One way to reduce friction is to use lubricants (LOO bri kuhnts). *Lubricants* are substances that are applied to surfaces to reduce the friction between them. Some examples of lubricants are motor oil, wax, and grease.

Friction can also be reduced by switching from sliding friction to rolling friction. Ball bearings are placed between the wheels and axles of in-line skates and bicycles to reduce friction and to make turning the wheels easier.

Another way to reduce friction is to make the surfaces that rub against each other smoother. For example, rubbing a park bench with sandpaper makes it smoother and more comfortable to sit on. The bench is more comfortable because the friction between your leg and the bench is reduced.

Some Ways to Increase Friction

One way to increase friction is to make surfaces rougher. For example, sand scattered on icy roads helps keep cars from skidding. Baseball players sometimes wear textured batting gloves to increase the friction between their hands and the bat.

Another way to increase friction is to increase the force pushing the surfaces together. For example, you can ensure that your magazine will not blow away at the park by putting a heavy rock on it. The added mass of the rock increases the friction between the magazine and the ground. Or if you are sanding a piece of wood, you can sand the wood faster by pressing harder on the sandpaper. **Figure 15** shows another situation in which friction is increased by pushing on an object.

Figure 15 *No one enjoys cleaning pans with baked-on food! To make this chore pass quickly, press down with the scrubber to increase friction.*

SECTION REVIEW

❶ Explain why friction occurs.

❷ Name two ways in which friction can be increased.

❸ Give an example of each of the following types of friction: sliding, rolling, and fluid.

❹ A hockey puck slides off the ice onto concrete. Describe how the change in friction affects the speed of the hockey puck. ⭐TEKS

❺ **Applying Concepts** Name two ways that friction is harmful and two ways that friction is helpful to you when you are riding a bicycle.

Terms to Learn

gravity
weight
mass

What You'll Do

- Define gravity.
- Describe the changes in direction or position of an object affected by gravity. ⊙ TEKS
- State the law of universal gravitation.
- Describe the difference between mass and weight.

Biology

C O N N E C T I O N

Scientists think seeds can "sense" gravity. The ability to sense gravity is what causes seeds to always send roots down and send the green shoot up. But scientists do not understand just how seeds sense gravity. Astronauts have grown seedlings during space shuttle missions to see how seeds respond to changes in gravity. So far, there are no definite answers from the results of these experiments.

Gravity: A Force of Attraction

Have you ever seen a videotape of astronauts on the moon? They bounce around like beach balls even though they wear heavy spacesuits. Why is leaping on the moon easier than leaping on Earth?

The answer has to do with gravity. **Gravity** is the force of attraction between objects that is due to their masses. The force of gravity can affect the position of an object or the direction of its motion. In this section, you will learn about the effects of gravity on objects, such as the astronaut in **Figure 16**.

All Matter Is Affected by Gravity

All matter has mass. Gravity is a result of mass. Therefore, all matter is affected by gravity. That is, all objects experience an attraction toward all other objects. Gravitational force "pulls" objects toward each other. Right now, because of gravity, you are being pulled toward this book, your pencil, and every other object around you.

The objects around you are also being pulled toward you and toward each other because of gravity. So, why don't you notice objects moving toward each other? The mass of most objects is too small to cause an attraction large enough to move objects toward each other. But, you are familiar with one object that is massive enough to cause a noticeable attraction—the Earth.

Figure 16 *Because gravity is less on the moon than on Earth, walking on the moon's surface was a very bouncy experience for the Apollo astronauts.*

Self-Check

How does gravity affect the path of a ball when you throw it? *(See page 640 to check your answer.)* ★TEKS

Figure 17 *Sir Isaac Newton realized that an unbalanced force was needed to make an apple fall from a tree.*

Earth's Gravitational Force Is Large

Compared with all the objects around you, Earth has an enormous mass. Therefore, Earth's gravitational force is very large. You must apply forces to overcome Earth's gravitational force any time you lift objects or even parts of your body.

Earth's gravitational force pulls everything toward the center of Earth. As a result, the books, tables, and chairs in the room stay in place, and dropped objects fall to Earth rather than moving together or toward you.

The Law of Universal Gravitation

For thousands of years, two very puzzling questions were, Why do objects fall toward Earth, and what keeps the planets in motion in the sky? The two questions were treated as separate topics until a British scientist named Sir Isaac Newton (1642–1727) realized that they were two parts of the same question.

The Core of an Idea

Legend has it that Newton made the connection when he observed a falling apple one night, as illustrated in **Figure 17.** He knew that unbalanced forces are necessary to move or change the motion of objects. He concluded that an unbalanced force has to act on the apple to make it fall. In the same way, an unbalanced force has to act on the moon to keep it moving around Earth. He proposed that these two forces are actually the same force—a force of attraction called gravity.

A Law Is Born

Newton generalized his observations on gravity in a law now known as the *law of universal gravitation*. This law describes the relationships between gravitational force, mass, and distance. It is called universal because it applies to all objects in the universe.

The law of universal gravitation states the following: All objects in the universe attract each other through gravitational force. The size of the force depends on the masses of the objects and the distance between them. The examples in **Figure 18** show the effects of the law of universal gravitation. Understanding the law is easier if you consider it in two parts.

Part 1: Gravitational Force Increases as Mass Increases

Imagine an elephant and a cat. An elephant has a larger mass than a cat. So, the amount of gravity between an elephant and Earth is greater than the amount of gravity between a cat and Earth. A cat is much easier to pick up than an elephant! Gravity between the cat and the elephant is very small. That's because the cat's mass and the elephant's mass are so much smaller than Earth's mass.

The moon has less mass than Earth. Therefore, the moon's gravitational force is less than Earth's. Do you remember the astronauts on the moon? They bounced around as they walked because they were not being pulled down with as much force as they would have been on Earth.

Astronomy CONNECTION

Black holes are formed when massive stars collapse. Black holes are 10 times to 1 billion times more massive than our sun. Thus, their gravitational force is incredibly large. The gravity of a black hole is so large that an object that enters a black hole can never get out. Even light cannot escape from a black hole. Because black holes do not emit light, they cannot be seen.

Figure 18 | **Gravitational Force Between Objects**

The arrows indicate the gravitational force between the objects.
The width of the arrows indicates the size of the force.

a Gravitational force is small between objects with small masses.

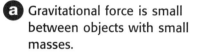

b Gravitational force is larger between objects with larger masses.

c If the distance between two objects increases, the gravitational force pulling them together decreases.

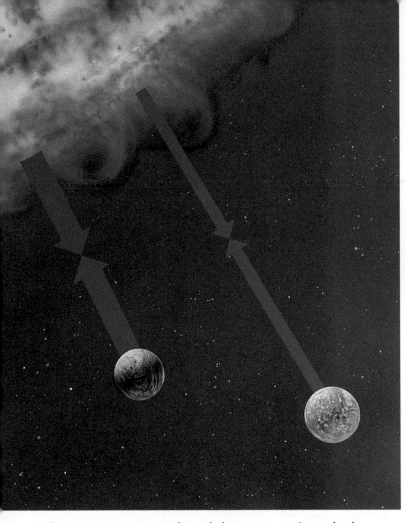

Figure 19 *Venus and Earth have approximately the same mass. However, Venus is closer to the sun. Thus, the gravity between Venus and the sun is greater than the gravity between Earth and the sun.*

Part 2: Gravitational Force Decreases as Distance Increases

The gravity between you and Earth is large. Whenever you jump up, you are pulled back down by Earth's gravitational force. On the other hand, the sun is more than 300,000 times as massive as Earth. So why doesn't the sun's gravitational force affect you more than Earth's does? The reason is that the sun is so far away.

You are about 150 million kilometers away from the sun. At this distance, the gravity between you and the sun is very small. If there were some way you could stand on the sun (and not burn up!), you would find jumping or even walking impossible. The sun is so massive that the gravitational force acting on you would be too large for your muscles to lift any part of your body!

The sun's gravitational force does not have much of an effect on your body here on Earth. However, it does have a big effect on Earth and the other planets, as illustrated in **Figure 19.** The gravity between the sun and the planets is large because the objects have large masses. If the sun's gravitational force did not have such an effect on the planets, the planets would not stay in orbit around the sun.

·····Activity·····

Suppose you had a device that could increase or decrease the gravitational force of objects around you (including small sections of Earth). In your ScienceLog, describe what you might do with the device, what effect the device would have on the weight of objects, and how changes in gravity would affect the speed of objects.

Weight Is a Measure of Gravitational Force

You have learned that gravity is a force of attraction between objects that is due to their masses. **Weight** is a measure of the gravitational force exerted on an object. The word *weight* usually refers to Earth's gravitational force on an object. But weight can also be a measure of the gravitational force exerted on objects by the moon or other planets.

You have learned that the unit of force is a newton (N). Because weight is a measure of gravitational force, weight is also expressed in newtons. On Earth, an object with a mass of 100 g, such as a medium-sized apple, weighs approximately 1 N.

Weight and Mass Are Different

Weight is related to mass. However, the two are not the same. Weight changes when gravitational force changes. **Mass** is the amount of matter in an object, and its value does not change. Imagine that an object is moved to a place with a greater gravitational force—such as the planet Jupiter. Its weight will increase, but its mass will remain the same. **Figure 20** shows the weight and mass of an astronaut on Earth and on the moon. The moon's gravitational force is about one-sixth of Earth's.

Gravitational force is about the same everywhere on Earth. So, the weight of any object is about the same everywhere. Because mass and weight are constant on Earth, the terms are often used to mean the same thing. Be sure you understand the difference!

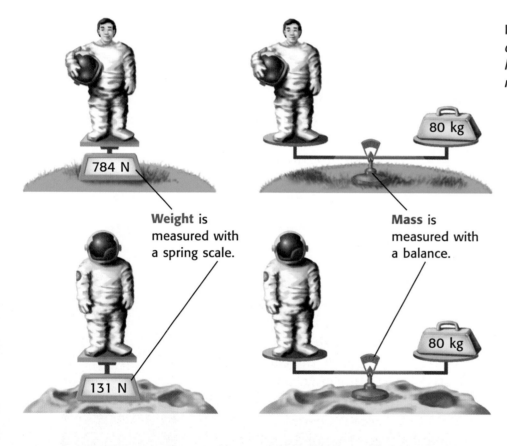

Weight is measured with a spring scale.

Mass is measured with a balance.

Figure 20 *The astronaut's weight on the moon is about one-sixth of his weight on Earth, but his mass remains constant.*

SECTION REVIEW

1. Describe how gravity affects a basketball when you throw it toward the basket. ⭐TEKS

2. How does the distance between objects affect the gravity between them?

3. **Comparing Concepts** Explain why your weight would change but your mass would not if you orbited Earth in the space shuttle.

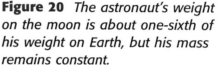

internetconnect

SCLINKS
NSTA **GO TO:** www.scilinks.org

TOPIC: Matter and Gravity
***sci*LINKS NUMBER:** HSTP115

Detecting Acceleration ⭐TEKS

Have you ever noticed that you can "feel" acceleration? In a car or in an elevator, you notice the change in speed or direction—even with your eyes closed! Inside your ears are tiny hair cells. These cells can detect the movement of fluid in your inner ear. When you accelerate, the fluid does, too. The hair cells detect this acceleration in the fluid and send a message to your brain. This message allows you to sense acceleration. In this activity, you will build a model of an accelerometer—a device that detects acceleration.

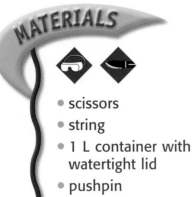

MATERIALS

- scissors
- string
- 1 L container with watertight lid
- pushpin
- small cork or plastic-foam ball
- modeling clay
- water

Procedure

1 Cut a piece of string that is just long enough to reach three-quarters of the way inside the container.

2 Use a pushpin to attach one end of the string to the cork or plastic-foam ball.

3 Use modeling clay to attach the other end of the string to the center of the inside of the container lid. Be careful not to use too much string—the cork (or ball) should hang no farther than three-quarters of the way into the container.

4 Fill the container to the top with water.

5 Put the lid tightly on the container with the string and cork (or ball) on the inside.

6 Turn the container upside down (lid on the bottom). The cork should float about three-quarters of the way up inside the container, as shown at right. You are now ready to use your accelerometer to detect acceleration by following the steps on the next page.

7 Put the accelerometer lid side down on a tabletop. Notice that the cork floats straight up in the water.

8 Now start gently pushing the accelerometer across the table at a constant speed. Notice that the cork quickly moves in the direction you are pushing and then swings backward. If you did not see this motion, try the same thing again until you are sure you can see the first movement of the cork.

9 When you are familiar with how to use your accelerometer, try the following changes in motion. Record your observations of the cork's first motion for each change in your ScienceLog.

a. While moving the device across the table, push a little faster.

b. While moving the device across the table, slow down.

c. While moving the device across the table, change the direction that you are pushing. (Try changing both to the left and to the right.)

d. Make any other changes in motion you can think of. You should change only one part of the motion at a time.

Analysis

10 The cork moves forward (in the direction you were pushing the bottle) when you speed up but backward when you slow down. Explain why. (Hint: Think about the changes in direction of motion of an object when acted on by a force.)

11 When you start pushing the bottle and then push it at a constant speed, why does the cork quickly swing back after it shows the direction of acceleration?

12 Imagine you are standing on a corner and watching a car that is waiting at a stoplight. A passenger inside the car is holding some helium balloons. Based on what you observed using your accelerometer, what do you think will happen to the balloons when the car begins moving?

Going Further
If you move the bottle in a circle at a constant speed, what do you predict the cork will do? Try it, and check your answer.

Highlights

Section 1

Vocabulary

motion *(p. 86)*
speed *(p. 87)*
velocity *(p. 88)*
acceleration *(p. 89)*

Section Notes

- An object is in motion if it changes position over time relative to a reference point.

- The speed of a moving object depends on the distance traveled by the object and the time taken to travel that distance.

- Speed and velocity are not the same. Velocity is speed in a given direction. Acceleration is the rate at which velocity changes.

- An object can accelerate by changing speed, changing direction, or both.

LabBook ✪TEKS

Built for Speed *(p. 607)*

Section 2

Vocabulary

force *(p. 92)*
newton *(p. 92)*
net force *(p. 93)*

Section Notes

- A force is a push or a pull.

- Forces are expressed in newtons.

- Force is always exerted by one object on another object.

- Net force is determined by combining forces.

- Unbalanced forces produce a change in motion. Balanced forces produce no change in motion. ✪TEKS

Section 3

Vocabulary

friction *(p. 96)*

Section Notes

- Friction is a force that opposes motion. Friction can change the speed of a moving object. ✪TEKS

- Friction is caused by "hills and valleys" touching on the surfaces of two objects.

- The amount of friction depends on factors such as the roughness of the surfaces and the force pushing the surfaces together.

- Four kinds of friction that affect your life are sliding friction, rolling friction, fluid friction, and static friction.

- Friction can be harmful or helpful.

LabBook ✪TEKS

Science Friction *(p. 608)*

Section 4

Vocabulary

gravity *(p. 101)*
weight *(p. 104)*
mass *(p. 105)*

Section Notes

- Gravity is a force of attraction between objects that is due to their masses. Gravity can change the position of an object or the direction of its motion. ✪TEKS

- The law of universal gravitation states that all objects in the universe attract each other through gravitational force. The size of the force depends on the masses of the objects and the distance between them.

- Weight and mass are not the same. Mass is the amount of matter in an object; weight is a measure of the gravitational force on an object.

LabBook ✪TEKS

Relating Mass and Weight *(p. 609)*

USING VOCABULARY

Complete the following sentences by choosing the correct term from each pair of terms.

1. __?__ opposes motion between surfaces that are touching. *(Friction or Gravity)*

2. Forces are expressed in __?__. *(newtons or grams)*

3. A __?__ is determined by combining forces. *(net force or newton)*

4. __?__ is the rate at which __?__ changes. *(Velocity or Acceleration/velocity or acceleration)*

UNDERSTANDING CONCEPTS

Multiple Choice

5. A student riding her bicycle on a straight, flat road covers one block every 7 seconds. If each block is 100 m long, she is traveling at
   a. a constant speed.
   b. a constant velocity.
   c. 10 m/s.
   d. Both (a) and (b)

6. Friction is a force that ⭐TEKS
   a. decreases an object's speed.
   b. does not exist when surfaces are very smooth.
   c. decreases with larger mass.
   d. All of the above

7. Rolling friction
   a. is usually less than sliding friction.
   b. makes moving objects on wheels difficult.
   c. is usually greater than sliding friction.
   d. is the same as fluid friction.

8. If Earth's mass doubled, your weight would
   a. increase because gravity increases.
   b. decrease because gravity increases.
   c. increase because gravity decreases.
   d. not change because you are still on Earth.

9. A force ⭐TEKS
   a. is expressed in newtons.
   b. can cause an object to speed up, slow down, or change direction.
   c. is a push or a pull.
   d. All of the above

10. The amount of gravity between 1 kg of lead and Earth is __?__ the amount of gravity between 1 kg of marshmallows and Earth.
    a. greater than   c. the same as
    b. less than   d. None of the above

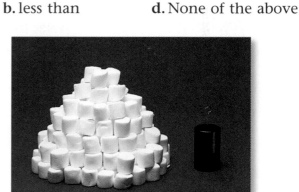

Short Answer

11. Describe the relationship between motion and a reference point.

12. How is it possible to be accelerating and traveling at a constant speed?

13. Explain the difference between mass and weight.

14. Describe how friction affects a person swimming across a lake. ⭐TEKS

CONCEPT MAPPING

15. Use the following terms to create a concept map: *speed, velocity, acceleration, force, direction,* and *motion.* ⭐TEKS

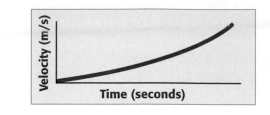

CRITICAL THINKING AND PROBLEM SOLVING

Write one or two sentences to answer the following questions:

16. Your family is moving, and you are asked to help move some boxes. One box is so heavy that you must push it across the room rather than lift it. What are some ways you could reduce friction to make moving the box easier?

17. Explain how using the term *accelerator* when talking about a car's gas pedal can lead to confusion, considering the scientific meaning of the word *acceleration.*

18. Explain why it is important for airplane pilots to know wind velocity, not just wind speed, during a flight.

MATH IN SCIENCE

19. After stopping at a lake for a drink of water, a kangaroo starts hopping again to the south. Every second, the kangaroo's velocity increases 2.5 m/s. Draw a graph showing the kangaroo's velocity over a period of 5 seconds. What is the kangaroo's average acceleration after 5 seconds? ⭐TEKS

INTERPRETING GRAPHICS

20. Does this graph show positive or negative acceleration? How can you tell?

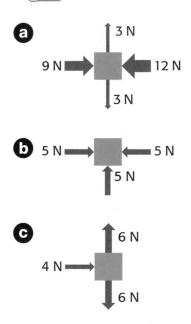

21. You know how to combine two forces that act in one or two directions. The same method you learned can be used to combine several forces acting in several directions. Examine the diagrams below, and predict with how much force and in what direction the object will move. ⭐TEKS

a 3 N ↑ 9 N → 12 N ← 3 N ↓

b 5 N → 5 N ← 5 N ↑

c 6 N ↑ 4 N → 6 N ↓

Reading Check-up

⭐TEKS

Take a minute to review your answers to the Pre-Reading Questions found at the bottom of page 84. Have your answers changed? If necessary, revise your answers based on what you have learned since you began this chapter.

Chapter 4

1 How will the motion of a ball rolling on the ground change if the ball encounters a frictional force that opposes its motion?

  A The ball will speed up.

  B The ball will slow down.

  C The ball's speed will not change.

  D Not Here

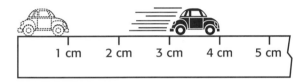

2 What is the *speed* of the toy car above if it moves through the distance shown in 2 seconds?

  F 2 cm/s

  G 2 cm/s²

  H 1.5 cm/s

  J 1.5 cm

3 Two of your classmates are playing tug of war with a piece of rope. Which of the following combinations of forces would cause the rope to move to the left?

  A 75N to the left and 85N to the right

  B 65N to the left and 75N to the right

  C 75N to the left and 65N to the right

  D 75N to the left and 75N to the right

4 Which will fly farther, a cannonball fired on Earth or a cannonball fired on the moon?

  F A cannonball fired on the moon

  G A cannonball fired on Earth

  H Neither

  J Cannonballs are too heavy to fly on the moon.

5 Sam rolls the same ball down two ramps (A and B) and finds that the ball rolls farther when rolled down ramp A. Which of the following is NOT a reasonable hypothesis?

  A A is steeper than B.

  B The ball weighs less on A than on B.

  C A is smoother than B.

  D A is longer than B.

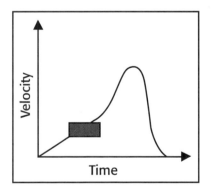

6 The graph above represents a bird's motion. During the shaded time interval, the bird

  F accelerates.

  G slows down.

  H flies higher.

  J decelerates.

Chapter 4

Math

1 Which of the following is equivalent to $\frac{3}{2}$?

A $1\frac{1}{3}$

B 1.5

C $2\frac{1}{2}$

D 0.67

2 Which of the following describes the angle marked in the triangle below?

F Obtuse

G Right

H Not an angle

J Acute

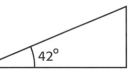

3 What is the mode of the following set of numbers: 4, 4, 5, 6, 6, 8, 9, 9, 9, and 10?

A 7

B 9

C 6

D 10

4 Which is in correct order from smallest fraction to largest fraction?

F $\frac{1}{2}, \frac{4}{5}, \frac{2}{3}, \frac{8}{9}$

G $\frac{2}{3}, \frac{5}{4}, \frac{7}{6}, \frac{10}{8}$

H $\frac{2}{3}, \frac{4}{5}, \frac{3}{2}, \frac{5}{3}$

J $\frac{1}{2}, \frac{1}{3}, \frac{1}{4}, \frac{1}{5}$

Reading

Read the passage. Then read each question that follows the passage. Decide which is the best answer to each question.

If you look closely at the surface of a golf ball, you'll see dozens of tiny dimples. When air flows past these dimples, it gets stirred up. By keeping air moving near the surface of the ball, the dimples help the golf ball move faster and farther through the air. Jeff DiTullio, a teacher at MIT, in Cambridge, Massachusetts, decided to apply this same idea to a baseball bat. When DiTullio tested his dimpled bat in a wind tunnel, he found that it could be swung 3 to 5 percent faster. That increase may not sound like much, but it could add about 5 m of distance to a fly ball!

1 Who is Jeff DiTullio?

A The inventor of the dimpled golf ball

B A teacher at Cambridge University

C The inventor of the dimpled bat

D A professional baseball player

2 Which of the following is NOT stated in the passage?

F Dimples make DiTullio's bat move faster.

G MIT is in Cambridge, Massachusetts.

H Stirred-up air near the surface of DiTullio's bat makes it easier to swing fast.

J DiTullio will make a lot of money from his invention.

The Golden Gate Bridge

Have you ever relaxed in a hammock? If so, you may have noticed how tense the strings got when the hammock supported your weight. Now imagine a hammock 1,965 m long supporting a 20-ton roadway with more than 100,000 cars traveling along its length each day. That describes the Golden Gate Bridge! Because of the way the bridge is built, it is very much like a giant hammock.

Tug of War

The bridge's roadway is suspended from main cables 2.33 km long that sweep from one end of the bridge to the other and that are anchored at each end. Smaller cables called *hangers* connect the main cables to the roadway. Tension, the force of being pulled apart, is created as the cables are pulled down by the weight of the roadway while being pushed up by the two main towers.

▲ *The Golden Gate Bridge spans the San Francisco Bay.*

Towering Above

Towers 227 m tall support the cables over the long distance across San Francisco Bay, which makes the Golden Gate Bridge the tallest bridge in the world. The towers receive a force that is the exact opposite of tension—compression.

Compression is the force of being pushed together. The main cables holding the weight of the roadway push down on the top of the towers while Earth pushes up on the bottom.

Stretching the Limits

Tension and compression are elastic forces, which means they are dependent on elasticity, the ability of an object to return to its original shape after being stretched or compressed. If an object is not very elastic, it breaks easily or becomes permanently deformed when subjected to an elastic force. The cables and towers of the Golden Gate Bridge are made of steel, a material with great elastic strength. A single steel wire 2.54 mm thick can support over half a ton without breaking!

On the Road

The roadway of the Golden Gate Bridge is subjected to multiple forces, including friction, gravity, and elastic forces, at the same time. Rolling friction is caused by the wheels of each vehicle moving across the roadway's surface. Gravity pulls down on the roadway but is counteracted by the support of the towers and cables. This causes each roadway span to bend slightly and experience both tension and compression. The bottom of each span is under tension because the cables and towers pull up along the road's sides, while gravity pulls down at its center. These same forces cause compression at the top of each span. Did you know that so many forces were at work on a bridge?

Bridge the Gap

▶ Find out more about another type of bridge, such as an arch, a beam, or a cable-stayed bridge. How do forces such as friction, gravity, tension, and compression affect this type of bridge?

UNIT 2

A World of Energy

SCIENCE

Place to Visit

Kilgore ★

The discovery of oil in Texas was one of the most important events in the history of the Lone Star State. The "oil boom" that started near the town of Nacogdoches spread quickly throughout East Texas. People flocked to the area with the hope of striking it rich. Since the early 1900s, the oil industry has become very important in Texas. Oil is a big reason why many towns and cities have thrived. At the East Texas Oil Museum in Kilgore, Texas, you can see what life was like for men and women in the oil "boomtowns" of East Texas during the 1930s.

A scene from the East Texas Oil Museum in Kilgore, Texas

Scientific Research

Near the small town of Bushland, near Amarillo, Texas, tall towers with propellers reach into the sky. The nearly constant wind spins the propellers of wind turbines to generate electrical energy. At the Alternative Energy Institute at West Texas A&M University in Canyon, Texas, scientists are researching wind energy. These scientists not only measure wind speed in Texas throughout the year but also study and test designs for wind turbines. The goal is to find more-efficient ways of using wind energy as a source for generating electrical energy.

Bushland

Science Career

Austin

David Turner is a civil engineer for the Lower Colorado River Authority in Austin, Texas. He designs high-voltage power lines and the supporting towers that carry electrical energy from the generating stations to the users around central Texas. Turner uses his knowledge of electric power to design the lines that carry the electric current. His understanding of properties of materials such as steel, aluminum, concrete, and wood helps him design the support towers. Turner's work helps electric companies supply people and businesses with the electrical energy they need.

internetconnect

go.hrw.com

go to: go.hrw.com
KEYWORD: HTXU62

Pre-Reading
Questions

1. What is energy? ⭐TEKS
2. How do machines help humans use energy? ⭐TEKS
3. What is an energy resource? ⭐TEKS

Energy and Energy Resources

THE RACE IS ON!

Imagine that you're a driver in this race. Your car will need a lot of energy to finish, so you should make sure your car is fueled up and ready. You'll probably need a lot of gasoline, right? Nope—just a lot of sunshine! The cars in this photo are solar powered, which means energy from the sun makes them go. In this chapter, you'll learn about different types of energy. You'll also learn where the energy used to run our cars and our appliances comes from.

ENERGY SWINGS! ⭐TEKS

All matter has energy. But what is energy? In this activity, you'll observe a moving pendulum to learn about energy.

Procedure

1. Make a pendulum by tying a **15 cm long string** around the hook of the **100 g hooked mass.**

2. Hold the string with one hand. Pull the mass slightly to the side, and let go of the mass without pushing it. Watch at least 10 swings of the pendulum.

3. In your ScienceLog, record your observations. Be sure to note how fast and how high the pendulum swings.

4. Repeat step 2, but pull the mass farther to the side.

5. Record your observations, noting how fast and how high the pendulum swings.

Analysis

6. Do you think the pendulum has energy? Explain your answer.

7. What causes the pendulum to move?

8. Do you think the pendulum had energy before you let go of the mass? Explain your answer.

READING WARM-UP

Terms to Learn

energy
kinetic energy
potential energy

What You'll Do

● Define energy. ⭐TEKS
● Explain how energy and work are related.
● Describe the different forms of energy.

What Is Energy?

It's match point. The tennis player tosses the ball into the air and then slams it with her racket. The ball flies toward her opponent, who swings her racket at the ball. Suddenly, THWOOSH!! The ball goes into the net, causing the net to shake. Game, set, and match!!

The tennis player needs energy to slam the ball with her racket. The ball also must have energy in order to cause the net to shake. Energy is around you all the time. But what, exactly, is energy? Read on to find out!

Energy and Work—Working Together

In science, you can think of **energy** as the ability to do work. *Work* happens when a force causes an object to move in the direction of the force. How are energy and work involved in playing tennis? Look at **Figure 1.** The tennis player does work on her racket by exerting a force on it. The racket moves in the direction of that force. The racket then does work on the ball, and the ball does work on the net. In each case, something is given by one object to another that allows the second object to do work. That "something" is energy. Figure 1 shows how energy can be transferred from one thing to another. The units of energy are called joules (J).

Figure 1 *Energy is the ability to do work. When one object does work on another, energy is transferred.*

a The tennis player has energy that she transfers to the racket.

b Energy is transferred from the racket to the ball when the racket hits the ball.

Kinetic Energy Is Energy of Motion

Energy is transferred from the racket to the ball during a game of tennis. As the ball flies over the net, it has kinetic energy. **Kinetic** (ki NET ik) **energy** is the energy of motion. All moving objects, even the slow-moving tortoise in **Figure 2,** have kinetic energy.

Kinetic Energy Depends on Speed and Mass

The amount of kinetic energy a moving object has depends on its speed and mass. The faster something is moving, the more kinetic energy it has. If the tortoise in Figure 2 sped up, its kinetic energy would increase. Also, the more massive a moving object is, the more kinetic energy it has. A car moving at the same speed as a tortoise would have more kinetic energy than the tortoise. An object's kinetic energy can be found using the following equation:

$$kinetic\ energy = \frac{mv^2}{2}$$

Figure 2 *As long as this tortoise is moving, it has kinetic energy.*

In this equation, *m* stands for an object's mass and *v* stands for an object's speed. As you can see, speed is squared. So speed has a greater effect on kinetic energy than mass does. You can practice using this equation in the MathFocus below.

MathFocus

Kinetic Energy

What is the *kinetic energy* of a car with a *mass* of 1,200 kg moving at a *speed* of 20 m/s?

Step 1: Write the equation for kinetic energy (*KE*).

$$KE = \frac{mv^2}{2}$$

Step 2: Replace *m* and *v* with the measurements given in the problem, and solve.

$$KE = \frac{1{,}200\ \text{kg} \times (20\ \text{m/s})^2}{2}$$

$$KE = \frac{1{,}200\ \text{kg} \times 400\ \text{m}^2/\text{s}^2}{2}$$

$$KE = \frac{480{,}000\ \text{kg} \bullet \text{m}^2/\text{s}^2}{2}$$

$$KE = 240{,}000\ \text{kg} \bullet \text{m}^2/\text{s}^2 = 240{,}000\ \text{J}$$
(Note: 1 kg•m^2/s^2 = 1 J)

Now It's Your Turn

1. What is the kinetic energy of a car with a mass of 1,200 kg moving at 25 m/s?

2. What is the kinetic energy of a 4,000 kg elephant running at 3 m/s? at 4 m/s?

3. What is the kinetic energy of a bus with a mass of 2,000 kg moving at 30 m/s?

Potential Energy Is Energy of Position

Not all energy involves motion. **Potential energy** is the energy an object has because of its position or shape. Look at **Figure 3.** The wound-up rubber band in this model airplane has potential energy. When the rubber band is released, the plane uses that energy to fly.

Gravitational Potential Energy Depends on Weight and Height

To lift an object, you do work on it by using a force that opposes gravitational force. Lifting the object gives it *gravitational potential energy.* The amount of gravitational potential energy the object has depends on its height and weight. If two objects with different weights are placed at the same height, the object that weighs more has more gravitational potential energy. If two objects with equal weights are placed at different heights, the object at the greater height has more gravitational potential energy. You can find an object's gravitational potential energy by using the following equation:

gravitational potential energy = weight × height

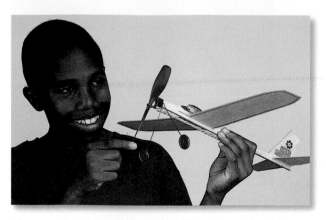

Figure 3 *The wound-up rubber band in this photo has potential energy because its shape has been changed.*

MathFocus ·

Gravitational Potential Energy

What is the *gravitational potential energy* of a book with a *weight* of 13 N at a *height* of 1.5 m off the ground?

Step 1: Write the equation for gravitational potential energy (*GPE*).

$GPE = weight \times height$

Step 2: Replace the weight and height with the measurements given in the problem, and solve.

$GPE = 13 \text{ N} \times 1.5 \text{ m}$

$GPE = 19.5 \text{ N•m}$

$GPE = 19.5 \text{ J}$

(Note: 1 N•m = 1 J)

Now It's Your Turn

1. What is the gravitational potential energy of a cat that weighs 40 N standing on a table 0.8 m above the ground?

2. What is the gravitational potential energy of a diver who weighs 500 N standing on a platform 10 m off the ground?

Forms of Energy

All energy involves either motion or position. But energy takes different forms. In the next few pages, you will learn more about the different forms of energy.

Thermal Energy

All matter is made of particles that are always moving. Because the particles are moving, they have kinetic energy. The particles also have energy because of how they are arranged. *Thermal energy* is the total energy of the particles that make up an object. At higher temperatures, particles move faster. The faster the particles move, the more kinetic energy they have and the greater the object's thermal energy is. In addition, particles of a substance that are farther apart have more energy than particles of the same substance that are closer together. Look at **Figure 4.** Thermal energy also depends on the number of particles in a substance.

Figure 4 *The particles in steam have more energy than the particles in ice or ocean water. But the ocean has the most thermal energy because it has the most particles.*

The particles in an **ice cube** vibrate in fixed positions and therefore do not have a lot of energy.

The particles in **ocean water** are not in fixed positions and can move around. They have more energy than the particles in an ice cube.

The particles in **steam** are far apart. They move rapidly, so they have more energy than the particles in ocean water.

Chemical Energy

During a chemical change, substances react to form new substances. The new substances have different amounts of chemical energy than the original substances. *Chemical energy* is the energy stored in a substance that can be released when the substance reacts.

Some examples of chemical energy are shown in **Figure 5.** When wood is burned, chemical energy is released. You can use this energy to toast a marshmallow. The sugar in the marshmallow also has chemical energy. After you eat the marshmallow, your body can use that energy.

Figure 5 *Both wood and a marshmallow have chemical energy.*

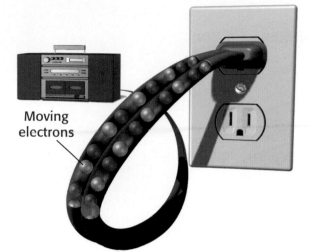

Figure 6 *A stereo uses electrical energy to produce sound.*

Moving electrons

Electrical Energy

The electrical outlets in your home allow you to use electrical energy, which is generated at electric power plants. *Electrical energy* is the energy of moving electrons. Electrons are negatively charged particles.

Look at **Figure 6.** Suppose you plug in a portable stereo and turn it on. The electrons in the wires will move back and forth, changing directions 120 times per second. As the electrons move, energy is transferred to different parts inside the stereo. The electrical energy created by moving electrons is used to do work. The work of a stereo is to make sound.

Sound Energy

To play a guitar like the one shown in **Figure 7,** you pluck the strings. The strings vibrate, or move back and forth. *Sound energy* is caused by an object's vibrations. When a guitar string vibrates, energy is transferred from the moving guitar string to the air particles around it. The air particles then vibrate and transmit energy from particle to particle. When the vibrating air particles cause your eardrum to vibrate, you hear the sound of the guitar. In the same way, sound can be transmitted through other materials, such as water or wood.

Figure 7 *Vibrations that produce sound are transmitted through the air.*

Quick Lab

Hear That Energy! Ⓣᴇᴋˢ

1. Make a simple drum by covering the open end of an **empty coffee can** with **wax paper.** Use a **rubber band** to hold the wax paper in place.

2. Using the eraser end of a **pencil,** tap lightly on the wax paper. In your ScienceLog, describe what happens to the paper. What do you hear?

3. Repeat step 2, but tap the paper a bit harder. In your ScienceLog, compare your results with those of step 2.

4. Cover half of the wax paper with one hand. Now tap the paper. What happened to the sound? How is sound energy related to kinetic energy? to potential energy?

TRY at HOME

Light Energy

Light allows us to see, but did you know that not all light can be seen? Microwave ovens, such as the one in **Figure 8,** use a type of light that we can't see. *Light energy* is caused by the vibrations of electrically charged particles. Like sound vibrations, light vibrations cause energy to be transmitted. But unlike sound vibrations, the vibrations that transmit light energy do not require particles to transmit energy. So light energy can be transmitted through a vacuum (the absence of matter).

Figure 8 *The energy used to cook food in a microwave is a form of light energy.*

Nuclear Energy

What form of energy can come from a tiny amount of matter, can be used to generate electrical energy, and gives the sun its energy? It's *nuclear* (NOO klee uhr) *energy,* the energy that can be caused by changes in the nucleus (NOO klee uhs) of an atom. An *atom* is the smallest particle into which an element can be divided and still remain that element. The nucleus is the center of an atom. Nuclear energy is produced in two ways—when two or more nuclei (NOO klee ie) join together or when the nucleus of an atom splits apart.

In the sun, shown in **Figure 9,** small nuclei join together to make a larger nucleus. This reaction gives off a huge amount of energy that allows the sun to light and heat the Earth. The nuclei of some atoms store a lot of potential energy. When work is done to split these nuclei apart, that energy is given off. This type of nuclear energy is used to create electrical energy at nuclear power plants.

Figure 9 *Without the nuclear energy from the sun, life on Earth would not be possible.*

SECTION REVIEW

1. Define the term energy. ⭐TEKS

2. How are energy and work related?

3. What determines an object's thermal energy?

4. Explain how sound energy is produced when you beat a drum.

5. **Analyzing Relationships** Explain why a high-speed crash might cause more damage to automobiles than a low-speed crash.

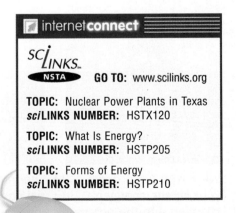

internet**connect**

SC*LINKS*
NSTA　　GO TO: www.scilinks.org

TOPIC: Nuclear Power Plants in Texas
*sci*LINKS NUMBER: HSTX120

TOPIC: What Is Energy?
*sci*LINKS NUMBER: HSTP205

TOPIC: Forms of Energy
*sci*LINKS NUMBER: HSTP210

Energy and Energy Resources　　**123**

READING WARM-UP

Terms to Learn

energy conversion
friction
law of conservation of energy

What You'll Do

- Give examples of energy conversions.

- Identify energy conversions that occur during the production of energy for human use. ⭐TEKS

- Explain the law of conservation of energy and why perpetual motion is impossible.

Energy Conversions

Imagine you're in art class, finishing a clay mug. You turn around and your elbow knocks the mug off the table. Luckily, you catch the mug before it hits the ground. Whew!

While sitting on the table, the mug has gravitational potential energy. As the mug falls, its gravitational potential energy changes into kinetic energy. This change is an example of an energy conversion. An **energy conversion** is a change from one form of energy to another. (An energy conversion can also be referred to as an energy transformation.) Any form of energy can be changed into any other form of energy. Often, one form of energy is changed into more than one form.

From Kinetic to Potential and Back

Take a look at **Figure 10.** Have you ever jumped on a trampoline? Because you're moving when you jump, you have kinetic energy. Each time you jump into the air, your position above the ground changes. So you also have gravitational potential energy. Another kind of potential energy is involved too—that of the trampoline stretching when you jump on it.

Figure 10   Energy Conversions on a Trampoline

1 When you jump down, your kinetic energy is changed into the potential energy of the stretched trampoline.

2 The trampoline's potential energy is changed into kinetic energy, which is transferred to you, making you bounce up.

3 At the top of your jump, all of your kinetic energy has been changed into potential energy.

4 Right before you hit the trampoline, all of your potential energy has been changed back into kinetic energy.

Energy Conversions in a Pendulum

Another example of the energy conversions between kinetic and potential energy is shown in **Figure 11.** A pendulum (PEN dyoo luhm) is a mass hung from a fixed point so that it can swing freely. When you lift the mass to one side, the energy used to move it is stored as potential energy. When you let the mass go, it swings because the Earth exerts a force on it. As the mass swings down, its potential energy is changed into kinetic energy. The total energy of a pendulum at any time is called its mechanical energy. *Mechanical energy* is the sum of an object's kinetic and potential energy.

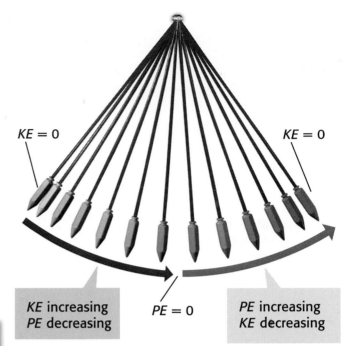

$KE = 0$ $KE = 0$

KE increasing
PE decreasing

$PE = 0$

PE increasing
KE decreasing

Figure 11 *A pendulum's mechanical energy is all kinetic (KE) at the bottom of its swing and all potential (PE) at the top of its swing.*

> ### ✔ Self-Check
>
> At what point does a roller coaster have the greatest potential energy? the greatest kinetic energy? *(See page 640 to check your answers.)*

Conversions Involving Chemical Energy

You've probably heard the saying "Breakfast is the most important meal of the day." Why does eating breakfast help you start the day? Look at **Figure 12.** As your body digests food, chemical energy can be used by your body.

Figure 12 *Your body carries out energy conversions.*

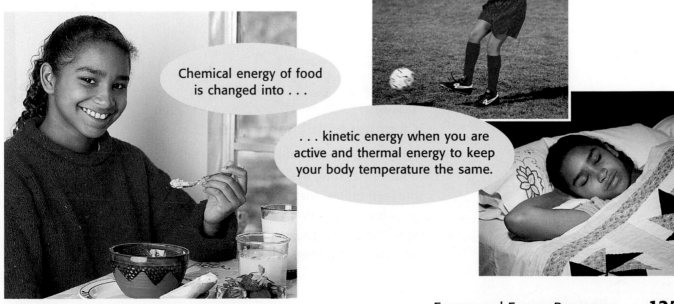

Chemical energy of food is changed into . . .

. . . kinetic energy when you are active and thermal energy to keep your body temperature the same.

Energy Conversions in Plants

Would you believe that the chemical energy in the food you eat comes from the sun's energy? It's true! When you eat fruits, vegetables, grains, or meat from animals that ate plants, you are taking in chemical energy. The chemical energy in food comes from a chemical change that uses the sun's energy. Look at **Figure 13.** Photosynthesis (FOHT oh SIN thuh sis) uses light energy to create new substances with chemical energy. In this way, light energy is changed into chemical energy.

Figure 13 *Green plants use chlorophyll and light energy from the sun to make the chemical energy in food.*

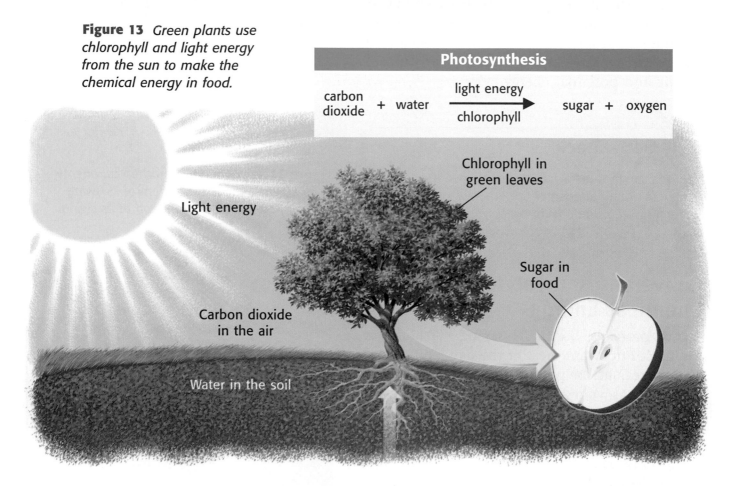

Photosynthesis

carbon dioxide + water $\xrightarrow[\text{chlorophyll}]{\text{light energy}}$ sugar + oxygen

Light energy

Chlorophyll in green leaves

Carbon dioxide in the air

Sugar in food

Water in the soil

Camping with Energy ⭐TEKS

When you go camping, you probably use a stove, such as the one shown here, to prepare meals. Identify some of the energy transformations that take place when you light the stove, cook the food, eat the meal, and then go hiking.

Conversions Involving Electrical Energy

You use electrical energy all the time. When you listen to the radio, make toast, or take a picture with a camera, you use electrical energy. Electrical energy can easily be changed into other forms of energy. **Figure 14** shows how electrical energy is changed in a hair dryer.

Why Energy Conversions Are Important

Everything we do is related to energy conversions. Heating our homes, getting energy from a meal, growing plants, and doing many other activities require energy conversions. You can think of energy conversions as a way of getting energy in the form that you need. Machines, such as a hair dryer, help harness energy and make that energy work for you. Electrical energy won't dry your hair. But you can use a hair dryer to change electrical energy into the thermal energy that will help you dry your hair. The chart at the bottom of the page lists some other energy conversions that involve electrical energy.

Self-Check

When you make toast, what energy conversions take place? *(See page 640 to check your answer.)* ⊛TEKS

Figure 14 | **Energy Conversions in a Hair Dryer**

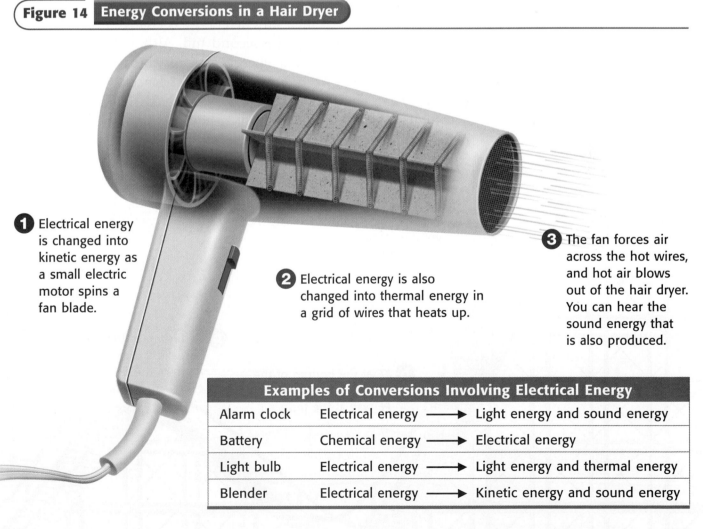

❶ Electrical energy is changed into kinetic energy as a small electric motor spins a fan blade.

❷ Electrical energy is also changed into thermal energy in a grid of wires that heats up.

❸ The fan forces air across the hot wires, and hot air blows out of the hair dryer. You can hear the sound energy that is also produced.

Examples of Conversions Involving Electrical Energy		
Alarm clock	Electrical energy ⟶	Light energy and sound energy
Battery	Chemical energy ⟶	Electrical energy
Light bulb	Electrical energy ⟶	Light energy and thermal energy
Blender	Electrical energy ⟶	Kinetic energy and sound energy

Conservation of Energy

As the cars go up and down the hills on a roller coaster track, their potential energy is changed into kinetic energy and back again. But the cars never return to the same height from which they started. Does energy get lost along the way? No, keep reading to learn why.

Overcoming Friction

Friction is a force that opposes motion between two surfaces that are touching. For the roller coaster to move, energy must be used to overcome the friction between the wheels of the cars and the track and between the cars and the surrounding air. As a result, not all of the potential energy of the cars is changed into kinetic energy as the cars go down the first hill. Likewise, as you can see in **Figure 15,** not all of the kinetic energy of the cars is changed back into potential energy.

Energy Is Conserved in a Closed System

When energy is used to overcome friction, it is changed into thermal energy. Some of the potential energy of the roller coaster cars is changed into thermal energy on the way down the first hill. Then some of their kinetic energy is changed into thermal energy on the way up the second hill. Although the amounts of kinetic and potential energy change, the total amount of energy does not. According to the **law of conservation of energy,** energy can be neither created nor destroyed. The total amount of energy in a closed system is always the same. The roller coaster cars, the track, and the surrounding air make up a closed system. The amounts of kinetic, potential, and thermal energy will always add up to the same amount of total energy.

Figure 15 *A roller coaster must overcome friction. For this reason, the second hill of a roller coaster will always be shorter than the first.*

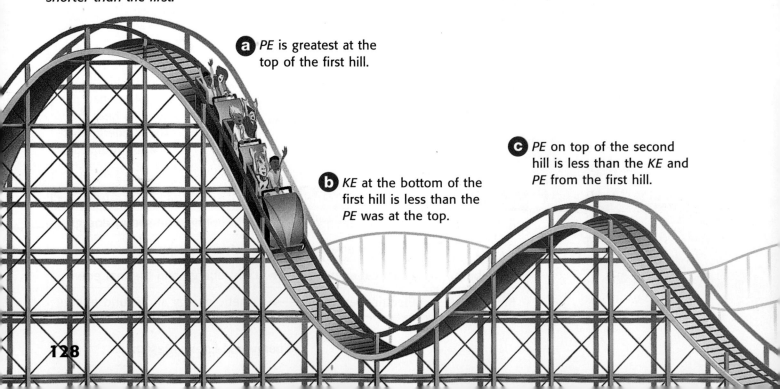

a *PE is greatest at the top of the first hill.*

b *KE at the bottom of the first hill is less than the PE was at the top.*

c *PE on top of the second hill is less than the KE and PE from the first hill.*

Energy Conversions and Efficiency

During any energy conversion, some energy is always changed into thermal energy as a result of overcoming friction. The thermal energy due to friction is not useful because it is not used to do work. *Energy efficiency* (e FISH uhn see) compares the amount of energy before a conversion with the amount of useful energy after a conversion. The less energy that must be used to overcome friction, the more efficient the energy conversion.

Making Conversions Efficient

More energy efficient conversions mean less wasted energy. Look at **Figure 16.** New cars tend to be more energy efficient than old cars. One reason is the smooth, aerodynamic (ER oh die NAM ik) shape of newer cars. The smooth shape reduces friction between the car and the surrounding air. Because these cars move through the air more easily, they use less energy to overcome friction. So they are more efficient.

No Such Thing As Perpetual Motion

A *perpetual* (puhr PECH oo uhl) *motion machine* is a machine that runs forever without any added energy. Such a machine would be 100 percent efficient. In other words, the machine would put out exactly as much energy as it takes in. But because all energy conversions result in some form of energy that isn't useful, perpetual motion is impossible. The only way a machine can keep moving is to have energy constantly delivered to it.

Figure 16 *The shape of newer cars reduces friction between the cars and the air.*

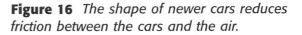

More aerodynamic

Less aerodynamic

SECTION REVIEW

1. What is an energy conversion?
2. Identify three energy transformations occurring during the production of energy for human use. ⭐TEKS
3. Describe the energy conversions that take place when you ride in a car. ⭐TEKS
4. **Analyzing Viewpoints** Imagine that you drop a ball. It bounces a few times, but then it stops. Your friend says that the ball has lost all of its energy. Using what you know about the law of conservation of energy, reply to your friend.

internet**connect**

SciLINKS
NSTA
GO TO: www.scilinks.org

TOPIC: Energy Conversions
*sci*LINKS NUMBER: HSTP215

TOPIC: Law of Conservation of Energy
*sci*LINKS NUMBER: HSTP217

READING WARM-UP

〔 *Terms to Learn* 〕

machine

〔 *What You'll Do* 〕

- Describe how machines transfer and convert energy.
- Give examples of how energy conversions help humans use energy. ★TEKS
- Compare energy conversions used for heating and cooling. ★TEKS

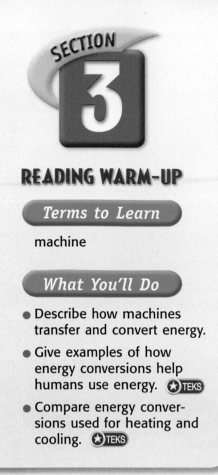

Using Energy

Beep! Beep! Beep! Your alarm clock wakes you up. You turn it off and then flip on the light. You get out of bed and stretch. It's time to get ready for a new day.

You've been awake for only 5 minutes, and several energy conversions have already happened. You've been learning about energy, its different forms, and the way it can change forms. Now you'll look at some of the ways energy conversions help make energy useful to you.

Energy and Machines

A **machine** is a device that can make work easier by changing the direction or size of force needed to do work. When you use a machine, you transfer your energy to it. The machine can then transfer energy to something else. It can also change the energy into another form. Just remember that machines cannot transfer or change more energy than you transfer to them. Look at **Figure 17**. Bicycles are machines that transfer energy to get you from place to place.

〔 **Figure 17** **Energy Transfer in a Bicycle** 〕

1 Chemical energy in your body is changed into kinetic energy by your muscles.

2 Your legs transfer this kinetic energy to the pedals, pushing the pedals around in a circle.

4 The chain moves and transfers energy to the back wheel, which gets you moving!

3 The pedals transfer this kinetic energy to the gear wheel, which transfers kinetic energy to the chain.

Machines Are Energy Converters

When machines transfer energy, energy conversions can often result. For example, you can hear the sounds that your bike makes when you pedal it, change gears, or brake quickly. Some of the kinetic energy being transferred gets changed into sound energy as the bike moves. Some machines are very useful to humans because they are energy converters. A digital alarm clock, a telephone, and a lawn mower are machines that perform energy conversions. Look at **Figure 18.** In a car's engine, chemical energy is changed into thermal and mechanical energy that is used to put the car into motion.

Figure 18 Energy Conversions in a Car Engine

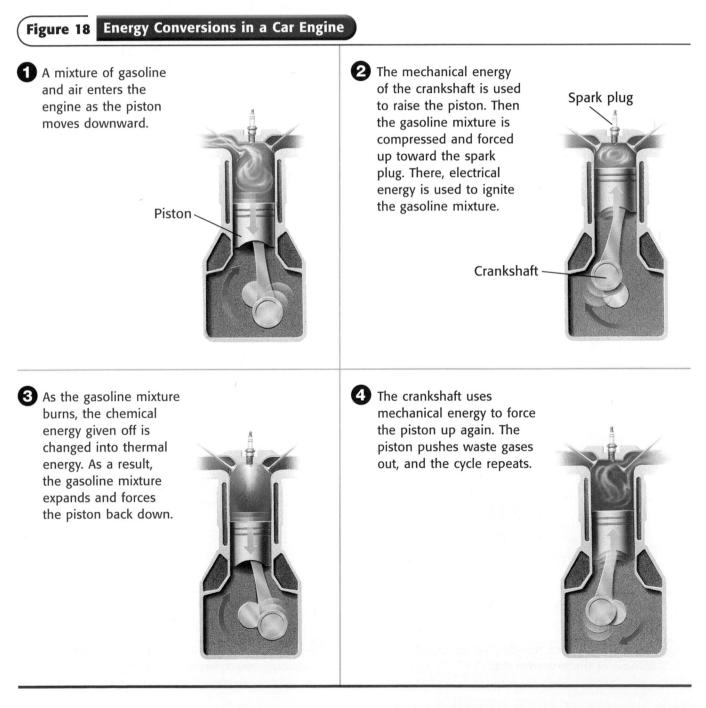

❶ A mixture of gasoline and air enters the engine as the piston moves downward.

Piston

❷ The mechanical energy of the crankshaft is used to raise the piston. Then the gasoline mixture is compressed and forced up toward the spark plug. There, electrical energy is used to ignite the gasoline mixture.

Spark plug

Crankshaft

❸ As the gasoline mixture burns, the chemical energy given off is changed into thermal energy. As a result, the gasoline mixture expands and forces the piston back down.

❹ The crankshaft uses mechanical energy to force the piston up again. The piston pushes waste gases out, and the cycle repeats.

Heating and Cooling Systems

Another way to use energy is in heating and cooling systems. In the next few pages, you'll learn about how energy is transferred and converted in machines such as heaters, air conditioners, and refrigerators.

Hot-Water and Warm-Air Heating

Heating systems move thermal energy to an area that is too cool. Look at **Figure 19.** In a *hot-water heating system,* thermal energy is given off by burning fuel. This thermal energy is transferred to the water in a hot-water heater. The hot water is then pumped through pipes that lead to radiators in each room. The hot water transfers thermal energy to the radiators. Then the radiators transfer thermal energy to the colder air around them. The water returns to the hot-water heater to be heated again. A *warm-air heating system* works like a hot-water heating system, except that air is used in place of water.

Self-Check

What energy conversions occur when fuel is burned in a heating system? (*See page 640 to check your answer.*) ⊛ TEKS

Figure 19 Heating Systems

Hot-Water Heating System	Warm-Air Heating System

Hot-Water Heating System

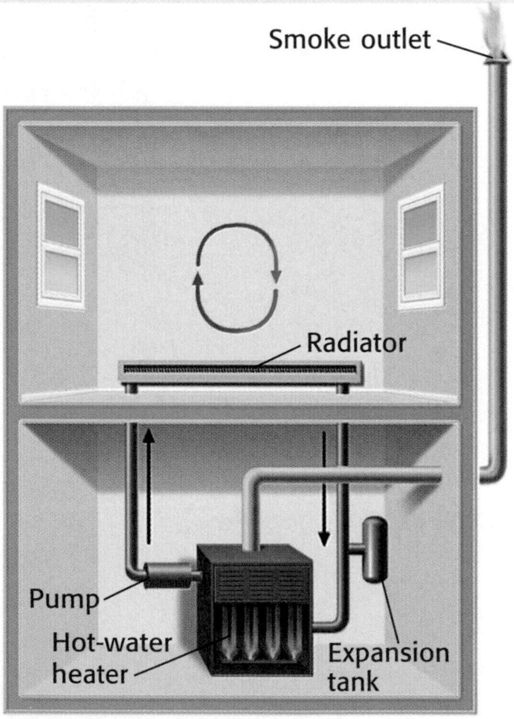

Smoke outlet

Radiator

Pump

Hot-water heater

Expansion tank

❶ The radiators transfer thermal energy to the surrounding air, which makes the room feel warmer.

❷ An expansion tank handles the increased volume of the heated water.

Warm-Air Heating System

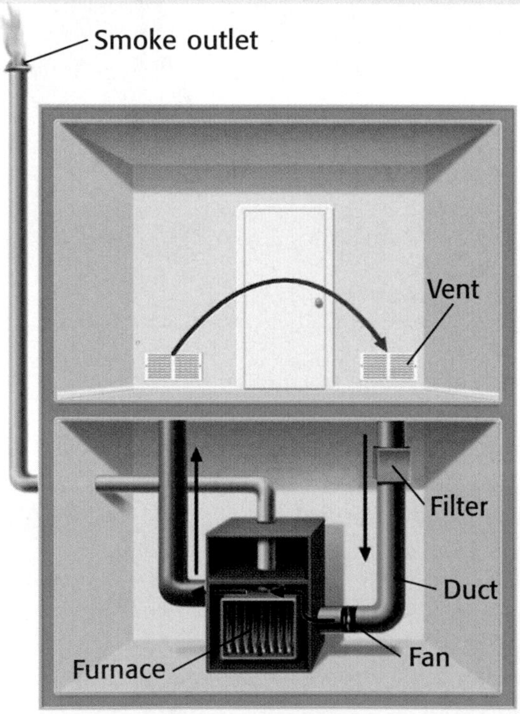

Smoke outlet

Vent

Filter

Duct

Furnace

Fan

❶ Fans blow warmed air into the room. Cooler air sinks and enters a vent that leads to a furnace, where the air will be warmed again.

❷ An air filter cleans the air as it circulates through the system.

Solar Heating

The sun gives off a huge amount of energy. Solar heating systems convert light energy from the sun into thermal energy. *Passive solar heating systems* rely on what shape the building has and what the building is made of to capture the sun's energy. *Active solar heating systems* have moving parts. They use machines to move the sun's energy throughout a building.

Look at the house in **Figure 20.** This house uses both forms of solar heating systems. The large windows on its south side allow large amounts of the sun's energy to heat the rooms. Thick, insulated concrete walls trap energy. That energy is used to keep the house warm at night or when it is cloudy. In the active solar heating system, water is pumped toward the solar energy collector. There the water is heated by solar energy. The hot water is pumped through pipes and transfers its thermal energy to them. A fan blowing over the pipes helps the pipes' thermal energy move to the air. Warm air is then sent into rooms through vents. Cooler water returns to the water storage tank. Then the water is pumped back through the solar collector.

Figure 20 *Passive and active solar heating systems use the sun's energy to heat an entire house.*

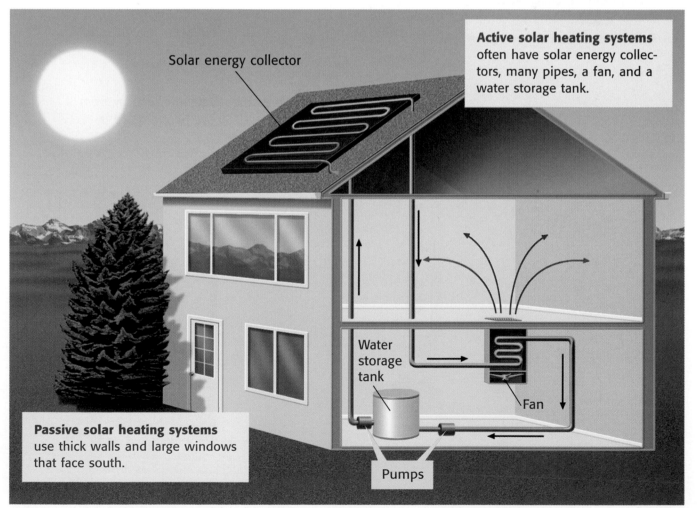

Solar energy collector

Active solar heating systems often have solar energy collectors, many pipes, a fan, and a water storage tank.

Water storage tank

Fan

Passive solar heating systems use thick walls and large windows that face south.

Pumps

Cooling Systems

Imagine that it's a hot summer day. You've been outside with your friends, and you walk into an air-conditioned store. The cool air feels great, but how can it be so much cooler inside? Unlike a heating system, a cooling system moves thermal energy out of a particular area. Look at **Figure 21.** An air conditioner moves thermal energy from a warm area inside a house or a car to an area outside. Outside, however, it is often even warmer. To move thermal energy from a cool area to a warm area, the cooling system must do work.

Cooling Takes Energy

Most cooling systems use electrical energy to do the work of cooling. The electrical energy is used by a machine called a compressor. The compressor does the work of compressing the refrigerant. The refrigerant is a gas that can easily change state to become a liquid.

To keep many foods fresh, you store them in a refrigerator. A refrigerator is a cooling system. **Figure 22,** on the next page, shows how a refrigerator works. A refrigerator constantly moves thermal energy from inside the refrigerator to the condenser coils on the outside of the refrigerator. That's why the area near the back of a refrigerator feels warm.

Self-Check

Compare methods used for transforming energy in a heating system and a cooling system. *(See page 640 to check your answer.)* ⊛TEKS

Figure 21 *This air conditioner moves thermal energy from inside the building to the outside. So the temperature is lower inside than it is outside.*

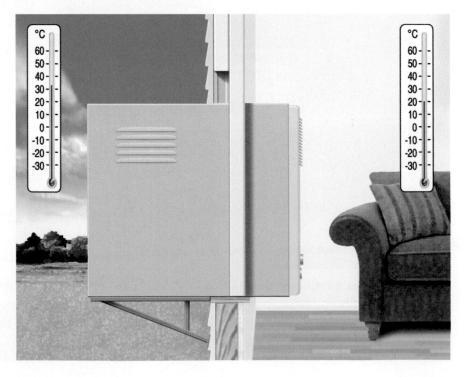

Figure 22 **How a Refrigerator Works**

1. The compressor changes electrical energy into mechanical energy, which the compressor uses to compress the refrigerant gas. The pressure and temperature of the gas increase.

2. The hot gas flows through the condenser coils on the outside of the refrigerator. The gas condenses into a liquid and transfers some of its thermal energy to the coils and surrounding air.

3. When the liquid passes through the expansion valve, it goes from a high-pressure area to a low-pressure area. As a result, the temperature of the liquid decreases.

4. The cold liquid refrigerant moves through the evaporating coils. It absorbs thermal energy from the refrigerator compartment and makes the inside of the refrigerator cold. As a result, the temperature of the refrigerant increases, and the refrigerant changes into a gas.

5. The gas is then returned to the compressor, and the cycle repeats.

SECTION REVIEW

1 What is the role of machines in energy transfer?

2 Compare a hot-water heating system and an active solar heating system. ⊛TEKS

3 **Analyzing Relationships** Describe how a car engine produces energy for human use. In your description, identify the energy conversions that take place during this process. ⊛TEKS

☐ internet**connect**

SCI**LINKS**
NSTA   **GO TO:** www.scilinks.org

TOPIC: Heating Systems
sciLINKS NUMBER: HSTP252

Terms to Learn

energy resource
nonrenewable resources
fossil fuels
renewable resources

What You'll Do

- Describe several energy resources from their source to their use. ⊗TEKS
- Determine whether energy resources are renewable or nonrenewable. ⊗TEKS
- Explain how the sun is the source of most energy on Earth.

Energy Resources

We use energy to light and warm our homes, to grow food, to make clothing, and to move people and things from place to place. Where does all of this energy come from?

An **energy resource** is a natural resource that people can turn into other forms of energy in order to do useful work. In this section, you will learn about several energy resources, including the sun, the source of most other energy resources.

Nonrenewable Resources

Some energy resources, called **nonrenewable resources,** cannot be replaced after they are used or can be replaced only over thousands or millions of years. Fossil fuels are the most important nonrenewable resources.

Fossil Fuels

Look at **Figure 23.** Coal, petroleum, and natural gas are the best known fossil fuels. **Fossil fuels** formed from the buried remains of plants and animals that lived millions of years ago. These plants used photosynthesis to store energy from the sun. Animals used and stored this energy by eating the plants or by eating other animals that ate plants. So fossil fuels are really forms of stored energy from the sun. Now, millions of years later, energy from the sun is given off when fossil fuels are burned. **Figure 24,** on the next page, shows how fossil fuels are used in our everyday lives.

Figure 23 Formation of Fossil Fuels

This piece of **coal** contains a fern fossil. This fossil shows that coal formed from plants that lived millions of years ago.

Petroleum, or **oil,** formed from organisms that lived in lakes and seas millions of years ago. Crushed by sediment and heated by the Earth, the remains were slowly changed into petroleum.

Natural gas formed in much the same way that petroleum formed. It is often found with petroleum deposits.

Figure 24 | Everyday Use of Fossil Fuels

Coal

Most coal used in the United States is burned in power plants to generate electrical energy.

U.S. Coal Use

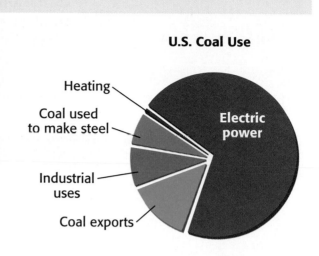

- Heating
- Coal used to make steel
- Electric power
- Industrial uses
- Coal exports

Petroleum

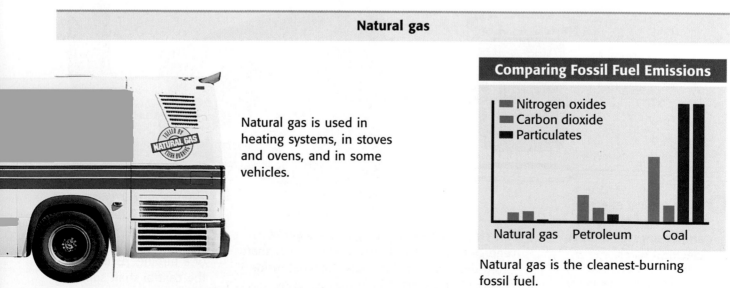

Gasoline, kerosene, wax, and petrochemicals come from petroleum.

Annual Oil Production—Past and Predicted

Oil production

1930   1970   2010   2050
Year

Finding other energy resources will become more important in years to come.

Natural gas

Natural gas is used in heating systems, in stoves and ovens, and in some vehicles.

Comparing Fossil Fuel Emissions

- Nitrogen oxides
- Carbon dioxide
- Particulates

Natural gas   Petroleum   Coal

Natural gas is the cleanest-burning fossil fuel.

Electrical Energy from Fossil Fuels

One way to generate electrical energy is to burn fossil fuels. In the United States, fossil fuels are the main source of electrical energy. Mechanical energy can be changed into electrical energy by an electric generator. This energy conversion is part of a larger process. **Figure 25** shows how the chemical energy in fossil fuels is changed into the electrical energy you use every day.

Figure 25 Converting Fossil Fuels into Electrical Energy

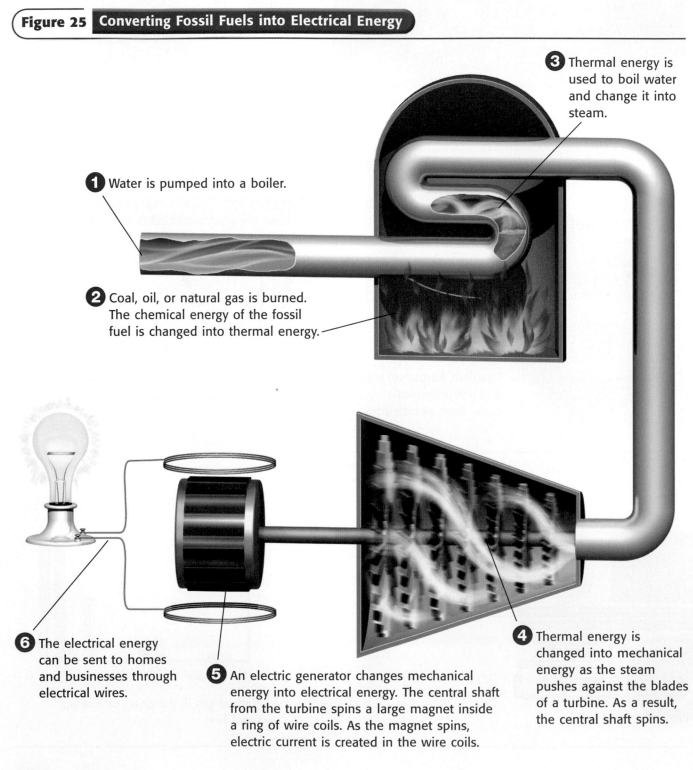

1 Water is pumped into a boiler.

2 Coal, oil, or natural gas is burned. The chemical energy of the fossil fuel is changed into thermal energy.

3 Thermal energy is used to boil water and change it into steam.

4 Thermal energy is changed into mechanical energy as the steam pushes against the blades of a turbine. As a result, the central shaft spins.

5 An electric generator changes mechanical energy into electrical energy. The central shaft from the turbine spins a large magnet inside a ring of wire coils. As the magnet spins, electric current is created in the wire coils.

6 The electrical energy can be sent to homes and businesses through electrical wires.

Nuclear Energy

Another way to generate electrical energy is to use nuclear energy. Like fossil-fuel power plants, a nuclear power plant generates thermal energy that boils water to produce steam. However, the fuels used in nuclear power plants are different from fossil fuels. Nuclear energy is generated from radioactive elements. One such element, uranium, is shown in **Figure 26.** In a nuclear power plant, a special process splits the nucleus of a uranium atom in two. Nuclear energy is given off as the nucleus splits. Because there is only a certain amount of radioactive elements, nuclear energy is thought of as nonrenewable.

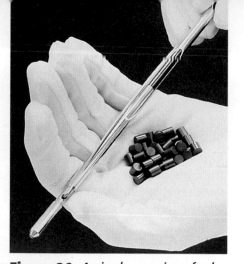

Figure 26 *A single uranium fuel pellet has the same amount of energy as about 1 metric ton of coal.*

Renewable Resources

Some energy resources, called **renewable resources,** are used and replaced over a relatively short period of time. Sunlight, wind, and trees are examples of renewable resources. Sunlight and wind have the added benefit of being in such large supply that they cannot be used up. For this reason, such energy resources are often referred to as *inexhaustible resources.*

Solar Energy

Sunlight can be changed into electrical energy through solar cells. These cells can be used in devices such as calculators, like the one shown in **Figure 27.** Solar cells can also be placed on the roof of a house to provide electrical energy. Some houses allow sunlight into the house through large windows. The sunlight is changed into thermal energy, which is used to heat the house.

Figure 27 *These solar cells can convert sunlight into electrical energy.*

Solar cells

Energy from Water

The sun causes water to evaporate and fall again as rain that flows through rivers. The potential energy of water in a reservoir can be changed into kinetic energy as the water flows downhill through a dam.

Figure 28 shows a hydroelectric dam. Falling water turns turbines in a dam. The turbines are connected to a generator that changes mechanical energy into electrical energy.

Figure 28 *This dam converts the energy from falling water into electrical energy.*

Figure 29 *These wind turbines are converting wind energy into electrical energy.*

Wind Energy

Wind is caused by the sun's heating of the Earth's surface. Because the surface is not heated evenly, wind is created. The kinetic energy of wind can turn the blades of a windmill. Wind turbines are shown in **Figure 29.** A wind turbine changes the kinetic energy of the air into electrical energy by turning a generator.

Geothermal Energy

Thermal energy caused by the heating of Earth's crust is called *geothermal energy*. Ground water that moves into hot spots near the surface of the Earth can form geysers.

Some geothermal power plants, such as the one shown in **Figure 30,** pump water underground into areas of hot rock. The water returns to the surface as steam. The steam can then be used to turn a generator to change mechanical energy into electrical energy.

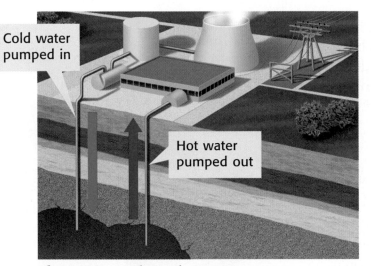

Cold water pumped in

Hot water pumped out

Figure 30 *Geothermal energy can be changed into electrical energy.*

Biomass

Plants use and store energy from the sun. Organic matter, such as plants, wood, and waste, that can be burned to release energy is called *biomass*. Some countries depend on biomass for energy.

Look at **Figure 31.** Certain plants can be turned into liquid fuel. Corn can be used to make ethanol. *Ethanol* is an alcohol that is often mixed with gasoline to make a cleaner-burning fuel for cars.

Figure 31 *This corn can be used to make fuel for cars.*

The Two Sides to Energy Resources

All energy resources have advantages and disadvantages. How can you decide which energy resource to use? The table below compares several energy resources. Depending on where you live, why you need energy, and how much energy you need, one energy resource may be a better choice than another.

A Comparison of Energy Resources		
Energy resource	**Advantages**	**Disadvantages**
Fossil fuels	◆ Fossil fuels provide a large amount of thermal energy per unit of mass. ◆ Fossil fuels are easy to transport. ◆ Fossil fuels can be used to generate electrical energy and to make products, such as plastic.	◆ Fossil fuels are nonrenewable. ◆ Fossil fuels produce smog when burned. ◆ Burning coal releases substances that can cause acid precipitation. ◆ Fossil fuels cause damage if spilled in transport.
Nuclear	◆ Nuclear resources are very concentrated forms of energy. ◆ Nuclear power plants do not produce smog.	◆ Nuclear resources produce radioactive waste. ◆ Radioactive elements are nonrenewable.
Solar	◆ Solar energy provides an inexhaustible source of energy. ◆ Solar energy does not produce pollution.	◆ Solar energy is expensive to use for large-scale energy production. ◆ Solar energy is practical only in sunny areas.
Water	◆ Water is renewable. ◆ Water does not produce smog.	◆ Dams disrupt a river's ecosystem. ◆ Water as an energy resource is available only in areas that have rivers.
Wind	◆ Wind energy is inexhaustible. ◆ Wind energy is relatively inexpensive to generate. ◆ Wind energy does not produce pollution.	◆ Wind as an energy resource is practical only in windy areas.
Geothermal	◆ Geothermal energy provides an inexhaustible source of energy. ◆ Geothermal power plants require little land.	◆ Geothermal energy is practical only in locations near hot spots. ◆ Geothermal waste water can damage soil.
Biomass	◆ Biomass is renewable.	◆ Biomass requires large areas of farmland. ◆ Biomass produces smoke.

SECTION REVIEW

1. Describe fossil fuels and biomass from their source to their use. ⭐TEKS

2. Determine whether the following energy types are renewable, nonrenewable, or inexhaustible: nuclear energy, solar energy, and biomass. Explain your answers. ⭐TEKS

3. **Comparing Concepts** Describe the similarities and differences between transforming energy in a hydroelectric dam and a wind turbine. ⭐TEKS

Discovery Lab

Finding Energy ★TEKS

When you coast down a big hill on a bike or skateboard, you may notice that you pick up speed. Because you are moving, you have kinetic energy—the energy of motion. Where does that energy come from? In this lab, you will find out.

MATERIALS

- 2 or 3 books
- wooden board
- masking tape
- meterstick
- metric balance
- rolling cart
- stopwatch
- computer (optional)

Form a Hypothesis

1 Where does the kinetic energy come from when you roll down a hill? Write your hypothesis in your ScienceLog.

Conduct an Experiment

2 Copy Table 1 into your ScienceLog, or use a computer to construct a similar table.

3 Create a model of a bike on a hill. First, make a ramp using the books and board.

4 Use masking tape to make a starting line. Be sure the starting line is far enough from the top so that the cart can be placed behind the line.

5 Place a strip of masking tape at the bottom of the ramp to mark the finish line.

6 Determine the height of the ramp by measuring the height of the starting line and subtracting the height of the finish line. Record the height of the ramp in meters in Table 1.

7 Measure the distance in meters between the starting and the finish lines. Record this distance as the length of the ramp in Table 1.

8 Use the metric balance to find the mass of the cart in grams. Convert to kilograms by dividing by 1,000. Record the mass in kilograms in Table 1.

Table 1 Data Collection							
Height of ramp (m)	Length of ramp (m)	Mass of cart (kg)	Weight of cart (N)	Time of trial (s)			Average time (s)
				1	2	3	
			DO NOT WRITE IN BOOK				

9 Multiply the mass by 10 to get the weight of the cart in newtons. Record the weight in Table 1.

Collect Data

10 Set the cart behind the starting line, and release it. Use the stopwatch to time how long the cart takes to reach the finish line. Record the time in Table 1.

11 Repeat step 10 twice more, and average the results. Record the average time in Table 1.

Analyze the Results

12 Copy Table 2 into your ScienceLog, or use a computer to construct a similar table.

Table 2 Calculations			
Average speed (m/s)	Final speed (m/s)	Kinetic energy at bottom (J)	Gravitational potential energy at top (J)
	DO NOT WRITE IN BOOK		

13 Using your data and the following equations, calculate and record the quantities for the cart in Table 2:

a. $average\ speed = \dfrac{length\ of\ ramp}{average\ time}$

b. $final\ speed = 2 \times average\ speed$

(This equation works because the cart accelerates smoothly from 0 m/s.)

c. $kinetic\ energy = \dfrac{mass \times (final\ speed)^2}{2}$

(Remember that $1\ kg \cdot m^2/s^2 = 1\ J$, the unit used to express energy.)

d. $gravitational\ potential\ energy = weight \times height$

(Remember that $1\ N = 1\ kg \cdot m/s^2$, so $1\ N \times 1\ m = 1\ kg \cdot m^2/s^2 = 1\ J$.)

Draw Conclusions

14 How does the cart's gravitational potential energy at the top of the ramp compare with its kinetic energy at the bottom? Communicate a valid conclusion about whether or not your hypothesis was supported.

15 You probably found that the gravitational potential energy of the cart at the top of the ramp was close but not exactly equal to the kinetic energy of the cart at the bottom. Analyze this information to construct a reasonable explanation for this finding using direct evidence.

16 While riding your bike, you coast down both a small hill and a large hill. Compare your final speed at the bottom of the small hill with your final speed at the bottom of the large hill. Explain your answer.

CHAPTER 5

Highlights

Section 1

Vocabulary

energy *(p. 118)*
kinetic energy *(p. 119)*
potential energy *(p. 120)*

Section Notes

- Energy is the ability to do work. Energy is expressed in joules. ⊛TEKS

- Kinetic energy is energy of motion and depends on speed and mass.

- Potential energy is energy of position or shape. Gravitational potential energy depends on weight and height.

- Thermal energy, sound energy, electrical energy, light energy, chemical energy, and nuclear energy are types of energy.

Section 2

Vocabulary

energy conversion *(p. 124)*
friction *(p. 128)*
law of conservation of energy
  (p. 128)

Section Notes

- An energy conversion is a change from one form of energy to another. Any form of energy can be converted into any other form of energy.

- Energy conversions help make energy useful by changing energy into the form you need. ⊛TEKS

- Because of friction, some energy is always converted into thermal energy during an energy conversion.

- Energy is conserved within a closed system. According to the law of conservation of energy, energy can be neither created nor destroyed.

LabBook ⊛TEKS

Energy of a Pendulum *(p. 610)*
Eggstremely Fragile *(p. 611)*
Battery Power *(p. 612)*

Section 3

Vocabulary

machine *(p. 130)*

Section Notes

- Machines can transfer energy and convert energy into a more useful form. ⊛TEKS

- Central heating systems include hot-water heating systems and warm-air heating systems.

- Solar heating systems can be passive or active.

- A cooling system transfers thermal energy from cooler temperatures to warmer temperatures by doing work.

Section 4

Vocabulary

energy resource *(p. 136)*
nonrenewable resources
  (p. 136)
fossil fuels *(p. 136)*
renewable resources *(p. 139)*

Section Notes

- An energy resource is a natural resource that can be converted into other forms of energy in order to do useful work.

- Nonrenewable resources cannot be replaced after they are used or can be replaced only after very long periods of time. They include fossil fuels and nuclear energy. ⊛TEKS

- Renewable resources can be used and replaced in nature over a relatively short period of time. They include solar energy, wind energy, energy from water, geothermal energy, and biomass. ⊛TEKS

- The sun is the source of most energy on Earth. ⊛TEKS

Review

USING VOCABULARY

For each pair of terms, explain how the meanings of the terms differ.

1. potential energy/kinetic energy

2. friction/energy conversion

3. energy conversion/law of conservation of energy

4. energy resources/fossil fuels ★TEKS

5. renewable resources/nonrenewable resources ★TEKS

UNDERSTANDING CONCEPTS

Multiple Choice

6. Which of the following is NOT a fossil fuel?
   a. gasoline
   b. coal
   c. firewood
   d. natural gas

7. Which of the following is NOT a renewable resource? ★TEKS
   a. wind energy
   b. nuclear energy
   c. solar energy
   d. geothermal energy

8. Which of the following is a conversion from chemical energy to thermal energy? ★TEKS
   a. Food is digested and used to regulate body temperature.
   b. Charcoal is burned in a barbecue pit.
   c. Coal is burned to boil water.
   d. all of the above

9. Machines can
   a. increase energy.
   b. transfer energy.
   c. convert energy.
   d. Both (b) and (c)

10. Kinetic energy depends on
    a. mass and volume.
    b. speed and weight.
    c. weight and height.
    d. speed and mass.

11. In an air conditioner, thermal energy is
    a. moved from warm areas to cooler areas.
    b. moved from warm areas inside to an area outside.
    c. used to do work.
    d. taken from air outside a building and transferred to air inside the building.

12. An object that has kinetic energy must be
    a. at rest.
    b. lifted above the Earth's surface.
    c. in motion.
    d. None of the above

13. In every energy conversion, some energy is always converted into
    a. kinetic energy.
    b. potential energy.
    c. thermal energy.
    d. mechanical energy.

Short Answer

14. Compare passive and active solar heating. ★TEKS

15. How can wind be used to run an electric stove? ★TEKS

16. Explain how energy is conserved within a closed system.

17. How are fossil fuels formed? ★TEKS

CONCEPT MAPPING

18. Use the following terms to create a concept map: *energy, machines, energy conversions, thermal energy,* and *friction.*

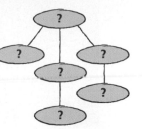

CRITICAL THINKING AND PROBLEM SOLVING

Write one or two sentences to answer the following questions:

19. What happens when you blow up a balloon and release it? Describe what you would see in terms of energy.

20. After you coast down a hill on your bike, you eventually come to a complete stop unless you keep pedaling. Relate this result to the reason why perpetual motion is impossible.

21. Look at the photo of the pole-vaulter below. Trace the energy conversions involved in this event, beginning with the pole-vaulter's breakfast of an orange-banana smoothie. ⭐TEKS

22. If the sun's nuclear energy were exhausted, what would happen to our energy resources on Earth? ⭐TEKS

MATH IN SCIENCE

23. A box has 400 J of gravitational potential energy.
   a. How much work had to be done to give the box that energy?
   b. If the box weighs 100 N, how far was it lifted?

INTERPRETING GRAPHICS

24. Look at the illustration below, and answer the questions that follow.
   a. What is the skier's gravitational potential energy at point **A**?
   b. What is the skier's gravitational potential energy at point **B**?
   c. What is the skier's kinetic energy at point **B**? (Hint: *mechanical energy = potential energy + kinetic energy*)

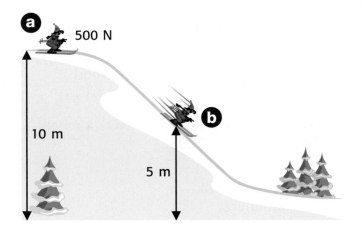

Reading Check-up ⭐TEKS

Take a minute to review your answers to the Pre-Reading Questions found at the bottom of page 116. Have your answers changed? If necessary, revise your answers based on what you have learned since you began this chapter.

Chapter 5

1 Which of the following provides the best definition of energy?

  A Energy is the flow of small particles in space.

  B Energy is the ability to do work.

  C Energy is the transfer of work.

  D Energy is useful only in the form of electrical energy.

2 Which of the following energy conversions does NOT take place in a hair dryer?

  F chemical energy to light energy

  G electrical energy to kinetic energy

  H electrical energy to thermal energy

  J kinetic energy to sound energy

3 Ariana put a piece of bread in the electric toaster, and pushed the lever down. After 2 minutes, the warm toast popped up. Which of the following best describes the energy conversion necessary to make Ariana's toast in the toaster?

  A electrical energy to thermal energy

  B thermal energy to electrical energy

  C light energy to electrical energy

  D sound energy to chemical energy

4 When burned, wood gives off energy that can be used to make electrical energy. New trees can be grown to replace the trees burned. Therefore, trees are a(n)

  F inexhaustible resource.

  G renewable resource.

  H nonrenewable resource.

  J Not Here

5 Coal is a fossil fuel that came from the remains of once-living plants. The energy in coal can ultimately be traced to

  A geothermal energy.

  B animals.

  C plants.

  D the sun.

U.S. Energy Sources

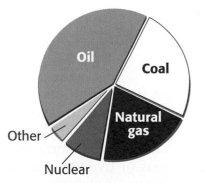

6 According to the graph, the United States relies on fossil fuels for about what percentage of its energy?

  F 30%

  G 45%

  H 60%

  J 80%

Chapter 5

Math

1 Which point best represents the ordered pair (3,2)?

A J

B K

C L

D M

2 Gerald bought 2.5 kilograms of apples. How many *grams* of apples did he buy?

F 0.0025 g

G 0.25 g

H 25 g

J 2500 g

3 Which group contains ratios that are all equivalent to $\frac{3}{8}$?

A $\frac{6}{16}$, $\frac{9}{24}$, $\frac{12}{32}$

B $\frac{6}{16}$, $\frac{12}{24}$, $\frac{12}{32}$

C $\frac{6}{24}$, $\frac{12}{32}$, $\frac{15}{40}$

D $\frac{6}{9}$, $\frac{9}{24}$, $\frac{15}{40}$

4 Carmen went to a bookstore. She bought 3 books for $7.99 each and 4 books for $3.35 each. Which number sentence can be used to find *c*, the total cost of the books?

F $c = 3 + (7.99 \times 1) + (4 \times 3.35)$

G $c = (1 \times 7.99) + (3 \times 3.35)$

H $c = (3 \times 7.99) + (4 \times 3.35)$

J $c = (3 + 7.99) \times (4 + 3.35)$

Reading

Read the passage. Then read each question that follows the passage. Decide which is the best answer to each question.

Gas hydrates are icy formations of water and methane. Methane is the main component of natural gas. The methane in gas hydrates is made by bacteria in the ocean. Large areas of hydrates have been found off the coasts of North Carolina and South Carolina in marine sediments. In just two areas that are each about the size of Rhode Island, scientists think there may be 70 times the amount of natural gas used by the United States in 1 year. The energy from gas hydrates could be used to drive machinery or to generate electrical energy.

1 How large are each of the two gas hydrate deposits mentioned in this article?

A About the size of the United States

B About the size of South Carolina

C About the size of North Carolina

D About the size of Rhode Island

2 What are the main components of gas hydrates?

F Bacteria and sediments

G Water and methane

H Natural gas and water

J Ice and sediments

CAREERS

POWER-PLANT MANAGER

Cheryl Mele is manager of the Decker Power Plant in Austin, Texas. She is in charge of almost 1 billion watts of electric power generation. More than 700 MW are made using a steam-driven turbine system with natural gas fuel. Oil is used as a backup fuel. Another 200 MW are created by gas turbines. Together the systems provide enough electrical energy for many homes and businesses.

Cheryl Mele says her job as plant manager is to do "anything that needs doing." Her training as a mechanical engineer allows her to run tests and to find problems at the plant. Mele runs the plant carefully in order to protect the environment. Mele states, "It is very important to keep the plant running properly and burning as efficiently as possible." Previously, she had a job in which she helped design more-efficient gas turbines. That job helped make her ready for the job of plant manager.

The Team Approach

Mele uses the team approach to keep the power plant in good repair. She says, "We think better as a team." Different members of a team have different strengths. Mele says that working together makes everyone's job easier.

Advice to Young People

Mele believes that mechanical engineering and managing a power plant are interesting jobs. In these jobs, you get to work with many exciting new technologies. These jobs are great choices for both men and women. You interact with creative people as you try to improve equipment to make it more efficient and to help protect the environment. Mele thinks young people should pursue what interests them. "Be sure to connect the math you learn to the science you are doing," she says. "This will help you to understand both."

A Challenge

▶ With the help of an adult, research the electrical energy used in your home from its source to its use. Then research the energy resources used to produce the electrical energy from their source to their use. ⭐TEKS

▶ *Cheryl Mele manages the Decker Power Plant in Austin, Texas.*

CHAPTER 6

Introduction to Electricity

IT'S ELECTRIFYING!

This student is not having a bad hair day. She is learning firsthand about electrical energy. Her hands are on a Van de Graaf generator, a device that produces a positive electric charge on the metal globe. By touching the globe, the girl— and all her hair—becomes positively charged. And because like charges repel each other, each of the girl's hairs repels all the others. The result is an electrified hairstyle! The Van de Graaf generator is a fun way to learn about electrical energy. In this chapter, you'll learn more about what electrical energy is and how you use it every day.

Pre-Reading
Questions

1. What is the difference between static electricity and electric current?

2. How is electrical energy produced for human use? ⊛TEKS

3. What is a circuit, and what are the parts of a circuit?

CHARGE OVER MATTER ⭐TEKS

In this activity, you will electrically charge an object and will use it to pick up other objects.

Procedure

1. Your teacher will give you **6 to 8 small squares of tissue paper.** Place the tissue-paper squares on your desk.

2. Hold a **plastic comb** close to the paper squares. Record what, if anything, happens.

3. Now rub the comb with a **piece of silk cloth** for about 30 seconds.

4. Hold the comb close to the tissue-paper squares, but don't touch them. Record your observations. If nothing happens, rub the comb for a little while longer and try again.

Analysis

5. When you rubbed the comb with the cloth, you gave the comb a negative electric charge. Why do you think this charge allowed you to pick up tissue-paper squares?

6. What other objects do you think you can use to pick up tissue-paper squares?

Terms to Learn

law of electric charges
electric force
electric field
conductor
insulator
static electricity
electric discharge

Electric Charge and Static Electricity

Have you ever reached out to open a door and received a shock from the knob? Or maybe you were petting a cat and heard some crackling sounds. What's going on?

On dry days, you can give yourself a shock by shuffling your feet on a carpet and then lightly touching something metal. The same thing happens when you rub a cat's fur. These shocks come from static electricity. But what is static electricity? To answer this question, you need to learn about charge.

Atoms and Charge

To learn about charge, you must know a little about matter. All matter is composed of very small particles called atoms. Atoms are made of even smaller particles called protons, neutrons, and electrons. Look at **Figure 1.** One important difference between protons, electrons, and neutrons is that protons and electrons are charged particles and neutrons are not.

Charges Can Exert Forces

Charge is a physical property of objects. Charge is best understood by describing how charged objects interact. There are two types of charge: positive and negative. Charged objects exert a force—a push or a pull—on other charged objects. Whether the force between two charged objects is a push or a pull depends on whether the objects have the same type of charge or opposite charges. Look at **Figure 2** on the next page. The **law of electric charges** states that like charges repel and opposite charges attract.

Protons are positively charged, and electrons are negatively charged. Because protons and electrons have opposite charges, they are attracted to each other. Without this attraction, electrons would fly away from the nucleus of an atom.

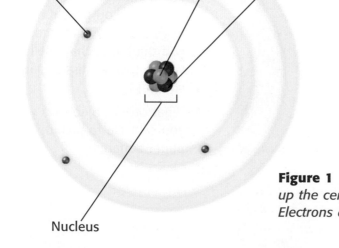

Electron
Proton
Neutron
Nucleus

Figure 1 *Protons and neutrons make up the center of the atom, the nucleus. Electrons are found outside the nucleus.*

Figure 2 — The Law of Electric Charges

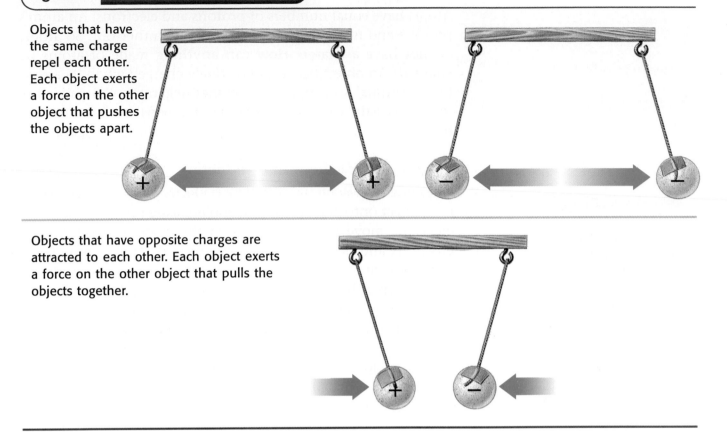

Objects that have the same charge repel each other. Each object exerts a force on the other object that pushes the objects apart.

Objects that have opposite charges are attracted to each other. Each object exerts a force on the other object that pulls the objects together.

The Electric Force and the Electric Field

Charged objects exert a force on each other and can cause each other to move. The force between charged objects is an **electric force.** The strength of the electric force is determined by two factors. One factor is the size of the charges. The greater the charges are, the greater the electric force. The other factor that determines the strength of the electric force is the distance between the charges. The closer together the charges are, the greater the electric force.

Charged objects are affected by electric force because charged objects have an electric field around them. An **electric field** is the region around a charged object in which an electric force is exerted on another charged object. A charged object in the electric field of another charged object is attracted to or repelled by the electric force exerted on it. Look again at the photograph that opens this chapter. Positively charged particles on the globe and negatively charged particles on the girl exert a force on each other through their electric fields. Negative charges leave the girl because they are attracted to the positive charges on the globe. So, her hair becomes positively charged. You can see the result in the picture!

BRAIN FOOD

Car makers use the law of electric charges when painting cars. The car bodies are given a positive charge. Paint droplets are given a negative charge as they exit the spray gun. The negatively charged paint droplets are attracted to the positively charged car body. Less paint is wasted because most of the paint droplets hit the car body.

Charge It!

Atoms have equal numbers of protons and electrons. An atom's positive and negative charges cancel each other out. So atoms do not have a charge. How can anything made of atoms be charged? An object becomes positively charged when its atoms lose electrons. And an object becomes negatively charged when its atoms gain electrons. Charging happens in three ways— friction, conduction, and induction—as shown in **Figure 3.**

Friction, Conduction, and Induction

Charging by *friction* happens when electrons are "wiped" from one object onto another. If you rub a plastic ruler with a cloth, electrons move from the cloth to the ruler. The ruler gains electrons and becomes negatively charged. At the same time, the cloth loses electrons and becomes positively charged.

Charging by *conduction* happens when electrons move from one object to another by direct contact. Suppose you touch an uncharged piece of metal with a positively charged glass rod. Electrons from the metal will move to the glass rod. The metal loses electrons and becomes positively charged.

Charging by *induction* happens when charges in an uncharged object are rearranged without direct contact with a charged object. Suppose you hold a neutral object near a positively charged object. The electrons in the neutral object are attracted to the positively charged object and move toward it. This movement induces an area of negative charge on the neutral object.

Self-Check

Plastic wrap clings to food containers (and to itself) because the wrap has a charge. Explain how plastic wrap becomes charged. *(See page 640 to check your answer.)*

Figure 3 **Three Ways to Charge an Object**

Friction	Conduction	Induction

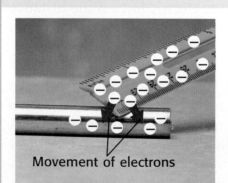
Movement of electrons

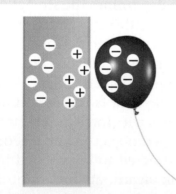

Electrons are transferred from your hair to the balloon because of **friction.** Your hair and the balloon are attracted to each other because the balloon is negatively charged and your hair is positively charged.

When a negatively charged plastic ruler touches an uncharged metal rod, the electrons in the ruler travel to the rod. The rod becomes negatively charged by **conduction.**

A negatively charged balloon **induces** a positive charge on a small section of a wall because the electrons in the wall are repelled and move away from the balloon.

Conservation of Charge

When an object is charged by any method, no charges are created or destroyed. The numbers of electrons and protons stay the same. Electrons simply move from one atom to another, creating regions with different charges. Because charges are not created or destroyed, charge is said to be conserved.

Detecting Charge

You can use a device called an electroscope to see if an object is charged. An *electroscope* is a glass flask that contains a metal rod inserted through a rubber stopper. There are two metal leaves at the bottom of the rod. The leaves hang straight down when the electroscope is not charged. When a negatively charged object, such as the ruler in **Figure 4,** is touched to the rod, electrons move from the object to the electroscope. The leaves become negatively charged, repel each other, and spread apart. If a positively charged object, such as a glass rod, is touched to the rod, electrons leave the electroscope. As electrons move away from the two leaves, the leaves both become positively charged and repel each other.

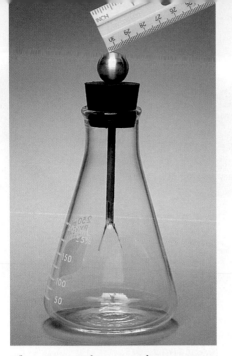

Figure 4 *When an electroscope is charged, the metal leaves have the same charge and repel each other.*

Quick Lab

Detecting Charge ⭐TEKS

1. Use **scissors** to cut **two strips of aluminum foil,** 1 × 4 cm each.

2. Bend a **paper clip** to make a hook. (The clip will look like an upside-down question mark.)

3. Push the end of the hook through the middle of an **index card,** and tape the hook so that it is hanging straight down from the card.

4. Lay the two foil strips on top of one another, and hang them on the hook by gently pushing the hook through them.

5. Lay the card over the top of a **glass jar.**

6. Bring **various charged objects** near the top of the paper-clip hook, and observe what happens. Explain your observations in your ScienceLog.

MID-SECTION REVIEW

1. What is the law of electric charges? Give examples.

2. True or false: The force between charged objects can cause the objects to change position. Explain your answer. ⭐TEKS

3. **Inferring Conclusions** Suppose you are using an electroscope. You touch an object to the top of the electroscope, and the metal leaves spread apart. You know the object has a charge. Do you know whether the charge is positive or negative? Explain your answer.

Moving Charges

Have you ever noticed that cords that connect electrical devices to outlets are always covered in plastic or rubber? And the prongs that fit into the socket are always metal. Look at **Figure 5.** Cords are made from different materials because electric charges move through some materials more easily than others. In fact, most materials can be divided into two groups based on how easily charges move through the material.

Conductors and Insulators

A **conductor** is a material in which charges can move easily. Most metals, such as copper, silver, aluminum, and mercury, are good conductors. For example, a lamp cord has metal wire and metal prongs. Charges move easily in the wire and prongs and transfer energy to light the lamp.

An **insulator** is a material in which charges cannot easily move. Wires used to conduct electric charges are usually covered with an insulator. The insulator prevents charges from leaving the wire and protects you from electric shock. Plastic, rubber, glass, wood, and air are good insulators.

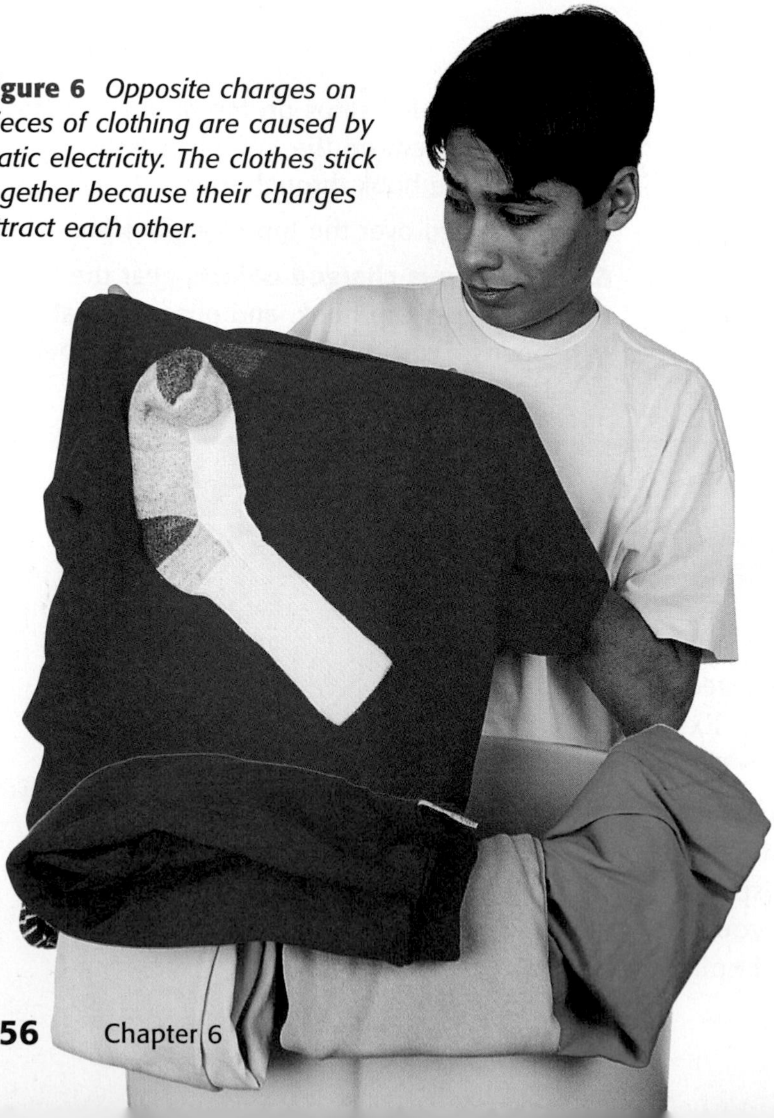

Figure 5 *The outer covering of an electrical cord is an insulator. The wire inside and the prongs are conductors.*

Figure 6 *Opposite charges on pieces of clothing are caused by static electricity. The clothes stick together because their charges attract each other.*

Static Electricity

After taking your clothes out of the dryer, you sometimes find clothing stuck together, as shown in **Figure 6.** You might say that the clothes stick together because of static electricity. **Static electricity** is the buildup of electric charges on an object.

When something is *static,* it is not moving. The charges that create static electricity do not move away from the object they build up on. Therefore, the object remains charged. For example, your clothes are charged by friction as they rub against each other inside a dryer. As the clothes tumble, negative charges are lost by some clothes and build up on other clothes. When the dryer stops, the transfer of charges also stops. And because clothing is an insulator, the built-up electric charges stay on each piece of clothing. The result? Static cling!

Electric Discharge

Charges that build up as static electricity on an object eventually leave the object. The loss of static electricity as charges move off an object is called **electric discharge.** Sometimes electric discharge happens slowly. For example, clothes stuck together by static electricity will eventually separate on their own. Over time, their electric charges move to water molecules in the air.

Sometimes electric discharge happens quickly. It may happen with a flash of light, a shock, or a crackling noise. For example, when you walk on a carpet with rubber-soled shoes, negative charges build up on your body. When you touch a metal doorknob, the negative charges on your body move quickly to the doorknob. Because the electric discharge happens quickly, you feel a small shock.

One of the most dramatic examples of electric discharge is lightning. How does lightning form from a buildup of static electricity? **Figure 7** shows the answer.

BRAIN FOOD

Although 70 to 80 percent of people struck by lightning survive, many suffer from long-term physical side effects such as memory loss, dizziness, and sleep disorders.

Figure 7 **How Lightning Forms**

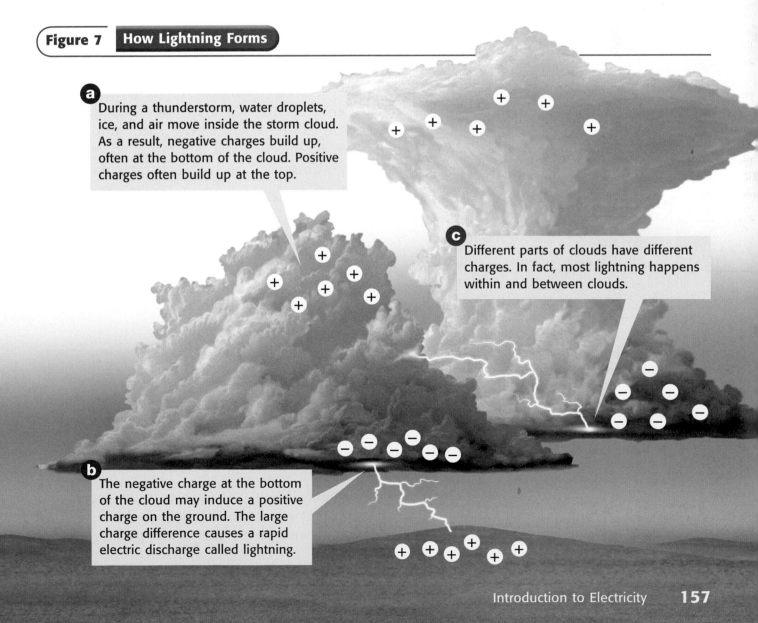

a During a thunderstorm, water droplets, ice, and air move inside the storm cloud. As a result, negative charges build up, often at the bottom of the cloud. Positive charges often build up at the top.

c Different parts of clouds have different charges. In fact, most lightning happens within and between clouds.

b The negative charge at the bottom of the cloud may induce a positive charge on the ground. The large charge difference causes a rapid electric discharge called lightning.

Lightning Dangers

Lightning usually strikes the highest point in a charged area because that point provides the easiest path for the charges to reach the ground. Anything that sticks up or out in an area can provide a path for lightning. Trees and people in open areas are at risk of being struck by lightning. For this reason, it is particularly dangerous to be at the beach or on a golf course during a lightning storm. And standing under a tree during a storm is dangerous because the charges from lightning striking a tree can jump to your body.

Lightning Rods

A lightning rod is a pointed rod connected to the ground by a wire. Lightning rods are always mounted so that they "stick out" and are the tallest point on a building, as shown in **Figure 8.**

Objects that are in contact with the Earth, such as a lightning rod, are *grounded*. Any object that is grounded provides a path for electric charges to travel to the Earth. Because the Earth is so large, it can give up or absorb electric charges without being damaged. When lightning strikes a lightning rod, the electric charges are carried safely to the Earth through the rod's wire. By directing the lightning's charge to the Earth, lightning rods prevent lightning damage to buildings.

Figure 8 *Lightning strikes the lightning rod rather than the building because the lightning rod is the tallest point on the building.*

SECTION REVIEW

❶ What is static electricity? Give an example of static electricity.

❷ How is the shock you receive from a metal doorknob similar to a bolt of lightning?

❸ **Applying Concepts** When you use an electroscope, why is it important to touch the charged object to the metal rod and not to the rubber stopper?

READING WARM-UP

Terms to Learn

cell   photocell
battery   thermocouple
potential
  difference

What You'll Do

- Identify the energy conversion that happens when a cell produces an electric current. ⭐TEKS 6.9A

- Describe how the potential difference is related to electric current.

- Compare the methods used for converting energy in photocells and thermocouples. ⭐TEKS 6.9B

Electrical Energy

How would your life be different without electrical energy? You couldn't watch television, use a computer, or even turn on a light bulb!

Electrical energy is the energy of electric charges. Electrical energy is used for many things. In most of the devices that use electrical energy, the electric charges flow through wires. As you read on, you will learn more about how this flow of charges—called *electric current*—is produced and how it is controlled to operate the devices you rely on every day.

Batteries Are Included

In science, *energy* is defined as the ability to do work. You know that energy cannot be created or destroyed. It can only be *converted,* or changed, into other types of energy. One way to generate electrical energy is through chemical changes in a cell. A **cell** is a device that produces an electric current by converting chemical energy into electrical energy. A **battery** is made of one or more cells and also converts chemical energy into electrical energy.

Parts of a Cell

A cell, such as the one in **Figure 9,** contains a mixture of chemicals called an *electrolyte* (ee LEK troh LIET). Electrolytes conduct electric current. Every cell also contains a pair of electrodes made from two different conducting materials. An *electrode* (ee LEK TROHD) is the part of a cell through which charges enter or exit. The electrodes are in contact with the electrolyte. Chemical changes between the electrolyte and the electrodes convert chemical energy into electrical energy.

Figure 9 *This cell has a zinc electrode and a copper electrode dipped in a liquid electrolyte.*

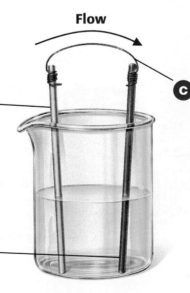

a A chemical change leaves extra electrons on the zinc electrode. This makes the zinc electrode negatively charged.

b A different chemical change pulls electrons off the copper electrode. This makes the copper electrode positively charged.

Flow

c If the electrodes are connected by a wire, charges will flow from the negative zinc electrode through the wire to the positive copper electrode. This flow of charges is an electric current.

Figure 10 *This cell uses the juice of a lemon as an electrolyte and uses strips of zinc and copper as electrodes.*

Types of Cells

Cells are divided into two groups—wet cells and dry cells. Wet cells, such as the cell shown in Figure 9, have liquid electrolytes. A car battery is made of several wet cells that use sulfuric acid as the electrolyte.

Dry cells work in a similar way, but dry cells have electrolytes that are solid or pastelike. Cells used in flashlights and portable radios are types of dry cells.

You can make your own cell by sticking strips of zinc and copper into a lemon. The electric current made when the metal strips are connected is strong enough to power a small clock, as shown in **Figure 10**.

Bring On the Potential

Now you know that cells and batteries are sources of electric current. But *why* is there an electric current between the two electrodes? The current is there because chemical changes in the cell cause a difference in charge between the two electrodes. So, charges will flow between the electrodes to provide energy. Each charge has a certain amount of energy. The energy per unit charge is called the **potential difference**. Potential difference is expressed in volts (V).

As long as there is a potential difference between the electrodes of a cell and there is a wire connecting them, charges will flow through the cell and the wire. These flowing charges are an electric current. The size of the current depends on the potential difference. The greater the potential difference is, the greater the current. **Figure 11** shows batteries and cells with different potential differences.

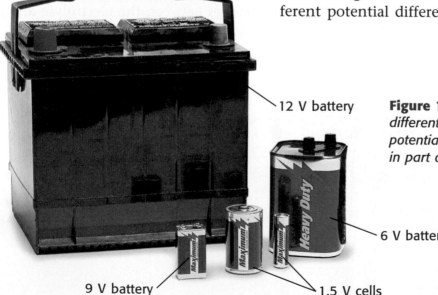

12 V battery

9 V battery

1.5 V cells

6 V battery

Figure 11 *Batteries are made with different potential differences. The potential difference of a battery depends in part on the number of cells it has.*

Other Ways of Generating Electrical Energy

You learned that batteries convert chemical energy into electrical energy. But there are many devices that change different types of energy into electrical energy. A common one is a generator, which converts mechanical energy into electrical energy. Read on to learn about two other common devices that generate electrical energy—photocells and thermocouples.

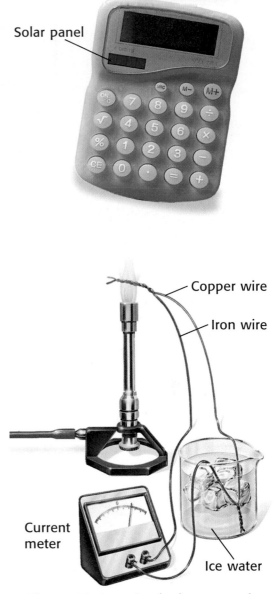

Photocells

Have you ever wondered how a solar-powered calculator works? Look at the calculator at right. Below the display you can see a dark strip called a solar panel. This panel is made of several photocells. A **photocell** is the part of a solar panel that converts light energy into electrical energy.

Most photocells contain silicon atoms. When light strikes the photocell, electrons are ejected from the silicon atoms. As long as light shines on the panel, electrons will be emitted. The free electrons are gathered into a wire to create an electric current.

Thermocouples

Thermal energy can be converted into electrical energy by a **thermocouple.** A simple thermocouple is shown in **Figure 12.** It is made by joining wires of two different metals into a loop. The temperature difference within the loop causes charges to flow through the loop. The greater the temperature difference is, the greater the current. Thermocouples are used to monitor the temperature of car engines, furnaces, and ovens.

Figure 12 *In a simple thermocouple, one section of the loop is heated and one section is cooled.*

SECTION REVIEW

❶ Name the parts of a cell, and explain how they work together to produce an electric current. ⭐TEKS

❷ How do the currents produced by a 1.5 V flashlight cell and a 12 V car battery compare?

❸ Compare the way thermocouples convert energy with the way batteries convert energy. ⭐TEKS

❹ **Inferring Conclusions** Why do you think some solar calculators contain batteries?

internet connect

SCI LINKS
NSTA   GO TO: www.scilinks.org

TOPIC: Electrical Energy
*sci*LINKS NUMBER: HSTP410

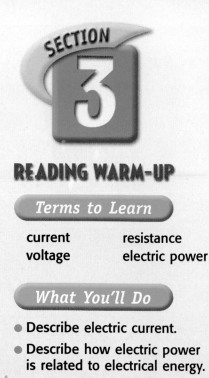

Electric Current

You have read about some ways to produce electrical energy and electric current. But what is electric current? Read on to learn more!

Cells and batteries are good sources of electrical energy for some things. But electric power plants provide most of the electrical energy you use every day. In this section, you will learn more about electric current and about the electrical energy you use at home.

Current Revisited

In the last section, you learned that electric current is a continuous flow of charge. **Current** is more precisely defined as the rate at which charge passes a given point. The higher the current is, the more charge passes the point each second. Current is expressed in units called *amperes* (AM pirz). The abbreviation for ampere, which is often shortened to amp, is A.

Charge Ahead!

When you flip a light switch, the light comes on instantly. Do charges flow that fast? No, they don't. But when you flip the switch, an electric field is set up in the wire at the speed of light. The electric field causes the free electrons in the wire to move, as illustrated in **Figure 13.** This field is created so quickly that all electrons start moving through the wire at the same instant. Think of the electric field as a command to the electrons to "Charge ahead!" The light comes on instantly because all the electrons obey this command at the same time. So the current that lights the bulb is established very quickly, even though each electron moves quite slowly. A single electron may take more than an hour to move 1 m through a wire.

Figure 13 *Electrons moving in a wire make up current, a continuous flow of charge.*

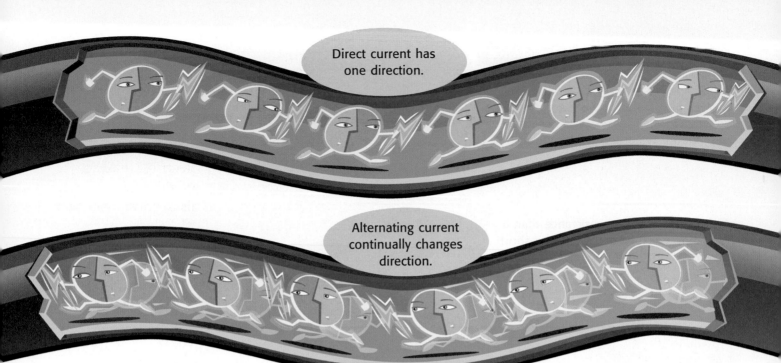

Direct current has one direction.

Alternating current continually changes direction.

Figure 14 *Charges move in one direction in DC, but charges continually change direction in AC.*

Let's See, AC/DC . . .

There are two different kinds of electric current—direct current (DC) and alternating current (AC). Look at **Figure 14.** In direct current, the charges always flow in the same direction. In alternating current, the charges continually switch from flowing in one direction to flowing in the reverse direction.

The electric current produced by batteries and cells is DC. The electric current from outlets in your home is AC. Both kinds of current can give you electrical energy. For example, if you connect a flashlight bulb to a battery, the light bulb will light. You can light a household light bulb by putting it in a lamp and turning the lamp on.

Voltage

Two factors determine the current in a wire. One factor is voltage. **Voltage** is the difference in energy per unit charge as a charge moves between two points in the path of a current. Voltage is another word for potential difference and is expressed in volts (V). The higher the voltage is, the more energy is released per charge. Therefore, the greater the voltage is, the greater the current. In the United States, most electrical outlets carry a voltage of 120 V.

Resistance

Resistance is the second factor that determines the current in a wire. **Resistance** is the opposition to the flow of electric charge. So, for a given voltage, the lower the resistance is, the greater the current. Resistance is expressed in *ohms* (Ω, the Greek letter *omega*).

Biology

CONNECTION

In your heart, some cells called pacemaker cells produce low electric currents at regular intervals to make the heart beat. During a heart attack, pacemaker cells do not work together and the heart beats irregularly. To correct this problem, doctors sometimes "jump start" the heart by creating a high voltage across a person's chest. This high voltage forces the pacemaker cells to act together and restores a regular heartbeat.

Introduction to Electricity **163**

Figure 15 A Model of Resistance

A big pipe has less resistance than a small pipe because there are more spaces between pieces of gravel in a big pipe for water to flow through.

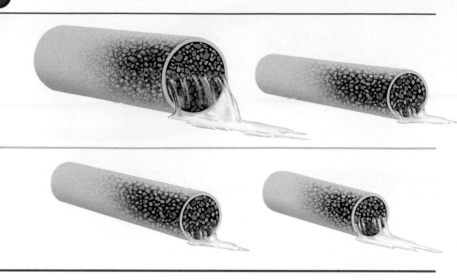

A short pipe has less resistance than a long pipe because the water in a short pipe does not have to work its way around as many pieces of gravel.

One way to think of electrical resistance is to use a model such as the gravel-filled water pipe shown in **Figure 15.** Notice that both the small pipe and the long pipe have more resistance to the flow of water than the big pipe and the short pipe. The same is true for electrical conductors. Think of resistance as "electrical friction" in a conductor. A thin conductor, such as a wire, will have more resistance to the flow of charges than a thick one will. Likewise, a long wire will have more resistance than a short one. Resistance also varies depending on the material and its temperature.

Electric Power

Often the word *power* is used in different ways. Power is often used to mean force, strength, or energy. In science, though, power is the rate at which work is done. **Electric power** is the rate at which electrical energy is used to do work. The unit for power is the watt (W).

Watt Is a Power Rating?!

Have you ever changed a light bulb? Then you are probably familiar with watts. Light bulbs have labels, such as "60 W," "75 W," or "100 W." A bulb with a higher power rating burns brighter because more electrical energy is converted into light energy per second. So, a 100 W light bulb is brighter than a 60 W light bulb.

Another common unit of power is the kilowatt (kW). One kilowatt is equal to 1,000 W. Kilowatts are used to express high values of power, such as the power needed to heat a house. The table on the next page shows the power ratings of some appliances you use every day.

Measuring Electrical Energy

Electric power companies sell electrical energy to homes and businesses. Power companies determine how much a home or business has to pay based on power and time. For example, the amount of electrical energy used by a household depends on the power of the electrical devices in the house and the length of time those devices are on.

Measuring Household Energy Use

Electric power companies use electric meters such as the one shown in **Figure 16.** The meter records the amount of energy a household uses. Electric meters are often on the outside of houses and apartment buildings so that someone from the power company can read them.

Households use different amounts of electrical energy in a day. Electric companies calculate electrical energy use by multiplying the power in kilowatts by the time in hours. The usual unit of electrical energy is kilowatt-hours (kWh). If a family uses 2,000 W (2 kW) of power for 3 hours, it uses 6 kWh of energy.

Figure 16 *An electric meter is used by electric power companies to measure electrical energy use.*

How to Save Energy

The amount of electrical energy an appliance uses depends on what the appliance's power rating is and how long the appliance is on. For example, a clock has a power rating of 3 W. If the clock is on 24 hours a day, it uses 72 Wh (3 W × 24 hours), or 0.072 kWh, of energy per day. Estimate how long each appliance listed in the chart is on during a day. Then determine how much electrical energy each appliance uses per day. Finally, describe what you can do to use less electrical energy.

Power Ratings of Household Appliances	
Appliance	**Power (W)**
Clothes dryer	4,000
Toaster	1,100
Refrigerator	600
Color television	200
Radio	100
Clock	3

SECTION REVIEW

1. What is electric current?

2. How does an electric power company calculate electrical energy?

3. **Applying Concepts** Explain why increasing the voltage in a wire can have the same effect as decreasing the resistance in the wire.

internet connect

SC*LINKS*
NSTA   GO TO: www.scilinks.org

TOPIC: Superconductor Research in Texas
*sci*LINKS NUMBER: HSTX190

TOPIC: Electric Current
*sci*LINKS NUMBER: HSTP415

READING WARM-UP

Terms to Learn

circuit   series circuit
load   parallel circuit

What You'll Do

● Name the three necessary parts of a circuit.

● Compare series circuits with parallel circuits.

● Explain how fuses and circuit breakers protect your home against short circuits and circuit overloads.

Electric Circuits

Think about a roller coaster. You start out nice and easy. Then the ride roars around the track. A couple of exciting minutes later, you are right back where you started! Fun!

A roller-coaster car follows a fixed pathway. The ride's starting point and ending point are the same place. This kind of closed pathway is called a circuit.

Parts of a Circuit

An electric circuit always forms a loop. Just like a roller coaster, it begins and ends in the same place. Because a circuit forms a loop, a circuit is a closed path. So an electric **circuit** is a complete, closed path through which electric charges flow.

All circuits need three basic parts. A circuit must have an energy source, a load, and wires to connect the source to the load. A **load** is a device that uses electrical energy to do work. All loads offer some resistance to electric currents. Loads can change electrical energy into other forms of energy, such as thermal energy, light energy, or mechanical energy. **Figure 17** shows examples of the necessary parts of a circuit.

| **Figure 17** | **Necessary Parts of a Circuit** |

Energy Source	Wires	Load
The **energy source** can be a battery, a photocell, a thermocouple, or an electric generator at a power plant.	**Wires** connect the other parts of a circuit together. Wires are made of conducting materials with low resistance, such as copper.	Examples of **loads** are light bulbs, appliances, televisions, and motors.

Opening and Closing a Circuit

Sometimes a circuit also uses a switch. A switch opens and closes a circuit. A switch is made of two pieces of conducting material. One piece can be moved, as shown in **Figure 18.** For charges to flow through a circuit, the switch must be closed, or "turned on." If a switch is open, or "off," the loop of the circuit is broken. No charges can flow through an open circuit. Light switches and power buttons on radios are switches. Even the keys on calculators and computers work like switches.

Figure 18 *You can turn a light bulb on and off by using a switch to close and open a circuit.*

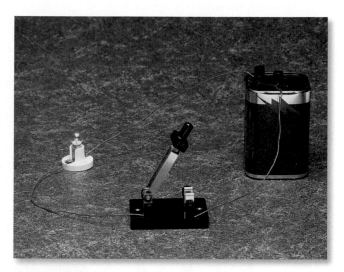

When the **switch is closed,** the two pieces of conducting material touch. This allows the electric charges to flow through the circuit. As a result, the bulb lights up.

When the **switch is open,** there is a gap between the two pieces of conducting material. This prevents the electric charges from traveling through the circuit. As a result, the bulb does not light up.

Types of Circuits

Look around the room for a moment, and count the number of objects that use electrical energy. You probably found several, such as lights, a clock, and maybe a computer. All of the objects you counted are loads on a large circuit. This one circuit may even go through several rooms in the building. Most circuits have more than one load. The loads in a circuit can be connected in two different ways—in series or in parallel.

✓ Self-Check

Is a microwave oven a load? Explain why or why not. *(See page 640 to check your answer.)*

Biology CONNECTION

Believe it or not, your body is controlled by a large electric circuit. Electrical impulses from your brain control all the muscles and organs in your body. The food you eat is the energy source for your body's circuit, your nerves are the wires, and your muscles and organs are the loads.

Series Circuits

A **series circuit** is a circuit in which all parts are connected in a single loop. The charges traveling through a series circuit must flow through each part. They can follow only one path. **Figure 19** shows a series circuit.

All the loads in a series circuit share the same current. Because the current in all the light bulbs in Figure 19 is the same, the light bulbs glow with the same brightness. If you add more light bulbs, the resistance of the entire circuit would increase. As a result, the current would decrease. All the bulbs would be dimmer.

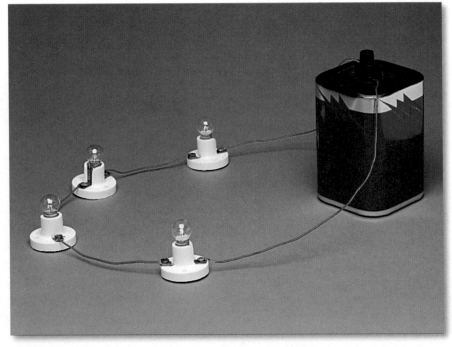

Figure 19 *The charges flow from the battery through each light bulb (load) and finally back to the battery.*

A Series of Circuits

1. Connect a **6 V battery** and **two flashlight bulbs** in a series circuit. Draw a picture of your circuit in your ScienceLog.

2. Add **another flashlight bulb** in series with the other two bulbs. How does the brightness of the light bulbs change?

3. Replace one of the light bulbs with a **burned-out light bulb.** What happens to the other lights in the circuit? Explain the result.

★TEKS

Uses for Series Circuits

Series circuits are usually used in circuits with a single load, such as in a flashlight or an electric fan. Several series circuits may be combined in larger devices, such as an electric stove. Each heating coil is connected in a series circuit with a control knob. When the control is set on "Low," the current to the coil is low and the coil gets warm. When the control is set on "High," the current is increased and the coil gets hot. When the control is turned off, the coil receives no current at all.

A series circuit has only one pathway for the current, so any break in the circuit causes the current to stop. For example, if one of the bulbs in Figure 19 burned out, it would cause a break in the circuit. The break would stop current throughout the circuit, and none of the bulbs would light.

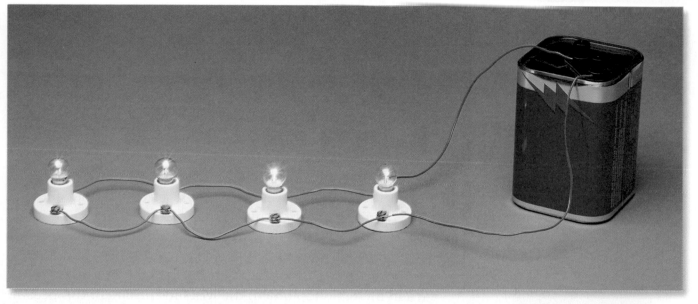

Figure 20 *The electric charges flow from the battery to each of the bulbs separately and then flow back to the battery.*

Parallel Circuits

Think about what would happen if all the lights in your home were connected in series. If you needed a light on in your room, all the other lights in the house would have to be turned on too! But circuits in buildings are wired in parallel rather than in series. A **parallel circuit** is a circuit in which each load is placed on a separate branch. Because there are separate branches, the charges can go through more than one path. **Figure 20** shows a parallel circuit.

Unlike the loads in a series circuit, the loads in a parallel circuit do not have the same current in them. Instead, each load in a parallel circuit uses the same voltage. For example, the full voltage of the battery is applied to each bulb in Figure 20. As a result, each light bulb glows at full brightness no matter how many bulbs are connected in parallel. You can connect loads that need different currents to the same parallel circuit. For example, you can have a hair dryer, which needs a high current to run, on the same circuit as a lamp, which needs less current.

Uses for Parallel Circuits

In a parallel circuit, each branch of the circuit can function by itself. If one load is broken or missing, charges will still run through the other branches. The loads on those branches will continue to work. In your home, each electrical outlet is usually on its own branch and has its own on-off switch. It would be inconvenient if each time a light bulb went out, your television or stereo stopped working. With parallel circuits, you can use one light or appliance at a time even if another load fails.

A Parallel Lab

1. Connect a **6 V battery** and **two flashlight bulbs** in a parallel circuit. Draw a picture of your circuit in your ScienceLog.

2. Add **another flashlight bulb** in parallel with the other two bulbs. How does the brightness of the light bulbs change?

3. Replace one of the light bulbs with a **burned-out light bulb.** What happens to the other lights in the circuit? Explain the result.

TEKS

Household Circuits

In every home, several circuits connect all the lights, major appliances, and outlets. Most home circuits are parallel circuits that can have several loads on them. The circuits branch out from a breaker box or a fuse box. This box acts as the "electrical headquarters" for the building. Each branch receives a standard voltage, which is 120 V in the United States.

Mayday! Circuit Failure!

Broken insulation or water can cause electrical appliances to short-circuit. A short circuit happens when charges do not go through one or more loads in the circuit. When charges do not go through the loads, the circuit's resistance drops. When resistance drops, the current in the circuit increases. If the current increases too much, the wires in the circuit can become hot enough to start a fire. **Figure 21** explains one way that a short circuit might occur.

Circuits also may fail if they are overloaded. A circuit is overloaded when too many loads, or electrical devices, are attached to it. Each time you add a load to a parallel circuit, the entire circuit draws more current. If too many loads are attached to one circuit, the current increases to a dangerous level that can cause wires to become hot enough to cause a fire. **Figure 22** shows a case that can cause a circuit overload.

Figure 21 *If the insulating plastic around a cord is broken, the two wires inside can touch. The charges can then bypass the load and travel from one wire to the other, resulting in a short circuit.*

Figure 22 *Plugging too many things into one outlet can cause a circuit to overload.*

Circuit Safety

Short circuits and circuit overloads can be very dangerous. Circuits in your home have built-in safety features. The two safety devices most often used are fuses and circuit breakers.

Fuses

A fuse, located in a fuse box, contains a thin strip of metal. The charges in the circuit flow through the fuse. If the current in the circuit is too high, the metal strip gets hot and melts, as shown in **Figure 23.** As a result, the circuit is broken, and the charges stop flowing. This break is referred to as "blowing a fuse." After a fuse is blown, you must replace it with a new fuse for the charges to flow through the circuit again.

Figure 23 *The blown fuse (left) must be replaced with a new fuse (right).*

Circuit Breakers

Circuit breakers are located in a breaker box. A circuit breaker is a switch that automatically opens if the current in the circuit is too high. A strip of metal in the breaker warms up and bends, which causes the switch to open the circuit. Charges stop flowing. Open circuit breakers can be closed by flipping a switch to reset the breaker once the problem has been corrected.

A device that acts like a circuit breaker is a ground fault circuit interrupter (GFCI). A GFCI, shown in **Figure 24,** compares the current in one side of an outlet with the current in the other side. If there is even a small difference, the GFCI opens the circuit. The charges stop flowing. To close the circuit, you must push the RESET button.

Figure 24
GFCI devices are often found in bathrooms and kitchens to protect you from electric shock.

SECTION REVIEW

1. Describe the three necessary parts of a circuit, and explain why they are important.

2. What are the differences between series and parallel circuits?

3. How do fuses and circuit breakers protect your home against electrical fires?

4. **Developing Hypotheses** Whenever you turn on the portable heater in your room, the circuit breaker for the circuit in your room opens and all the lights go out. Propose two possible reasons that explain why.

internet**connect**

SC/LINKS.
NSTA   GO TO: www.scilinks.org

TOPIC: Electric Circuits
*sci*LINKS NUMBER: HSTP420

Skill Builder Lab

Circuitry 101 ⊛TEKS

You have learned that there are two basic types of electric circuits. A series circuit connects all the parts to the power source in a single loop. A parallel circuit connects all the parts to the power source on separate branches. If you want to control the whole circuit, the loads and the switch must be wired in series. If you want parts of the circuit to operate independently, the loads must be wired in parallel. In this lab, you will construct both a series circuit and a parallel circuit. You will use an ammeter to measure current and a voltmeter to measure voltage.

MATERIALS

- power source—dry cell(s)
- switch
- 3 light-bulb holders
- 3 light bulbs
- insulated wire, cut into 15 cm lengths with both ends stripped
- ammeter
- voltmeter

Part A—Series Circuit

Procedure

1 Construct a series circuit with a power source, a switch, and three light bulbs. Draw your circuit in your ScienceLog.
Caution: Always leave the switch open when constructing or changing the circuit. Close the switch only when testing or taking a reading.

2 Test your circuit. Do all three bulbs light up? Are they all the same brightness? What happens if you carefully unscrew one light bulb? Does it make any difference which bulb you unscrew? Record your observations in your ScienceLog.

3 Connect the ammeter between the power source and the switch. Close the switch, and record the current on your diagram in your ScienceLog. Use a label to show where you measured the current and what the value was.

4 Reconnect the circuit. Place the ammeter between the first and second bulbs. Record the current, as you did in step 3.

5 Move the ammeter. Place it between the second and third bulbs. Record the current again. Remove the ammeter from the circuit.

6 Connect the voltmeter to the two ends of the power source. Label the voltage on your diagram.

7 Use the voltmeter to measure the voltage across each bulb. Label the voltage across each bulb on your diagram.

8 Add the voltages measured across each bulb, and record the total in your ScienceLog.

Part B—Parallel Circuit
Procedure

9 Take apart your series circuit. Reassemble the same power source, switch, and three light bulbs so that the bulbs are wired in parallel. (Note: The switch must remain in series with the power source to be able to control the whole circuit.)

10 Draw a diagram of your parallel circuit in your ScienceLog.

11 Test your circuit, and record your observations, as you did in step 2.

12 Connect the ammeter between the power source and the switch. Record the reading on your diagram.

13 Reconnect the circuit so that the ammeter is right next to one of the three bulbs. Record the current on your diagram.

14 Repeat step 13 for the remaining bulbs. Remove the ammeter from your circuit.

15 Connect the voltmeter to the two ends of the power source. Record this voltage.

16 Measure and record the voltage across each light bulb. Add and record the voltages as you did in step 8.

Analysis—Parts A and B

17 Was the current the same everywhere in the series circuit? Was it the same everywhere in the parallel circuit?

18 For each circuit, compare the voltage across each light bulb with the voltage across the power source.

19 For each circuit, compare the sum of the voltages across the light bulbs with the voltage across the power source.

20 Why did the bulbs differ in brightness?

21 Consider your results. What do you think might happen if too many loads are plugged into the same series circuit? the same parallel circuit?

22 Compare your results with the results of your classmates.

Section 1

Vocabulary

law of electric charges *(p. 152)*
electric force *(p. 153)*
electric field *(p. 153)*
conductor *(p. 156)*
insulator *(p. 156)*
static electricity *(p. 156)*
electric discharge *(p. 157)*

Section Notes

- The law of electric charges states that like charges repel and opposite charges attract.

- The size of the electric force between two objects depends on the size of the charges exerting the force and the distance between the objects.

- Charged objects exert a force on each other and can cause each other to move. ⭐TEKS

- Objects become charged when they gain or lose electrons. Objects may become charged by friction, conduction, or induction.

- Charges are not created or destroyed and are said to be conserved.

- Charges move easily in conductors but do not move easily in insulators.

- Static electricity is the buildup of electric charges on an object. It is lost through electric discharge.

LabBook ⭐TEKS

Stop the Static Electricity! *(p. 613)*

Section 2

Vocabulary

cell *(p. 159)*
battery *(p. 159)*
potential difference *(p. 160)*
photocell *(p. 161)*
thermocouple *(p. 161)*

Section Notes

- Cells convert chemical energy into electrical energy. A battery is a collection of one or more cells. ⭐TEKS

- Electric current can be produced when there is a potential difference between two electrodes.

- Photocells and thermocouples are devices used to generate electrical energy. ⭐TEKS

LabBook ⭐TEKS

Potato Power *(p. 614)*

Section 3

Vocabulary

current *(p. 162)*
voltage *(p. 163)*
resistance *(p. 163)*
electric power *(p. 164)*

Section Notes

- Electric current is a continuous flow of charge caused by the motion of electrons.

- Voltage is the same as potential difference. As voltage increases, current increases.

- An object's resistance varies depending on the object's material, thickness, length, and temperature.

- As resistance increases, current decreases.

- Electric power is the rate at which electrical energy is used to do work. It is expressed in watts or kilowatts.

Section 4

Vocabulary

circuit *(p. 166)*
load *(p. 166)*
series circuit *(p. 168)*
parallel circuit *(p. 169)*

Section Notes

- Circuits consist of an energy source, a load, wires, and sometimes a switch.

- All parts of a series circuit are connected in a single loop.

- The loads in a parallel circuit are on separate branches.

- Circuits can fail because of a short circuit or circuit overload.

- Fuses or circuit breakers protect your home against circuit failure.

USING VOCABULARY

Complete the following sentences by choosing the correct term from each pair of terms.

1. A __?__ converts thermal energy into electrical energy. *(thermocouple or photocell)* ⭐TEKS

2. Charges flow easily in a(n) __?__. *(insulator or conductor)*

3. __?__ is the opposition to the flow of electric charge. *(Resistance or Electric power)*

4. A __?__ is a complete, closed path through which charges flow. *(load or circuit)*

5. Lightning is a form of __?__. *(electric discharge or electric power)*

UNDERSTANDING CONCEPTS

Multiple Choice

6. If two charges repel each other, the two charges must be
   a. positive and positive.
   b. positive and negative.
   c. negative and negative.
   d. Either (a) or (c)

7. A device that can convert chemical energy into electrical energy is a ⭐TEKS
   a. lightning rod.
   b. cell.
   c. light bulb.
   d. All of the above

8. An object's resistance depends on which of the following?
   a. mass, density, temperature, and length
   b. material, thickness, length, and temperature
   c. height, weight, temperature, and thickness
   d. material, density, color, and length

9. An object becomes charged when the atoms in the object gain or lose
   a. protons.   c. electrons.
   b. neutrons.   d. All of the above

10. A device used to protect buildings from electrical fires is a(n)
    a. electric meter.   c. fuse.
    b. circuit breaker. d. Both (b) and (c)

11. For a cell to produce current, the electrodes of the cell must
    a. have a potential difference.
    b. be in a liquid.
    c. be exposed to light.
    d. be at two different temperatures.

12. What type of current comes from the outlets in your home?
    a. direct current
    b. alternating current
    c. electric discharge
    d. static electricity

Short Answer

13. List and describe the three necessary parts of a circuit.

14. Name the two factors that affect the strength of electric force, and explain how they affect electric force.

15. Describe how direct current differs from alternating current.

16. Use the following terms to create a concept map: *electric current, battery, charges, photocell, thermocouple, circuit, parallel circuit,* and *series circuit.*

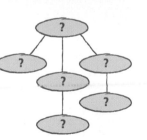

CRITICAL THINKING AND PROBLEM SOLVING

Write one or two sentences to answer the following questions:

17. Compare the methods used by photocells and batteries to transform energy in a calculator. ⭐TEKS

18. Explain how to make a cell using an apple, a strip of copper, and a strip of silver. Identify the parts of the cell. What type of cell is formed? Explain your answer. ⭐TEKS

19. Your friend shows you a magic trick. She rubs a plastic comb with a piece of silk and holds the comb close to a stream of water. When the comb is close to the water, the water bends toward the comb. Explain how this trick works. (Hint: Think about how objects become charged.)

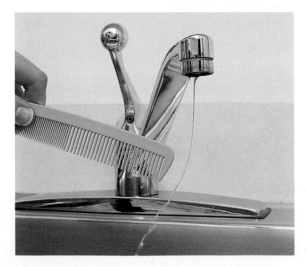

20. A solar panel converts light energy into electrical energy. Can you think of other devices that convert electrical energy into light energy? that convert electrical energy into thermal energy? ⭐TEKS

MATH IN SCIENCE

21. How much does it cost to operate a 200 W color television for 24 hours if electrical energy costs $0.15 per kWh? Show your calculations.

INTERPRETING GRAPHICS

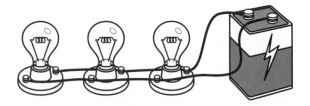

22. Use the circuit diagram for lights shown above to answer the following questions:
  a. Which kind of circuit is shown?
  b. What would happen if one of the lights burned out? if three lights burned out? Explain why.
  c. What would happen to the brightness of each bulb if a fourth bulb is added to the circuit? Explain why.

Reading Check-up Take a minute to review your answers to the Pre-Reading Questions ⭐TEKS found at the bottom of page 150. Have your answers changed? If necessary, revise your answers based on what you have learned since you began this chapter.

Chapter 6

Number of windmill blades	Average number of rotations per minute
2	15
4	18
6	21
8	31
10	21

1 The picture shows a model of a windmill. When the wind blows and spins a windmill's blades, the windmill can convert the kinetic energy of wind into electrical energy. The faster a windmill's blades spin, the more electrical energy the windmill produces. Some students made a hypothesis that the more blades a windmill had, the faster the blades would spin at a particular wind speed. The students tested their model with different numbers of blades. They used an electric fan to provide the "wind." For each number of blades, the students counted the number of rotations. The table shows their results. Given those results, which statement is the best analysis of the students' hypothesis?

A The hypothesis is supported because adding more blades always makes the blades spin faster.

B The hypothesis is supported because increasing the wind speed makes the blades spin faster.

C The hypothesis is not supported because adding more blades makes the blades spin faster only up to a certain number of blades.

D The hypothesis is not supported because not enough blades were added.

2 Putting two north poles or two south poles of two magnets together makes the magnets push each other apart. Putting a north pole with a south pole makes the magnets stick together. For which of the following could the magnets serve as a simple model?

F Parallel circuit

G Voltage

H Law of electric charges

J Potential difference

3 Using batteries in a portable stereo at the lake involves which energy conversions?

A Kinetic energy into electrical energy into sound energy

B Chemical energy into electrical energy into sound energy

C Electrical energy into sound energy into kinetic energy

D Sound energy into chemical energy into electrical energy

4 A thermocouple can be made by joining wires of two different metals into a loop. A thermocouple is used to

F convert electrical energy into thermal energy.

G convert thermal energy into electrical energy.

H convert electrical energy into mechanical energy.

J convert mechanical energy into thermal energy.

Chapter 6

Math

1 Look at triangle ABC. If you want to draw a square, ADBC, what would be the coordinates of D?

A (1, 5)

B (3, 3)

C (5, 5)

D (5, 1)

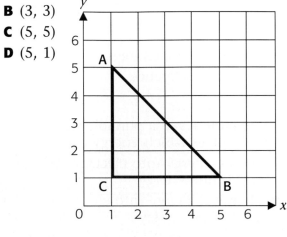

2 The radius of a family's circular swimming pool is 2 meters. What is the approximate *circumference* of the pool? (π = 3)

F 3 m

G 6 m

H 9 m

J 12 m

3 Heather has 6 large dogs. In 1 day, each of the dogs eats 2.1 kilograms of dog food. Which is the best estimate of the total number of *kilograms* of food all of the dogs eat in 4 weeks?

A Less than 150 kg

B Between 150 and 200 kg

C Between 200 and 250 kg

D Between 250 and 300 kg

E More than 300 kg

Reading

Read the passage. Then read each question that follows the passage. Decide which is the best answer to each question.

In 1888, Frank J. Sprague developed a way to operate trolleys with electrical energy. These electric trolleys ran on a metal track and were connected by a pole to an overhead power line. Electric charges flowed down the pole to motors in the trolley. A wheel at the top of the pole, called a <u>shoe</u>, rolled along the power line and allowed the trolley to move along its track without losing contact with its source of electrical energy. The charges passed through the motor and then returned to a generator by way of the metal track.

1 In this passage, the word <u>shoe</u> means

A a type of covering that you wear on your feet.

B a device that allowed a trolley to get electrical energy.

C a flat, U-shaped metal plate nailed to a horse's hoof.

D the metal track on which trolleys ran.

2 The main purpose of this passage is to

F inform the reader.

G influence the reader's opinion.

H express the author's opinion.

J make the reader laugh.

Sprites and Elves

Imagine you are a pilot flying a plane on a moonless night. About 80 km away, you notice a powerful thunderstorm. You see the lightning flash between the clouds and the Earth. You expect this because you know that weather activity takes place in the troposphere, the lowest layer of Earth's atmosphere. But all of a sudden, a ghostly red glow stretches many kilometers above the storm clouds and into the stratosphere! You did not expect that!

Capturing Sprites

In 1989, scientists at the University of Minnesota followed the trail of many such reports. They captured the first image of this strange, red-glowing lightning using a video camera. Since then, photographs from space shuttles, airplanes, telescopes, and observers on the ground have identified several types of wispy electrical glows. Two of these types were named sprites and elves because, like the mythical creatures, they disappear just as the eye begins to see them. Sprites and elves last only a few thousandths of a second.

Sprites and elves occur only when ordinary lightning is discharged from a cloud. Sprites are very large. They extend from the cloud tops at an altitude of about 15 km to as high as 95 km. They are up to 50 km wide. Elves are expanding disks of red light, probably caused by an electromagnetic pulse from lightning or sprites. Elves can be 200 km across, and they appear at altitudes above 90 km.

What Took So Long?

Sprites and elves have likely been occurring for thousands of years. They have been unrecorded for several reasons. For one, they are produced with only about 1 percent of lightning flashes. Sprites and elves also disappear quickly and are very faint. Finally, because they occur above thunderclouds, where few people can see,

observers are more often distracted by the brighter lightning below.

▼ *Sprites (left) and elves (right) are strange electric discharges in the atmosphere.*

Still, scientists are not surprised to learn that electric discharges extend up from clouds. There is a large potential difference between thunderclouds and the ionosphere, an atmospheric level above the clouds. The ionosphere is electrically conductive and provides a path for these electric discharges.

Search and Find

▶ Would you like to find sprites on your own? (Elves disappear too quickly.) Go with an adult, avoid being out in a thunderstorm, and remember:

- It must be completely dark, and your eyes must adjust to the total darkness.
- Viewing is best when a large thunderstorm is 45 to 100 km away, with no clouds in between.
- Block out the lightning below the clouds with dark paper so that you can still see above the clouds.
- Be patient.

Report sightings to a university geophysical department. Scientists use the information to help explain how sprites and elves are part of the chemical and electrical workings of our atmosphere.

SCIENCE

Living Things

Place to Visit

Visit the Gladys Porter Zoo in Brownsville, Texas, and you might see jaguars, Galápagos tortoises, orangutans, Bactrian camels, Sumatran tigers, kookaburras, white rhinoceroses, and Arabian oryxes all in one afternoon! The zoo has carefully recreated habitats of Africa, tropical America, Indo-Australia, and Asia. Each area has rocks, streams, and native plants so that you can see the animals in their natural environment. The zoo has more than 1,500 animals representing about 400 species. Visit the zoo, and see how many species you can spot!

Brownsville

The Gladys Porter Zoo, Brownsville, Texas

ACROSS TEXAS

Scientific Research

College Station

What color are bluebonnets? According to Texas A&M University, bluebonnets are the school's color—maroon! In nature, bluebonnets are usually blue. However, in some locations, people have found white bluebonnets. There are also very rare pink varieties. Scientists at Texas A&M and the Texas Agricultural Extension created maroon bluebonnets by selectively breeding bluebonnets of various colors. Maroon bluebonnets! Now that's school spirit.

SCIENCE FACT

South Padre Island

You may have heard of organ transplants, but have you ever heard of turtle transplants? In 1977, scientists realized that sea turtles' breeding grounds in Mexico were being destroyed. Since then, the Kemp's Ridley Sea Turtle Restoration and Enhancement Project has been moving eggs from Mexico to a protected beach on South Padre Island, Texas, each year. Because sea turtles return to their birth site to lay eggs, scientists hope that the Texas-born ridleys will return after they mature. So far, more than 18,000 eggs have hatched!

internet connect

go.hrw.com

go to: go.hrw.com
KEYWORD: HTXU63

Cells: The Basic Units of Living Things

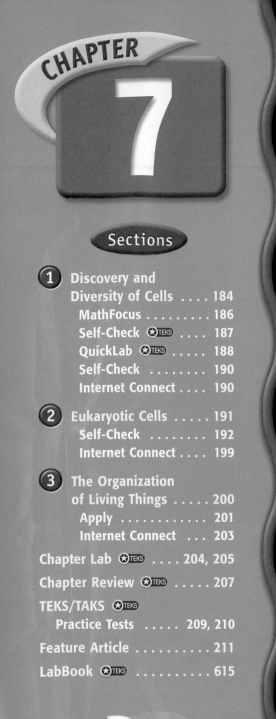

Pre-Reading Questions

1. All organisms are made of what building block? ⊛TEKS

2. What life-sustaining functions do cells carry out? ⊛TEKS

3. Where is the genetic material in an organism located? ⊛TEKS

TINY DEFENDERS

Invading bacteria have entered your body. These foreign cells are about to make you sick. But wait—your white blood cells come to the rescue! In this microscopic image, a white blood cell is reaching out its "arms" to destroy bacteria, shown in purple. In this chapter, you will learn about bacteria, blood cells, and other cells.

START-UP Activity

WHAT ARE PLANTS MADE OF? ⭐TEKS

All living things, including plants, are made of cells. What do plant cells look like? Do this activity to find out.

Procedure

1. Tear off a small leaf near the tip of an *Elodea* sprig.

2. Using **tweezers,** place the whole leaf in a **drop of water** on a **plastic microscope slide.**

3. Place a **plastic coverslip** on top of the water drop. Put one edge on the slide, and then slowly lower the coverslip over the drop to prevent air bubbles.

4. Place the slide on your **microscope.** Find the cells. You may have to use the highest-powered lens to see them.

5. Draw a picture of what you see.

Analysis

6. Describe the shape of the *Elodea* cells. Are they all the same?

7. Do you think your cells look like *Elodea* cells? Explain your answer.

READING WARM-UP

Terms to Learn

cell
cell membrane
cytoplasm
organelle

DNA
nucleus
eukaryote
prokaryote

What You'll Do

- State the parts of the cell theory.
- Explain why cells are small.
- Identify cells as structures containing genetic material. ⊙TEKS
- Explain the differences between the three basic types of cells.

Discovery and Diversity of Cells

Most cells are so small that they can't be seen by the naked eye. So how did scientists find the first cells? By accident, that's how! The first person to see cells wasn't even looking for them.

All living things are made of cells. **Cells** are membrane-covered structures that contain all the materials necessary for life. Cells also carry out many functions that sustain life. Because of their size, cells weren't discovered until microscopes were invented in the mid-1600s.

The Discovery of Cells

Robert Hooke was the first person to describe cells. In 1665, he built a microscope, shown in **Figure 1,** to look at tiny objects. One day, he looked at a thin slice of cork. Cork, shown in **Figure 2,** is found in the bark of cork trees. The cork looked like it was made of little boxes. Hooke named these boxes *cells,* which means "little rooms" in Latin. Hooke's cells were really the outer layers of dead cork cells.

Hooke also looked at thin slices of living plants. He saw that they too were made of cells. Some were even filled with "juice." The "juicy" cells were living cells.

Hooke also used his microscope to look at feathers, fish scales, and the eyes of houseflies. But he spent most of his time looking at plants and fungi. The cells of plants and fungi have cell walls. This makes them easy to see. Animal cells do not have cell walls. So it is harder to see the outline of animal cells. Because Hooke couldn't see their cells, he thought that animals weren't made of cells.

Figure 1 *This is the microscope Hooke used when he discovered cells.*

Figure 2 *Here is Hooke's drawing of cork cells and a picture of the type of tree they come from.*

Finding Cells in Other Organisms

Anton van Leeuwenhoek (LAY vuhn HOOK) was a Dutch merchant who made his own microscopes. A few years after Hooke's discovery, Leeuwenhoek looked at pond scum under one of his microscopes. Leeuwenhoek saw small organisms in the water. He named these organisms *animalcules*, which means "little animals." Today we call these single-celled organisms *protists*. Pond scum and some protists that live in ponds are shown in **Figure 3.**

Leeuwenhoek also looked at animal blood. He saw differences in the shape of blood cells from different animals. For example, blood cells in fish, birds, and frogs are oval shaped. Blood cells in humans and dogs are flatter. Leeuwenhoek was also the first person to see bacteria. And he discovered that the yeasts used to make bread dough rise are actually single-celled organisms.

Figure 3 *This pond has a layer of pond scum. These organisms, called protists, live in ponds.*

Euglena

Microcystis

Stentor

Spirogyra

The Cell Theory

Almost 200 years passed before scientists realized that cells are present in all living things. Matthias Schleiden studied plants. In 1838, he concluded that all plant parts were made of cells. Theodor Schwann studied animals. In 1839, he concluded that all animal tissues were made of cells. Nineteen years later, Rudolf Virchow, a doctor, saw that cells formed only from other cells. Together, the observations of these three German scientists form the *cell theory:*

◆ All organisms are made of one or more cells.
◆ The cell is the basic unit of all living things.
◆ All cells come from existing cells.

Cells Are Small

Most cells are too small to be seen without a microscope. It would take 50 human cells to cover up the dot on this letter *i*.

Why Are Cells So Small?

There is a physical reason why most cells are so small. Cells take in food and get rid of wastes through their outer surface. As a cell gets larger, it needs more food and produces more waste. Therefore, more materials have to pass across its outer surface.

As the cell's volume increases, its surface area grows too. But its volume grows faster than its surface area. If a cell gets too large, the cell's surface area will not be large enough to take in enough nutrients or pump out enough wastes. So, the area of a cell's surface—compared to the volume of the cell—limits the cell's size. The ratio of the cell's outer surface area to its volume is called the *surface-to-volume ratio,* which can be calculated using the following equation:

$$surface\text{-}to\text{-}volume\ ratio = \frac{surface\ area}{volume}$$

A Few Cells Are Big

Most cells are small. A few, however, are big. A chicken egg, shown in **Figure 4,** is one big cell. It can be this large because it does not take in nutrients.

Figure 4 *The white and yolk of this chicken egg are part of a single cell. The largest cells on Earth are bird eggs.*

MathFocus ··········

Surface-to-Volume Ratio

Calculate the *surface-to-volume ratio* of a cube whose *sides* measure 2 cm.

Step 1: Calculate the surface area.

surface area of cube = number of sides × area of square
surface area of cube = 6 × (2 cm × 2 cm)
surface area of cube = 24 cm^2

Step 2: Calculate the volume.

volume of cube = side × side × side
volume of cube = 2 cm × 2 cm × 2 cm = 8 cm^3

Step 3: Calculate the surface-to-volume ratio.

surface-to-volume ratio = $\frac{surface\ area}{volume}$ = $\frac{24}{8}$ = $\frac{3}{1}$

Now It's Your Turn

1. Calculate the surface-to-volume ratio of a cube whose sides are 3 cm long.

2. Calculate the surface-to-volume ratio of a cube whose sides are 4 cm long.

3. Of the cubes from questions 1 and 2, which has the greater surface-to-volume ratio?

4. What is the relationship between size and the surface-to-volume ratio of a cell?

Parts of a Cell

There are many kinds of cells. Different cells perform different functions, but all cells have the following things in common.

The Cell Membrane and Cytoplasm

Cells are surrounded by a **cell membrane.** This membrane acts as a barrier. It separates the cell's contents from its environment. The cell membrane also controls the passage of materials into and out of the cell. Inside the cell is a fluid. This fluid and almost all of its contents are called the **cytoplasm** (SIET oh PLAZ uhm).

Organelles

Cells have organelles. **Organelles** are structures that enable cells to live and reproduce. Different types of cells have different organelles. Most organelles are surrounded by membranes. For example, the algal cell in **Figure 5** has membrane-bound organelles. Some organelles float in the cytoplasm. Others are attached to membranes or other organelles.

Genetic Material

All cells contain DNA (**d**eoxyribo**n**ucleic **a**cid) at some point in their life. **DNA** is the genetic material. It contains the information needed to make new cells and new organisms. DNA is passed on from parent cells to new cells and controls the activities of a cell. **Figure 6** shows the DNA of a bacterium.

In some cells, the DNA is enclosed inside an organelle called the **nucleus.** For example, your cells have a nucleus. In contrast, bacterial cells do not have a nucleus.

In humans, mature red blood cells do not have DNA. Red blood cells are made inside bones. When red blood cells are made, they have a nucleus with DNA. But before they enter the bloodstream, red blood cells lose their nucleus. They must then survive with no new instructions from their DNA.

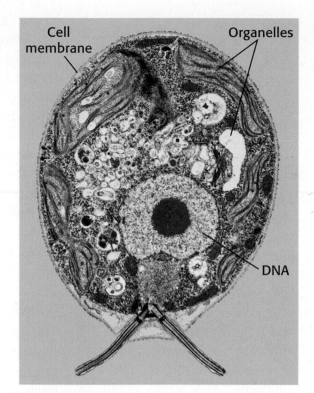

Figure 5 *This green algae has organelles. The organelles and the fluid surrounding them make up the cytoplasm.*

Figure 6 *This photo shows DNA spilling out of a bacterium,* E. coli, *which is found in your gut.*

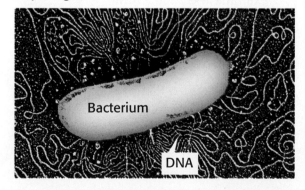

Self-Check

What is the genetic material, and where is it found? *(See page 640 to check your answer.)* ⭐TEKS

Bacteria in Your Lunch?

Most of the time, you don't want bacteria in your food. Many bacteria make toxins that will make you sick. However, some foods—such as yogurt—are supposed to have bacteria in them! The bacteria in these foods are not dangerous.

In yogurt, masses of rod-shaped bacteria feed on the sugar (lactose) in milk. The bacteria convert the sugar into lactic acid. Lactic acid causes milk to thicken. This thickened milk makes yogurt.

1. Using a **cotton swab,** put a **small dot of yogurt** on a **plastic microscope slide.**

2. Add a **drop of water.** Use the cotton swab to stir.

3. Add a **plastic coverslip.**

4. Use a **microscope** to examine the slide. Draw what you observe.

TEKS

Three Types of Cells

There are three basic types of cells on Earth: *eubacteria* (YOO bak TIR ee uh), *archaebacteria* (AHR kee bak TIR ee uh), and *eukaryotes* (yoo KAR ee OHTS). All these cells have some things in common. For example, they all have a cell membrane and contain genetic material (DNA). However, they also differ from each other in important ways.

One important difference is whether a cell has a nucleus. **Eukaryotes** are organisms whose cells have a nucleus. Many eukaryotes are multicellular organisms. *Multicellular* means "many cells."

Prokaryotes (proh KAR ee OHTS) do not have a nucleus. Prokaryotes are also called bacteria. All bacteria are single-celled organisms. Some bacteria may form chains or clusters, but none form a true multicellular organism.

Eubacteria

The most common type of bacteria are *eubacteria.* These organisms live almost everywhere on Earth. Some live in the soil or water. Others live on, or in, other organisms. For example, you have bacteria living on your skin and teeth. You also have bacteria in your gut. A eubacterial cell is shown in **Figure 7.**

Eubacteria are smaller than eukaryotic cells. They do not have a nucleus, and they do not have any membrane-bound organelles. Bacterial DNA forms a loop. Eubacteria also have a cell wall. The cell wall helps a bacterium retain its shape.

Figure 7 *This diagram shows the DNA, cell membrane, and cell wall of a eubacterial cell. The "tail" of this bacterium is called a* flagellum.

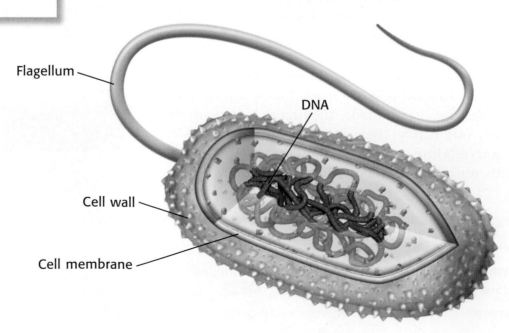

Flagellum

DNA

Cell wall

Cell membrane

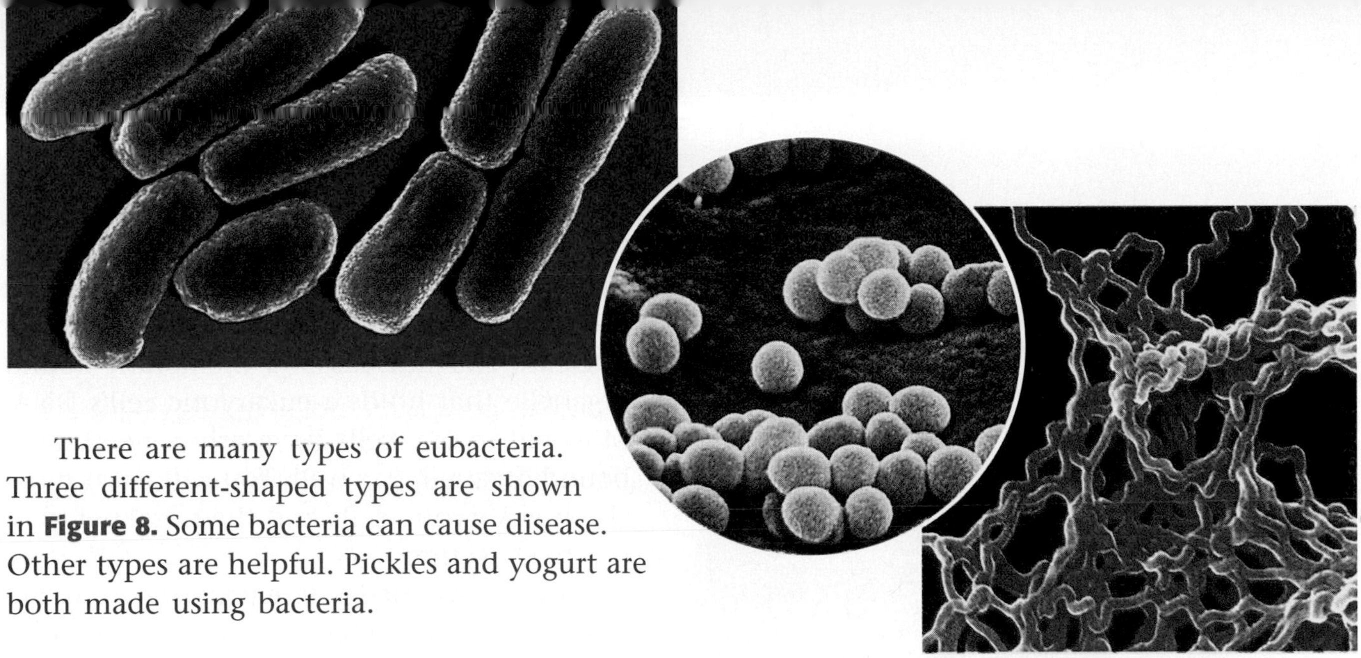

There are many types of eubacteria. Three different-shaped types are shown in **Figure 8.** Some bacteria can cause disease. Other types are helpful. Pickles and yogurt are both made using bacteria.

Figure 8 *Eubacteria can have many different shapes.*

Archaebacteria

Another type of bacteria, *archaebacteria* are not as common as eubacteria. Archaebacteria are similar to eubacteria in some ways. For example, both are single-celled organisms. They both have circular DNA, and both lack a nucleus and membrane-bound organelles.

Archaebacteria are similar to eukaryotes in some ways, too. Both have similar ribosomes, a kind of organelle. But archaebacteria also have some features that no other cells have. For example, their cell wall is made from different materials than other cell walls are.

Most archaebacteria live in places where other bacteria could not survive. For example, many live in hot springs. Others live in very salty water. There are three types of archaebacteria: "heat-loving," "salt-loving," and "methane-making" archaebacteria. Methane is a kind of gas frequently found in swamps. The biologist in **Figure 9** is working with archaebacteria.

Figure 9 *This biologist is working with archaebacteria.*

Eukaryotic Cells

Eukaryotic cells are the largest cells. Most eukaryotic cells are 10 times larger than most bacterial cells. A eukaryotic cell is shown in **Figure 10.**

Unlike bacteria, eukaryotic cells have a nucleus. The nucleus is a membrane-bound organelle that holds a eukaryotic cell's DNA. Most eukaryotic cells have other membrane-bound organelles as well. You will learn more about eukaryotic cells and their organelles in the next section.

Organisms made of eukaryotic cells are called eukaryotes. Many eukaryotes are multicellular organisms. So, most organisms you can see with your naked eye are eukaryotes. There are many types of eukaryotes. Animals, including humans, are eukaryotes. So are plants. Some protists, such as amoebas, are single-celled eukaryotes. Other protists, such as green algae, are multicellular eukaryotes. Fungi are organisms such as mushrooms or yeasts. Mushrooms are multicellular eukaryotes. Yeasts are single-celled eukaryotes.

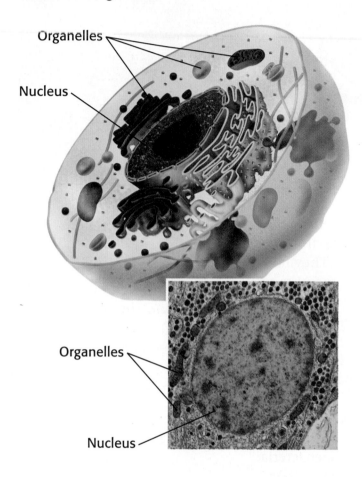

Figure 10 *This eukaryotic cell has several organelles.*

Organelles

Nucleus

Organelles

Nucleus

Self-Check

What does a eukaryotic cell have that other cells don't? *(See page 640 to check your answer.)*

internet**connect**

SCILINKS.
NSTA   **GO TO:** www.scilinks.org

TOPIC: Prokaryotic Cells
*sci*LINKS NUMBER: HSTL065

SECTION REVIEW

❶ What basic structure carries out functions to sustain life? ★TEKS

❷ Why are cells so small?

❸ What are the three basic types of cells, and how are they different?

❹ **Applying Concepts** A scientist is looking at a cell under a microscope. The cell has a nucleus. What type of cell is it?

Eukaryotic Cells

Eukaryotic cells are larger than prokaryotic cells. But most eukaryotic cells are still so small that they can be seen in detail only with a microscope.

For a long time after the discovery of cells, scientists did not really know what cells were made of. We now know that eukaryotic cells are very complex. They have many parts that work together to keep the cell alive.

Cell Wall

Some eukaryotes have cell walls. A **cell wall** provides strength and support to a cell membrane. A cell wall is the outermost structure of a cell. Plants and algae have cell walls made of cellulose. *Cellulose* is a type of complex sugar that most animals can't digest.

The cell walls of a plant allow it to stand upright. In some plants, the cells need to have water to inflate the cell wall. Without enough water, plant cells wilt and the plant droops. **Figure 11** shows a cross section of a plant cell with a close-up of the cell wall. When you are looking at dried hay or wood, you are seeing the cell walls of dead plant cells.

Fungi, including yeasts and mushrooms, also have cell walls. Some fungi have cell walls made of *chitin* (KIE tin). Chitin is a material also found in the shell of insects. Other fungi have cell walls made from a chemical like chitin. Eubacteria and archaebacteria also have cell walls. But their cell walls are different from plant or fungal cell walls.

Cell wall

Cell membrane

Figure 11 *The cell walls of plants help plants retain their shape. Plant cell walls are made of cellulose.*

Cellulose fibers

Cell Membrane

All cells have a cell membrane. The *cell membrane* is a barrier between the contents of the cell and the outside environment. For cells without a cell wall, the cell membrane is the outermost structure. For cells with cell walls, the membrane lies just inside the cell wall.

The cell membrane also controls the movement of things into and out of the cell. The cell membrane pumps nutrients in and keeps them in. It pumps waste products out and keeps them out. **Figure 12** shows the cell membrane.

The cell membrane has two layers. Each layer is made of lipids. *Lipids* are a kind of fat. Proteins float in the two layers of the cell membrane. Some of these proteins form passageways. Nutrients move into the cell and wastes move out of the cell through these protein passageways.

Self-Check

What types of cells have cell walls? *(See page 640 to check your answer.)*

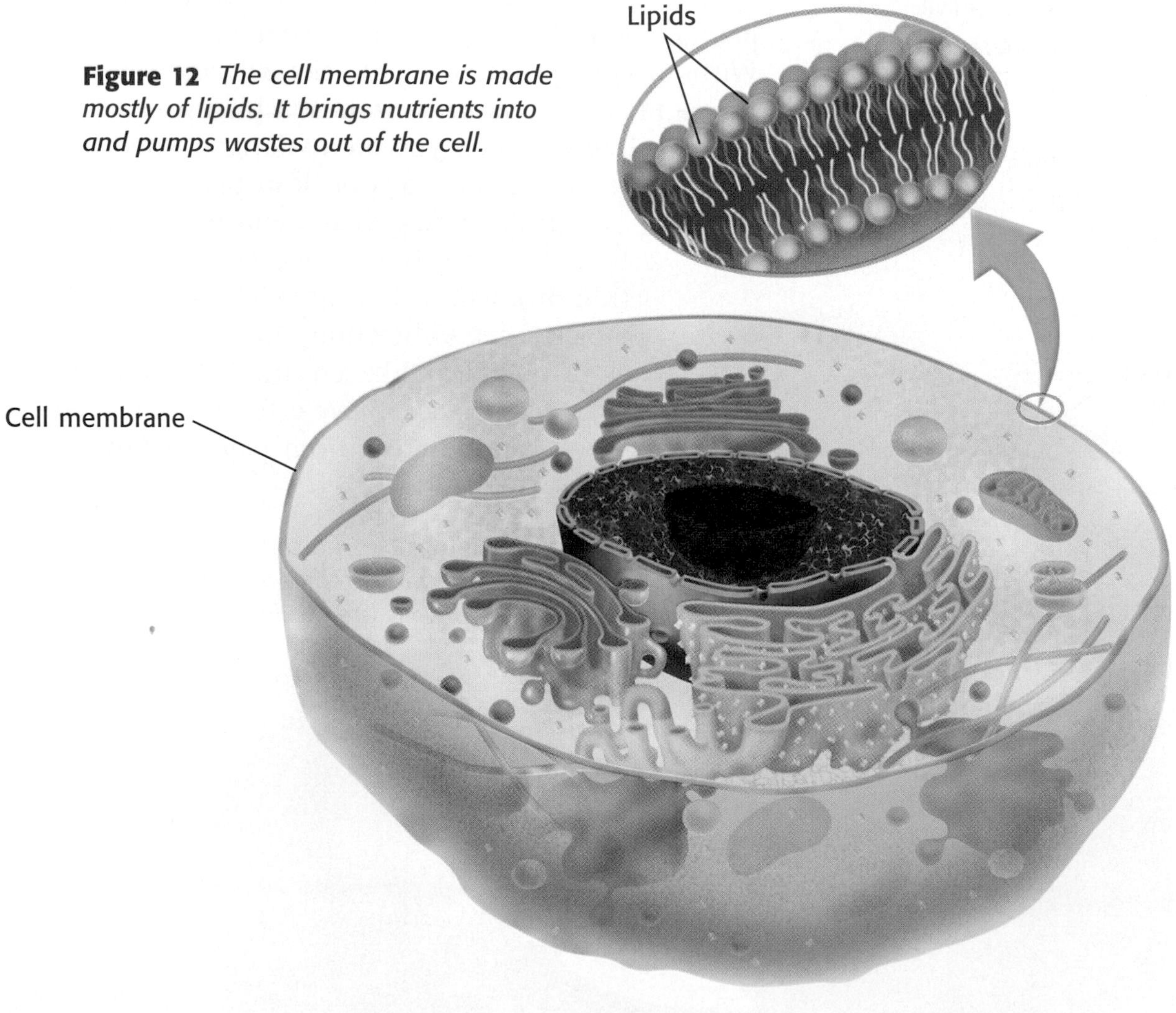

Figure 12 *The cell membrane is made mostly of lipids. It brings nutrients into and pumps wastes out of the cell.*

Lipids

Cell membrane

The Cell's Scaffold

The **cytoskeleton** (SIET oh SKEL uh tuhn) is a web of proteins located in the cytoplasm. The cytoskeleton helps a cell keep its shape. It also helps a cell move. The cytoskeleton is shown in **Figure 13.**

The cytoskeleton is made of proteins. These proteins form hollow tubes and long strings or fibers. One of the "stringy" proteins is also found in your muscle cells.

The Cell's Library

The nucleus is a large organelle in a eukaryotic cell. The nucleus is covered by two membranes. Materials can get across this double membrane by passing through pores. You can see the nucleus and the nuclear pores in **Figure 14.** Often a dark spot is found in the nucleus. This spot is called the nucleolus (noo KLEE uh luhs). The *nucleolus* contains materials that will be used to make ribosomes.

The nucleus contains the genetic material, DNA. DNA contains the information on how to make the cell's proteins. Proteins control the chemical reactions in a cell. They also provide structural support for cells and tissues.

The nucleus contains the instructions on how to make proteins. But proteins are not made in the nucleus. Messages for how to make proteins are copied from the DNA. These messages are then sent out of the nucleus through the pores.

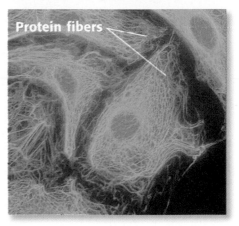

Figure 13 *The cytoskeleton helps a cell retain its shape. Some cells also use their cytoskeleton to move.*

Protein fibers

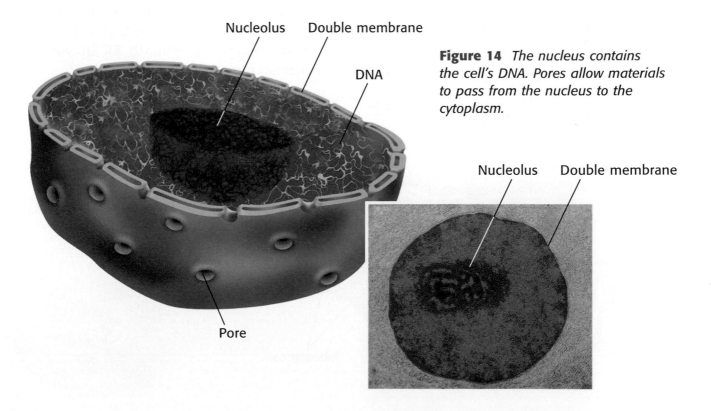

Nucleolus   Double membrane

DNA

Pore

Figure 14 *The nucleus contains the cell's DNA. Pores allow materials to pass from the nucleus to the cytoplasm.*

Nucleolus   Double membrane

Protein Factories

Ribosomes are organelles that make proteins. They make proteins by joining amino acids together. Amino acids are the building blocks of proteins. All cells have ribosomes because all cells need proteins to live.

Ribosomes are the smallest organelles, and there are more ribosomes in a cell than any other organelle. Some ribosomes float freely in the cytoplasm. Others are attached to membranes or the cytoskeleton. Unlike most organelles, ribosomes are not covered with a membrane.

The Cell's Delivery System

Many chemical reactions occur in a cell. Many of these reactions occur on, or in, the endoplasmic reticulum (EN doh PLAZ mik ri TIK yuh luhm). The **endoplasmic reticulum,** or ER, makes lipids and other materials. The ER also breaks down chemicals that can damage a cell.

The ER is the internal delivery system of the cell. It is a folded membrane that contains many tubes and passageways. Substances can move through the ER to different places within the cell. The ER is shown in **Figure 15.**

ER is called either rough ER or smooth ER depending on if it is covered in ribosomes. Rough ER is ER covered with ribosomes. Rough ER is usually found near the nucleus. Many proteins are made by ribosomes on rough ER. These proteins move into the ER's tubes and are delivered to where they are needed. ER without ribosomes is called smooth ER. Smooth ER in your liver breaks down toxic materials.

Figure 15 *Smooth ER is made of membrane. In rough ER, the membrane is covered with ribosomes.*

Rough ER

Smooth ER

Ribosomes

Endoplasmic reticulum

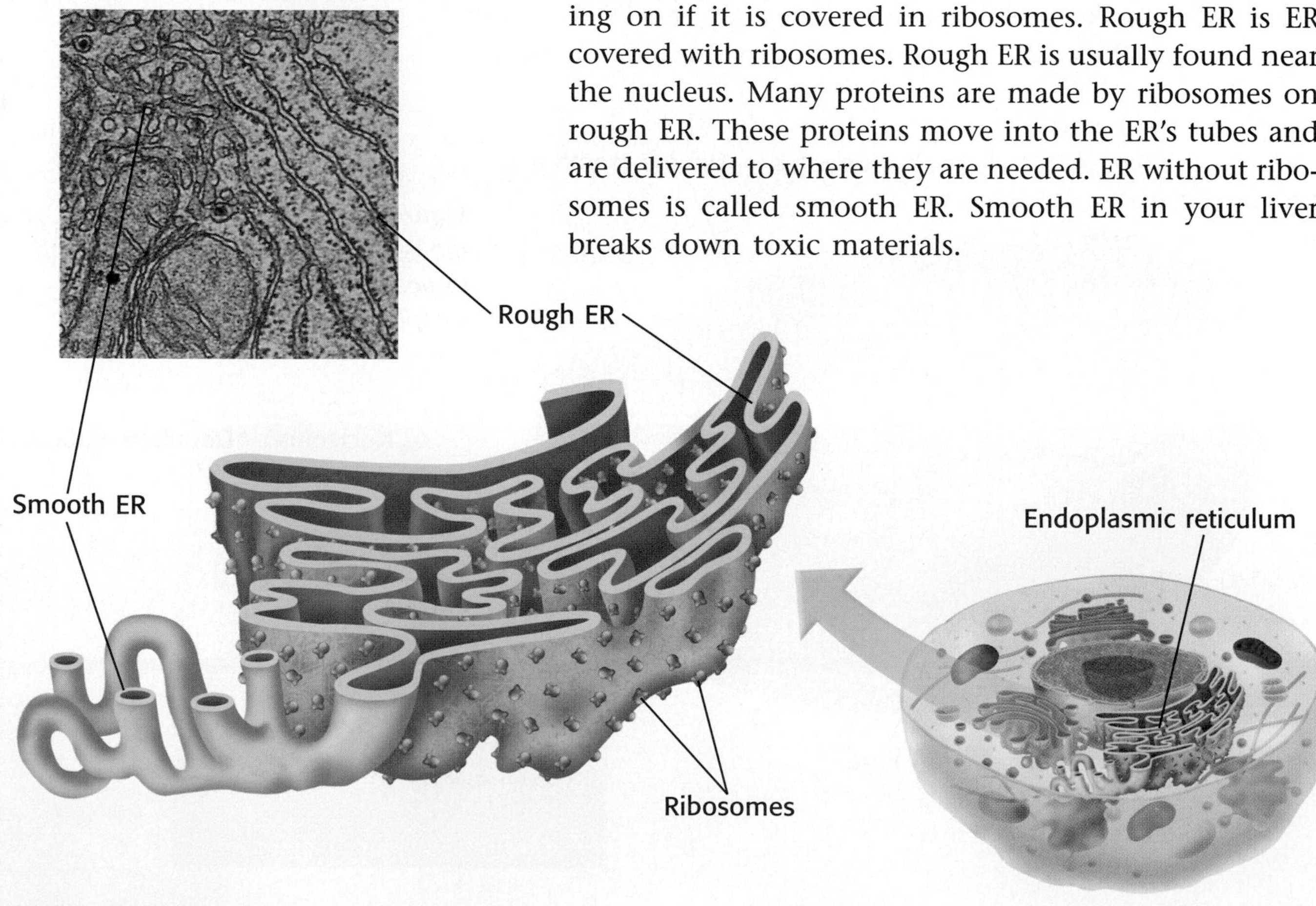

The Cell's Power Plants

Mitochondria (MIET oh KAHN dree uh) are the powerhouses of a cell. These organelles "burn" food molecules to release energy. The energy is transferred to a special substance called ATP. The cell uses ATP to do work. ATP can be made at several locations within a cell. But most of it is produced in the inner membrane of mitochondria.

Most eukaryotic cells have mitochondria. Mitochondria are the size of some bacteria and divide within the cell. Like bacteria, mitochondria have their own DNA. Mitochondria are covered by two membranes. See **Figure 16** for a picture of a mitochondrion.

Food Factories

Inside mitochondria, cells break down food for energy. But most cells do not make their own food. Food for cells is made in organelles called **chloroplasts** (KLAWR uh PLASTS). Plants and algae have chloroplasts in some of their cells. Like mitochondria, chloroplasts are surrounded by two membranes and have their own DNA. A chloroplast is shown in **Figure 17.**

Chloroplasts are green because they contain *chlorophyll,* a green pigment. Chlorophyll is found in membrane-covered sacs that look like stacks of coins. Chlorophyll traps the energy of sunlight and uses this energy to make sugar, which stores chemical energy. This process is called *photosynthesis.* The sugar that is produced is then used by mitochondria to make ATP.

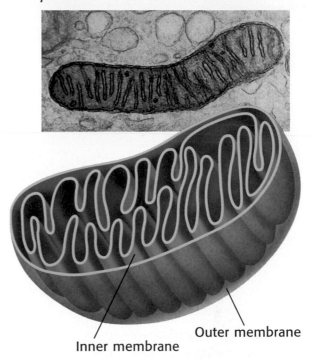

Figure 16 *Mitochondria break down food molecules and make ATP. ATP is produced on the inner membrane.*

Outer membrane

Inner membrane

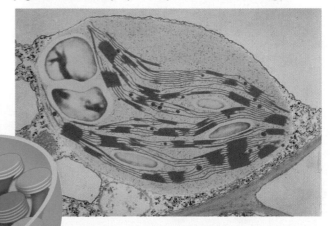

Figure 17 *Chloroplasts harness the energy of the sun and use it to make sugar. A green pigment—chlorophyll—traps the sun's energy.*

Inner membrane

Outer membrane

The Cell's Packaging Center

The **Golgi** (GAWL jee) **complex** ships proteins out of a eukaryotic cell. The structure is named after Camillo Golgi, the Italian scientist who first identified it.

The Golgi complex looks like ER. But it is located closer to the cell membrane. The Golgi complex of a cell is shown in **Figure 18.** Lipids and proteins from the ER are delivered to the Golgi complex. There the lipids and proteins may be modified for different functions. The final products are enclosed in a piece of the Golgi complex's membrane. This membrane pinches off to form a small bubble. The bubble transports its contents to other parts of the cell or outside of the cell.

Cell Compartments

All eukaryotic cells have membrane-covered compartments called **vesicles** (VES i kuhlz). Some vesicles form when part of the membrane pinches off the ER or the Golgi complex. Others form when part of the cell membrane surrounds an object outside the cell.

Figure 18 *The Golgi complex processes proteins. It ships proteins where they are needed, even out of the cell.*

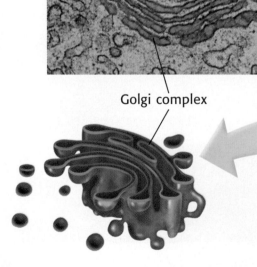

Golgi complex

Golgi complex

Packages of Destruction

Lysosomes (LIE suh SOHMZ) are vesicles that contain enzymes. Lysosomes destroy worn-out or damaged organelles. They also get rid of waste materials and protect the cell from foreign invaders. Lysosomes are shown in **Figure 19.**

Lysosomes are found in animal and fungal cells. When a cell engulfs a particle, it encloses the particle in a vesicle. Lysosomes bump into these vesicles and pour enzymes into them. The particles in the vesicles are then digested by the enzymes.

Water Storage and Hydraulic Support

Vacuoles (VAK yoo OHLZ) are large vesicles found in plant cells. They store water and other liquids. Vacuoles that are full of water help support the cell, as seen in **Figure 20.** Some plants wilt when their cells' vacuoles lose water.

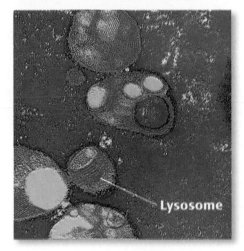

Figure 19 *Lysosomes digest materials inside other vesicles.*

Lysosome

Vacuole

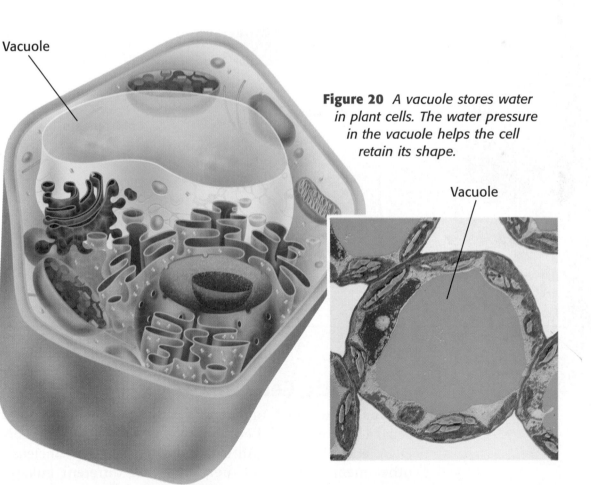

Figure 20 *A vacuole stores water in plant cells. The water pressure in the vacuole helps the cell retain its shape.*

Vacuole

Figure 21 Eukaryotic Cells and Their Organelles

Cell Type	Organelles

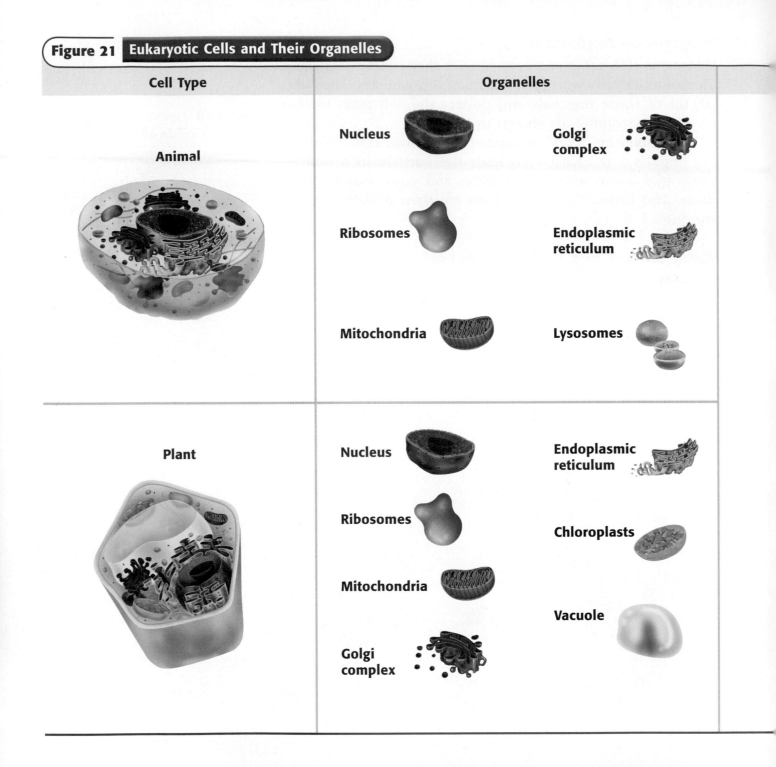

Animal

Nucleus

Golgi complex

Ribosomes

Endoplasmic reticulum

Mitochondria

Lysosomes

Plant

Nucleus

Endoplasmic reticulum

Ribosomes

Chloroplasts

Mitochondria

Vacuole

Golgi complex

Eukaryotic Cells and Their Organelles

Do you know which organelles are found in which eukaryotic cells? Like bacteria, all eukaryotic cells have a cell membrane, DNA, and ribosomes. All eukaryotes also have a nucleus and other membrane-bound organelles. But different eukaryotes have different organelles. You can see which organelles are found in animal, plant, fungal, and protist cells in **Figure 21.**

Cell Type	Organelles	
Fungi	Nucleus	Golgi complex
	Ribosomes	Endoplasmic reticulum
	Mitochondria	Lysosomes
Protist 1	Nucleus	Golgi complex
	Ribosomes	Endoplasmic reticulum
	Mitochondria	Vacuole
Protist 2	Nucleus	Golgi complex
	Ribosomes	Endoplasmic reticulum
	Mitochondria	Chloroplasts

SECTION REVIEW

1. What organelles do all organisms have? What organelles do only eukaryotic organisms have?

2. What is DNA, and where is it found? ⭐TEKS

3. **Applying Concepts** In humans, mature red blood cells do not have a nucleus. Do you think red blood cells live a long time or a short time? Explain your answer.

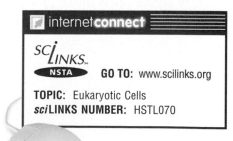

internet**connect**

SCI**LINKS**
NSTA
GO TO: www.scilinks.org

TOPIC: Eukaryotic Cells
sciLINKS NUMBER: HSTL070

Terms to Learn

tissue	organism
organ	structure
organ system	function

What You'll Do

- Describe the difference between single-celled organisms and multicellular organisms.
- Explain how life is organized, from a single cell to an organism.
- Relate structure to function in living things. ★TEKS

The Organization of Living Things

In some ways, organisms are like machines. Most machines have many different parts. Each part has a function in the machine. Do you know what the different parts of your body are and what they do for you?

A cell is smaller than the period at the end of this sentence. Yet a single cell has all the items necessary to carry out life's activities. Every living thing has at least one cell. Many living things exist as a single cell, while others have trillions of cells.

The Benefits of Being Multicellular

You are not made up of one large cell. A cell as big as you would have a small surface-to-volume ratio. This cell could not survive because its outer surface would be too small. You are a *multicellular organism,* which means you are made up of many cells.

Multicellular organisms grow by producing more small cells. They don't grow by making their existing cells larger. An elephant is bigger than you are. But its cells are about the same size as yours. An elephant just has more cells.

A single cell cannot do all the things that many different cells working together can do. In multicellular organisms, each type of cell is specialized to do a particular job. For example, the cardiac muscle cell in **Figure 22** is part of a heart. Heart muscle cells contract and make the heart pump blood. Having many different cells that are specialized for specific jobs allows multicellular organisms to perform more functions than single-celled organisms.

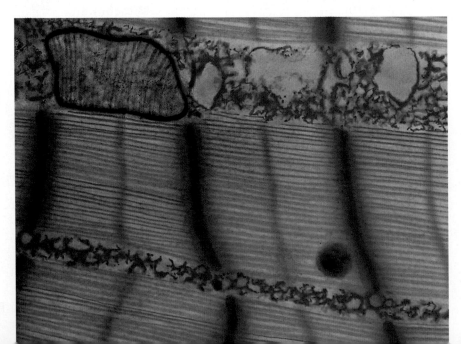

Figure 22 *This is a cardiac cell. Many cardiac cells make up heart muscle tissue.*

A Pet *Paramecium*

Imagine that you have a pet *Paramecium*, a type of protist. To properly care for your pet, you have to figure out how much to feed it. The dimensions of your *Paramecium* are roughly 125 × 50 × 2 μm. If seven food particles per second can enter through each square micrometer of surface area, how many particles can your *Paramecium* eat in 1 minute?

Cells Working Together

A **tissue** is a group of cells that work together to perform a specific job. The material around and between the cells is also part of the tissue. The cardiac muscle tissue, shown in **Figure 23,** is made of cardiac muscle cells. Cardiac muscle tissue is one type of tissue in a heart.

Animals have four basic types of tissues: nerve tissue, muscle tissue, connective tissue, and protective tissue.

Plants have three types of tissues: transport tissue, protective tissue, and ground tissue. Transport tissue moves water and nutrients through the plant. Protective tissue covers the plant. It helps the plant retain water and protects the plant against damage. Ground tissue is where photosynthesis takes place.

Figure 23 *This cardiac muscle tissue is made of cardiac muscle cells.*

Tissues Working Together

When two or more tissues work together to perform a specific job, the group of tissues is called an **organ.** Your stomach is an organ. So are your intestines, heart, and lungs. The heart, as shown in **Figure 24,** is made up of different kinds of tissues. These tissues include cardiac muscle tissue, nerve tissue, and the tissues of the blood vessels.

Plants also have different kinds of tissues that work together. A leaf is a plant organ that contains tissue that traps light energy to make food. Other examples of plant organs are stems and roots.

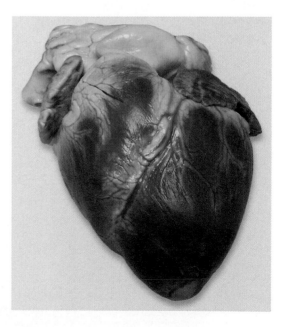

Figure 24 *The human heart is made of cardiac muscle tissue and other tissues.*

Organs Working Together

Organs work together in groups to perform particular jobs. These groups are called **organ systems.** Each system has a specific job to do in the body.

For example, your digestive system is made up of several organs, including your stomach and intestines. Your digestive system's job is to break down food into very small particles. These small particles can be used by other parts of your body that do not break down food. In return, your digestive system relies on oxygen in order to function. Oxygen is brought to cells in the digestive system by the cardiovascular system. Your cardiovascular system, shown in **Figure 25,** includes organs such as your heart and all the blood vessels in your body.

Plants also have organ systems. They include leaf systems, root systems, and stem systems.

Figure 25 **Levels of Organization in the Cardiovascular System**

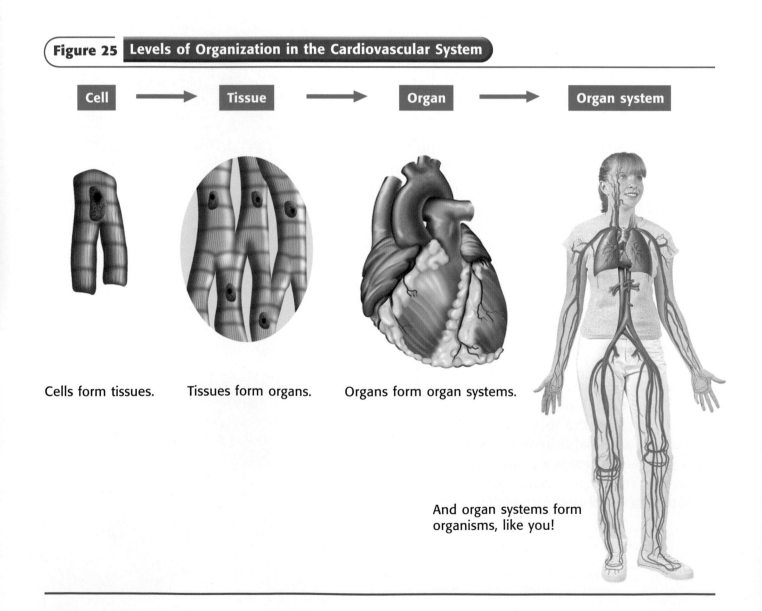

Cell ➞ Tissue ➞ Organ ➞ Organ system

Cells form tissues.   Tissues form organs.   Organs form organ systems.

And organ systems form organisms, like you!

Organisms

Anything that can live on its own is called an **organism.** If the organism is only a single cell, it is called a *unicellular organism.* Bacteria, most protists, and some fungi are unicellular. Some organisms live in colonies, but all their cells are the same. They are still considered unicellular because each cell does the same thing. A colonial protist, *Volvox,* is shown in **Figure 26.** Multicellular organisms are composed of many different cells, tissues, organs, and organ systems.

Structure and Function

In organisms, structure determines function. **Structure** is the shape of a part and the material the part is made of. **Function** is the job the part does. For example, the structure of the lungs is a large, spongy sac. Passages leading into the lungs branch many times until they end in many small sacs, called alveoli. Blood vessels lie right next to the alveoli, as shown in **Figure 27.** Here, oxygen from the air enters the blood. The blood flows through blood vessels and brings oxygen to tissues inside our body. The tissues could not get oxygen if it were not for blood. Thus, the structure of the lungs and blood vessels affects their function—to move oxygen from the air to tissues that need oxygen.

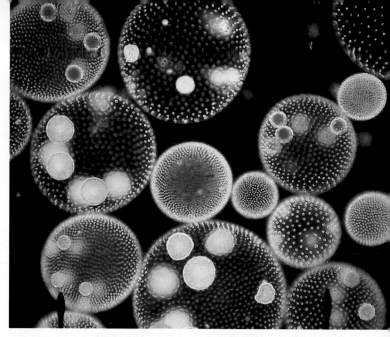

Figure 26 Volvox *is a colonial organism.*

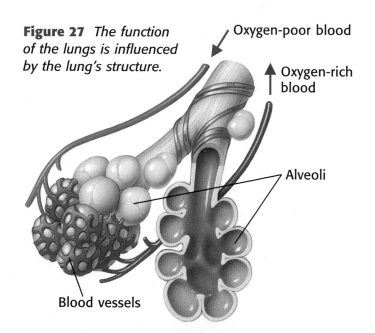

Figure 27 *The function of the lungs is influenced by the lung's structure.*

Oxygen-poor blood

Oxygen-rich blood

Alveoli

Blood vessels

SECTION REVIEW

1. What are tissues made of? What are organs made of?

2. Name an organ system in your body.

3. **Applying Concepts** Differentiate between structure and function in organ systems using the lungs and heart as examples. ⭐TEKS

Skill Builder Lab

Cells Alive! ⭐TEKS

Single-celled organisms can be found in many places. Using a microscope and some other materials, you can see some of these organisms. In the following exercise, you will look at *Protococcus*—algae that form a green stain on tree trunks, wooden fences, flowerpots, and buildings.

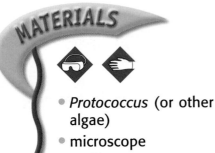

MATERIALS

- *Protococcus* (or other algae)
- microscope
- eyedropper
- water
- microscope slide
- coverslip

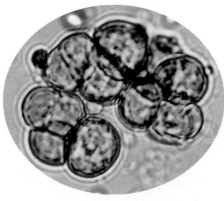

Protococcus

Procedure

1. Locate some *Protococcus*. Scrape a small sample into a container. Bring the sample to the classroom, and make a slide of it as directed by your teacher. If you can't find *Protococcus* outdoors, look for algae on the glass in an aquarium. Such algae may not be *Protococcus*, but they will be a very good substitute.

2. Set the microscope on low power to examine the algae. Draw the cells that you see.

3. Switch to high power to examine a single cell. Draw the cell.

4. You will probably notice that each cell contains several chloroplasts. Label a chloroplast on your drawing. What is the function of the chloroplast?

5. Another structure that should be clearly visible in all the algae cells is the nucleus. Find the nucleus in one of your cells, and label it on your drawing. What is the function of the nucleus?

6. What does the cytoplasm look like? Describe any movement you see inside the cells.

Analysis

7. Are *Protococcus* single-celled organisms or multicellular organisms?

8. How are *Protococcus* different from multicellular organisms?

Skill Builder Lab

Name That Part!

Plant cells and animal cells have many organelles and other parts in common. For example, both plant and animal cells contain a nucleus and mitochondria. But plant cells and animal cells differ in several ways. In this exercise, you will investigate the similarities and differences between animal cells and plant cells.

MATERIALS

• colored pencils or markers
• white, unlined paper

Procedure

1. Using colored pencils or markers and white, unlined paper, trace or draw the plant cell and animal cell shown below. Draw each cell on a separate piece of paper. You may color each organelle a different color.

2. Label the parts of each cell.

3. Below each drawing, list all the parts that you labeled and describe their function.

Analysis

4. List at least four structures that plant cells and animal cells have in common.

5. List three structures that plant cells have that animal cells do not have.

Plant cell

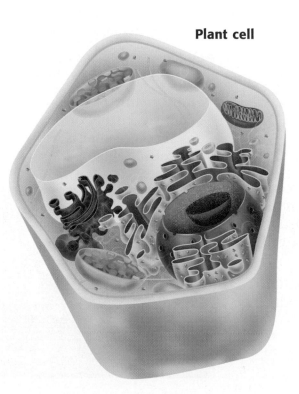

Animal cell

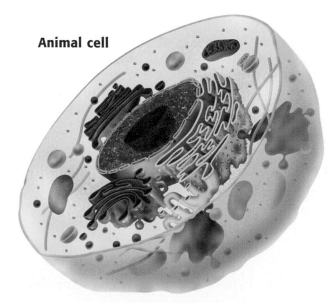

Section 1

Vocabulary

cell *(p. 184)*
cell membrane *(p. 187)*
cytoplasm *(p. 187)*
organelle *(p. 187)*
DNA *(p. 187)*
nucleus *(p. 187)*
eukaryote *(p. 188)*
prokaryote *(p. 188)*

Section Notes

● The cell theory states that all organisms are made of cells. The cell is the basic unit of life. All cells come from other cells. ⭐TEKS

● All cells have a cell membrane, DNA, cytoplasm, and organelles.

● Most cells are too small to be seen with the naked eye.

● The surface-to-volume ratio is a comparison of the cell's outer surface to the cell's volume. A cell's surface-to-volume ratio decreases as the cell grows.

● There are three basic types of cells: eubacteria, archaebacteria, and eukaryotes.

LabBook ⭐TEKS

Elephant-Sized Amoebas?
(p. 615)

Section 2

Vocabulary

cell wall *(p. 191)*
cytoskeleton *(p. 193)*
ribosome *(p. 194)*
endoplasmic reticulum *(p. 194)*
mitochondria *(p. 195)*
chloroplast *(p. 195)*
Golgi complex *(p. 196)*
vesicle *(p. 196)*
lysosome *(p. 197)*
vacuole *(p. 197)*

Section Notes

● Cells have organelles that perform functions that help cells remain alive.

● All cells have a cell membrane. Some cells have a cell wall. Some have a cytoskeleton.

● The nucleus of a eukaryotic cell contains the cell's genetic material, DNA. ⭐TEKS

● Ribosomes are the sites where amino acids are linked together to form proteins. Ribosomes are not covered by a membrane.

● The endoplasmic reticulum (ER) and the Golgi complex make and process proteins before they are transported to other parts of the cell or out of the cell.

● Mitochondria and chloroplasts are energy-producing organelles.

● Vesicles and vacuoles are membrane-bound compartments that store materials.

● Different types of eukaryotic cells have different sets of organelles.

Section 3

Vocabulary

tissue *(p. 201)*
organ *(p. 201)*
organ system *(p. 202)*
organism *(p. 203)*
structure *(p. 203)*
function *(p. 203)*

Section Notes

● Different cells within multicellular organisms perform different functions.

● Tissues are made up of cells.

● Organs are made from two or more tissues.

● Organ systems are groups of organs working together.

● The structure of an organelle, tissue, or organ complements its function. ⭐TEKS

Review

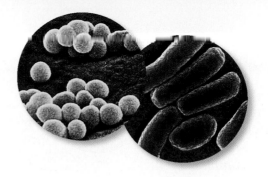

USING VOCABULARY

Complete the following sentences by choosing the correct term from each pair of terms.

1. All organisms are composed of ___?___, structures that carry on processes that sustain life. (cells or cellulose) ⭐TEKS

2. The cell wall of plant cells is made of ___?___. (lipids or cellulose)

3. ___?___ cells have membrane-bound organelles. (Prokaryotic or Eukaryotic)

4. The information for how to make proteins is located in the ___?___. (Golgi complex or nucleus)

5. Vesicles that will transport materials out of the cell are formed at the ___?___. (Golgi complex or cell membrane)

UNDERSTANDING CONCEPTS

Multiple Choice

6. Which of the following is NOT found in animal cells?
   a. cell wall
   b. cell membrane
   c. lysosomes
   d. vesicle

7. Different ___?___ work together in an organ.
   a. organ systems
   b. tissues
   c. organisms
   d. prokaryotes

8. The scientist who said that all cells come from cells was named ⭐TEKS
   a. Virchow.
   b. Schleiden.
   c. Hooke.
   d. Schwann.

9. Which organelles are NOT covered by a membrane?
   a. Golgi complex   c. ribosomes
   b. mitochondria   d. chloroplasts

10. Mitochondria make ATP by
    a. photosynthesis.
    b. binary fusion.
    c. using the power of sunlight.
    d. breaking down food molecules.

11. DNA, the genetic material, is found in ⭐TEKS
    a. stars.   c. rocks.
    b. cells.   d. water.

12. Which organisms have a nucleus?
    a. prokaryotes   c. archaebacteria
    b. eukaryotes   d. eubacteria

13. Photosynthesis occurs in
    a. the nucleus.
    b. mitochondria.
    c. chloroplasts.
    d. the ER.

14. Which organelles have two membranes?
    a. nuclei   c. chloroplasts
    b. mitochondria   d. all of the above

Short Answer

15. Why are most cells so small?

16. In what ways are mitochondria and chloroplasts similar?

17. Differentiate between the structure and the function of a part of an organism. ⭐TEKS

18. In your own words, list the three parts of the cell theory.

CONCEPT MAPPING

19. Use the following terms to create a concept map: *cells, organisms, Golgi complex, organ systems, organs, endoplasmic reticulum, nucleus,* and *tissues.*

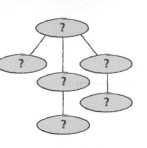

CRITICAL THINKING AND PROBLEM SOLVING

Write one or two sentences to answer the following questions:

20. What would happen if the sun stopped shining? (Hint: Think about photosynthesis.)

21. Pick an organelle and describe what would happen to a cell if that organelle were removed.

MATH IN SCIENCE

22. Assume that a cell is shaped like a cube whose sides are 2 units long. Three food molecules per cubic unit of volume per minute are required for the cell to survive. If one molecule can enter through each square unit of surface per minute, this cell is
   a. too big and would starve.
   b. too small and would starve.
   c. at a size that would allow it to survive.

23. Calculate the surface area of a cube whose sides are 5 cm long.

INTERPRETING GRAPHICS

Look at the cell diagrams below, and answer the questions that follow.

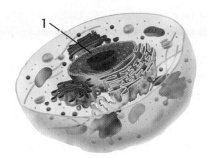

Cell A

Cell B

24. Name the organelle labeled "1" in Cell A.

25. Is Cell A a bacterial cell, a plant cell, or an animal cell? Explain your answer.

26. What is the name and function of the organelle labeled "2" in Cell B?

27. Is Cell B a prokaryotic cell or a eukaryotic cell? Explain your answer.

Reading Check-up

★TEKS

Take a minute to review your answers to the Pre-Reading Questions found at the bottom of page 182. Have your answers changed? If necessary, revise your answers based on what you have learned since you began this chapter.

Chapter 7

1 In the diagrams below, both items are

  A cells, structures that contain genetic material.

  B organelles, structures without genetic material.

  C nuclei, structures that contain genetic material.

  D multicellular organisms, organisms composed of many cells.

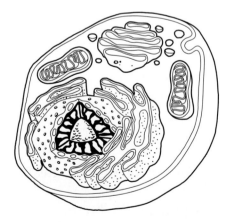

2 The structure of a part of an organism refers to

  F the size of the part.

  G the job the part performs.

  H the shape of the part and the material it is made from.

  J the number and types of organelles the part contains.

3 The function of a part of an organism refers to

  A the size of the part.

  B the job the part performs.

  C the shape of the part and the material it is made from.

  D the number and types of organelles the part contains.

4 Which structures are all living things composed of?

  F Organs

  G Prokaryotes

  H Eukaryotes

  J Cells

Chapter 7

Math

1 There are about 6000 species of living reptiles. If 2700 of them are snakes, what percentage of reptiles are snakes?

A 3300

B 45

C 2.2

D 8700

2 If ribosomes make 50 proteins per second and a piece of ER has 50 ribosomes on it, how many proteins can be made on this stretch of ER in 1 second?

F 100

G 2500

H 0

J 1

3 What is the surface-to-volume ratio of a cube whose sides are 5 meters long?

A 1:1

B 1:5

C 6:5

D 6:1

4 If there are 200 cells in an organ and only 50 of the cells are part of a connective tissue, how many cells are NOT a part of the connective tissue?

F 250

G 150

H 4

J 10,000

Reading

Read the passage. Then read each question that follows the passage. Decide which is the best answer to each question.

An injury to the skin, such as a scraped knee, triggers skin cells to produce and release a steady stream of proteins that heal the injury. These naturally occurring proteins are called *human growth factors,* or just *growth factors*. Growth factors specialize in rebuilding the body. Some reconstruct connective tissue that provides structure for new skin, some help rebuild blood vessels in a wounded area, and still others stimulate the body's immune system. Thanks to growth factors, scraped skin usually heals in just a few days.

1 What proteins are released in response to injury?

A Growth factors

B Shock factors

C Ribosomes

D DNA

2 How do these proteins help heal a wound?

F They stimulate the brain.

G They regenerate neurons.

H They rebuild blood vessels.

J They alert predators.

N
Nitrogen
14.0067

Battling Cancer with Pigs' Blood and Laser Light

What do you get when you cross pigs' blood and laser beams? Would you believe that you get a treatment for cancer? Medical researchers have developed a new cancer treatment. It is called photodynamic therapy, or PDT. It combines laser beams with a drug from pigs' blood to combat the disease.

▲ *Blood from pigs provides substances used to fight cancer.*

Pigs' Blood to the Rescue

The first step in PDT involves a light-sensitive substance called porphyrin. Porphyrins are chemicals found in blood cells that bind to lipoproteins. Lipoproteins carry cholesterol in our blood. All cells use lipoproteins in their cell membranes. But cells that divide quickly, such as cancer cells, make membranes faster than normal cells. Since they use more lipoproteins, they also accumulate more porphyrins.

Scientists have developed a synthetic porphyrin, called Photofrin®. It is made from natural porphyrins found in pigs' blood. Photofrin can absorb energy from light. The Photofrin is injected into a patient's bloodstream. There it acts the same way natural porphyrins do—it becomes part of the cell membranes formed by

cancer cells. The patient then visits a surgeon's office for step two of PDT. In this step, the diseased tissue is zapped with a laser beam.

Hitting the Target

A surgeon threads a long, thin, laser-tipped tube into the cancerous area. The Photofrin has accumulated there. When the laser beam hits the cancerous tissue, Photofrin absorbs the light energy. Then, in a process similar to photosynthesis, Photofrin releases oxygen. The type of oxygen released damages the cancer cells. This damage kills off the cells in the treated area. But it doesn't kill healthy cells. Photofrin is more sensitive to certain wavelengths of light than natural porphyrins are. And the intense beam of laser light can be precisely focused on the cancerous tissue without affecting nearby healthy tissue.

An Alternative?

PDT is an important medical development because it kills cancer cells without causing many of the harmful side effects caused by other cancer therapies. However, PDT does have some side effects. Until the drug wears off, in about 30 days, the patient is susceptible to severe sunburn. Researchers are working to develop a second-generation drug, called BPD (benzoporphyrin derivative), that will have fewer side effects and respond to different wavelengths of lasers. BPD is also being tested as a treatment for certain eye diseases and for psoriasis, a skin condition.

Find Out for Yourself

▶ Do some research. Find out why scientists used pigs' blood to create Photofrin.

Population Changes and Heredity

Pre-Reading Questions

1. What is evolution?
2. Why don't all humans look exactly alike?

HIDDEN TREASURE

Can you see the fish in this picture? Look closer. The fish are coral blennies, and they are hard to see against the background of coral. Their coloring makes them likely to live longer and to have more offspring than blennies that don't blend in as well. In this chapter, you will learn how some characteristics help organisms survive and reproduce. You will also learn how these characteristics are passed from parents to offspring.

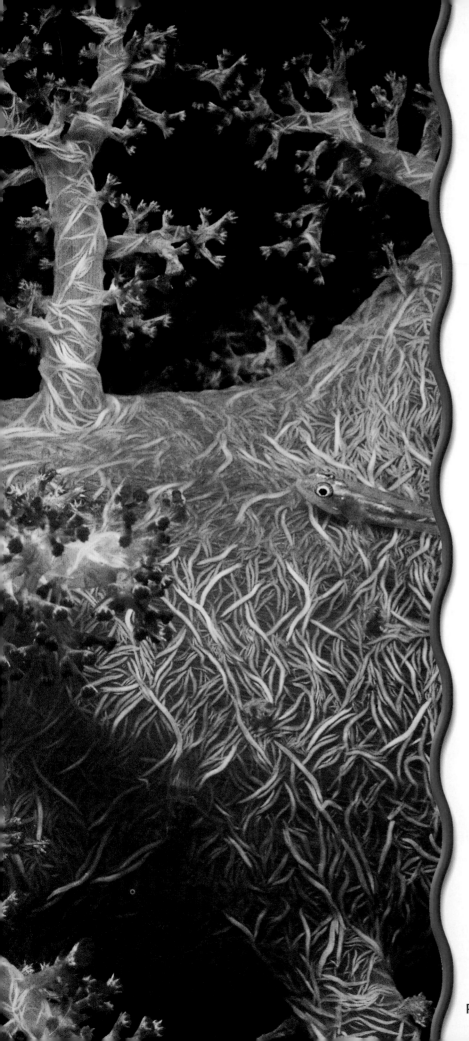

MAKING A FOSSIL ⭐TEKS

In this activity, you will make a model of a fossil.

Procedure

1. Get a **paper plate**, some **modeling clay**, and a **leaf** or a **shell** from your teacher.

2. Flatten some of the modeling clay on the paper plate. Push the leaf or shell into the clay. Be sure that your leaf or shell has made a mark in the clay. Remove the leaf or shell carefully.

3. Ask your teacher to cover the clay completely with **plaster of Paris.** Allow the plaster to dry overnight.

4. Carefully remove the paper plate and the clay from the plaster the next day.

Analysis

5. Which of the following do you think would make good fossils—a clam, a jellyfish, a crab, or a mushroom? Explain your answer.

6. Real fossils are usually formed when a dead organism is covered by tiny bits of sand or dirt. Oxygen cannot be present when fossils are being formed. What are some limitations of your fossil model?

READING WARM-UP

Terms to Learn

evolution
fossil
adaptation

What You'll Do

- Explain how fossils provide evidence that organisms have changed over time.
- Define adaptation.

Change over Time

Have you ever wondered what happened to the dinosaurs or how they are similar to the animals on Earth today? How has life on Earth changed over time?

Earth is very old. In fact, scientists think that it is about 4.6 billion years old! Earth has changed a lot during its history. And fossil evidence suggests that living things, or *organisms*, have also changed. **Figure 1** shows some of the organisms that have lived during Earth's history.

Populations Change

Since life first appeared on Earth, many kinds of living things have died out and many new kinds have appeared. What has caused all of these changes?

Different individuals have different characteristics. Characteristics that can be passed from one generation to the next are called *inherited* characteristics. Most scientists think that the inherited characteristics in a population change over time. A *population* is a group of the same kind of organism living in the same place.

Some characteristics help individuals in the population survive and reproduce. Individuals with these characteristics will pass them to the next generation. Individuals who do not have these favorable characteristics are likely to die early or to produce fewer offspring. Therefore, the favorable characteristics will become more and more common in the population. The theory that the inherited characteristics in a population change over time is called the theory of **evolution.**

Figure 1 *This diagram shows many different kinds of organisms that have lived on Earth.*

Fossils

Scientists use fossils to study organisms that lived in the past. Fossils have given scientists information about how living things have changed over millions of years.

What Is a Fossil?

A **fossil** is physical evidence of a living thing, such as its remains or imprints found in rock. Fossils, such as those shown in **Figure 2,** can be of complete organisms, of parts of organisms, or even of a set of footprints.

Where are Fossils Found?

The Earth's crust is arranged in layers. These layers are formed when small pieces of sand, dust, or larger particles are carried by wind and water and are deposited in an orderly fashion. Older layers were deposited before newer layers. So older layers are usually buried deeper inside the Earth. Older fossils are found in these older layers of rock.

Why do scientists think that the older rock layers are deeper inside the Earth's crust? Think of a pile of newspapers. Your friend reads the paper every day. When she is finished, she puts the paper on top of the stack. Last week's papers are deeper in the pile than yesterday's paper. Rock layers, such as those shown in **Figure 3,** are stacked like those newspapers. The older rocks and the fossils buried in them are found deeper in the "pile."

Figure 2 *The fossil on the left is of a trilobite (TRIE loh BIET), an animal that once lived in water. The fossils on the right are of seed ferns.*

Figure 3 *Layers of rock are formed over time. The deeper layers are older than the layers near the surface.*

Modeling Fossils

1. Flatten some **modeling clay** into the bottom of a **paper cup.** Press a **seashell** into the modeling clay.

2. Ask your teacher to pour **plaster of Paris** into the cup on top of the shell. Allow the plaster to dry overnight.

3. Carefully remove the cup, the shell, and the clay from the plaster the next day.

4. What kind of fossil did you make in this activity?

TEKS

Kinds of Fossils

There are several kinds of fossils. *Trace fossils* are evidence of animal activity. For example, a footprint is a trace fossil. A *mold* is a cavity in rock where a plant or animal was buried. When these cavities are filled with minerals, sand, dust, or soil, a *cast* of the original organism may be made. Sometimes whole skeletons are preserved as fossils. In such cases, the pores in the bones are filled with hard minerals. Read on to learn about one example.

A New Discovery

A family in Poughkeepsie, New York, made an amazing discovery in the summer of 1999. When beginning to deepen the backyard pond, the family found an enormous bone. What's so special about a big bone? Well, this wasn't just any bone. It was a very old bone—about 11,000 years old! Since the discovery of that first bone, scientists have discovered a skeleton of a mastodon, an extinct relative of elephants. The scientists expect to find almost every bone in the skeleton. By September 2000, they had already found 180 of the 220 bones. **Figure 4** shows one of the scientists as she uncovers the skeleton.

Scientists think that there were many mastodons in North America 10,000 years ago. These enormous mammals became extinct at the end of the last Ice Age. The mastodon found in Poughkeepsie probably weighed about 5,000 kg!

Figure 4 *Scientists and volunteers have removed almost an entire mastodon skeleton from a backyard pond in Poughkeepsie, New York.*

The Fossil Record

From studying fossils, scientists have made a timeline of life known as the *fossil record*. The fossil record organizes fossils by their estimated ages. Fossils found near the surface of the Earth's crust tend to look like present-day organisms. This similarity might suggest that these organisms were closely related to present-day living things. The deeper in the Earth's crust fossils are found, the less they tend to look like present-day organisms. These fossils are of earlier forms of life that may not exist anymore.

Gaps in the Fossil Record

Although scientists have described and named 300,000 different kinds of fossil organisms, empty spaces still remain in the fossil record. Specific conditions are necessary for fossils to form. For example, organisms without bones or shells must be buried in very fine sand or dust with little or no oxygen present. Very few places on Earth are free of oxygen. The conditions that help fossils form are more often found on the ocean floor than on land. So, the fossil record is more complete for ocean life than for land-dwelling organisms.

If every living thing left a fossil behind, scientists would better understand if and how organisms are related to each other. Even though there are gaps, the fossil record suggests certain relationships. **Figure 5** shows how many questions are still left to answer about the relationships between organisms. Scientists will probably never be able to fill all of the gaps in the fossil record.

Geology

CONNECTION

Wind and water deposit small pieces of rock, called sediment, in layers on Earth's surface. Over time, layers of sediment pile up. Lower layers are compacted and slowly change into rock. When the remains of organisms are preserved within these layers, they form fossils.

Self-Check

What conditions are necessary for a fossil of an organism without bones or shells to form? *(See page 640 to check your answer.)*

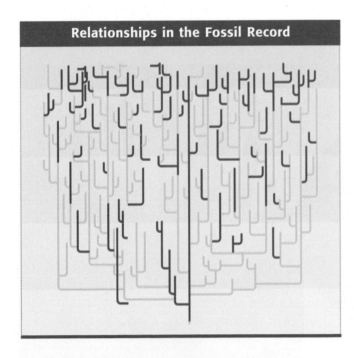

Relationships in the Fossil Record

Figure 5 *This diagram shows relationships among organisms based on the fossil record. The dark lines show the relationships scientists think they understand. The lighter lines show how many questions have not yet been answered.*

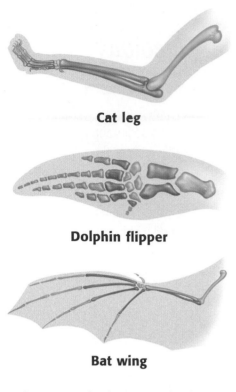

Cat leg

Dolphin flipper

Bat wing

Figure 6 *The bones in the front limbs of these animals are similar. Similar bones are shown in the same color.*

Figure 7 *Compare the stems of the spurge (left) and the cactus (right). They look very similar, but they have different origins.*

Comparing Organisms

Scientists compare different groups of living organisms to study how living things have changed. Scientists have found some similarities that they use to support the theory of evolution.

Similarities in Structures

What do the front leg of a cat, the front flipper of a dolphin, and the wing of a bat have in common? At first glance, you might think that they have very little in common. After all, these structures don't really look alike and are not used in the same way. But the structure and order of the bones in the front limbs of these different animals are in fact similar. This is shown in **Figure 6.**

Some scientists think that these similarities suggest that animals as different as a dolphin, a bat, and a cat may have an ancestor in common. Over millions of years, these bones may have been modified by the evolutionary process, and now they perform different functions.

Differences in Structures

Making evolutionary connections based on physical similarities can be misleading. For example, the thick, water-storing stems of the cactus and spurge in **Figure 7** are similar structures with similar functions. However, evidence suggests that these stems have different origins. In other words, similar structures do not necessarily point to a common ancestor.

Likewise, similar function does not always point to a common ancestor. Although the wings of birds and the wings of insects have similar functions, scientists think that they have different origins. Bird wings and insect wings are both used for flight. However, they have very different structures.

Changing Characteristics

Populations are constantly responding to a changing environment. Some individuals in a population may have characteristics that help them survive and reproduce. Over many years, these characteristics may become more and more common in the population.

Scientists call some of these characteristics adaptations. **Adaptations** are characteristics that help an organism survive and reproduce in its environment. Adaptations can include structures and behaviors for finding food, for protecting oneself, and for attracting mates. For example, take a look at the smoky jungle frog in **Figure 8.** The colors of this frog make it difficult to see against the forest floor. As a result, it is harder for other animals to catch a smoky jungle frog. Such coloring may help the frogs survive long enough to reproduce. The frogs in **Figures 9** and **10** also have characteristics that may help them survive and reproduce.

Figure 8 *The smoky jungle frog blends into the forest floor.*

Figure 9 *The red-eyed tree frog hides among a tree's leaves during the day and comes out at night.*

Figure 10 *The strawberry dart-poison frog's coloring warns predators that the frog is poisonous. This may prevent other animals from eating the frog.*

Quick Lab

Out of Sight, Out of Mind ⊙TEKS

1. Count out **25 colored marshmallows** and **25 white marshmallows.** Ask your partner to look away while you spread the marshmallows out on a **white cloth.** Do not make a pattern with the marshmallows.

2. Now ask your partner to turn around and pick the first marshmallow he or she sees. Repeat this activity 10 times.

3. How many white marshmallows did your partner pick?

4. How many colored marshmallows did your partner pick?

5. What did the marshmallows and the cloth represent in your investigation?

6. Did the color of the cloth affect the color of the marshmallows chosen?

7. When an animal blends into its environment, it is *camouflaged.* How does this activity model camouflage in the wild? What are some weaknesses of this model?

Did You See That?

Imagine that you and a friend are walking through the forest. You are startled when you hear several deer bounding away from you. You didn't even see them until they were running away. Your friend thinks that deer are camouflaged so that they can sneak up on kids and scare them. Might there be another explanation? How do you think this adaptation might help the deer survive?

Standing Out in the Crowd

You know from your own experience that individuals in a population are not exactly the same. Just look around the room, and you will see a lot of differences between your classmates. You may have even noticed that no two dogs or two cats are exactly the same. Not every individual has exactly the same adaptations. For example, one cat may be better at catching mice, while another is better at running away from dogs. Because adaptations help an organism survive and reproduce, the individuals that are better adapted to their environment are more likely to pass their traits to future generations. You will read more about the importance of adaptations in the next section.

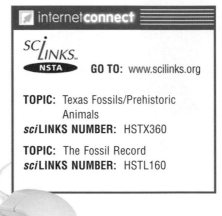

internetconnect

SCiLINKS.
NSTA GO TO: www.scilinks.org

TOPIC: Texas Fossils/Prehistoric Animals
*sci*LINKS NUMBER: HSTX360

TOPIC: The Fossil Record
*sci*LINKS NUMBER: HSTL160

SECTION REVIEW

1. How can the fossil record be used to suggest that living things have changed over time?

2. In your own words, give a one- or two-sentence definition of the word *adaptation*.

3. **Interpreting Graphics** Imagine that you took the photograph at left while you were studying rocks at a local quarry. It shows layers of sedimentary rock. You found the fossil of an organism that lived 200 million years ago in the layer marked **b.** Its ancestor, which lived 201 million years ago, would most likely be found in which layer, **a** or **c?** Explain your answer. ⭐TEKS

Terms to Learn

trait
selective breeding
natural selection

What You'll Do

- Describe the process of natural selection.
- Identify some changes in traits that can occur through natural selection and selective breeding. ⭐TEKS

How Do Populations Change?

Imagine that you are a scientist in the 1800s. Some fossils of very strange animals have been found. And some familiar fossils were found where you would least expect them. Who has ever heard of seashells at the top of mountains?

The early 1800s was a time of great scientific discovery. Geologists learned that Earth was much older than anyone had ever thought. Evidence showed that slow processes had shaped Earth's surface over millions of years. Earth suddenly seemed to be a place where great change was possible. Charles Darwin had a good idea of how living things had changed.

Charles Darwin

In 1831, 21-year-old Charles Darwin, shown in **Figure 11,** had just finished college. His father wanted him to become a doctor, but seeing blood made Darwin sick. He earned a degree in religion, but he was *really* interested in plants and animals.

So Darwin signed up for a 5-year trip around the world. He served as the naturalist (a scientist who studies nature) on a British ship, the HMS *Beagle*. During this trip, Darwin made observations that later helped him form his ideas about natural selection.

Figure 11 *Charles Darwin, shown at left, sailed around the world on a ship a lot like this one.*

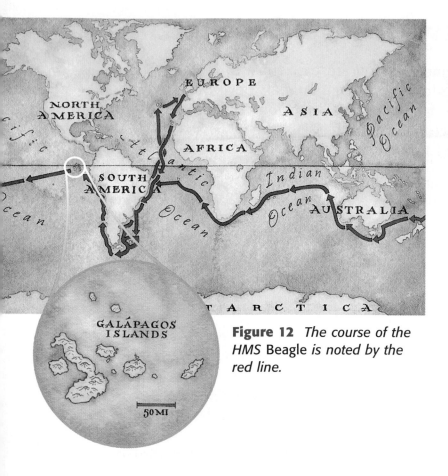

Figure 12 *The course of the* HMS Beagle *is noted by the red line.*

GALÁPAGOS ISLANDS

50 MI

Darwin's Excellent Adventure

Darwin collected many samples of plants and animals from around the world. He kept good notes of his observations along the way. The *Beagle*'s journey is charted in **Figure 12.** During the journey, the ship visited the Galápagos (guh LAH puh GOHS) Islands, which are 965 km west of Ecuador, a country in South America.

Darwin's Finches

Darwin noticed that the animals and plants on the Galápagos Islands were a lot like the animals and plants in Ecuador. However, they were not exactly the same. For example, the finches living on the Galápagos Islands looked a little different from the finches in Ecuador. And the finches on each island were different from the finches on the other islands. As you can see in **Figure 13,** the finches' beaks are adapted to the different ways the birds get food.

Figure 13 | Galápagos Finches

Large ground finch

The **large ground finch** has a heavy, strong beak that is good for cracking big, hard seeds. This finch's beak works like a nutcracker.

Cactus finch

The **cactus finch** has a tough beak that is good for eating cactus and its nectar. This beak works like a pair of needle-nosed pliers.

Warbler finch

The **warbler finch's** small, pointed beak is good for reaching into cracks to catch small insects. This beak works like a pair of tweezers.

Darwin Does Some Thinking

Darwin thought that the island finches descended from finches on the South American mainland. The first finches on the islands may have been blown from South America by a storm. Over many generations, the finches may have adapted to different ways of life on the islands.

After Darwin returned to England, he spent many years working on his ideas. During this time, he gathered ideas from many different people.

Darwin Learned from Animal and Plant Breeders

In Darwin's time, farmers and breeders had produced many different kinds of farm animals and plants. Farmers only bred the plants and animals that had certain desired traits. **Traits** are distinguishing qualities that can be passed from parent to offspring. When humans, not nature, select which plants or animals will reproduce based on certain desired traits, the process is called **selective breeding.** The dogs in **Figure 14** have been bred for several different traits.

In addition to dogs, you can see the results of selective breeding in many other kinds of organisms. For example, people have bred horses to get breeds that are particularly fast or strong. Crops have been bred to improve their resistance to pests and drought.

Self-Check

What is selective breeding? *(See page 640 to check your answer.)*

Figure 14 *Over the past 12,000 years, dogs have been selectively bred to produce more than 150 different breeds.*

Even roses have been altered by selective breeding, as shown in **Figure 15.** Wild roses have only five petals. But when you buy a rose at the local flower shop, it will have many more petals. Flower breeders have selectively bred roses for many generations to increase the number of petals on each flower. Each generation, the breeders allowed only the flowers with many petals to breed. Flowers with only five petals were not allowed to breed. Therefore, the trait for flowers with many petals was passed to future generations more often and became more and more common.

Individuals in a population have many different traits. Darwin was impressed that farmers could make large changes in just a few generations. He thought that wild organisms could also change but that the process would take much longer.

Figure 15 *Breeders have used selective breeding to grow roses with many petals. Wild roses have five petals.*

MathBreak

Cellular Calculations

Scientists think that the Earth is about 4.6 billion years old. Many also think that the first cells appeared on Earth about 3.5 billion years ago. How long do these scientists think Earth existed before the first cells appeared?

Darwin Learned from Geologists

Darwin thought that populations changed very slowly, but people had always thought that Earth was only a few thousand years old. However, geologists were beginning to find evidence that Earth was much older than anyone had ever imagined. Geologist Charles Lyell thought that geologic changes happened over millions of years. If Lyell was right, then it seemed more possible that Darwin's theory could also be true.

Darwin Learned from Thomas Malthus

Thomas Malthus studied the population growth in Europe during the late 1700s. He thought that humans could have so many children that there would not be enough food. His ideas are described in **Figure 16.** Malthus thought that hunger, sickness, and war keep human populations from expanding too rapidly.

Darwin knew that the same thing could happen with other organisms. Hunger, sickness, and predators affect their populations. Only a few survive to reproduce. There must be something different about the survivors. Darwin thought that the survivors must carry traits that help them survive. They then pass these traits to their offspring.

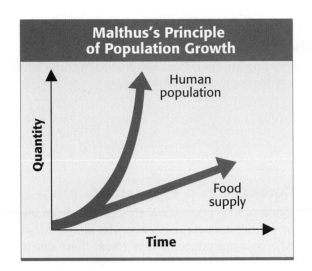

Figure 16 *Malthus thought the human population would get so large that there would not be enough food to feed everyone.*

Natural Selection

In 1859, Darwin wrote a book called *On the Origin of Species.* In this book, Darwin said that evolution happens through a process he called natural selection. In **natural selection,** organisms that are best adapted to their environment are more likely to survive and reproduce.

Some traits, such as the ability to outrun predators, improve an individual's chance of survival or reproduction. Such traits are selected and passed to future generations. Natural selection, described in **Figure 17** on the next page, can be divided into four steps.

QuickLab

Modeling Malthus's Principle TEKS

1. Get **two empty egg cartons** and a **bag of rice.** Label one carton "Food" and the second carton "Population growth."

2. Place one grain of rice in the first cup. Add one more grain to each subsequent cup. (Put two grains in the second cup, three in the third cup, and so on.) Each grain represents a unit of food.

3. In the other carton, place one grain of rice in the first cup and double the number of grains of rice in each subsequent cup. Stop after you have added rice to the sixth cup. Calculate how many grains of rice would go into each of the last six cups. This rice represents people.

4. How many "people" are in the twelfth cup?

5. How many "units of food" are in the twelfth cup?

6. What conclusion can you draw?

Figure 17 Natural Selection in Four Steps

1. Overproduction

More offspring are born than will live to become adults.

2. Differences in a Population

The individuals in a population are different from one another. Some of the different traits improve the chances that the individual will survive and reproduce. Others lower these chances. For example, rabbits that are stronger or faster are more likely to survive and reproduce than weaker or slower rabbits.

3. Struggle to Survive

An environment might not have enough food or water for every individual born. Many individuals are killed by other organisms. Still others cannot find mates. Only some individuals survive and reproduce.

4. Successful Reproduction

Successful reproduction is the key to natural selection. The individuals that have better traits for living in their environment and for finding mates are more likely to reproduce. Those that are not well adapted to their environment are more likely to die early or to have few offspring.

---

internet connect

SCI LINKS

NSTA GO TO: www.scilinks.org

TOPIC: The Galápagos Islands
sciLINKS NUMBER: HSTL165

TOPIC: Darwin and Natural Selection
sciLINKS NUMBER: HSTL170

SECTION REVIEW

① What traits changed in the Galápagos finches as they adapted to the different islands? ★TEKS

② How do farmers get animals and plants with desired traits, such as plumpness in corn kernels? ★TEKS

③ **Summarizing Data** What did Darwin think happened over several generations to the finches that first reached the Galápagos Islands from South America?

READING WARM-UP

Terms to Learn

species

What You'll Do

- Give two examples of natural selection in action. ★TEKS
- Outline the process of speciation.

Natural Selection in Action

Have you ever had to take an antibiotic? Antibiotics kill bacteria. But sometimes bacteria are not killed by the medicine. Do you know why?

A population of bacteria might develop this adaptation through natural selection. Most bacteria are killed by the medicine. But naturally *resistant* bacteria are not killed immediately by antibiotics. If these bacteria survive, they can pass the resistance trait on to their offspring.

Population Changes

Bacteria that are resistant to antibiotics are more likely to survive and pass their traits to future generations. This is how natural selection works. Read on to learn how natural selection can affect cockroaches and moths.

Insecticide Resistance

Farmers use insecticides to keep crops safe from insects. But some insecticides do not work as well as they did when they were first used. More than 500 kinds of insects are now resistant to certain insecticides.

Insects quickly develop resistance to insecticides because insects produce many offspring and usually have short generation times. *Generation time* is the period between the beginning of one generation and the beginning of the next. **Figure 18** shows how cockroaches can become insecticide resistant.

Figure 18 | **Resistance to Insecticides**

Most insects are killed by an insecticide. But a few are naturally resistant to the chemical. These few will survive when an insecticide is used.	The survivors then pass the trait for insecticide resistance to their offspring.	In time, the population is made up mostly of insects that are resistant to the insecticide.	When the same insecticide is used again, only a few insects are killed because most of them are resistant.

Adaptation to Pollution

As shown in **Figure 19,** European peppered moths can be either dark- or light-colored. Dark peppered moths were rare before 1850. There were many more light-colored peppered moths. After the 1850s, however, dark moths became more common in certain areas.

Figure 19 *Against a dark tree trunk (left), the light peppered moth stands out. Against a light tree trunk (above), the dark peppered moth stands out.*

What caused this change in the moth population? Several kinds of birds eat peppered moths that are resting on tree trunks. Before the 1850s, the trees were gray and light peppered moths were hard to see against the bark. Dark peppered moths were easier for the birds to see and were eaten more often. During the 1850s, smoke from new factories blackened nearby trees. The dark moths became harder to see on the dark tree trunks. The light moths stood out against the dark background and became easy prey for birds. More dark moths survived and had more dark offspring. Thus, the population changed from mostly light-colored moths to mostly dark-colored moths.

✓ Self-Check

Cities in Europe have begun to clean up air pollution. As they succeed, how might the traits of peppered moths change throughout the population? *(See page 640 to check your answer.)*

Figure 20 *The Grand Canyon separates two populations of squirrels.*

Forming a New Species

Sometimes, drastic changes take place that can form a new species. In the animal kingdom, a **species** is a group of organisms that can mate with one another to produce fertile offspring. A new species may form after a group becomes separated from the original population. This group forms a new population. Over time, the two populations adapt to their different environments. Eventually, they can become so different that they can no longer mate. At this point, the two groups are no longer the same species. When a single species divides into two, the process is called speciation (SPEE shee AY shuhn). The following steps explain one way that scientists think this process may happen.

Separation

When the Grand Canyon, shown in **Figure 20,** was forming, a single population of tassel-eared squirrels may have been separated. Today, descendants of the tassel-eared squirrels live on both sides of the canyon. Although the two groups share many characteristics, they look very different. The Albert squirrels live on the south rim of the Grand Canyon. The Kaibab squirrels live on the north rim. Both squirrels are shown in **Figure 21.**

Figure 21 *Two populations of tassel-eared squirrels were divided by the Grand Canyon, and two new species were formed—the Albert squirrel (left) and the Kaibab squirrel (above).*

Adaptation and Division

The environments on the two sides of the Grand Canyon are different. The north rim is about 370 m higher than the south rim. Almost twice as much precipitation falls on the north rim than on the south rim every year. Over many generations, the two groups of squirrels have adapted to their new environments. Eventually, the groups became so different that they could no longer interbreed. At this point, they were no longer the same species. **Figure 22** describes how the Galápagos finches might have followed a similar pattern.

Figure 22 *Separation and adaptation may have caused speciation on the Galápagos Islands. This pattern would have to be repeated several times before the population divided into separate species.*

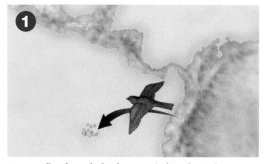

Some finches left the mainland and reached one of the islands (separation).

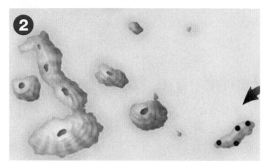

The finches reproduced and adapted to their new environment (adaptation).

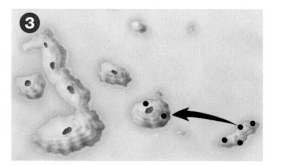

Some finches flew to a second island (separation).

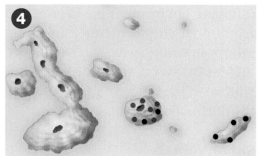

The finches reproduced and adapted to the different environment (adaptation).

internet**connect**

SCI*LINKS*
NSTA   GO TO: www.scilinks.org

TOPIC: Species and Adaptation
*sci*LINKS NUMBER: HSTL155

SECTION REVIEW

1. How did the traits of the peppered moth population in industrial areas of Europe change after 1850? ⊛TEKS

2. In your own words, explain how speciation may have affected the Galápagos finches.

3. **Applying Concepts** Most cactuses have spines, which are leaves that protect the plant. The spines cover a juicy stem that stores water. Explain how cactus leaves and stems might have changed through natural selection.

READING WARM-UP

Terms to Learn

heredity   gene
mutation   sex cell
DNA

What You'll Do

- Define heredity.
- Interpret the role of genes in inheritance. ⭐TEKS

Inheritance

Look around the room. You probably do not look exactly like anyone else. There are more than 6 billion people on Earth. But no two people are exactly the same. Have you ever wondered how this happens?

Darwin's theory of natural selection was partly based on his observation that parents pass traits to their offspring. But Darwin did not know *how* inheritance happens. Little was known about this process until Gregor Mendel's work was discovered in 1900. Mendel studied garden pea plants and worked out a theory of inheritance. His work was later used to support Darwin's theory of evolution.

Who Was Gregor Mendel?

Gregor Mendel, shown in **Figure 23,** was born in 1822 in Heinzendorf, Austria. Growing up on his family's farm, Mendel learned a lot about flowers and fruit trees. After completing his studies at college, he entered a monastery. He worked in the garden, where he used plants to study heredity. **Heredity** is the passing of traits from one generation to the next.

Strange Patterns

Mendel knew that sometimes the patterns of inheritance seemed simple and sometimes they did not. For example, sometimes a trait that appeared in one generation did not appear in the next one. In the third generation, though, the trait showed up again. Mendel noticed similar patterns in many living things. He wanted to find out why.

Peas in a Pod

To find out, Mendel decided to study one kind of living thing. He had already worked with the garden pea plant, so he chose it as his subject again. He also decided to study one characteristic, such as plant height, at a time. Mendel chose plants that had two forms for each of the characteristics he studied. For example, when Mendel studied plant height, he used plants that were either tall or short. **Figure 24** on the next page shows some of the characteristics Mendel studied.

Figure 23 Gregor Mendel

Figure 24 Characteristics Studied by Mendel

Seed shape		Plant height		Flower color	
Round	Wrinkled	Tall	Short	Purple	White

Mendel's Experiments

In his first experiments, Mendel bred plants that had different traits for each characteristic. For example, he bred plants that made round seeds with plants that made wrinkled seeds. The offspring are known as the *first generation*. His results are shown in **Figure 25.** Do the results surprise you? What do you think happened to the trait for wrinkled seeds in the first generation?

Mendel got the same results for each characteristic. One trait always appeared, and the other trait seemed to vanish. Mendel chose to call the trait that appeared the *dominant trait*. He called the trait that seemed to disappear the *recessive trait*.

Later, Mendel discovered that the recessive trait did not vanish altogether. When pollen fertilizes an egg on the same plant, the plant has *self-pollinated*. When Mendel allowed the first generation of plants to self-pollinate, some of the offspring had the recessive trait. These offspring are also shown in Figure 25.

Figure 25 *A plant that makes wrinkled seeds is fertilized with pollen from a plant that makes round seeds.*

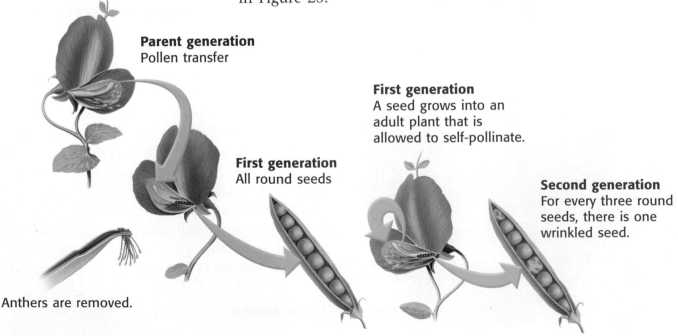

Parent generation
Pollen transfer

First generation
A seed grows into an adult plant that is allowed to self-pollinate.

First generation
All round seeds

Second generation
For every three round seeds, there is one wrinkled seed.

Anthers are removed.

APPLY

Curly Eared Cat

A curly eared cat, such as the one at right, mated with a cat that had normal ears. If all of the kittens had curly ears, which is the recessive trait—curly ears or normal ears? If these kittens grew up to have more kittens, would all of the offspring have curly ears?

Darwin and Mendel

Scientists have used Mendel's research to explain natural selection. Before Mendel's work was found in 1900, scientists did not understand inheritance. Mendel's studies gave them a place to start.

During the 1930s and 1940s, scientists combined the principles of inheritance with Darwin's ideas on natural selection. Together, these ideas explain that the differences Darwin noticed within a population could be caused by mutations. A **mutation** is a change in an organism's hereditary information.

New evidence has been gathered from many fields of science. Scientists now think that additional mechanisms play a part in population changes. However, natural selection provides a basic explanation for the many different kinds of life on Earth.

MID-SECTION REVIEW

1 In your own words, give a one- or two-sentence definition of the term *recessive trait*.

2 What were the results of Mendel's first experiments? What happened when Mendel allowed his first-generation plants to self-pollinate?

3 **Math Practice** After Mendel allowed the first-generation plants to self-pollinate, he counted the number of offspring with each trait. For example, when he counted the offspring of the first-generation plants, he found that 6,002 of them had yellow seeds and 2,001 had green seeds. What was the ratio of yellow seeds to green seeds?

It's in Your Cells

But how does inheritance work? How are traits passed from parents to offspring? The answer is in a molecule called **d**eoxyribo**n**ucleic (dee AHKS ee RIE boh noo KLEE ik) **a**cid, or DNA. **DNA** is the hereditary material in cells. The color of your hair, the kind of blood cells you make, and many other characteristics are determined by DNA.

DNA and Proteins

Your DNA came from your parents, half from your mother and half from your father. This DNA is passed on as cells divide. Parts of DNA called **genes** give the instructions for making proteins. Proteins determine traits.

You may be wondering, "What do proteins have to do with who I am or what I look like?" Proteins are found throughout cells. Proteins act as chemical messengers, and they help determine how tall you will grow, what colors you can see, and whether your hair is curly or straight. Human cells contain about 100,000 genes, and each gene spells out sequences of amino acids for specific proteins. Proteins are the reason for the many different shapes, sizes, and colors found in living things. **Figure 26** shows just one of the traits determined by proteins and your genes.

Figure 26 *The color of your eyes is just one trait determined by your DNA.*

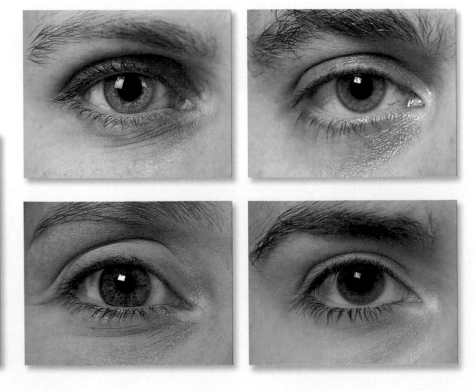

Two Kinds of Reproduction

Living things make other living things like themselves. Organisms reproduce in one of two ways: by asexual reproduction or by sexual reproduction.

One Makes Two

In *asexual reproduction,* a single parent cell produces offspring that are exactly like the parent. First the structures of the cell are copied. Then the cell divides, making new cells that are exact copies of the parent cell. Most single-celled organisms reproduce in this way. The hydra in **Figure 27** is a multicellular organism that reproduces asexually.

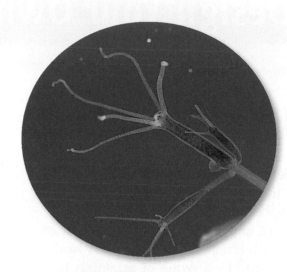

Figure 27 *This hydra is reproducing asexually.*

Two Make One

On the other hand, most animals reproduce by sexual reproduction. In *sexual reproduction,* two parent cells join together and develop into a new individual. The offspring are not exactly like either parent. Instead, they share traits of both parents.

The parent cells are known as **sex cells.** Each body cell usually has two copies of the genes for every trait. But sex cells have only one copy. When sex cells combine to form a new cell, the new cell gets half of its genes from the mother and half of its genes from the father. For any trait, the two copies may be identical or different. There are usually many forms of any one trait. This is why offspring do not look exactly like their parents, as shown in **Figure 28.**

Figure 28 *Humans and most animals reproduce sexually.*

SECTION REVIEW

① What are genes, and what role do they play in inheritance? ⭐TEKS

② Mendel used the term recessive to describe traits that seemed to disappear in his first-generation plants. How did he know that those traits did not vanish altogether?

③ **Analyzing Relationships** How is reproduction related to heredity?

Design Your Own Lab

Mystery Footprints ★TEKS

Sometimes scientists find evidence of past life in clues preserved in rocks. Evidence such as preserved footprints can give important information about an organism. Imagine that your class has been asked by a group of scientists to help study some footprints. These footprints were found in rocks just outside of town.

MATERIALS

- large box of damp sand, at least 1 m² (large enough to hold three or four footprints)
- metric ruler or meterstick

Form a Hypothesis

1 Your teacher will give you some mystery footprints in sand. Study the footprints. Brainstorm about what you might learn about the people who walked on this patch of sand. As a class, formulate as many testable hypotheses as possible about the people who left the footprints.

2 Form groups of three people, and choose one hypothesis for your group to investigate.

Test the Hypothesis

3 Use a computer or graph paper to construct a table for organizing your data. If you have two sets of mystery footprints, your table might look like the one below.

Mystery Footprints		
	Footprint set 1	**Footprint set 2**
Length		
Width		
Depth of toe		
Depth of heel		
Length of stride		

DO NOT WRITE IN BOOK

4 With the help of your group, you may first want to look at your own footprints to help you draw conclusions about the mystery footprints. For example, use a meterstick to measure your stride when you are running. How long is it when you are walking? Does your weight affect the depth of the footprint? What part of your foot touches the ground first when you are running? What part touches the ground first when you are walking? When you are running, which part of your footprint is deeper? Make a list of the kind of footprint each activity makes. For example, you might write, "When I am running, my footprints are deep near the toe. These footprints are 110 cm apart."

Analyze the Results

5 Compare the data from your footprints with the data from the mystery footprints. How are the footprints alike? How are they different?

6 Were the footprints made by one person or more than one person? Explain your interpretation.

7 Can you tell if the footprints were made by men, women, children, or a combination? Explain your interpretation.

Draw Conclusions

8 Based on your analysis of your own footprints, would you conclude that the people who made the mystery footprints were standing still, walking, or running?

9 Do your data support your hypothesis? Explain.

10 How could you improve your experiment?

Communicate Results

11 Outline your group's conclusions in a letter addressed to the scientists who asked for your help. Begin by stating your hypothesis. Then tell them how you gathered information from the study of your own footprints. Include the comparisons you made between your footprints and the mystery footprints. Before stating your conclusions, offer some suggestions about how you could improve your investigation.

12 Make a poster or chart, or use a computer if one is available, to present your findings to the class.

Section 1

Vocabulary

evolution *(p. 214)*
fossil *(p. 215)*
adaptation *(p. 219)*

Section Notes

- The theory of evolution states that populations accumulate inherited changes over time.

- The fossil record can be used to study how living things have changed over millions of years. Gaps still remain in the fossil record.

- Adaptations are characteristics that help an organism survive and reproduce.

Section 2

Vocabulary

trait *(p. 223)*
selective breeding *(p. 223)*
natural selection *(p. 225)*

Section Notes

- Charles Darwin developed his ideas on natural selection after years of studying the organisms he observed on the voyage of the HMS *Beagle.* ⭐TEKS

- Darwin's study was influenced by the concepts of selective breeding, the age of the Earth, and the idea that organisms produce more offspring than they can feed. ⭐TEKS

- In selective breeding, people breed only those plants or animals that have certain desirable traits. ⭐TEKS

- Darwin explained that evolution happens through natural selection. Natural selection can be divided into four steps:

  1. More offspring are born than will survive to reproduce.

  2. Individuals within a population are different from one another.

  3. Only some individuals within a population will survive and reproduce.

  4. Individuals that are better adapted to an environment are more likely to survive and reproduce.

Section 3

Vocabulary

species *(p. 229)*

Section Notes

- Natural selection allows a population to adapt to changes in environmental conditions.

- Evidence of natural selection can be seen in organisms that have developed resistance to an insecticide. ⭐TEKS

LabBook ⭐TEKS

Survival of the Chocolates *(p. 617)*

Section 4

Vocabulary

heredity *(p. 231)*
mutation *(p. 233)*
DNA *(p. 234)*
gene *(p. 234)*
sex cell *(p. 235)*

Section Notes

- Heredity is the passing of traits from parents to offspring.

- Mendel used pea plants to study heredity. ⭐TEKS

- Offspring inherit two sets of instructions for each characteristic, one set from each parent.

- Genes are made of DNA and provide instructions for making proteins. ⭐TEKS

CHAPTER 8
Review

USING VOCABULARY

The statements below are false. For each statement, replace the underlined word to make a true statement.

1. <u>Genes</u> are characteristics that help an organism survive and reproduce.

2. <u>Natural selection</u> is the process by which populations accumulate inherited changes over time.

3. From studying fossils, scientists have made a timeline of life known as <u>heredity</u>.

4. A group of organisms that can mate and produce fertile offspring is called a <u>population</u>.

5. Sections of DNA that provide instructions for making proteins are called <u>fossils</u>.

6. <u>Mutation</u> is the hereditary material in cells.

UNDERSTANDING CONCEPTS

Multiple Choice

7. While working on his theory of natural selection, Charles Darwin gathered information and ideas from many people. Which of the following people did NOT influence Darwin? ⊛TEKS
   a. Gregor Mendel
   b. plant and animal breeders
   c. Thomas Malthus
   d. Charles Lyell

8. The passing of traits from parents to offspring is called
   a. recessive.   c. evolution.
   b. heredity.   d. adaptation.

9. Although Darwin did not know it, the differences he observed among the individuals in a population of finches were probably caused by
   a. resistance.   c. fossils.
   b. mutations.   d. selective breeding.

Short Answer

10. Why are there gaps in the fossil record?

11. What are some of the traits that have been exaggerated through selective breeding in dogs? ⊛TEKS

12. Describe the four parts of Darwin's theory of natural selection.

CONCEPT MAPPING

13. Use the following terms to create a concept map: *struggle to survive, Darwin, differences in a population, overproduction, natural selection,* and *successful reproduction.*

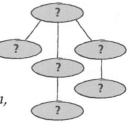

Write one or two sentences to answer the following questions:

14. In selective breeding, humans may decide that they would like a dog's fluffy tail or a flower's red petals to be passed to the next generation. Identify some changes in traits that can happen through natural selection. ⭐TEKS

15. Many rats have developed resistance to rat poison. Based on what you know about how insects develop resistance to insecticides, how might rats develop resistance to poisons?

16. In your own words, explain the theory of evolution. What are some of its strengths? What are some of its weaknesses? (Hint: What evidence do scientists use to support it? What evidence is missing?) ⭐TEKS

17. How do genes relate to proteins and to traits? ⭐TEKS

MATH IN SCIENCE

18. When Mendel allowed his first-generation plants to self-pollinate, he found that some of the offspring showed the recessive trait and some showed the dominant trait. In fact, for every three offspring with the dominant trait, one had the recessive trait. So, out of 900 second-generation plants, how many would you expect to be tall (dominant trait) and how many would you expect to be short (recessive trait)?

19. Imagine that you repeated Mendel's experiments with garden pea plants. If there were 450 purple-flowered plants in your second generation, how many white-flowered plants would you expect to have?

INTERPRETING GRAPHICS

Use the following graphs to answer the questions that follow.

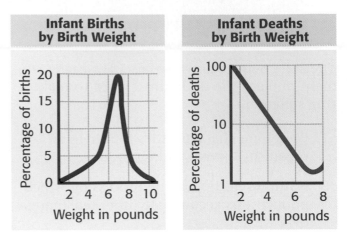

Infant Births by Birth Weight

Infant Deaths by Birth Weight

20. What is the most common birth weight?

21. At what birth weight are babies most likely to survive?

22. How do the principles of natural selection help explain why there are more deaths among babies with low birth weights than among babies with average birth weights?

Reading Check-up

Take a minute to review your answers to the Pre-Reading Questions found at the bottom of page 212. Have your answers changed? If necessary, revise your answers based on what you have learned since you began this chapter.

Chapter 8

	Paleozoic	Mesozoic	Cenozoic	
540 mya	248 mya	65 mya	present	

mya = million years ago

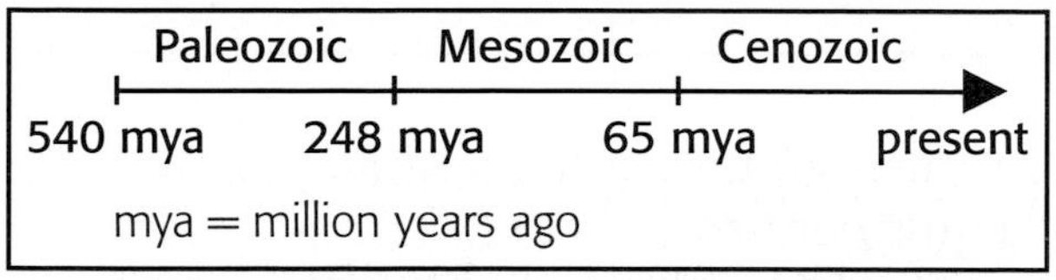

1 The diagram above represents life on Earth for the past 540 million years. Organisms that lived 286 million years ago lived in which of the following time periods?

A Mesozoic era

B Present time

C Cenozoic era

D Paleozoic era

2 When farmers allow only cows that produce a lot of milk to breed with a bull, the process is called

F natural selection.

G selective breeding.

H evolution.

J heredity.

3 In a population of smoky jungle frogs, several individuals are showing new traits. Which of the following is most likely to increase the frogs' chances of survival?

A A bright-red line down a frog's back

B A distinct odor that a predator can smell from a distance

C Coloring that blends into the forest floor even better than the coloring of the other frogs in the population does

D Feet that are more likely to make noise as the frog hops along the forest floor

4 Tamara repeated some of Mendel's experiments. Her results are shown in the chart below. Use the chart to answer the question that follows.

Results		
Characteristic	Dominant trait	Recessive trait
Flower color	600 purple	200 white
Seed color	750 yellow	250 green
Pod color	450 green	150 yellow

What percentage of the offspring expressed the dominant trait?

F 100%

G 75%

H 50%

J 25%

5 Genes provide instructions to the cell for making

A traits.

B DNA.

C proteins.

D adaptations.

Chapter 8

Math

1 Melissa decided to try Mendel's experiments on her own. In the second step in her experiments, she got 15 plants with purple flowers and 5 plants with yellow flowers. What is the ratio of yellow flowers to purple flowers?

A $\frac{1}{3}$

B $\frac{1}{4}$

C $\frac{1}{5}$

D $\frac{2}{5}$

2 Which group contains ratios that are all equivalent to $\frac{3}{5}$?

F $\frac{5}{10}, \frac{6}{15}, \frac{12}{20}$

G $\frac{6}{10}, \frac{7}{15}, \frac{10}{20}$

H $\frac{6}{10}, \frac{9}{15}, \frac{12}{20}$

J $\frac{4}{10}, \frac{6}{15}, \frac{8}{20}$

3 Last week, Bryan bought 10 pea plants for his garden. Each plant cost $3.50. Which is the best estimate of the cost of all of the plants?

A $20

B $40

C $60

D $80

Reading

Read the passage. Then read the questions that follow the passage. Decide which is the best answer to each question.

Fossils are most likely to be found in sedimentary rock. Sedimentary rock is a type of rock that forms as the surfaces of rocks are worn away by wind, rain, and ice. The particles from these rock surfaces then collect in low-lying areas. As these layers build up, their combined weight <u>compacts</u> the particles, and chemical reactions cement them together. After thousands of years, the layers of particles become solid rock—and so do parts of any organisms that have been trapped in the layers.

1 According to the passage, where are fossils most likely to be found?

A On rock surfaces

B Underwater

C In sedimentary rock

D In ice

2 You can tell from this passage that <u>compacts</u> means

F presses together.

G washes away.

H pulls apart.

J cleans.

EYE ON THE ENVIRONMENT

Saving at the Seed Bank

A very unusual laboratory can be found in Fort Collins, Colorado. There, sealed in test tubes, locked in special drawers, and even frozen at −196°C, are hundreds of thousands of seeds and plants. These plants are only being stored right now, but some day they may help prevent world hunger. They may also provide enough medicine to go around. Sound serious? Well, it is.

This place is called the National Seed Storage Lab, and it is the largest seed bank in the world. The seeds and plant cuttings stored in these seed banks represent almost every plant grown for food, clothing, and medicine.

No More Pizza!

Imagine heading out for pizza only to discover a sign on the door that says, "Closed today because there is not enough flour." Not enough flour? How can that be? What about burritos? When you get to the burrito stand, the sign is the same, "Closed—no flour." Think this sounds far-fetched? Well, it really isn't.

If wheat crops around the world are killed by a disease, we could have a flour shortage. And the best way to prevent such a terrible problem is by making new kinds of wheat. Through selective breeding, many plants have been improved to grow better and to be more resistant to disease and insects. But to breed new crops, plant breeders need lots of different genetic material. Where do they get this genetic material? At the seed bank, of course!

Why We'll Never Know

But what if some plants never make it to the seed bank? We have the new and improved kinds, so why does it matter if we keep the old ones? It matters because these lost plants often have important traits, such as resistance to disease and drought, that might be useful later. Once a plant is improved, need for the old one can drop to nothing. If an old plant is no longer grown, it may become extinct if it is not placed in the seed bank. In fact, many kinds of plants have already been lost forever. We'll never know if one of those lost varieties was able to resist a severe drought.

It's All in the Bank

Fortunately, seed banks have gathered seeds and plants for more than a hundred years. They preserve the genetic diversity of crop plants while allowing farmers to grow the most productive varieties in their fields. As long as there are seed banks across the world, it is not likely that there will be a flour shortage. Let's go out for pizza!

Going Further

▶ Many seed banks are in danger of going out of business. Why? Find out by doing research to learn more about the complicated and costly process of operating a seed bank.

Senses and Responses of Living Things

Pre-Reading Questions

1. What are some senses, and how are they helpful?

2. What causes responses in organisms?

3. How do organisms respond to stimuli? ⊛TEKS

AIRBORNE ARMADILLOS!!

When an armadillo is frightened, it jumps straight up in the air. Some jump as high as 4 ft! This reflex helps protect the armadillo. Jumping sometimes scares off predators and gives the armadillo time to run away. Animals and plants spend their lives sensing and responding to their environments and their neighbors. In this chapter, you'll learn more about the ways that organisms sense and respond.

START-UP Activity

SENSING CENTS ⭐TEKS

In this activity, you will learn to identify coins using sound and touch.

Procedure

1. Choose a partner. With your eyes closed, have your partner hand you a **penny,** a **nickel,** a **dime,** and a **quarter,** one at a time. Examine each coin with your hands. Is the coin small or large? Is the edge rough or smooth? Is the coin thin or thick?

2. Try to identify each coin. Have your partner correct you if you guess incorrectly.

3. Listen to the sound each coin makes as your partner drops it onto the floor. Try to figure out which coin makes which noise. Have your partner correct you until you can match the sounds to the coins.

4. Switch places with your partner so that your partner can identify the coins by touch and by sound.

Analysis

5. What is distinctive about the feel and sound of each coin? Write your answers in your ScienceLog.

6. Did you learn to identify the coins without looking? How did you do it? Write your answers in your ScienceLog, and share them with the class.

READING WARM-UP

Terms to Learn

stimulus
sensory receptor
nerve
olfactory cells

What You'll Do

- Define stimulus.
- Describe five senses.
- Compare the means of sensing among organisms.

Animals Sense

What happens when you get really cold? Do you shiver so much that your teeth start chattering? If so, your brain is responding to the cold by causing your muscles to twitch rapidly and warm you up.

The rapid twitching, commonly called shivering, is a response to a cold environment. Anything that causes a response in an organism is a **stimulus** (plural *stimuli*). There are *internal stimuli,* such as hunger and thirst, and *external stimuli* such as light and sound. For all organisms, living in the world means detecting these stimuli and reacting to them.

Senses and Nerves

How do you know what's going on around you? Your five senses—sight, hearing, smell, taste, and touch—let you know. Each sense provides a different kind of information, but all sensing begins the same way. First, a stimulus activates sensory receptors in your body. **Sensory receptors** are special cells that detect internal and external stimuli. Animals have receptors for many stimuli, including light, sound, odor, taste, and texture. After a receptor is stimulated, a message in the form of an impulse is sent to the brain along nerve pathways. A **nerve** is a group of cells that carries impulses from one place in the body to another.

Even Worms Can Sense

The flatworm has a very simple system of nerves, but it still can detect and respond to some stimuli. For example, some flatworms have eyespots, as shown in **Figure 1.** These eyespots are made up of light-absorbing pigments and nerves. Eyespots cannot focus, but they can determine the direction of the light.

Figure 1 *This kind of flatworm is called a planarian. A planarian's eyespots are made up of pigments and nerve cells.*

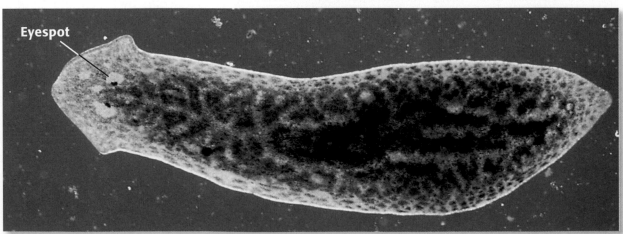

Eyespot

The Eyes Have It

Animals sense light energy using light receptors. Some animals have simple eyes that can detect light but cannot form images. Other animals, such as bees, see different kinds of light than we see. Many insects have *compound eyes*, which allow them to see images, but differently than human eyes do. A *compound eye* is made of many identical light-sensitive cells, as shown in **Figure 2.**

The Human Eye

Figure 3 shows a human eye. The human eye is a complex organ. The front of the human eye is covered by the *cornea*, a clear membrane that protects the eye while letting light enter. The light you can see is called visible light. Visible light is reflected by objects around you and enters your eye through an opening at the front. This opening is called the *pupil*. The light that comes through the pupil is focused by a *lens*. The light is then detected by receptors lining the back of your eye on a layer called the *retina*. When these receptors detect light, they trigger nerve impulses. These impulses leave the back of each eye through an *optic nerve* and travel to the brain.

Figure 2 *Ants have large, compound eyes. Scientists think that compound eyes can form images, but differently than human eyes do.*

Figure 3 *The human eye not only detects light but also perceives images.*

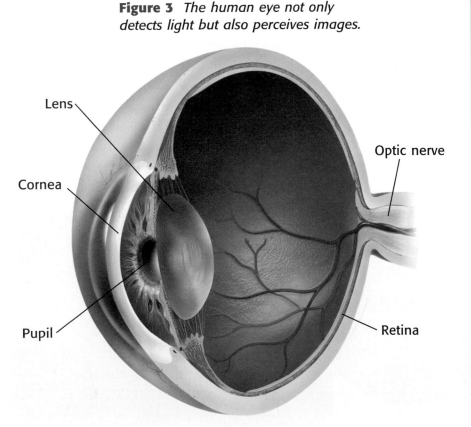

Lens

Cornea

Pupil

Optic nerve

Retina

Quick Lab

Agreeable Pupils

Caution: Do not use the sun as a light source in this exercise.

1. Hold the open end of a prepared **film canister** over your right eye.
2. With both eyes open, face an **indoor light source.**
3. What do you see through your right eye?
4. Still facing the light source, close your left eye.
5. What do you see now?
6. What was the stimulus? What was the response?

★ TEKS

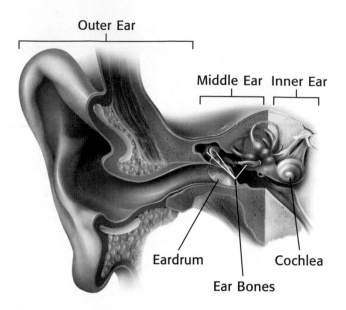

Outer Ear

Middle Ear   Inner Ear

Eardrum   Cochlea

Ear Bones

Figure 4 *The human ear detects sound waves and converts them to nerve impulses.*

Sounds Good to Me

Animals sense sound, or "hear," using sound receptors. Some animals have very simple sound receptors. Other animals have sound receptors so sensitive that they can navigate and find food using only their hearing.

What Is a Sound?

Sound travels as vibrations or waves. A sound begins when an object, such as a bell, begins to vibrate. The vibrations push on the matter, such as air or water, that touches the bell. As a result, sound waves move from the bell through the matter around it. If the sound waves reach a sound receptor, the organism can sense the bell ringing.

The Human Ear

The human ear, shown in **Figure 4,** has three sections: *the outer ear, the middle ear,* and *the inner ear.* When sound waves get to the outer ear, they are directed into the middle ear, where they cause the eardrum to vibrate. The *eardrum* is a thin membrane that is very sensitive to sound waves. It is connected to three small bones. The vibrating eardrum makes these tiny bones vibrate. One of the tiny bones vibrates against the *cochlea* (KAHK lee uh), a tiny fluid-filled part of the inner ear. These vibrations cause waves in the cochlea. Sound receptors in the cochlea change these waves to nerve impulses and send them to the brain.

Ears on Legs?

Many animals have ears on their head, but sound detectors are found in other places, too. Some insects, such as the cricket in **Figure 5,** use receptors on their legs to pick up sounds.

Figure 5 *Some crickets have sound receptors in a membrane on their front legs. They can find the direction a sound is coming from by moving their legs.*

— Membrane

Getting Nosy

Light receptors detect light energy, whereas sound receptors detect energy of tiny vibrations. Receptors for smell and taste detect chemicals. Smells are picked up by receptors called **olfactory** (ohl FAK tuh ree) **cells** in the nasal cavity, shown in **Figure 6.** In humans and dogs, such as those in **Figure 7,** these cells are in the space behind the nose. Other organisms have olfactory cells elsewhere. Male silkworm moths have olfactory cells on their antennae. Snakes, such as the viper in **Figure 8,** have olfactory cells in their nose and in a structure called the Jacobson's organ.

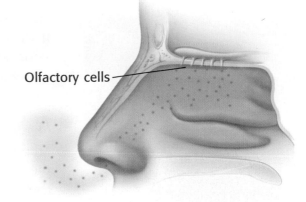

Olfactory cells

Figure 6 *Olfactory cells in the nasal cavity are what give you a sense of smell. They are located in the area marked in blue.*

Figure 7 *A dog's sense of smell is about 1,000 times more sensitive than a human's. A search and rescue dog can often tell if a person buried under snow or rubble is still alive.*

Figure 8 *This viper is not tasting the air. It is smelling by using its tongue to deliver chemicals to the Jacobson's organ.*

QuickLab

Smells Tell

1. In a small group, have each person put a **piece of fruit** in a **paper cup** and cover the cup with **foil.**

2. Close your eyes, and exchange cups with another member of the group. Lift the foil from each cup, and see if you can identify which kind of fruit is inside.

3. How many fruits could you identify?

4. Did any of the fruit samples smell similar to other samples?

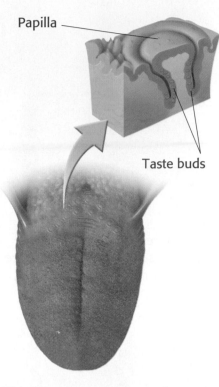

Papilla

Taste buds

Figure 9 *Taste buds are located within tiny bumps called papillae on your tongue.*

Smell and Taste

Have you ever tried to eat when you had a stuffy nose? Was it difficult to taste your food? Your sense of taste is linked to your sense of smell. Your brain uses information from your olfactory cells and your taste buds to give you a sense of flavor.

A Matter of Taste

Like the sense of smell, the sense of taste requires that a tiny piece of an object touch the receptor. In humans, taste receptors are located on *taste buds.* When you bite into a sweet apple, you know it is sweet because juice from the apple touches receptors for sugar on your tongue.

If you look at your tongue in the mirror, you'll notice that it is covered with tiny bumps. These tiny bumps are called *papillae* (puh PIL ee). Taste buds are located within the papillae (singular *papilla*), as shown in **Figure 9.** Taste buds have receptors for four basic tastes: sweet, sour, salty, and bitter.

Animals taste in different ways. Butterflies have receptors for taste on their feet. Catfish, such as the one in **Figure 10,** learn about what is near them from the taste buds on their skin.

Figure 10 *A catfish searches for food using the 600,000 taste buds that cover much of the outside of its body.*

MathBreak

Taste-Bud Tally

A 30 cm catfish may have 600,000 taste buds. Humans have around 10,000 taste buds. How many more taste buds does a catfish have than a human? What is the factor of difference between the number of taste buds in a catfish and the number of taste buds in a human?

How Touching

In humans, the sense of touch results from a mixture of stimuli: heat, pain, and pressure. We have receptors for these stimuli all over our skin, but we have more of them in some places than in others. For example, you have more receptors on your face and fingers than on your elbows and knees. It's helpful to have a good sense of touch in places that provide warning and in places that get information. Human touch in the fingers is so sensitive that people can learn to read Braille, as shown in **Figure 11.** Braille is a system of writing that uses small bumps instead of ink to form letters.

Feeling Well

Many animals have an excellent sense of touch. Octopuses can find a meal just by feeling for it with their tentacles. Insects, such as the cockroach, often investigate their environment using the sense of touch on their antennae. The star-nosed mole in **Figure 12** uses the star on its sensitive snout not to smell, but to feel for food.

Figure 11 *The skin of human fingers has many receptors that give us a sense of touch. Blind students use their sense of touch to read Braille.*

Figure 12 *Star-nosed moles have an excellent sense of touch in their snout. This enables them to search for food by feeling for it.*

SECTION REVIEW

1. What is a stimulus?

2. List five senses. What does each sense detect?

3. How do humans sense smells? What organ do snakes use to sense smells?

4. **Inferring Relationships** How many types of sensory receptors are found on the human head? What might be some advantages to having them there?

internet**connect**

*sci*LINKS.
NSTA   GO TO: www.scilinks.org

TOPIC: Animal Senses
*sci*LINKS NUMBER: HSTL337

READING WARM-UP

Terms to Learn

internal stimulus
hormone
external stimulus

echolocation
migrate
hibernation

What You'll Do

- Identify animal responses to internal stimuli. ⭐TEKS
- Identify animal responses to external stimuli. ⭐TEKS
- Identify animal responses to seasonal changes. ⭐TEKS

Animals Respond

When you are hungry, you search for food. You might sniff to find out if something is cooking or open the refrigerator and look for a snack.

Your responses and those of all other organisms are caused by internal and external stimuli. Hunger is an **internal stimulus** because it is a stimulus that comes from inside your body.

When you search for food, you are responding to hunger. The daily lives of most animals are filled with many different survival responses. Animals have to find food and water, avoid being eaten, and find a place to live. All of these activities depend on an animal's ability to sense the world around it and use what it learns to stay alive.

Responding to Internal Stimuli

Sometimes you respond to internal stimuli by taking action. Sometimes you respond to internal stimuli without even knowing it. Both kinds of responses are important.

I'm So Thirsty!

Why do you get thirsty when you exercise? When you exercise, your body loses a lot of water as sweat through the pores in your skin. As you continue to sweat, the amount of water in your blood decreases. Salivary glands in your mouth make less saliva when the water level in your body is low. Without saliva, your mouth feels dry. Your dry mouth reminds you that it's time for a drink of water. As shown in **Figure 13,** people who exercise must be sure to get enough water.

Is Supper Ready?

You feel hungry when your brain receives signals that your cells need energy. After you have eaten and have begun digesting your food, the hunger signals stop until you need to eat again.

Figure 13 *A dry mouth is an internal stimulus that signals a need for water.*

A Breath of Fresh Air

We need oxygen to live, and we get oxygen by breathing. Even the swimmer in **Figure 14** is breathing. Do you have to remember to breathe while you sleep? No, your brain sends internal stimuli to keep you breathing at all times. Parts of the brain control many body functions so that you don't have to think about them.

Hormones

How does your body send internal messages? Sometimes, it uses nerve pathways, as in breathing. Another way the body sends signals is through hormones. **Hormones** are chemicals made in one part of the body that cause a change in another part of the body. For example, when your body needs energy, a hormone causes some of the sugars you have stored in your liver to be released.

Growth is also controlled by the internal stimulus of hormones. Your muscles grow as you get bigger because your body sends hormonal signals that stimulate growth. Hormones also control the internal signals for different stages of human development. *Puberty* (PYOO buhr tee) is the time when the reproductive system of a human being becomes mature. During puberty, a person begins to look less like a child and more like an adult. Hormones are responsible for signaling many of these changes.

Figure 14 *The brain sends internal signals that regulate breathing so that you get a constant supply of oxygen. This diver is breathing through a snorkle.*

Changing Form

Humans aren't the only living things that respond to internal stimuli. Treehoppers are insects that go through several big changes during their lives. Each change is a response to internal stimuli. First a nymph hatches from an egg. Later, internal stimuli direct the nymph to develop into an adult. When fully formed, an adult treehopper emerges from the skin of the nymph. You can see an adult treehopper emerging in **Figure 15.**

Figure 15 *Internal stimuli control growth and development. This treehopper has finished developing into an adult.*

Responding to External Stimuli

External stimuli are stimuli that come from outside the body. Animals respond to external stimuli in a number of ways. Some responses are fairly predictable. For example, moths will almost always fly toward light. Other responses are less automatic. Animals respond to the sight or smell of food differently when they are hungry than when they have just eaten.

Having You for Dinner

Animals must respond to external stimuli in order to survive. Survival for animals often depends on finding food and not becoming food for another animal. An animal that eats another animal is called a *predator*. An animal that gets eaten is called *prey*. Animals use their senses to pick up external stimuli to find a meal and to avoid becoming one.

A Sound Diet

Many bats are excellent predators. They find food using echolocation (EK oh loh KAY shuhn). **Echolocation** is the process of using reflected sound waves to find objects. To use echolocation, bats, such as the one in **Figure 16,** make a very high pitched sound. The sound waves bounce off any object they hit and make an echo. If the sound waves hit a flying insect, an echo returns from the insect to the bat's ears. The echo is an external stimulus. The information travels to the bat's brain, which tells the bat where to fly to capture dinner.

BRAIN FOOD

Honeybees have a great sense of smell that they use to find nectar. Some scientists are now experimenting with using bees to sniff out buried land mines.

Figure 16 *Some bats can use echolocation to find and eat up to half their weight in insects every night!*

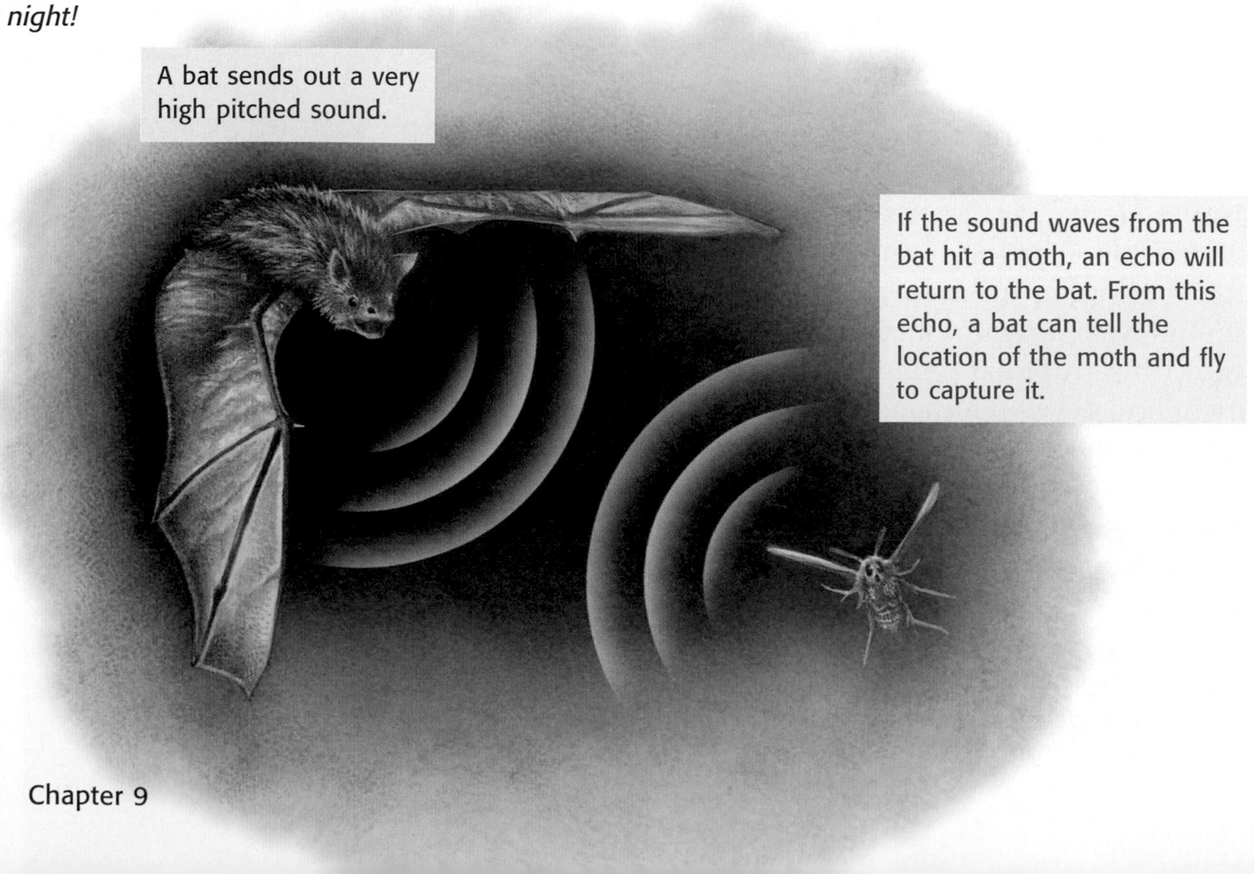

A bat sends out a very high pitched sound.

If the sound waves from the bat hit a moth, an echo will return to the bat. From this echo, a bat can tell the location of the moth and fly to capture it.

Figure 17 *Some species of octopuses can change color in response to external stimuli. Blending in with their environment helps them avoid danger.*

Who Goes There?

Animals that sense they are being sized up for dinner also have responses. Sometimes they fight, run, or swim away. Rabbits that see, smell, or hear predators will often freeze so that they will not be noticed. An octopus, such as the one in **Figure 17,** can change its skin color to blend in and avoid danger. If you have ever approached a wasps' nest, you may have noticed that some wasps stand guard. The closer you get, the more alert the guards become. If you get too close, they will attack.

Communication

Communication is another way that animals use their senses. We often think of the sense of hearing when we think of communication. But animals communicate in many ways. Have you ever left your jacket on a seat to let people know you'd like to sit there? When other people see your jacket, they usually choose another seat. Your jacket is an external stimulus that marks your place. People respond by sitting somewhere else. Marking a territory is just one kind of communication. Animals also communicate in order to share resources, scare off predators, and find a family member or a mate. Animals communicate using sight, sound, smell, and touch.

Other Senses and Responses

Many animals have senses that humans don't have. The monarch butterfly can detect changes in the magnetic fields of Earth. They use this sense to find their migration route. The duckbill platypus has sensors in its bill that can detect very tiny nerve impulses. A platypus uses this sense when it roots around in the mud searching for worms.

Self-Check

When elephants sense that they need minerals, they seek minerals from the rocks and soil in their environment. What is the stimulus and what is the response? Is the stimulus internal or external? Explain your answers. *(See page 640 to check your answers.)* ⓉEKS

Astronomy
CONNECTION

The seasons are caused by Earth's tilt and its orbit around the sun. We have summer when the Northern Hemisphere is tilted toward the sun and the sun's energy falls more directly on the Northern Hemisphere. While the Northern Hemisphere experiences the warm season, the Southern Hemisphere experiences the cold season. The opposite occurs when the Northern Hemisphere is tilted away from the sun.

Figure 18 *Whooping cranes migrate with the seasons. They return to the same area every winter.*

Responding to Seasonal Changes

Another set of external stimuli that animals respond to comes with the change of seasons. Winter is very harsh in some areas of the world. It gets very cold, and food is scarce. Animals respond to these conditions in a number of ways. Some move to a warmer place. Others store food. Some rest deep in the mud, in the snow, or in some other safe place and wait for spring.

Telling Time

Animals need to know when to store food and when to move south for the winter. How do they know what time it is? The internal clocks and calendars that animals use are called biological clocks. A *biological clock* is an internal control of a natural cycle. Animals may use clues from their surroundings, such as the length of the day and the temperature, to "set" their biological clocks. Sensing these stimuli in the environment, an animal's body begins responding to seasonal changes.

All Aboard!

When food is scarce because of winter or dry weather, many animals migrate. To **migrate** is to move from one place to another. Animals migrate to find food, water, or safe nesting grounds. Whales, salmon, bats, and even chimpanzees migrate. Each winter, whooping cranes, such as those shown in **Figure 18,** fly from Canada to the Texas Gulf Coast to eat crabs and find mates.

Hibernation

Some animals deal with dramatic food and water shortages by hibernating. **Hibernation** (HIE buhr NAY shuhn) is a period of inactivity and lowered body temperature that some animals undergo in winter. Hibernating animals use stored body fat as their food. Many animals, including mice, squirrels, and skunks, hibernate. While an animal hibernates, its body changes. Its temperature, heart rate, and breathing rate decrease. The body temperature of some hibernating animals goes down to a few degrees above freezing. These animals do not wake for weeks at a time. Texas horned lizards, such as the one shown in **Figure 19,** hibernate from early fall to late spring. Other animals, such as bears, do not enter deep hibernation. Their body temperatures do not drop as severely, and they sleep for shorter periods of time.

Estivation

Winter is not the only time that resources can be scarce. Many desert squirrels and mice experience a similar internal slowdown in the hottest part of the summer, when they run low on water and food. This period of reduced activity in the summer is called *estivation* (ES tuh VAY shuhn). California ground squirrels, such as the one shown in Figure 19, are estivators.

Texas horned lizard

Figure 19 *California ground squirrels estivate when Texas horned lizards are active. When the horned lizards are hibernating, the squirrels are active.*

California ground squirrel

SECTION REVIEW

1. Identify two internal stimuli for animals and responses to them. Identify two external stimuli for animals and responses to them. ⭐TEKS

2. What are two ways that animals respond to a change in seasons? ⭐TEKS

3. **Applying Concepts** Explain the following sentence: "Animal responses are caused by internal or external stimuli."

🖬 internet**connect**

SC*LINKS*
NSTA   GO TO: www.scilinks.org

TOPIC: Responding to Stimuli
*sci*LINKS NUMBER: HSTL343

READING WARM-UP

Terms to Learn

tropism
thigmotropism
phototropism
gravitropism
chlorophyll

What You'll Do

- Describe how plants may respond to touch, light, and gravity. ⊛TEKS
- Explain how some plants flower in response to night length. ⊛TEKS
- Describe how some plants are adapted to survive cold weather.

Plants Sense and Respond

Do plants respond to stimuli? They sure do! Plants respond to stimuli, such as touch, light, gravity, and changing seasons, just to name a few.

Plants are not just standing there! Plants sense stimuli and are active responders. Plants sense using chemicals inside their cells. Stimuli change the chemistry of plant cells. In response, those cells can grow differently or can change the chemistry of other cells.

Plants Respond to External Stimuli

Plant growth in response to an external stimulus is called a **tropism** (TROH PIZ uhm). Plant growth toward a stimulus is a *positive tropism*. Plant growth away from a stimulus is a *negative tropism*. There are several specific kinds of tropisms. All are responses to different kinds of stimuli.

Responding to Touch

Thigmotropism (thig MAH truh PIZ uhm) is a plant's response to touch. It is especially easy to see in tendrils. *Tendrils* are plant parts that hold onto other things. The vine in **Figure 20** has tendrils that are very sensitive to touch. The cells on the twig side of each tendril sense contact with the twig and cause the entire tendril to grow in a coil around the twig. Using the twig as a support, the vine grows upward and outward.

Figure 20 *This vine has tendrils that are sensitive to touch. When the tendrils sense pressure on one side, they grow toward the pressure. As a result, the tendrils wrap around supports.*

Responding to Light

If you place a houseplant so that it gets light from only one direction, such as from a window, the plant will grow toward the light. A change in the growth of a plant in response to the direction of light is called **phototropism** (foh TAH troh PIZ uhm). As shown in **Figure 21,** the bending happens because cells on one side of the shoot grow longer than cells on the other side of the shoot.

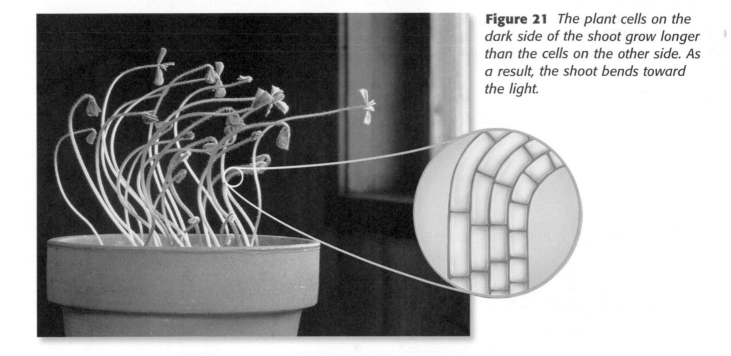

Figure 21 *The plant cells on the dark side of the shoot grow longer than the cells on the other side. As a result, the shoot bends toward the light.*

Responding to Gravity

A change in a plant's direction of growth due to the effect of gravity is **gravitropism** (GRAV i TROH PIZ uhm). The plant in **Figure 22** shows the effect of gravitropism. A few days after a plant is placed on its side or turned upside down, the roots and shoots change their direction of growth. Most shoot tips have negative gravitropism—they grow upward, away from the center of the Earth. In contrast, most root tips have positive gravitropism—they grow downward, toward the center of the Earth.

Figure 22 *The shoot tip of this plant has grown upward, away from the pull of gravity.*

Self-Check

Use the following terms in one or two sentences: *tropism, stimulus, light, gravity, phototropism,* and *gravitropism. (See page 640 to check your answer.)* ★TEKS

QuickLab

Grow Thataway!

Will a potted plant grow sideways? You will need **several potted plants** to find out.

1. Use **duct tape** to secure **cardboard** around the base of each plant so that the soil will not fall out.

2. Turn the plants on their sides, and observe what happens over the next few days.

3. Describe two stimuli that might have influenced the direction of growth.

4. How might gravitropism benefit this plant?

★TEKS

Plants Respond to Seasonal Changes

What would happen if a plant living in an area that has severe winters flowered in October? Would the plant be able to successfully produce seeds and fruits? If your answer is no, you're correct. If the plant produced any flowers at all, the flowers would probably freeze and die before they had the chance to produce mature seeds. Plants living in regions with cold or dry winters can detect the change in seasons. How do plants detect seasonal changes? Keep reading to find out.

As Different as Night and Day

Think about what happens as the seasons change. For example, what happens to the length of days and nights? As autumn and winter approach, the days get shorter and the nights get longer. The opposite happens when spring and summer approach.

Night length is an important external stimulus for many plants. This stimulus can cause plants to begin reproducing. Some plants make flowers only in late summer or early autumn, when night length is longer. These plants are called short-day plants. Examples of short-day plants are poinsettias (shown in **Figure 23**) and ragweed. Other plants flower in spring or early summer, when night length is short. These plants are called long-day plants. Clover, spinach, and lettuce are examples of long-day plants.

Figure 23 | **Poinsettia Flowering Response**

In the early summer, night length is short. At this time, poinsettia leaves are all green and there are no flowers.

Poinsettias flower in the fall, when nights are long. The leaves surrounding the flower clusters turn red.

Seasonal Changes in Leaves

Some trees, such as maple trees, lose all their leaves at the same time each year. These trees usually lose their leaves before winter begins. In tropical climates that have wet and dry seasons, trees that lose their leaves do so before the dry season. Plants lose water through their leaves. Having bare branches during the winter or during the dry season reduces the amount of water plants lose. The loss of leaves helps plants survive low temperatures or long periods without rain.

Figure 24 *The leaves of some trees, such as the maple shown here, change from green to orange in autumn. In winter the maple is bare.*

An Autumn Show

As shown in **Figure 24,** leaves sometimes change color before they fall. As autumn approaches, **chlorophyll,** the green pigment plants use to make food, breaks down. As chlorophyll is lost, other yellow and orange pigments can be seen. These pigments were always present in the leaves but were hidden by the green chlorophyll. Some leaves also have red pigments, which also become visible when the green pigment is gone.

SECTION REVIEW

1. What are the effects caused by touch, light, and gravity on plant growth? Are these effects responses to internal or external stimuli? ⭐TEKS

2. How does the loss of leaves help a plant survive winter or long periods without rain?

3. **Applying Concepts** If a plant does not flower when exposed to 12 hours of darkness but does flower when exposed to 9 hours of darkness, is it a short-day plant or a long-day plant?

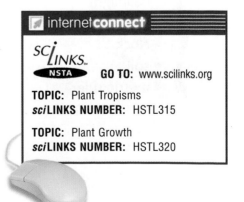

internetconnect

SciLINKS.
NSTA GO TO: www.scilinks.org

TOPIC: Plant Tropisms
*sci*LINKS NUMBER: HSTL315

TOPIC: Plant Growth
*sci*LINKS NUMBER: HSTL320

Skill Builder Lab

Wet, Wiggly Worms! ⭐TEKS

In this activity, you will observe the behavior of a live earthworm. Remember that earthworms are living animals that deserve to be handled gently. Be sure to keep your earthworm moist during this activity. The skin of the earthworm must stay moist so that the worm can get oxygen. If the earthworm's skin dries out, the worm will suffocate and die. Use a spray bottle to moisten the earthworm with water.

MATERIALS

- spray bottle
- dissecting pan
- paper towels
- water
- live earthworm
- probe
- celery leaves
- flashlight
- shoe box with lid
- clock
- soil
- metric ruler

Procedure

1 Place a wet paper towel in the bottom of a dissecting pan. Put a live earthworm on the paper towel, and observe how the earthworm moves. Record your observations in your ScienceLog.

2 Use the probe to carefully touch the anterior end (head) of the worm. Gently touch other areas of the worm's body with the probe. Record the kinds of responses you observe.

3 Place celery leaves at one end of the pan. Record how the earthworm responds to the presence of food.

4 Shine a flashlight on the anterior end of the earthworm. Record the earthworm's reaction to the light.

5 Line the bottom of the shoe box with a damp paper towel. Cover half of the shoe box with the box top.

6 Place the worm in the uncovered side of the shoe box in the light. Record your observations of the worm's behavior for 3 minutes.

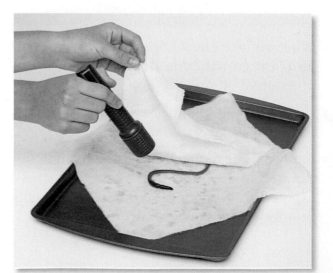

7 Place the worm in the covered side of the box. Record your observations for 3 minutes.

8 Repeat steps 6–7 three times.

9 Spread some loose soil evenly in the bottom of the shoe box so that it is about 4 cm deep. Place the earthworm on top of the soil. Observe and record the earthworm's behavior for 3 minutes.

10 Dampen the soil on one side of the box, and leave the other side dry. Place the earthworm in the center of the box between the wet and dry soil. Cover the box, and wait 3 minutes. Uncover the box, and record your observations. Repeat this procedure three times. (You may need to search for the worm!)

Analysis

11 How did the earthworm respond to being touched? Were some areas more sensitive than others?

12 How is the earthworm's behavior influenced by light? Based on your observations, describe how an animal's response to a stimulus might provide protection for the animal.

13 How did the earthworm respond to the presence of food?

14 When the worm was given a choice of wet or dry soil, which did it choose? Explain this result.

Going Further

Based on your observations of an earthworm's behavior, draw a conclusion about where you might find earthworms. Prepare a poster that illustrates your conclusion. Draw a picture with colored markers, or cut out pictures from magazines. Include all the variables that you used in your experiment, such as soil or no soil, wet or dry soil, light or dark, and food. At the bottom of your poster, write a caption describing where earthworms might be found in nature.

Highlights

Section 1

Vocabulary

stimulus (p. 246)

sensory receptor (p. 246)

nerve (p. 246)

olfactory cells (p. 249)

Section Notes

- A stimulus is anything that causes a response in an organism.

- Animals sense stimuli through a variety of sensory receptors.

- Sensory receptors send messages to the brain along nerve pathways.

- Planaria have eyespots. Insects have compound eyes. Human eyes are composed of a cornea, pupil, lens, retina, and optic nerve.

- Sound travels as waves caused by vibrations in matter. We hear a sound when these waves reach our ears, and our ears send a signal to our brain.

- Olfactory cells detect tiny pieces of the things that we smell.

- Taste receptors are located on taste buds.

- Human touch is a mixture of the senses pressure, heat, and pain.

Section 2

Vocabulary

internal stimulus (p. 252)

hormone (p. 253)

external stimulus (p. 254)

echolocation (p. 254)

migrate (p. 256)

hibernation (p. 257)

Section Notes

- Internal stimuli, such as hunger and thirst, are signals inside your body that cause you to respond. ⭐TEKS

- External stimuli, such as light and heat, are signals outside your body that cause you to respond. ⭐TEKS

- Hormones are chemicals that are made in one part of the body and cause a change in another part. ⭐TEKS

- Predators are animals that eat other animals. Prey are animals that get eaten by other animals.

- Animals respond to seasonal changes. To migrate is to change location with the seasons. To hibernate is to experience a period of inactivity during a cold season. ⭐TEKS

Section 3

Vocabulary

tropism (p. 258)

thigmotropism (p. 258)

phototropism (p. 259)

gravitropism (p. 259)

chlorophyll (p. 261)

Section Notes

- Plants respond to stimuli. ⭐TEKS

- Plant growth in response to an external stimulus is called a tropism. ⭐TEKS

- Thigmotropism is a response to touch in part of a plant. Phototropism is a response to the direction of light in part of a plant. Gravitropism is a response to gravity in part of a plant. ⭐TEKS

- Plants respond to seasonal changes. Some plants respond to the difference between day length and night length. Some trees lose their leaves before winter to prevent water loss. ⭐TEKS

- When the green pigment, chlorophyll, breaks down in the leaves of some plants, the colors of other pigments show.

LabBook ⭐TEKS

Weepy Weeds (p. 618)

Review

Use the following terms in a sentence to show that you know what they mean:

1. stimulus/sensory receptor

2. nerve/olfactory cell

3. predator/prey

4. migrate/hibernate ⭐TEKS

5. phototropism/tropism ⭐TEKS

UNDERSTANDING CONCEPTS

Multiple Choice

6. Something that causes a response in an organism is a
   a. receptor.
   b. nerve.
   c. stimulus.
   d. retina.

7. Compound eyes are found on
   a. plants.
   b. flatworms.
   c. humans.
   d. insects.

8. When you are thirsty and get a drink of water, you are responding to a(n) ⭐TEKS
   a. external stimulus.
   b. internal stimulus.
   c. communication.
   d. tropism.

9. Hormones are
   a. sound receptors.
   b. tropisms.
   c. chemicals made in the body.
   d. predators.

10. Taste buds can detect the tastes salty, sweet, bitter, and
    a. fishy.
    b. sour.
    c. spoiled.
    d. creamy.

11. When a snake gets too warm because of sunshine, it needs to move to a cooler place. This movement is a response to ⭐TEKS
    a. an external stimulus.
    b. an internal stimulus.
    c. communication.
    d. a tropism.

12. Thigmotropism is a response in plants to ⭐TEKS
    a. sound.
    b. smell.
    c. taste.
    d. touch.

13. Some trees lose their leaves before winter or a dry season. This loss helps
    a. make room for new leaves.
    b. prevent water loss.
    c. phototropism.
    d. keep predators away.

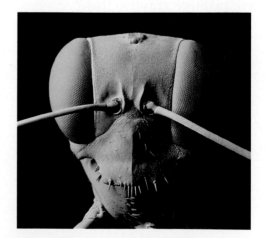

Short Answer

14. Describe echolocation, and explain how bats use it. ⭐TEKS

15. What is the difference between hibernation and estivation?

16. What is a positive tropism? Give an example. Is a tropism a response to an internal or external stimulus? ⭐TEKS

CONCEPT MAPPING

17. Use the following terms to create a concept map: *animals, plants, seasonal changes, hibernate, stimuli, estivate, migrate,* and *lose leaves.*

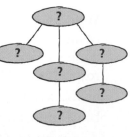

CRITICAL THINKING AND PROBLEM SOLVING

Write one or two sentences to answer the following questions.

18. What are the similarities and differences between migration and hibernation? ⭐TEKS

19. If you wanted to make poinsettias bloom and turn red in the summer, what would you have to do? ⭐TEKS

20. What benefits are there for a plant's shoots to have positive phototropism? What benefit is there for a plant's roots to have positive gravitropism?

MATH IN SCIENCE

21. The compound eyes of dragonflies have 28,000 sections. The eyes of butterflies have 14,000, and houseflies have 4,000. How many times more sections do dragonflies have than butterflies and houseflies?

INTERPRETING GRAPHICS

The following graph shows the rise and fall in the total mass of leaves on a particular maple tree.

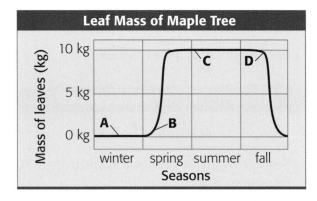

22. When does the tree have the most leaves? When does it have the fewest?

23. What is the change in the tree at **B**? What are the stimuli that might cause this change? ⭐TEKS

24. If these leaves change color, at what point in the graph would this change happen? ⭐TEKS

Reading Check-up

⭐TEKS

Take a minute to review your answers to the Pre-Reading Questions found at the bottom of page 244. Have your answers changed? If necessary, revise your answers based on what you have learned since you began this chapter.

Chapter 9

1 Which of the following best defines an external stimulus?

A All things

B Something outside an organism that causes a response in an organism

C Always light

D Something that only affects plants

2 Which of the following is NOT an example of an external stimulus?

F Hunger

G Sound

H Heat

J Light

3 According to the chart below, which of the following is true?

A Plants sense and respond to external stimuli.

B Plants never change.

C Plants respond to touch.

D Animals and plants have the same responses to stimuli.

Stimulus	Response
Light	The plant bends toward the light.
Gravity	The plant roots grow down, and the stems grow up.
Seasonal changes	The plant loses leaves.

4 What is the stimulus?

F The light

G A moth

H Flying

J A wing

5 Information about tropisms would most likely be found under which heading in the table of contents?

A Plant Responses to External Stimuli

B How Animals Hear

C Seasonal Responses in Plants

D Seasonal Responses in Animals

6 While you sleep your brain regulates your breathing. This is an example of a(n)

F external stimulus.

G tropism.

H internal stimulus.

J tendril.

Chapter 9

Math

1 What letter best represents $2\frac{1}{3}$ on the number line?

A R

B S

C T

D U

2 There are 12 marbles in a bag. All the marbles are the same except for the color. There are 6 blue marbles, 2 red marbles, and 4 green marbles. If someone selects a marble at random from the bag, what is the probability that the marble will be blue?

F $\frac{1}{5}$

G $\frac{1}{4}$

H $\frac{1}{3}$

J $\frac{1}{2}$

Reading

Read the passage. Then read each question that follows the passage. Decide which is the best answer to each question.

When a corn plant is being eaten by a caterpillar, chemicals in the mouth of the caterpillar cause the corn plant to release a second chemical into the air. Certain wasps sense the corn's response and make a beeline for the infested plant. The wasps dive for the caterpillars and lay eggs under their skin. The eggs hatch in a short time, and the wasp larvae eat the insides of the caterpillars.

1 What alerts the wasps to the presence of caterpillars?

A The corn plants release a chemical into the air.

B Wasps hear the caterpillars eating the corn plants.

C Caterpillars release a chemical that wasps can smell.

D Caterpillars trick the wasps into coming and then eat them.

2 You can tell from the passage that wasp larvae

F eat corn.

G are chemicals that wasps inject into caterpillars.

H are not alive.

J are a stage that wasps go though after hatching.

EYE ON THE ENVIRONMENT

Do Not Disturb!

Did you know that bats are the only mammals that can fly? Unlike many birds, most bat species in the northern and central parts of the United States don't fly south for the winter. Instead of migrating, many bat species go into hibernation. But if their sleep is disturbed too often, the bats may die.

Long Winter's Nap

Most bats eat insects, but winter is a time of food shortage. In late summer, many North American bats begin to store up extra fat. These fat reserves help them survive the winter. For the stored fat to last until spring, bats must hibernate. They travel to caves where winter temperatures are low enough—0°C to 9.5°C—and stable enough for the bats to hibernate comfortably.

The body temperature of hibernating bats drops to almost the same temperature as the surrounding cave. Their heart rate, normally about 400 beats per minute, slows to about 25 beats per minute. With these changes, the stored fat will usually last all winter, unless human visitors wake the bats from their deep sleep.

No Admittance!

Even with their slowed metabolism, bats must wake up occasionally. They still need to drink water every so often. Sometimes they move to a warmer or cooler spot in the cave. But bats usually have enough fat stored so that they can wake up a few times each winter and then go back to sleep.

People visiting the caves force the bats to wake up unnecessarily. As a result, the bats use up the fat that they have stored more quickly than they can afford. For example, a little brown bat consumes 67 days' worth of stored fat each time it awakes. And with no insects around to eat, it cannot build up its fat reserve again.

▲ *These little brown bats are roosting in a cave.*

Most species of hibernating bats can survive the winter after waking about three extra times. But frequent intrusions can lead to the death of a whole colony of bats. Thousands of these interesting and extremely beneficial mammals may die when people carelessly or deliberately disturb them as they hibernate.

Increase Your Knowledge

▶ Using the Internet or the library, find out more about bats. Learn how they are beneficial to the environment and what threatens their survival. Discuss with your classmates some ways to protect bats and their habitats. ⭐TEKS

Connections in the Environment

Pre-Reading Questions

1. What are three parts of the environment to which organisms can respond? ⊛TEKS

2. Where do plants get energy?

3. How does energy flow through the living environment? ⊛TEKS

Midnight Snack

The bat responds to the movement of the centipede on the sand, flying down and catching it in near darkness. The pallid bat, which lives in West Texas, will eat the centipede to get the energy it needs to live. These animals are part of the same environment. In this chapter, you will learn about the structure of the environment and how the organisms that live there are connected to each other.

WHO EATS WHOM? ⭐TEKS

In this activity, you will learn how organisms interact when finding (or becoming) the next meal.

Procedure

1. On each of **four index cards,** print the name of one of the following organisms: white-tailed deer, turkey vulture, oak tree, and cougar.

2. Arrange the cards on your desk in a chain to show who eats whom.

3. List the order of your cards in your ScienceLog.

4. In nature, would you expect to see more cougars, more deer, or more oak trees? Arrange the cards in order of most individuals to fewest.

Analysis

5. What might happen to the other organisms if the oak trees were removed from this group? What might happen if the cougars were removed?

6. Are there any organisms in this group that eat more than one kind of food? (Hint: What else might a deer, a cougar, or a turkey vulture eat?) How could you change the order of your cards to show this information? How could you use pieces of string to show these relationships?

READING WARM-UP

Terms to Learn

environment   community
ecology   ecosystem
population   biosphere

What You'll Do

- Recognize and name the five levels of the environment.
- Identify components of an ecosystem to which organisms may respond. **★TEKS**
- Explain how organisms respond to their environment.

Life in the Environment

How are you connected to the spider weaving a web in the corner of your room? You both breathe the same air. The spider may one day catch a mosquito that could have sucked your blood. You and the spider are separate but are part of the same environment.

The **environment** is everything that affects an organism. Think about your environment. You are affected by the other people around you. You are affected by the weather. Even the plants and animals that you get food from affect you. Everything in your environment is connected to everything else. Scientists who study these connections specialize in ecology. **Ecology** (ee KAHL uh jee) is the study of the relationships between organisms and their environment.

How the Environment Works

Take a look at the lizard, called an iguana, in **Figure 1.** What is this animal's environment? Its environment is made up of the vines and the trees. The soil and the water are also parts of its environment. So are the insects that it eats and the air that it breathes. The iguana's environment can be sorted into two parts. The *nonliving* part includes water, sunlight, air, and rocks. The trees and the other organisms in the area make up the *living* part. How many living and nonliving parts can you name in your environment?

Figure 1 *The iguana affects and is affected by all of the parts of its environment.*

The Environment Has Structure

At first glance, the environment may seem a bit messy. But take a closer look. You will find that it can be broken down into different levels. **Figure 2** shows you these different levels.

The first level of the environment is the single organism. The second level is made up of a group of similar organisms that share the same area. This is called a **population.** The third level, the **community,** is made up of the different populations that live in the same area. The fourth level, the **ecosystem,** is a community together with its nonliving environment. Finally, the fifth level is made up of all of the ecosystems on Earth. This level is called the **biosphere** (BIE oh SFIR).

Figure 2 **The Five Levels of the Environment**

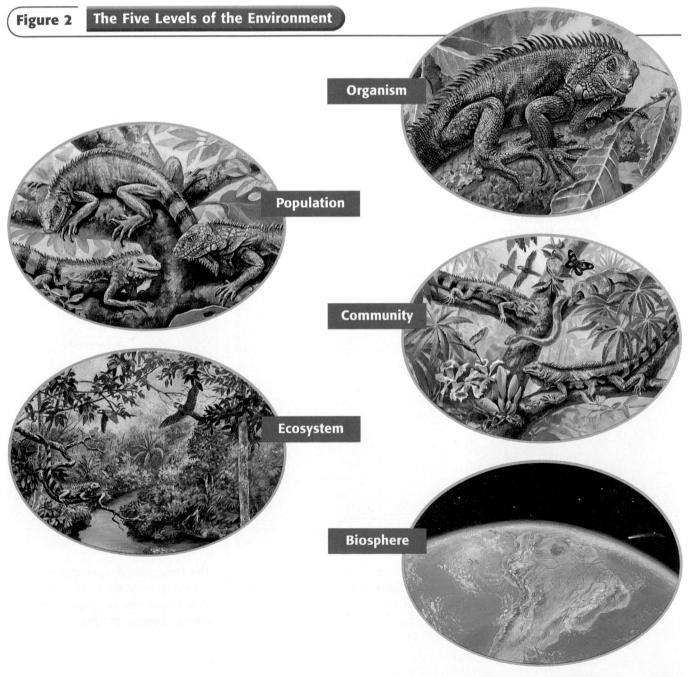

Organism

Population

Community

Ecosystem

Biosphere

Everything Is Connected

The natural environment in which an organism lives is its ecosystem. An organism interacts with the parts of its ecosystem by responding to them. All organisms, including humans, respond to both the nonliving and living environment.

Responding to the Nonliving Environment

The nonliving environment includes everything that is not alive. This includes the rocks in the ground, sunlight, water, wind, and the temperature of the air. An organism is affected by each of these things. Organisms respond to these things as well. You can see examples of these responses in **Figure 3.**

Plants have many kinds of responses to the nonliving environment. For example, they respond to light by making food. They use the food to live and to grow. Some plants respond to rain by flowering and making seeds. Once a seed falls to the ground, it may grow in response to water in the soil, temperature, and light.

Figure 3 **Responses to the Nonliving Environment**

This tree is using sunlight to make food for itself.

Bluebonnets grow in response to sunlight and the minerals and water in the soil.

The Peringuey's viper moves in a unique way across the sand. This snake can be found in the Namib Desert, in Africa.

The Peringuey's viper, a snake, has an interesting response to the sand of its desert home. The snake moves using a sideways motion. Only a small part of its body touches the ground at any one time. This response helps it move through very loose sand. It also keeps the snake from burning itself, much like running on the tips of your toes.

The temperature of the air is a very important part of the nonliving environment. Animals, such as the Texas horned lizard, respond to air temperature. As the air gets colder, the lizard's body processes slow down. In order to stay alert, it will lie on a warm, sunny rock. Crickets respond to higher temperatures as well. They tend to chirp faster when the air is warmer! Think about how dogs respond on hot days. Dogs are not the only animals that pant. On very hot days, birds will open their beaks to cool themselves off.

Several birds, such as turkey vultures, use visual landmarks to guide themselves while flying. They respond to their nonliving environment—the mountains, rivers, and other parts of the landscape—and use it in the same way that we would use a map.

Organisms also respond to the amount of water in their environment. A cactus in the desert is able to live with very small amounts of water. During the spring, the cactus responds to rainwater by blooming right after a desert rain.

····Activity····

Think of your favorite animal or an animal that you would like to learn more about. Do some research on this animal at the library or on the Internet. Where does it live? What types of relationships does it have with its nonliving environment? Record your findings in your ScienceLog.

TRY at HOME

Texas horned lizards lie flat against a warm rock when they get too cold.

Turkey vultures use landmarks when they fly south for the winter.

Desert cactuses bloom shortly after it rains.

Figure 4 Responses to the Living Environment

Badgers instinctively dig or find dens to protect their young.

Tropical plants compete for the small amount of light that comes through the rain-forest canopy.

Chemistry
C O N N E C T I O N

Plants often compete with each other for nutrients and living space. Many plants use chemicals to stop other plants from growing near them. Juniper trees, which are native to Texas, release chemicals into the soil. These chemicals make it hard for other plants to grow near the tree. This way, the juniper keeps more living space and nutrients for itself.

Responding to the Living Environment

Have you ever noticed how animals interact with each other? Think of a cat and a mouse. What is the first thing these animals will do when they see each other? You probably think that the cat will chase the mouse. But animals respond to their living environment in other ways as well.

Responding to Internal Stimuli

One way an organism interacts with its living environment is by responding to itself. Organisms respond to themselves by reacting to internal stimuli. When your stomach growls, you are reacting to your own hunger. Organisms respond to other internal stimuli as well, like the natural drive to protect their young. As shown in **Figure 4,** one way badgers respond to this stimulus is by finding or digging a den.

Responding to Population Members

An organism can also respond to other members of its population. The members of a population often try to use the same resource, such as water or light. Figure 4 shows forest plants competing with each other for light. Animals respond to other members of their population too. A cat will defend its food and the area that it considers home. It will often fight or chase away another cat that wanders into its home area.

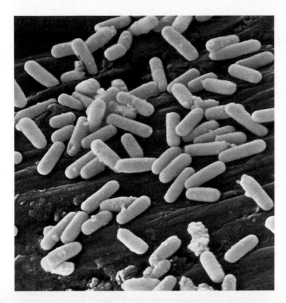

The bacterium *Escherichia coli* lives in your intestines and helps you to digest your food.

In response to danger, the caterpillar of the spicebush swallowtail butterfly puffs up its back to make itself look like a snake.

Responding to Different Organisms

An organism will also respond to other kinds of organisms. A spider will try to catch a fly. And the fly will try to get away from the spider. Some animals respond to an attacker by playing dead. Others will try to scare the other animal away. The animal being attacked, such as the caterpillar in Figure 4, may pretend it is more dangerous than it really is.

Different kinds of organisms may help each other as well. You and a kind of bacterium that lives in your intestines have such a relationship. The bacterium gets a food supply from you. It responds by making a vitamin that your body needs. Crocodiles and certain birds help each other too. When a crocodile opens its mouth wide, the bird responds by picking food from its teeth. The crocodile gets a teeth cleaning, and the bird gets a meal!

SECTION REVIEW

❶ What is the environment?

❷ Explain the difference between the living and the nonliving environment.

❸ **Applying Concepts**   Identify three components of an ecosystem to which organisms may respond. ⭐TEKS

internet**connect**

*sci*LINKS.
NSTA   GO TO: www.scilinks.org

TOPIC: Texas Ecosystems
*sci*LINKS NUMBER: HSTX330

TOPIC: Organization in the Environment
*sci*LINKS NUMBER: HSTL435

Terms to Learn

producer   food chain
consumer   food web
scavenger   energy pyramid
decomposer

What You'll Do

● Describe the functions of producers, consumers, and decomposers.
● Distinguish between a food web and a food chain.
● Explain how energy flows through a food chain and a food web. ⭐TEKS

Living Things Need Energy

Do you think you could survive on water and vitamins alone? Why not? Eating food satisfies your hunger for a reason. It provides something else you cannot live without.

All living things need energy to survive. For example, black-tailed prairie dogs eat grass and seeds to get the energy they need. They use this energy to grow, move, and reproduce. Everything a prairie dog does uses energy. The same is true for the plants that grow in the prairies. Coyotes, which eat prairie dogs, need energy too. So do the bacteria and worms that live in the prairie soil.

The Energy Connection

Organisms in any community can be divided into three groups based on how they get energy. These groups are producers, consumers, and decomposers. Look at **Figure 5** to see how energy passes through these groups in an ecosystem.

Producers

Organisms that use sunlight directly to make food are called **producers.** They do this using a process called photosynthesis. Most producers are plants, but algae and some bacteria are also producers. Grasses are the main producers in the prairie. Producers in other ecosystems include cordgrass in a salt marsh and trees in a forest. Algae are the main producers in the ocean.

Figure 5 *Follow the path of energy as it moves from the sun through an ecosystem.*

Energy
Sunlight is the source of energy for almost all living things.

Producer
Plants use energy from the sun to make food.

Consumer
Prairie dogs eat plants and seeds to get energy. This prairie dog is an *herbivore.*

Consumer
Coyotes get energy from the animals they eat. Sometimes, a prairie dog is the food for a coyote. This consumer is a *carnivore.*

Herbivore

Carnivore

Consumers

Organisms that eat other organisms are called **consumers.** They cannot use the sun's energy directly like producers can. Instead, consumers must eat producers or other organisms to get energy.

There are several kinds of consumers. An *herbivore* is a consumer that eats plants. Herbivores in the prairie ecosystem include grasshoppers, gophers, prairie dogs, bison, and pronghorn antelope. A *carnivore* is a consumer that eats animals. Carnivores in the prairie ecosystem include spiders, snakes, coyotes, hawks, and owls. Consumers known as *omnivores* eat both plants and animals. The grasshopper mouse is an example of an omnivore in the prairie. It eats insects, scorpions, lizards, and grass seeds. **Scavengers** are animals that feed on the bodies of dead animals. The turkey vulture is a scavenger in the prairie. Scavengers in aquatic ecosystems include catfish, snails, worms, and crabs.

Decomposers

Organisms that get energy by breaking down the remains of other organisms are called **decomposers.** Bacteria and fungi are kinds of decomposers. Living material that can supply energy is called *biomass*. Decomposers break down biomass in a process called *decay*. In this process, they rearrange the matter in biomass into simpler compounds, such as water and carbon dioxide. This releases energy, which decomposers can then use. Decay also releases other substances in the biomass, such as nitrogen and calcium. All of these materials can then be used again by plants and other living things.

Self-Check

Are you a herbivore, a carnivore, or an omnivore? Explain. *(See page 640 to check your answer.)*

BRAIN FOOD

There are a few organisms that are both producers *and* consumers. One example is *Euglena,* a type of one-celled organism. Like a plant, *Euglena* can use the sun's energy to make its own food. But like an animal, it can hunt and eat small prey.

Consumer
A turkey vulture gets its energy from eating the leftovers from the coyote's meal. This consumer is a *scavenger.*

Decomposer
Bacteria and fungi in the soil break down any prairie dog remains that aren't eaten by the coyote or turkey vulture. These organisms put nutrients back into the ecosystem.

Scavenger

Food Chains

Energy flows through an ecosystem as one organism eats another. You can think of these organisms as links in a chain. A **food chain** is the path of energy from one feeding level to another. The food chain in **Figure 6** shows the energy flow through part of a woodland ecosystem.

The grass uses light energy from the sun to make food for itself. A grasshopper eats the grass and uses the energy to live. Then, the grasshopper becomes food for a frog. The frog uses this energy to live. The frog is then eaten by a snake. The snake uses this energy for itself. Finally, the snake becomes food for an owl. The owl then uses the energy for its own processes. Energy flows from one organism to another in every step of this food chain.

There are many food chains in an ecosystem. Another food chain may begin with a plant. A small rabbit eats the plant and gets energy. In turn, the rabbit is eaten by an owl. The owl is part of *both* food chains. Most organisms are part of more than one food chain. So how are all of these food chains related to each other? Keep reading!

Figure 6 A Woodland Food Chain

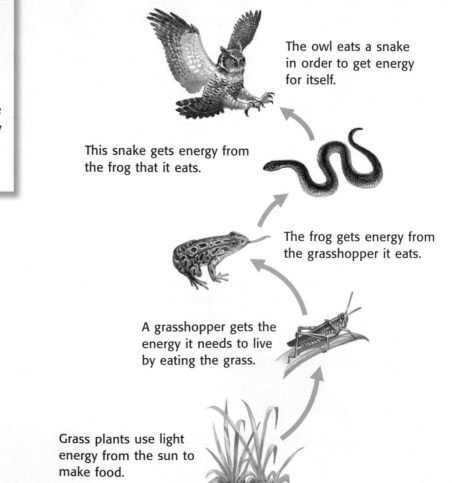

The owl eats a snake in order to get energy for itself.

This snake gets energy from the frog that it eats.

The frog gets energy from the grasshopper it eats.

A grasshopper gets the energy it needs to live by eating the grass.

Grass plants use light energy from the sun to make food.

Food Webs

An owl eats many different animals, such as mice, snakes, and rabbits. Therefore, an owl is part of many food chains. All of the food chains in a community link together to form a **food web.** A food web shows the many ways energy can flow through an ecosystem. Food webs, like the one in **Figure 7,** give a more realistic idea of the energy flow than a simple food chain. Look at Figure 7 carefully to see how food chains link together to form a food web.

Figure 7 *Energy flows in many ways in an ecosystem. In this woodland, several food chains join together to form a food web.*

Energy Pyramids

Energy moves from one organism to another in food chains and food webs. But most of it is used up along the way. Very little of the energy captured by plants ever makes it to carnivores. Think again about a prairie ecosystem as an example.

A prairie community includes grass, prairie dogs, and coyotes. A grass plant uses most of the energy it gets from the sun for its own life processes. But some of the energy is stored in its tissues. Prairie dogs get this energy when they eat the grass. The animals use most of the energy in the grass to live and stay warm. Only a little of the energy is stored in their tissues. Coyotes get this energy when they eat prairie dogs. Coyotes need even more energy than prairie dogs do. Therefore, it takes a lot of prairie dogs to support a coyote. In turn, a coyote uses most of the energy it gets as well.

This loss of energy along a food chain can be represented by an **energy pyramid,** as shown in **Figure 8.** The size of each level shows how much energy is available at that step in the food chain. The amount of energy becomes smaller at each higher level as energy is lost. Organisms use up most of the energy they take in, or they give it off as thermal energy. Only energy stored in their tissues can be passed on to the next level. So it takes much more energy to support organisms at higher feeding levels.

MathBreak

Energy Pyramids

Draw an energy pyramid for a river ecosystem that contains four levels: river plants, insects, little fish, and big fish. Assume the plants get 1,000 units of energy from the sun. If each level uses $\frac{9}{10}$ of the energy it receives from the previous level, how many units of energy are available to the big fish?

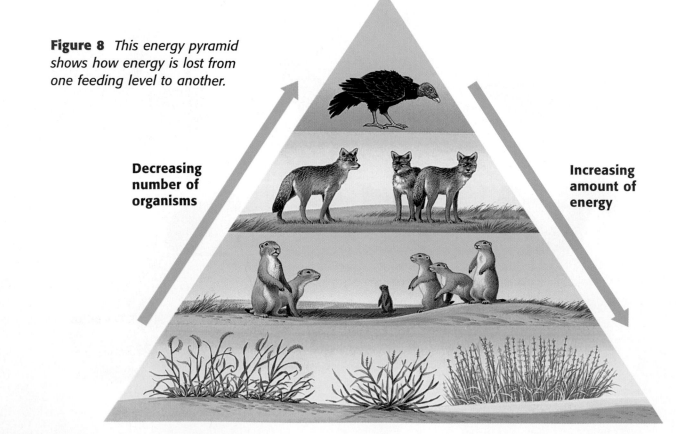

Figure 8 *This energy pyramid shows how energy is lost from one feeding level to another.*

Decreasing number of organisms

Increasing amount of energy

The Gray Wolf, A Case Study

A single species can be very important to the flow of energy in an environment. Gray wolves, for example, are consumers that affect the populations of many other species. The diet of a gray wolf includes everything from lizards to moose.

Gray wolves were once common throughout much of the United States. They were almost wiped out as the wilderness was settled. You can see a pair of gray wolves in **Figure 9.** Without wolves, some populations, such as elk, became very large. Because the elk population was so large, many areas became overgrazed. The elk also began to die of starvation.

Gray wolves were recently put back in Yellowstone National Park. The U.S. Fish and Wildlife Service hopes that this will restore the natural energy flow in this area. But not everyone is happy. Ranchers near Yellowstone are worried about the safety of their livestock.

Figure 9 *As the wilderness was settled, the gray wolf population in the United States declined.*

Gray Wolves Are Consumers

Wolves are carnivores, as shown in **Figure 10.** Their diet includes large animals, such as deer, moose, reindeer, sheep, and elk. They also eat small animals, such as birds, lizards, snakes, and fish.

Gray Wolves Are Needed in the Food Web

If wolves again become part of Yellowstone, they will reduce the elk population. They will eat mainly the old, hurt, and diseased elk. This in turn will allow more plants to grow. Once there are more plants, herbivore populations, like that of the snowshoe hare, will begin to grow. This will allow the animals that eat the hares, such as foxes, to increase in number as well.

Figure 10 *Wolves are carnivores—they feed on elk, deer and moose.*

SECTION REVIEW

1. Why is the role of a decomposer important to a community?

2. Describe how energy flows through both food chains and food webs. ⭐TEKS

3. **Analyzing Ideas** Explain why there is a loss of energy at each level of an energy pyramid.

Making Models Lab

Adaptation: It's a Way of Life ★TEKS

Did you know that organisms have special characteristics called *adaptations* that help them survive changes in their environment? These changes can be climate changes, food shortages, or disease. These things can cause a population to die out unless some members have adaptations that help them survive. For example, a bird may have an adaptation for eating sunflower seeds and ants. If the ants die out, the bird can still eat seeds in order to live.

In this activity, you will design an organism with special adaptations. Then you will describe how these adaptations help the organism live.

- poster board
- colored markers
- magazines for cutouts
- other arts-and-crafts materials
- scissors

Procedure

1 Study the chart below. Choose one adaptation from each column. For example, an organism might be a scavenger that burrows underground and has spikes on its tail!

Adaptations		
Diet	**Type of transportation**	**Special adaptation**
• Carnivore	• Flies	• Uses sensors to detect heat
• Herbivore	• Glides through the air	• Is active only at night and has excellent night vision
• Omnivore	• Burrows underground	• Changes colors to match its surroundings
• Scavenger	• Runs fast	• Has armor
• Decomposer	• Swims	• Has horns
	• Hops	• Can withstand extreme temperature changes
	• Walks	• Secretes a terrible and sickening scent
	• Climbs	• Has poison glands
	• Floats	• Has specialized front teeth
	• Slithers	• Has tail spikes
		• Stores oxygen in its cells so that it does not have to breathe continuously
		• Has an adaptation of your own invention

2 Design an organism that has the three adaptations you have chosen. Use poster board, colored markers, picture cutouts, construction paper, or anything of your choice to create your organism.

3 Write a caption on your poster describing your organism. Describe its appearance, where it lives, and how its adaptations help it survive. Give your animal a two-part "scientific" name based on its characteristics.

4 Display your creation in your classroom. Share with class-mates how you chose the adaptations for your organism.

Analysis

5 What does your imaginary organism eat?

6 In what environment would your organism be most likely to survive—a desert, a tropical rain forest, plains, icecaps, mountains, or an ocean? Explain your answer.

7 What kind of animal is your organism (mammal, insect, reptile, bird, fish)? What modern organism (on Earth today) or ancient organism (extinct) is your imaginary organism most like? Explain the similarities between the two organisms. Do some research outside of class about a real organism that your imaginary organism may resemble.

8 If a sudden climate change occurred, such as daily down-pours of rain in a desert, would your imaginary organism survive? What adaptations does it have for surviving such a change?

CHAPTER 10
Highlights

Section 1

Vocabulary

environment (p. 272)
ecology (p. 272)
population (p. 273)
community (p. 273)
ecosystem (p. 273)
biosphere (p. 273)

Section Notes

- Ecology is the study of relationships between organisms and their environment.

- The environment is everything that affects an organism. The environment consists of both nonliving and living parts.

- The environment can be organized into five levels: organism, population, community, ecosystem, and biosphere.

- An ecosystem includes a community of organisms and its nonliving environment.

- Organisms respond to both their living and nonliving environment. ⭐TEKS

Section 2

Vocabulary

producer (p. 278)
consumer (p. 279)
scavenger (p. 279)
decomposer (p. 279)
food chain (p. 280)
food web (p. 281)
energy pyramid (p. 282)

Section Notes

- Organisms can be divided into three groups based on how they obtain energy: producers, consumers, and decomposers.

- Producers are organisms that get their energy directly from sunlight. Consumers are organisms that eat other organisms to get energy.

- Decomposers are organisms that break down the remains of dead organisms to get energy.

- A food chain shows how energy flows fom one organism to the next. ⭐TEKS

- Because most organisms eat more than one kind of food, there are many energy pathways possible; these are represented by a food web. ⭐TEKS

- Energy pyramids demonstrate that most of the energy at each level of the food chain is used up at that level and is unavailable for organisms higher on the food chain.

CHAPTER 10 Review

USING VOCABULARY

For each pair of terms, explain how the meanings of the terms differ.

1. herbivore/carnivore

2. food web/food chain

3. scavenger/decomposer

4. producer/consumer

5. population/community

Complete the following sentences by choosing the correct term from each pair of terms.

6. A(n) __?__ shows how energy is lost at each level of the food chain. *(food web* or *energy pyramid)*

7. The __?__ is everything that affects an organism. *(environment* or *community)*

UNDERSTANDING CONCEPTS

Multiple Choice

8. Water, land, air, and light are part of
   a. communities.
   b. populations.
   c. the nonliving environment.
   d. the living environment.

9. Ecology is the study of the relationships between
   a. consumers and decomposers.
   b. an organism and its environment.
   c. carnivores and herbivores.
   d. food webs and wolves.

10. Energy is __?__ at each level of an energy pyramid.
    a. doubled   c. gained
    b. lost   d. constant

11. Organisms may respond to
    a. themselves.
    b. other organisms.
    c. the air.
    d. water.
    e. All of the above ★TEKS

12. A carnivore
    a. uses sunlight to make food.
    b. is a consumer that eats animals.
    c. is a producer that eats plants.
    d. is a consumer that eats flowers.

13. Food webs show that
    a. energy flows in many ways through an ecosystem.
    b. most animals eat only one type of food.
    c. energy is gained at each level of an energy pyramid.
    d. organisms respond to their environment. ★TEKS

14. Gray wolves play an important role in their community because
    a. they are producers, and they provide most of the energy in the community.
    b. they are consumers, and they help control the size of certain populations, such as those of elk or deer.
    c. they nurture their young.
    d. they are considered endangered in most parts of the world.

Connections in the Environment   **287**

Short Answer

15. Name and describe two parts of an ecosystem. ⭐TEKS

16. Do organisms respond to these parts? Explain. ⭐TEKS

17. Explain how energy flows through a food chain. How does this differ from energy flow through a food web? ⭐TEKS

CONCEPT MAPPING

18. Use the following terms to create a concept map: *individual organisms, producers, populations, ecosystems, consumers, herbivores, biosphere, carnivores,* and *communities.*

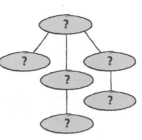

CRITICAL THINKING AND PROBLEM SOLVING

Write one or two sentences to answer the following questions:

19. Could a balanced ecosystem contain producers and consumers but no decomposers? Explain your answer.

20. Some ecologists think that certain organisms, such as wolves, help maintain a variety of organisms in their ecosystem. Predict what might happen to other organisms, such as rabbits or deer, if wolves were to become extinct.

21. Explain why it is important to have a variety of organisms in a community. Give an example.

22. Draw a diagram that illustrates the interactions between matter and energy in the decay of biomass. Explain your answer. ⭐TEKS

MATH IN SCIENCE

23. The plants in an ecosystem obtained 20,810 Cal of energy from the sun in 1 year. The herbivores in the ecosystem ate all of the plants but only obtained 3,370 Cal of energy. How much energy did the plants use for their own life processes?

INTERPRETING GRAPHICS

24. Is it possible for an inverted energy pyramid to exist, as shown in the figure below? Explain your answer.

Reading Check-up

Take a minute to review your answers to the Pre-Reading Questions found at the bottom ⭐TEKS of page 270. Have your answers changed? If necessary, revise your answers based on what you have learned since you began this chapter.

Chapter 10

1 Which of the following parts of an eco-system can an organism respond to?

A Itself

B Other members of its population

C The nonliving parts

D All of the above

2 In a food chain, energy could flow

F from plants to small fish to humans.

G from humans to small fish to plants.

H from small fish to plants to humans.

J from small fish to humans to plants.

3 Organisms may respond to other parts of the living environment, such as

A moonlight and sunlight.

B ocean water.

C other organisms in the community.

D the temperature of the air.

4 A company selling food supplements includes the following claim on bottles of their garlic capsule pills: "Taken daily, garlic has been shown to reduce cholesterol levels 5 percent or more in clinical studies." Which statement draws the most accurate inference about this claim?

F The garlic pills will help lower your cholesterol.

G Garlic pills work as well as garlic at lowering cholesterol.

H Garlic pills are not useful for people who have low cholesterol.

J Garlic pills are a good substitute for garlic in your diet.

5 Which of the following statements best describes how energy flows through the many organisms in an ecosystem?

A Energy flows in a chain-shaped manner through an ecosystem.

B Energy flows in a web-shaped manner through the many organisms in an ecosystem.

C Energy flows outward from a central point, in a fan-shaped manner.

D Energy flows through an ecosystem like water down a drain.

6 A compost bin holds biomass, such as lawn clippings and kitchen leftovers, while they decay into soil fertilizer. Which statement best explains the interactions between matter and energy during this process.

F The biomass decays into energy and elements, such as carbon and nitrogen.

G Decomposers release matter, using up the energy in the biomass.

H Decomposers break the biomass into compounds plants can use, releasing energy in the process.

J The energy in the biomass changes into compounds plants can use.

7 You have just finished using wood and aluminum fence posts during a field investigation. Make the wisest choice for recycling the materials in the posts.

A Leave the posts to decay on their own.

B Reuse the wood and recycle the aluminum.

C Decompose the aluminum in a compost heap and recycle the wood.

D Recycle the aluminum and burn the wood.

Chapter 10

Math

1 In a meadow ecosystem, the grass plants in the area receive 42,870 units of energy from the sun in 1 month. The prairie dogs in this community eat all of the grass in the area. The prairie dogs receive only 4200 units of energy. How much energy did the grass use up or give off as thermal energy?

A 16,110 units

B 40,220 units

C 38,670 units

D 356 units

2 The figure below is a map of a forest ecosystem. What is the *area* of this ecosystem?

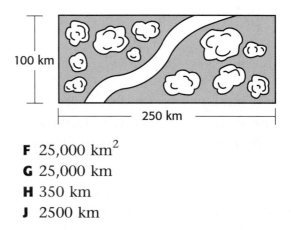

F 25,000 km²

G 25,000 km

H 350 km

J 2500 km

Reading

Read the passage. Then read each question that follows the passage. Decide which is the best answer to each question.

In 1859, settlers released 12 rabbits in Australia. Before this time, rabbits did not exist in Australia. There were no <u>predators</u> to control the rabbit populations, and there was plenty of food. The rabbit population increased so fast that the country was soon overrun by rabbits. To control the rabbit population, the government introduced a virus that makes rabbits sick. The first time the virus was used, more than 99 percent of the rabbits died. The survivors reproduced, and the rabbit population grew large again.

1 According to this passage, a <u>predator</u> is

A an animal that lives only in Australia.

B an organism that hunts other organisms for food.

C a type of rabbit.

D a virus introduced by the government.

2 Based on information in this passage, the reader can conclude that

F rabbits are a vital part of the natural Australian environment.

G rabbits can resist any virus.

H Australians do not appreciate their government's rabbit control efforts.

J the Australian government considers rabbits to be pests.

LIFE SCIENCE • EARTH SCIENCE

Ocean Vents

▲ *"They're very slim, fuzzy, flattened-out worms. Really hairy,"* says scientist Bob Feldman about tube worms.

Picture the extreme depths of the ocean. There is no light at all, and it is very cold. But in the cracks between the plates on the bottom of the ocean floor, sea water trickles deep into the Earth. On the way back up from these cracks, the heated water collects metals, sulfuric gases, and enough heat to raise the temperature of the chilly water to 360°C. That is hot enough to melt lead! This heated sea water blasts up into the ocean through volcanic vents. And when this hot and toxic brew collides with icy ocean waters, the metals and sulfuric gases *precipitate,* that is, they settle out of the heated ocean water as solids.

These solids form tubes, called black smokers, that extend up through the ocean floor. To humans, this dark, cold, and toxic environment would be deadly. But to a community of about 300 species, including certain bacteria, clams, mussels, and tube worms, it is home. For these species, black smokers make life possible.

Life Without Photosynthesis

For a long time, scientists believed that energy from sunlight was the basis for all of Earth's food chains and for life itself. But in the last 15 years, researchers have discovered ecosystems that challenge this belief. We now know of organisms around black smokers that can live without sunlight. One type of bacterium uses toxic gases from a black smoker in the same way that plants use sunlight. In a process called *chemosynthesis,* these bacteria convert energy in sulfur compounds into energy the bacteria can use.

These bacteria are producers, and the mussels and clams are the consumers in this deep-sea food web. The bacteria use the mussels and clams as a sturdy place to live. The mussels and clams, in turn, feed off the bacteria. This kind of relationship between organisms is called *symbiosis.* The closer to the vent the clams and mussels are, the more likely the bacteria are to grow. As a result, the mussels and clams frequently move to spots near the black smokers.

What Do You Think?

▶ Conditions near black smokers are similar to conditions on other planets. Do some research on these extreme environments, both on Earth and elsewhere. Then discuss with your classmates where and how you think life on Earth may have started.

Classification of Living Things

Pre-Reading
Questions

1. What is classification?

2. How do people use classification in their everyday lives?

3. Why do scientists classify living things?

A Name Game

Suppose you discovered an insect that nobody had ever seen before. How would you go about naming it? You might give it a name based on its features. Or you could give it a name based on how you think that insect is related to other insects. Whatever name you choose, you want it to be as unique as the insect itself. That way, no one would confuse your insect with another insect. In this chapter, you will learn about how scientists name, organize, and classify living things.

CLASSIFYING SHOES

In this activity, you will develop a system of classification for shoes.

Procedure

1. Gather **10 different shoes.** Use **masking tape** and a **marker** to label each sole with a number (1–10).

2. Make a list of shoe features such as left or right, color, size, and laces or no laces. In your ScienceLog, make a table with a column for each feature. Complete the table by describing each shoe.

3. Use the data in the table to make a shoe identification key. The key should be a list of steps. Each step should have two statements about the shoes. The statements will lead you to two more statements. For example, step 1 might be:
   1a. This is a red sandal. Shoe #4
   1b. This isn't a red sandal. Go to step 2.

4. Each step should eliminate more shoes until only one shoe fits the description, such as in 1a, above. Check the number on the sole of the shoe to see if you are correct.

5. Trade keys with another student. How well does that key help you to identify the shoes?

Analysis

6. Could you identify the shoes using another person's key? Explain.

7. How helpful was it to list the shoe features before making the key?

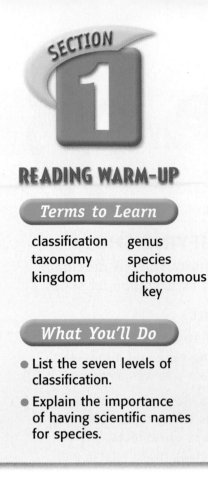
Terms to Learn

classification   genus
taxonomy   species
kingdom   dichotomous
               key

What You'll Do

• List the seven levels of classification.

• Explain the importance of having scientific names for species.

Classification: Sorting It All Out

Imagine that you live in a tropical rain forest and must get your own food, shelter, and clothing from the forest. If you are going to survive, what do you need to know?

You need to know which plants are safe to eat and which are not. You need to know which animals you can eat and which might eat you. In other words, you need to organize the living things around you into categories, or *classify* them. **Classification** means putting things into orderly groups based on how they are alike.

Why Classify?

For thousands of years, humans have classified living things based on their usefulness. The Chácabo people of Bolivia know of 360 different plants in the forest where they live. Of these plants, they have uses for 305.

Biologists also classify organisms—both living and extinct. They do this because there are countless different living things in the world. Making sense and order of them requires classification. Classifying living things makes it easier for biologists to find the answers to many important questions, such as the following:

◆ How many known species are there?
◆ What are the characteristics of each?
◆ What are the relationships between these species?

Biologists, such as the ones in **Figure 1,** use a system to classify living things. This system groups organisms according to the characteristics they share.

Figure 1 *These botanists are sorting rain forest plant material.*

What Is the Basis for Classification?

Until the 1700s, scientists divided organisms into two groups, plants and animals. But scientists found that some living things did not fit into either group. In the 1700s, a Swedish physician and botanist named Carolus Linnaeus (li NEE uhs) solved the problem. Linnaeus, shown in **Figure 2,** founded taxonomy. **Taxonomy** (taks AHN uh mee) is the science of identifying, classifying, and naming living things. Linnaeus tried to classify all known living things based on their shape and structure. He came up with a seven-level system of classification, which is still used today.

Figure 2 *Carolus Linnaeus classified more than 7,000 species of plants.*

Classification Today

Taxonomists classify living things based on their shared characteristics. Scientists also use shared characteristics to hypothesize how closely related living things are. The more characteristics the organisms share, the more closely related they may be. The platypus, brown bear, lion, and house cat are thought to be related because they share many characteristics. These animals have hair and mammary glands, so they are grouped together as mammals.

A brown bear, lion, and house cat share more characteristics with each other than they do with the platypus. Therefore, brown bears, lions, and house cats are labeled as part of a smaller group of mammals called Carnivora.

Look at the branching diagram in **Figure 3.** Several characteristics are listed along the line that points to the right. Each characteristic is shared by the animals to the right of it. All of the animals shown have hair and mammary glands. But only the brown bear, lion, and house cat give birth to live young. The lion and the house cat have retractable claws, which the other animals do not have. Thus, the lion and the house cat are more closely related to each other than to the other animals.

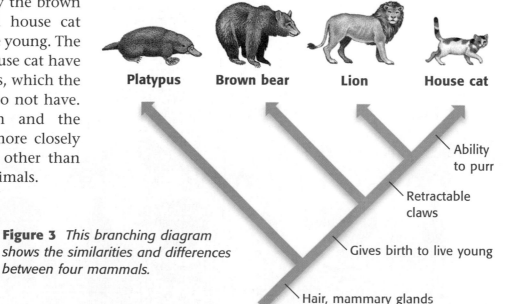

Figure 3 *This branching diagram shows the similarities and differences between four mammals.*

Levels of Classification

Every living thing is classified into one of six kingdoms. **Kingdoms** are the largest, most general groups. All living things in a kingdom are then sorted into several *phyla* (singular, *phylum*). The members of one phylum are more like each other than they are like members of other phyla. All of the living things in a phylum are further sorted into *classes*. Each class is divided into one or more *orders*. Orders are separated into *families*. Families are broken into genera (singular, **genus**). And genera are sorted into **species. Figure 4** below shows the classification of a house cat from kingdom Animalia to genus and species *Felis domesticus*.

Naming Names

By classifying organisms, biologists are able to give them scientific names. A scientific name is always the same for a specific organism no matter how many common names it might have. Before Linnaeus's time, however, scholars used names up to 12 words long to identify species. The names were hard to work with because they were so long. And different scientists named organisms differently, so an organism could have more than one name.

| Figure 4 | Seven Levels of Classification |

Kingdom Animalia	Phylum Chordata	Class Mammalia	Order Carnivora
All animals are in **kingdom Animalia.**	All animals in **phylum Chordata** have a hollow nerve cord. Most have a backbone.	Animals in the **class Mammalia** have a backbone. They also nurse their young.	Animals in the **order Carnivora** have a backbone and nurse their young. They also have special teeth for tearing meat.

Linnaeus made the naming of living things simpler by giving each species a two-part scientific name. The scientific name for the Indian elephant, for example, is *Elephas maximus*. The first part of the name, *Elephas*, is the genus. The second part, *maximus*, is the species. The genus name always begins with a capital letter. The species name always begins with a lowercase letter. Both words are underlined or italicized. No other species has this name. And all scientists understand that *Elephas maximus* refers to the Indian elephant. That is because all scientists now use the above rules for naming organisms.

It's All Greek (or Latin) to Me

Scientific names might seem difficult to understand because they are in Latin or Greek. But the scientific name can tell you a lot about an organism. You probably know the name of the animal shown in **Figure 5.** It's *Tyrannosaurus rex*! The first word combines two Greek words meaning "tyrant lizard." The second word is Latin for "king." You may have heard *Tyrannosaurus rex* called *T. rex*. This is okay in science as long as the genus name is spelled out the first time it is used. The scientific name is not correct without the genus name or its abbreviation.

Figure 5 *You would never call* Tyrannosaurus rex *just rex!*

Family *Felidae*	Genus *Felis*	Species *Felis domesticus*
Animals in the **family Felidae** are cats. They have a backbone, nurse their young, and have special teeth for tearing meat. Their claws can be drawn back into their paws.	Animals in the **genus Felis** have traits of other animals in the same family. However, these cats cannot roar; they can only purr.	**Species *Felis domesticus*** is the common house cat. It has traits of all the levels above it, but it also has other special traits.

Figure 6 *Using a two-part scientific name is a sure way for scientists to know they are discussing the same living thing.*

Why Are Scientific Names So Important?

Look at the cartoon in **Figure 6.** What do you call the small, black and white, sometimes smelly animal pictured? The skunk has several common names in English. It also has names in many other languages! All of these names can be confusing to biologists from different parts of the world who want to discuss the skunk. They need to know that they are all talking about the same animal. To do this, they use the skunk's scientific name, *Mephitis mephitis.* All known living things have a two-part scientific name.

Dichotomous Keys

Taxonomists have made special guides known as **dichotomous** (die KAHT uh muhs) **keys** to help identify unknown organisms. A dichotomous key has several pairs of descriptive statements. The person trying to make an identification looks at the first pair of statements. They choose the statement that best describes the organism. From there, the person is directed to another pair of statements. By working through the statements in the key, the person will be able to identify the organism. Use the dichotomous key on the next page to identify the two animals shown.

internet connect

SCILINKS
NSTA   GO TO: www.scilinks.org

TOPIC: The Basis for Classification
*sci*LINKS NUMBER: HSTL205

TOPIC: Levels of Classification
*sci*LINKS NUMBER: HSTL210

TOPIC: Dichotomous Keys
*sci*LINKS NUMBER: HSTL215

Dichotomous Key to 10 Common Mammals in the Eastern United States

1. a. This mammal flies. Its "hand" forms a wing. **b.** This mammal does not fly.	**Little brown bat** **Go to step 2.**
2. a. This mammal has no hair on its tail. **b.** This mammal has hair on its tail.	**Go to step 3.** **Go to step 4.**
3. a. This mammal has a short, naked tail. **b.** This mammal has a long, naked tail.	**Eastern mole** **Go to step 5.**
4. a. This mammal has a black mask across its face. **b.** This mammal does not have a black mask across its face.	**Raccoon** **Go to step 6.**
5. a. This mammal has a tail that is flat and paddle shaped. **b.** This mammal has a tail that is not flat or paddle shaped.	**Beaver** **Opossum**
6. a. This mammal is brown with a white underbelly. **b.** This mammal is not brown with a white underbelly.	**Go to step 7.** **Go to step 8.**
7. a. This mammal has a long, furry tail that is black on the tip. **b.** This mammal has a long tail without much fur.	**Longtail weasel** **White-footed mouse**
8. a. This mammal is black with a narrow white stripe on its forehead and broad white stripes on its back. **b.** This mammal is not black with white stripes.	**Striped skunk** **Go to step 9.**
9. a. This mammal has long ears and a short, cottony tail. **b.** This mammal has short ears and a medium-length tail.	**Eastern cottontail** **Woodchuck**

SECTION REVIEW

1 Why do scientists use scientific names for organisms?

2 List the seven levels of classification.

3 Describe how a dichotomous key helps to identify unknown organisms.

4 **Interpreting Illustrations** Study the figure at right.

    a. Which plant is the most similar to the hibiscus?

    b. Which plant is the least similar to the hibiscus?

    c. Which plants have seeds?

Moss   **Fern**   **Pine**   **Hibiscus**

Flowers

Seeds

Tissues that carry materials

Ability to live on land

Classification of Living Things   **299**

Terms to Learn

Archaebacteria   Plantae
Eubacteria   Fungi
Protista   Animalia

What You'll Do

● Explain how the kingdom system changed as greater numbers of different organisms became known.

● List the six kingdoms.

The Six Kingdoms

What do you call an organism that is green, makes its own food, lives in pond water, and moves? *Euglena*!

For over 2,000 years, all living things were classified as either plants or animals. These two kingdoms, Plantae and Animalia, included all living things until organisms like *Euglena* were discovered. *Euglena*, which is described above, is shown in **Figure 7.** If you were a taxonomist, how would you classify it?

Figure 7 *How would you classify this organism?* Euglena, *shown here magnified 1,000 times, has characteristics of both plants and animals.*

What Is It?

As you know, living things are classified by their characteristics. Being a good taxonomist, you decide to list the characteristics of *Euglena.*

◆ *Euglena* is a single-celled organism that lives in pond water.

◆ *Euglena* is green. Like most plants, it can make its own food through photosynthesis.

"Aha!" you think to yourself. "*Euglena* is a plant." Not so fast! There are other important characteristics to think about:

◆ *Euglena* can move about from place to place by whipping its "tail." The tail is called a *flagellum.*

◆ Sometimes *Euglena* gets its food from other living things.

Plants don't move around. And most plants do not eat other living things. Does this mean that *Euglena* is an animal? As you can see, it doesn't seem right to call *Euglena* a plant or an animal. Scientists ran into the same problem. So they decided to add a kingdom for classifying organisms such as *Euglena*. This kingdom is known as Protista. Most of the living things classified in Protista are very small, like *Euglena*.

BRAIN FOOD

If *Euglena*'s food-making parts, called chloroplasts, are shaded from light or are removed, the protist will begin to hunt for food, like an animal. If the chloroplasts are shaded long enough, they break down and never come back.

More Kingdoms

As scientists learned more about living things, they added more kingdoms. They did this because many organisms did not fit well into the existing kingdoms. Most scientists now agree that the six-kingdom classification system works best. There is still some disagreement, however, and there is still more to be learned about living things. In the following pages, you will learn about each kingdom.

Figure 8 *The water in the Grand Prismatic Spring, in Yellowstone National Park, is about 90°C (194°F). The spring is home to heat-loving archaebacteria.*

The Two Kingdoms of Bacteria

Bacteria are very small and have only one cell. They are different from all other living things because they are *prokaryotes*. This means they do not have nuclei. Many biologists divide bacteria into two kingdoms, Archaebacteria (AHR kee bak TIR ee uh) and Eubacteria (YOO bak TIR ee uh).

Archaebacteria have been on Earth for at least 3 billion years. The prefix *archae-* comes from a Greek word meaning "ancient." Today you can find archaebacteria in places where most living things could not survive. **Figure 8** shows a hot spring in Yellowstone National Park. Notice the yellow and orange rings around the edge of the hot spring. The rings are formed by the billions of archaebacteria that live there.

Most of the other thousands of kinds of bacteria are eubacteria. **Eubacteria** are tiny organisms that live almost every place on and near Earth's surface. They even live on and inside the human body! For example, the eubacterium *Escherichia coli* lives in great numbers in human intestines. It makes a chemical that helps your blood clot. *E. coli* is shown in **Figure 9.** Another kind of eubacterium changes milk to yogurt. And another species causes ear and sinus infections and pneumonia.

Figure 9 E. coli, *such as those shown here on the point of a pin, can be seen with a scanning electron microscope. These eubacteria live in the intestines of animals. They break down undigested food.*

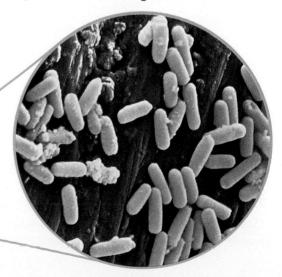

Kingdom Protista

Members of the kingdom Protista, or protists, are single-celled or simple, many-celled living things. Unlike bacteria, protists are *eukaryotes*. This means that their cells have a nucleus and other organelles surrounded by a membrane. Kingdom **Protista** includes all eukaryotes that are not plants, animals, or fungi. Scientists think the first protists appeared about 2 billion years ago.

Kingdom Protista contains many different kinds of living things. Protozoa (PROHT oh ZOH uh) are animal-like protists. Algae are plantlike protists. Slime molds and water molds are funguslike protists. *Euglena,* which you read about on page 300, is a protist. So are the *Paramecium* and the slime mold pictured in **Figures 10** and **11.** Most protists have only one cell, but some have many cells. An example is the giant kelp shown in **Figure 12.**

Figure 10 Paramecium *usually moves about rapidly.* ▼

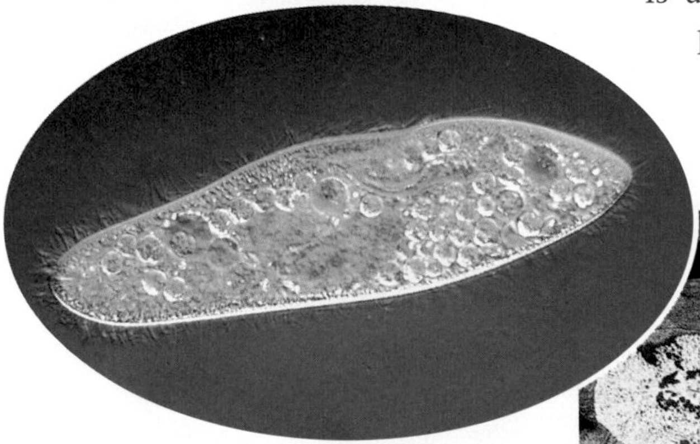

Figure 11 *A slime mold spreads over a fallen log on the forest floor.* ▶

Figure 12 *This giant kelp is a many-celled protist.* ▶

Self-Check

1. How are the two kingdoms of bacteria different from all other kingdoms?

2. Explain why protists are eukaryotes.

(See page 640 to check your answers.)

Kingdom Plantae

Although plants range greatly in size and form, most people can quickly spot members of the kingdom **Plantae.** Plants are complex and have many cells. Most plants tend to be green. They use the sun's energy to make sugar by a process called *photosynthesis.* Take a look at the giant sequoias and the flowering plants shown in **Figures 13** and **14.** They are examples of the many species in the kingdom Plantae.

Figure 13 *A giant sequoia can measure 30 m around its base. It can also grow to more than 91.5 m tall.*

MathBreak

Building a Human Chain Around a Giant Sequoia

How many students would it take to form a human chain around a giant sequoia that is 30 m in circumference? Assume that the average student's arms can span about 1.3 m. (Note: You can't have a fraction of a student, so be sure to round your answer up to the next whole number.)

Environment CONNECTION

Giant sequoia trees, *Sequoiadendron giganteum,* are very rare. They grow only in California and are a protected species. Some are over 3,000 years old.

Figure 14 *Plants such as these are common in the rain forest.*

Kingdom Fungi

Molds and mushrooms are members of the kingdom Fungi. Nearly all members of kingdom **Fungi** have many cells. They were once grouped as plants. But unlike plants, fungi (singular, *fungus*) do not make their own food. They also have few animal-like characteristics. Because fungi are so different from plants and animals, they have been placed in a separate kingdom.

Instead of making food or eating, fungi soak up what they need from their surroundings. They do this after using their digestive juices to break down dead or living matter into nutrients. The mushrooms in **Figure 15** and the the black bread mold in **Figure 16** absorb nutrients from their surroundings. Where have you seen fungi growing?

Figure 15 *These beautiful mushrooms of the genus* Amanita *are poisonous.*

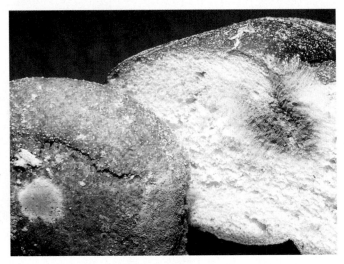

Figure 16 *Don't take a whiff of this black bread mold! Some molds are dangerous. Other molds can be used to make life-saving drugs.*

Classify This! ⭐TEKS

You and a friend are walking through the forest, and you find the living thing shown at right. You think it is a plant, but you are not sure. It has a flower and seeds, very small leaves, and roots growing into a rotting log. It's also white from petals to roots! To which kingdom do you think this organism belongs? Give a reasonable explanation of your answer. What other information would you need to be sure of your answer?

Kingdom Animalia

Animals belong to the kingdom **Animalia.** Their bodies have many cells, and most animals can move about. They also have nervous systems that help them sense and react to their surroundings. At the microscopic level, animal cells are different from the cells of fungi, plants, most protists, and bacteria. This is because most animal cells do not have cell walls. **Figure 17** shows some members of the kingdom Animalia.

Figure 17 *The kingdom Animalia contains many different organisms. These are just a few of them.*

Giant tortoise

Northern mockingbird

Bead coral

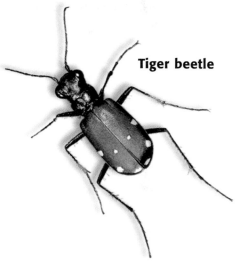

Tiger beetle

SECTION REVIEW

❶ Name the six kingdoms.

❷ Explain how the kingdom system changed as greater numbers of organisms became known.

❸ Explain the different ways that plants, fungi, and animals obtain nutrients.

❹ Why are protists placed in their own kingdom?

❺ **Applying Concepts** What is the kingdom to which humans belong? Explain your answer.

☑ internet**connect**

SC*i*LINKS.
NSTA GO TO: www.scilinks.org

TOPIC: The Six Kingdoms
*sci*LINKS NUMBER: HSTL220

Skill Builder Lab

Shape Island

You are a biologist looking for new animal species. You sailed for days across the ocean and finally found an uncharted island hundreds of miles south of Hawaii. You decide to call it Shape Island. This island has some very unusual organisms. Each of them has some variation of a geometric shape. You have spent over a year collecting specimens and classifying them according to Linnaeus's system. You have given a scientific name to most species you have collected. You must give names to the last 12 specimens before you sail for home.

Procedure

1 In your ScienceLog, draw each of the organisms shown below. Beside each one, draw a line for its name, as shown on the following page. The first one has been named for you, but you have 12 more to name. Use the glossary of Greek and Latin prefixes, suffixes, and root words on page 307 to help you name the organisms.

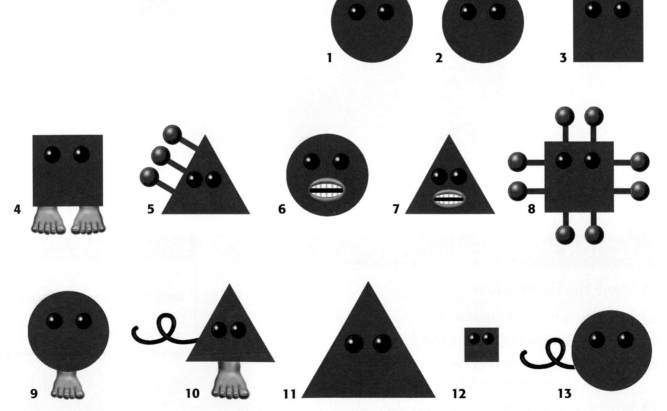

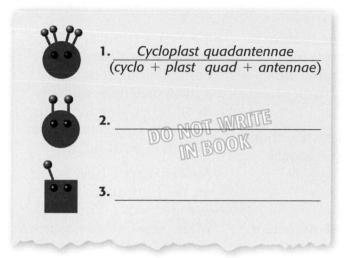

1. *Cycloplast quadantennae*
   (*cyclo* + *plast* *quad* + *antennae*)

2. _____ DO NOT WRITE IN BOOK

3. _____

Glossary	
Greek and Latin roots, prefixes, and suffixes	**Meaning**
ankylos	angle
antennae	external sense organs
tri-	three
bi-	two
cyclo-	circle
macro-	large
micro-	small
mono-	one
peri-	all around
-plast	body
-pod	foot
quad-	four
stoma	mouth
uro-	tail

2 One more organism lives on Shape Island, but you have not been able to capture it. Unfortunately, your supplies are running out, and soon you must sail home. You have had a good look at the unusual animal and can draw it in detail. In your ScienceLog, draw an animal that is different from all the others. Then use the glossary at right to help you give the animal a two-part scientific name.

Analysis

3 If you gave species 1 a common name, such as round-face-no-nose, would other scientists know which new organism you were referring to? Explain.

4 Describe two characteristics shared by all of your specimens from Shape Island.

Going Further

Look up the scientific names listed below. You can use the library, the Internet, a taxonomy index, or field guides.

- *Mertensia virginica*
- *Porcellio scaber*

For each organism, answer the following questions: Is it a plant or an animal? How many common names does it have? How many scientific names does it have?

Think of the name of your favorite fruit or vegetable. Find out if it has other common names, and find out its two-part scientific name.

Highlights

Vocabulary

classification *(p. 294)*
taxonomy *(p. 295)*
kingdom *(p. 296)*
genus *(p. 296)*
species *(p. 296)*
dichotomous key *(p. 298)*

Section Notes

- Classification refers to the arrangement of things into orderly groups based on their similarities.

- Biologists classify living things to organize their number and variety. Each type of classified organism is given a unique scientific name.

- The classification system used today is based on the work of Carolus Linnaeus. Linnaeus founded taxonomy, the science of identifying, classifying, and naming living things. ★TEKS

- Modern classification takes into account shared characteristics among organisms.

- Today's living things are classified using a seven-level system of organization. The seven levels are kingdom, phylum, class, order, family, genus, and species. The genus and species of an organism make up its two-part scientific name.

- A scientific name is always the same for a specific organism, no matter how many common names the organism has.

- Dichotomous keys are tools for identifying unknown organisms.

LabBook ★TEKS

Voyage of the USS *Adventure* *(p. 620)*

Vocabulary

Archaebacteria *(p. 301)*
Eubacteria *(p. 301)*
Protista *(p. 302)*
Plantae *(p. 303)*
Fungi *(p. 304)*
Animalia *(p. 305)*

Section Notes

- At first, living things were classified as either plants or animals. As scientists learned more about living things and discovered more organisms, they added more kingdoms to classify organisms that were not plants or animals. ★TEKS

- Most biologists today recognize six kingdoms—Archaebacteria, Eubacteria, Protista, Plantae, Fungi, and Animalia.

- Bacteria are prokaryotes, which means they have one cell and do not have a nucleus. The organisms in all other kingdoms are eukaryotes, organisms that have cells with nuclei.

- Archaebacteria have been on Earth for more than 3 billion years. They live where most other organisms cannot survive.

- Most bacteria are eubacteria and live almost everywhere. Some are harmful and some are helpful to humans.

- Plants, most fungi, and animals are complex, many-celled living things. Plants perform photosynthesis. Fungi break down material outside their body and then absorb the nutrients. Animals eat food, which is digested inside their body.

USING VOCABULARY

Complete the following sentences by choosing the correct term from each pair of terms.

1. Linnaeus founded the science of __?__. (*dichotomous keys* or *taxonomy*) ⭐TEKS

2. All of the organisms classified into a single kingdom are then divided into one of several __?__. (*phyla* or *classes*)

3. The narrowest level of classification is the __?__. (*genus* or *species*)

4. Linnaeus began naming organisms using __?__. (*two-part scientific names* or *structures*) ⭐TEKS

5. Archaebacteria and eubacteria are __?__. (*prokaryotes* or *eukaryotes*)

UNDERSTANDING CONCEPTS

Multiple Choice

6. When scientists classify organisms, they
   a. arrange them in orderly groups.
   b. give them a common name.
   c. decide whether they are useful.
   d. ignore physical characteristics.

7. When the seven levels of classification are listed from broadest to narrowest, which level is listed fifth?
   a. class
   b. order
   c. genus
   d. family

8. The scientific name for the European white waterlily is *Nymphaea alba*. What is the genus to which this plant belongs?
   a. *Nymphaea*
   b. *alba*
   c. waterlily
   d. alba lily

9. A dichotomous key does NOT contain
   a. steps that lead to earlier steps.
   b. steps that lead to later steps.
   c. pairs of descriptive statements.
   d. characteristics of some living things.

10. Most bacteria alive today are classified in which kingdom?
    a. Archaebacteria
    b. Eubacteria
    c. Protista
    d. Fungi

11. What kind of organism thrives in hot springs and other extreme environments?
    a. archaebacteria
    b. eubacteria
    c. protists
    d. fungi

Short Answer

12. Why is the use of scientific names so important in biology? ⭐TEKS

13. What kind of evidence is used by modern taxonomists to classify organisms?

14. Is a eubacterium, such as the *E. coli* shown below, a type of eukaryote? Explain your answer.

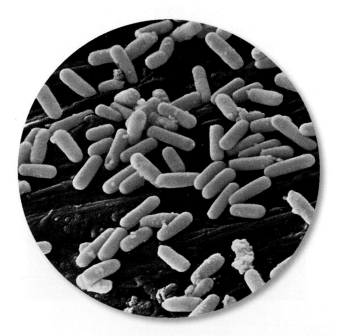

CONCEPT MAPPING

15. Use the following terms to create a concept map: *kingdom, fern, lizard, Animalia, Fungi, algae, Protista, Plantae,* and *mushroom.*

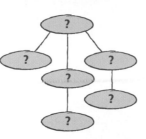

CRITICAL THINKING AND PROBLEM SOLVING

Write one or two sentences to answer the following questions:

16. Explain how the seven levels of classification depend on the similarities and differences between organisms. ⭐TEKS

17. Explain why two species that belong to the same genus, such as white oak (*Quercus alba*) and cork oak (*Quercus suber*), also belong to the same family.

18. What characteristic do the members of all six kingdoms have in common?

MATH IN SCIENCE

19. Scientists estimate that out of the millions of species on Earth, only 1.5 million, or one-tenth, of all species have been discovered and classified. How many species do scientists think exist on Earth?

20. Sequoia trees can grow to more than 90 m in height. There are 3.28 ft in a meter. How many feet are in 90 m?

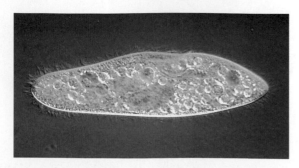

INTERPRETING GRAPHICS

Use the branching diagram below to answer the questions that follow.

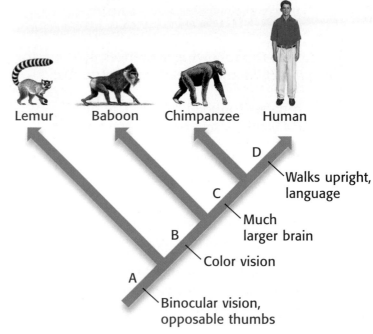

21. Which animal shares the most traits with humans? ⭐TEKS

22. Do lemurs share the characteristics listed at point D with humans? Explain your answer. ⭐TEKS

23. What characteristic do baboons have that lemurs do not have? Explain your answer. ⭐TEKS

Reading Check-up

Take a minute to review your answers to the Pre-Reading Questions found at the bottom of page 292. Have your answers changed? If necessary, revise your answers based on what you have learned since you began this chapter.

Chapter 11

1 Assume that you are a scientist who is studying how the bones of a fossilized dinosaur fit together. You might use a computer to examine the data by drawing which of the following?

A Graphs that have *x*- and *y*-axes

B Tables that have rows and columns

C Maps that show locations

D Charts that show pictures

2 In the history of classification, which of the following happened FIRST?

F *Euglena* was discovered.

G Linnaeus gave each species a 2-part name.

H Species were identified with up to 12 words.

J A sixth kingdom was added.

3 Below is part of a field guide that several students have been using to identify trees in a local park. The students noticed that one plant has thin 1.20 centimeter needles that occur in clusters. Which of the following conclusions is correct?

A The plant is deciduous.

B The plant is an Eastern white pine.

C The plant is a *Pinus rigida*.

D The plant cannot be identified from the information provided.

A Dichotomous Key to Common Trees of the Northeastern United States

1. a. Leaves are thin and needlelike (coniferous) . . . . Go to 2
   b. Leaves are broad and fanlike (deciduous) . . . . Go to 6

2. a. Needles are over 2.5 cm long and are clustered . . . . Go to 3
   b. Needles are 1.25 cm long or less . . . . Go to 4

3. a. Needles occur in clusters of 3 . . . . Pitch pine *(Pinus rigida)*
   b. Needles occur in clusters of 5 . . . . Eastern white pine
      (Pinus strobus)

Chapter 11

Math

1 Which group contains ratios that are all equivalent to $\frac{5}{6}$?

A $\frac{10}{12}, \frac{15}{18}, \frac{20}{24}$

B $\frac{5}{12}, \frac{10}{24}, \frac{24}{30}$

C $\frac{3}{12}, \frac{20}{24}, \frac{30}{36}$

D $\frac{10}{18}, \frac{15}{24}, \frac{20}{30}$

2 The city zoo collected $3616 from entrance fees over the weekend. If admission was $8 per person, how many people visited the zoo over the weekend?

F 442

G 452

H 458

J 462

3 How is the product $3 \times 3 \times 3 \times 3 \times 7 \times 7$ expressed in exponential notation?

A 63^2

B $4^3 \times 2^7$

C $3^4 \times 7^2$

D $3 \times 4 \times 7 \times 2$

4 Jeanne is standing under a basketball hoop that is 3.05 meters above the ground. Jeanne is 1.7 meters tall. How far above Jeanne's head is the basketball hoop?

F 1.35 m

G 1.45 m

H 1.8 m

J 2.05 m

Reading

Read the passage. Then read each question that follows the passage. Decide which is the best answer to each question.

Skunks were once thought to be most closely related to weasels, ferrets, minks, badgers, and otters. Those furry, short-legged, long-bodied, meat-eating mammals are grouped together in a <u>family</u> called *Mustelidae. Mustelidae* comes from the Latin word for "mouse." The animals listed above were put in the Mustelidae family because they all share several physical characteristics with mice, such as short, round ears and short legs. But a researcher discovered that the DNA of skunks is very different from the DNA of other members of that family. Now skunks are classified in their own family, *Mephitidae,* from the Latin word that means "bad odor."

1 Skunks were classified in their own family because they

A have a bad odor.

B have shorter legs than weasels.

C have different DNA from members of Mustelidae.

D do not look like mice.

2 In this passage, the word <u>family</u> means

F a group of animals that have fur, short legs, and long bodies.

G a group of animals that share certain characteristics.

H a group of animals that are related to weasels.

J a group of animals that smell bad.

It's a Bird, It's a Plane, It's a *Dinosaur*?

It may seem hard to believe, but at one time there were no birds. So where did they come from? When did birds appear? Trying to answer these questions has fueled a heated debate among scientists. The debate began when the fossil remains of a 150-million-year-old dinosaur with wings and feathers—*Archaeopteryx* (AHR kee AHP tuh riks)—were found in Germany in 1860 and 1861.

▲ *Was* Archaeopteryx *the first true bird?*

Birds Are Dinosaurs!

Some scientists think that birds evolved from small, meat-eating dinosaurs like *Velociraptor* about 115 million to 150 million years ago. Their claim relies on similarities between modern birds and these small dinosaurs. Both have a similar size, shape, and number of toes and "fingers." The location and shape of the breastbone and shoulder are similar as well. Both also have a hollow bone structure and wrist bones that "flap" for flight. To many scientists, this evidence can lead to only one conclusion: Modern birds are descendants of dinosaurs.

No They Aren't!

"Not so fast!" says a smaller group of scientists. They think that birds developed 100 million years before *Velociraptor* and its relatives. They point out that all of these dinosaurs were ground dwellers. Also, they were the wrong shape and size for flying and would never get off the ground! In addition, these dinosaurs were missing at least one of the bones that today's birds need to fly.

Thecodonts, small tree-dwelling reptiles, lived about 225 million years ago. One thecodont, a small, four-legged tree dweller called *Megalancosaurus,* had the right bones and body shape—and the right center of gravity—for flight. And fossils of the oldest known bird, *Protoavis,* are estimated to be 225 million years old. The evidence is clear, say these scientists, that birds flew long before dinosaurs even existed!

So Who Is Right?

Both sides are debating about fossils 65 million years to 225 million years old. Some species left many fossils, while some left just a few. In the

▲ *This small tree-dwelling reptile,* Megalancosaurus, *had many similar characteristics to the birds we know today.*

last few years, new fossils discovered in China, Mongolia, Texas, and Argentina have added fuel to the fire. *Archaeoraptor liaoningensis,* once believed to be the missing link between dinosaurs and birds, was later found to be a fake. It was actually a fossilized dinosaur tail glued onto the body of a fossilized bird. The debate rages on!

Decide for Yourself

▶ Find photographs of *Protoavis* and *Archaeopteryx* fossils, and compare them. How are they similar? How are they different? Do you think birds could be modern dinosaurs? Debate your idea with someone who holds the opposite view.

UNIT 4

The Animal Kingdom

SCIENCE

Place to Visit

Fairfield ★

Gather 'round! Come see the amazing bald eagles! The bald eagle is one of the most recognizable birds in the country. But where do you go to see live ones? Texas, of course! One of the best places to see bald eagles is Fairfield Lake State Park. Many bald eagles spend the winter months there, eating local fish. You can take boat tours in the park between November and February. While you are watching the beautiful birds, your tour guide will tell you what the Texas Parks and Wildlife Department is learning about the health and populations of the bald eagles.

Bald eagle, Fairfield Lake State Park

Scientific Research

David Bamberger built a home for a million of his friends near Johnson City, Texas. The home he built is a cave, and his friends are bats! The 800 m² cave was designed as a habitat for bats. It has special lighting, crevices for bats, and an observation area for scientists. Nearby ponds and farmland have a lot of insects for the bats to eat. Bamberger hopes that about 1 million bats will move into his cave so that scientists can observe the bats over long periods of time.

Johnson City

Science Career

Brownsville

Linda Laack dedicates her time to preserving and studying the endangered ocelot. Ocelots are spotted cats that are a little larger than house cats. Laack works as a biologist for the Laguna Atascosa National Wildlife Refuge near Brownsville, Texas. She works with ranchers to protect ocelot habitats. She also traps ocelots to make sure they are healthy and to fit them with radio collars. The collars send out signals that give Laack data about the cats' whereabouts. The radio-collar data, combined with her years of experience with ocelots, allow Laack to help these beautiful cats survive.

Pre-Reading Questions

1. How are sponges different from other invertebrates?

2. What characteristics do all insects have?

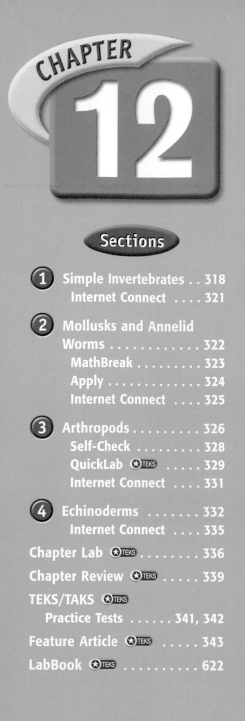

CLASSIFY IT! ⭐TEKS

Animals are classified according to their different characteristics, including their internal and external features. In this activity, you will try your hand at classification.

Procedure

1. Look at the **pictures** that your teacher has provided. Scientists group all of these animals together because these animals do not have backbones.

2. Which animals are the most alike? Put them in the same group.

3. For each group, decide which animals within the group are the most alike. Put these animals into smaller groups inside the larger group.

4. In your ScienceLog or using a computer, construct a table that organizes your classification groups.

Analysis

5. What features did you use to classify these animals into groups? Explain why you think these features are the most important.

6. What features did you use to place the animals in smaller groups? Explain your reasoning.

7. Compare your table with those of your classmates. What similarities or differences do you find?

A SCI-FI SLUG?

No, this isn't an alien! It's a sea slug, a close relative of garden slugs and snails. This sea slug lives in the cold Pacific Ocean near the coast of California. Its bright coloring comes from the food that the slug eats. This animal doesn't use lungs to breathe. Instead, it brings oxygen into its body through the spikes on its back.

Sea slugs don't have a backbone. In this chapter, you will discover many other animals that do not have backbones.

Terms to Learn

invertebrate
bilateral symmetry
radial symmetry
asymmetry

What You'll Do

● Describe the different types of symmetry found in invertebrates.

● Explain how a sponge feeds.

● Identify a cnidarian's response to an external stimulus. ⭐TEKS

Simple Invertebrates

Humans and snakes have them, but octopuses and butterflies don't. What are they? Backbones!

Animals that don't have backbones are known as **invertebrates** (in VUHR tuh brits). They make up about 96 percent of all animal species. So far, more than 1 million invertebrates have been discovered and named.

No Backbones Here!

Invertebrates come in many different shapes and sizes. Grasshoppers, clams, earthworms, and jellyfish are examples of invertebrates. They are all very different from each other. But like all organisms, invertebrates have cells that carry out functions that sustain life. Invertebrates also have many special structures that help them function in their environment.

Invertebrates have two basic body plans, or types of *symmetry*. Symmetry can be bilateral (bie LAT uhr uhl) or radial (RAY dee uhl). Some animals have no symmetry at all. Animals that don't have symmetry are said to have *asymmetry* (ay SIM uh tree). **Figure 1** shows examples of these types of symmetry.

Figure 1 **Animal Body Plans**

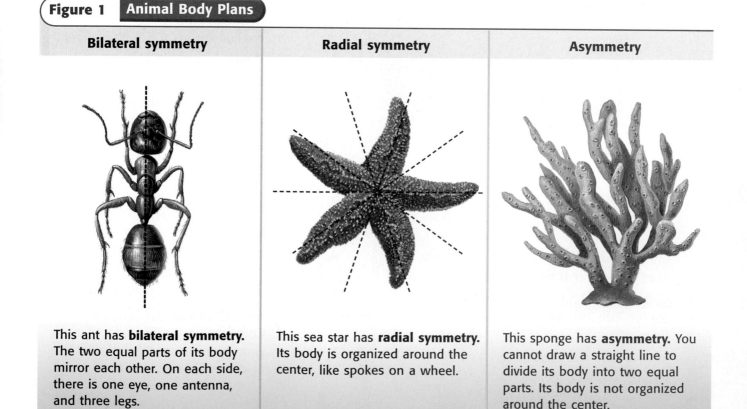

Bilateral symmetry	Radial symmetry	Asymmetry
This ant has **bilateral symmetry.** The two equal parts of its body mirror each other. On each side, there is one eye, one antenna, and three legs.	This sea star has **radial symmetry.** Its body is organized around the center, like spokes on a wheel.	This sponge has **asymmetry.** You cannot draw a straight line to divide its body into two equal parts. Its body is not organized around the center.

Sponges

Sponges are the simplest invertebrates. They are asymmetrical and have no head or nerves. Some sponges can move, but they do so very slowly. In fact, sponges were once thought to be plants!

How Do Sponges Eat?

Unlike plants, sponges cannot make their own food. They must eat other organisms. That's one reason why sponges are classified as animals. Sponges use special cells to filter food from their surroundings.

Sponges feed on small pieces of plants and animals in the water. The structure of a sponge is shown in **Figure 2.** A sponge sweeps water into its body through its *pores*. Pores are the holes on the outside of the sponge's body. Inside the body are cells called *collar cells*. Their function is to remove food from the water and to digest food. Water flows into a central cavity in the middle of the body and then leaves through a hole at the top of the sponge's body. This hole is called the *osculum* (AHS kyoo luhm).

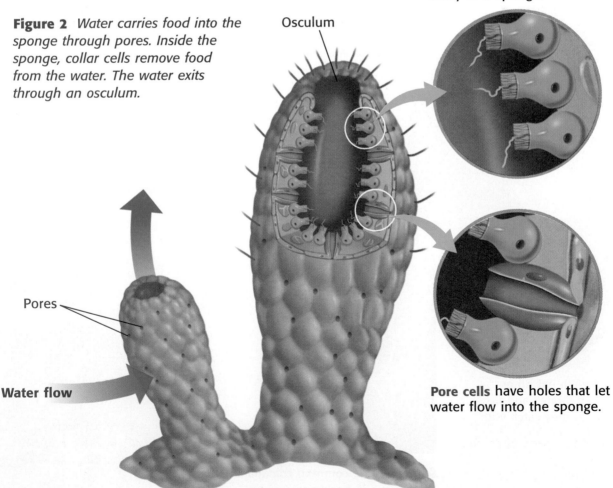

Figure 2 *Water carries food into the sponge through pores. Inside the sponge, collar cells remove food from the water. The water exits through an osculum.*

Osculum

Collar cells line the central cavity of a sponge.

Pores

Water flow

Pore cells have holes that let water flow into the sponge.

Cnidarians

Take a look at the organisms shown in **Figure 3.** They look very different from one another. But all of these animals are simple invertebrates called *cnidarians* (ni DER ee uhnz). They all have radial symmetry.

Cnidarians are more complex than sponges. They have tissues and a gut for digesting food. They also have a simple nervous system. Many cnidarians can move.

All cnidarians have tentacles covered with stinging cells. When another organism brushes against the cnidarian, these cells respond by firing into the enemy. Each stinging cell uses water pressure to fire a tiny, poisonous spear.

Figure 3 **Kinds of Cnidarians**

Corals are tiny cnidarians that live in colonies on *reefs.* Reefs are rocky, underwater structures formed from the remains of corals and algae. ▶

Sea anemones look like brightly colored flowers. Like flowers, most sea anemones stay in one place. But some species can crawl or swim. ▼

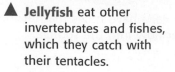

▲ **Jellyfish** eat other invertebrates and fishes, which they catch with their tentacles.

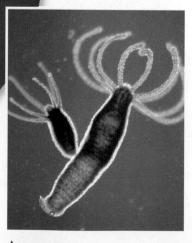

▲ **Hydras** are common cnidarians that live in fresh water.

Flatworms

When you think of worms, you probably think of earthworms. But there are many kinds of worms besides earthworms. Most worms are too tiny to see without a microscope. The simplest group of worms are flatworms. They have bilateral symmetry. These worms are divided into three classes: planarians (pluh NER ee uhnz), flukes, and tapeworms.

Planarians

As you can see in **Figure 4,** *planarians* have a clearly defined head and two large eyespots. The head has flaps called *sensory lobes* on each side. The flaps help the worm find food by smell. Most planarians eat other animals.

Flukes and Tapeworms

The two other groups of flatworms are *flukes* and *tapeworms*. These animals are parasites. A *parasite* is a living thing that feeds on another living thing, called the *host.* Most of the time, the parasite does not kill the host. Most flukes and all tapeworms live inside the bodies of host animals.

Flukes and tapeworms have tiny heads without eyespots or sensory lobes. They use special suckers and hooks to fasten themselves onto the host.

Roundworms

Roundworms have bodies that are long, slim, and round like spaghetti. Like other worms, they have bilateral symmetry. Most roundworms are tiny. Many break down dead plants and animals and help build rich soils. Other roundworms are parasites of plants or animals. **Figure 5** shows a roundworm.

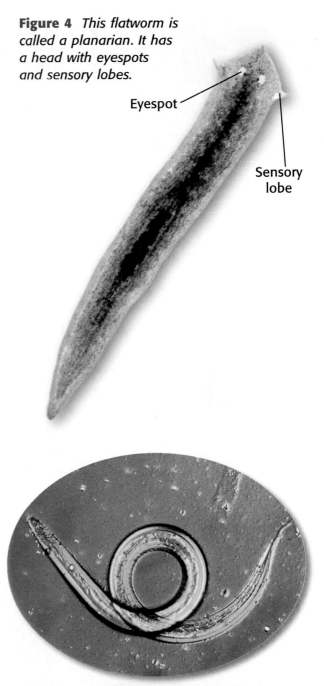

Figure 4 *This flatworm is called a planarian. It has a head with eyespots and sensory lobes.*

Eyespot

Sensory lobe

Figure 5 *Roundworms have tubelike bodies.*

SECTION REVIEW

1. Explain how sponges feed.

2. Identify one response in cnidarians to an external stimulus, such as being touched by a fish. **⊙**TEKS

3. **Inferring Conclusions** Explain why the host's survival is important to a parasite.

internetconnect

*sci*LINKS.
NSTA   GO TO: www.scilinks.org

TOPIC: Sponges
*sci*LINKS NUMBER: HSTL355

TOPIC: Roundworms
*sci*LINKS NUMBER: HSTL360

READING WARM-UP

Terms to Learn

open circulatory system
closed circulatory system
segment

What You'll Do

● Compare and contrast the classes of mollusks.

● Explain the differences between an open circulatory system and a closed circulatory system.

● Identify how a radula's structure complements its function. ⭐TEKS

Mollusks and Annelid Worms

Have you ever eaten clams or calamari? Have you ever seen earthworms on the sidewalk after it rains?

If you have, then you already know a thing or two about mollusks and annelid worms. These animals are more complex than the invertebrates you have read about. For example, mollusks and annelid worms have a circulatory system that moves materials throughout their bodies.

Mollusks

Snails, slugs, clams, oysters, squids, and octopuses are all mollusks. Most of these animals live in the ocean. But some live in fresh water, and a few even live on land.

Most mollusks fit into three classes. The *gastropods* (GAS troh PAHDZ) include slugs and snails. The *bivalves* include clams and other shellfish that have two shells. *Cephalopods* (SEF uh loh PAHDZ) include squids and octopuses.

How Do Mollusks Eat?

Each kind of mollusk has its own way of eating. Clams and oysters sit in one place and use gills to filter tiny plants, bacteria, and other particles from the water. Snails and slugs eat with a ribbonlike organ—a tongue covered with curved teeth. This organ is called a radula (RAJ oo luh). **Figure 6** shows a close-up of a slug's radula. Slugs and snails use the radula to scrape algae off rocks, chunks of tissue from seaweed, or pieces from the leaves of plants. Octopuses and squids use tentacles to grab their food and place it in their powerful jaws.

Figure 6 *The rows of teeth on a slug's radula help scrape food from surfaces.*

Have a Heart

Most mollusks have an open circulatory system. In an **open circulatory system,** a simple heart pumps blood through blood vessels that empty into spaces in the animal's body called *sinuses*. This is very different from the human circulatory system. Humans have a closed circulatory system. In a **closed circulatory system,** a heart circulates blood through a network of blood vessels that form a closed loop. Squids and octopuses also have a closed circulatory system.

It's a Brain!

Cephalopods have a more complex nervous system than do other mollusks. Octopuses and squids have the most advanced nervous system of all invertebrates. They have a large brain, which makes these animals the smartest invertebrates.

Mollusk Bodies

A snail, a clam, and a squid look quite different from one another. Yet if you look closely, you will see that their bodies all have similar structures. A mollusk has a soft body. In most cases, it is covered by a shell. All mollusks also have a foot, a visceral (VIS uhr uhl) mass, and a mantle. The body parts of mollusks are described below in **Figure 7.**

MathBreak

Speeding Squid

If a squid is swimming at 30 km/h, how many kilometers can it go in 1 minute?

Figure 7 — Body Parts of Mollusks

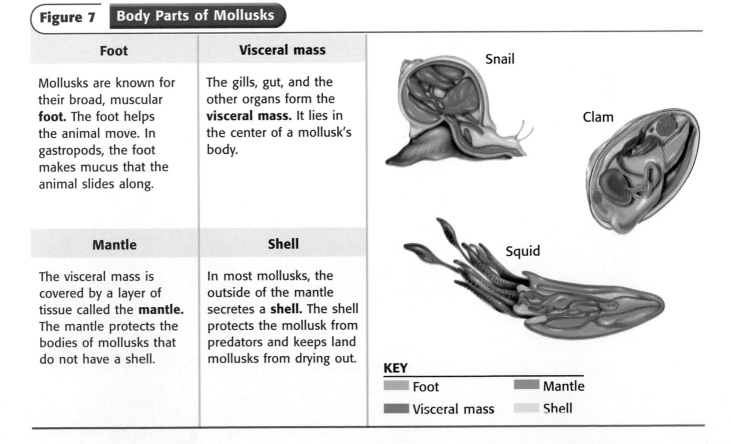

Foot	Visceral mass
Mollusks are known for their broad, muscular **foot.** The foot helps the animal move. In gastropods, the foot makes mucus that the animal slides along.	The gills, gut, and the other organs form the **visceral mass.** It lies in the center of a mollusk's body.

Mantle	Shell
The visceral mass is covered by a layer of tissue called the **mantle.** The mantle protects the bodies of mollusks that do not have a shell.	In most mollusks, the outside of the mantle secretes a **shell.** The shell protects the mollusk from predators and keeps land mollusks from drying out.

Snail

Clam

Squid

KEY

Foot   Mantle

Visceral mass   Shell

Annelid Worms

Earthworms are annelid worms. Annelid worms are often called segmented worms because their bodies have segments. **Segments** are identical, or almost identical, repeating body parts. You can see the segments of an earthworm in **Figure 8.**

Like roundworms and flatworms, annelid worms have bilateral symmetry. But these worms are more complex than flatworms and roundworms. For example, annelid worms have a closed circulatory system.

Annelid worms live in salt water, in fresh water, or on land. They eat plant material or animals. Annelid worms fall into three classes: earthworms, bristle worms, and leeches.

More Than Just Bait

Earthworms are the most common annelid worms. Each one has 100 to 175 segments, most of which are identical. Some segments look different from the others. They have special jobs, such as eating or reproducing.

Earthworms eat soil. They break down plant and animal matter in the soil and leave behind wastes called *castings*. Castings make the soil richer for plants to grow in. Earthworms also improve the soil by digging tunnels. The tunnels allow air and water to reach deep into the soil.

Earthworms have stiff bristles on the outside of their bodies that help them move. The bristles hold the back part of the worm in place while the front part pushes through the soil.

Figure 8 *Except for the head, tail, and reproductive segments, all the segments of this earthworm are identical.*

Tail

Reproductive segments

Head

APPLY

Do Worms Make Good Neighbors?

Your friend has decided to start a new hobby, organic gardening. People who grow organic gardens don't use human-made chemicals to fertilize or to control weeds and pests. Write a letter to your friend, and explain how invertebrates can help out in the garden.

Bristles Can Be Beautiful

If there were a beauty contest for worms, bristle worms would win. These outstanding worms come in many colorful varieties. **Figure 9** shows a bristle worm. All bristle worms live in water. Some crawl along the bottom of the ocean. There they eat mollusks and other small animals. Others dig through wet sand and mud and eat whatever small animals and pieces of food they find.

Blood Suckers and More

Leeches are known mostly as parasites that suck other animals' blood. This is true of some leeches. But some leeches are not parasites. Some leeches are scavengers that eat dead animals. Others are predators that prey on insects, slugs, and snails.

But leeches aren't all bad. They can even be useful. After surgery, doctors sometimes use leeches to prevent dangerous swelling near a wound, as shown in **Figure 10.** These worms also make a chemical that keeps blood from forming clots. Modern doctors often give heart attack patients medicines that contain this chemical to prevent and break down blood clots.

Figure 9 *This bristle worm feeds by filtering particles from the water with its bristles. Can you see the segments on this worm?*

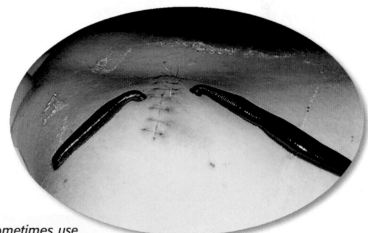

Figure 10 *Doctors sometimes use leeches to reduce swelling after surgery.*

SECTION REVIEW

1. Name the three classes of mollusks. How are they alike? How are they different?

2. Explain the differences between an open circulatory system and a closed circulatory system.

3. How does a radula's structure complement its function? ★TEKS

4. **Analyzing Relationships** How are annelid worms different from flatworms and roundworms? What characteristics do these worms share?

READING WARM-UP

Terms to Learn

exoskeleton
compound eye
antennae
metamorphosis

What You'll Do

- Describe how an arthropod's body structure complements its function. ⭐TEKS
- Identify an arthropod based on its features.
- Explain the two kinds of metamorphosis in insects.

Arthropods

Do you get a fright at the sight of creepy, crawly critters? Do bugs bug you? Maybe you look away before you have a chance to get a really good look at them. But insects really aren't that bad. In fact, we couldn't live without them.

They have lived here for hundreds of millions of years and have adapted to nearly every environment. An acre of land has millions of them. You know them by their everyday names, such as insects, spiders, crabs, and centipedes. They are *arthropods,* the largest group of animals on Earth. Seventy-five percent of all animal species are arthropods.

Characteristics of Arthropods

All arthropods share four characteristics: a segmented body with specialized parts, jointed limbs, an exoskeleton, and a well-developed nervous system.

Segmented and Specialized

Like annelid worms, arthropods are *segmented.* In some arthropods, such as centipedes, nearly every segment is identical. Only the segments at the head and tail are different from the rest. However, most species of arthropods have segments that include specialized parts, such as wings, antennae, gills, pincers, and claws. These parts form during the animal's development, as segments grow together to form a *head,* a *thorax,* and an *abdomen.* You can see these parts in **Figure 11.**

Figure 11 *The segments of this arthropod grew together during the early stages of its life. A head, a thorax, and an abdomen formed as a result.*

Jointed Limbs

Jointed limbs give arthropods their name. *Arthro* means "joint," and *pod* means "foot." Jointed limbs are legs or other body parts that bend at the joints. Jointed limbs make it easier for arthropods to move.

An External Skeleton

Arthropods, such as the crabs in **Figure 12,** have a hard **exoskeleton.** This skeleton covers the outside of the body. It is made of protein and a special substance called *chitin* (KIE tin). This skeleton does some of the same things that an internal skeleton does. It serves as a stiff frame that supports the animal's body. The exoskeleton also allows the animal to move. All of the muscles connect to different parts of the skeleton. When the muscles contract, they move the exoskeleton, which moves the parts of the animal.

But the exoskeleton also does things that internal skeletons don't do well. The exoskeleton acts like a suit of armor to protect organs and other structures inside the body. It also allows arthropods to live on land without drying out.

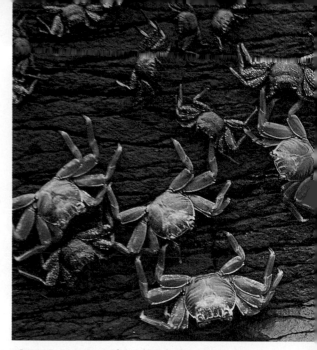

Figure 12 *A crab's exoskeleton protects its body from enemies and from dryness.*

They've Got Smarts

All arthropods have a head and a well-developed brain. The brain receives information from many sense organs, including eyes and bristles on the exoskeleton. Some arthropods, such as the tarantula in **Figure 13,** use bristles to sense motion, vibration, pressure, and chemicals.

The eyes of some arthropods are very simple. They can detect light but cannot see an image. But most arthropods have compound eyes. They can see images, but not as well as we do. A **compound eye** is made of many identical, light-sensitive units. The fly in **Figure 14** has two compound eyes.

Figure 13 *This tarantula's body is covered with bristles. The bristles gather information about the tarantula's surroundings.*

Figure 14 *Compound eyes are made of many identical, light-sensitive units that work together.*

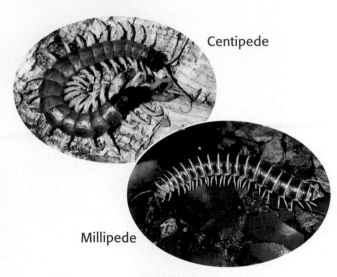

Centipede

Millipede

Figure 15 *Most body segments of centipedes and millipedes have legs. But in many species, the last few segments are legless.*

Self-Check

What is the difference between a segmented worm and a centipede? *(See page 640 to check your answer.)*

Kinds of Arthropods

Arthropods are classified by the kinds of body parts they have. You can tell the difference between arthropods by looking at the number of legs, eyes, and antennae they have. **Antennae** are feelers that sense touch, taste, or smell.

Centipedes and Millipedes

Centipedes and millipedes have one pair of antennae, a hard head capsule, and one pair of jaws called *mandibles*. One way to tell these animals apart is to count the number of legs on each segment. Centipedes have one pair of legs on each segment. They can have 30 to 354 legs. Millipedes have two pairs of legs on each segment. The record number of legs on a millipede is 752! Look at **Figure 15.** How many legs can you count?

Crustaceans

Shrimps, barnacles, crabs, and lobsters are crustaceans. All crustaceans live in water and have *gills* for breathing in the water. Unlike other arthropods, crustaceans have two pairs of antennae. Crustaceans also have mandibles. They have two compound eyes, usually on the end of eye stalks. The lobster in **Figure 16** shows some of these traits.

Figure 16 *The labeled features of this lobster are common to most crustaceans.*

Eye stalk

Antenna

Arachnids

Spiders, scorpions, mites, and ticks are arachnids (uh RAK nidz). **Figure 17** shows the two main body parts of an arachnid: the *cephalothorax* (SEF uh loh THAWR AKS) and the abdomen. The cephalothorax is made of both a head and a thorax.

Most arachnids have four pairs of legs. Spiders not only have eight legs but also have eight eyes. These animals have no antennae. Instead of mandibles, they have mouthparts called chelicerae (kuh LIS uhr EE).

The chelicerae of small garden spiders cannot pierce human skin. A few kinds of spider bites do need medical treatment, but these bites are usually not fatal. Spiders can use their chelicerae in a way that is quite useful to humans: they kill more insect pests than any other animal does.

Ticks live in forests, brush, and even country lawns. Their small bodies are up to 2 cm long. Their body segments are joined into one part. Ticks are parasites. They use their sharp chelicerae to slice into the host's skin. They attach onto the host and feed on the host's blood. Ticks that bite humans can carry diseases, such as Lyme disease and Rocky Mountain spotted fever. But most people who are bitten by ticks do not get sick. **Figure 18** shows an American dog tick.

Insects

The largest group of arthropods is the insects. If you put all of the insects in the world together, they would weigh more than all of the other animals combined! You can learn more about insects by reading the next few pages.

Figure 17 *The bodies of arachnids have two main parts: the abdomen and the cephalothorax. The chelicerae are mouthparts found on the cephalothorax.*

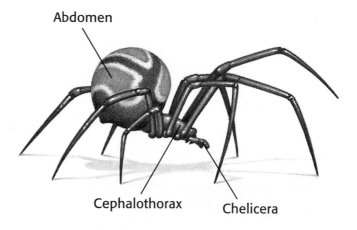

Abdomen

Cephalothorax   Chelicera

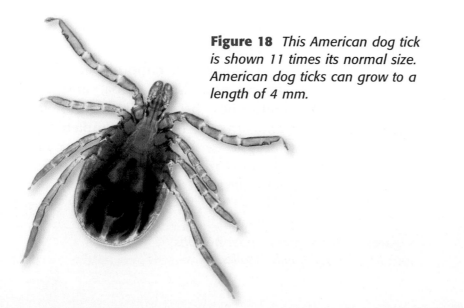

Figure 18 *This American dog tick is shown 11 times its normal size. American dog ticks can grow to a length of 4 mm.*

Quick Lab

Sticky Webs

1. Place a **piece of tape** on your desk sticky side up. The tape represents a web. Your fingers will represent an insect.

2. Holding the tape in place by the edges, "walk" your fingers across the tape. What happens?

3. Dip your fingers in **cooking oil,** and walk them across the tape again. What happens this time? Explain.

4. How might this experiment explain why spiders don't get stuck in their webs?

★ TEKS   *TRY at HOME*

The World of Insects

Insects live on land, in every freshwater environment, and at the edges of the sea. The only place on Earth insects do not live is in the ocean.

Many insects are beneficial. Most flowering plants depend on bees, butterflies, and other insects to carry pollen from one plant to another. Farmers depend on insects to pollinate hundreds of fruit crops, such as apples, cherries, and tomatoes.

Many insects are also pests. Fleas, lice, mosquitoes, and flies burrow into our flesh, suck our blood, and make us itch. Some of them carry diseases that make us sick. Plant-eating insects eat or spoil up to one-third of crops in this country.

Figure 19 *Insects' bodies follow this basic body plan.*

Insect Bodies

As shown in **Figure 19,** an insect's body has three parts: the head, the thorax, and the abdomen. On the head, insects have one pair of antennae, one pair of compound eyes, and mandibles. The thorax is made of three segments, each of which has one pair of legs.

Many insects have no wings. Others may have one or two pairs of wings on the thorax.

Insect Development

As an insect develops from an egg to an adult, it changes form. This process is called **metamorphosis** (MET uh MAWR fuh sis). There are two main kinds of metamorphosis, incomplete and complete. Grasshoppers and cockroaches go through incomplete metamorphosis. As shown in **Figure 20,** incomplete metamorphosis has three stages: egg, nymph, and adult.

Complete metamorphosis has four stages: egg, larva, pupa, and adult. Butterflies, beetles, flies, bees, wasps, and ants go through complete metamorphosis. As shown in **Figure 21** on the next page, the butterfly larva looks very different from the adult.

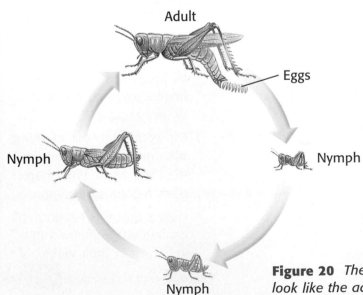

Figure 20 *These grasshopper nymphs look like the adult, only smaller.*

Figure 21 The Stages of Complete Metamorphosis

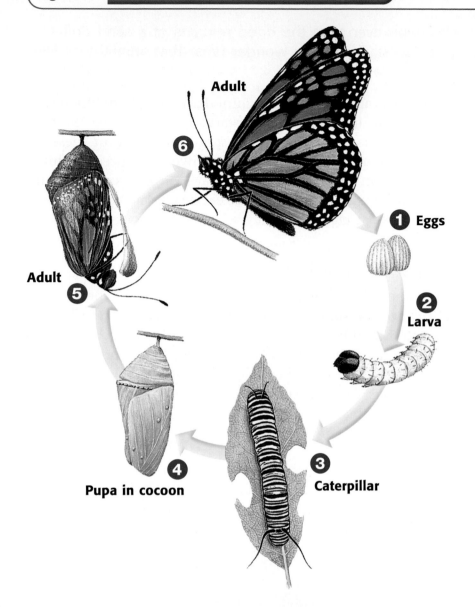

Adult

6

Adult

5

Pupa in cocoon

4

Caterpillar

3

Larva

2

Eggs

1

1. An adult lays **eggs.** The embryo forms inside the egg.

2. A **larva** hatches from the egg. Butterfly and moth larvae are called caterpillars. The caterpillar eats leaves and grows rapidly.

3. As the **caterpillar** grows, it sheds its outer skin several times. This process is called molting.

4. After its final molt, the caterpillar forms a cocoon and becomes a **pupa.** Depending on the insect, the pupal stage may last a few days or several months. During this stage, the butterfly is inactive.

5. **Adult** body parts replace the larval body parts. The adult splits its cocoon.

6. The adult butterfly pumps blood into its wings until they are full-sized. The butterfly is now strong enough to fly.

SECTION REVIEW

❶ How does a tick's body structure complement the function of drinking blood? ⭐TEKS

❷ What is the difference between complete metamorphosis and incomplete metamorphosis?

❸ **Applying Concepts** Suppose you have found an arthropod in a swimming pool. The creature has compound eyes, antennae, and wings. Is it a crustacean? How do you know?

🖅 internet**connect**

SC*i*LINKS.
NSTA   **GO TO:** www.scilinks.org

TOPIC: Fire Ants: A Texas Terror
*sci*LINKS NUMBER: HSTX065

TOPIC: Texas Honeybees
*sci*LINKS NUMBER: HSTX380

TOPIC: Arthropods
*sci*LINKS NUMBER: HSTL370

READING WARM-UP

Terms to Learn

endoskeleton
water vascular system

What You'll Do

- Describe three main characteristics of echinoderms.
- Describe how an echinoderm's symmetry changes with age.
- Identify how the structure of an echinoderm's water vascular system complements its function. ⭐TEKS

Echinoderms

Have you ever seen the dried remains of a sand dollar or a sea star? Did you wonder what that animal was like when it was alive?

Sand dollars and sea stars are echinoderms (ee KIE noh DUHRMZ). Echinoderms include sea stars (starfish), sea urchins, sea lilies, sea cucumbers, brittle stars, and sand dollars. All of these are marine animals. That means that they live in the ocean. Echinoderms live on the sea floor in all parts of the world's oceans. Some of them eat shellfish, some eat dead plants and animals, and others eat algae that they scrape off of rocks.

Spiny Skinned

The name *echinoderm* means "spiny skinned." But the animal's skin is not the spiny part. The spiny part is the **endoskeleton** (EN doh SKEL uh tuhn)—the skeleton inside an echinoderm's body. Some of these animals have hard, bony endoskeletons. Others have stiff but flexible endoskeletons. Sharp spines or bumps cover the endoskeleton and give the animal its spiny look. The animal's skin covers the endoskeleton.

Bilateral or Radial?

Adult echinoderms have radial symmetry. But they start out as larvae that have bilateral symmetry. Notice in **Figure 22** how the two sides of the sea urchin larva look alike.

Figure 22 *The sea urchin larva has bilateral symmetry. The adult sea urchin has radial symmetry.*

Larva

Adult

The Nervous System

All echinoderms have a simple nervous system. Around the mouth is a circle of nerve fibers called the *nerve ring*. In sea stars, a *radial nerve* runs from the nerve ring to the tip of each arm, as shown in **Figure 23.** The radial nerves control the motion of the sea star's arms.

At the tip of each arm is a simple eye that senses light. The rest of the body is covered with cells that sense touch and chemical signals in the water.

Water Vascular System

One system that is unique to echinoderms is the **water vascular system.** This system uses water to help the animal move, eat, and breathe. **Figure 24** shows the water vascular system of a sea star. Notice how water pressure from the system is used for many functions.

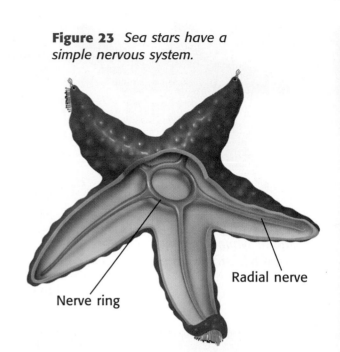

Figure 23 *Sea stars have a simple nervous system.*

Radial nerve

Nerve ring

Figure 24 **The Water Vascular System**

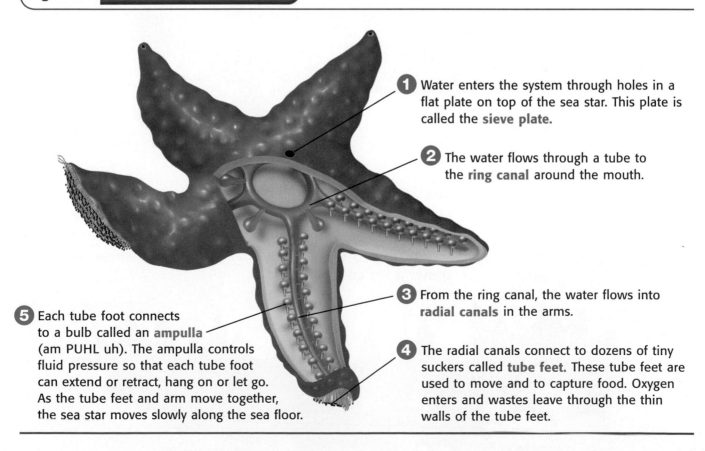

1. Water enters the system through holes in a flat plate on top of the sea star. This plate is called the **sieve plate.**

2. The water flows through a tube to the **ring canal** around the mouth.

3. From the ring canal, the water flows into **radial canals** in the arms.

4. The radial canals connect to dozens of tiny suckers called **tube feet.** These tube feet are used to move and to capture food. Oxygen enters and wastes leave through the thin walls of the tube feet.

5. Each tube foot connects to a bulb called an **ampulla** (am PUHL uh). The ampulla controls fluid pressure so that each tube foot can extend or retract, hang on or let go. As the tube feet and arm move together, the sea star moves slowly along the sea floor.

Kinds of Echinoderms

Scientists divide echinoderms into several classes. Sea stars, as shown in **Figure 25,** are the most familiar class of echinoderms. There are other classes of echinoderms that may not be as familiar to you.

Sea Urchins and Sand Dollars

Sea urchins and sand dollars are round, and their skeletons form a solid endoskeleton. As you can see in **Figure 26,** sea urchins have no arms. They use their tube feet to move in the same way as sea stars. Some sea urchins also walk on their spines. Sea urchins feed on algae they scrape from rocks and other objects. They chew the algae with special teeth. Sand dollars dig into soft sand or mud, as shown in **Figure 27.** They eat tiny pieces of food that they find in the sand.

Figure 25 *This adult sea star has radial symmetry. Larval sea stars have bilateral symmetry.*

▲ **Figure 26** *A sea urchin uses its spines for defense.*

▼ **Figure 27** *A sand dollar uses its spines to move from place to place.*

Sea Cucumbers

Like sea urchins and sand dollars, sea cucumbers have no arms. A sea cucumber has a soft, leathery body. Unlike sea urchins, sea cucumbers are long and have a wormlike shape. **Figure 28** shows a sea cucumber.

Figure 28 *Like other echinoderms, sea cucumbers move using their tube feet.*

Brittle Stars and Basket Stars

Brittle stars and basket stars look like sea stars with long, slim arms. They do not have suckers on their tube feet. These delicate animals tend to be smaller than sea stars. **Figure 29** shows a brittle star and a basket star.

Figure 29 *Brittle stars (above) and basket stars (left) move about more than other echinoderms do.*

Sea Lilies and Feather Stars

Sea lilies and feather stars may have 5 to 200 feathery arms. Their arms stretch away from their bodies and trap small pieces of food. A sea lily's cup-shaped body sits on top of a long stalk, which sticks to a rock. Sea lilies live at ocean depths of 100 m or more. Feather stars live on reefs at depths up to 100 m. Feather stars, such as the one shown in **Figure 30,** do not have a stalk.

Figure 30 *Like sea stars, brittle stars, and basket stars, feather stars can regrow lost arms.*

SECTION REVIEW

❶ Describe three main characteristics of echinoderms.

❷ How does an echinoderm's symmetry change with age?

❸ **Interpreting Graphics** Look at Figure 24. Identify how the structure of a sea star's water vascular system complements its function. ⭐TEKS

internetconnect

SCI LINKS
NSTA   GO TO: www.scilinks.org

TOPIC: Echinoderms
*sci*LINKS NUMBER: HSTL375

Skill Builder Lab

Soaking Sponges ★TEKS

Early biologists thought that sponges were plants because sponges are like plants in some ways. In many species, the adults stick to a surface and stay there. They cannot chase their food. Instead sponges absorb and filter a lot of water to get food.

In this activity, you will observe the structure of a sponge. You will also consider how the size of the sponge's holes affects the amount of water the sponge can hold.

MATERIALS

- natural sponge
- kitchen sponge
- paper towel
- balance
- bowl (large enough for sponge and water)
- water
- graduated cylinder
- funnel
- calculator (optional)

Make Observations

1 Observe the natural sponge. Identify the pores on the outside of the sponge. See if you can find the central cavity and oscula. Record your data in your ScienceLog.

2 Notice the size and shape of the holes in the kitchen sponge and in the paper towel. How do their holes compare with the natural sponge's holes? Record your data in your ScienceLog.

Form a Hypothesis

3 Which item do you think can hold the most water per gram of dry mass? Formulate a testable hypothesis and record it in your ScienceLog.

Test the Hypothesis

4 Read steps 5–9. Using a computer or your Science-Log, design and draw a data table.

5 Use the balance to measure the mass of the natural sponge. Record the mass.

6 Place the natural sponge in the bowl. Use the graduated cylinder to add water to the sponge, 10 mL at a time, until the sponge is completely soaked. Record the amount of water added.

7 Gently remove the sponge from the bowl. Use the funnel and the graduated cylinder to measure the amount of water left in the bowl. Calculate how much water the sponge absorbed. Record your data.

8 Calculate how many milliliters of water your sponge holds per gram of dry sponge. For example, if your sponge's dry mass is 12 g and your sponge holds 59.1 mL of water, then your sponge holds 4.9 mL of water per gram.

$$\frac{59.1 \text{ mL}}{12 \text{ g}} = 4.9 \text{ mL/g}$$

9 Repeat steps 5–8 using the kitchen sponge and the paper towel.

Analyze the Results

10 Compare your results from steps 5–9. Which item held the most water per gram of dry mass?

Draw Conclusions

11 Did your results support your hypothesis? Explain your answer.

Going Further
Consider how the size and structure of a sponge's pores affect its feeding ability. Ask a question about how a sponge's body structure complements the sponge's feeding function. Then use the Internet to see if scientists have done research that answers your question. Record your findings in your ScienceLog.

Section 1

Vocabulary

invertebrate *(p. 318)*
bilateral symmetry *(p. 318)*
radial symmetry *(p. 318)*
asymmetry *(p. 318)*

Section Notes

- Invertebrates are animals without a backbone.

- Almost all animals have radial symmetry or bilateral symmetry.

- Unlike other animals, sponges have no symmetry.

- Sponges have special cells called collar cells that digest food. ⭐TEKS

- Cnidarians respond to touch by firing stinging cells. ⭐TEKS

- Planarians, flukes, and tapeworms are three classes of flatworms.

Section 2

Vocabulary

open circulatory system *(p. 323)*
closed circulatory system *(p. 323)*
segment *(p. 324)*

Section Notes

- Mollusks are divided into three classes: gastropods, bivalves, and cephalopods.

- The structure of a radula helps the organ scrape up food. ⭐TEKS

- All mollusks have a foot, a visceral mass, and a mantle. Most mollusks have one or more shells.

- Mollusks and annelid worms have a circulatory system.

- In an open circulatory system, the heart pumps blood through vessels into spaces called sinuses. In a closed circulatory system, the blood is pumped through a closed network of vessels.

- Segments are identical or nearly identical repeating body parts.

Section 3

Vocabulary

exoskeleton *(p. 327)*
compound eye *(p. 327)*
antennae *(p. 328)*
metamorphosis *(p. 330)*

Section Notes

- Seventy-five percent of all animal species are arthropods.

- The four main characteristics of arthropods are jointed limbs, an exoskeleton, segments, and a well-developed nervous system.

- The four kinds of arthropods are centipedes and millipedes, crustaceans, arachnids, and insects.

- Insects can undergo complete or incomplete metamorphosis.

LabBook ⭐TEKS

The Cricket Caper *(p. 622)*

Section 4

Vocabulary

endoskeleton *(p. 332)*
water vascular system *(p. 333)*

Section Notes

- Echinoderms are marine animals that have an endoskeleton and a water vascular system.

- Echinoderms have a simple nervous system consisting of a nerve ring and radial nerves.

- The water vascular system allows echinoderms to move by means of tube feet, which act like suction cups. ⭐TEKS

Complete the following sentences by choosing the correct term from each pair of terms.

1. Animals without a backbone are called __?__. *(invertebrates* or *vertebrates)*

2. A sponge uses __?__ to move water in and releases water out through __?__. *(an osculum* or *pores; pores* or *an osculum)*

3. Cnidarians have __?__ symmetry, and flatworms have __?__ symmetry. *(radial* or *bilateral; radial* or *bilateral)*

4. The shell of a snail is secreted by the __?__. *(radula* or *mantle)*

5. Annelid worms have __?__. *(jointed limbs* or *segments)*

Multiple Choice

6. Invertebrates make up what percentage of all animal species?
   a. 4 percent
   b. 50 percent
   c. 85 percent
   d. 96 percent

7. Which of the following describes the body plan of a sponge?
   a. radial symmetry
   b. bilateral symmetry
   c. asymmetry
   d. partial symmetry

8. What cells do sponges have that no other animal has?
   a. blood cells
   b. collar cells
   c. nerve cells
   d. none of the above

9. Both tapeworms and leeches are
   a. annelid worms.
   b. parasites.
   c. flatworms.
   d. predators.

10. Some arthropods do not have
    a. jointed limbs.
    b. antennae.
    c. an exoskeleton.
    d. segments.

11. Which is NOT a function of a sea star's nervous system? ★TEKS
    a. sensing chemicals
    b. sensing light
    c. controlling movement
    d. controlling stinging cells

12. Which of the following eating structures is NOT used by mollusks?
    a. mandibles
    b. gills
    c. a radula
    d. tentacles

Short Answer

13. How are arachnids different from insects?

14. How do insects help farmers?

15. How does an echinoderm move?

16. Use what you know about sponges to explain the following statement: "All organisms are composed of cells that carry on functions to sustain life." ★TEKS

17. Using examples from this chapter, explain the difference between *structure* and *function.* ★TEKS

18. Use the following terms to create a concept map: *insect, sponges, sea anemone, invertebrates, arachnid, sea cucumber, crustacean, centipede, cnidarians, arthropods,* and *echinoderms.*

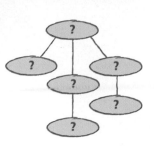

CRITICAL THINKING AND PROBLEM SOLVING

Write one or two sentences to answer the following questions:

19. You have discovered a new animal that has radial symmetry and tentacles with stinging cells. Can this animal be classified as a cnidarian? Explain your answer.

20. Unlike other mollusks, cephalopods can move quickly. Based on what you know about the structure and function of mollusks, why do you think that cephalopods have this ability? 🟠TEKS

21. Why don't roundworms, flatworms, and annelid worms belong to the same group?

MATH IN SCIENCE

22. If 75 percent of all animal species are arthropods, what ratio describes the proportion of arthropods to animals?

INTERPRETING GRAPHICS

23. Name the body segments labeled **A**, **B**, and **C**.

24. How many legs does this arthropod have?

25. This arthropod's legs are attached to which segment?

26. What kind of arthropod is this?

Reading Check-up

Take a minute to review your answers to the Pre-Reading Questions found at the bottom of page 316. Have your answers changed? If necessary, revise your answers based on what you have learned since you began this chapter.

Chapter 12

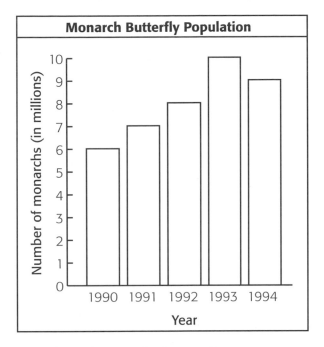

Monarch Butterfly Population

1 Look at the graph above. Compare the ranges of the number of monarch butterflies born from 1990–1991, 1991–1992, and 1992–1993. Identify the statement that best describes the pattern for those ranges of information.

A The ranges increase.

B The ranges remain the same.

C The ranges decrease.

D The ranges double yearly.

2 Determine which word set best completes the following sentence:

All organisms are composed of _____ that carry on functions to _____.

F Organ systems; provide oxygen

G Organs; remove waste

H Tissues; digest food

J Cells; sustain life

3 Which is NOT an example of a structure?

A Chelicerae

B Digestion

C Mandible

D Collar cell

4 The following information concerns the promotional material for a product:

The label on the bag of candies says, "Fat free."

The ingredients listed on the label are sugar, corn syrup, citric acid, and food coloring.

Assuming these data provided by the label are true, what can you infer?

F Because the candy is fat free, it is healthy to eat.

G Because the candy is fat free, it is low in Calories.

H The candy once contained fat, but it was removed at the factory.

J Sugar, corn syrup, citric acid, and food coloring do not contain fat.

5 Your class is conducting laboratory investigations about how rainfall affects mosquito growth. How much rainwater is in the graduated cylinder at right?

A 1 mL

B 3 mL

C 5 mL

D 7 mL

Chapter 12

Math

1 Choose the list in which the numbers are in order from smallest to largest.

A 0.016, 0.061, 0.160, 0.610

B 0.160, 0.016, 0.610, 0.061

C 0.061, 0.016, 0.016, 0.061

D 0.610, 0.160, 0.061, 0.016

2 Which number is NOT a multiple of 32?

F −32

G 0

H 32

J 98

Reading

Read the passage. Then read each question that follows the passage. Decide which is the best answer to each question.

Giant squids are very similar to their smaller relatives. They have a torpedo-shaped body, two tentacles, eight arms, a mantle, and a beak. All of their body parts are much larger, though. A giant squid's eyes may be as large as a volley-ball! Given the size of giant squids, it's hard to imagine that they have any ene-mies in the ocean, but they do.

Toothed sperm whales eat giant squids. How do we know this? As many as 10,000 squid beaks have been found in the stomach of a single sperm whale. The hard beaks of giant squids are <u>indigestible</u>. This typical meal can result in some bat-tle scars. Many whales bear ring marks on their forehead and fins that match the size of the suckers found on giant squids.

1 You can tell from this passage that the word <u>indigestible</u> describes

A something that cannot be digested.

B something that causes indigestion.

C something that one cannot dig out.

D something that one cannot guess.

2 The reader of this passage can infer that

F giant squids only imagine that they have enemies.

G a toothed sperm whale can eat 10,000 giant squids in one meal.

H giant squids defend themselves against toothed sperm whales.

J giant squids and sperm whales battle over food.

WATER BEARS

You're alive and you know it, but how? Well, eating, breathing, and moving are all pretty sure signs of life. And once something stops eating or breathing, the end is near. Or is it? This is not true for one group of invertebrates—the water bears.

Grin and Bear It

When the going gets rough—too hot, too cold, or too dry to survive—a water bear shuts down its body processes. This action is like a bear going into hibernation, but to a greater extreme. When a water bear dries out, it coats its cells with sugar. Scientists think this coating may keep the cells from breaking down. It may be the water bear's key to survival.

In this state, *cryptobiosis* (KRIP toh bie OH sis), the water bear doesn't eat, move, or breathe. And it doesn't die, either. Just add water, and the water bear returns to normal life!

Hard to Put a Finger On

Scientifically called *tardigrades* (TAHR di GRAYDZ), water bears were hard to classify. The 700 species of water bears are probably most closely related to arthropods. Most live on wet mosses and lichens. Some water bears eat roundworms and other tiny wormlike animals. Most feed on the juice of mosses.

From the tropics to the poles, the world is full of water bears. None are much larger than a grain of sand. All have a slow, stomping walk. Some water bears live at the bottom of the ocean, more than 4,700 m below sea level. Others live at 6,600 m above sea level, well above the tree line. And they can survive temperatures as cold as −270°C and as hot as 151°C.

On Your Own

▶ What impact can water bear research have on the environment, society, or scientific thought? Brainstorm three reasons why studying water bears may be worthwhile. ⊛TEKS

Water bear

Pre-Reading
Questions

1. What does it mean to
say that an animal is
coldblooded?

2. What is the difference
between a reptile and
an amphibian?

A BLAST FROM THE PAST!

In December 1938, Marjorie Courtenay Latimer made an amazing discovery. On a fishing dock in South Africa, she found an unusual fish. She sent a sketch of the fish to her friend J.L.B. Smith, an expert on fish. Smith recognized the fish as a coelacanth (SEE luh kahnth) right away. So what's so amazing about a coelacanth? Scientists had thought that coelacanths became extinct about 70 million years ago! In this chapter, you will learn about other fishes as well as about amphibians and reptiles.

START-UP Activity

OIL ON TROUBLED WATERS ⭐TEKS

To stay afloat, sharks store a lot of oil in their liver. In this activity, you will build a model of an oily liver to see how an oily liver helps to keep a shark afloat.

Procedure

1. Use **two beakers** to measure out equal amounts of **water** and **cooking oil.**

2. Fill **one balloon** with the water.

3. Fill a **second balloon** with the cooking oil.

4. Tie the balloons so that no air remains inside. Float each balloon in a **bowl half full of water.** Observe what happens to the balloons.

Analysis

5. Compare how the two balloons floated.

6. The function of an oily liver is to keep the fish from sinking. How does the structure of the liver complement its function?

Fishes, Amphibians, and Reptiles   **345**

READING WARM-UP

Terms to Learn

vertebrate   endotherm
vertebrae   ectotherm

What You'll Do

- List the four common body parts of chordates.
- Describe the main characteristics of vertebrates.
- Explain the difference between an ectotherm and an endotherm.

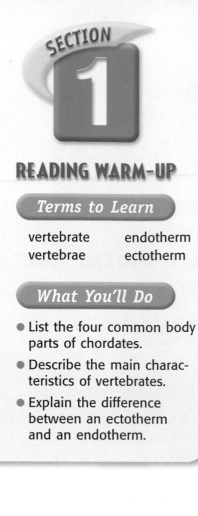

What Are Vertebrates?

You may have seen a dinosaur skeleton at a museum. Have you ever stopped to think that you might have something in common with these animals?

Dinosaur bones are often put back together to show what the animal looked like. Most dinosaur skeletons are huge compared with the skeletons of the humans who view them. But you have many of the same kinds of bones that dinosaurs had; yours are just smaller. For example, your backbone is very much like the one in a dinosaur. Animals with a backbone are called **vertebrates** (VUHR tuh brits).

Vertebrates Are Chordates

Vertebrates belong to a group of animals called *chordates* (KAWR DAYTS). Vertebrates make up the largest group of chordates. But there are two other chordate groups—lancelets (LANS lits) and tunicates (TOO ni kits). These chordates are very simple compared with vertebrates. They do not have a backbone or a well-developed head. A tunicate and a lancelet are shown in **Figure 1.**

The three groups of chordates share certain characteristics. At some point in their life, all chordates have four special body parts that are shown in **Figure 2** on the next page.

Figure 1 *Tunicates, like the sea squirt at left, and lancelets, like the one below, are chordates.*

Figure 2 | Chordate Body Parts

Tail	Notochord	Hollow nerve cord	Pharyngeal pouches
Chordates have a **tail** that begins behind the anus. Some chordates have a tail only in the embryo stage.	A stiff but flexible rod called a **notochord** (NOHT uh KAWRD) gives the body support. In most vertebrates, the embryo's notochord disappears and a backbone grows in its place.	A **hollow nerve cord** runs along the back and is full of fluid. In vertebrates, this nerve cord is called the *spinal cord.*	**Pharyngeal** (fuh RIN jee uhl) **pouches** are found in all chordate embryos. These pouches develop into gills or other body parts as the embryo matures.

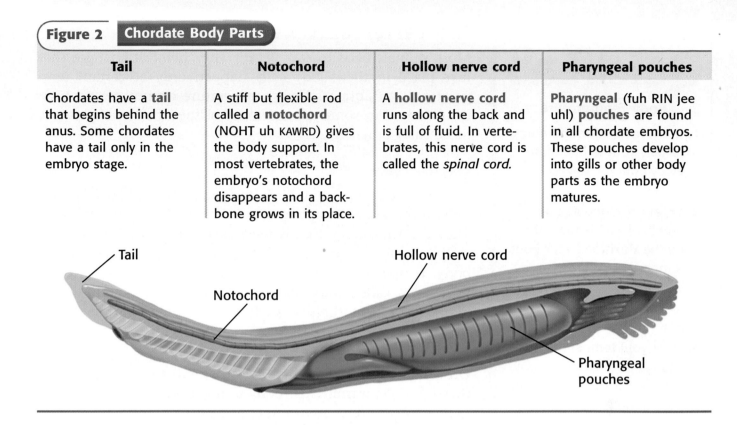

Tail

Notochord

Hollow nerve cord

Pharyngeal pouches

Getting a Backbone

Many things set vertebrates apart from lancelets and tunicates. For example, vertebrates have a backbone. A *backbone* is a column of bones along an animal's back. These bones are called **vertebrae** (VUHR tuh BREE). You can see the vertebrae of a human in **Figure 3.** These bones surround and protect the spinal cord. Vertebrates also have a head protected by a skull.

The skull and vertebrae are made of either cartilage or bone. *Cartilage* forms the flexible parts of your ears and nose. The skeletons of all vertebrate embryos are made of cartilage. But as most vertebrates grow, the cartilage is changed to bone. Bone is much harder than cartilage.

Figure 3 *The vertebrae interlock to form a strong but flexible column of bone. The backbone protects the spinal cord and helps to hold the rest of the body up.*

Are Vertebrates Warm or Cold?

Most animals need to stay warm. The chemical changes that take place in their body cells happen only at certain temperatures. An animal's body temperature cannot be too high or too low. But some animals control their body temperature more than others do.

Staying Warm

The body temperature of birds and mammals does not change much even as the temperature of their environment changes. They use the energy that is released by the chemical changes in their cells to warm their bodies. Animals that have a stable body temperature are called **endotherms.** Endotherms are sometimes called *warmblooded.* Because of their stable body temperature, endotherms can live in cold environments.

Cold Blood?

On sunny days, lizards, such as the one in **Figure 4,** lie out in the sun to get warm. Their body temperature changes with the temperature of their environment. Animals that do not control their body temperature through the chemical changes of their cells are called **ectotherms.** Ectotherms are sometimes called *coldblooded.* Nearly all fishes, amphibians, and reptiles are ectotherms.

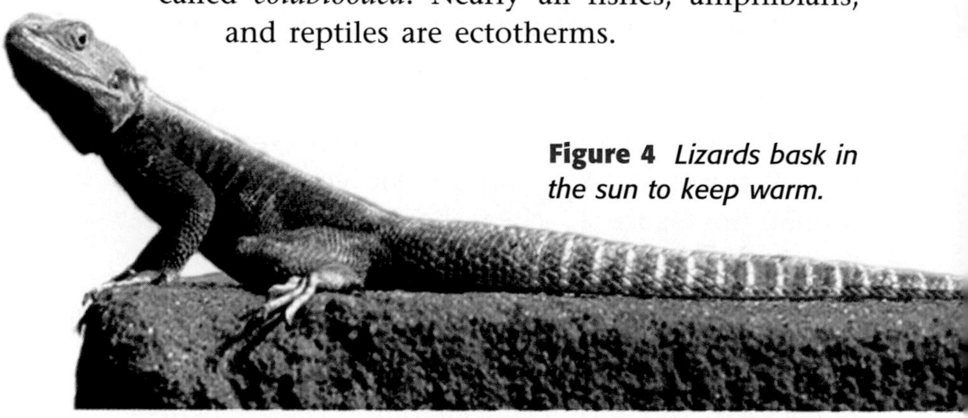

Figure 4 *Lizards bask in the sun to keep warm.*

QuickLab

Body Temperature

1. Use a **fever thermometer** to take your temperature every hour for at least 6 hours.
2. Organize your data into a graph. Place the time of day on the *x*-axis and your body temperature on the *y*-axis. You may want to use a computer to construct your graph.
3. Does your temperature change throughout the day? How much does it change?
4. Do you think your body temperature changes after exercise?
5. How do you think your answers would be different if you were an ectotherm?

TEKS

TRY at HOME

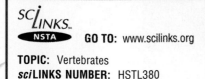

SECTION REVIEW

1. How are vertebrates the same as other chordates? How are they different?
2. Describe the structure and function of vertebrae. TEKS
3. How are endotherms and ectotherms different?
4. **Applying Concepts** Your pet lizard is not moving very much. Your sister tells you to put a heat lamp in the cage because the lizard is cold. Why might this help?

internet connect

sciLINKS NSTA GO TO: www.scilinks.org

TOPIC: Vertebrates

sciLINKS NUMBER: HSTL380

READING WARM-UP

Terms to Learn

fin   gills
scales   swim bladder
lateral line system

What You'll Do

- Describe the three classes of living fishes, and give an example of each.
- Explain how the structure of a swim bladder complements its function. ★TEKS
- Explain the difference between internal fertilization and external fertilization.

Fishes

Find a body of water, and you'll probably find fish. How many different kinds of fishes do you think there are? Can you even imagine what they could all look like?

Fossil evidence indicates that fish appeared on Earth about 500 million years ago. Today Earth's saltwater and freshwater fishes make up more species than all other vertebrates combined. There are more than 25,000 species of fishes, and more are being discovered all the time. A few are shown in **Figure 5.**

Fish Characteristics

Although the fishes on this page look very different from each other, they share many characteristics that help them live in water. For example, most fishes are ectotherms. Fishes also have characteristics that help them catch other animals or find plants for food. Because fishes must actively search for food, they need a strong body, well-developed senses, and a brain.

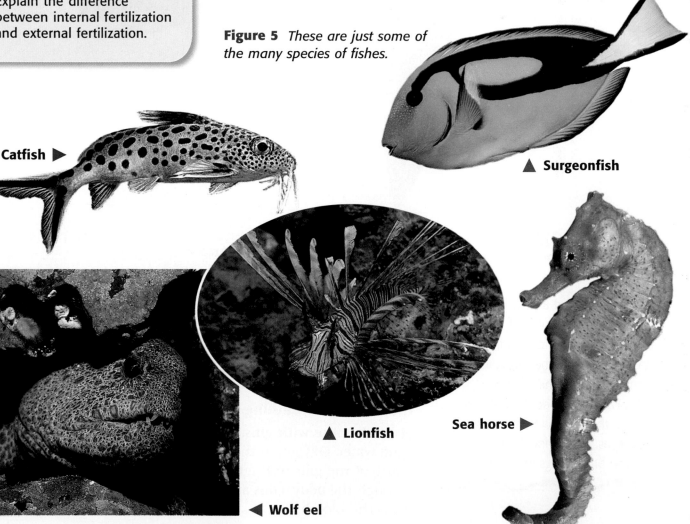

Figure 5 *These are just some of the many species of fishes.*

◄ **Catfish** ▶

▲ **Surgeonfish**

▲ **Lionfish**

Sea horse ▶

◄ **Wolf eel**

Fishes, Amphibians, and Reptiles · **349**

Born to Swim

Fishes swim through the water by moving their fins. **Fins** are fan-shaped structures that help fish move, steer, stop, and balance. Many fishes have bodies covered by scales. **Scales** are bony structures that protect the body. Scales also lower the friction as fish swim through the water. **Figure 6** shows some of the body parts of a typical fish.

Figure 6 *Fishes come in many shapes and sizes, but all have gills, fins, and a tail.*

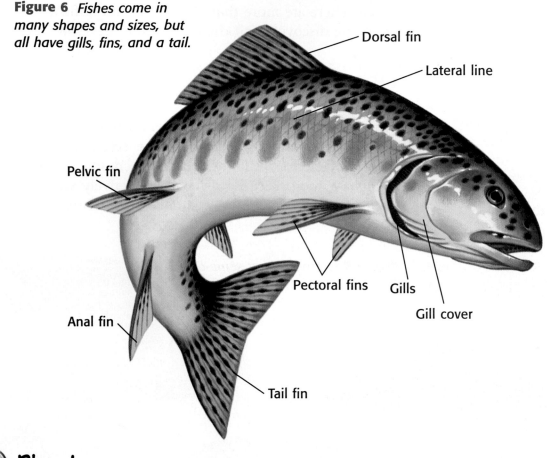

Dorsal fin

Lateral line

Pelvic fin

Pectoral fins   Gills

Gill cover

Anal fin

Tail fin

Physics CONNECTION

When you look at an object through a magnifying lens, you have to move the lens back and forth in front of your eye to bring the object into focus. The same thing happens in fish eyes. Fish have special muscles to change the position of the lenses of their eyes. By moving the eye lenses, fish can bring things into focus.

Making Sense of the World

Most fishes have a lateral line system. The **lateral line system** is a row or rows of tiny organs that sense water vibrations, such as those caused by another fish swimming nearby. These organs are lined up along each side of the body and are often found along the side of the head. Fishes have a brain that keeps track of all the information coming in from these organs.

Underwater Breathing

Fishes breathe with gills. **Gills** are organs that remove oxygen from water. Oxygen in the water passes through the thin membrane of the gills to the blood. The blood then carries oxygen through the body. Gills are also used to remove carbon dioxide from the blood.

Making More Fish

Most fishes reproduce by *external fertilization*. The female lays unfertilized eggs in the water, and the male drops sperm on them. But some fishes reproduce by internal fertilization. In *internal fertilization*, the male deposits sperm inside the female. In most cases, the female then lays eggs with the developing embryos inside. Baby fish hatch from the eggs. But in some cases, the embryos grow inside the mother, and the baby fish are born live.

Kinds of Fishes

There are five very different classes of fishes. Two classes are now extinct, but scientists have been able to study their fossils. The three classes of fishes living today are jawless fishes, cartilaginous (KART'L AJ uh nuhs) fishes, and bony fishes.

Jawless Fishes

Modern *jawless fishes* are eel-like. They have smooth, slimy skin and a round, jawless mouth. Their skeleton is made of cartilage, and they have a notochord but no backbone. Jawless fishes have a skull, a brain, and eyes. There are two kinds of modern jawless fishes—lampreys and hagfish. Both kinds of jawless fishes are shown in **Figure 7.**

Figure 7 | **Jawless Fishes**

Lampreys use their suckers to attach themselves to other fishes. ▶

▼ **Hagfish** can tie their flexible bodies into knots. They slide the knot from their tail end to their head to remove slime from their skin or to escape from predators.

Cartilaginous Fishes

Did you know that a shark is a fish? Sharks belong to a class of fishes called *cartilaginous fishes*. In most vertebrates, soft cartilage in the embryo is slowly replaced by bone. But in sharks, skates, and rays, the skeleton never changes from cartilage to bone. That is why they are called cartilaginous fishes.

Cartilaginous fishes have fully functional jaws. These fishes are strong swimmers and expert predators. Many have excellent senses of sight and smell, and they have a lateral line system. **Figure 8** shows some cartilaginous fishes.

Some cartilaginous fishes need to swim to keep water flowing over their gills. If these fishes stop swimming, they will suffocate. Other cartilaginous fishes do not have to swim. They can lie on the ocean floor and pump water across their gills.

Figure 8   **Cartilaginous Fishes**

Rays, like this **stingray,** feed on shellfish and worms on the sea floor. A ray swims by moving its fins up and down. ▶

◀ Unlike rays, **skates** have small dorsal fins.

▼ Sharks, like this **hammerhead shark,** rarely prey on humans. They would rather eat their normal food—other fish.

Figure 9   Bony Fishes

▼ Lungfishes have air sacs, which are like lungs, and can gulp air. They live in shallow waters that often dry up in the summer.

▲ Masked butterfly fish live in waters around coral reefs.

▼ A **pike** can swim faster than the fastest humans can run, about 48 km/h.

Bony Fishes

When you think of a fish, you probably think of a bony fish. Goldfish, tuna, catfish, and cod are all *bony fishes,* the largest class of fishes. Ninety-five percent of all fishes are bony fishes. They range in size from 1 cm long to more than 6 m long. Some bony fishes are shown in **Figure 9.**

As you might have guessed, bony fishes have a skeleton made of bone. The body of a bony fish is covered by scales.

Unlike cartilaginous fishes, bony fishes can float in one place without swimming. This is because they have a swim bladder that keeps them from sinking. The **swim bladder** is a balloon-shaped organ that is filled with oxygen and other gases from the bloodstream. These gases are lighter than water. So the swim bladder helps the fish float.

MathBreak

A Lot of Bones

If there are 30,000 species of fishes and 95 percent of all fishes are bony fishes, how many species of bony fishes are there?

● ● ● ● ● ● ● ● ● ● ● ● ● ● ● ●

SECTION REVIEW

1. How does the structure of a fish's swim bladder complement its function? ⊛TEKS

2. Most bony fishes reproduce by external fertilization. What does this mean?

3. **Applying Concepts** What is the structure of the lateral line system, and what is its function? ⊛TEKS

Terms to Learn

lung
tadpole
metamorphosis

What You'll Do

● Explain how amphibians breathe.

● Describe metamorphosis in amphibians.

● Describe the three groups of amphibians, and give an example of each.

Amphibians

Did you know that some animals are able to breathe through their skin? Would you think these animals would live on land or in the water? Actually, they live part of their life on land and part in the water.

About 350 million years ago, fishes lived wherever there was water. But none of these vertebrates could live on land. And the land was a wonderful place for a vertebrate. It had thick green forests, many tasty insects, and few predators. But for vertebrates to adapt to life on land, they needed lungs for breathing and legs for walking.

Moving to Land

Amphibians (am FIB ee UHNZ) are able to live part of their life in the water and part on land. Most amphibians have lungs to get oxygen from the air. A **lung** is a saclike organ that takes oxygen from the air and delivers it to the blood.

Most of the amphibians living on Earth today are frogs or salamanders, such as those in **Figure 10.** But the early amphibians looked much different. Many were very large—up to 10 m long—and could stay on dry land longer than today's amphibians can. But early amphibians still had to return to the water to keep from drying out, to keep from overheating, and to lay their eggs.

Figure 10 *Frogs and salamanders are just some of the many amphibians on Earth today.*

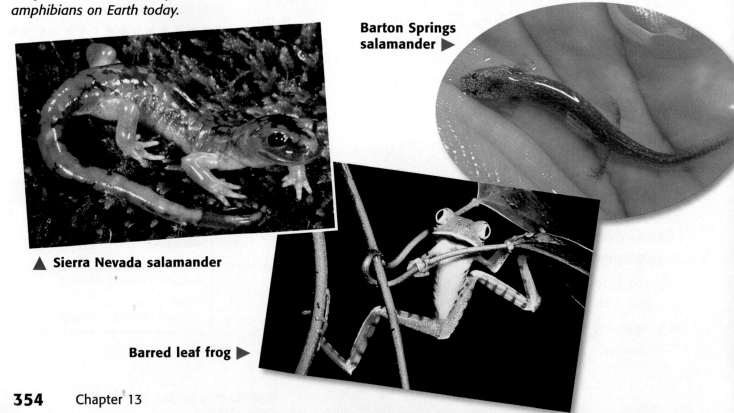

Barton Springs salamander ▶

▲ **Sierra Nevada salamander**

Barred leaf frog ▶

Characteristics of Amphibians

Amphibian means "double life." Most amphibians have two parts to their life. Because their eggs do not have a shell or a special membrane to stop water loss, the embryos must develop in a very wet environment. After amphibians hatch from an egg, they live in the water, like fishes do. Later they are able to live on land. But even adult amphibians are only partly adapted to life on land, and they must always live near water.

Amphibians are ectotherms. Like the body of a fish, the body of an amphibian changes temperature as the temperature of its environment changes.

Thin Skinned

Most amphibians do not have scales. Their skin is thin, smooth, and moist. They do not drink water. Instead, they absorb water through their skin. Because their skin is so thin and moist, these animals can lose water through their skin and easily become dehydrated. For this reason, most amphibians live in water or in damp habitats.

Amphibians can breathe air into their lungs. But many also get oxygen through their skin, which is full of blood vessels. Some salamanders, such as the one in **Figure 11,** breathe only through their skin.

Many amphibians have brightly colored skin. The colors are often a warning to predators because the skin of many amphibians has poison glands. These poisons may simply be irritating, or they may be deadly. The skin of the dart-poison frog, shown in **Figure 12,** has one of the most deadly toxins known.

Figure 11 *The four-toed salamander has no lungs. It gets all of its oxygen through its skin.*

Figure 12 *The skin of this dart-poison frog is full of poison glands. Hunters in South America rub the tips of their arrows in the deadly toxin.*

Self-Check

How is amphibian skin like a lung? *(See page 640 to check your answer.)*

Figure 13 Amphibian Metamorphosis

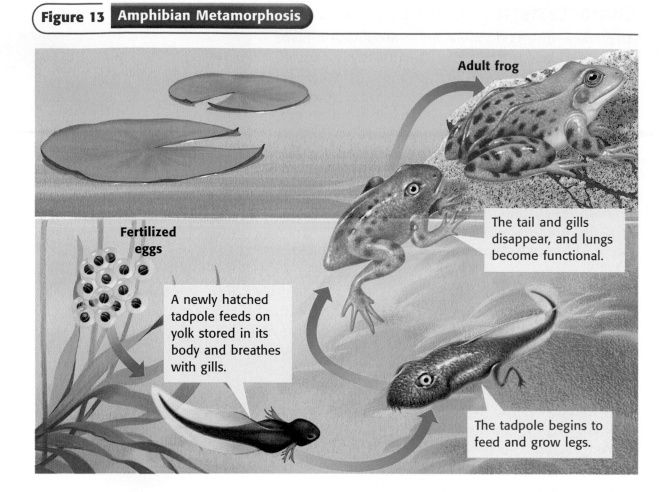

Adult frog

The tail and gills disappear, and lungs become functional.

Fertilized eggs

A newly hatched tadpole feeds on yolk stored in its body and breathes with gills.

The tadpole begins to feed and grow legs.

Leading a Double Life

Most amphibians change form as they grow into adults. After hatching, an amphibian embryo usually becomes a tadpole. **Tadpoles** are immature amphibians that must live in water. A tadpole gets oxygen through gills and uses its long tail to swim. Later the tadpole loses its gills and develops lungs and limbs. This change from an immature form to an adult form is called **metamorphosis** (MET uh MAWR fuh sis) and is shown in **Figure 13.** Most adult amphibians are able to live on land, but they still need to keep their skin moist.

A few amphibians skip the aquatic stage and develop directly into adult frogs or salamanders. For example, Darwin frogs lay eggs on moist ground. When an embryo begins to move, a male adult quickly takes it into its mouth and protects it inside his vocal sacs. When the embryo finishes developing, the adult frog opens his mouth and a tiny frog jumps out. You can see an adult Darwin frog in **Figure 14.**

Figure 14 *Darwin frogs live in Chile and Argentina. A male frog may carry 5 to 15 embryos in his vocal sacs until the young are about 1.5 cm long.*

Kinds of Amphibians

There are about 4,600 species of amphibians alive today. They belong to three groups: caecilians (see SIL ee uhns), salamanders, and frogs and toads.

Caecilians

Most people are not familiar with caecilians. These amphibians do not have legs and are shaped like worms or snakes. But they have the thin, moist skin of amphibians. Unlike other amphibians, some caecilians have bony scales. Many caecilians have very small eyes beneath their skin and are blind. Caecilians live in the tropical areas of Asia, Africa, and South America. About 160 different species are known. A caecilian is shown in **Figure 15.**

Figure 15 *Caecilians do not have legs. They live in damp soil in the Tropics. Caecilians eat small invertebrates in the soil.*

Salamanders

Of modern amphibians, salamanders are the most like prehistoric amphibians. Even though salamanders are much smaller than ancient amphibians, they have a similar body shape, a long tail, and four strong legs. They range in size from a few centimeters long to 1.5 m long.

There are about 390 known species of salamanders. Most of them live under stones and logs in the damp woods of North America. They eat small invertebrates. A few do not go through metamorphosis. They live their whole life in the water. Look at **Figure 16** to see some different kinds of salamanders.

Figure 16   Salamanders

The **marbled salamander** lives in damp places, such as under rocks or logs or among leaves.

This **axolotl** (AK suh LAHT′l) is an unusual salamander. It keeps its gills and never leaves the water.

Figure 17 Frogs and Toads

Frogs, such as this **bull frog,** have smooth, moist skin.

Toads, such as this **Fowlers toad,** spend less time in water than frogs do. Their skin is drier and bumpier.

Environment

C O N N E C T I O N

Amphibians are extremely sensitive to chemical changes in their surroundings. When large numbers of them begin to die or show deformities, this may indicate a problem with the environment. For this reason, amphibians are often called ecological indicators.

internetconnect

SCI*LINKS*

NSTA GO TO: www.scilinks.org

TOPIC: Texas Amphibians
*sci*LINKS NUMBER: HSTX225

TOPIC: Amphibians
*sci*LINKS NUMBER: HSTL390

Frogs and Toads

Ninety percent of all amphibians are frogs or toads. They are found all over the world, from deserts to rain forests. Frogs and toads are very similar to each other. In fact, toads are a kind of frog. You can see a frog and a toad in **Figure 17.**

Frogs and toads are highly adapted for life on land. Adults have powerful leg muscles for jumping. They have well-developed ears for hearing, and some have vocal cords for calling. They also have an extendible, sticky tongue. The tongue is attached to the front of the mouth so that it can be flipped out quickly to catch insects.

Frogs are well known for their nighttime choruses, but many frogs sing in the daytime too. Like humans, they force air from their lungs across vocal cords in the throat. But some frogs have something we lack. Surrounding their vocal cords is a thin sac of skin called the *vocal sac.* When these frogs vocalize, the sac inflates with air, like a balloon does, and vibrates. The vibrations of the sac increase the volume of the song so that it can be heard over long distances.

SECTION REVIEW

❶ Describe metamorphosis in amphibians.

❷ Why do most amphibians have to live near water or in a very wet habitat?

❸ Applying Concepts Name the three kinds of amphibians. How are they similar? How are they different?

Terms to Learn

amniotic egg

What You'll Do

● Explain the adaptations that allow reptiles to live on land.
● Describe the characteristics of an amniotic egg.
● Name the three orders of modern reptiles.

Reptiles

Have you ever wondered what the difference is between amphibians and reptiles? Amphibians need to spend part of their lives in the water. But reptiles can spend their whole lives on land. What is it about reptiles that makes this possible?

Reptiles were the first animals to live entirely out of the water. Several different kinds of reptiles are shown in **Figure 18.** Reptiles have many traits that allow them to live in a drier environment. They have thick, dry skin that protects them from water loss. They have strong legs, so they are better able to walk. And they have a special egg that can be laid on dry land.

Figure 18 *These are just a few of the many different kinds of reptiles on Earth today.*

▼ **Crocodile**

Panther ▶ **chameleon**

▲ **Giant tortoise**

◀ **South American emerald boa**

Fishes, Amphibians, and Reptiles   **359**

Characteristics of Reptiles

Reptiles are well adapted for life on land. Although crocodiles, turtles, and a few species of snakes live in the water, most reptiles live on land. To live on land, animals need to breathe air. All reptiles use lungs, just as you do.

Thick Skinned

Thick, dry skin is a very important adaptation for life on land. This skin forms a watertight layer and keeps cells from losing water by evaporation. Most reptiles cannot breathe through their skin the way that amphibians can. They depend entirely on their lungs for oxygen. Check out the snake's skin in **Figure 19.**

But Aren't They Cold?

Reptiles are ectotherms. They are active when it's warm outside, and they slow down when it's cool. A few reptiles can generate some warmth from their own body cells. For example, some lizards in the southwestern United States can keep their body temperature at about 34°C, even when the air temperature is cool. But most modern reptiles live in places where the climate is mild. They cannot handle the cold polar regions, where many mammals and birds thrive.

The Amazing Amniotic Egg

Among reptiles' many adaptations to life on land, the most important is the amniotic (AM nee AHT ik) egg. An **amniotic egg** holds fluid that protects the embryo and is usually surrounded by a shell. The shell protects the embryo and keeps the egg from drying out. An amniotic egg can be laid under rocks, in the ground, in forests, or even in the desert. The amniotic egg is so well suited for a dry environment that even crocodiles and turtles return to land to lay their eggs. Amniotic eggs are shown in **Figure 20.**

Figure 19 *Many people think snakes are slimy, but the skin of snakes and other reptiles is scaly and dry.*

Figure 20 *Compare these amphibian and reptile eggs. The reptile eggs are amniotic, and the amphibian eggs are not.*

Amphibian eggs

Reptile eggs

Figure 21 An Amniotic Egg

The **shell** protects the egg from damage and keeps the egg from drying out. The shell has small pores that allow oxygen to pass through to the growing embryo and allow carbon dioxide to be removed.

The **yolk** gives the embryo a rich supply of food.

The **albumen** (al BYOO muhn) provides water and protein to the embryo.

The **amniotic sac** is filled with fluid. The amniotic fluid surrounds and protects the embryo.

The **allantois** (uh LAN toh is) stores the embryo's wastes. It also passes oxygen to the embryo from the pores in the shell.

The shell is just one important part of an amniotic egg. The parts of an amniotic egg are described in **Figure 21.** The egg protects the embryo from predators, bacterial infections, and dehydration.

Reptile Reproduction

Almost all reptiles reproduce by internal fertilization. The egg is fertilized inside the female. A shell then forms around the egg, and the female lays the egg.

Most reptiles lay their eggs in soil or sand. A few do not lay eggs. Instead the embryos grow inside the mother, and the young are born live. In either case, the embryo develops into a tiny young reptile. Reptiles do not go through metamorphosis.

Kinds of Reptiles

In the age of the dinosaurs, from 300 million years ago until about 65 million years ago, most land vertebrates were reptiles. The 6,000 species of reptiles living today are only a handful of the many species of reptiles that once lived. Turtles and tortoises, crocodiles and alligators, and lizards and snakes are modern reptiles.

Self-Check

What characteristics of reptiles are important for living on dry land? *(See page 640 to check your answer.)*

Figure 22 Turtles and Tortoises

◄ Sea turtles, such as this **green sea turtle,** have a streamlined shell to help them swim and turn rapidly.

▲ The **Texas tortoise** lives in southern Texas and northern Mexico. It is one of only four living species of tortoises that are native to North America.

Turtles and Tortoises

The 250 species of turtles and tortoises are only distantly related to other reptiles. Generally, tortoises live on land, and turtles live in the water. **Figure 22** shows some examples.

What makes these animals unique is their shell. The shell makes a turtle slow and inflexible, so outrunning its predators is unlikely. But many turtles can draw their head and limbs into the armorlike shell to protect themselves.

Crocodiles and Alligators

Crocodiles and alligators are meat eaters. These reptiles spend most of their time in the water. Because their eyes and nostrils are on the top of their flat head, they can watch their surroundings while most of their body is hidden underwater. This gives them a great advantage over their prey. How can you tell the difference between an alligator and a crocodile? See for yourself in **Figure 23.**

Figure 23 Crocodiles and Alligators

An alligator, such as this **American alligator,** has a broad head and a rounded snout.

A crocodile, such as this **American crocodile,** has a narrow head and a pointed snout.

Lizards and Snakes

Lizards and snakes are the most common modern reptiles. Look at **Figure 24** for a few examples. Lizards live in deserts, grasslands, temperate forests, and rain forests. Most lizards eat small invertebrates, but many eat plants. The largest lizard is 3 m long. But most lizards are less than 30 cm long.

Snakes are carnivores. They eat small animals and eggs. Snakes have special jaws with five joints that allow them to open their mouth wide and swallow their prey whole. Some snakes kill their prey by squeezing it until it suffocates. Other snakes have poison glands and special fangs for injecting venom.

Snakes do not see or hear well, but they do smell very well. When a snake flicks its forked tongue out of its mouth, it is sampling the air. When the snake pulls its tongue inside its mouth, it places the tips of its tongue into two openings in the roof of its mouth. When the molecules from the air reach the roof of the snake's mouth, the snake can "smell" the air.

Figure 24 Lizards and Snakes

The **thorny devil** is a harmless lizard that lives in Australia. This lizard eats ants. ▶

◀ **Sinaloan (SEE nah LOH uhn) milk snakes** live in Mexico. They are not poisonous, but they look a lot like poisonous coral snakes.

The **Gila (HEE luh) monster** of the southwestern United States and northern Mexico is one of only two kinds of venomous lizards. ▶

SECTION REVIEW

❶ What characteristics set turtles apart from other reptiles?

❷ How does the structure of a snake's mouth relate to its function? ⭐TEKS

❸ **Applying Concepts** Like reptiles, mammals have an amniotic egg. But most mammals give birth to live young. The embryo develops from a fertilized egg inside the female's body. Which parts of a reptile's amniotic egg do you think a mammal could do without? Explain your answer.

📶 internet**connect**

SC*i*LINKS.
NSTA   GO TO: www.scilinks.org

TOPIC: Reptiles
*sci*LINKS NUMBER: HSTL395

Making Models Lab

Floating a Pipe Fish ⭐TEKS

Bony fishes control how deep or shallow they swim with an organ called a swim bladder. As gases are absorbed and released by the swim bladder, the fish rises or sinks in the water. In this activity, you will make a model of a fish with a swim bladder. Your challenge will be to make the fish float halfway between the top of the water and the bottom of the container. It will probably take several tries and a lot of observing and analyzing along the way.

Make a Prediction

1 Estimate how much air you will need in the balloon so that your pipe fish will float halfway between the top of the water and the bottom of the container. Will you need to inflate the balloon halfway, just a small amount, or all the way? The balloon will have to fit inside the pipe, but there will need to be enough air to make the pipe float. Write your prediction in your ScienceLog.

MATERIALS

- water
- container for water at least 15 cm deep
- slender balloon
- small cork
- PVC pipe, 12 cm long, $\frac{3}{4}$ in. diameter
- rubber band

Build a Model

2 Inflate your balloon. Hold the neck of the balloon so that no air escapes, and push the cork into the end of the balloon. If the cork is properly placed, no air should leak out when the balloon is held underwater.

3 Place your swim bladder inside the pipe, and place a rubber band along the pipe as shown below. The rubber band will keep the swim bladder from coming out of either end.

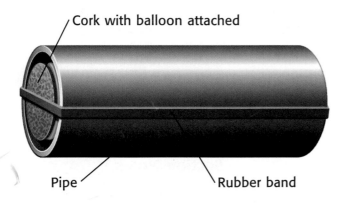

Cork with balloon attached

Pipe

Rubber band

Collect Data

4 Place your pipe fish in the water, and note where the fish floats. Record your observations in your ScienceLog.

5 If the pipe fish does not float where you want, take it out of the water, adjust the amount of air in the balloon, and try again.

6 You can release small amounts of air from the bladder by carefully lifting the neck of the balloon away from the cork. You can add more air by removing the cork and blowing more air into the balloon. Keep adjusting and testing until your fish floats halfway between the bottom of the container and the top of the water.

Analyze the Results

7 Was the prediction you made in step 1 correct? Explain your answer.

8 In relation to the length and volume of the entire pipe fish, how much air was needed to make the fish float? State your answer as a percentage.

9 Based on the amount of space the balloon took up in your model, how much space do you estimate is taken up by a swim bladder inside a living fish? Explain.

10 What are some limitations to your model?

Going Further

Some fast-swimming fishes, such as sharks, and marine mammals, such as whales and dolphins, do not have a swim bladder. Find out from the library or the Internet how these animals keep from sinking to the bottom of the ocean. Create a poster to explain your results. Include drawings of the fishes or marine mammals that you have researched.

Highlights

Section 1

Vocabulary

vertebrate *(p. 346)*
vertebrae *(p. 347)*
endotherm *(p. 348)*
ectotherm *(p. 348)*

Section Notes

- At some point during their development, chordates have a notochord, a hollow nerve cord, pharyngeal pouches, and a tail.

- Chordates include lancelets, tunicates, and vertebrates. Most chordates are vertebrates.

- Vertebrates differ from the other chordates in that they have a backbone and a skull made of bone or cartilage.

- The backbone is composed of units called vertebrae.

- Endotherms control their body temperature through the chemical reactions of their cells. Ectotherms do not.

Section 2

Vocabulary

fin *(p. 350)*
scales *(p. 350)*
lateral line system *(p. 350)*
gills *(p. 350)*
swim bladder *(p. 353)*

Section Notes

- There are three groups of living fishes: jawless fishes, cartilaginous fishes, and bony fishes.

- Most bony fishes have a swim bladder. The swim bladder helps bony fishes float. ⭐TEKS

- In external fertilization, eggs are fertilized outside the female's body. In internal fertilization, eggs are fertilized inside the female's body.

Section 3

Vocabulary

lung *(p. 354)*
tadpole *(p. 356)*
metamorphosis *(p. 356)*

Section Notes

- Amphibians were the first vertebrates to live on land.

- Amphibians breathe by gulping air into their lungs and by absorbing oxygen through their skin.

- Amphibians start life in water, where they breathe through gills. During metamorphosis, they lose their gills and develop structures that allow them to live on land.

- Modern amphibians include caecilians, salamanders, and frogs and toads.

LabBook ⭐TEKS

A Prince of a Frog *(p. 625)*

Section 4

Vocabulary

amniotic egg *(p. 360)*

Section Notes

- Reptiles have thick, scaly skin that protects them from drying out. ⭐TEKS

- A tough shell keeps the amniotic egg from drying out and protects the embryo. ⭐TEKS

- Amniotic fluid surrounds and protects the embryo in an amniotic egg.

- Modern reptiles include turtles and tortoises, crocodiles and alligators, and lizards and snakes.

USING VOCABULARY

Complete the following sentences by choosing the correct term from each pair of terms.

1. At some point in their development, all chordates have __?__. (*lungs and a notochord* or *a hollow nerve cord and a tail*)

2. Most fish are __?__. (*endotherms* or *ectotherms*)

3. When a frog lays eggs that are later fertilized by sperm, __?__ fertilization has taken place. (*internal* or *external*)

4. The vertebrae wrap around and protect the __?__ of vertebrates. (*notochord* or *spinal cord*)

UNDERSTANDING CONCEPTS

Multiple Choice

5. Which of the following is not a vertebrate?
   a. tadpole
   b. lizard
   c. lamprey
   d. tunicate

6. The swim bladder is found in
   a. jawless fishes.
   b. cartilaginous fishes.
   c. bony fishes.
   d. lancelets.

7. Tadpoles change into frogs by the process of
   a. adaptation.
   b. internal fertilization.
   c. metamorphosis.
   d. temperature regulation.

8. Which of the following organisms have amniotic eggs?
   a. bony fishes
   b. sharks
   c. reptiles
   d. amphibians

9. The yolk holds
   a. food for the embryo.
   b. amniotic fluid.
   c. wastes.
   d. oxygen.

10. Both bony fishes and cartilaginous fishes have
   a. scales.
   b. fins.
   c. an oily liver.
   d. a swim bladder.

11. Reptiles are adapted to a life on land because they
   a. can breathe through their skin.
   b. are endotherms.
   c. have thick, moist skin.
   d. have an amniotic egg.

Short Answer

12. How do amphibians breathe?

13. What characteristics allow fish to live in the water?

14. How does an embryo in an amniotic egg get oxygen?

CONCEPT MAPPING

15. Use the following terms to create a concept map: *turtle, reptiles, amphibians, fishes, shark, salamander,* and *vertebrates.*

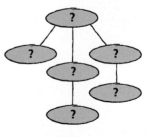

CRITICAL THINKING AND PROBLEM SOLVING

Write one or two sentences to answer the following questions:

16. Suppose you have found an animal that has a backbone and gills, but you can't find a notochord. Is it a chordate? How can you be sure?

17. Many fishes live in groups called schools. In this case, the structure of the population is that the fish live in groups that swim together. How might the structure of such a population relate to its function? ⭐TEKS

18. Describe amphibian skin. How does the structure of the skin relate to its function? ⭐TEKS

19. A rattlesnake does not see very well, but it can detect a temperature change of as little as 0.003°C. How is this ability useful to a rattlesnake?

20. It's 43°C outside, and the normal body temperature of a certain kind of dinosaur (a reptile) is 38°C. Are you most likely to find the dinosaur in the sun or in the shade? Explain.

MATH IN SCIENCE

21. A Costa Rican viper can eat a mouse that has one-third more mass than the viper. How much can you eat? Write down your mass in kilograms. To find your mass in kilograms, divide your mass in pounds by 2.2. If you were to eat a meal with a mass one-third larger than your mass, what would the mass of the meal be in kilograms?

INTERPRETING GRAPHICS

Your teacher measured the body temperature of two organisms for several hours and organized the data into the graph below. Examine the graph, and answer the questions that follow.

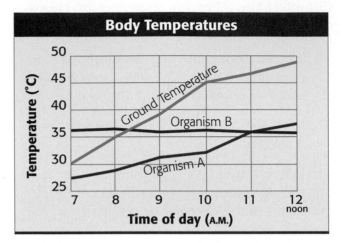

22. Explain how the body temperatures of organism A and organism B change with the ground temperature. ⭐TEKS

23. Which of these organisms is most likely an ectotherm? Explain. ⭐TEKS

24. Which of these organisms is most likely an endotherm? Explain. ⭐TEKS

25. What is the normal body temperature of organism B?

Reading Check-up

Take a minute to review your answers to the Pre-Reading Questions found at the bottom of page 344. Have your answers changed? If necessary, revise your answers based on what you have learned since you began this chapter.

Chapter 13

1 Which of the following best describes the structure of a backbone?

A A segmented column of bones

B A hollow cord filled with liquid

C Protecting the nerve cord

D Cartilage

2 Which of the following is a function of the shell of an amniotic egg?

F The shell has small pores in its surface.

G The shell is hard and brittle.

H The shell lets carbon dioxide into the egg and oxygen out of the egg.

J The shell lets oxygen into the egg and carbon dioxide out of the egg.

3 Which of the following correctly describes the structure and function of a fish's gills?

A Structure—bony scales
Function—to protect the fish's body

B Structure—thin membrane
Function—to help the fish float

C Structure—thin membrane
Function—to remove oxygen from the water

D Structure—floats
Function—to remove oxygen from the water

4 Ruth has a pet frog. For her science project, Ruth wanted to find out what the frog ate and why it chose its food. One day, she put a red ladybug in the cage with her frog. The frog didn't eat the ladybug. Which of the following would be a reasonable hypothesis to explain why the frog didn't eat the ladybug?

F The frog felt sorry for the ladybug and wanted to set it free.

G The ladybug reminded the frog of an old friend.

H The frog will not eat anything that is red.

J The ladybug was stronger than the frog.

5 Bill's teacher asked the class to perform experiments to see whether salamanders prefer light or darkness. At the beginning of class, Bill and his partner washed their hands. During the experiment, they wore protective gloves and handled the salamander very carefully. When Bill and his partner were finished, they put the salamander back in the aquarium, wiped their table, and got their books together to leave the classroom. Which step did they miss?

A Asking the teacher's permission to perform an experiment

B Cleaning up

C Washing their hands after handling the salamander

D Washing their hands before handling the salamander

Chapter 13

Math

1 What is the *area* of the shaded figure?

A 5 square units

B 10 square units

C 20 square units

D 30 square units

2 Which ordered pair is inside of both rectangles?

F (3, 2)

G (5, 4)

H (6, 6)

J (8, 2)

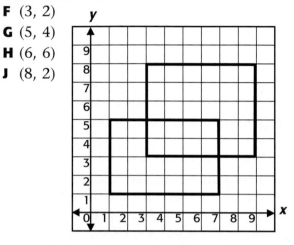

Reading

Read the passage. Then read each question that follows the passage. Decide which is the best answer to each question.

Most fish and marine animals are ectotherms. An ectotherm's body temperature closely matches the temperature of its surroundings. Endotherms, on the other hand, maintain a steady body temperature regardless of the temperature of their surroundings. Birds and mammals, such as dogs, elephants, and whales are endotherms. But only a few kinds of fish—tuna, for example—are endotherms. These fish can heat their eyes and brain. Endothermic fish can hunt for prey in extremely chilly water. Yet these fish pay a high price for their ability to inhabit very cold areas—they use a lot of energy.

1 Which of these is a FACT in this passage?

A It is better to be endothermic than ectothermic.

B An ectotherm's body temperature closely matches the temperature of its surroundings.

C Dogs and birds are ectotherms.

D Endothermic fish can hunt in warmer waters than ectothermic fish.

2 According to the passage, tuna are unusual because they are

F endotherms.

G ectotherms.

H fast swimmers.

J good hunters.

Robot Fish

When is a fish tail not a fish tail? When it's the tail of RoboTuna, a robotic fish made by scientists at the Massachusetts Institute of Technology (MIT).

Something Fishy Going On

Fish are certainly quicker and much more maneuverable than most ships and submarines. So why aren't ships and submarines built more like fish—with tails that flap back and forth? This question caught the attention of some scientists at MIT and gave them the idea to build RoboTuna, a model of a bluefin tuna. This robot fish is 124 cm long and has six motors, a skin of foam and Lycra™, and a skeleton of aluminum ribs and hinges connected by pulleys and strings.

A Tail of Force and Motion

The MIT scientists think that if ships were built more like fish, the ships would use much less energy. This would save money. A ship moving through water leaves a trail of little whirlpools called vortices behind it. These vortices increase the friction between the ship and the water. A fish, however, senses the vortices and flaps its tail, making vortices of its own. The fish's vortices counteract the effects of the original vortices, and the fish is pushed forward with much less effort.

RoboTuna measures changes in water pressure in much the same way that a living tuna senses vortices. Then the robot fish flaps its tail, allowing the robot to swim like a living fish. As strange as it may seem, RoboTuna may be the beginning of a new era in boat design.

Viewing Vortices

▶ Fill a roasting pan three-quarters full with water. Wait long enough for the water to stop moving. Then tie a 6 cm piece of yarn or ribbon to the end of a pencil. Drag the pencil through the water with the yarn or ribbon trailing behind it. What happens to the yarn or ribbon? Where are the vortices? ⭐TEKS

▶ *Inner workings of MIT's RoboTuna*

A strut supports the robot, encloses the tendons, and conveys control and sensor information.

A skin of foam and Lycra eliminates wrinkles or bulges and prevents the stray turbulence they would cause.

Ribs and flexible beams hold the skin in place while allowing the body to flex continuously.

Birds and Mammals

Pre-Reading Questions

1. How does the shape of a bird's wings help the bird fly? ⊛TEKS 6.10C

2. What makes a mammal a mammal?

PEST CONTROL FOR GIRAFFES!

Why is this bird riding on this giraffe? Well, this bird is more than a passenger. This bird and the giraffe on which it stands have a special relationship. The bird, called a tickbird, eats ticks and other pests off the giraffe. The tickbird also warns the giraffe when danger is near. In this chapter, you will learn more about different kinds of birds and mammals. You will also learn what makes birds and mammals so unique.

LET'S FLY! ✪TEKS

How do birds and airplanes fly? This activity will give you a few hints.

Procedure

1. Carefully fold a **piece of paper** to make a paper airplane. Make the folds even and the creases sharp.

2. Throw the plane very gently. What happened?

3. Take the same plane, and throw it more forcefully. Did anything change?

4. Reduce the size of the wings by folding them inward, toward the center crease. Make sure the two wings are the same size and shape.

5. Throw the airplane again, first gently and then with more force. What happened each time?

Analysis

6. Analyze what effect the force of your throw has on the paper airplane's flight. Do you think this is true of bird flight? Explain.

7. What happened when the wings were made smaller? Why do you think this happened? Do you think wing size affects the way a bird flies?

8. Based on your results, how would you design and throw the perfect paper airplane? Explain your answer.

READING WARM-UP

Terms to Learn

molting   preening
down feather   lift
contour feather   brooding

What You'll Do

● Describe the characteristics of birds.
● Explain lift.

Characteristics of Birds

What do a powerful eagle, a lumbering penguin, and a dainty finch have in common? Well, they all have feathers, wings, and a beak. These shared characteristics point to one answer—they are all birds!

Birds share many characteristics with reptiles. Like reptiles, birds are vertebrates. And birds' feet and legs, like those of reptiles, are covered by thick, dry scales. Even the skin around their beak is scaly. Birds also lay eggs that have an amniotic sac and a shell. But their eggshells are generally harder than the leathery shells of turtles and lizards.

Birds also have many characteristics that set them apart from other animals. Take a look at **Figure 1.** Birds have a beak instead of teeth and jaws. They also have feathers, wings, and many other adaptations for flight. And unlike most reptiles, fishes, and amphibians, birds maintain a constant body temperature.

Toucan

Figure 1 *Here are two of the almost 9,000 species of birds on Earth today.*

Hummingbird

Birds of a Feather

One of the most obvious characteristics of birds is feathers. Birds have two main types of feathers—down feathers and contour feathers. Examples of each are shown in **Figure 2.** Because feathers wear out, birds shed their worn feathers and grow new ones. Most birds shed their feathers at least once a year through a process called **molting.**

Figure 2 *Birds have light, fluffy down feathers and leaf-shaped contour feathers.*

Down feathers are the fluffy feathers that lie next to a bird's body. Their function is to keep a bird warm. When a bird fluffs these feathers, air is trapped close to its body. This helps keep the bird from losing body heat. **Contour feathers** are the stiff feathers that cover the body and wings of birds. They have a different structure and function than down feathers do. Take a look at **Figure 3.** Contour feathers have a stiff central *shaft*. The shaft has many side branches called *barbs*. The barbs hook together to form a smooth suface. Contour feathers fit together snugly over the body and wings. Together they form a streamlined surface that helps a bird fly. Their colors and shapes also help some birds attract mates.

Birds take good care of their feathers by preening. In **preening,** birds use their beaks to rub oil onto their feathers. The oil is made by a gland near the bird's tail. The oil waterproofs the feathers and helps keep them clean.

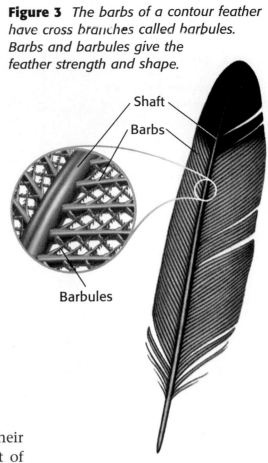

Figure 3 *The barbs of a contour feather have cross branches called barbules. Barbs and barbules give the feather strength and shape.*

Shaft
Barbs
Barbules

High-Energy Animals

Birds need a lot of energy to fly. To get this energy, their bodies break down food very quickly. This generates a lot of body heat. In fact, the average body temperature of a bird is 40°C—three degrees warmer than yours! Birds don't sweat to keep themselves cool like you do. When birds get too warm, they lay their feathers flat and pant like dogs do.

Eat Like a Bird?

Because birds need so much energy, they eat a lot. Hummingbirds eat almost constantly to maintain their energy! Most birds eat a high-protein, high-fat diet of insects, nuts, seeds, or meat. A few birds, such as geese, eat the leaves of plants. To break down so much food, birds have a special type of digestive system, shown in **Figure 4.**

Birds don't have teeth, so they can't chew. However, birds have beaks that fit their diet. They break or tear food into sizes they can gulp. The food then moves directly from the mouth to the crop, where it is stored. Birds also have an organ called a *gizzard*. This organ often contains small stones that grind up the food. Then the food can be fully digested in the intestine.

Figure 4 *A bird's digestive system allows food to be changed rapidly into usable energy.*

Crop
Gizzard
Intestine

Up, Up, and Away

Most birds fly. Even flightless birds, such as ostriches, have flying ancestors.

Birds have many adaptations for flight. To start with, all birds have wings. In addition, their hearts beat rapidly so that enough oxygen gets to their powerful flight muscles. Birds also have lightweight bodies so that they can get off the ground. Take a look at **Figure 5** on these two pages. It explains many of the bird characteristics that are important for flight.

Figure 5 Flight Adaptations of Birds

Most birds have **large eyes** and excellent eyesight. Large eyes allow birds to see objects and food from a distance. Some birds, such as hawks and eagles, can see eight times better than humans!

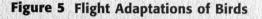

Lungs

Heart

Air sacs

Birds have special organs called **air sacs** attached to their lungs. The air sacs store air. So, a bird's lungs always have oxygen, whether the bird is inhaling or exhaling.

Birds have a **rapidly beating heart.** The heart pumps a fast, steady stream of oxygen-rich blood to the flight muscles. In small birds, the heart beats almost 1,000 times a minute! (Your heart beats about 70 times a minute.)

Wing shape is related to the kind of flying the bird does. Short, rounded wings allow a bird to quickly turn, drop, and pull up, much like a fighter plane moves. Long, narrow wings are best for soaring, just as a glider does.

Bird skeletons are compact and strong. Some of the vertebrae, ribs, and hip bones are fused together. This makes bird skeletons more rigid than those of other vertebrates. A **rigid skeleton** allows a bird to move its wings powerfully and efficiently.

Flight muscles

Keel

Birds that fly have **powerful flight muscles** that move the wings. These muscles are attached to a large breastbone called a **keel**. The keel anchors the flight muscles. It allows the bird to flap its wings with force and speed.

Birds have **hollow bones.** So birds have much lighter skeletons than other vertebrates do. The bones have thin cross supports that give strength, much like many bridges have.

Cross supports

Getting off the Ground

How do birds overcome gravity and fly? Birds flap their wings to get into the air. They keep flapping to push themselves through the air. Wings also provide lift. **Lift** is the upward pressure on the wing that keeps a bird in the air.

When air flows past a wing, some of the air is forced over the wing, and some is forced underneath it. Take a look at **Figure 6.** A bird's wing is curved on top. This means that the air moving over the wing moves *farther* than the air moving under it in the same amount of time. As a result, the air on top moves *faster* than the air underneath. Air pressure is lower in the faster-moving air over the wing. The higher air pressure under the wing pushes the wing toward the lower air pressure above it, creating lift.

The faster a bird flies, the greater the lift. So a bird flying fast will glide longer than a bird flying slowly. Wing size also affects lift. The larger the wing, the greater the lift. In fact, birds with large wings can soar long distances without flapping. An albatross, shown in **Figure 7,** can glide over the ocean for many hours without flapping its wings.

Figure 6 *A bird's wing is shaped to produce lift. Air moving over the wing moves faster than air moving under it. This creates a difference in air pressure that helps keep a bird in the air.*

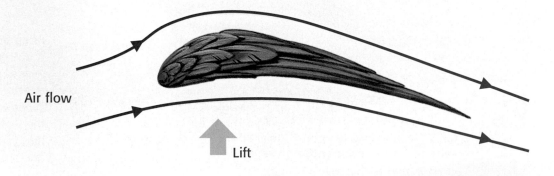

Air flow

Lift

Figure 7 *The wandering albatross has the largest wingspan of any living bird—3.5 m. This wingspan allows the albatross to glide for very long periods of time. An albatross comes ashore only to lay its eggs.*

Bringing Up Baby

Like most reptiles, birds reproduce sexually by internal fertilization. They lay eggs with the growing embryo inside. But unlike most reptiles, birds must keep their eggs warm for the embryo to live and grow.

Most birds build nests and lay their eggs inside them. **Figure 8** shows two of the many kinds of bird nests. Birds sit on and cover their eggs. They use their body heat to keep the eggs warm until they hatch. This is called **brooding.** The job of brooding is shared between the males and females of some kinds of birds, such as gulls. But among songbirds, the female broods the eggs. The male brings her food. In a few species, the male incubates the eggs.

Raising young birds is hard work. Some birds, such as cuckoos and cowbirds, make other birds do their work for them. A cuckoo lays its eggs in the nest of another kind of bird. When the cuckoo egg hatches, the young cuckoo is fed and protected by the foster parents.

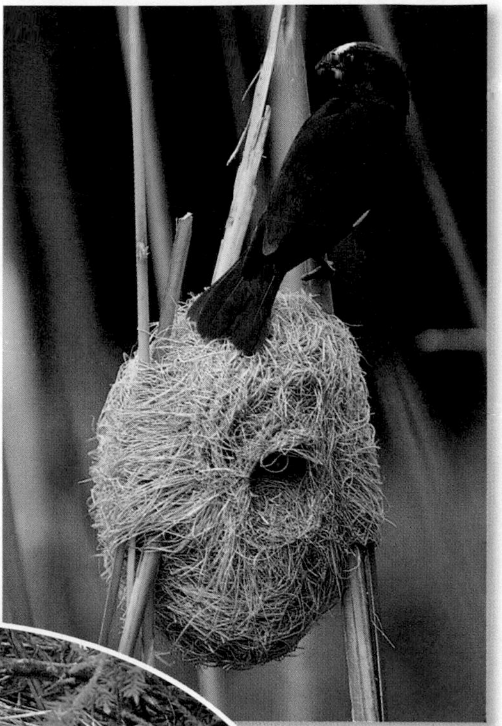

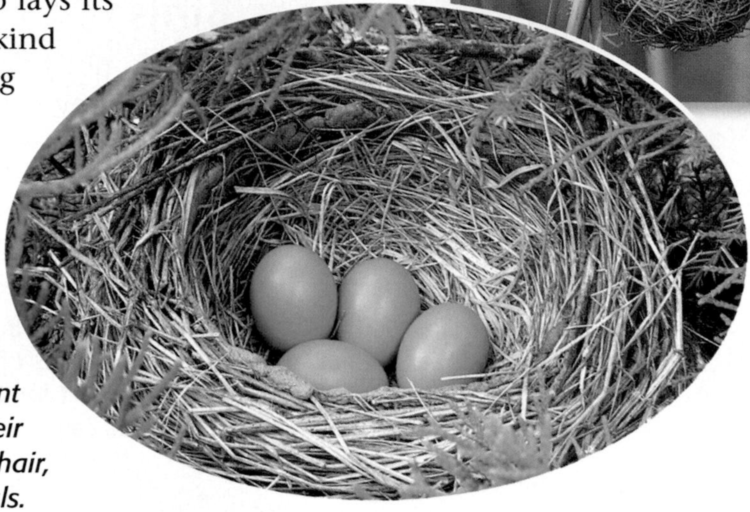

Figure 8 *There are many different types of bird nests. Birds build their nests with grass, branches, mud, hair, feathers, and many other materials.*

SECTION REVIEW

1. List three ways birds are similar to reptiles and three ways they are different.
2. People use the phrase "eats like a bird" to describe someone who eats very little. Is this saying accurate? Explain your answer.
3. How does the structure of a bird's digestive system complement its function? TEKS
4. **Applying Concepts** Would an airplane wing that is flat on top generate lift? Draw a picture to illustrate your explanation.

internet**connect**

sciLINKS NSTA **GO TO:** www.scilinks.org

TOPIC: Bird Characteristics
***sci*LINKS NUMBER:** HSTL405

Terms to Learn

waterfowl   bird of prey

What You'll Do

● Identify the differences between flightless birds, water birds, birds of prey, and perching birds.

Kinds of Birds

There are about 9,000 species of birds on Earth. Birds range in mass from the 1.6 g bee hummingbird to the 125 kg North African ostrich. The ostrich is almost 80,000 times more massive than the hummingbird!

Scientists divide living bird species into 28 different orders. Songbirds, such as robins or bluebirds, make up the largest order. This order includes 60 percent of all bird species. But birds are often grouped into four nonscientific categories: flightless birds, water birds, birds of prey, and perching birds. These categories don't include all birds. They do, however, show how different birds can be.

Flightless Birds

Most flightless birds do not have a large keel to anchor their flight muscles. Though they cannot fly, some flightless birds are fast runners. **Figure 9** shows three kinds of flightless birds.

| Figure 9 | Flightless Birds |

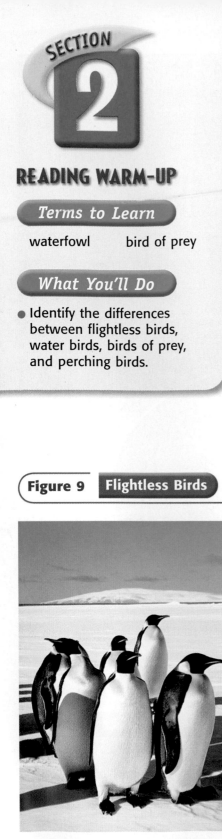

▲ Unlike other flightless birds, **penguins** have a large keel and very strong flight muscles. Their wings have changed over time to become flippers. They flap these wings to "fly" underwater.

The **ostrich** is the largest living bird. It can reach a height of 2.5 m and a mass of 125 kg. An ostrich's two-toed feet look almost like hoofs. These birds can run up to 64 km/h. ▶

▲ The **kiwi** is a small, chicken-sized bird from New Zealand. Kiwis sleep during the day. At night, they hunt for worms, caterpillars, and berries.

Figure 10 Water Birds

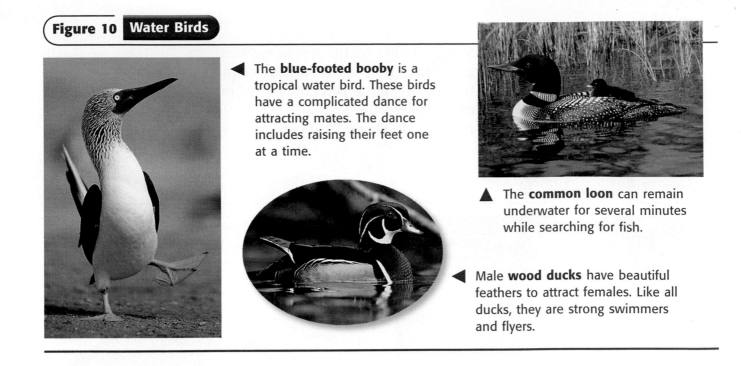

◄ The **blue-footed booby** is a tropical water bird. These birds have a complicated dance for attracting mates. The dance includes raising their feet one at a time.

▲ The **common loon** can remain underwater for several minutes while searching for fish.

◄ Male **wood ducks** have beautiful feathers to attract females. Like all ducks, they are strong swimmers and flyers.

Water Birds

Water birds are sometimes called **waterfowl.** Waterfowl include cranes, ducks, geese, swans, pelicans, loons, and many others. These birds usually have webbed feet for swimming or long legs for wading. Many are also strong flyers. **Figure 10** above shows three different water birds.

Birds of Prey

Birds that hunt and eat other vertebrates are called **birds of prey.** Take a look at the owl and the osprey in **Figure 11** below. Birds of prey have sharp claws on their feet and a sharp, curved beak. These traits help the birds catch and eat their prey. Birds of prey also have very good vision. Most of them, like the osprey, hunt during the day.

Figure 11 Birds of Prey

Owls, like this **northern spotted owl,** are the only birds of prey that hunt at night. They have a keen sense of hearing to help them find their prey. ▶

◄ **Ospreys** eat fish. They fly over the water and catch fish with their clawed feet.

Perching Birds

Songbirds, like robins, wrens, warblers, and sparrows, are perching birds. They have special adaptations for perching on a branch. When a perching bird lands, its feet automatically close around the branch. Even if the bird falls asleep, it will not fall off. **Figure 12** shows three types of perching birds.

Figure 12 Perching Birds

Parrots have special feet for perching and climbing. They open seeds and slice fruit with their strong, hooked beak.

Chickadees are lively little birds that often visit garden feeders. They can dangle underneath a branch while hunting for seeds, berries, or insects. ▶

Most tanagers are tropical birds. But the **scarlet tanager** spends the summer in North America. The male is red. The female is a yellow-green color that blends into the trees.

SECTION REVIEW

① Why do most flightless birds not need a large keel?

② Why are sharp claws and a sharp, curved beak important for birds of prey?

③ Analyzing Relationships How does the structure of a duck's foot complement its function? ⭐TEKS

READING WARM-UP

Terms to Learn

mammary gland
diaphragm

What You'll Do

- Learn about the origin of mammals.
- Describe common characteristics of mammals.

Characteristics of Mammals

What do you have in common with a bat, a donkey, a giraffe, and a whale? You're all mammals!

Mammals live in the coldest oceans, the hottest deserts, and almost every place in between. They range in form from the tiniest bats, which weigh less than a cracker, to the largest whales. The blue whale has a mass of more than 90,000 kg. It's the largest animal that has ever lived. **Figure 13** shows just a few of the many types of mammals.

Figure 13 *Even though these animals look very different, all of them are mammals.*

Beluga whale

Mandrill baboon

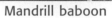
Rhinoceros

The First Mammals

Fossil evidence suggests that about 280 million years ago, reptiles called therapsids appeared. Fossils indicate that *therapsids* (thuh RAP sidz) had characteristics of both reptiles and mammals. An artist's idea of one of these reptiles is shown in **Figure 14.**

The first mammals appeared in the fossil record about 200 million years ago. They were about the size of mice. The early mammals were able to keep their body temperature constant. They did not depend on their surroundings to keep warm. This allowed them to look for food at night and to avoid being eaten by dinosaurs during the day.

When the dinosaurs died out, there was more land and food for the mammals. They began to spread out and live in many different environments.

Figure 14 *Therapsids had characteristics of both reptiles and mammals. They may have looked something like this.*

Birds and Mammals **383**

Common Characteristics

Dolphins and elephants are mammals, and so are monkeys, horses, and rabbits. You are too! All mammals share traits that make them unlike other animals.

Reproduction

All mammals reproduce sexually. Eggs are fertilized by sperm inside the female's body. Most mammals also give birth to live young. And all mammals nurse their young. Mammal parents are very protective. One or both parents care for their young until they are grown. **Figure 15** shows a brown bear with its young.

Figure 15 A mother bear will attack anything that threatens her cubs.

Figure 16 Like all mammals, this calf gets its first meals from its mother's milk.

Mother's Milk

All mammals have mammary glands. They are the only animals that have them. **Mammary glands** make a fluid called milk. Milk is made only in the glands of mature females. And all female mammals supply milk to their young. **Figure 16** shows a cow nursing her calf.

All milk is made of water, protein, fat, and sugar. The amount of each nutrient is different in different mammals. Human milk has half as much fat as cow's milk but twice as much sugar. Seal milk contains a high level of fat. A newborn elephant seal has a mass of 45 kg. After drinking its mother's rich milk for 3 weeks, it will have grown to 180 kg!

Getting Oxygen

All animals need oxygen to break down the food they eat. Like birds and reptiles, mammals use lungs to get oxygen from the air. But mammals also get help from a large muscle. This muscle, the **diaphragm** (DIE uh FRAM), helps bring air into a mammal's lungs. It lies at the bottom of the rib cage.

Cozy and Warm

Have you ever had a dog or cat sit in your lap, like in **Figure 17**? Then you know that mammals are very warm. Like birds, mammals need a lot of energy to survive. They eat a lot of food and use oxygen to break the food down. Then they use energy from the food to keep warm. Usually a mammal keeps its body temperature constant. This helps it survive in cold areas and stay active when the weather is cool.

Staying Warm

Mammals also have special characteristics to help them keep warm. One way they stay warm is by having hair. Having hair makes mammals different from other animals. Even whales have hair. Mammals that live in cold climates usually have thick coats of hair, or *fur*. The fox in **Figure 18** has very thick fur to keep itself warm. Large mammals that live in warm climates, like elephants, have less hair. Gorillas and humans have similar amounts of hair on their bodies. But human hair is finer and shorter.

Most mammals also have a layer of fat under their skin. The layer of fat helps them save body heat. Whales and other mammals that live in cold oceans have a thick layer of fat to keep themselves warm. This layer is called *blubber*.

Figure 17 *Mammals feel warm to the touch. This is because they use energy to keep themselves warm.*

·····Activity·····

Like all other mammals, you have a diaphragm. Place your hand below your rib cage. What happens as you breathe in and out? You are feeling the motion of your abdominal muscles. Those muscles are connected to your diaphragm. Contract and relax your abdominal muscles. What happens?

TRY at HOME

Figure 18 *The thick fur of this arctic fox keeps the fox warm in the coldest winters.*

Figure 19
Mountain lions have sharp canines for grabbing their prey.

Figure 20 *A horse cuts plants with the sharp incisors in the front of its mouth. It grinds the plants with flat molars in the back of its mouth.*

Crunch!

Another characteristic that makes mammals different from other animals is their teeth. Birds don't have teeth. Fish and reptiles do, but all of their teeth tend to be alike. Most mammals have teeth with different shapes and sizes for different jobs.

Look at your teeth, for example. You have cutting teeth, called *incisors,* in the front of your mouth. Most people have four on top and four on the bottom. The next teeth are stabbing teeth, called *canines.* Canines help you grab food and hold onto it. Farther back in your mouth are flat teeth for grinding, called *molars.*

A mammal's teeth match the kind of food it eats. Meat-eating mammals have large canines. Plant-eating mammals have larger incisors and molars. Look at **Figures 19** and **20.** They show the teeth of a meat-eating mammal and a plant-eating mammal.

Unlike other vertebrates, mammals have two sets of teeth. The first set of teeth are called *baby teeth.* These smaller teeth are replaced by a set of larger, permanent teeth. The second set grows in after the animal begins eating solid food and its jaw grows larger.

The Brainy Bunch

A mammal's brain is much larger than that of another animal the same size. The larger brain allows a mammal to learn and think quickly. It also allows the animal to respond quickly to events around it.

Mammals use their senses of vision, hearing, smell, touch, and taste to find out about the world around them. The importance of each sense often depends on a mammal's surroundings. For example, mammals that are active at night depend on their hearing more than their vision.

SECTION REVIEW

1. Name three characteristics that are unique to mammals.

2. What is the purpose of a diaphragm?

3. **Making Inferences** Suppose you found a mammal skull while on a hike. How would the teeth give you clues about the mammal's diet? ⭐TEKS

READING WARM-UP

Terms to Learn

monotreme   gestation
marsupial   echolocation
placental
    mammal

What You'll Do

- Explain the difference between the three groups of mammals.
- Give some examples of each type of mammal.
- Explain how bats use echolocation to find their way and their food.

Kinds of Mammals

Did you know that not all mammals develop in the same way? Some even hatch from eggs!

There are over 4,500 species of mammals. Mammals are divided into three groups based on the way their young develop. These groups are monotremes, marsupials, and placental mammals.

Monotremes

Mammals that lay eggs are called **monotremes.** Monotremes have all the traits of mammals, including mammary glands and hair. And like other mammals, they keep their body temperature constant.

A female monotreme lays eggs with thick, leathery shells. She uses her body's energy to keep the eggs warm. After the young hatch, the mother takes care of them and feeds them milk. Monotremes do not have nipples like other mammals. Baby monotremes lick milk from the skin and hair around their mother's mammary glands.

The three species of living monotremes are found only in Australia and New Guinea. Two of these species are shown below, in **Figure 21.**

Figure 21   Monotremes

Two of the species of monotremes are **echidnas** (ee KID nuhz). These spine-covered animals are about the size of a house cat. The echidna digs up ants and termites with its long nose and sharp claws. Then it catches the insects with its long, sticky tongue. ▼

▲ The third species of monotreme is the platypus. The **platypus** lives in rivers and ponds. It has webbed feet and a flat tail, which help it move through the water. It uses its flat, rubbery bill to dig for food. It also uses its bill to dig tunnels in riverbanks to lay its eggs.

Marsupials

You probably know that kangaroos have pouches. Kangaroos are **marsupials** (mar SOO pee UHLZ)—mammals with pouches. Like other mammals, marsupials have mammary glands, hair, and teeth. Unlike monotremes, marsupials give birth to live young. **Figure 22** shows some kinds of marsupials.

Newborn marsupials are not fully developed. At birth, kangaroos are as small as bumblebees. They drag themselves through their mother's fur to a pouch on her belly. Inside the pouch are mammary glands. The newborn kangaroo climbs in, latches onto a nipple, and starts drinking milk. The baby stays in the mother's pouch until it can move around by itself and leave the pouch for short periods. Young kangaroos are called *joeys*.

There are about 280 species of marsupials. Most of them live in Australia, New Guinea, and South America. The only living marsupial in North America is the opossum (uh PAHS uhm). Other marsupials include Tasmanian devils, wallabies, and koalas.

Figure 22 Marsupials

▲ **Koalas** sleep in trees during the day and are active at night. They eat only eucalyptus leaves.

When in danger, an **opossum** will lie perfectly still. It "plays dead" so predators will ignore it. ▶

◀ After birth, a **kangaroo** continues to grow in its mother's pouch. Older youngsters leave the pouch but return if there is any sign of danger.

Placental Mammals

Most mammals are placental mammals. In **placental mammals,** the embryos grow and develop inside the mother's body. They do this in an organ called the *uterus*. The embryos form a special attachment to the uterus called a *placenta*. The placenta brings food and oxygen from the mother's blood to the growing embryo. It also takes wastes away from the embryo.

An embryo develops within the mother during a time called **gestation** (jes TAY shuhn). Gestation in placental animals ranges from a few weeks in mice to as long as 23 months in elephants. Humans have a gestation of about 9 months.

Over 90 percent of all of the mammals on Earth are placental mammals. Living placental mammals are divided into 18 orders. The characteristics of the most common orders are given on the following pages.

✔ Self-Check

Explain the difference between monotremes, marsupials, and placental mammals. *(See page 640 to check your answer.)*

MathBreak

Ants for Dinner!

The giant anteater can stick its tongue out 150 times a minute. Count how many times you can stick out your tongue in a minute. Imagine that you are an anteater and you need 1,800 Cal a day to survive. If you need to eat 50 ants to get 1 Cal, how many ants would you have to eat per day? If you could catch two ants every time you stuck your tongue out, how many times a day would you have to stick out your tongue? How many hours a day would you have to eat?

Toothless Mammals

This group includes anteaters, armadillos, and sloths. Two closely related orders include aardvarks and pangolins. These mammals are called "toothless," but only anteaters have no teeth. The others have small teeth. Most toothless mammals eat insects they catch with their long, sticky tongues. Two kinds of toothless mammals are shown in **Figure 23.**

Figure 23 Toothless Mammals

Armadillos eat insects, frogs, mushrooms, and roots. When threatened, an armadillo rolls up into a ball. It is protected by its tough plates.

The largest anteater is the 40 kg **giant anteater** of South America. Anteaters never destroy the nests of the insects they eat. They open a nest and eat a few ants or termites. Then they move on to another nest.

Figure 24 **Insect Eaters**

Hedgehogs live throughout Europe, Asia, and Africa. Their spines keep them safe from most predators. ▶

◀ The **star-nosed mole** has sensitive feelers on its nose. These help the mole find insects and feel its way while burrowing underground. Moles have tiny eyes, but they cannot see.

Insect Eaters

Insect eaters, or *insectivores,* live on every continent except Australia and Antarctica. Most insectivores are small and have long, pointed noses to dig into the soil for food. They have very small brains and few teeth. Insectivores include moles, shrews, and hedgehogs. Some eat fruit as well as snakes and other animals. **Figure 24** above shows two different insectivores.

Rodents

More than one-third of all mammal species are rodents. Rodents can be found on every continent except Antarctica. They include squirrels, mice, rats, guinea pigs, porcupines, and chinchillas. Most rodents are small animals with long, sensitive whiskers. All rodents have sharp front teeth for gnawing and chewing. Because rodents chew so much, their teeth wear down. A rodent's front teeth grow continuously, just like your fingernails do. Two of the many kinds of rodents are shown below in **Figure 25.**

Figure 25 **Rodents**

Like all rodents, **porcupines** have gnawing teeth. ▶

◀ The **capybara** (KAP i BAH ruh) of South America is the largest rodent in the world. Females have a mass of up to 70 kg— as much as a grown man.

Figure 26 Lagomorphs

▼ **Pikas** are small animals that live high in the mountains. Pikas gather plants and pile them into "haystacks" to dry. In the winter, they use the dry plants for food and insulation.

◄ The large ears of this **black-tailed jack rabbit** help it to hear well and keep cool. Rabbits and hares have long, powerful hind legs for jumping. They also have sensitive noses and large ears and eyes that keep them alert to danger.

Lagomorphs

Rabbits, hares, and pikas are placental mammals called *lagomorphs* (LAG uh MAWRFS). Two lagomorphs are shown above in **Figure 26.** Like rodents, they have sharp, gnawing teeth. But unlike rodents, lagomorphs have two sets of sharp, front teeth in their upper jaw. They also have a short tail.

Flying Mammals

Bats are the only mammals that fly. You can see two kinds of bats in **Figure 27** below. Bats are active at night. They sleep in protected areas during the day. Most bats eat insects or other small animals. Some bats eat fruit or plant nectar. A few bats, called vampire bats, drink the blood of birds or mammals.

Most bats find their food and their way using echolocation. **Echolocation** means using echoes to find things. Bats make clicking noises when they fly. The clicks echo off trees, rocks, insects, and other objects. Echoes from a big, hard tree sound very different from echoes from a small, soft moth. Bats often have very large ears to hear the echoes of their clicks.

Figure 27 Flying Mammals

Fruit bats, also called flying foxes, live in tropical regions. They pollinate plants as they go from one plant to another picking fruit. ▶

◄ Most bats eat flying insects. Bats use their sensitive ears during echolocation. The **spotted bat** is found in parts of the American southwest.

Figure 28 Carnivores

Coyotes are members of the dog family. They live throughout North America and in parts of Central America. ▶

◀ Walruses, like all pinnipeds, eat in the ocean but sleep and mate on land. They use their enormous canines to defend themselves, to dig for food, and to climb on ice.

Carnivores

Carnivores are mammals that have large canines and special teeth for slicing meat. The name *carnivore* means "meat eater." Some carnivores also eat plants. For example, black bears eat grass, nuts, and berries and rarely eat meat. But many carnivores eat nothing but other animals. Look at **Figure 28** above. Carnivores include coyotes, cats, dogs, otters, bears, raccoons, and hyenas. A group of fish-eating ocean mammals, called *pinnipeds,* are also carnivores. Seals, sea lions, and walruses are pinnipeds.

Hoofed Mammals

Horses, pigs, deer, and rhinoceroses are some of the many mammals that have thick hoofs. A *hoof* is a thick pad that covers a mammal's toe. Most hoofed mammals are fast runners. They also have large, flat molars that help them grind plants.

Hoofed mammals are actually made up of two different orders—odd-toed and even-toed. An example from each order is shown below in **Figure 29.** Odd-toed hoofed mammals have one or three toes on each foot. Horses and zebras have a single, large hoofed toe. Rhinoceroses have three toes. Even-toed hoofed mammals have two or four toes on each foot. Pigs, cattle, camels, deer, hippopotamuses, and giraffes are even-toed.

Figure 29 Hoofed Mammals

Tapirs are large, three-toed mammals. They can be found in Central America, South America, and Southeast Asia. ▶

◀ Giraffes are the tallest living mammals. They have long necks, long legs, and are two-toed.

Trunk-Nosed Mammals

Elephants are the only mammals with a trunk. The trunk is a combination of an upper lip and a nose. Elephants use their trunk the same way we use our hands, lips, and nose. The trunk is powerful enough to lift a tree. It can also pick up small objects with fingerlike parts near its tip. Elephants use their trunk to put food in their mouth. They also use it to spray their back with water to cool off.

There are two species of elephants, African elephants and Indian elephants. Both are shown below in **Figure 30.** African elephants are larger and have bigger ears and tusks. Both kinds of elephants eat plants.

Elephants are the largest land animals. Male African elephants can grow to a mass of more than 6,000 kg! Elephants are very intelligent and may live for more than 60 years. They live in groups of related females. The oldest and largest female is usually in charge of where the herd moves. Once male elephants are grown, they leave the herd and live alone.

Environment
CONNECTION

Both species of elephants are endangered. For centuries, humans have hunted elephants for their long teeth, called tusks. Tusks are made of ivory, a hard material often made into carvings. Because of the high demand for ivory, much of the elephant population has been wiped out. Today elephant hunting is illegal in some countries, such as Kenya.

✔ Self-Check

1. Why are bats classified as mammals and not as birds?
2. How are rodents and lagomorphs similar? How are they different?

(See page 640 to check your answers.)

Figure 30 **Trunk-Nosed Mammals**

Elephants are social animals. They live in herds of mothers, daughters, and sisters. This is a herd of **African elephants.** ▼

▲ **Indian elephants** have smaller ears and tusks than African elephants.

Figure 31 Cetaceans

Spinner dolphins spin like a football when they leap from the water. Like all dolphins, they are intelligent and highly social. ▼

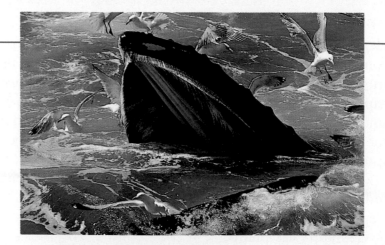

▲ **Humpback whales,** like this one, are toothless. Like all toothless whales, they strain sea water through special plates called *baleen,* which are shown here. The baleen trap tiny sea life for the whale to eat.

Cetaceans

Whales, dolphins, and porpoises make up a group of mammals called *cetaceans* (suh TAY shuhnz). All cetaceans live in the water. Take a look at **Figure 31** above. At first glance, they may look more like fish than mammals. But unlike fish, cetaceans have lungs and nurse their young. Most of the largest whales are toothless. They strain tiny, shrimplike animals from the sea water. Dolphins, porpoises, sperm whales, and killer whales all have teeth to help them eat. Like bats, these animals use echolocation to find fish and other animals.

Sirenia

The smallest group of mammals that live in the water is called *sirenia* (sie REE nee uh). Sirenia includes three species of manatees and the dugong. A manatee is shown in **Figure 32.** All sirenia live along coasts and in large rivers. They are large, quiet animals that eat seaweed and water plants.

Figure 32 Sirenia

Manatees are also called sea cows. They spend all of their time in the water, but they lift their noses from the water to breathe. ▼

Primates

Scientists classify prosimians, monkeys, apes, and humans as *primates*. There are about 160 species of primates. Two examples are shown in **Figure 33.** All primates have forward-facing eyes that can focus on a single point. Most primates have five fingers on each hand and five toes on each foot. Their thumbs allow them to make complicated movements, like holding objects. Most primates also have flat fingernails instead of claws. Primates have a larger brain than other mammals the same size. Many are considered highly intelligent mammals.

Many primates live in trees. They have flexible shoulder joints and grasping hands and feet. These traits allow primates to climb trees and to swing from branch to branch. Most primates eat leaves and fruits. Some also eat animals.

Figure 33 Primates

◀ **Spider monkeys,** like most monkeys, have grasping tails. Their long arms, legs, and tails help them move among the trees.

Orangutans and other apes often walk upright. Apes usually have larger brains and bodies than monkeys do. ▶

SECTION REVIEW

❶ If you saw only the feet of a hippopotamus and those of a rhinoceros, could you tell the difference between the two? Explain your answer.

❷ How are monotremes different from all other mammals? How are they similar?

❸ **Analyzing Relationships** How does the structure of an elephant herd help the herd survive? ⭐TEKS

❹ **Making Inferences** What is gestation? Why do you think dogs have a longer gestation than mice do?

internet connect

SC*LINKS*
NSTA   **GO TO:** www.scilinks.org

TOPIC: Texas Birds and Mammals
*sci***LINKS NUMBER:** HSTX275

TOPIC: Kinds of Mammals
*sci***LINKS NUMBER:** HSTL425

Making Models Lab

What? No Dentist Bills? ⭐TEKS

When you eat, you must chew your food well. Chewing food into small bits is the first part of digestion. But birds don't have teeth. How do birds make big chunks of food small enough to begin digestion? In this activity, you will develop a hypothesis about how birds digest their food. Then you will build a model of a bird's digestive system to test your hypothesis.

Ask a Question

1 How are birds able to begin digestion without having any teeth?

Form a Hypothesis

2 Look at the diagram below of a bird's digestive system. Form a hypothesis that answers the question above. Write your hypothesis in your ScienceLog.

MATERIALS

- several resealable plastic bags of various sizes
- birdseed
- aquarium gravel
- water
- string
- drinking straw
- transparent tape
- scissors or other materials as needed

Crop

Gizzard

Intestine

Test the Hypothesis

3 Design a model of a bird's digestive system using the materials listed on page 396. Label the following parts: crop, gizzard, and intestine.

4 Using the materials you selected, build your model.

5 Test your model with the birdseed. Record your observations.

Analyze the Results

6 Did your "gizzard" grind the food?

7 What do you think *gizzard stones* are? How do you think they help a bird?

8 Does the amount of material added to your model gizzard change its ability to work effectively? Explain your answer.

9 Birds can break down food particles without using teeth. What conclusions can you draw about how they do this?

Draw Conclusions

10 Analyze the strengths and weaknesses of your hypothesis based on your results. Was your hypothesis correct? Explain your answer.

11 What are some limitations of your model? How do you think you could improve it?

Going Further
Did you know that scientists have found "gizzard stones" with fossilized dinosaur skeletons? Look in the library or on the Internet for information about the relationship between dinosaurs and birds. List the similarities and differences you find between these two types of animals.

Highlights

Section 1

Vocabulary

molting (p. 374)

down feather (p. 375)

contour feather (p. 375)

preening (p. 375)

lift (p. 378)

brooding (p. 379)

Section Notes

- Like reptiles, birds lay amniotic eggs and have thick, dry scales.

- Unlike reptiles, birds have feathers and keep their body temperature constant.

- Because flying requires a lot of energy, birds must eat a high-energy diet and breathe efficiently.

- Birds' bodies are lightweight to help with flying. The structure of a bird's skeleton complements this function. The skeleton is rigid, and the bones are hollow and compact. ⊛TEKS

- The structure of birds' wings is related to their function. Their shape helps create lift. Lift helps keep a bird in the air during flight. ⊛TEKS

- The difference in air pressure above and below a bird's wings helps create lift.

- Birds reproduce by internal fertilization. Birds brood their eggs, keeping the eggs warm until they hatch.

Section 2

Vocabulary

waterfowl (p. 381)

bird of prey (p. 381)

Section Notes

- Most flightless birds do not have a large keel like other birds.

- Water birds are strong flyers. Most have webbed feet.

- Birds of prey have a sharp beak and claws for catching and eating their prey.

- The structure of a perching bird's feet relates to their function. When the bird lands, its feet automatically close around the branch.

Section 3

Vocabulary

mammary gland (p. 384)

diaphragm (p. 385)

Section Notes

- Mammals nurse their young.

- Female mammals have mammary glands, which make milk.

- A muscle called a diaphragm helps mammals breathe.

- Mammals keep their body temperature constant. All mammals have hair. Most have a layer of fat under their skin for warmth. ⊛TEKS

- Mammals have different kinds of teeth for chewing different kinds of food. Plant eaters have large incisors and molars for cutting and grinding plants. Carnivores have large canines for grabbing and tearing their prey. ⊛TEKS

- Mammals' large brains allow them to respond quickly to their environment.

Section 4

Vocabulary

monotreme (p. 387)

marsupial (p. 388)

placental mammal (p. 389)

gestation (p. 389)

echolocation (p. 391)

Section Notes

- Mammals are divided into monotremes, marsupials, and placental mammals.

- Monotremes lay eggs. They have mammary glands but no nipples.

- Marsupials give birth to tiny live young. The embryo climbs into its mother's pouch, which holds and protects the embryo. There the embryo drinks milk and develops. ⊛TEKS

- Placental mammals develop inside of the mother for a period of time called gestation. Placental mothers nurse their young after birth.

LabBook ⊛TEKS

Wanted: Mammals on Mars (p. 627)

USING VOCABULARY

Complete the following sentences by choosing the correct term from each pair of terms.

1. The time a mammal develops within its mother is called __?__. *(fertilization or gestation)*

2. The __?__ helps mammals breathe. *(diaphragm or air sac)*

3. The __?__ allows some mammals to supply nutrients to young in the mother's uterus. *(mammary gland or placenta)*

4. Birds take care of their feathers by __?__. *(molting or preening)*

5. A lion belongs to a group of mammals called __?__. *(carnivores or primates)*

6. __?__ are fluffy feathers that help keep birds warm. *(Contour feathers or Down feathers)*

UNDERSTANDING CONCEPTS

Multiple Choice

7. Both birds and reptiles
   a. lay eggs.
   b. brood their young.
   c. have air sacs.
   d. have feathers.

8. The rigid structure of a bird's skeleton helps the bird ⭐TEKS
   a. anchor its feathers.
   b. maintain impressively good posture.
   c. resist attacks from predators.
   d. move its wings powerfully enough to fly.

9. Only mammals
   a. have glands.
   b. nurse their young.
   c. lay eggs.
   d. have teeth.

10. Monotremes do NOT
    a. have mammary glands.
    b. care for their young.
    c. have pouches.
    d. have hair.

11. Lift is
    a. air that travels over the top of a wing.
    b. provided by air sacs.
    c. created by force from the diaphragm.
    d. the upward force on a wing that keeps a bird in the air.

12. Which of the following is NOT a primate?
    a. prosimian
    b. human
    c. pika
    d. chimpanzee

Short Answer

13. How are marsupials different from other mammals? How are they similar?

14. Both birds and mammals can keep their body temperature constant. How do they stay warm?

15. How does the structure of a bird's body complement its ability to fly? ⭐TEKS

16. What function do a bat's large ears serve? ⭐TEKS

CONCEPT MAPPING

17. Use the following terms to create a concept map: *monotremes, animals, constant body temperature, birds, mammals, mammary glands, placental mammals, marsupials, feathers,* and *hair.*

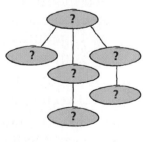

CRITICAL THINKING AND PROBLEM SOLVING

Write one or two sentences to answer each of the following questions:

18. Bird and monotreme eggs have a yolk, which provides nutrients. The eggs of placental mammals and marsupials do not. How do the embryos of marsupials and placental mammals get their nutrients?

19. Most bats and cetaceans use echolocation to find their prey and examine their surroundings. Why is it not enough for bats and cetaceans to rely on sight to do these things?

20. Suppose you are working at a museum and are making a display of bird skeletons. Unfortunately, the skeletons have lost their labels. How can you separate the skeletons of flightless birds from those of birds that fly? Will you be able to tell which birds could fly rapidly and which birds could soar? Explain your answer.

MATH IN SCIENCE

21. A bird is flying at a speed of 35 km/h. At this speed, its body uses 60 Cal/g of body mass per hour. Suppose the bird has a mass of 50 g. How many Calories will the bird use if it flies for 30 minutes at this speed?

22. Cecilia's kitten weighed two pounds when she brought him home from the animal shelter. The cat gained about $\frac{1}{2}$ pound each month for the next 11 months. It is reasonable to assume that at the end of the 11 months, the cat weighed—
    a. less than 5 lb.
    b. between 5 and 6 lb.
    c. between 6 and 7 lb.
    d. between 7 and 8 lb.
    e. more than 8 lb.

INTERPRETING GRAPHICS

Animals that keep their body temperature constant use a lot of energy when they run or fly. The graph below shows how many Calories a small dog uses while running at different speeds. Use this graph to answer the questions below.

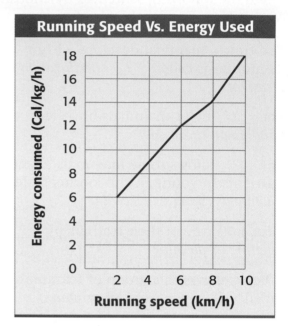

Running Speed Vs. Energy Used

23. As the dog runs faster, how does the amount of energy it consumes per hour change? ⭐TEKS

24. How much energy will this dog consume per hour if it is running at 4 km/h? at 9 km/h?

25. Energy consumed is given in Calories per kilogram of body mass per hour. If the dog has a mass of 6 kg and is running at 7 km/h, how many Calories per hour will it use?

Reading Check-up

⭐TEKS

Take a minute to review your answers to the Pre-Reading Questions found at the bottom of page 372. Have your answers changed? If necessary, revise your answers based on what you have learned since you began this chapter.

Chapter 14

1 Which of the following best describes the structure of a contour feather?

A Smooth, fluffy surface and inter-locking barbs

B No central shaft, fluffy, light

C Central shaft, interlocking barbs, smooth surface

D Fluffy to hold air near the body

2 Which of the following best describes the function of a contour feather?

F To make a bird look sleek

G To provide a streamlined flying surface

H To trap air close to a bird's body

J To keep oil on the bird's body

3 According to the graph below, which of the following mammals can tolerate the narrowest range of temperatures before being affected?

A Human

B Night monkey

C Marmoset

D Arctic fox

4 According to the graph below, which of the following mammals would be least likely to survive in freezing temperatures?

F Eskimo dog

G Ground squirrel

H Polar bear cub

J Arctic fox

The graph below shows the range of temperatures over which various mammals can perform normal body functions, such as digestion and respiration.

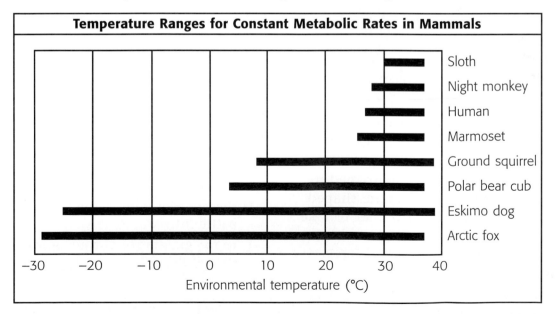

Chapter 14

Math

1 Gina has a bird cage. She bought a pair of parakeets for $31.96, a box of bird-seed for $1.69, and some parakeet treats for $3.98. What is the best estimate of the total cost of Gina's purchase before tax was added?

  A Between $35 and $36

  B Between $36 and $37

  C Between $37 and $38

  D More than $38

2 Sean kept a log of how many rabbits he counted in his garden for 1 week. On each of 5 days, he counted 5 rabbits. On each of the other 2 days, he counted 3 rabbits. Which number sentence can be used to find C, the total number of rabbits Sean counted that week?

  F $C = (5 \times 5) + (2 \times 3)$

  G $C = (5 + 5) \times (2 + 3)$

  H $C = 5 + 5 + 2 + 3$

  J $C = (5 \times 5) - (2 \times 3)$

Reading

Read the passage. Then read each question that follows the passage. Decide which is the best answer to each question.

For centuries, people have tried to imitate a spectacular <u>feat</u> that birds perfected millions of years ago—flight! It was not until 1903 that the Wright brothers were able to fly in a heavier-than-air flying machine. Their first flight lasted only 12 seconds, and they traveled only 37 m. Although modern airplanes are much more sophisticated, they still rely on the same principles of flight.

The sleek body of a jet is shaped to battle drag, while the wings are shaped to battle Earth's gravity. In order to take off, airplanes must pull upward with a force greater than gravitational force. This upward force is called *lift*.

1 In this passage, the word <u>feat</u> means

  A thing.

  B achievement.

  C perfection.

  D feature.

2 Based on information in the passage, the reader can conclude that

  F engineers model jet planes after birds.

  G the principles of flight have not changed over time.

  H the body of a jet is shaped to battle lift.

  J to fly, gravitational force must exceed lift.

NAKED MOLE-RATS

What do you call a nearly blind, 7 cm long rodent that looks like an overcooked hot dog? A naked mole-rat! This mammal makes its home in the hot, dry regions of Kenya, Ethiopia, and Somalia. For over 150 years, this animal has puzzled scientists by its strange appearance and odd habits.

What's Hair Got to Do with It?

Naked mole-rats have some strange characteristics. It's surprising that they are mammals at all! Their grayish pink skin hangs loosely on their body. It allows them to move through their home of narrow underground tunnels. At first glance, naked mole-rats appear to be hairless. (Remember, hair is an important mammal trait.) Though naked mole-rats don't have fur, they do have hair. Their whiskers guide them through the dark tunnels. Hair between their toes sweeps up loose dirt like tiny brooms. They even have hair on their lips. It keeps dirt from getting into their mouth while they dig!

Is It Cold in Here?

Most mammals keep their body temperature somewhat constant. This is not true of naked mole-rats. Their body temperature stays close to the air temperature in their tunnels. That's a cool 31°C—more than 5°C cooler than your body temperature. At night they huddle to prevent the loss of more body heat. Fortunately, the temperature does not change very much in their tunnels.

Who's in Charge?

Naked mole-rats form communities like bees and wasps do. They are the only mammals known to do this. A community has between 20 and 300 members. Each community has a queen. All females can reproduce, but only the queen is allowed to breed. She has up to three mates. The other members of the colony divide up tasks, such as finding food and digging or clearing tunnels.

Think About It!

At first glance, naked mole-rats are missing several important characteristics of mammals. Do further research to find out what characteristics they have that make them mammals.

▲ *Naked mole-rats are so unique that they have become a popular attraction at zoos.*

SCIENCE

Exploring Earth's Surface

Place to Visit

Fredericksburg ★

That's one big rock! Rising 122 m from Earth's surface, Enchanted Rock, located near Fredericksburg, Texas, has been a source of mystery and fun for visitors for thousands of years. At one time, Enchanted Rock was entirely underground. After thousands of years, water and wind have worn away rock and soil to uncover the tip of Enchanted Rock. Enchanted Rock is a protected state natural area, which means that only a certain number of people are allowed to visit each day. So, pack your backpack, and head for Fredericksburg. You might want to get there early to make sure you get a place on the rock!

Enchanted Rock, Fredericksburg Texas

Scientific Discovery

With the help of mapping technology, the Texas Historical Commission solved a mystery that was more than 300 years old. In 1686, the French explorer La Salle lost one of his ships, *La Belle,* during a storm. In 1995, using the Global Positioning System (GPS) and electronic survey tools, archeologists found *La Belle* resting in silt and sand about 4 m below the surface of Matagorda Bay, Texas. After the ship was found, archeologists mapped the location of every artifact that was recovered. Using the maps of the artifacts, archeologists can determine how the ship was built and what happened to it when it sank.

Matagorda Bay

Science Career

Austin

Cynthia Banks is a GIS data librarian with the Texas Parks and Wildlife Department in Austin, Texas. GIS, or Geographic Information Systems, is a type of computer software that allows people to analyze many different kinds of geographic data to answer questions. Banks helps manage a digital archive of GIS information. Using GIS data, Banks helps scientists and other researchers study and protect ecologically sensitive zones and archeological sites on Texas park land. Banks enjoys working with a wide range of people and says, "The software is continually changing so I'm in a learning mode all of the time."

Pre-Reading
Questions

1. Do all maps represent the world accurately? ✪TEKS
2. How is information shown on maps?
3. What information must every map have?

A Picture of the World

During ancient times, maps of the world were often based on imagination, guesswork, and travelers' tales. Areas of the world that had not yet been visited and explored were sometimes filled in with scenes of mythical places and monsters. Today computer technology and satellite images are used to make maps that are very accurate. In this chapter, you will learn about different kinds of maps and the things that go into making a map.

FOLLOW THE YELLOW BRICK ROAD ⭐TEKS

In this activity, you will not only learn how to read a map but also make a map that someone else can read.

Procedure

1. With a **computer drawing program or colored pencils and paper,** draw a map showing how to get from your classroom to another place in your school, such as the gym. Make sure you include enough information for someone unfamiliar with your school to find his or her way.

2. After you finish drawing your map, switch maps with a partner. Examine your classmate's map, and try to figure out where the map is leading you.

Analysis

3. Is your map an accurate representation of your school? Explain your answer.

4. How do you think your map could be made better? What are some limitations of your map?

5. Compare your map with your partner's map. How are your maps alike? How are they different?

READING WARM-UP

Terms to Learn

map   latitude
true north   equator
magnetic   longitude
   declination   prime meridian

What You'll Do

● Explain how a magnetic compass is used to find directions on Earth.

● Explain the difference between true north and magnetic north.

● List differences between latitude and longitude.

● Describe how latitude and longitude are used to find places on Earth.

You Are Here

Have you ever noticed the curve of the Earth's surface? You probably haven't. When you walk across the Earth, it does not appear to be curved. It looks flat.

Over time, ideas about Earth's shape have changed. Maps reflected the time's views of the world as well as the current technology. A **map** is a model of Earth's surface. If you look at Ptolemy's (TAHL uh meez) world map from the second century, shown in **Figure 1**, you might not know what you are looking at. Today satellites in space give true pictures of what Earth looks like. In this section, you will learn how early scientists knew Earth was round long before pictures from space were taken. You will also learn how to find location and direction on Earth's surface.

What Does Earth Really Look Like?

The Greeks thought of Earth as a sphere almost 2,000 years before Christopher Columbus made his trip in 1492. The observation that a ship sinks below the horizon as it moves farther away supported the idea of a round Earth. If the Earth were flat, the ship would appear smaller as it moved away.

Figure 1 *This map shows what people thought the world looked like 1,800 years ago.*

Eratosthenes (ER uh TAHS thuh NEEZ), a Greek mathematician, wanted to know how big Earth was. About 240 BCE, he calculated Earth's circumference using math and observations of the sun. We now know his estimation was off by 6,250 km, an error of 15 percent. That's not bad for someone who lived in a time when computer and satellite technologies were not around!

Finding Direction on Earth

How would you give a friend from school directions to your home? You might name a landmark, such as a grocery store, as a reference point. A *reference point* is a fixed place on Earth's surface from which direction and location can be described.

Because Earth is round, it has no top, bottom, or sides for people to use as reference points. Earth does, however, turn on its axis. Earth's *axis* is an imaginary line that runs through the Earth. At either end of the axis is a geographic pole. The North and South Poles, shown in **Figure 2,** are often used as reference points.

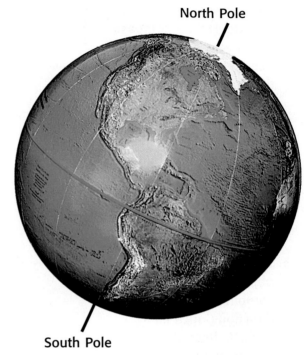

Figure 2 *The North Pole is a good reference point for describing a location in North America.*

Cardinal Directions

North, south, east, and west are called *cardinal directions*. **Figure 3** shows these cardinal directions and combinations of these directions. Using these directions is much more exact than using directions such as turn left, go straight, and turn right. For most of us, using cardinal directions requires the use of a compass.

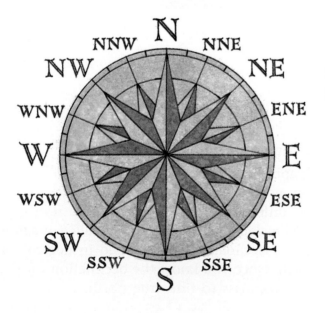

Figure 3 *A compass rose helps you orient yourself on a map.*

Using a Compass

One way to find north is to use a magnetic compass. A *compass* is a tool that uses the natural magnetism of the Earth to show direction. A compass needle points to the magnetic north pole. Earth has two different sets of poles—the geographic poles and the magnetic poles, as shown in **Figure 4.**

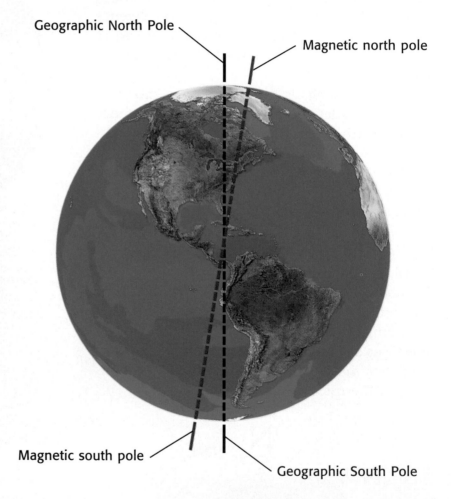

Figure 4 *You can see that the magnetic poles are in a slightly different place than the geographic poles.*

Geographic North Pole

Magnetic north pole

Magnetic south pole

Geographic South Pole

True North and Magnetic Declination

Because the geographic North Pole never changes, it is called **true north.** When using a compass, you need to make a correction for the difference between geographic north and magnetic north. The angle of correction is called **magnetic declination.** Magnetic declination is measured in degrees east or west of true north. Once you know the declination for your area, you can use a compass to find true north.

This correction is like the correction you would make to the handlebars of a bicycle with a bent front wheel. You have to turn the handlebars a certain amount to make the bicycle go straight. Look at **Figure 5.** A compass needle at Pittsburgh, Pennsylvania, points 5° west of true north. Can you find the magnetic declination of San Antonio?

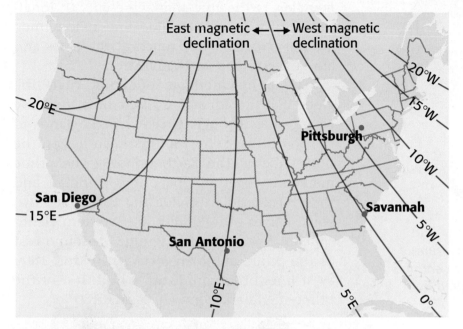

Figure 5 *The red lines on the map connect points with the same magnetic declination.*

Finding Locations on Earth

All of the houses and buildings in your neighborhood have addresses that give their location. But how would you find the location of a city or an island? These places can be given an "address" using latitude and longitude. Latitude and longitude are lines that cross on a globe or map and allow you to find exact locations. They are used together to make global addresses.

Latitude

Imaginary lines drawn around the Earth parallel to the equator are called lines of latitude, or *parallels.* **Latitude** is the distance north or south from the equator. Latitude is expressed in degrees, as shown in **Figure 6.** The **equator** is a circle halfway between the poles that divides the Earth into the Northern and Southern Hemispheres. It represents 0° latitude. The North Pole is 90° north latitude, and the South Pole is 90° south latitude.

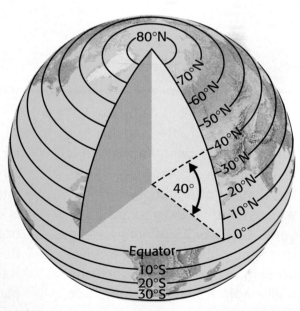

Figure 6 *Degrees latitude are a measure of the angle made by the equator and the location on Earth's surface, as measured from the center of the Earth.*

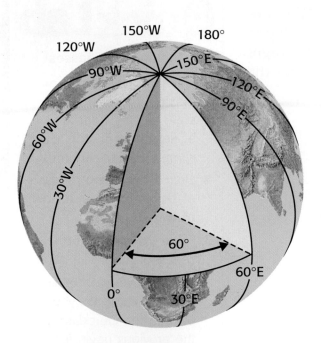

Figure 7 *Degrees longitude are a measure of the angle made by the prime meridian and the location on Earth's surface, as measured from the center of Earth.*

Longitude

Lines of longitude, or *meridians,* are imaginary lines that pass through the poles. **Longitude** is the distance east and west from the prime meridian. Like latitude, longitude is expressed in degrees, as shown in **Figure 7.** The **prime meridian** is the line that represents 0° longitude. Unlike lines of latitude, lines of longitude are not parallel. They touch at the poles and are farthest apart at the equator.

The prime meridian does not circle the globe like the equator does. It runs from the North Pole through Greenwich, England, to the South Pole. The 180° meridian lies on the other side of the Earth opposite the prime meridian. Together, the prime meridian and the 180° meridian divide the Earth into two equal halves—the Eastern and Western Hemispheres. East lines of longitude are found east of the prime meridian, between 0° and 180°. West lines of longitude are found west of the prime meridian, between 0° and 180°.

Using Latitude and Longitude

Points on Earth's surface can be found using latitude and longitude. Lines of latitude and lines of longitude cross to form a grid system on globes and maps. This grid system can be used to find places north or south of the equator and east or west of the prime meridian.

Spotlight On . . .

GPS

Have you ever been lost? There is no need to worry anymore. With the Global Positioning System (GPS), you can find where you are on Earth. GPS has 25 orbiting satellites that send radio signals to receivers on Earth. The receivers calculate a given place's latitude, longitude, and elevation.

GPS was invented in the 1970s by the U.S. Department of Defense for military use. During the last 20 years, GPS has made its way into people's daily lives. Today GPS is used in many ways. Airplane and boat pilots use it for navigation. Businesses and state agencies use it for mapping and environmental planning. Even some cars have a GPS unit that can show the car's location on a computer screen on the dashboard.

Using latitude and longitude, try finding the location of a Texas city shown in **Figure 8.** First choose a city, and find the dot representing the city on the map. Find the lines of latitude and longitude closest to the city. From here you can estimate the city's latitude and longitude.

Many people have problems remembering which lines are latitude and which lines are longitude. If you find yourself getting confused, try this memory device: lines of latitude go across the map like rungs of a ladder. Lines of longitude are long.

Figure 8 *The grid formed by lines of latitude and longitude allows you to pinpoint any place on Earth's surface.*

SECTION REVIEW

❶ Explain the difference between true north and magnetic north.

❷ In what three ways is the equator different from the prime meridian?

❸ Describe how the grid system that is used to locate places on Earth is a combination of two systems. ⭐TEKS

❹ **Applying Concepts** While digging through an old trunk, you find a treasure map. The map shows that the treasure is buried at 97° north and 188° east. Explain why this location is impossible.

SECTION 2

READING WARM-UP

Terms to Learn

Mercator projection
conic projection
azimuthal projection
aerial photograph
remote sensing

What You'll Do

- Describe a globe and identify its limitations as a model. ⭐TEKS
- Describe three map projections and identify their limitations as models. ⭐TEKS
- Describe technology that has helped improve mapmaking.
- List the parts of a map.

Mapping Earth's Surface

What do a teddy bear, a toy airplane, and a plastic doll have in common, besides all being toys? They are all models that represent real things.

Scientists also use models to represent real things, but their models are not toys. Globes and maps are examples of models that scientists use to help them study the Earth's surface.

Because a globe is a sphere, a globe is the most accurate model of Earth. A globe accurately shows the sizes and shapes of the continents and oceans in relation to one another. But a globe is not always the best model to use when studying Earth's surface. For example, a globe is too small to show a lot of detail, such as roads and rivers. It is much easier to show details on maps. Maps can show the whole Earth or parts of it. But how do you show Earth's curved surface on a flat map? Keep reading to find out.

A Flat Sphere?

A map is a flat representation of Earth's curved surface. However, when you move information from a curved surface to a flat surface, you lose some accuracy. Changes called *distortions* happen in the shapes and sizes of landmasses and oceans. These distortions make some landmasses appear larger than they really are. Direction and distance can also be distorted. Think about the example of the orange peel shown in **Figure 9.**

Figure 9 *If you remove and flatten the peel from an orange, the peel will stretch and tear. Notice how shapes are distorted, as are distances between points on the peel.*

Map Projections

Mapmakers use map projections to move the image of Earth's curved surface onto a flat surface. No map projection of Earth can show the surface of a sphere exactly. All flat maps have distortion. However, a map showing a smaller area, such as a city, has less distortion than a map showing a larger area, such as the world.

To understand how map projections are made, think of Earth as a clear globe with a light inside. If you hold a piece of paper against the globe, shadows appear on the paper. These shadows show marks on the globe, such as continents, latitude, and longitude. The way the paper is held against the globe determines the kind of projection that is made. The most common projections are based on three shapes—cylinders, cones, and planes.

Mercator Projection

A **Mercator** (muhr KAYT uhr) **projection** is a map projection that is made when the contents of the globe are moved onto a cylinder of paper. The Mercator projection shows Earth's latitude and longitude as straight lines. Lines of longitude are shown with an equal amount of space between each line. Lines of latitude are spaced farther apart north and south of the equator. As a result, areas near the poles look wider and longer than they really are. Look at **Figure 10.** Greenland appears almost as large as Africa. Africa is actually 15 times larger than Greenland.

Figure 10 *A Mercator projection is accurate near the equator but distorts distances and sizes of areas near the poles.*

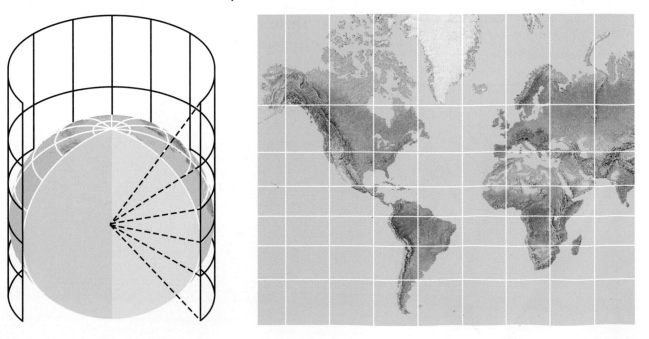

Conic Projection

A **conic projection** is a map projection that is made by moving the contents of the globe onto a cone, as shown in **Figure 11.** The cone touches the globe at each line of longitude but at only one line of latitude. There is no distortion along the line of latitude where the globe touches the cone. Places near this line of latitude are distorted the least amount. Because the cone touches many lines of longitude and only one line of latitude, conic projections are best for mapping land that has more area east to west. A conic projection is often used to map the United States.

Figure 11 *On a conic projection, distortion increases as you move away from the line of latitude where the globe touches the cone.*

Azimuthal Projection

An **azimuthal** (AZ uh MYOOTH uhl) **projection** is a map projection that is made by moving the contents of the globe onto a plane. Look at **Figure 12.** The plane touches the globe at only one point. There is little distortion at this point. However, distortion increases as you move away from the point where the plane touches the globe.

Figure 12 *On this azimuthal projection, distortion increases as you move farther away from the North Pole.*

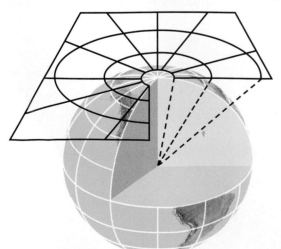

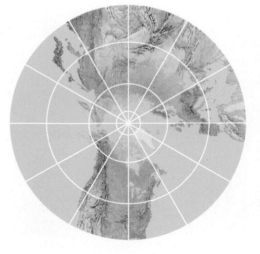

Modern Mapmaking

Mapmaking has changed more since the beginning of the 1900s than during any other time in history. Changes have been due to many technological advances, such as the airplane, cameras, computers, and space travel.

Airplanes and Cameras

The airplane and better cameras have had the biggest effect on mapmaking. Airplanes give people a bird's-eye view of the Earth's surface. Photographs from the air are called **aerial photographs.** These photographs are important in helping mapmakers make accurate maps.

Remote Sensing

The use of airplanes and cameras led to the science of remote sensing. **Remote sensing** is the gathering of information about something without being there. Remote sensing can be as basic as putting cameras in airplanes or as sophisticated as launching satellites that can sense and record what our eyes cannot see. Remotely sensed images allow a mapmaker to map the surface of Earth more accurately.

Our eyes can see only a small part of the sun's energy. The part we see is called visible light. Remote sensors on satellites can sense energy that we cannot see. Satellites do not take photographs with film like cameras do. A satellite gathers information about energy coming from Earth's surface and sends it back to receiving stations on Earth. A computer is then used to process the information to make a picture we can see, such as the picture shown in **Figure 13.**

Figure 13 *The satellite that took this picture of the University of Texas campus in Austin, Texas, was 264 km above Earth's surface!*

Information Shown on Maps

As you have already learned, there are many different ways to make maps. There are also many kinds of maps. You might have used a road map or other type of map. But regardless of the kind of map, each map should have the information shown in **Figure 14.** But don't be surprised if the next map you use is missing some of this information. Some maps are more carefully made than others. The better the map, the more information it will provide.

Figure 14 Road Map of West Texas

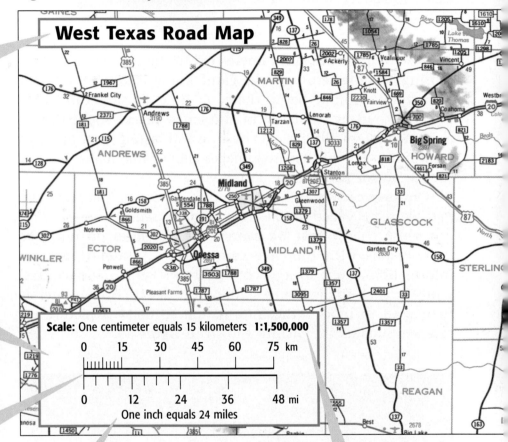

The **title** gives you information about the subject of the map.

West Texas Road Map

A **map's scale** shows the relationship between the distance on Earth's surface and the distance on the map.

A **graphic scale** is like a ruler. It is a bar showing units of distance that represent the distance on Earth's surface.

Scale: One centimeter equals 15 kilometers **1:1,500,000**

| 0 | 15 | 30 | 45 | 60 | 75 km |

| 0 | 12 | 24 | 36 | 48 mi |
One inch equals 24 miles

A **verbal scale** is a sentence that compares the distance on the map with the distance on Earth's surface.

A **representative fraction** is a fraction or ratio that shows the relationship between the distance on the map and the distance on Earth's surface. A representative fraction has no units, which means it stays the same no matter what unit of measure you are using.

Reading a Map

Imagine that you are planning a trip for a car club. Two people come in who want to drive from Midland, Texas, to Big Spring, Texas. Using the map in Figure 14, describe the shortest route between the two cities. List the roads the travelers would take, the direction they would drive, and the towns they would pass through. Use the map scale to figure out about how many miles there are between Midland and Big Spring.

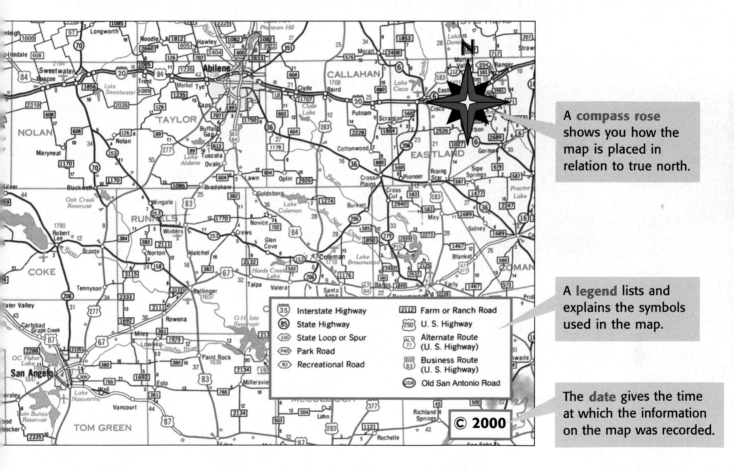

A **compass rose** shows you how the map is placed in relation to true north.

A **legend** lists and explains the symbols used in the map.

The **date** gives the time at which the information on the map was recorded.

SECTION REVIEW

1 A globe is a fairly accurate model of Earth, yet it has some limitations. What is one limitation? ⭐TEKS

2 Describe three map projections. Explain their limitations as models. ⭐TEKS

3 What is remote sensing? How has it changed mapmaking?

4 **Summarizing Data** List five things found on maps. Explain how each thing is important to reading a map.

📶 internet**connect**

SC*i*LINKS.
NSTA   GO TO: www.scilinks.org

TOPIC: Texas Maps
*sci*LINKS NUMBER: HSTX400

TOPIC: Mapmaking
*sci*LINKS NUMBER: HSTE040

Maps as Models of the Earth   **419**

Terms to Learn

topographic map
elevation
contour line
contour interval
relief
index contour

What You'll Do

● Describe how contour lines show elevation and landforms on a map.

● List the rules of contour lines.

● Read a topographic map.

Topographic Maps

Imagine you are going on a wilderness camping trip. To be prepared, you want to take a compass and a map. But what kind of map should you take? Because there won't be any roads in the wilderness, you can forget about a road map. Instead, you will need a topographic map.

A **topographic** (TAHP uh GRAF ik) **map** is a map that shows surface features, or topography (tuh PAHG ruh fee), of Earth. Topographic maps show both natural features, such as rivers, lakes, and mountains, and features made by humans, such as cities, roads, and bridges. Topographic maps also show elevation. **Elevation** is an object's height above sea level. The elevation at sea level is 0. In this section, you will learn how to read a topographic map.

Elements of Elevation

The United States Geological Survey (USGS), a federal government agency, has made topographic maps for all of the United States. Each of these maps shows a small area of Earth's surface. Because the topographic maps made by the USGS use feet rather than meters, we will follow their example for this discussion.

Contour Lines

On a topographic map, contour lines are used to show elevation. **Contour lines** are lines that connect points of equal elevation. For example, one contour line would connect points on a map that have an elevation of 100 ft. Another line would connect points on a map that have an elevation of 200 ft. **Figure 15** shows how contour lines appear on a map.

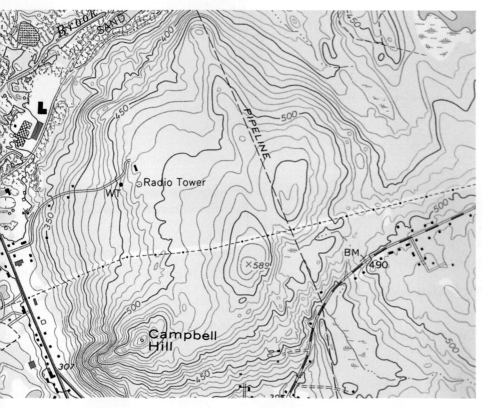

Figure 15 *The shape of the contour lines shows the shape of the land.*

Contour Interval

The difference in elevation between one contour line and the next is called the **contour interval.** A map with a contour interval of 20 ft would have contour lines every 20 ft of elevation change, such as 0 ft, 20 ft, 40 ft, and so on. A mapmaker chooses a contour interval based on the area's relief. **Relief** is the difference in elevation between the highest and lowest points of the area being mapped. Because the relief of an area with mountains is high, the area might be shown on a map using a large contour interval, such as 100 ft. However, a flat area has low relief and might be shown on a map using a small contour interval, such as 10 ft.

The spacing of contour lines also shows slope. Look at the two maps in **Figure 16.** Contour lines that are close together show a steep slope. Contour lines that are spaced far apart show a gentle slope.

MathBreak

Counting Contours

Calculate the contour interval for the map shown in Figure 15 on page 420. (Hint: Find the difference between two bold lines found next to each other. Subtract the lower marked elevation from the higher marked elevation. Divide by 5.)

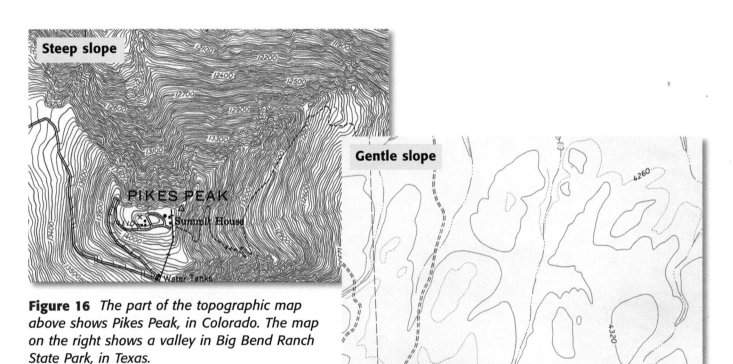

Figure 16 *The part of the topographic map above shows Pikes Peak, in Colorado. The map on the right shows a valley in Big Bend Ranch State Park, in Texas.*

Index Contour

On USGS topographic maps, an index contour is used to make reading the map easier. An **index contour** is a darker, heavier contour line that is usually every fifth line and is marked by elevation. Find an index contour on both of the topographic maps above.

 **Self-Check**

If elevation is not labeled on a map, how can you decide if the mapped area is steep? *(See page 640 to check your answer.)*

Reading a Topographic Map

Topographic maps, like other maps, use symbols to represent parts of Earth's surface. **Figure 17** shows a USGS topographic map and its legend. The legend shows some of the symbols that represent features in topographic maps.

Colors are also used to represent features of Earth's surface. In general, buildings, roads, bridges, and railroads are black. Contour lines are brown. Major highways are red. Bodies of water, such as rivers, lakes, and oceans, are shown in blue. Cities and towns are pink, and wooded areas are green.

Figure 17 *All USGS topographic maps use the same legend to show natural and human-made features.*

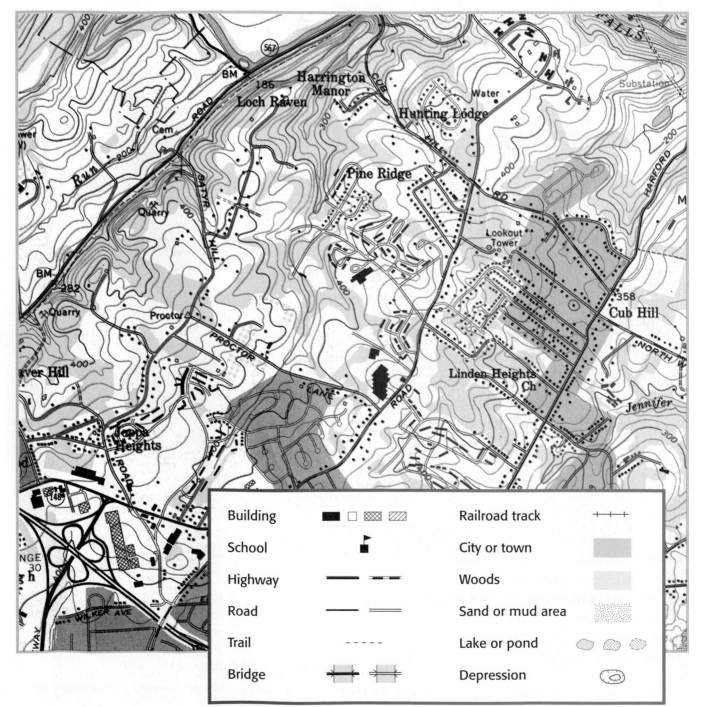

Building	▰ ▢ ▨ ▨	Railroad track	┼─┼─┼
School	⚑	City or town	
Highway	▬▬▬ ▬▬	Woods	
Road	─── ═══	Sand or mud area	
Trail	- - - - -	Lake or pond	⬭ ⬭ ⬭
Bridge	╪══╪ ╪═╪	Depression	⬭

The Golden Rules of Contour Lines

Contour lines are the key to explaining the size and shape of landforms on a topographic map. When you first look at a topographic map, it might seem puzzling. To read a topographic map, you need training and practice. The following rules will help you understand how to read topographic maps:

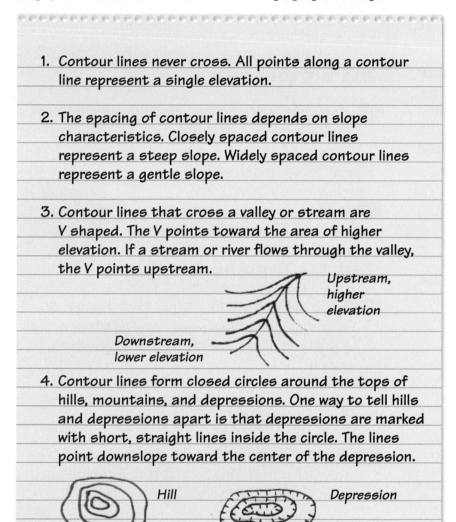

1. Contour lines never cross. All points along a contour line represent a single elevation.

2. The spacing of contour lines depends on slope characteristics. Closely spaced contour lines represent a steep slope. Widely spaced contour lines represent a gentle slope.

3. Contour lines that cross a valley or stream are V shaped. The V points toward the area of higher elevation. If a stream or river flows through the valley, the V points upstream.

   Upstream, higher elevation

   Downstream, lower elevation

4. Contour lines form closed circles around the tops of hills, mountains, and depressions. One way to tell hills and depressions apart is that depressions are marked with short, straight lines inside the circle. The lines point downslope toward the center of the depression.

   Hill   Depression

Environment
CONNECTION

The Texas Parks and Wildlife Department uses topographic maps to mark where endangered plant and animal species are. By marking the location of these animals and plants on a map, the Texas Parks and Wildlife Department can record and protect these places.

SECTION REVIEW

❶ How do topographic maps show Earth's surface? ⭐TEKS

❷ If a contour map shows streams, can you tell where the higher ground is even if all of the numbers are removed?

❸ Why can't contour lines cross?

❹ **Inferring Conclusions** Why isn't the highest point on a hill or a mountain shown by a contour line?

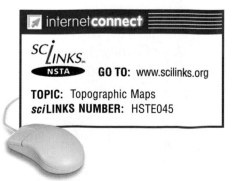

Skill Builder Lab

Round or Flat? ⭐TEKS

Eratosthenes thought he could measure the circumference of Earth. He came up with the idea while reading that a well in southern Egypt was entirely lit by the sun at noon once each year. He realized that for this to happen, the sun must be directly over the well! But at the same time, in a city just north of this well, a tall monument cast a shadow. Eratosthenes reasoned that the sun could not be directly over both the monument and the well at noon on the same day. In this experiment, you will test his idea and see for yourself how his investigation works.

MATERIALS

- basketball
- 2 books or notebooks
- modeling clay
- 2 unsharpened pencils
- metric ruler
- meterstick
- masking tape
- flashlight or small lamp
- string, 10 cm long
- protractor
- tape measure
- calculator (optional)

Ask a Question

1. How could I use Eratosthenes' investigation to measure the size of Earth?

Form a Hypothesis

2. In your ScienceLog, formulate a hypothesis that answers the question above.

Test the Hypothesis

3. Set the basketball on a table. Place a book or notebook on either side of the basketball to hold the ball in place. The ball represents Earth.

4. Use modeling clay to attach a pencil to the "equator" of the ball so that the pencil points away from the ball.

5. Attach the second pencil to the ball 5 cm above the first pencil. This second pencil should also point away from the ball.

6. Using a meterstick, mark a position 1 m away from the ball with masking tape. Label the position "Sun." Place the flashlight here.

7. When your teacher turns out the lights, turn on your flashlight and point it so that the pencil on the equator does not cast a shadow. Ask a partner to hold the flashlight in this position. The second pencil should cast a shadow on the ball.

8 Tape one end of the string to the top of the second pencil. Hold the other end of the string against the ball at the far edge of the shadow. Make sure that the string is tight. Be careful not to pull the pencil over.

9 Use a protractor to measure the angle between the string and the pencil. Record this angle in your ScienceLog.

10 Use the following formula to calculate the *experimental circumference* of the ball:

$$circumference = \frac{360° \times 5 \text{ cm}}{\textit{angle between pencil and string}}$$

Record this circumference in your ScienceLog.

11 Wrap the tape measure around the ball's equator to measure the *actual circumference* of the ball. Record this circumference in your ScienceLog.

Analyze the Results

12 In your ScienceLog, compare the experimental circumference with the actual circumference.

13 What could have caused your experimental circumference to be different from the actual circumference?

14 What are some of the advantages and disadvantages of taking measurements this way?

Draw Conclusions

15 Was this method an effective way for Eratosthenes to measure Earth's circumference? Explain your answer.

Section 1

Vocabulary

map *(p. 408)*
true north *(p. 410)*
magnetic declination *(p. 410)*
latitude *(p. 411)*
equator *(p. 411)*
longitude *(p. 412)*
prime meridian *(p. 412)*

Section Notes

- The North and South Poles are used as reference points for describing direction and location on Earth.

- Magnetic compasses are used to find direction on Earth's surface. The north needle on the compass points to the magnetic north pole.

- Because the geographic North Pole never changes location, it is called true north. The magnetic poles are different from Earth's geographic poles.

- Latitude and longitude help you find locations on a map or a globe. Lines of latitude run east-west. Lines of longitude run north-south through the poles.

- The magnetic declination is the difference between magnetic north and geographic north.

LabBook ★TEKS

Orient Yourself! *(p. 628)*

Section 2

Vocabulary

Mercator projection *(p. 415)*
conic projection *(p. 416)*
azimuthal projection *(p. 416)*
aerial photograph *(p. 417)*
remote sensing *(p. 417)*

Section Notes

- A globe is the most accurate model of Earth. A globe is limited in that it is too small to show detail. ★TEKS

- Maps have built-in distortion because some information is lost when mapmakers move images from a curved surface to a flat surface. ★TEKS

- Mapmakers use map projections to transfer images of Earth's curved surface to a flat surface.

- The most common map projections are based on three geometric shapes—cylinders, cones, and planes.

- Remote sensing has allowed mapmakers to make more accurate maps.

- All maps should have a title, date, scale, legend, and compass rose.

Section 3

Vocabulary

topographic map *(p. 420)*
elevation *(p. 420)*
contour line *(p. 420)*
contour interval *(p. 421)*
relief *(p. 421)*
index contour *(p. 421)*

Section Notes

- Topographic maps use contour lines to show a mapped area's elevation and the shape and size of landforms.

- The shape of contour lines reflects the shape of the land.

- The contour interval and the spacing of contour lines indicate the slope of the land.

- Like all maps, topographic maps use a set of symbols to represent features of Earth's surface.

- Contour lines never cross. Contour lines that cross a valley or stream are V shaped. Contour lines form closed circles around the tops of hills, mountains, and depressions.

LabBook ★TEKS

Topographic Tuber *(p. 630)*

Review

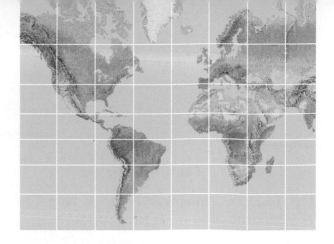

USING VOCABULARY

For each pair of terms, explain how the meanings of the terms differ.

1. true north/magnetic north

2. latitude/longitude

3. equator/prime meridian

4. Mercator projection/azimuthal projection

5. contour interval/index contour

6. elevation/relief

UNDERSTANDING CONCEPTS

Multiple Choice

7. A point whose latitude is 0° is located on the
   a. North Pole.
   b. equator.
   c. South Pole.
   d. prime meridian.

8. The distance in degrees east or west of the prime meridian is
   a. latitude.
   b. declination.
   c. longitude.
   d. projection.

9. The needle of a magnetic compass points toward the
   a. meridians.
   b. parallels.
   c. geographic North Pole.
   d. magnetic north pole.

10. The most common map projections are based on three geometric shapes. Which of the following geometric shapes is NOT one of them?
    a. cylinder
    b. square
    c. cone
    d. plane

11. A Mercator projection is distorted near the ⊕TEKS
    a. equator.
    b. poles.
    c. prime meridian.
    d. date line.

12. What kind of scale does not have written units of measure?
    a. representative fraction
    b. verbal
    c. graphic
    d. mathematical

13. What is the relationship between the distance on a map and the actual distance on Earth called?
    a. legend
    b. elevation
    c. relief
    d. scale

14. The latitude of the North Pole is
    a. 100° north.
    b. 90° north.
    c. 180° north.
    d. 90° south.

15. Widely spaced contour lines indicate a
    a. steep slope.
    b. gentle slope.
    c. hill.
    d. river.

16. __?__ is an object's height above sea level.
    a. Contour interval
    b. Elevation
    c. Declination
    d. Index contour

Short Answer

17. How can a magnetic compass be used to find direction on Earth's surface?

18. Why is a map legend important?

19. Why does Greenland appear so large in relation to other landmasses on a map with a Mercator projection? ⭐TEKS

20. What is the function of contour lines on a topographic map?

CONCEPT MAPPING

21. Use the following terms to create a concept map: *maps, legend, map projection, map parts, scale, cylinder, title, cone, plane, date,* and *compass rose.*

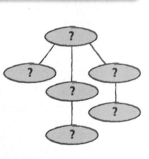

CRITICAL THINKING AND PROBLEM SOLVING

Write one or two sentences to answer the following questions:

22. One of the important parts of a map is its date. Why is the date so important?

23. A mapmaker has to draw one map for three countries that do not share a common unit of measure. What type of scale would this mapmaker use? Explain your answer.

24. How would a topographic map of the Rocky Mountains differ from a topographic map of the Great Plains?

MATH IN SCIENCE

25. A map's verbal scale shows that 1 cm equals 200 m. If the actual distance between two points is 12,000 m, how far apart will the points appear on the map?

26. On a topographic map, the contour interval is 50 ft. The bottom of a mountain begins on a contour line marked with a value of 1,050 ft. The top of the mountain is within a contour line that is 12 lines higher than the bottom of the mountain. What is the elevation of the top of the mountain?

INTERPRETING GRAPHICS

Use the topographic map below to answer the questions that follow.

27. What is the elevation change between two adjacent lines on this map?

28. What type of relief does this area have?

29. What surface features are shown on this map?

30. What is the elevation at the top of Ore Hill?

Reading Check-up

⭐TEKS

Take a minute to review your answers to the Pre-Reading Questions found at the bottom of page 406. Have your answers changed? If necessary, revise your answers based on what you have learned since you began this chapter.

Chapter 15

1 Evaluate the impact of technology on society. Which has been a benefit of remote sensing?

  A More accurate maps

  B Preventing bad weather

  C New computer technology

  D Advancements in photography

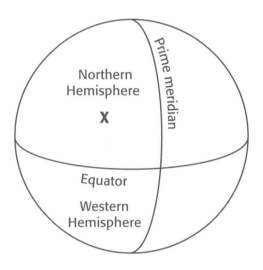

2 During a field investigation, the map above was made showing the location of the study site. Which of these descriptions accurately describes the location of the *x* on the map?

  F Northern Hemisphere; Eastern Hemisphere

  G Northern Hemisphere; Western Hemisphere

  H Southern Hemisphere; Eastern Hemisphere

  J Southern Hemisphere; Western Hemisphere

3 Which of the following is the most accurate model of Earth?

  A Mercator projection

  B Conic projection

  C Azimuthal projection

  D Globe

4 During a field investigation, the map below was made showing the distance from point A to point B. According to this map, what is the actual distance from point A to point B?

  F 1 km

  G 2 km

  H 3 km

  J 4 km

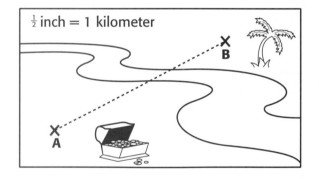

$\frac{1}{2}$ inch = 1 kilometer

Chapter 15

Math

1 How is the product $4 \times 4 \times 4 \times 4 \times 4 \times 8 \times 8 \times 8$ expressed in exponential notation?

A $4^8 \times 8^8$

B $4^5 \times 8^3$

C $5^4 \times 3^8$

D 32^8

2 What is the *area* of the shaded figure?

F 16 square units

G 24 square units

H 25 square units

J 30 square units

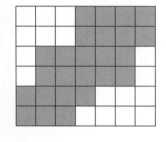

3 Jeremy hiked 10 kilometers. How many *centimeters* did he hike?

A 100 cm

B 1000 cm

C 10,000 cm

D 1,000,000 cm

4 Which group contains ratios that are all equivalent to $\frac{3}{6}$?

F $\frac{1}{2}, \frac{4}{8}, \frac{6}{12}$

G $\frac{2}{5}, \frac{4}{7}, \frac{5}{8}$

H $\frac{9}{12}, \frac{12}{15}, \frac{15}{18}$

J $\frac{2}{3}, \frac{4}{12}, \frac{6}{24}$

Reading

Read the passage. Then read each question that follows the passage. Decide which is the best answer to each question.

Many urban planners use Geographic Information System (GIS) maps to determine types of vegetation and the functions of different sections of land. GIS is a computer-based tool that allows people to store, <u>access</u>, and display geographic information collected through remote sensing, fieldwork, global positioning systems, and other sources. Maps and mapping systems play an important role in identifying land areas with water problems. Maps tell urban planners whether an area has problems with soil erosion, which could threaten water quality. Often the type of soil plays an important role in erosion.

1 In this passage, the word <u>access</u> means

A get.

B change.

C remove.

D process.

2 From information in the passage, the reader can conclude that

F GIS is not used very often.

G GIS is a mapping system.

H GIS is a new technology.

J urban planners are the only people who use GIS.

Science, Technology, and Society

The Lost City of Ubar

Can you imagine tree sap being more valuable than gold? Well, about 2,000 years ago, a tree sap called frankincense was just that! Frankincense was used to treat illnesses and to hide body odor. Ancient people from Rome to India treasured it. While the name of the city that was the center of frankincense production and export had been known—Ubar—there was just one problem. No one knew where it was! But now the mystery is solved. Using remote sensing, scientists have found clues hidden beneath the desert sand.

Using Eyes in the Sky

Remote sensing uses satellites to take pictures of large areas of land. The satellite records pictures as sets of data and sends these data to a receiver on Earth. A computer processes the data and makes a picture. These remote-sensing pictures can then be used to show differences that can't be seen by the human eye.

Remote-sensing pictures show modern roads as well as ancient roads hidden beneath the sand in the Sahara Desert. But how can researchers tell the difference between the two? Everything on Earth reflects or radiates energy. Soil, plants, cities, and roads all send out a unique wavelength of energy. The problem is, sometimes modern roads and ancient roads are hard to tell apart. To tell how similar things are different, researchers can give color to an area and can show the area on a computer screen.

Researchers used differences in color to tell the roads of Ubar apart from modern roads. When researchers found ancient roads and discovered that all the roads met at one place, they knew they had found the lost city of Ubar!

Continuing Discovery

Archeologists are still studying the region around Ubar. They believe that the great city may have fallen into a cave under its foundation. Researchers use remote sensing to study more pictures for clues to aid their investigation.

Think About It!

▶ Do modern civilizations value certain resources enough to start complex trade routes to move them? If so, what makes these resources so valuable? Record your thoughts in your ScienceLog.

Roads appear as purple lines on this computer-generated remote-sensing image. ▼

Rocks

Pre-Reading
Questions

1. What are the three
types of rock, and how
do they form?

2. What properties are used
to classify rocks? ✪TEKS

3. How does the rock
cycle change rock from
one type to another
type? ✪TEKS

STEPS FOR A GIANT

Irish legend claims that the mythical hero Finn MacCool built the Giant's Causeway, shown here, as stepping stones to cross the sea to invade a neighboring island. Actually, this rock formation is the result of the cooling of huge amounts of molten rock. As the molten rock cooled, it formed tall, hexagonal pillars separated by cracks called *columnar joints*. Columnar joints can be seen in basalt rocks around the world. In this chapter, you will learn more about how rocks form.

CLASSIFYING OBJECTS ⭐TEKS

Scientists use the physical and chemical properties of rocks to classify them. Classifying objects such as rocks requires close attention to many properties. Do this activity to get some practice classifying objects.

Procedure

1. Your teacher will give you a **bag containing several objects.** Examine the objects and note features such as size, color, shape, texture, smell, and any unique properties.

2. Invent three different ways to sort these objects. You may have only one group or as many as 14.

3. With a **computer program or colored pencils and paper,** create an identification chart explaining how you organized the objects into each group.

Analysis

4. What properties did you use to sort the items?

5. Were there any objects that could fit into more than one group? How did you solve this problem?

6. Which properties might you use to classify rocks? Explain your answer.

Terms to Learn

rock
mineral
igneous rock
sedimentary rock
metamorphic rock
composition
texture

What You'll Do

● Classify rocks by their physical properties. ⊙TEKS
● List the three different types of rock.
● Explain how the three different types of rock form.

Types of Rock

When you sort your socks, how do you decide which socks belong together? Would you use the same properties to classify rocks? Why do scientists classify rocks?

Believe it or not, some of the properties you use to sort your socks are used by scientists to classify rocks! Scientists classify rocks to learn more about how the rocks formed. But what exactly is rock? **Rock** is a solid mixture of crystals of one or more minerals. To learn how to classify rocks, you'll need to learn about minerals.

Minerals

So, what is a mineral? A **mineral** is naturally formed solid matter with a crystal structure. Every mineral has a unique set of physical properties, which can include color, hardness, and the way the mineral breaks. These properties are determined by the chemical makeup of the mineral. **Figure 1** shows several minerals. Can you tell these minerals apart?

Mineral crystals often form as a result of heat or pressure. Crystals can grow as melted rock material cools or as cooler rock material is heated. Minerals combine in many ways to form rock. Rock is often *classified,* or sorted into groups, depending on the minerals it contains.

Figure 1 *These minerals show various physical properties.*

Quartz is a very hard mineral that does not break along flat surfaces.

Galena is a metallic-looking mineral that breaks in three directions.

Biotite mica is a dark-brown mineral that breaks in only one direction. ▶

Orthoclase, a type of feldspar, commonly has a pink color and breaks in two directions.

▲ **Calcite** is a very soft mineral that also breaks in three directions.

The Nitty-Gritty on Rock Classification

Scientists classify all rocks into three main types based on how they form. The three major types of rock are igneous rock, sedimentary rock, and metamorphic rock. **Igneous rock** forms when hot, liquid rock cools and hardens. **Sedimentary rock** forms when rocks are broken down into smaller pieces that harden into new rock. **Metamorphic rock** forms when rock is heated or squeezed. Each of these rock types can be broken into smaller groups based on composition and texture.

What Is It Made Of?

The **composition** of a rock is its chemical makeup, or the combination of minerals of which it is made. The granite in **Figure 2** is a combination of quartz, feldspar, and biotite mica. The composition of a rock tells only half the story. Its texture tells the other half.

What Does It Look Like?

The **texture** of a rock depends on the sizes, shapes, and positions of the minerals in the rock. Some rocks are made of crystals that fit together like the pieces of a puzzle. Rock can also be made of fragments of rock or mineral, called *grains*. Grains range in size from very fine dust to boulders measuring several meters across.

Rocks with a *fine-grained* texture are made of small crystals or grains. *Coarse-grained* rocks are made of large crystals or grains larger than pebbles. Rocks that have a texture between fine and coarse grained are said to have a *medium-grained* texture. Examples of these textures are shown in **Figure 3.**

MathBreak

What's in It?

Imagine that a granite rock you are studying is made of 40 percent quartz and 45 percent feldspar. The rest is biotite mica. What percentage of the rock is biotite mica?

Figure 2 *The overall composition of a rock depends on the minerals it contains.*

Granite

10% Biotite mica

35% Quartz

55% Feldspar

| Figure 3 | Examples of Rock Textures |

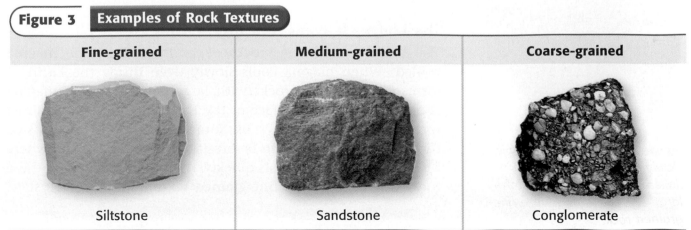

Fine-grained	Medium-grained	Coarse-grained
Siltstone	Sandstone	Conglomerate

Metamorphic Rock

Metamorphic rock forms when rocks *metamorphose,* or change, as they are heated or squeezed. Metamorphic rock generally contains crystals or mineral grains that are fused together by heat and pressure. **Figure 8** shows two examples of metamorphic rock.

Figure 8 *Gneiss (nies) is a metamorphic rock with a foliated, or banded, texture. Quartzite has no bands, so it has a nonfoliated texture.*

Gneiss

Quartzite

Dough Goes In, Bread Comes Out

The minerals in metamorphic rock depend on the type of rock that is being changed. Minerals in the original rock form new minerals when heated and squeezed. The depth and temperature of the rock determine which new minerals form.

Rocks Can Change Their Stripes

The texture of metamorphic rock depends on how the mineral grains are arranged. During metamorphism, the pressure on the rock causes the mineral grains to form bands. Rocks made of many different minerals often have a *foliated,* or banded, texture as shown in Figure 8. Rocks that contain grains of very few different minerals commonly have a *nonfoliated* texture, which means that the mineral grains do not line up.

internet connect

*sci*LINKS.

NSTA   GO TO: www.scilinks.org

TOPIC: Texas Rocks
*sci*LINKS NUMBER: HSTX455

TOPIC: Types of Rocks
*sci*LINKS NUMBER: HSTE091

SECTION REVIEW

1. What physical properties are used to classify rocks?

2. How do the three types of rock form?

3. Describe how sedimentary rocks get their textures.

4. **Making Inferences** If a rock is made of large particles with rough, angular edges, was the sediment deposited close to or far from its source? Explain. ⭐TEKS

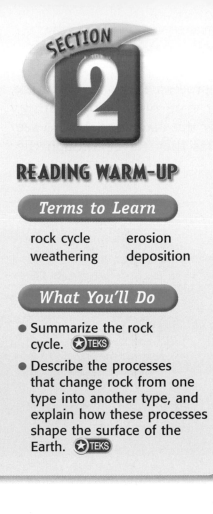

SECTION

2

READING WARM-UP

Terms to Learn

rock cycle   erosion
weathering   deposition

What You'll Do

● Summarize the rock
  cycle. ⊛TEKS

● Describe the processes
  that change rock from one
  type into another type, and
  explain how these processes
  shape the surface of the
  Earth. ⊛TEKS

The Rock Cycle

You know how important it is to recycle paper, plastics, and aluminum. But did you know that the Earth also recycles? As strange as it may sound, one of the things the Earth recycles is rock.

It may be hard to believe, but the Earth's rocks are always changing. The **rock cycle** is the continual process by which new rock forms from old rock material. Read on to learn about how rock changes as it moves through the rock cycle.

Round and Round It Goes

Through the rock cycle, each type of rock can become any other type of rock. All three rock types can melt to form magma. The magma cools to form igneous rock. All three rock types can be heated and squeezed to create metamorphic rock. All three rock types can break down to form sediment. When the sediment is deposited, buried, and cemented, it forms sedimentary rock. **Figure 9** shows the paths that rock material can take as it changes from one form to another.

Figure 9 *The rock cycle changes rock from one type to another.*

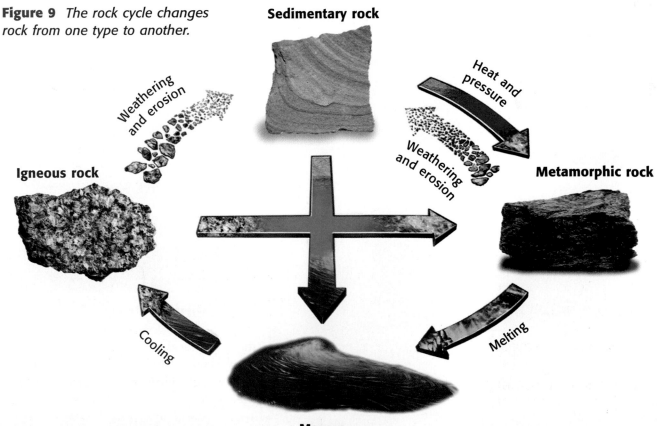

Sedimentary rock

Weathering and erosion

Heat and pressure

Igneous rock

Weathering and erosion

Metamorphic rock

Cooling

Melting

Magma

The Rock Cycle

The rock cycle is not a one-way process. Every type of rock can be changed into every other type of rock by heating, melting, or breaking down. Follow the diagram below to see one way sand grains can change as they travel through the rock cycle.

❶ Sedimentary Rock Grains of sand and other sediment are removed from the mountains and wash down a river to the sea. Over time, the sediment forms thick layers on the ocean floor. The sediment is squeezed and cemented together to form sedimentary rock.

❷ Metamorphic Rock As more sediment piles up, the rock is forced downward. At these greater depths, heat and pressure "cook" and squeeze the sedimentary rock, but they do not melt it. The sedimentary rock changes into metamorphic rock.

5

Sediment When overlying rock is worn away, the igneous rock is exposed at the Earth's surface. The igneous rock then wears away into grains of sand and clay. These grains of sediment are then carried and dropped elsewhere.

4

Igneous Rock The original sand grains from step 1 have changed a lot, but they're not done yet! Magma is usually less dense than the surrounding rock, so it tends to rise to higher levels of the Earth's crust. Once there, it cools and hardens to become igneous rock.

3

Magma The hot liquid that forms when rock melts is called magma. With the correct balance of heat and pressure, the metamorphic rock melts. The material that began as a bunch of sand grains now becomes part of the magma.

Figure 10 *Bryce Canyon, in Utah, provides beautiful examples of the results of weathering and erosion.*

Processes That Shape the Earth

What causes rocks to break down, heat up, melt, and cool? What processes help make and destroy rock? Water, ice, wind, and gravity all play parts in the processes that change rocks from one form to another.

Weathering and Erosion

When water, ice, wind, and heat break down rocks, the process is called **weathering.** Weathering is very important because it breaks rocks into smaller pieces. These pieces make up the sediment that forms sedimentary rock. Grains of rock are removed from their source by a process called **erosion.** Water and ice break off and carry away grains of rock. Wind can lift very small particles of dust and sand and can carry them long distances. Gravity can cause mudflows and rock slides. Erosion moves the sediment to a place where the sediment can collect. **Figure 10** shows one example of how land looks after weathering and erosion.

Deposition

Figure 11 *Sediment can take many forms, including sludgy mud, as seen in the lower left, and boulder-sized rubble, as seen in the lower right.*

The process in which water, ice, wind, and gravity drop newly formed sediments is called **deposition.** Sediment is deposited in lakes, oceans, rivers, streams, and other low-lying areas. **Figure 11** shows an example of deposition. Water carries dissolved minerals that can be deposited with the sediment. These substances glue the grains together to form sedimentary rock.

Heat and Pressure

Sedimentary rock can also form when the sediment is squeezed by the weight of overlying layers of sediment. If the temperature and pressure are high enough at the bottom of the stack, the rock can change into metamorphic rock.

The buried rock is also affected by heat, which can cause rock to metamorphose. In some cases, the rock gets hot enough to melt. This melting creates the magma that cools to form igneous rock.

The Cycle Begins Again

Buried rock is brought to the surface again in two ways. Sometimes rock is shoved to the surface by uplift. *Uplift* is the process by which regions of the Earth's crust rise to higher elevations. Buried rock is also brought to the surface when overlying rocks erode away. When the rock is at the Earth's surface, weathering, erosion, and deposition begin again. **Figure 12** shows that uplifted areas supply large amounts of sediment.

Biology
CONNECTION

Plants can cause a lot of weathering! When a tree grows, its roots can anchor into small cracks in rock. As the tree grows, the roots get larger. The expanding roots force the cracks in the rock to get larger. In time, a tree root can break solid rock!

Figure 12 *Mountains are uplifted areas that supply huge amounts of sediment. Sediment piles up at the base of the mountain in large, triangular formations called alluvial fans.*

SECTION REVIEW

1. Where do the grains that make up sedimentary rock come from?

2. Describe how the rock cycle changes rock from one type to every other type. ⭐TEKS

3. What processes affect rocks at the Earth's surface? ⭐TEKS

4. **Analyzing Relationships** If a rock is buried deep inside the Earth, which processes cannot change the rock? Explain your answer. ⭐TEKS

internet**connect**

SC*i*LINKS.
NSTA   GO TO: www.scilinks.org
TOPIC: The Rock Cycle
*sci*LINKS NUMBER: HSTE092

Making Models Lab

Round and Round in Circles ⭐TEKS

The rocks that make up the Earth are constantly being recycled. One form of rock is often broken down and changed into another form of rock. Do this activity to learn what happens to rocks as they change from one rock type to another.

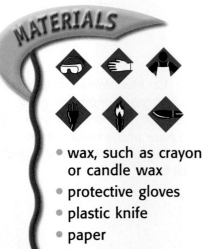

MATERIALS

- wax, such as crayon or candle wax
- protective gloves
- plastic knife
- paper
- heavy book
- heat-resistant gloves
- hot plate
- small pan or aluminum can
- wax mold

Procedure

1 Choose several pieces of wax. Each piece should be a different color. Carefully scrape the wax with the edge of a plastic knife to form a pile of shavings on a piece of paper. These shavings will represent tiny grains of rock or sand.

2 When you have made a large pile of wax shavings, cover it with a piece of paper and a heavy book. Gently press down on the book until the wax shavings stick together. This mixture of mineral grains will represent sedimentary rock. Write a description of the "rock" in your ScienceLog. How is it different from the tiny shavings you started with?

3 Now take your "sedimentary rock" and warm it in your hands for a while. Place the paper and the book on top of the warm wax. Press down on the wax a little harder than you did in the first step. Fold the warmed wax in half, and press down some more. This second type of rock represents metamorphic rock. Describe this new rock in your ScienceLog.

4 Place the wax in the pan. Put on heat-resistant gloves. Turn on the hot plate, and place the pan on the hot plate. Observe the wax as it melts. In this state, what does the wax represent?

5 Turn off the hot plate. Carefully pour the melted wax into a mold. Observe the wax as it cools and hardens. Carefully touch the wax with the eraser end of your pencil. Record your observations. The newly cooled wax represents igneous rock. Describe how this rock is different from the first two rocks you modeled.

6 Finally, take the cooled wax and scrape off bits of the rock to form grains of rock or sand. If you have time, go back to step 2.

Analysis

7 Review your descriptions of each type of rock that you modeled. Which rock do you think resembles the rock that forms from erupting volcanoes?

8 Which rock is formed from pieces of broken-down rock? How do these rock fragments harden into rock?

9 In step 6 you were asked to go back to step 2. Explain how this lab activity can be described as a rock cycle.

10 Does this model of the rock cycle have any limitations? Explain your answer.

Section 1

Vocabulary

rock *(p. 434)*
mineral *(p. 434)*
igneous rock *(p. 435)*
sedimentary rock *(p. 435)*
metamorphic rock *(p. 435)*
composition *(p. 435)*
texture *(p. 435)*

Section Notes

- Rocks are classified into three main types—igneous, sedimentary, and metamorphic— depending on how they form. Rocks are further classified by their composition and texture. ★TEKS

- Igneous rock forms when liquid magma cools and hardens.

- The texture of igneous rock depends on how quickly the magma cools. The slower the magma cools, the larger the crystals are.

- Sedimentary rock is made of grains of rock that are cemented together.

- The texture of sedimentary rock depends on the size and shape of the grains that the rock contains.

- Metamorphic rock forms when rocks are heated and squeezed deep inside the Earth.

- The texture of metamorphic rock depends on how the minerals in the rock line up when heated and pressed together. Texture of metamorphic rock depends in part on the composition.

Section 2

Vocabulary

rock cycle *(p. 439)*
weathering *(p. 442)*
erosion *(p. 442)*
deposition *(p. 442)*

Section Notes

- The rock cycle is the continual process by which new rock forms from old rock material. Each type of rock can be turned into all three types of rock depending on the processes that act on the rock. ★TEKS

- Weathering, erosion, heating, melting, and squeezing are processes that change one rock into another type of rock.

- Weathering is the process by which rocks at the Earth's surface are broken down by wind, water, and ice. ★TEKS

- Particles of rock are removed from their source by erosion. As sediments are transported, the size and shape of the grains change. ★TEKS

- Deposition happens when water, ice, wind, or gravity drops the sediment it is moving.

- When sediment or rock is buried, it is affected by heat and pressure. The heat and pressure can cause sediment and rock to harden, metamorphose, or melt.

- Rocks can be returned to the Earth's surface through erosion of overlying rock and by uplift. ★TEKS

USING VOCABULARY

Complete the following sentences by choosing the correct term from each pair of terms.

1. When metamorphic rock has a banded texture with mineral grains that are arranged in layers, it is called ___?___. *(foliated or nonfoliated)*

2. When grains of sand become cemented together, ___?___ rock forms. *(sedimentary or igneous)*

3. The texture of ___?___ rock depends upon how the rock cools. *(metamorphic or igneous)*

4. During ___?___, particles of rock are removed from their source. *(deposition or erosion)*

5. Rock changes from one form to another as it moves through ___?___. *(the rock cycle or composition)*

UNDERSTANDING CONCEPTS

Multiple Choice

6. A type of rock that forms when hot, liquid rock hardens is called
   a. sedimentary.　　c. fine grained.
   b. metamorphic.　　d. igneous.

7. A type of rock that forms as a result of heat and pressure but does not melt is called
   a. sedimentary.　　c. fine grained.
   b. metamorphic.　　d. igneous.

8. Sedimentary rocks can be made of particles from which of the following?
   a. sedimentary rocks　c. igneous rocks
   b. metamorphic rocks　d. all of the above

9. An igneous rock with a coarse-grained texture forms when
   a. magma cools very slowly.
   b. magma cools very quickly.
   c. magma cools quickly, then slowly.
   d. magma cools slowly, then quickly.

10. Rock can be brought to Earth's surface by uplift and by
    a. water.
    b. ice.
    c. wind.
    d. the erosion of overlying rock.

11. The arrangement of minerals in a rock determines the rock's
    a. texture.　　　c. composition.
    b. deposition.　　d. cycle.

12. When sediment or rock is buried deep inside the Earth, it is affected by
    a. heat and pressure.
    b. heat only.
    c. pressure only.
    d. heat, pressure, and erosion.

Short Answer

13. How do sandstone and conglomerate differ from one another? How are they similar?

14. In one or two sentences, explain how the composition of a sedimentary rock affects the composition of the metamorphic rock that it becomes.

15. Summarize the rock cycle. ⭐TEKS

16. Use the following terms to create a concept map: *rocks, rock cycle, cooling, metamorphic, igneous, heat, pressure, melting, deposition, erosion,* and *sedimentary.*

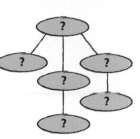

Write one or two sentences to answer the following questions:

17. Suppose you were asked to identify an unknown rock. Describe what physical and chemical properties you would use to classify the rock. ★TEKS

18. At the peak of a mountain, you find a rock containing fossils of plants that lived only at low elevations. How did the rock get to the top of a mountain? ★TEKS

19. At the base of the same mountain as in item 18, you find a rock like the one from the peak. The rock from your base camp is smaller and more rounded than the rock from the peak, but it has the same texture and composition. How did a rock from the top of the mountain get to the bottom? ★TEKS

20. Imagine that you have found a rock that contains igneous, metamorphic, and sedimentary rock fragments. In which group would you classify this rock? Explain.

21. A 60 kg granite boulder was broken down into sand grains. If quartz makes up 35 percent of the boulder's mass, how many kilograms of the resulting sand are quartz grains?

Imagine that you have a sample of granite, and you analyzed it to find out what it is made of. The results of your analysis are shown below.

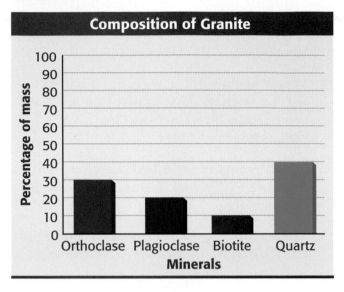

22. Your sample is made of four minerals. What percentage of each mineral is your sample made of? ★TEKS

23. Both plagioclase and orthoclase are feldspar minerals. What percentage of the minerals in the granite are NOT feldspar minerals? ★TEKS

24. If your rock sample has a mass of 10 g, how many grams of quartz does it contain?

25. Using graph paper or a computer, make a pie chart showing how much of each of the four minerals the granite contains. (You will find help on making pie charts in the Appendix of this book.) ★TEKS

Reading Check-up

★TEKS

Take a minute to review your answers to the Pre-Reading Questions found at the bottom of page 432. Have your answers changed? If necessary, revise your answers based on what you have learned since you began this chapter.

Chapter 16

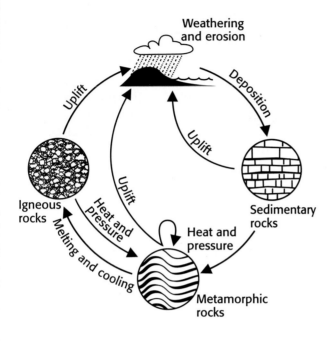

Weathering and erosion

Uplift

Deposition

Uplift

Igneous rocks

Uplift

Heat and pressure

Melting and cooling

Heat and pressure

Sedimentary rocks

Metamorphic rocks

1 According to the rock cycle diagram above, which of the following is NOT true?

A Only sedimentary rock gets weathered and eroded.

B Sedimentary rocks are made from metamorphic, igneous, and sedimentary rock fragments and minerals.

C Melting and cooling create igneous rocks.

D Metamorphic rock is created by the effects of heat and pressure.

2 Which of the following processes brings rocks to Earth's surface, where they can be eroded?

F Burial

G Deposition

H Uplift

J Weathering

3 Volcanoes erupt hot, liquid rock. What type of rock is produced by volcanoes?

A Metamorphic

B Sedimentary

C Both metamorphic and igneous

D Igneous

4 Which of the following is the best summary of the rock cycle?

F All three rock types get weathered to create sedimentary rock. All three rock types melt to form magma. Magma forms igneous rock. All three types of rock form metamorphic rock due to heat and pressure.

G Each type of rock gets melted; then the magma turns into igneous, sedimentary, and metamorphic rock.

H Magma cools to form igneous rock. Then the igneous rock becomes sedimentary rock. Sedimentary rock is heated and forms metamorphic rock. Metamorphic rock melts to form magma.

J Igneous rock gets weathered to create sedimentary rock. Sedimentary rock is melted to form igneous rock. Metamorphic rock is melted to form igneous rock.

5 A rock exists at the surface of the Earth. Predict the next step in the rock cycle.

A Cooling

B Erosion

C Melting

D Metamorphism

Chapter 16

Math

1 Eric has a box of rocks that contains 25 rocks. Nine rocks are sedimentary, 10 are igneous, and 6 are metamorphic. If Eric chooses a rock at random, what is the probability that he will choose an igneous rock?

A $\frac{1}{2}$

B $\frac{2}{5}$

C $\frac{3}{8}$

D $\frac{1}{15}$

2 At the rock and mineral show, Elizabeth bought 2 quartz crystals that cost $2.00 each and 4 trilobite fossils that cost $3.50 each. Which number sentence can be used to describe *c*, the total cost of her purchases?

F $c = (2 \times 4) + (2.00 \times 3.50)$

G $c = (2 \times 2.00) - (4 \times 3.50)$

H $c = (2 \times 2.00) + (4 \times 3.50)$

J $c = (4 \times 2.00) + (2 \times 3.50)$

K $c = (2 + 2.00) \times (4 + 3.50)$

Reading

Read the passage. Then read each question that follows the passage. Decide which is the best answer to each question.

The texture and composition of a rock can provide good clues about how and where the rock formed. Scientists use both texture and composition to understand the origin and history of rocks. For example, marble is a rock that is made when limestone is metamorphosed. Only limestone contains the right minerals to change into marble. Therefore, wherever scientists find marble, they know that the sediment that created the original rock was deposited in a warm ocean or lake environment.

1 In this passage, the word <u>origin</u> means

A size or appearance.

B age.

C location or surroundings.

D source or formation.

2 From the information in the passage, the reader can conclude that

F marble is a sedimentary rock.

G limestone is deposited in warm ocean or lake environments.

H the marble is 25 million years old.

J in identification, the texture of a rock is more important than the composition.

3 What is the main idea of the paragraph?

A Scientists like to find marble.

B Scientists study the texture and composition of the rock to decide how the rock formed and what happened after it formed.

C Some sediments are deposited in warm oceans and lakes.

D When limestone metamorphoses, it creates marble.

Science, Technology, and Society

Rock City

Today when we dig into a mountainside to build a highway or make room for a building, we use heavy machinery and explosives. Can you imagine doing the same job using just a hammer and chisel? Well, between about 300 BCE and 200 CE, an Arab tribe called the Nabateans (NAB uh TEE uhns) did just that. In fact, the tribe carved a whole city—homes, storage areas, monuments, administrative offices, and temples—right into the mountainsides!

▲ *Petra's most famous building, the Treasury, was shown in the movie* Indiana Jones and the Last Crusade.

Rose-Red City

This amazing city in southern Jordan is Petra (named by the Roman emperor Hadrian Petra during a visit in 131 CE). A poet once described Petra as "the rose-red city" because all of the buildings and monuments were carved from the pink sandstone mountains surrounding Petra.

Using this reddish stone, the Nabateans lined the main street in the center of the city with tall stone columns. The street ends at what was once the foot of a mountain but is now known as the Great Temple—a two-story stone religious complex larger than a football field!

The High Place of Sacrifice, another site near the center of the city, was a mountaintop. The Nabateans leveled the top and created a place of worship more than 1,000 m above the valley floor. Today, visitors climb stairs to the top. Along the way, they pass dozens of tombs carved into the pink rock walls.

Tombs and More Tombs

There are more than 800 other tombs dug into the mountainsides in and around Petra. One of them, the Treasury (created for a Nabatean ruler), stands more than 40 m high! It is a magnificent building with an elaborate facade. Behind the massive stone front, the Nabateans carved one large room and two smaller rooms deeper into the mountain.

Petra Declines

The Nabateans once ruled an area extending from Petra to Damascus. They grew wealthy and powerful by controlling important trade routes near Petra. But their wealth attracted the Roman Empire, and in 106 CE, Petra became a Roman province. Though the city prospered under Roman rule for almost another century, a gradual decline in Nabatean power began. The trade routes by land that the Nabateans controlled for hundreds of years were abandoned in favor of a route by the Red Sea. People moved and the city faded. By the seventh century, nothing was left of Petra but empty stone structures.

Think About It!

▶ Petra is sometimes referred to as a city "from the rock as if by magic grown." Why might such a city seem "magic" to us today? What might have encouraged the Nabateans to create this city? Share your thoughts with a classmate.

UNIT 6

SCIENCE

Earth Systems and Structure

Place to Visit

Pine Springs

Desert mountains or ocean reef? The Guadalupe Mountains are actually both. About 250 million years ago, the Capitan Reef was deep under a vast tropical ocean that covered much of what is now Texas. Long after the reef was buried and the ocean evaporated, the rocks that make up the Guadalupe Mountains were uplifted to the Earth's surface. Now you can visit Guadalupe Mountains National Park in Pine Springs, Texas, and see part of the world's most extensive Permian limestone fossil reef, as well as the highest point in Texas—Guadalupe Peak, which stands 2,667 m (or 8,750 ft) high.

The Guadalupe Mountains, Pine Springs, Texas

Scientific Research

★ Lubbock

Texas Tech University in Lubbock, Texas, is the home of the Wind Engineering Research Center (WERC). The WERC has been conducting research and on-site documentation of windstorms since 1970. The WERC faculty and students conduct research on damage caused by winds from windstorms, tornadoes, and hurricanes. They also use the research facilities at Texas Tech to design buildings and structures that resist damage from high winds. The WERC has designed an above-ground, in-residence tornado shelter that is approved and endorsed by the Federal Emergency Management Agency (FEMA).

Science Career

San Antonio ★

Dr. George Veni is a hydrogeologist and the owner of a hydrological and environmental consulting firm in San Antonio, Texas. Dr. Veni uses his knowledge and experience in caves and karst areas to consult on issues related to ground-water quality and quantity, cave-adapted endangered species, and geologic structures. His services are needed when construction projects are planned for areas with caves and sinkholes. He has also become somewhat of an expert on cave-dwelling creatures that may be endangered by construction projects in environmentally sensitive areas.

internet connect

go. hrw .com

go to: go.hrw.com
KEYWORD: HTXU66

Pre-Reading
Questions

1. Explain the two models
   that scientists use to
   describe the interior of
   the Earth.

2. What are tectonic plates?

3. Explain how compression
   and tension affect rocks.

4. How does uplift shape
   features of the surface
   of the Earth? ★TEKS

ROAD CLOSED FOR REPAIRS!

This damaged California freeway didn't fall because of poor construction. This freeway and many others fell as a result of an earthquake that occurred in Northridge, California, on January 19, 1994. It took months to repair all the damage. Although earthquakes can be dangerous, they also provide important information about the planet we live on. In this chapter, you will learn how earthquakes have helped scientists learn more about the interior of the Earth.

START-UP Activity

WHAT'S IT LIKE ON THE INSIDE? ⭐TEKS

In this activity, you will compare slices of different foods to determine which one most closely resembles a cross section of the interior of the Earth.

Procedure

1. Get one half of each of the following items from your teacher—a **hard-boiled egg,** an **apple,** and an **orange.**

2. Study the cross section of each item for a few minutes. What can you tell about the inside of the item by looking at it that you cannot tell by just looking at its surface? Record your answer in your ScienceLog.

3. Sketch the cross section of each item in your ScienceLog. Be sure to label on your chart any layers you can see in the items.

Analysis

4. In your ScienceLog, explain which food's cross section most closely resembles what you think a profile of the Earth might look like.

5. What do you think the inside of the Earth is made of?

6. Are there things that happen on the surface of the Earth that give you a hint about what the inside of the Earth is made of?

The Restless Earth

SECTION 1

READING WARM-UP

Terms to Learn

crust	asthenosphere
mantle	mesosphere
core	outer core
lithosphere	inner core

What You'll Do

- Identify the layers of the Earth by their composition.
- Classify the layers of the Earth by their physical properties.
- Explain how scientists know about the structure of Earth's interior.

Inside the Earth

If you tried to dig to the center of the Earth, what do you think you would find? Would the Earth be solid? Would it be hollow? Would it be made of the same material all the way through?

Actually, the Earth is made of several layers. Each of these layers is made of different materials that have different properties. Scientists think about the Earth's layers in two ways—by their composition and by their physical properties.

The Composition of the Earth

Earth's layers differ in composition because they are made of different mixtures of substances. The least dense substances make up the outermost layer, and the densest substances make up the inner layers. This is because as the Earth formed, the denser substances such as iron sank to the center of the planet. The Earth is divided into three layers—the *crust,* the *mantle,* and the *core*—based on what each layer is made of.

The Crust

The **crust** is the outermost layer of the Earth. Ranging from 5 to 100 km thick, it is also the thinnest layer of the Earth. And because it is the layer we live on, we know more about the crust than the mantle and the core.

As you can see in **Figure 1,** there are two types of crust—continental and oceanic. *Continental crust* is made of light substances such as silicon, oxygen, and aluminum. It has an average thickness of 30 km. *Oceanic crust* contains more heavy substances such as iron, calcium, and magnesium. It is generally between 5 and 8 km thick. Because it contains a larger amount of heavy substances, oceanic crust is denser than continental crust.

Figure 1 *Oceanic crust is thinner but denser than continental crust.*

Continental crust

Oceanic crust

The Mantle

The **mantle** is the layer of the Earth between the crust and the core. Compared with the crust, the mantle is very thick and contains most of the Earth's mass.

No one has ever seen what the mantle really looks like. It is too far down to drill for a sample. We must infer the composition and other characteristics of the mantle by looking at the Earth's surface. In some places, mantle rock has been pushed up to the surface, allowing scientists to study the rock directly.

Another place we can look for clues about the mantle is the ocean floor. Hot, liquid rock called magma comes from the mantle and flows out of active volcanoes on the ocean floor. These underwater volcanoes are like windows through the crust into the mantle. These "windows" have given us strong clues about the composition of the mantle. Scientists have learned that the rocks in the mantle are made up of large amounts of iron and magnesium.

The Core

The **core** is the layer of the Earth that begins at the bottom of the mantle and ends at the center of the Earth. The Earth's core is made mostly of iron, with smaller amounts of nickel and perhaps some sulfur and oxygen. As you can see in **Figure 2,** the core makes up roughly one third of the Earth's mass.

Figure 2 *Based on composition, the Earth is divided into three layers. The innermost layer, the core, is about the same size as the planet Mars.*

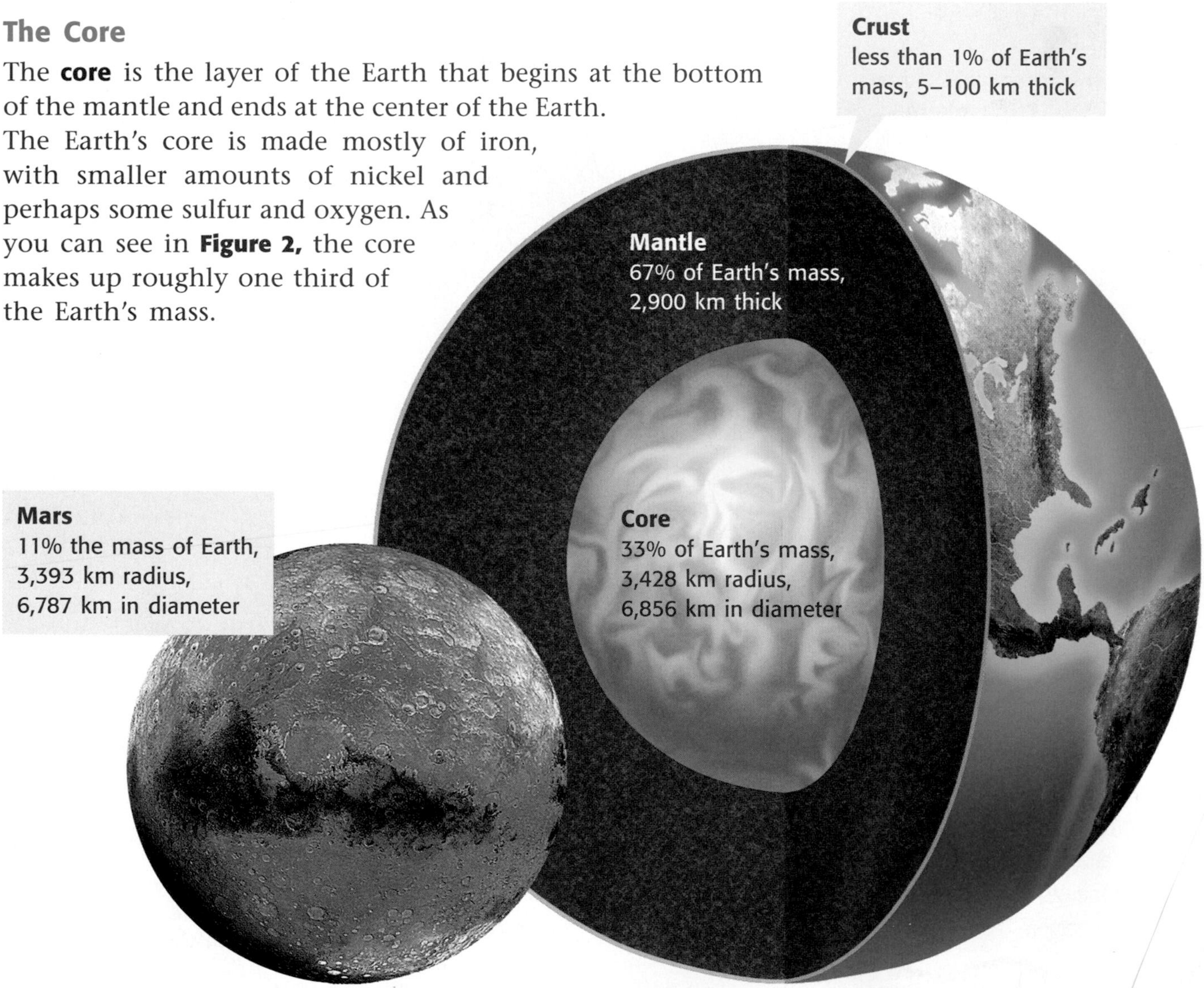

Crust
less than 1% of Earth's mass, 5–100 km thick

Mantle
67% of Earth's mass, 2,900 km thick

Core
33% of Earth's mass, 3,428 km radius, 6,856 km in diameter

Mars
11% the mass of Earth, 3,393 km radius, 6,787 km in diameter

The Structure of the Earth

Another way to look at what the Earth is made of is to study the physical properties of its layers. These properties include temperature, density, and ability to flow. The Earth is divided into five main physical layers—the *lithosphere*, the *asthenosphere*, the *mesosphere*, the *outer core*, and the *inner core*. As shown in **Figure 3,** each layer has a different thickness. Each layer also has its own set of physical properties, which are explained on the next page.

Figure 3 *Based on physical properties, the Earth is divided into five layers. Physical properties include density, temperature, and melting point.*

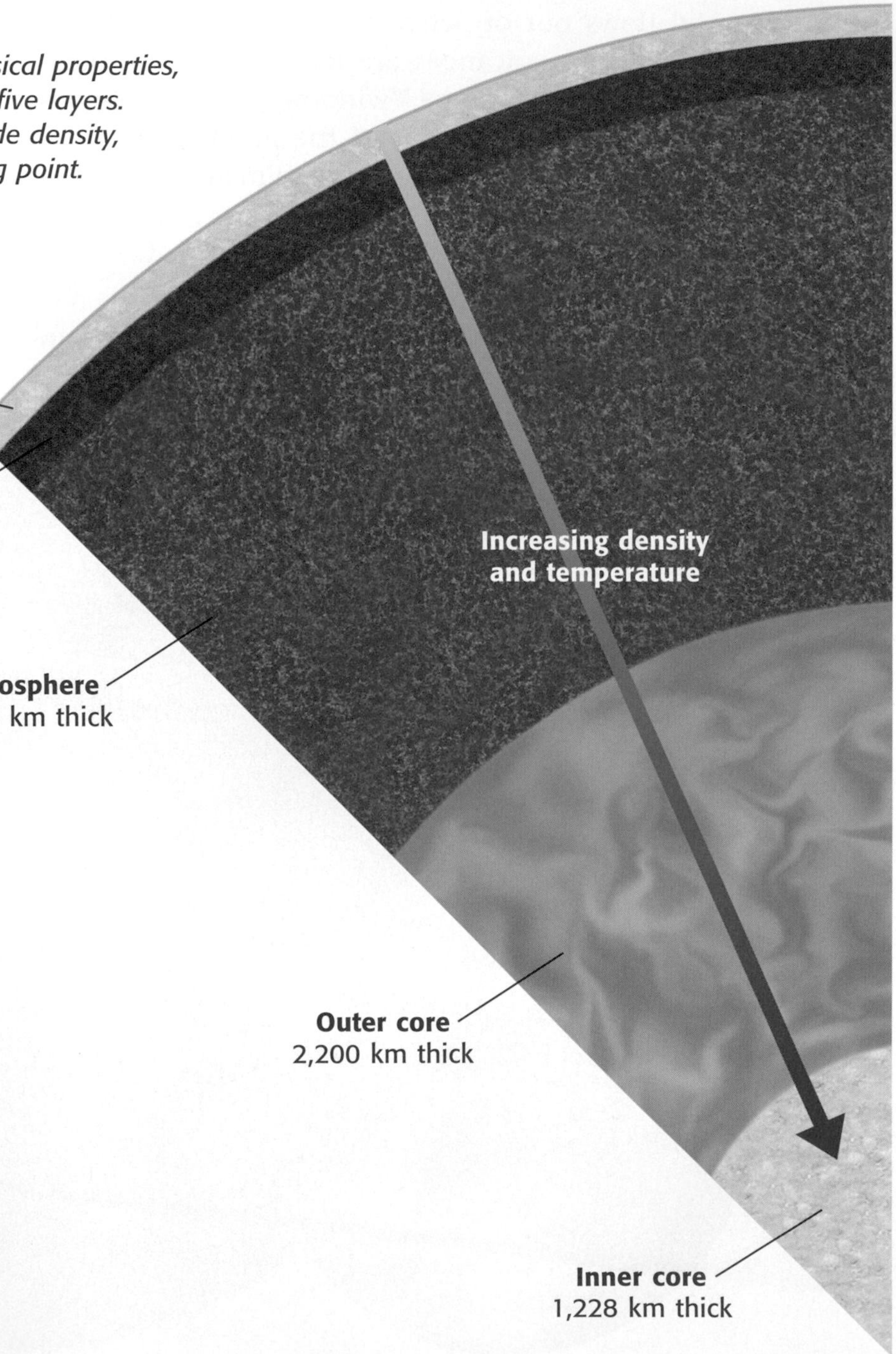

Lithosphere
60–300 km thick

Asthenosphere
250 km thick

Increasing density and temperature

Mesosphere
2,550 km thick

Biology CONNECTION

The part of the Earth where life is possible is called the *biosphere.* The biosphere is the layer of the Earth above the crust and below the uppermost part of the atmosphere. The oceans, dry land, and the lower part of the atmosphere are also parts of the biosphere.

Outer core
2,200 km thick

Inner core
1,228 km thick

The Earth's Physical Layers

The hard, outermost layer of the Earth is called the **lithosphere.** *Lithosphere* is a Greek word meaning "rock sphere." It is made up of two parts—the crust and the rigid, upper part of the mantle, as shown in **Figure 4.** The lithosphere is divided into pieces called *tectonic plates.* You'll learn more about tectonic plates in the next section.

The **asthenosphere** is a soft layer of the mantle on which the tectonic plates move. *Asthenosphere* is a Greek word meaning "weak sphere." The asthenosphere is made of solid rock that, like putty, flows very slowly. The asthenosphere is the layer between the lithosphere and the mesosphere.

Beneath the asthenosphere is the strong, lower part of the mantle called the **mesosphere.** *Mesosphere* is a Greek word meaning "middle sphere." The mesosphere lies between the asthenosphere and the Earth's core.

The Earth's core is divided into two parts—the outer core and the inner core. The **outer core** is the liquid layer of the Earth's core that lies beneath the mantle and surrounds the inner core. The **inner core** is the solid, dense center of our planet. It begins at the bottom of the outer core and goes all the way down to the center of the Earth, some 6,378 km beneath the surface.

MathBreak

Using Models

Imagine that you are building a model of the Earth that has a radius of 1 m. You find out that the average radius of the Earth is 6,378 km and that the thickness of the lithosphere is about 150 km. What percentage of the Earth's radius is the lithosphere? How thick (in centimeters) should you make the lithosphere in your model?

Figure 4 *The lithosphere is made of both the crust and the uppermost part of the mantle.*

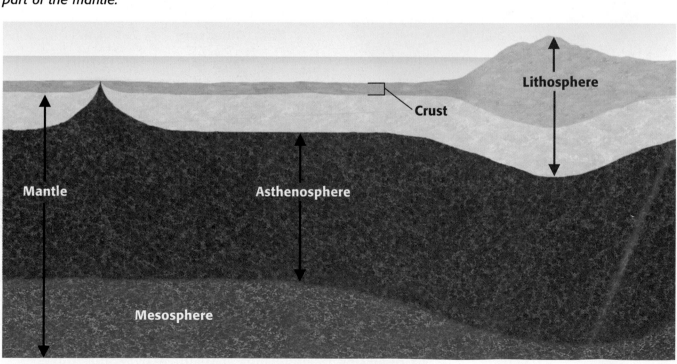

Mapping the Earth's Interior

No one has ever drilled all the way through the Earth's crust, which is only a thin skin on the surface of the Earth. So how do we know all these things about the deepest parts of the Earth, where no one has ever been?

Would you be surprised to know that the answers come from earthquakes? When there is an earthquake, vibrations called *seismic waves* are produced. Seismic waves travel at different speeds through the Earth. Their speed depends on the density and the strength of the material that they pass through. For example, a seismic wave traveling through solid rock will go faster than a seismic wave moving through a liquid.

When there is an earthquake, machines called *seismographs* measure the times at which different seismic waves arrive, and they record the differences in their speeds. Scientists then use these measurements to find the density and thickness of each physical layer of the Earth. **Figure 5** shows how one seismic wave moves through the Earth.

Figure 5 *The speed of seismic waves depends on the density of the material they move through. The denser the material is, the faster seismic waves move.*

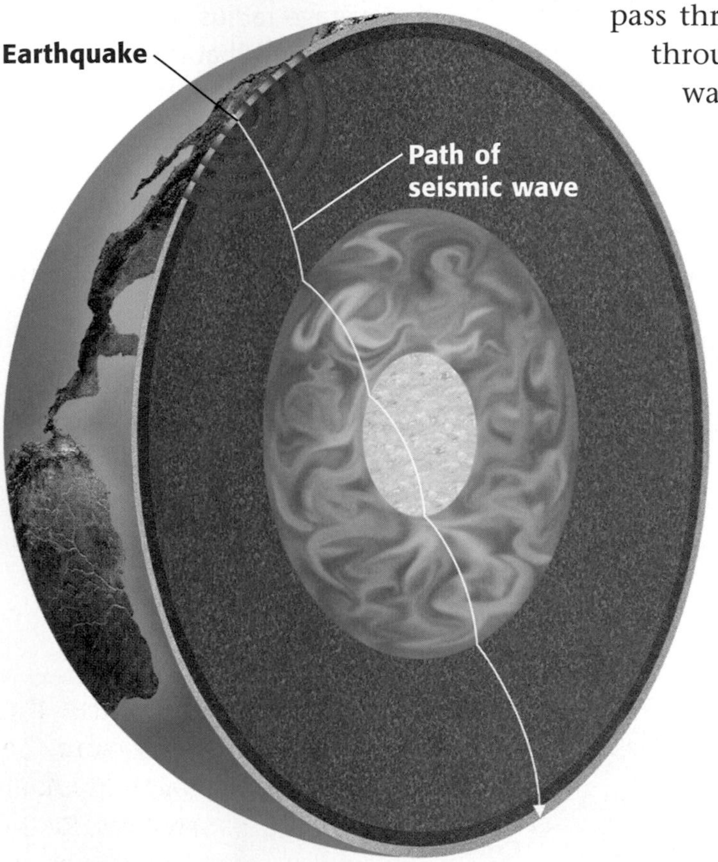

Earthquake

Path of seismic wave

	Lithosphere	7–8 km/s
	Asthenosphere	7–11 km/s
	Mesosphere	11–13 km/s
	Outer core	7–10 km/s
	Inner core	11–12 km/s

SECTION REVIEW

1. What is the difference between continental and oceanic crust?

2. How is the lithosphere different from the asthenosphere?

3. Explain the difference between the crust and the lithosphere.

4. **Analyzing Relationships** Explain why seismic waves travel more rapidly through the mesosphere than through the outer core. ⭐TEKS

READING WARM-UP

Terms to Learn

tectonic plates
Global Positioning System

What You'll Do

- Define tectonic plate.
- Explain how scientists measure the rate at which tectonic plates move.

Continents on the Move

Did you know that the continent you are on is moving? How can a continent be moving if you can't feel it?

All of the Earth's continents are part of the tectonic plates that move very slowly around the Earth's surface. **Tectonic plates** are the large slabs of lithosphere that move around on the asthenosphere. Tectonic plates move so slowly that you generally can't see or feel the movements. The amount of motion is measured in centimeters per year. How the plates move depends on many things, such as the kind and shape of the plate and the way a plate interacts with the plates around it.

Tracking Tectonic Plate Motion

The place where two tectonic plates meet is called the *plate boundary*. The type of boundary that forms depends mainly on the directions the plates are moving. Most plates do not move smoothly along the boundary, though. As the plates pass each other, they put pressure on the rocks at their edges. When enough pressure builds up on these rocks, earthquakes happen. Large shifts that occur along some boundaries can be seen right on the surface. However, most movements of tectonic plates are very small, so they are difficult to measure. So how do scientists do it?

Figure 6 *The picture below shows the orbits of the GPS satellites.*

The Global Positioning System

Scientists use a network of satellites called the **Global Positioning System** (GPS) to measure the rate of tectonic plate movement. Take a look at **Figure 6** to see the orbits of these satellites. Radio signals are continuously beamed from the satellites to GPS ground stations, which record the exact distance between the satellites and the ground station. Over time, these distances change a little. By recording the time it takes for the GPS ground stations to move a given distance, scientists can measure how fast each tectonic plate moves.

Tectonic Plates

What exactly does a tectonic plate look like? How big are tectonic plates? To answer these questions, start by thinking of the lithosphere as a giant puzzle.

A Giant Puzzle

Look at the world map in **Figure 7.** All of the plates have names, some of which you may already be familiar with. Some of the major tectonic plates are named on the map below. Notice that each tectonic plate fits together with the other tectonic plates that surround it, just like the pieces of a puzzle.

You will also notice that not all tectonic plates are the same. For example, compare the size of the South American plate with that of the Cocos plate. Tectonic plates are different in other ways too. For example, the South American plate has an entire continent on it, while the Cocos plate has only oceanic crust. Like the South American plate, some tectonic plates include both continental *and* oceanic crust.

Figure 7 *Tectonic plates fit together like the pieces of a puzzle.*

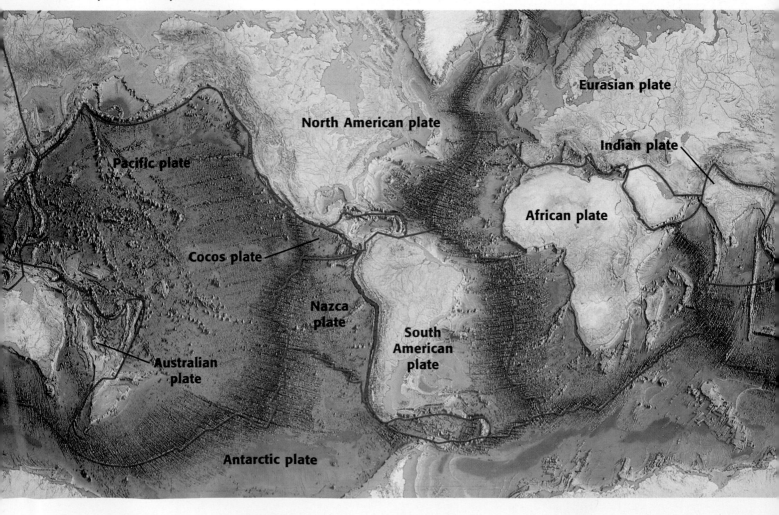

A Tectonic Plate Close-up

What would a tectonic plate look like if you could lift it out of its place? **Figure 8** shows what a cross section of the South American plate might look like. Notice that this tectonic plate consists of both oceanic and continental lithosphere. The thickest part of this tectonic plate is under the continental crust. The thinnest part is in the ocean near a mid-ocean ridge. A *mid-ocean ridge* is a long mountain chain that forms on the ocean floor where tectonic plates pull apart.

Like Ice Cubes in a Bowl of Punch

Think about ice cubes floating in a bowl of punch. If there are enough cubes, they will cover the surface of the punch and bump into one another. Parts of the ice cubes rest below the surface of the punch and displace the punch. Large pieces of ice displace more punch than small pieces of ice. Tectonic plates "float" on the asthenosphere in a similar way. The plates cover the surface of the asthenosphere, and they touch one another and move around. The lithosphere that rests below the Earth's surface displaces the asthenosphere. Thick tectonic plates, such as those made of continental lithosphere, displace more asthenosphere than do thin plates, such as those made of oceanic lithosphere.

Tectonic Ice Cubes

1. Take the bottom half of a clear, **3 L soda bottle** that has been cut in half. Make sure that the label has been removed.

2. Fill the bottle with **water** to about 1 cm below the top edge of the bottle.

3. Get **3 pieces of irregularly shaped ice** that are small, medium, and large.

4. Float the ice in the water, and note how much of each piece sits below the surface of the water.

5. Do all pieces of ice have more material below the surface than above? Which has the most? Why?

⭐TEKS   *TRY at HOME*

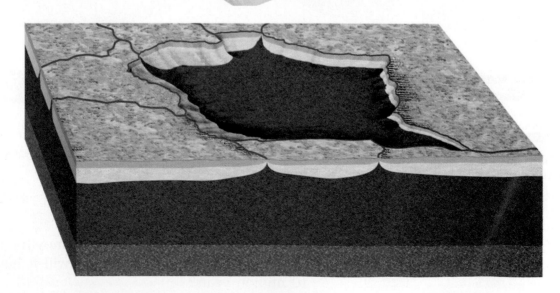

Figure 8 *This is what you might see if you could lift a plate out of its position between the other plates.*

The Changing Earth

Now that you know that the continents are on the move, it might not surprise you to learn that they have been moving for a long time. Many millions of years ago, the continents we see today were joined together into one large continent called a *supercontinent*. This supercontinent was called *Pangaea* (pan JEE uh). Over time, Pangaea broke up and formed into the continents we have today. Because Earth's tectonic plates are always moving, some scientists think that the continents may one day form another supercontinent. The idea that supercontinents form and break apart over time is called the *supercontinent cycle*. Forming a new supercontinent would take millions of years, though. Some scientists have an idea of what the next supercontinent might look like. Take a look at **Figure 9** to see an example of the supercontinent cycle.

Figure 9 *Note the outline of each continent as shown in today's map, then try to identify the modern continents on the supercontinent maps.*

The continents today

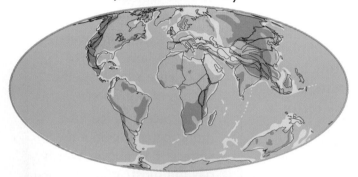

The supercontinent 245 million years ago

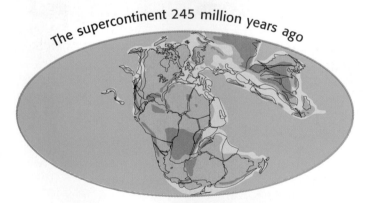

A supercontinent 250 million years from now

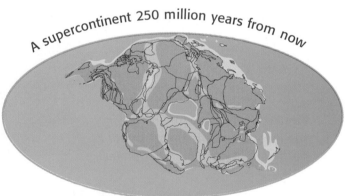

SECTION REVIEW

1. What are tectonic plates?

2. Why is it that some tectonic plates are not the same thickness all over?

3. How do scientists measure the rate at which tectonic plates move?

4. **Math Practice**   A tectonic plate is moving at a rate of 2 cm/year. How many kilometers will it have moved in 10 million years?

READING WARM-UP

Terms to Learn

stress	fault
compression	normal fault
tension	reverse fault
folding	strike-slip fault

What You'll Do

- Identify the forces that cause folding and faulting. ⭐TEKS
- Describe major types of folds.
- Explain how the three major types of faults differ.

Tectonic Forces

Have you ever tried to "stress out" a handful of spaghetti?

Try this: Take a bunch of long, uncooked pieces of spaghetti, and bend it very slowly, and only a little. Now bend it again, but this time go much farther and faster. What happened to the spaghetti the second time? How can the same material bend at one time and break at another? The answer is that the *stress* you put on it was different. **Figure 10** shows what stress can do to spagetti. Read on to learn what stress does to rocks.

Rocks Get Stressed

Stress is the amount of force per unit area that is put on a given material. The same principle that affects the spaghetti also works on the rocks in the Earth's crust. When the shape of a rock changes because of stress, the process is called *deformation*. Rock layers can bend when stress is placed on them. When enough stress is placed on rocks, they can break. The rock's composition and temperature and the amount of pressure on the rock determine how much stress the rock can handle before it bends or breaks.

The type of stress in which an object is squeezed, as when two tectonic plates collide, is called **compression.** Another type of stress is tension. **Tension** is the type of stress in which forces act to stretch an object. As you might guess, tension is what happens when two tectonic plates pull away from each other. Compression and tension bend and break rock to form some of the landforms with which you may be familiar. Read on to learn more about the deformation caused by stress.

Figure 10 *With a small amount of stress, uncooked spaghetti bends. More stress causes the spaghetti to break.*

Figure 11 | **Folding: When Rock Layers Bend Because of Stress**

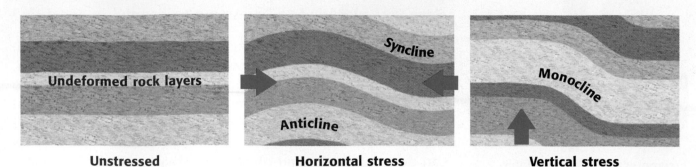

Undeformed rock layers

Unstressed

Syncline

Anticline

Horizontal stress

Monocline

Vertical stress

Folding

Folding is what happens when rock layers bend because of stress in the Earth's crust. Folds are good clues that rocks have been placed under stress. Depending on the type of stress placed on the rock layers, different types of folds are made. **Figure 11** above shows the two most common forms of folds—anticlines and synclines. *Anticlines* are arch-shaped folds. *Synclines* are trough-shaped folds. Anticlines and synclines form together when horizontal compression acts on rock.

Another type of fold is a *monocline.* In a monocline, rock layers are folded so that both ends of the fold are still horizontal. Monoclines generally form when vertical stress acts on rock. Imagine taking a stack of paper and laying it on a tabletop. Think of all the sheets of paper as different rock layers. Now imagine putting a book under one end of the stack. The ends of the sheets would still be horizontal, but all the sheets would be bent in the middle. Look again at Figure 11 to see an example of a monocline.

Folds can be large or small. The largest folds are measured in kilometers. They can make up the entire side of a mountain. Other folds are easy to see but are much smaller. **Figure 12** shows examples of large and small folds.

Figure 12 *Folds can be as big as mountains or smaller than a penknife.*

Faulting

While some rock layers bend and fold when stress is put on them, other rock layers break. The surface along which rocks break and slide past each other is called a **fault.** The blocks of crust on each side of the fault are called *fault blocks.*

When a fault is not vertical, understanding the difference between its two sides—the hanging wall and the footwall—is useful. **Figure 13** shows the difference between a hanging wall and a footwall. Depending on how the hanging wall and footwall move, one of two main types of faults can form. The two types are a *normal fault* and a *reverse fault.*

Figure 13 *The position of a fault block determines if it is a hanging wall or a footwall.*

Fault

Footwall

Hanging wall

Normal Faults

A normal fault is shown in **Figure 14.** When a **normal fault** moves, it causes the hanging wall to move down relative to the footwall. This motion is considered "normal" to the pull of gravity. These faults usually form when tectonic forces cause tension that pulls the crust apart.

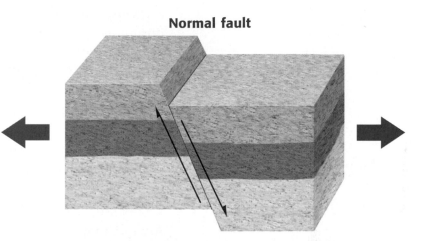

Normal fault

Figure 14 *When rocks are pulled apart by tension, normal faults often form.*

Reverse Faults

A reverse fault is shown in **Figure 15.** When a **reverse fault** moves, it causes the hanging wall to move up relative to the footwall—the "reverse" of a normal fault. Reverse faults usually form when tectonic forces cause compression that pushes the crust together.

Self-Check

Identify the two main types of stress that shape the features of the Earth. *(See page 640 to check your answer.)* ⭐TEKS

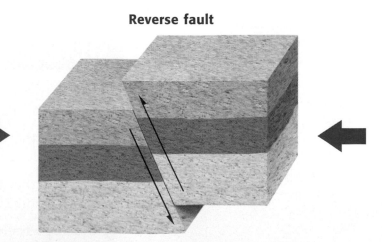

Reverse fault

Figure 15 *When rocks are pushed together by compression, reverse faults often form.*

Figure 16 *The photo at left shows a normal fault. The photo at right shows a reverse fault.*

Telling the Difference

It's easy to tell the difference between a normal fault and a reverse fault in drawings with arrows. But can you tell the difference between the faults in **Figure 16**? You can certainly see the faults, but which one is a normal fault, and which one is a reverse fault? Take a look at the photo on the left. One side has clearly moved relative to the other. You can tell that this is a normal fault by looking at the order of the sedimentary rock layers. If you compare the two dark layers near the surface, you can see that the hanging wall has moved down relative to the footwall.

Strike-Slip Faults

A third major type of fault is called a strike-slip fault. **Strike-slip faults** form when opposing forces cause rock to break and move horizontally. If you were standing on one side of a strike-slip fault looking across the fault when it moved, the ground on the other side would appear to move to your left or right.

SECTION REVIEW

1. Name two types of stress, and describe how they affect the Earth's surface. ⊛TEKS

2. What is the difference between an anticline and a syncline?

3. What is the difference between a normal fault and a reverse fault? ⊛TEKS

4. **Making Predictions** If you find evidence that rocks in an area are being compressed, which type of deformation is likely to happen there? Explain why. ⊛TEKS

READING WARM-UP

Terms to Learn

uplift
folded mountains
fault-block mountains
volcanic mountains

What You'll Do

● Define uplift, and describe how it shapes the Earth's surface. ⭐TEKS

● Name and describe the most common types of mountains.

● Explain how different types of mountains form.

● Explain how volcanic mountains change Earth's surface. ⭐TEKS

Building Mountains

Have you ever watched a mountain grow? Even though you can't really see them growing, many mountains are!

You have just learned about several ways the Earth's crust changes because of the forces of plate tectonics. When tectonic plates collide, land features that start out as small folds and faults can one day become great mountain ranges.

Uplift

Tectonic plates are always moving around and interacting with each other. This is why there are mountains on the Earth's surface. Most major mountain ranges form at the edges of tectonic plates. When two tectonic plates collide, the place where they meet is called a *convergent boundary*. It is at these boundaries that you can find some of the tallest mountain ranges on Earth, such as the Himalayas in India, Tibet, and Nepal.

When tectonic plates collide, the crust is uplifted. **Uplift** is the process by which regions of the crust are raised to a higher elevation. This happens because of the stress created when the plates push against each other. Remember that compression is the type of stress in which an object is squeezed. **Figure 17** is an example of the result of uplift.

Stress between tectonic plates causes mountains to form in several different ways. Let's take a look at three of the most common types of mountains—folded mountains, fault-block mountains, and volcanic mountains.

Figure 17 *Uplift raises the crust to a higher elevation.*

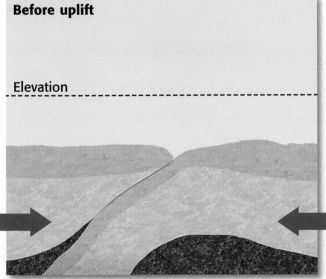

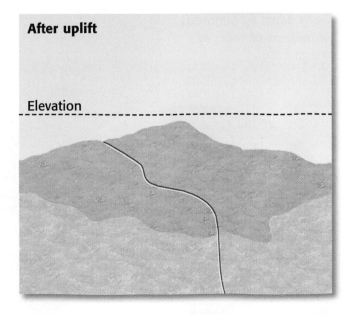

Folded Mountains

Folded mountains form when rock layers are squeezed together and pushed upward. If you make a pile of paper on a table-top and push on both ends of the pile, you will see how a folded mountain forms. **Figure 18** shows how the layers of rock might look in a folded mountain range. **Figure 19** shows an example of a folded mountain range that formed at a convergent boundary.

Figure 18 *In a folded mountain range, the rock layers are rumpled up like a rug.*

Figure 19 *Once as mighty as the Himalayas (inset), the Appalachian Mountains have been worn down by hundreds of millions of years of weathering.*

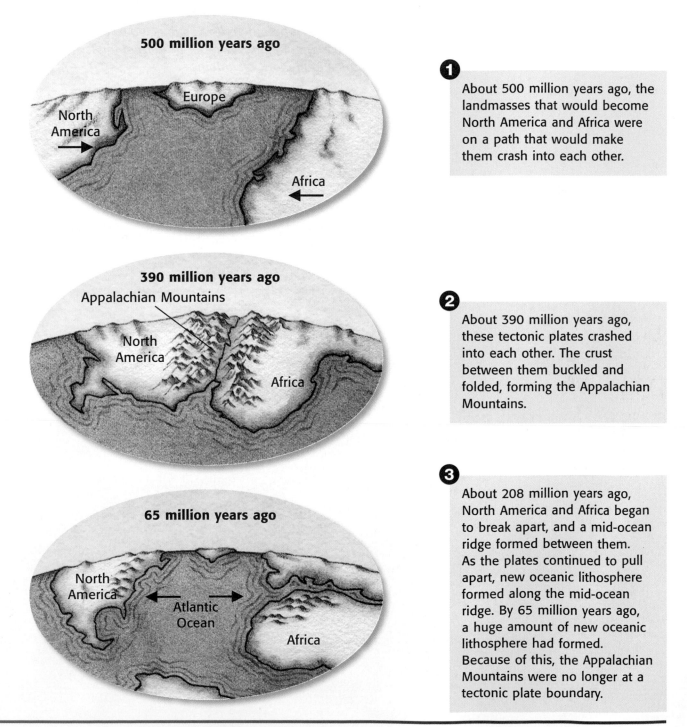

Spotlight On...

The Appalachian Mountains

Most of the world's major mountain ranges form at tectonic plate boundaries. The Appalachian Mountains, however, are located in the middle of the North American plate. How can this be? Shouldn't they be at the edge of a tectonic plate? Read below to find the answer.

500 million years ago

Europe

North America

Africa

1 About 500 million years ago, the landmasses that would become North America and Africa were on a path that would make them crash into each other.

390 million years ago

Appalachian Mountains

North America

Africa

2 About 390 million years ago, these tectonic plates crashed into each other. The crust between them buckled and folded, forming the Appalachian Mountains.

65 million years ago

North America

Atlantic Ocean

Africa

3 About 208 million years ago, North America and Africa began to break apart, and a mid-ocean ridge formed between them. As the plates continued to pull apart, new oceanic lithosphere formed along the mid-ocean ridge. By 65 million years ago, a huge amount of new oceanic lithosphere had formed. Because of this, the Appalachian Mountains were no longer at a tectonic plate boundary.

Fault-Block Mountains

When tectonic forces put enough tension on the Earth's crust, a large number of normal faults can result. **Fault-block mountains** form when this faulting causes large blocks of the Earth's crust to drop down relative to other blocks. **Figure 20** shows one way this can happen.

When rock layers are tilted up by faulting, they can produce mountains with sharp, jagged peaks. As you can see in **Figure 21,** the Tetons, in western Wyoming, are a wonderful example of this type of mountain.

Figure 20 *When the crust is subjected to tension, the rock can break into a number of normal faults. This creates fault-block mountains.*

Figure 21 *The Tetons formed as a result of tectonic forces that stretched the Earth's crust, causing it to break into a series of normal faults.*

Tectonics and Natural Gas

Natural gas is used in many homes and factories as a source of energy. Some companies search for sources of natural gas just as other companies search for oil and coal. Like oil, natural gas travels upward through rock layers until it hits a layer through which it cannot travel and it becomes trapped. Imagine that you are searching for pockets of trapped natural gas. Would you expect to find these pockets associated with anticlines, synclines, or faults? Explain your answer in your ScienceLog. Include drawings to help in your explanation.

Volcanic Mountains

Volcanic mountains form when molten rock erupts onto the Earth's surface, as shown in **Figure 22.** Unlike folded and fault-block mountains, volcanic mountains form from new material being added to the Earth's surface. Most volcanic mountains form along convergent boundaries where oceanic lithosphere is being pulled under continental lithosphere. There are so many volcanic mountains around the rim of the Pacific Ocean that it has become known as the *Ring of Fire.*

Figure 22 *Volcanic mountains are often cone-shaped, and they often form along convergent boundaries.*

SECTION REVIEW

❶ Name and describe the type of tectonic stress that forms folded mountains. ✪TEKS

❷ Name and describe the type of tectonic stress that forms fault-block mountains. ✪TEKS

❸ Explain how volcanic mountains change the surface of the Earth. ✪TEKS

❹ **Analyzing Relationships** Explain how plate tectonics has helped create the Earth that exists today. ✪TEKS

🖅 internet**connect**

*SCi*LINKS.
NSTA **GO TO:** www.scilinks.org

TOPIC: Mountain Building
*sci***LINKS NUMBER:** HSTE175

Section 1

Vocabulary

crust *(p. 456)*
mantle *(p. 457)*
core *(p. 457)*
lithosphere *(p. 459)*
asthenosphere *(p. 459)*
mesosphere *(p. 459)*
outer core *(p. 459)*
inner core *(p. 459)*

Section Notes

- The Earth is made up of three main compositional layers—the crust, the mantle, and the core. ⭐TEKS

- The Earth is made of five main structural layers—the lithosphere, the asthenosphere, the mesosphere, the outer core, and the inner core. ⭐TEKS

- Scientists learn about the structure of the Earth by studying seismic waves caused by earthquakes.

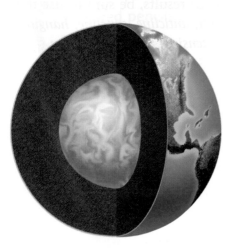

Section 2

Vocabulary

tectonic plates *(p. 461)*
Global Positioning System *(p. 461)*

Section Notes

- Tectonic plates are large pieces of the lithosphere that move around on the Earth's surface.

- Data from satellite tracking show how tectonic plates move over time.

- The continents of today once formed one large supercontinent called Pangaea.

Section 3

Vocabulary

stress *(p. 465)*
compression *(p. 465)*
tension *(p. 465)*
folding *(p. 466)*
fault *(p. 467)*
normal fault *(p. 467)*
reverse fault *(p. 467)*
strike-slip fault *(p. 468)*

Section Notes

- As tectonic plates move around, a great amount of stress is placed on the rocks at the plate boundaries.

- Folding takes place when rock layers bend because of compressional stress. ⭐TEKS

- Faulting takes place when rock layers break because of compressional and tensional stresses. ⭐TEKS

Section 4

Vocabulary

uplift *(p. 469)*
folded mountains *(p. 470)*
fault-block mountains *(p. 472)*
volcanic mountains *(p. 473)*

Section Notes

- Uplift takes place when tectonic plates collide and the rocks near the plate boundary are raised to higher elevations. ⭐TEKS

- Mountains are classified as either folded, fault-block, or volcanic, depending on how they form.

- Mountain building is caused by the movement of tectonic plates. Different types of movement cause different types of mountains. ⭐TEKS

- Volcanic mountains add material to the surface of the Earth. ⭐TEKS

Review

USING VOCABULARY

For each pair of terms, explain how the meanings of the terms differ.

1. oceanic crust/continental crust

2. lithosphere/asthenosphere

3. outer core/inner core

4. compression/tension

5. folding/faulting

6. normal fault/reverse fault

UNDERSTANDING CONCEPTS

Multiple Choice

7. The part of the Earth that is a liquid is the
   a. crust.
   c. outer core.
   b. mantle.
   d. inner core.

8. The part of the Earth on which the tectonic plates are able to move is the
   a. lithosphere.
   c. mesosphere.
   b. asthenosphere.
   d. core.

9. The lower part of the mantle is called the
   a. asthenosphere.
   c. mesosphere.
   b. lithosphere.
   d. crust.

10. Millions of years ago all the continents formed one landmass called a
    a. supercontinent.
    c. cyclecontinent.
    b. ultracontinent.
    d. pancontinent.

11. What type of tectonic plate boundary involves a collision between two tectonic plates?
    a. divergent
    c. convergent
    b. transform
    d. normal

12. When a fold is shaped like an arch, it is called a(n)
    a. monocline.
    c. syncline.
    b. anticline.
    d. decline.

13. In which type of fault does the hanging wall move down relative to the footwall? ★TEKS
    a. strike-slip
    c. normal
    b. reverse
    d. fault-block

14. The type of fault in which opposing forces cause rock to move horizontally is called ★TEKS
    a. strike-slip.
    c. normal.
    b. fault-block.
    d. reverse.

15. The Appalachian Mountains are an example of
    a. plate mountains.
    b. volcanic mountains.
    c. folded mountains.
    d. fault-block mountains.

16. Volcanic mountains ★TEKS
    a. are the same as fault-block mountains.
    b. create synclines and anticlines.
    c. are found only in Hawaii.
    d. add new material to the Earth's surface.

Short Answer

17. What is a tectonic plate?

18. What types of stress cause changes in the Earth's crust? ★TEKS

19. Describe the supercontinent cycle.

CONCEPT MAPPING

20. Use the following terms to create a concept map: *convergent boundary, tectonic plates, compression, tension, normal fault, reverse fault, folded mountains, fault-block mountains,* and *volcanic mountains.*

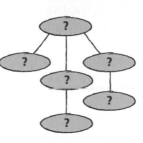

CRITICAL THINKING AND PROBLEM SOLVING

Write one or two sentences to answer the following questions:

21. Why is it necessary to think about the different layers of the Earth in terms of both their composition and their physical properties?

22. Folded mountains usually form at the edge of a tectonic plate. How can you explain old folded mountain ranges located in the middle of a tectonic plate?
★TEKS

23. Explain how the movement of tectonic plates shapes the surface of the Earth.
★TEKS

MATH IN SCIENCE

24. Look back at "Spotlight On: The Appalachian Mountains" on page 471. About 200 million years ago, the North American and African landmasses we have today were side by side. Approximately how many centimeters per year did the landmasses move away from one another if they are now 6,000 km apart?

INTERPRETING GRAPHICS

Imagine that you could travel to the center of the Earth. The diagram below lists the average thickness or radius of each layer of the Earth. Use the diagram to answer the questions that follow.

Crust (50 km)	
	Lithosphere (150 km)
Mantle (2,900 km)	Asthenosphere (250 km)
	Mesosphere (2,550 km)
Core (3,428 km)	Outer core (2,200 km)
	Inner core (1,228 km)

25. How far from the center of the Earth would you be if you were leaving the lithosphere and entering the asthenosphere?

26. How far beneath Earth's surface would you have to go to find the liquid material in the Earth's core?

27. At what range of depth would you find mantle material but still be within the lithosphere?

Reading Check-up

★TEKS Take a minute to review your answers to the Pre-Reading Questions found at the bottom of page 454. Have your answers changed? If necessary, revise your answers based on what you have learned since you began this chapter.

Chapter 17

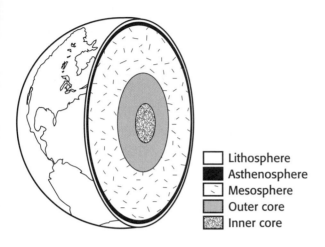

- Lithosphere
- Asthenosphere
- Mesosphere
- Outer core
- Inner core

1 Scientists have created the diagram above from data collected from studying seismic waves. According to the diagram, which of the following layers is the thickest?

A Outer core

B Mesosphere

C Asthenosphere

D Lithosphere

2 Which of the following adds material to the surface of the Earth?

F Volcanoes

G Tornadoes

H Uplift

J Folding

3 What type of stress causes uplift?

A Tension

B Compression

C Normal

D Not Here

4 According to the collected data listed in the table below, through which layer of the Earth could a seismic wave move the fastest?

F Asthenosphere

G Lithosphere

H Mesosphere

J Outer core

Layer	Speed of seismic waves
Lithosphere	7–8 km/s
Asthenosphere	7–11 km/s
Mesosphere	11–13 km/s
Outer core	7–10 km/s
Inner core	11–12 km/s

5 Which of the following is NOT explained by plate tectonics?

A Earthquakes

B Mountain building

C The layers of the Earth

D The supercontinent cycle

6 Which of the following does NOT act to shape the surface of the Earth?

F Volcanic activity

G Uplift

H Folding

J Global Positioning System

Chapter 17

Math

1 Sandra is measuring the growth of the Himalaya Mountains using a GPS recorder. If the mountains grow 6 cm per year, on average, what fraction of a centimeter do they grow every month?

A $\frac{1}{4}$

B $\frac{3}{4}$

C $\frac{1}{2}$

D $\frac{1}{3}$

2 How is the product $5 \times 5 \times 5 \times 5 \times 8 \times 8 \times 8$ expressed in exponential notation?

F $5^4 \times 8^3$

G 40^7

H $4^5 \times 3^7$

J $5^7 \times 8^7$

3 Mark wants to buy a ticket to a 3-day geology camp that costs $35. If he earns $5 a week, how many weeks will it be before he has enough money to buy his ticket to the camp?

A 4 weeks

B 5 weeks

C 6 weeks

D 7 weeks

4 If no digit appears more than once, how many 3 digit numbers can be formed from the digits 7, 8, and 9?

F 3

G 6

H 9

J 27

Reading

Read the passage. Then read each question that follows the passage. Decide which is the best answer to each question.

It was a <u>grueling</u> climb to the top of Mount Everest. The temperature was well below freezing, and the blinding snow made it difficult to see. These harsh conditions and the extreme altitude are what make Mount Everest one of the most difficult mountains to climb. But these conditions did not stop a professional mountain climber by the name of Wally Berg. He was on a mission—a scientific mission that had been years in the planning.

1 You can tell from the passage that a <u>grueling</u> climb is

A an easy climb.

B a hard climb.

C a fun climb.

D a cold weather climb.

2 Which of these is a FACT in this passage?

F Wally Berg climbed Mount Everest because of difficult conditions.

G Mount Everest is an easy mountain to climb.

H Wally Berg was on a scientific mission.

J The temperature was 32°C.

Europa: Life on a Moon?

Smooth and brownish white, Europa, one of Jupiter's moons, has fascinated scientists and science-fiction writers for decades. More recently, scientists were excited by tantalizing images from the Galileo Europa mission. Could it be that life is lurking (or sloshing) beneath Europa's surface?

An Active History

Slightly smaller than Earth's moon, Europa is the fourth largest of Jupiter's moons. It is unusual among other bodies in the solar system because of its extraordinarily smooth surface. The ridges and brownish channels that crisscross Europa's smooth surface may tell a unique story—the surface appears to be a slushy combination of ice and water. Some scientists think that the icy ridges and channels are ice floes left over from ancient volcanoes that erupted water. The water flowed over Europa's surface and froze, in the same way that lava flows and cools on Earth's surface.

A Slushy Situation

Scientists speculate that Europa's surface consists of thin tectonic plates of ice floating on a layer of slush or water. These plates, which would look like icy rafts floating in an ocean of slush, have been compared to giant glaciers floating in polar regions on Earth.

▼ *Europa looks like a cracked cue ball.*

Where plates push together, the material of the plates may crumple, forming an icy ridge. Where plates pull apart, warmer liquid mixed with darker silicates may erupt toward the surface and freeze, forming the brownish icy channels that create Europa's cracked cue-ball appearance.

Life on Europa?

These discoveries have led scientists to consider an exciting possibility: Does Europa have an environment that could support primitive life-forms? In general, at least three things are necessary for life as we know it to develop—water, organic compounds (substances that contain carbon), and heat. Europa has water, and organic compounds are fairly common in the solar system. But is Europa hot enough? Europa's slushy nature suggests a warm interior. One theory is that the warmth is the result of Jupiter's strong gravitational pull on Europa. Another theory is that warmth is brought to Europa's surface by convection heating.

So does Europa truly satisfy the three requirements for life? The answer is still unknown, but the sloshing beneath Europa's surface has sure heightened some scientists' curiosity!

If You Were in Charge . . .

▶ If you were in charge of NASA's space-exploration program, would you send a spacecraft to look for life on Europa? (Remember that this would cost billions of dollars and would require sacrificing other important projects!) Explain your answer. ⭐TEKS

The Flow of Fresh Water

Pre-Reading
Questions

1. What happens to the rainwater that soaks into the Earth? ⊛TEKS

2. How does the movement of water shape features of the Earth? ⊛TEKS

3. How do caves form?

THE SOUND IS DEAFENING

You can hear the thundering roar of Iguaçu (EE gwah SOO) Falls for miles. The Iguaçu River travels more than 500 km across Brazil before it tumbles off the edge of a volcanic plateau in a series of 275 individual waterfalls. Over the past 20,000 years, erosion has caused the falls to move 28 km upstream. Where will they be 20,000 years from now? In this chapter, you will learn how flowing water shapes the Earth's surface.

STREAM WEAVERS ⊘TEKS

How do streams and river systems develop? Do the following activity to find out.

Procedure

1. Begin with a **bucket of sand** and enough **gravel** to fill the bottom of a **rectangular plastic washtub.**

2. Spread the gravel in a layer at the bottom of the washtub. Place 4 to 6 cm of sand on top of the gravel. Form a slope by adding more sand to one end of the washtub.

3. Make a small hole in the bottom of a **paper cup.** Attach the cup to the inside of the tub with a **clothespin.** The cup should be placed at the end that has more sand. Fill the cup with **water,** and observe the water as it moves over the sand. Use a **magnifying lens** to observe features of the stream more closely.

4. Record your observations in your ScienceLog.

Analysis

5. At the start of your experiment, how did the moving water affect the sand?

6. As time passed, how did the moving water affect the sand?

7. Explain how this activity modeled the development of streams. In what ways was it accurate? How was it inaccurate?

Terms to Learn

erosion   divide
water cycle   channel
tributary   load
watershed

What You'll Do

● Explain the interactions between matter and energy in the water cycle. ⭐TEKS

● Describe how moving water shapes the surface of the Earth by the process of erosion. ⭐TEKS

● Explain the major factors that affect the rate of stream erosion.

● Describe a watershed, and identify the stages of river development.

The Active River

If you had fallen asleep with your toes dangling in the Rio Grande 2 million years ago and you had woken up today, your toes would be hanging about 518 m (1,700 ft) above the river!

The Rio Grande carved the canyon shown in **Figure 1** by washing billions of tons of soil and rock from its riverbed. This process is a form of erosion. **Erosion** is the removal and transport of rock and soil by the flow of water and by the actions of wind and ice. In this section, you will learn about stream development, river systems, and the different factors that affect the rate of stream erosion.

Figure 1 *The Rio Grande flows through Big Bend National Park in West Texas. The river, which forms the border between Texas and Mexico, is one of the youngest in the United States—it reached the Gulf of Mexico only 2 million years ago!*

The Water Cycle

Have you ever wondered what happens to the water that falls during a rainstorm? How does it end up in rivers? Does water travel through the ground beneath your feet? Where does the water in clouds come from? Learning about the water cycle will help you answer these questions. The **water cycle** is the continuous movement of water between the Earth and its atmosphere. The water cycle is driven by energy from the sun.

Self-Check

What role does the sun's energy play in the water cycle? *(See page 640 to check your answer.)* ⭐TEKS

Condensation takes place when water vapor cools and changes into liquid water droplets that form clouds.

Water loses energy during condensation.

Water gains energy during evaporation.

Precipitation is rain, snow, sleet, or hail that falls from clouds to the Earth's surface.

Evaporation takes place when liquid water from the Earth's surface changes into water vapor. Energy from the sun causes evaporation. Water vapor is also added to the air by plants.

Runoff is water that flows across the land and enters rivers and streams. It eventually flows into lakes and the ocean.

Percolation is the downward movement of water through soil and rock due to gravity.

River Systems

The next time you take a shower, notice how individual drops of water join together to become small streams. These streams join other small streams and form larger ones. Eventually all of the water flows down the drain. Every time you shower, you create a model *river system*—a network of streams and rivers that drain an area of its runoff. Just as the shower forms a network of flowing water, streams and rivers form a network of flowing water on land. Smaller streams or rivers that flow into larger ones are called **tributaries.**

Watersheds

Have you ever seen a sign like the one in **Figure 2**? A **watershed** is the region of land drained by a river system. The largest watershed in the United States is the Mississippi River watershed. It has hundreds of tributaries that extend from the Rocky Mountains, in the West, to the Appalachian Mountains, in the East.

The satellite photograph in **Figure 3** shows that the Mississippi River watershed covers more than one-third of the United States. Other major watersheds in the United States are the Columbia River, Rio Grande, and Colorado River watersheds. Watersheds are separated by an area of higher ground called a **divide.** In the photograph below, you can see that the Continental Divide is a major divide in North America. On which side of the divide do you live?

Figure 2 *This sign informs people that they are entering an environmentally sensitive area.*

····· Activity ·····

Imagine that you are planning a rafting trip down the Missouri and Mississippi Rivers. Use a computer or a map of the United States to trace the route of your trip. You will start in the Rocky Mountains in Montana and finish at the mouth of the Mississippi River in Louisiana. What major tributaries would you travel past? What cities would you pass through? Mark them on the map. How many kilometers would you travel on this trip?

·· ⭐TEKS ········· TRY at HOME ··

Figure 3 *The Continental Divide runs through the Rocky Mountains. It separates the watersheds that flow into the Atlantic Ocean and the Gulf of Mexico from those that flow into the Pacific Ocean.*

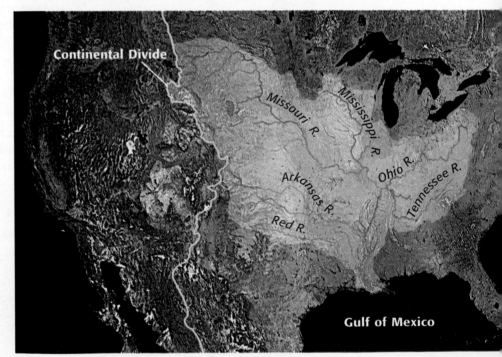

Stream Erosion

As a stream forms, it erodes soil and rock to form a channel. A **channel** is the path that a stream follows. At first, a stream channel is narrow and steep. As more rock and soil are carried down the stream, the channel becomes wider and deeper. When streams become longer and wider, they are called rivers.

Gradient

Have you ever wondered why some streams flow faster than others? The stream shown in **Figure 4** is flowing down a steep mountainside. That stream has a high gradient. *Gradient* is the measure of the change in elevation over a certain distance. A stream or river with a high gradient flows faster and has more energy to erode rock and soil. A river or stream with a low gradient, such as the one in **Figure 5**, flows slowly and has less erosive energy.

Discharge

The amount of water that a stream or river carries in a given amount of time is called *discharge*. A stream's discharge increases after a major rainstorm or when warm weather rapidly melts snow. As a stream's discharge increases, its erosive energy, its speed, and the amount of materials that it can carry also increase.

MathBreak

Calculating a Stream's Gradient

If a stream starts at an elevation of 4,900 m and travels 450 km to a lake that is at an elevation of 400 m, what is the stream's gradient? (Hint: Subtract the final elevation from the starting elevation, and divide by 450.)

Figure 4 *This mountain stream in Canada flows rapidly and has more erosive energy.*

Figure 5 *A river on a flat plain, such as this one in Arkansas, flows slowly and has less erosive energy.*

Load

You may think that rivers are mostly flowing water, but actually they carry an incredible amount of soil and rock as they flow. For example, the Mississippi River carries an average of 34,000 metric tons of sediment to the Gulf of Mexico every hour! The materials carried by a stream are referred to as the stream's **load.** The size of a stream's load is affected by the stream's speed. Fast-moving streams can carry large particles that bounce and scrape along the bottom and sides of the streambed. Thus, the size of a stream's load also affects its rate of erosion. The illustration below shows the three ways a stream can carry its load.

1 A stream can bounce large materials, such as pebbles and boulders, along the streambed. These materials are called the **bed load.**

2 A stream can carry small rocks and soil in suspension. These materials, called the **suspended load,** make the river look muddy.

3 Some material is carried in solution, meaning that it is dissolved in the water. The **dissolved load** is made of dissolved materials such as sodium and calcium.

✔ Self-Check

What would happen to the suspended load if a river slowed down? *(See page 640 to check your answer.)*

The Stages of a River

In the early 1900s, William Morris Davis developed a model of the stages of river development. In his model, rivers evolve from a youthful stage to an old-age stage. Davis thought that all rivers erode in the same way and at the same rate. Today scientists support a different model that considers the effects of a river's environment on its development. For example, because different materials erode at different rates, one river may develop more quickly than another river. Many factors, such as climate, gradient, and load, affect the development of a river. While scientists no longer use Davis's model, they still use many of his terms to describe a river. Remember, these terms do not tell the actual age of a river. Instead, they are used to describe a river's general features.

Youthful Rivers

A youthful river, such as the one in **Figure 6,** erodes its channel deeper rather than wider. The river flows quickly because of its steep gradient. Its channel is narrow and straight. The river tumbles over rocks in rapids and waterfalls. Youthful rivers have few tributaries.

Figure 6 *This youthful river is in Yellowstone National Park in Wyoming. Rapids and waterfalls are found where the river flows over hard, resistant rock.*

Mature Rivers

A mature river, as shown in **Figure 7,** erodes its channel wider rather than deeper. The gradient of a mature river is not as steep as that of a youthful river, and there are fewer waterfalls and rapids. A mature river is fed by many tributaries and has more discharge than a youthful river.

Figure 7 *A mature river, such as this one in Peru, begins to curve back and forth. The bends in the river's channel are called* meanders.

Figure 8 *This old river is in New Zealand.*

Old Rivers

An old river has a low gradient and little erosive energy. Instead of widening and deepening its channel, the river deposits sediment in its channel and along its banks. Old rivers, such as the one shown in **Figure 8,** often have valleys, wide *flood plains,* and more meanders. Also, an old river has fewer tributaries than a mature river because the smaller tributaries have joined.

Rejuvenated Rivers

Rejuvenated (ri JOO vuh NAYT id) rivers are found where the land is raised by tectonic activity. When land rises, the river's gradient becomes steeper. The increased gradient of a rejuvenated river allows the river to cut more deeply into the valley floor. Steplike *terraces* often form on both sides of a river valley as a result of rejuvenation. Can you find the terraces in **Figure 9**?

Figure 9 *This rejuvenated river is in Canyonlands National Park, in Utah.*

SECTION REVIEW

❶ Explain the interactions between matter and energy in the water cycle. ✪TEKS

❷ Describe the difference between a river system and a watershed. Explain how a river system can be a combination of several smaller systems. ✪TEKS

❸ List three factors that affect the rate of stream erosion.

❹ Describe the ways that youthful, mature, old, and rejuvenated rivers shape the Earth's surface. ✪TEKS

❺ **Analyzing Relationships** Explain why tectonic uplift produces terraces in rejuvenated rivers. ✪TEKS

Terms to Learn

deposition   alluvial fan
delta   flood plain

What You'll Do

● Describe the different types of stream deposits.

● Describe how the deposition of sediment shapes the surface of the Earth. ✪ TEKS

● Explain the relationship between fertile farming regions and river flood plains.

Stream and River Deposits

If you had to transport millions of tons of soil across the state of Texas, how would you do it? You might use bulldozers and dump trucks, but that would take a lot of time and energy. Did you know that Texas rivers do this job every day?

Rivers erode and transport an enormous amount of sediment and soil across the Earth's surface. Like liquid conveyer belts, rivers carry fertile soil to farmland and wetlands. While erosion is a serious problem, rivers also renew soils and form new land. As you will see in this section, rivers create some of the most impressive landforms on Earth.

Deposition in Water

You have learned how flowing water erodes the Earth's surface. But eventually a river's load must be dropped, or deposited. Imagine a mud puddle after a rainy day. If the water is not disturbed, it will settle and become clear again. **Deposition** is the process by which material is dropped, or settles. River deposition forms and renews some of the world's most fertile soils. In a river, sediment is deposited at places where the speed of the current decreases. **Figure 10** shows this type of deposition.

Figure 10 *This photo shows erosion and deposition at a bend, or meander, of a river in Alaska.*

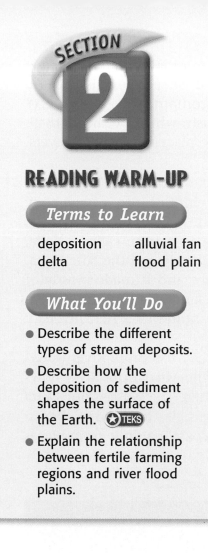

a Erosion happens on the outside bank, where the current is faster.

b Deposition happens along the inside bank, where the current is slower.

Figure 11 *Miners rushed to California in the 1850s to find gold. They often found it in placer deposits in river bends.*

Heavy minerals are sometimes deposited at places where a river's current slows down. This kind of sediment is called a *placer deposit.* Some placer deposits contain gold, as **Figure 11** shows. During the California gold rush, which began in 1849, many miners panned for gold in the placer deposits of rivers.

Deltas

A river's current slows when a river empties into a large body of water, such as a lake or an ocean. As this happens, rivers often deposit their load in a fan-shaped pattern called a **delta.** In **Figure 12,** you can see an astronaut's view of the Nile Delta. A delta usually forms on a flat surface and is made mostly of mud. These mud deposits form new land and cause the coastline to grow. The world's deltas are home to a rich diversity of plant and animal life.

If you look back at the photo of the Mississippi River watershed in Figure 3, you can see where the Mississippi River flows into the Gulf of Mexico. This is where the Mississippi Delta has formed. Each of the fine mud particles in the delta began its journey far upstream. Louisiana's coastline came from places as far away as Ohio, Illinois, Montana, and Minnesota!

Astronomy CONNECTION

Ancient riverbeds have been discovered on the surface of Mars. NASA images show stream channels and evidence of massive floods. Astronomers wonder why liquid water is no longer present on the surface of this dry and frozen planet.

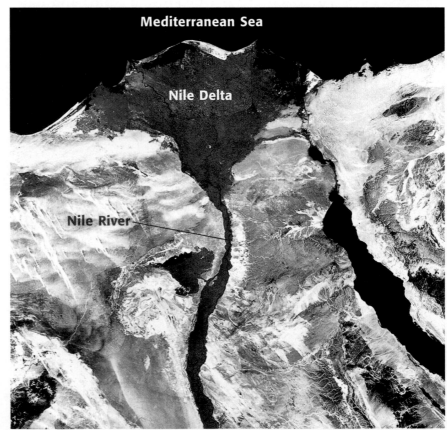

Figure 12 *Sediment dropped at the mouth of the Nile River, in Egypt, forms the Nile Delta. Unlike most major rivers of the world, the Nile River flows north.*

Deposition on Land

When a fast-moving mountain stream flows onto a flat plain, the stream slows down. As the stream slows down, it deposits sediment and forms an alluvial fan, such as the one shown in **Figure 13.** **Alluvial fans** are fan-shaped deposits like deltas, but they form on dry land.

During periods of high rainfall or rapid snowmelt, streams can overflow their banks and flood the surrounding land. This land is called a **flood plain.** When a stream floods, a layer of sediment is deposited across the flood plain. Every flood adds another layer of sediment.

Figure 13 *An alluvial fan, such as this one in the Sierra Nevada Mountains, forms when an eroding stream changes rapidly into a depositing stream. The sediment deposited by rivers and streams is called* alluvium.

Fatal Flooding

Flood plains are very productive farming areas because periodic flooding brings new soil to the land. This is one reason why many towns and cities are built on or near flood plains. When a river floods, however, the results can be disastrous. For example, many people live in the Mississippi River valley, a large flood plain with very fertile soil. When the Mississippi River flooded in 1993, farms were destroyed and entire towns were evacuated. The flood affected nine Midwestern states and was called by some "the flood of the century." **Figure 14** shows an area north of St. Louis, Missouri, that was flooded.

Figure 14 *The normal flow of the Mississippi River and the Missouri River is shown in black. The area that was flooded when both rivers spilled over their banks in 1993 is shaded red.*

SECTION REVIEW

❶ Describe how river deposition forms deltas, alluvial fans, and flood plains. ⭐TEKS

❷ How are alluvial fans and deltas similar? How are they different?

❸ Explain why flood plains are good farming areas.

❹ **Identifying Relationships** What factors increase the chance that a river's load will be deposited?

internetconnect

SC*i*LINKS.
NSTA   GO TO: www.scilinks.org

TOPIC: Texas Floods and Flood Management
*sci*LINKS NUMBER: HSTX350

TOPIC: Stream Deposits
*sci*LINKS NUMBER: HSTE263

Terms to Learn

ground water porosity
water table permeability
aquifer recharge zone

What You'll Do

- Identify and describe the location of the water table.
- Describe an aquifer.
- Identify the relationships between ground water and surface water in a watershed. ⭐TEKS
- Describe how underground water forms features such as caves. ⭐TEKS

Water Underground

Instead of pouring yourself a glass of water from a faucet, imagine pouring it from a chunk of solid rock! This idea may sound outrageous, but millions of people do it every day. Depending on where you live, the water that you drink may actually come from rock deep underground.

We can see surface water in rivers and lakes, but there is much more water flowing underground that we cannot see. Water beneath the Earth's surface is called **ground water.** Almost 97 percent of the world's liquid fresh water is stored underground. Ground water not only is a vital resource but also plays an important role in erosion and deposition.

The Location of Ground Water

As you know, surface water seeps into the soil and rock. This underground area is divided into two zones. After a rainstorm, water passes through the upper zone, called the *zone of aeration.* Farther down, the water collects in the *zone of saturation.* Here the spaces between rock particles are filled with water.

These two zones meet at a boundary known as the **water table,** shown in **Figure 15.** Imagine a cup of ice that is half-filled with water. For you to sip the water, your straw must reach the water table. The water table rises during wet seasons and falls during dry seasons. In wet regions, the water table can be at the Earth's surface. But in deserts, the water table may be hundreds of meters beneath the ground.

Figure 15 *The water table is the upper surface of the zone of saturation.*

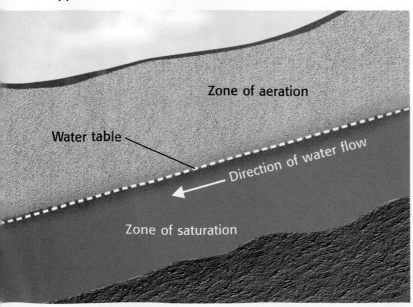
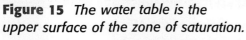

Zone of aeration

Water table

Direction of water flow

Zone of saturation

Aquifers

An **aquifer** is a rock layer that stores ground water and allows it to flow. Some types of rock can hold large amounts of water, while other types can hold little or no water. To qualify as an aquifer, a rock layer must have many open spaces. **Porosity** is the amount of space between the particles that make up a rock. Aquifers allow water to pass freely from one pore space to another. A rock's ability to allow water to pass through it is called **permeability.** Rock that tends to stop the flow of water is *impermeable.*

Aquifer Geology and Geography

The best aquifers usually form in permeable materials such as sandstone, limestone, or layers of sand and gravel. Some aquifers cover large underground areas and are an important source of water for cities and for agriculture. **Figure 16** shows the locations of aquifers in Texas.

Ogallala
Trinity
Carrizo-Wilcox
Edwards-Trinity
Gulf Coast
Edwards

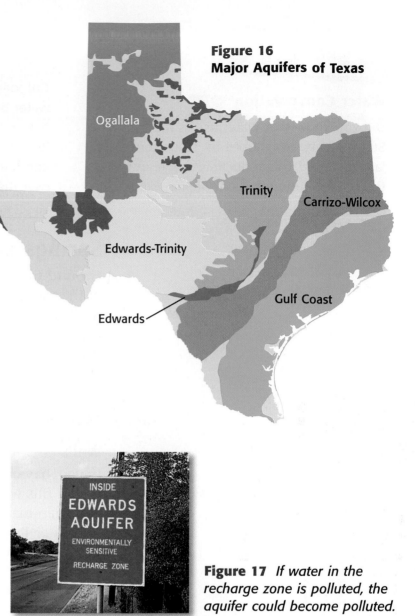

Figure 16
Major Aquifers of Texas

Recharge Zones

Like rivers, aquifers depend on the water cycle to maintain a constant flow of water. The ground surface where water enters an aquifer is called the **recharge zone.** Environmentally sensitive recharge zones are sometimes marked by signs, as shown in **Figure 17.** The size of the recharge zone varies depending on how permeable the rock is at the surface. If the surface rock is permeable, water can seep down into the aquifer. If the aquifer is covered by an impermeable rock layer, water cannot reach the aquifer. Construction on top of the recharge zone can also limit the amount of water that enters an aquifer.

INSIDE
EDWARDS
AQUIFER
ENVIRONMENTALLY
SENSITIVE
RECHARGE ZONE

Figure 17 *If water in the recharge zone is polluted, the aquifer could become polluted.*

QuickLab

Degree of Permeability TEKS

1. Begin with **five paper cups.**
2. Pack one cup halfway with **soil.** Pack a second cup halfway with **sand.**
3. Poke five holes in the bottom of each cup with a **sharpened pencil.**
4. Fill a third cup with **water.** Place an empty cup under the cup filled with soil. Pour the water into the top cup.
5. Put the cup aside, and allow it to drain.
6. Repeat steps 4 and 5 with the cup of sand and another empty cup. Compare the volumes of the two cups of water. The cup that allowed the most water to drain holds the more permeable sediment.

TRY at HOME

Springs and Wells

Ground-water movement is determined by the slope of the water table. Just like surface water, ground water tends to flow downslope, toward lower elevations. If the water table reaches the Earth's surface, water will flow out from the ground and form a *spring*. Springs are an important source of drinking water for humans and other animals. Lakes also form in areas where the water table is higher than the Earth's surface.

Wells

If you have ever dug a hole in the ground so deep that it fills with water, you have dug a well. A *well* is a human-made hole that is deeper than the level of the water table. Do you know why people can drink from wells but not from mud puddles? The answer lies in a very important quality of aquifers. As water travels through an aquifer, it is filtered and purified. Because wells extend below the water table, they fill with ground water. If a well is not deep enough, it will dry up when the water table falls below the bottom of the well, as shown in **Figure 18.** If the wells in an area remove ground water too rapidly, the water table will drop and all the wells will run dry.

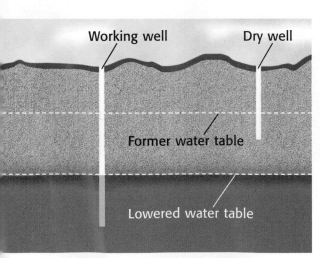

Figure 18 *A good well is drilled deep enough so that when the water table drops, the well still reaches below the water table.*

Underground Erosion and Deposition

As you know, sugar dissolves in water. But did you know that certain rocks also dissolve in water? One such rock is limestone, which is made of calcium carbonate. Most caves form as ground water dissolves limestone in the Earth's crust. Over thousands of years, ground water dissolves enough rock to form caves.

Figure 19 *At Harrison Cave, in Barbados, long passages and enormous chambers have been eroded beneath the Earth's surface.*

Cave Formations

Caves are formed by erosion, but they also show signs of deposition. Water that drips from a crack in a cave's ceiling leaves behind deposits of calcium carbonate. Sharp, icicle-shaped features that form on cave ceilings are known as *stalactites* (stuh LAK tiets). Water that falls to the cave's floor adds to cone-shaped features known as *stalagmites* (stuh LAG MIETS). If water drips long enough, stalactites and stalagmites join to form a *dripstone column*. See how many cave formations you can find in **Figure 19.** Limestone is very common in Texas, so there are many caves in the state. There may even be caves near you!

Environment
C O N N E C T I O N

Most bat species live in caves. Historically, bats have been the focus of much superstition and fear. Today, scientists know that bats play an extremely important role in the environment. Bat colonies consume vast quantities of insect pests, such as mosquitoes, and many bat species pollinate plants and distribute seeds.

SECTION REVIEW

❶ What is the source of the water in an aquifer? ⭐TEKS

❷ What are some of the features formed by underground erosion and deposition? ⭐TEKS

❸ **Analyzing Relationships** Identify the relationships between ground water and surface water in a watershed. How would the construction of a parking lot on top of a recharge zone affect the flow of surface water into an aquifer? ⭐TEKS

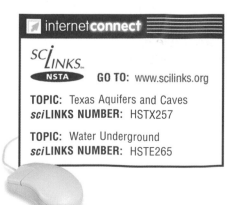

internetconnect

*SCI*LINKS.
NSTA   GO TO: www.scilinks.org

TOPIC: Texas Aquifers and Caves
*sci*LINKS NUMBER: HSTX257

TOPIC: Water Underground
*sci*LINKS NUMBER: HSTE265

Making Models Lab

Water Cycle—What Goes Up . . . ⊛TEKS

Why does a bathroom mirror fog up? Where does water go when it dries up? Where does rain come from, and why don't clouds run out of rain? These questions relate to the major parts of the water cycle—condensation, evaporation, and precipitation. In this activity, you will make a model of the water cycle, and you will watch water as it moves through the model.

MATERIALS

- graduated cylinder
- 50 mL of tap water
- beaker
- heat-resistant gloves
- hot plate
- glass plate or watch glass
- tongs or forceps

Procedure

1 Use the graduated cylinder to pour 50 mL of water into the beaker. Note the water level in the beaker.

2 Put on your safety goggles and gloves. Place the beaker securely on the hot plate. Turn the heat to medium, and bring the water to a boil.

3 While waiting for the water to boil, practice picking up and handling the glass plate or watch glass with the tongs. Hold the glass plate a few centimeters above the beaker, and tilt it so that the lowest edge of the glass is still above the beaker.

4 Observe the glass plate as the water in the beaker boils. In your ScienceLog, write down the changes you see in the beaker, in the air above the beaker, and on the glass plate. Write down any changes you see in the water.

5 Continue until you have observed steam rising off the water, the glass plate becoming foggy, and water dripping from the glass plate.

6 Carefully set the glass plate on a counter or other safe surface as directed by your teacher.

7 Turn off the hot plate, and allow the beaker to cool. If you are directed to do so by your teacher, use gloves or tongs to move the hot beaker.

8 In your ScienceLog, copy the illustration shown at right. On your sketch, draw and label the water cycle you observed in your model. Include arrows and labels for condensation, evaporation, and precipitation.

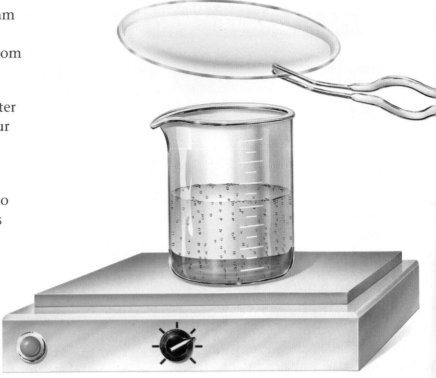

Analysis

9 Compare the water level in the beaker now with the water level at the beginning of the experiment. Was there a change? Explain why or why not.

10 If you had used a scale or a balance to measure the mass of the water in the beaker before and after this activity, would the mass have changed? Why or why not?

11 How is your model similar to the Earth's water cycle? On your sketch of the illustration above, label where the processes shown in the model are similar to the Earth's water cycle. Also indicate the interactions between water and thermal energy in the water cycle.

12 When you finished this experiment, the water in the beaker was still hot. What stores much of the energy in the Earth's water cycle?

Going Further

As rainwater runs over the land, the water picks up minerals and salts. Do these minerals and salts evaporate, condense, and precipitate as part of the water cycle? Where do they go?

If the average global temperature on Earth became warmer, how would you expect sea levels to change, and why? What would happen to sea levels if the average global temperature cooled?

Section 1

Vocabulary

erosion (*p. 484*)
water cycle (*p. 485*)
tributary (*p. 486*)
watershed (*p. 486*)
divide (*p. 486*)
channel (*p. 487*)
load (*p. 488*)

Section Notes

- Erosion is the removal and transport of soil and rock. River and stream erosion plays an important role in shaping the Earth's surface. ★TEKS

- The water cycle is the continuous movement of water between the Earth and its atmosphere. The water cycle is driven by energy from the sun. ★TEKS

- A watershed is the region of land drained by a river system.

- The rate of stream erosion is affected by many factors, including the stream's gradient, discharge, speed, and load.

- Gradient is the change in elevation over distance.

- Discharge is the volume of water moved by a stream in a given amount of time.

- A stream's load is the material it carries.

- Rivers can be described as youthful, mature, old, or rejuvenated.

Section 2

Vocabulary

deposition (*p. 491*)
delta (*p. 492*)
alluvial fan (*p. 493*)
flood plain (*p. 493*)

Section Notes

- Deposition happens when eroded soil and rock are dropped. Deposition by streams and rivers creates landforms such as deltas, alluvial fans, and flood plains. ★TEKS

- Deltas are fan-shaped deposits of sediment at a river's mouth.

- Alluvial fans are fan-shaped deposits of sediment on land.

- Flood plains are rich farming areas because flooding brings new soil to the area.

Section 3

Vocabulary

ground water (*p. 494*)
water table (*p. 494*)
aquifer (*p. 494*)
porosity (*p. 494*)
permeability (*p. 494*)
recharge zone (*p. 495*)

Section Notes

- Ground water is recharged by water from the Earth's surface. ★TEKS

- The zone of aeration and the zone of saturation meet at a boundary called the water table.

- An aquifer is a porous and permeable rock layer through which ground water flows.

- Ground water can dissolve rock, such as limestone, to form caves. ★TEKS

Review

For each set of terms, identify the term that doesn't belong, and explain why.

1. tributary/river/water table

2. load/recharge zone/aquifer

3. delta/alluvial fan/divide

4. porosity/permeability/deposition

5. stalactite/spring/stalagmite

6. divide/gradient/discharge

UNDERSTANDING CONCEPTS

Multiple Choice

7. Which of the following processes is NOT part of the water cycle?
   a. evaporation
   c. condensation
   b. percolation
   d. deposition

8. Which type of stream load makes a river look muddy?
   a. bed load
   b. dissolved load
   c. suspended load
   d. gravelly load

9. What features are common in youthful river channels? ⭐TEKS
   a. meanders
   b. flood plains
   c. rapids
   d. sandbars

10. Over time, erosion will cause a stream's channel to become
    a. narrower and shallower.
    b. narrower and deeper.
    c. wider and deeper.
    d. wider and shallower.

11. Which depositional feature is found at the coast? ⭐TEKS
    a. delta
    c. alluvial fan
    b. flood plain
    d. placer deposit

12. Caves are mainly a product of ⭐TEKS
    a. erosion by rivers.
    b. river deposition.
    c. water pollution.
    d. erosion by ground water.

13. The largest watershed in the United States is the
    a. Amazon.
    b. Columbia.
    c. Colorado.
    d. Mississippi.

14. An aquifer must be
    a. nonporous and nonpermeable.
    b. porous and permeable.
    c. porous and nonpermeable.
    d. nonporous and permeable.

15. The water in an aquifer comes from ⭐TEKS
    a. the percolation of surface water.
    b. evaporation within the Earth.
    c. a chemical reaction.
    d. the melting of ice.

Short Answer

16. What is the relationship between tributaries and rivers? ⭐TEKS

17. Explain how surface water enters an aquifer. ⭐TEKS

18. Why are caves usually found in limestone-rich regions?

19. Use the following terms to create a concept map: *zone of aeration, zone of saturation, water table, gravity, porosity,* and *permeability.*

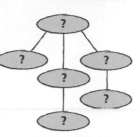

Write one or two sentences to answer the following questions:

20. What role does water play in erosion and deposition? ⭐TEKS

21. What are the features of a river channel that has a steep gradient?

22. Critique William Morris Davis's model of river development and explain its strengths and weaknesses. How has our understanding of the stages of river development changed? ⭐TEKS

23. Imagine that you are hiking beside a mature stream. What would the stream be like?

24. Does water vapor lose or gain energy during condensation? ⭐TEKS

25. A river has flooded a town with a population of 5,000. The town is declared a disaster area, and $2 million is given to the town by the federal government. The local government uses 60 percent of the money for repairs to city property, and the rest is given to the townspeople.

a. How much would each person receive?

b. If there are 2,000 families in the town, how much would each family receive?

c. Would each family receive enough money to rebuild a home? If not, how could the money be distributed more fairly?

The hydrograph below illustrates data collected on river flow during field investigations over a period of 1 year. The discharge readings are from the Yakima River, in Washington. The Yakima River flows eastward from the Cascade Mountains to the Columbia River.

26. During which months is river discharge highest? ⭐TEKS

27. Why is river discharge so high during these months? ⭐TEKS

28. What might cause the peaks in river discharge between November and March? ⭐TEKS

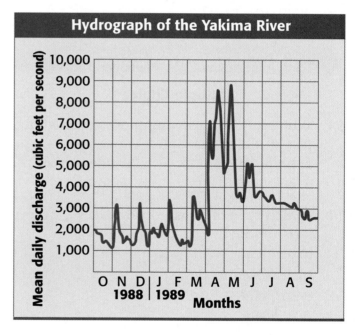

Hydrograph of the Yakima River

Reading Check-up

⭐TEKS Take a minute to review your answers to the Pre-Reading Questions found at the bottom of page 482. Have your answers changed? If necessary, revise your answers based on what you have learned since you began this chapter.

Chapter 18

1 Which one of the following landforms results from river and stream erosion?

A Mountains

B Glaciers

C River channels

D Aquifers

2 A well-drilling company offers the four types of wells shown below. Which well is most likely to be a reliable source of ground water?

F 1

G 2

H 3

J 4

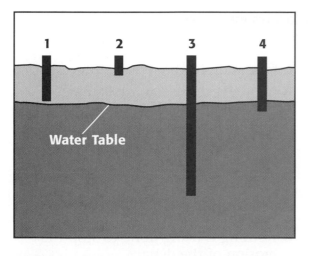

3 In the water cycle, the sun's energy causes

A evaporation.

B condensation.

C precipitation.

D percolation.

4 Lakes form in areas where

F wells are drilled.

G the water table is below the Earth's surface.

H the water table is above the Earth's surface.

J there are placer deposits.

5 Stream and river deposits include

A deltas.

B caves.

C alluvial fans.

D A and C

6 In the illustration of the water cycle below, at what point does water vapor gain energy?

F Evaporation

G Condensation

H Precipitation

J Not Here

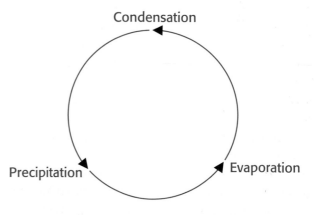

Chapter 18

Math

1 A river flows at a speed of 8 kilometers per hour. If you floated on a raft in this river, how far would you have traveled after 5 hours?

A 5 km

B 16 km

C 40 km

D 80 km

2 A river flows at a speed of 10 kilometers per hour. If a boat travels upstream at a speed of 15 kilometers per hour, how far will it travel in 3 hours?

F 10 km

G 15 km

H 20 km

J 25 km

Reading

Read the passage. Then read each question that follows the passage. Decide which is the best answer to each question.

The lush wetlands that make up the Mississippi Delta are eroding. The threat comes from efforts to make the Mississippi River more useful. Large portions of the river bottom were dredged to make the river deeper for ship traffic, and barriers were built to control flooding. As a result, much of the sediment that the Mississippi River carries is deposited in the ocean rather than in the delta. By 1995, more than half of the wetlands were already gone, swept out to sea by waves along the Louisiana coast. Fortunately, scientists, government leaders, and citizens are working together to help the Mississippi Delta recover.

1 Information in the passage suggests that

A efforts to make the Mississippi River more useful have also improved the delta.

B the Mississippi Delta is home to many kinds of wildlife.

C if the Mississippi River does not deposit enough sediment, the coastline will erode.

D nothing is being done to stop the erosion of the delta.

2 Which of these statements is NOT a fact in this passage?

F By 1995, more than half of the wetlands were gone.

G Currently no sediment is deposited in the delta.

H The river bottom was dredged.

J Barriers were built to control flooding.

BUBBLE, BOIL & SQUIRT

In parts of Yellowstone National Park, boiling water blasts into the sky, lakes of strange-colored mud boil and gurgle, and hot gases hiss from the ground. What are these strange geologic features? What causes them? The story begins deep inside the Earth.

Old Geysers

One of Yellowstone's main tourist attractions is a *geyser* called Old Faithful. Erupting every 60 to 70 minutes, Old Faithful sends a plume of steam and scalding-hot water as high as 60 m into the air. A geyser is formed when a narrow vent connects one or more underground chambers to the Earth's surface. These chambers are heated by rock that is nearly molten. As underground water flows into the vent and chambers, it is heated above 100°C. The superheated water quickly turns to steam and explodes first toward the surface and then into the air. And Old Faithful erupts right on schedule!

Nature's Hot Tub

A *hot spring* is a geyser without pressure. Its vents are wider than a geyser's, and they let the underground water cool a little and flow to the surface rather than erupt in a big fountain. To be called a hot spring, the water must be at least as warm as the temperature of the human body (37°C). Some underground springs are several hundred degrees Celsius.

Flying Mud Pies

Mud pots form when steam or hot water trickles to the surface and chemically weathers and dissolves surface features, such as rocks. The mixture of dissolved rock and water creates a boiling, bubbling pool of sticky liquid clay. But don't get too close! Occasionally, the steam will rise quickly and forcefully enough to make the mud pot behave like a volcano. When it does, a mud pot can toss car-sized gobs of mud high into the air!

Some mud pots become *paint pots* when microorganisms or brightly colored minerals are mixed in with the mud. For instance, if there is a lot of iron in the mud, the paint pot will turn reddish brown or yellowish brown. Other minerals and bacteria can make the mud white or bluish in color. Some paint pots may even gurgle up blobs in several different colors.

What Do You Think?

▶ Some people think that tapping geothermal energy sources such as geysers could harm the delicate ecology of those sources. Find out about the benefits and the risks of using geothermal energy. What is your opinion?

▲ *Mud pot in Yellowstone National Park*

The Earth's Atmosphere

Pre-Reading Questions

1. Describe the components of the Earth's atmosphere. ⊛TEKS
2. What is wind, and how does it affect the weather? ⊛TEKS

FLOATING ON AIR

These skydivers might have checked their parachutes at least a half-dozen times before they jumped. They probably also paid particular attention to the day's weather report. When skydiving, skydivers should know what to expect from the atmosphere. The atmosphere can be unpredictable and dangerous, but it also provides us with the gases needed for our survival on Earth. In this chapter, you will learn about the Earth's atmosphere and its effect on your life.

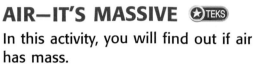

AIR—IT'S MASSIVE ★TEKS

In this activity, you will find out if air has mass.

Procedure

1. Use a **scale** to find the mass of a **ball,** such as a football or a basketball, with no air in it. Record the mass of the empty ball in your ScienceLog.

2. Pump up the ball with an **air pump.**

3. Use the scale to find the mass of the ball filled with air. Record the mass of the ball filled with air in your ScienceLog.

Analysis

4. Compare the mass of the empty ball with the mass of the ball filled with air. Did the mass of the ball change after you pumped it up?

5. Based on your results, does air have mass? Explain your answer.

READING WARM-UP

Terms to Learn

atmosphere   stratosphere
air pressure   ozone
altitude   mesosphere
troposphere   thermosphere

What You'll Do

● Describe components of the Earth's atmosphere. ⭐TEKS

● Explain why pressure changes with altitude.

● Explain how temperature changes with altitude.

● Describe the structure of the atmosphere. ⭐TEKS

Characteristics of the Atmosphere

If you were lost in the desert, you could live for a few days without food and water. But you wouldn't last more than 5 minutes without the atmosphere.

The **atmosphere** is a mixture of gases that surrounds the Earth. It has the oxygen you need to breathe, and it protects you from the sun's damaging rays. But the atmosphere is always changing. Every breath you take, every tree you plant, and every car you ride in affects the makeup of our atmosphere. Later you will find out how the atmosphere is changing. But first you need to learn about the atmosphere's makeup and structure.

Components of the Atmosphere

Figure 1 shows the amounts of the gases that make up the atmosphere. Besides gases, the atmosphere has small amounts of solids and liquids. Tiny solid particles, such as dust, volcanic ash, sea salt, dirt, and smoke, are carried in the air. The next time you turn off the lights at night, turn on a flashlight and you will see some of these tiny particles floating in the air. Water is the most common liquid in the atmosphere. Liquid water is found as drops of water in clouds. Water vapor, which is also found in the atmosphere, is a gas that you cannot see.

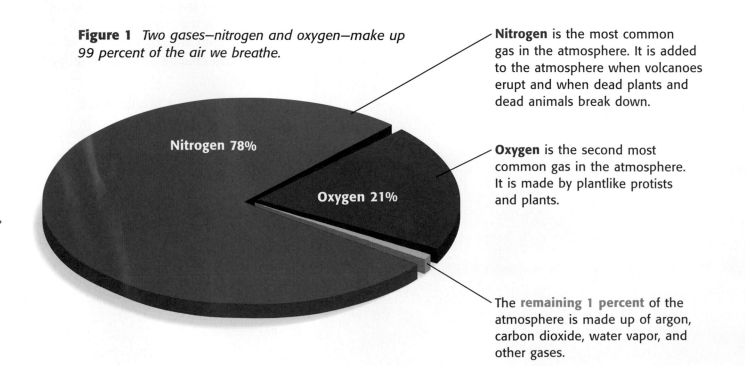

Figure 1 *Two gases—nitrogen and oxygen—make up 99 percent of the air we breathe.*

Nitrogen is the most common gas in the atmosphere. It is added to the atmosphere when volcanoes erupt and when dead plants and dead animals break down.

Oxygen is the second most common gas in the atmosphere. It is made by plantlike protists and plants.

Nitrogen 78%

Oxygen 21%

The **remaining 1 percent** of the atmosphere is made up of argon, carbon dioxide, water vapor, and other gases.

Atmospheric Pressure and Temperature

Have you ever been in an elevator in a tall building? If you have, you might remember the "popping" in your ears as you went up or down. In a moving elevator, the air pressure outside your ears changes, while the air pressure inside your ears stays the same. **Air pressure** is the measure of the force with which air particles push on a surface. Your ears pop when the pressure inside and outside of your ears suddenly becomes equal. Air pressure changes as you move through the atmosphere. Temperature and the kinds of gases present also change. Why do these changes happen? Read on to find out.

Chemistry

C O N N E C T I O N

Water is the only substance that can be found as a liquid, a solid, and a gas in the Earth's atmosphere.

Pressure

Look at **Figure 2.** Think of air pressure as a human pyramid. The people at the bottom of the pyramid can feel all the weight and pressure of the people on top. The person on top doesn't feel any weight because there isn't anyone above her. The atmosphere works in much the same way.

The Earth's atmosphere is held around the planet by gravity. The gas particles in the atmosphere are pulled toward the Earth's surface, which gives the particles weight. As you move farther away from the Earth's surface, air pressure decreases because fewer gas particles are above you to push down on you. **Altitude** is the height of an object above the Earth's surface. As altitude increases, air pressure decreases.

Figure 2 *Like in a human pyramid, pressure increases the closer you get to the Earth's surface.*

Lower pressure

Higher pressure

Temperature

Air temperature also changes as you increase altitude. As you pass through the atmosphere, air temperature alternates between warm and cold. The temperature differences result from the way the sun's energy is absorbed by gases as it moves through the atmosphere. Some parts of the atmosphere are warmer because they have gases that absorb the sun's energy. Other parts are cooler because they do not have these gases that absorb the sun's energy.

Structure of the Atmosphere

Based on temperature differences, the Earth's atmosphere is divided into four layers—the troposphere, stratosphere, mesosphere, and thermosphere. **Figure 3** shows the four atmospheric layers and describes their average altitude and temperature.

Figure 3 **Layers of the Earth's Atmosphere**

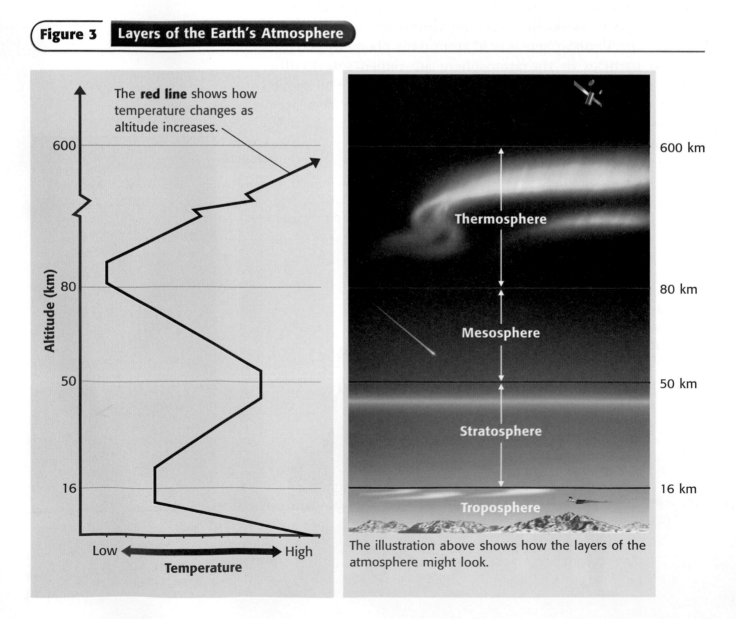

The **red line** shows how temperature changes as altitude increases.

Altitude (km)

600
80
50
16

Low ⟷ High

Temperature

600 km
Thermosphere
80 km
Mesosphere
50 km
Stratosphere
16 km
Troposphere

The illustration above shows how the layers of the atmosphere might look.

Troposphere

The **troposphere,** which lies next to the Earth's surface, is the lowest layer of the atmosphere. In the troposphere, the temperature generally drops as altitude increases. The troposphere has almost 90 percent of the atmosphere's mass. It is also the densest layer. *Density* is the amount of matter in a given space or volume. Almost all of Earth's carbon dioxide, water vapor, clouds, air pollution, weather, and life-forms are found in the troposphere. In fact, the troposphere is the layer in which you live.

Self-Check

Describe the components of the Earth's atmosphere. *(See page 640 to check your answer.)* TEKS

Stratosphere

The atmospheric layer above the troposphere is called the **stratosphere.** In the stratosphere, the air is very thin and has little moisture. The lower stratosphere is very cold—it is about –60°C. In the stratosphere, the temperature increases with altitude. The temperature increases because of ozone. **Ozone** is a substance that is made up of three oxygen atoms, as shown in **Figure 4.** Almost all of the ozone in the atmosphere is in the ozone layer of the stratosphere. The ozone layer absorbs some of the sun's damaging rays, known as ultraviolet radiation. The absorption of the sun's rays by the ozone layer warms the air and protects life on Earth.

Ozone   **Oxygen**

Figure 4 *While ozone is made up of three oxygen atoms, the oxygen in the air you breathe is made up of two oxygen atoms.*

UV and SPFs TEKS

People protect themselves from the hot Texas sun by putting on sunblock. Exposing unprotected skin to the sun's damaging ultraviolet rays over time can cause skin cancer. The breakdown of the ozone in the stratosphere is thinning the layer. The thinning of the ozone layer allows damaging ultraviolet radiation to reach the Earth's surface. Sunblocks have different ratings of SPFs, or skin protection factors. What do the SPF ratings mean? How accurate do you think SPF ratings are?

Mesosphere

Above the stratosphere is the mesosphere. The **mesosphere** is the coldest layer of the atmosphere. In the mesosphere, as in the troposphere, the temperature drops as altitude increases. Temperatures can be as low as –93°C at the top of the mesosphere. The mesosphere protects the Earth from meteoroids. A *meteoroid* is a very small rocky body found in space. Meteoroids usually burn up in the mesosphere.

Thermosphere

The uppermost atmospheric layer is the **thermosphere.** Here temperature again increases as altitude increases because many of the gases absorb the sun's energy. Temperatures in this layer can reach 1,700°C.

While the thermosphere has very high temperatures, it would not feel hot. How hot something feels has to do with not only temperature but also heat. And temperature and heat are not the same thing. Temperature is a measure of the average energy of moving particles in a substance. A high temperature means that the particles are moving very fast. Heat is the transfer of energy between objects at different temperatures. But in order for energy to move from one particle to another, particles must touch one another. **Figure 5** describes how the density of particles affects heat in the thermosphere compared with heat in the troposphere.

Figure 5 *Temperatures in the thermosphere are higher than those in the troposphere, but the air particles are too far apart to touch one another very often. So the thermosphere would not feel hot.*

The **thermosphere** is not very dense because there are few particles. The temperature of this layer is high because the particles move fast. But because the particles rarely touch one another, the particles do not transfer much energy.

The **troposphere** is denser because there are more particles. The temperature of this layer is lower than that of the thermosphere because the particles move more slowly. But because the particles are bumping into one another, the particles transfer much more energy.

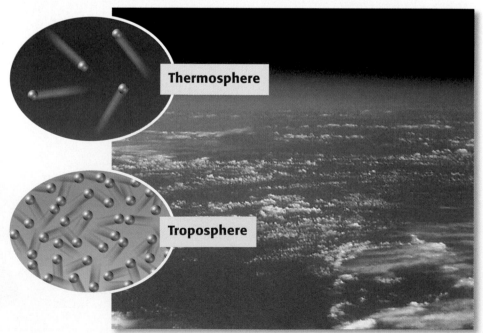

Ionosphere

In the upper part of the mesosphere and the lower thermosphere, certain gases absorb the sun's damaging rays. As a result, the thermosphere's temperature rises and the gas particles become electrically charged. These electrically charged particles are called *ions,* and this part of the thermosphere is called the *ionosphere.* Look at **Figure 6.** Sometimes these ions radiate energy as light of different colors.

The ionosphere also reflects certain radio waves, such as AM radio waves. If you have ever listened to an AM radio station, you can be sure that the ionosphere had something to do with how clear the station sounded. These radio signals bounce off the ionosphere and are sent back to Earth.

Figure 6 *Aurora borealis (northern lights) and aurora australis (southern lights) happen because of ions radiating energy.*

SECTION REVIEW

1. What causes air pressure?

2. Explain why pressure decreases but temperature can either increase or decrease as altitude increases.

3. How can the thermosphere have high temperatures but not feel hot?

4. **Analyzing Relationships** Describe one characteristic of each layer of the atmosphere. Explain how that characteristic affects life on Earth. **★TEKS**

internet connect

SCiLINKS

NSTA   GO TO: www.scilinks.org

TOPIC: Composition of the Atmosphere
*sci*LINKS NUMBER: HSTE355

The Earth's Atmosphere   **513**

Terms to Learn

radiation
conduction
convection
greenhouse effect
global warming

What You'll Do

● Describe what happens to energy that reaches the Earth.

● Explain radiation, conduction, and convection.

● Explain how the greenhouse effect could contribute to global warming.

Heating of the Atmosphere

Have you ever walked barefoot across a sidewalk on a sunny day? If so, your feet felt how hot the pavement was.

How did the sidewalk get so hot? The sidewalk was heated as it absorbed the sun's energy. The Earth's atmosphere is also heated by the sun. In this section, you will learn about the different ways that the sun's energy moves through the Earth's atmosphere. You will also find out why it seems to be getting hotter every year.

Energy in the Atmosphere

The Earth receives energy from the sun by radiation. **Radiation** is the transfer of energy through matter or space as waves. Although the sun releases a huge amount of energy, the Earth receives only about two-billionths of this energy. **Figure 7** shows what happens to the sun's energy once it enters the atmosphere.

When an object absorbs energy, its temperature can increase. For example, when you stand in the sunshine on a cool day, you can feel the sun's rays warming your body. As your skin absorbs the energy, particles in the surface of your skin start

Figure 7 *Energy from the sun is scattered, reflected, and absorbed by the atmosphere and the Earth.*

25 percent scattered and reflected by clouds and air
20 percent absorbed by ozone, clouds, and atmospheric gases

5 percent reflected by the Earth's surface
50 percent absorbed by the Earth's surface

to move faster. You feel this as an increase in temperature. The same thing happens when energy is absorbed by the Earth's surface. The energy from the Earth's surface can then be transferred to the atmosphere, which warms the atmosphere.

Conduction

Think back to the example about walking barefoot on a hot sidewalk. Energy is transferred from the sidewalk to your foot by conduction. **Conduction** is the transfer of energy from one substance to another by direct contact. Energy always moves from a warm area to a cold area. Just as your feet are heated by the sidewalk, the air is heated by land and ocean surfaces. When air particles come into direct contact with particles of a warmer surface, energy is transferred from the warmer surface to the atmosphere.

Convection

Most energy in the atmosphere moves by convection. **Convection** is the transfer of energy by the movement of a liquid or a gas. As air is heated, it becomes less dense and rises. Cool air is denser and sinks. The cool air is heated by the ground and again rises. Look at **Figure 8.** As the warm air rises and the cool air sinks, air moves in a circular pattern. This circular movement of air is called a *convection current*.

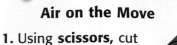

QuickLab

Air on the Move

1. Using **scissors,** cut a spiral shape out of a **piece of construction paper.** Poke a hole in the middle of the spiral.

2. Tie a **piece of string** about 40 cm long through the hole in the middle of the spiral.

3. Hold the spiral about 5 cm over a **hot light bulb.** Make sure not to touch the light bulb with the spiral.

4. What happened when you held the spiral over the light bulb? What do you think caused this result?

⊛ TEKS

TRY at HOME

Figure 8 *The Earth and its atmosphere are heated by radiation, conduction, and convection.*

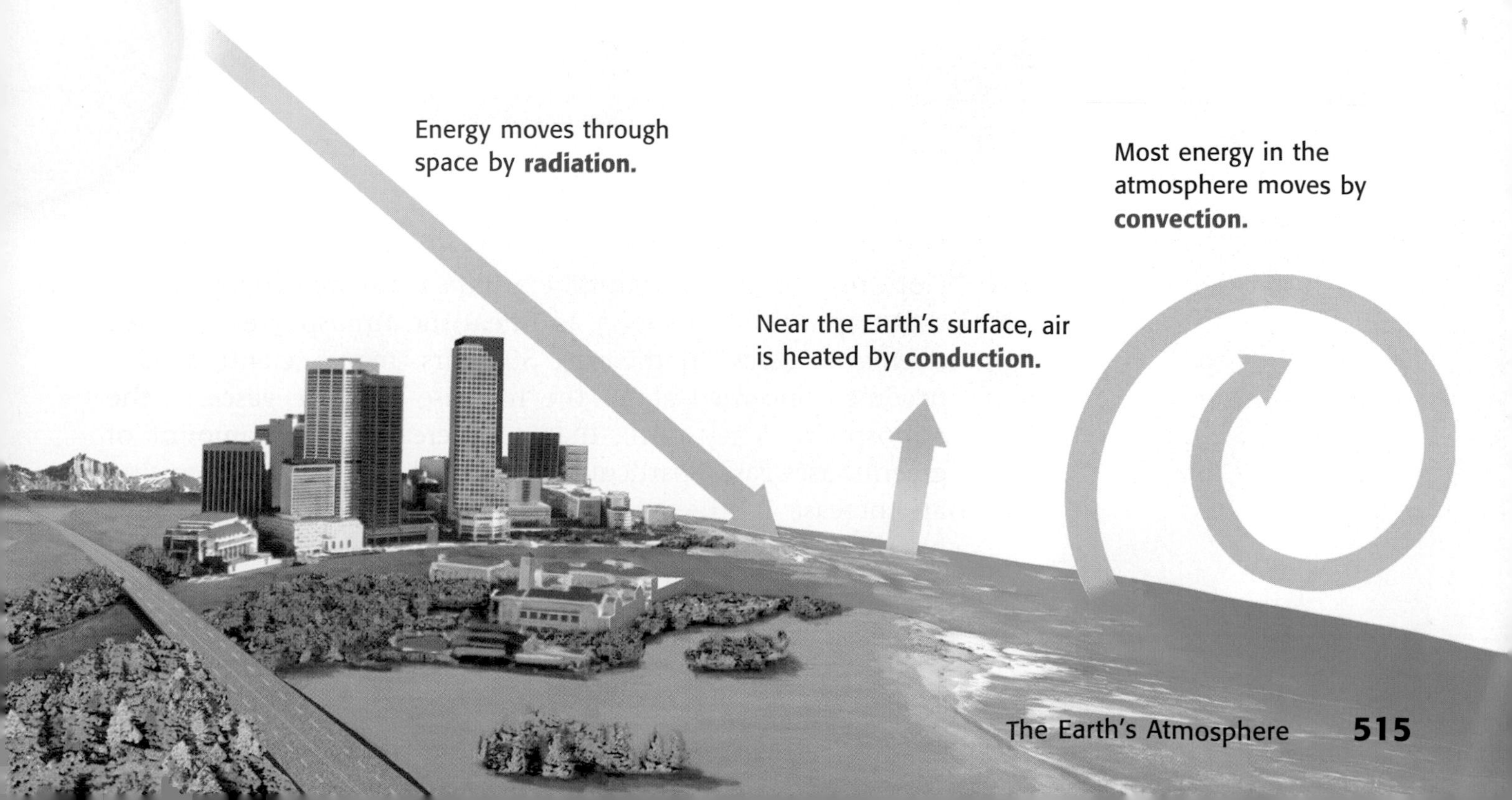

Energy moves through space by **radiation.**

Most energy in the atmosphere moves by **convection.**

Near the Earth's surface, air is heated by **conduction.**

The Greenhouse Effect

As you learned in Figure 7, 50 percent of the energy that enters the Earth's atmosphere is absorbed by the Earth's surface. This energy is then reradiated to the Earth's atmosphere. Gases can stop this energy from escaping into space by absorbing it and reradiating the energy back to the Earth's surface. As a result, the Earth's atmosphere stays warm. The way gases absorb energy and keep the Earth warm is like the way a blanket traps energy and keeps you warm at night. The way that gases in the Earth's atmosphere trap reradiated energy, heating the atmosphere, is known as the **greenhouse effect.** This term is used because the Earth's atmosphere works like a greenhouse. **Figure 9** shows how a greenhouse works.

Figure 9 *The gases in the atmosphere act like a layer of glass. The gases allow the sun's energy to pass through. But some of the gases trap reradiated energy.*

1 Sunlight streams through the glass into the greenhouse.

2 Sunlight is absorbed by objects inside the greenhouse. The objects reradiate the energy.

3 The glass stops the energy from escaping to the outside.

Global Warming

Not every gas in the atmosphere traps reradiated energy. Gases that trap reradiated energy and heat the atmosphere are called *greenhouse gases.* In the past 30 years, many scientists have become concerned about the increase of these gases in the atmosphere. They think that an increase in the amount of greenhouses gases, particularly carbon dioxide, may be causing an increase in the greenhouse effect. These scientists have hypothesized that a rise in carbon dioxide due to human activity has led to increased global temperatures. A rise in average global temperatures is called **global warming.** If an increase in the greenhouse effect occurred, global warming would happen.

The Radiation Balance

For you to be able to live on Earth, the amount of energy received from the sun must equal the amount of energy returned to space. About 30 percent of the incoming energy from the sun is reflected back into space. Most of the energy that is absorbed by the Earth and its atmosphere is also sent back into space. The balance between incoming energy and outgoing energy is known as the *radiation balance*. If greenhouse gases continue to increase in the atmosphere, the radiation balance may be affected. Some of the energy that once escaped into space could be trapped. The Earth's temperatures would continue to rise, and Earth would become a little less livable.

Keeping the Earth Livable

Some scientists think that recent global warming may be the result of natural processes. However, many of the world's nations have signed a treaty called the Kyoto Protocol to reduce activities that increase greenhouse gases in the atmosphere. One step that is being taken to lower high carbon dioxide levels in the atmosphere is the planting of millions of trees. Plants take in carbon dioxide and give off oxygen, which we need to breathe. Look at **Figure 10** to see what people your age are doing to protect their future.

·····Activity·····

Use your school library or the Internet to find out more about global warming. Using scientific evidence, review and analyze the hypothesis that human activity has led to global warming. Describe both strengths and weaknesses of the hypothesis.

·· ⭐TEKS ········· *TRY at HOME* ··

Figure 10 *By planting trees, these students hope to lower carbon dioxide levels in the atmosphere.*

internet connect

SC*i*LINKS™

NSTA   GO TO: www.scilinks.org

TOPIC: Texas and Global Warming
*sci*LINKS NUMBER: HSTX240

TOPIC: Texas and the Greenhouse Effect
*sci*LINKS NUMBER: HSTX245

TOPIC: Energy in the Atmosphere
*sci*LINKS NUMBER: HSTE360

SECTION REVIEW

1. Describe three things that can happen to energy when it enters the Earth's atmosphere.

2. How does energy move through the atmosphere?

3. What is the greenhouse effect?

4. **Inferring Relationships** How does convection depend on conduction?

Terms to Learn

wind	trade winds
Coriolis effect	westerlies
cyclone	polar easterlies
anticyclone	jet stream

What You'll Do

- Explain how air pressure causes wind direction.
- Identify the role of atmospheric movement in weather change. ✪TEKS
- Describe the global patterns of wind.
- Explain the causes of local wind patterns.

Atmospheric Pressure and Winds

Have you ever raked leaves into a pile just to have the wind blow away all your hard work?

Sometimes wind cools you. Other times wind scatters piles of newly raked leaves. Still other times wind blows down trees and squashes buildings, as shown in **Figure 11**. **Wind** is the movement of air as a result of differences in air pressure. In this section, you will learn about wind and its role in changing the weather.

Why Air Moves

Wind is produced by differences in air pressure. The greater the pressure difference is, the faster the wind moves. This difference in air pressure is generally caused by the unequal heating of the Earth. For example, the air at the equator is warmer and less dense than air at the poles. This warm, less dense air rises. As it rises, it creates an area of low pressure. At the poles, however, the air is cold and dense. Colder, denser air is heavier and sinks. This cold, sinking air creates areas of high pressure. Pressure differences in the atmosphere at the equator and at the poles cause air to move. Because air moves from areas of high pressure to areas of low pressure, winds generally move from the poles toward the equator.

Figure 11 In 1998, the winds from Hurricane Mitch reached speeds of 288 km/h and destroyed towns in Honduras.

Pressure Belts

You may be imagining wind moving in one huge circle from the poles to the equator. In fact, the pattern is much more complex. As warm air rises over the equator, it begins to cool. Eventually, it stops rising and moves toward the poles. At about 30° north and 30° south latitude, some of the cool air begins to sink. This cool, sinking air causes high-pressure belts near 30° north and 30° south latitude.

At the poles, cold air sinks. As this air moves away from the poles and along the Earth's surface, it begins to warm. As the air warms, the pressure drops, which makes low-pressure belts around 60° north and 60° south latitude. Look at **Figure 12.** You can see how the rising and sinking of air make circular patterns. These patterns are called *convection cells.*

Figure 12 *The unequal heating of the Earth makes pressure belts.*

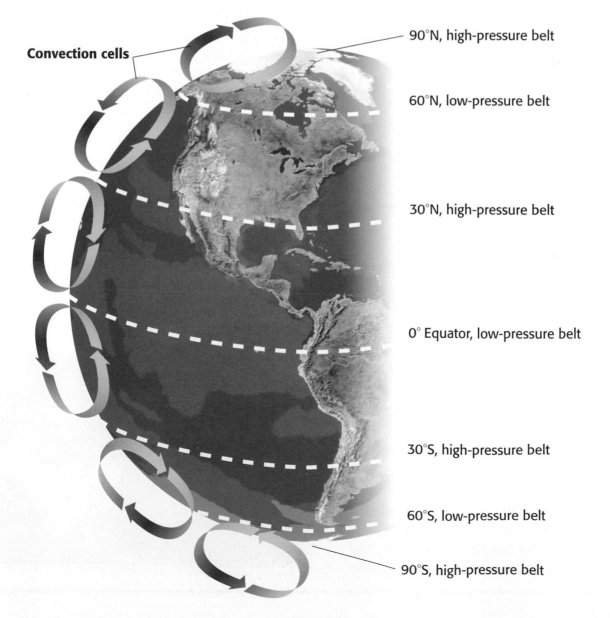

Convection cells

90°N, high-pressure belt

60°N, low-pressure belt

30°N, high-pressure belt

0° Equator, low-pressure belt

30°S, high-pressure belt

60°S, low-pressure belt

90°S, high-pressure belt

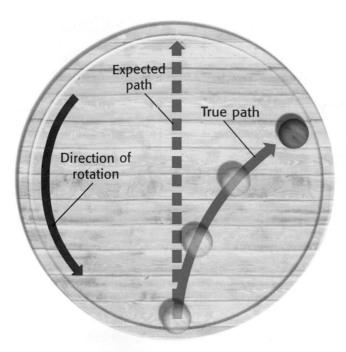

Figure 13 *A marble moving across a Lazy Susan is a good model for showing how wind curves because of the Earth's rotation.*

Coriolis Effect

Winds don't blow directly north or south. The way wind moves is affected by the *rotation,* or spinning, of the Earth. The Earth's rotation causes wind to move in a curved path rather than in a straight line. The curving of moving objects caused by the Earth's rotation is called the **Coriolis effect.** Because of the Coriolis effect, the winds in the Northern Hemisphere curve to the right. Winds in the Southern Hemisphere curve to the left.

To understand how the Coriolis effect works, imagine rolling a marble across a Lazy Susan while it is spinning. What you might see is shown in **Figure 13.** Because of the Lazy Susan's rotation, the marble curves instead of moving in a straight line. The Earth's rotation affects wind moving across its surface in much the same way.

Spotlight On . . .

The Coriolis Effect

A common myth about the Coriolis effect is that it affects the way water moves down a drain. Many people believe that if you flush a toilet in the Northern Hemisphere, the water will spin in a clockwise direction as it drains out of the bowl. The plumbing, not the Coriolis effect, is probably the reason that the water spins clockwise. If you are not convinced, try draining a sink.

The reason that you don't always see the clockwise spiral in your sink is because water or air must move a long distance before it is noticeably affected by the Coriolis effect. The Coriolis effect does affect an airplane pilot's flight path. Because the Earth is rotating, the pilot must make a correction because of the

Coriolis effect. If the pilot chooses not to make the correction, the plane and its passengers will land in a place far from their chosen destination.

Cyclones and Anticyclones

If you have listened to a weather report on the television, you might remember the weather reporter talking about areas of low pressure and high pressure. These areas affect the weather. Areas that have lower pressure than the surrounding areas are called **cyclones.** Warm, less-dense air at the center of a cyclone rises. As the air rises, the air pressure decreases. Areas that have high pressure are called **anticyclones.** Colder, denser air at the center of an anticyclone sinks. As the air sinks, the air pressure increases. Colder, denser air spirals out of the center of these high-pressure areas toward areas of lower pressure. **Figure 14** shows how winds spiral out of an anticyclone and into a cyclone. Because of the Coriolis effect, the winds spin like a wheel. In the Northern Hemisphere, air in a cyclone spins counter-clockwise. Air in an anticyclone spins clockwise.

Weather Wheels

The movement of air affects the weather. In the United States, cyclones and anticyclones play a major role in determining what the weather will be like. As the warm air in the center of a cyclone rises, it cools. As the air cools, clouds and rain form. The warm, rising air in a cyclone causes stormy weather. In an anticyclone, cold air sinks. As it sinks, it gets warmer and absorbs moisture. The cool, sinking air in an anticyclone brings dry, clear weather. By keeping track of cyclones and anticyclones, meteorologists can predict the weather.

Self-Check

Identify the role of air movement in weather change. *(See page 640 to check your answer.)* ⭐TEKS

BRAIN FOOD

Cyclone comes from a Greek word meaning "wheel."

Figure 14 | **Wind Patterns in Cyclones and Anticyclones in the Northern Hemisphere**

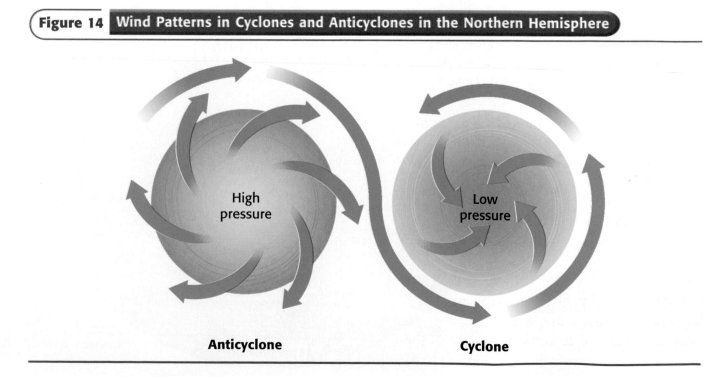

High pressure

Low pressure

Anticyclone

Cyclone

Full of "Hot Air"

Kinds of Winds

There are two kinds of winds—local winds and global winds. Both kinds are caused by the unequal heating of the Earth's surface and by pressure differences. *Local winds* generally move short distances and can blow from any direction. *Global winds* are part of a pattern of air flow that moves across the Earth. Global winds travel longer distances than local winds, and they each travel in a certain direction. **Figure 15** shows the locations of the major global wind systems. Keep in mind that most winds are named after the direction from which they flow. First, you will review the different kinds of global winds. Later in this section, you will learn about local winds.

Trade Winds

In both hemispheres, the winds that blow from 30° latitude to the equator are called **trade winds.** You can see how the Coriolis effect causes the trade winds to curve. Early traders used the trade winds to sail from Europe to the Americas. This is how they became known as "trade winds."

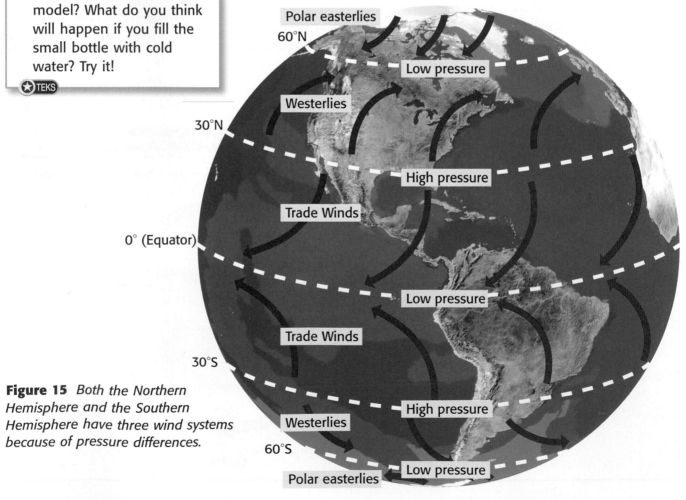

Figure 15 *Both the Northern Hemisphere and the Southern Hemisphere have three wind systems because of pressure differences.*

The Doldrums and Horse Latitudes

The trade winds of the Northern and Southern Hemispheres meet in an area of low pressure around the equator. This area is called the *doldrums*. In the doldrums, there is very little wind because of warm rising air. *Doldrums* comes from an Old English word meaning "foolish." Sailors were thought to be foolish if they got their ship stuck in this area.

At approximately 30° north and 30° south latitude, sinking air makes an area of high pressure. This area is called the *horse latitudes*. Here the winds are weak. Legend has it that the horse latitudes were named when sailing ships carried horses from Europe to the Americas. When the ships were stuck in this area because of little wind, horses were sometimes thrown overboard to save drinking water for the sailors.

Westerlies

The **westerlies** are the wind systems found in both hemispheres between 30° and 60° latitude. The westerlies flow toward the poles in the opposite direction of the trade winds. The westerlies helped early traders return to Europe. Sailing ships, such as the one in **Figure 16,** were designed to use the wind to move the ship forward.

Polar Easterlies

The **polar easterlies** are the wind systems that are found between the poles and 60° latitude in both hemispheres. The polar easterlies are formed from cold, sinking air moving from the poles toward 60° north and 60° south latitude.

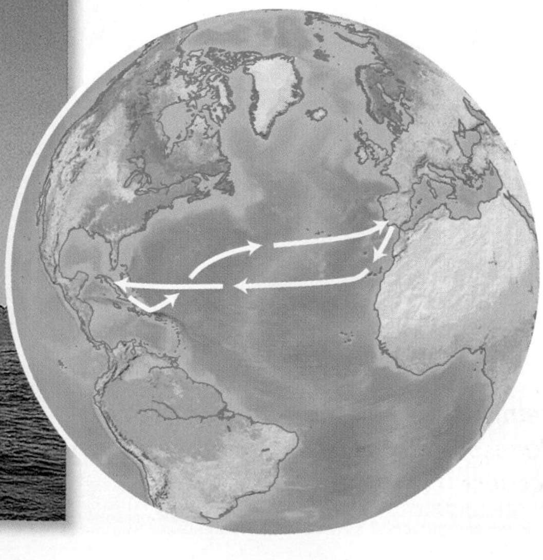

Environment CONNECTION

People have been using wind energy for thousands of years. Today, wind energy is being tapped to generate electrical energy at wind farms. Wind farms are made up of hundreds of wind turbines. These turbines look like giant airplane propellers attached to towers. Together they can generate enough electrical energy for a town.

Figure 16 *A ship in Columbus's day would have used the westerlies to return to Europe.*

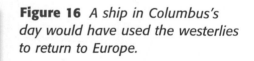

Jet Stream

The **jet stream** is a narrow belt of high-speed winds that blow in the upper troposphere and lower stratosphere. You can see the jet stream in **Figure 17.** These winds can reach speeds of 500 km/h. Unlike other global winds, the jet stream changes paths around the Earth.

Knowing the location of the jet stream is important to both meteorologists and airline pilots. Because the jet stream controls how storms move, meteorologists can track a storm. By flying in the direction of the jet stream, pilots can save time and fuel.

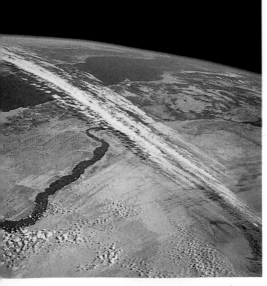

Figure 17 *The jet stream is the white line moving above the Earth.*

Local Winds

Local winds are influenced by an area's geography. Surface features, such as a shoreline or a mountain, sometimes create temperature differences that cause local winds. Land heats up and cools down more quickly than water does. **Figure 18** shows how this difference in heating characteristics causes sea and land breezes.

Figure 18 Sea and Land Breezes

Air over the water is cooler and makes an area of high pressure.

The cool air moves toward the land and causes a *sea breeze.*

As warm air rises, it makes an area of low pressure over the land.

Daytime

Air over the water is warmer and makes an area of low pressure.

Air over land is cooler and makes an area of high pressure.

The cool air moves toward the water and causes a *land breeze.*

Nighttime

Mountain and valley breezes are also caused by surface features, but in a slightly different way. During the day, a gentle breeze blows up the slopes. At night, cold air flows downslope and settles in the valley. **Figure 19** shows how the rising of warm air and the sinking of cool air form mountain and valley breezes.

MathBreak

Calculating Groundspeed

An airplane has an airspeed of 500 km/h and is moving into a 150 km/h head wind due to the jet stream. What is the groundspeed of the plane? Over a 3-hour flight, how far would the plane travel? (Hint: To calculate groundspeed, subtract head-wind speed from airspeed.)

Figure 19 **Valley and Mountain Breezes**

During the day, the sun heats the valley floor and warms the air above it. Warm air moves upslope and makes a *valley breeze.*

Warm air

Daytime

At night, the mountains cool more quickly than the valley. Cold air sinks and makes a *mountain breeze.*

Cool air

Nighttime

SECTION REVIEW

1. What causes winds?

2. How does the Coriolis effect affect the way wind moves?

3. How do winds affect the weather? TEKS

4. **Applying Concepts** Suppose you are vacationing at the beach. It is daytime, and you want to go swimming in the ocean. You know the beach is near your hotel, but you don't know which direction to go. How might the local wind help you find the ocean?

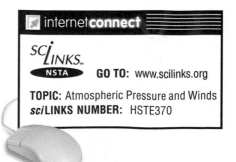

internet**connect**

SC/*LINKS*
NSTA   **GO TO:** www.scilinks.org

TOPIC: Atmospheric Pressure and Winds
*sci***LINKS NUMBER:** HSTE370

Discovery Lab

Under Pressure! ★TEKS

You are planning a picnic with your friends, so you look in the newspaper for the weather forecast. The temperature this afternoon should be in the low 80s. This temperature sounds quite comfortable! But you notice that the newspaper's forecast also includes the barometer reading. What's a barometer? And what does the reading tell you? In this activity, you will build your own barometer and will discover what this tool can tell you.

Ask a Question

1 How do changes in atmospheric pressure affect a barometer?

Form a Hypothesis

2 In your ScienceLog, write a few sentences that answer the question above.

Conduct an Experiment

3 Stretch and blow up the balloon. Then let the air out. This step will make your barometer more sensitive to changes in atmospheric pressure.

4 Cut off the end of the balloon that you put in your mouth to blow it up. Stretch the balloon over the mouth of the coffee can. Attach the balloon to the can with the tape or the rubber band.

MATERIALS

- balloon
- scissors
- large empty coffee can, 10 cm in diameter
- masking tape or rubber band
- drinking straw
- transparent tape
- index card

5 Cut one end of the straw at an angle to make a pointer.

6 Place the straw with the pointer directed away from the center of the stretched balloon. Look at the illustration below. Place the straw so that 5 cm of the end of the straw hang over the edge of the can. Tape the straw to the balloon.

7 Tape the index card to the can near the straw. Congratulations! You have just made a barometer!

8 Now, use your barometer to collect and record information about air pressure. Place the barometer outside for 3 or 4 days. On each day, mark on the index card where the straw points.

Analyze the Results

9 What atmospheric factors affect how your barometer works? Explain your answer.

10 What does it mean when the straw moves up?

11 What does it mean when the straw moves down?

Draw Conclusions

12 Compare your results with the barometric pressures listed in your local newspaper. What kind of weather is associated with high pressure? What kind of weather is associated with low pressure?

13 Does the barometer you built support your hypothesis? Explain your answer.

Going Further

Now you can use your barometer to measure the actual air pressure! Get the weather section from your local newspaper for the same 3 or 4 days that you were testing your barometer. Find the barometer reading in the newspaper for each day, and record it beside that day's mark on your index card. Divide the markings on the index card into equal spaces. Write the matching barometric pressures on the card.

Section 1

Vocabulary

atmosphere *(p. 508)*
air pressure *(p. 509)*
altitude *(p. 509)*
troposphere *(p. 511)*
stratosphere *(p. 511)*
ozone *(p. 511)*
mesosphere *(p. 512)*
thermosphere *(p. 512)*

Section Notes

- The atmosphere is a mixture of gases. ⭐TEKS

- Nitrogen and oxygen are the two most common atmospheric gases. ⭐TEKS

- Throughout the atmosphere, there are changes in air pressure, temperature, and gases.

- Air pressure decreases as altitude increases.

- Temperature differences in the atmosphere result from the way the sun's energy is absorbed as it moves through the atmosphere.

- The troposphere is the lowest layer of the atmosphere. It also has most of the atmosphere's mass. ⭐TEKS

- The stratosphere contains the ozone layer, which protects us from harmful ultraviolet radiation. ⭐TEKS

- The mesosphere is the coldest layer of the atmosphere. ⭐TEKS

- The uppermost atmospheric layer is the thermosphere. ⭐TEKS

Section 2

Vocabulary

radiation *(p. 514)*
conduction *(p. 515)*
convection *(p. 515)*
greenhouse effect *(p. 516)*
global warming *(p. 516)*

Section Notes

- The Earth receives energy from the sun by radiation.

- Energy that reaches the Earth's surface is absorbed, reflected, or reradiated.

- Energy is transferred through the atmosphere by radiation, conduction, and convection.

- The greenhouse effect is caused by gases in the atmosphere that trap energy reradiated by the Earth's surface.

Section 3

Vocabulary

wind *(p. 518)*
Coriolis effect *(p. 520)*
cyclone *(p. 521)*
anticyclone *(p. 521)*
trade winds *(p. 522)*
westerlies *(p. 523)*
polar easterlies *(p. 523)*
jet stream *(p. 524)*

Section Notes

- At the Earth's surface, winds blow from areas of high pressure to areas of low pressure.

- Pressure belts exist approximately every 30° of latitude.

- The Coriolis effect makes wind curve as it moves across the Earth's surface.

- Cyclones and anticyclones play a major role in weather change. ⭐TEKS

- Global winds are part of a pattern of air flow across the Earth and include the trade winds, the westerlies, and the polar easterlies.

- Local winds move short distances, can blow in any direction, and are influenced by geography.

LabBook ⭐TEKS

Gone with the Wind *(p. 632)*
Go Fly a Bike! *(p. 634)*

Review

USING VOCABULARY

For each pair of terms, explain how the meanings of the terms differ.

1. air pressure/altitude

2. troposphere/thermosphere

3. greenhouse effect/global warming

4. convection/conduction

5. cyclone/anticyclone

6. global wind/local wind

UNDERSTANDING CONCEPTS

Multiple Choice

7. What is the most common gas in the air that we breathe? ★TEKS
   a. oxygen   c. hydrogen
   b. nitrogen   d. carbon dioxide

8. The major source of oxygen for the Earth's atmosphere is
   a. sea water.   c. plants.
   b. the sun.   d. animals.

9. The bottom layer of the atmosphere is the ★TEKS
   a. stratosphere.
   b. troposphere.
   c. thermosphere.
   d. mesosphere.

10. About __?__ percent of the energy that reaches the outer atmosphere is absorbed at the Earth's surface.
    a. 20   c. 50
    b. 30   d. 70

11. The ozone layer is located in the ★TEKS
    a. stratosphere.   c. thermosphere.
    b. troposphere.   d. mesosphere.

12. How does most energy in the atmosphere move?
    a. conduction   c. advection
    b. convection   d. radiation

13. The balance between incoming energy and outgoing energy is called
    a. convection.
    b. conduction.
    c. the greenhouse effect.
    d. the radiation balance.

14. Stormy weather is associated with ★TEKS
    a. anticyclones.   c. doldrums.
    b. cyclones.   d. westerlies.

15. The wind systems found near the poles blow from the
    a. north.   c. west.
    b. south.   d. east.

16. Most of the United States is located in which prevailing wind system?
    a. westerlies
    b. northeast trade winds
    c. southeast trade winds
    d. doldrums

Short Answer

17. Why does the atmosphere become less dense as altitude increases?

18. Explain why air rises when it is heated.

19. What causes temperature changes in the atmosphere?

20. What is the relationship between the greenhouse effect and global warming?

21. Use the following terms to create a concept map: *altitude, air pressure, temperature,* and *atmosphere.*

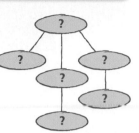

CRITICAL THINKING AND PROBLEM SOLVING

Write one or two sentences to answer the following questions:

22. Explain how atmospheric movement affects weather change. ★TEKS

23. How do you think the Coriolis effect would change if the Earth rotated twice as fast? Explain your answer.

24. Without the atmosphere, the Earth's surface would be very different. What are several ways that the atmosphere affects the Earth?

MATH IN SCIENCE

25. Wind speed is measured in miles per hour and in knots. One mile (statute mile or land mile) is 5,280 ft. One nautical mile (or sea mile) is 6,076 ft. Speed in nautical miles is measured in knots. Calculate the wind speed in knots if the wind is blowing at 25 mi/h.

INTERPRETING GRAPHICS

The windchill chart below was constructed from data collected by a weather center. Use the windchill chart to answer the questions that follow.

Windchill Chart						
		Actual thermometer reading (°F)				
Wind speed		40	30	20	10	0
Knots	mi/h	Equivalent temperature (°F)				
Calm		40	30	20	10	0
4	5	37	27	16	6	−5
9	10	28	16	4	−9	−21
13	15	22	9	−5	−18	−36
17	20	18	4	−10	−25	−39
22	25	16	0	−15	−29	−44
26	30	13	−2	−18	−33	−48
30	35	11	−4	−20	−35	−49

26. If the wind speed is 20 mi/h and the temperature is 40°F, how cold will the air seem? ★TEKS

27. If the wind speed is 30 mi/h and the temperature is 20°F, how cold will the air seem? ★TEKS

28. If the wind speed is 17 knots and the temperature is 30°F, how cold will the air seem? ★TEKS

29. The temperature is 10°F, and the wind speed is 13 knots. If the wind speed changes to 17 knots, how many degrees cooler will the air feel? ★TEKS

Reading Check-up

Take a minute to review your answers to the Pre-Reading Questions ★TEKS found at the bottom of page 506. Have your answers changed? If necessary, revise your answers based on what you have learned since you began this chapter.

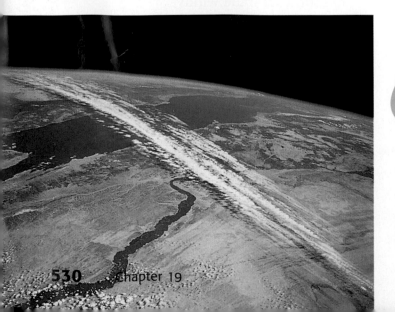

Chapter 19

1 The diagram below illustrates the results of a laboratory experiment. According to the diagram, which statement best describes what happens to gas particles as the gas is heated?

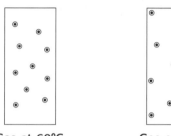

Gas at 60°C   Gas at 90°C

A They move farther apart.

B They move closer together.

C They increase in size.

D They move at a slower speed.

2 Liquids A, B, and C have different densities. Analyze the evidence in the diagram to determine which statement is NOT correct.

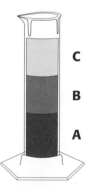

F Liquid A is denser than liquids B and C.

G Liquid B is denser than liquid A but less dense than liquid C.

H Liquid C is less dense than liquids B and A.

J Liquid B is less dense than liquid A but denser than liquid C.

3 Which gas is most common in the atmosphere?

A Oxygen

B Carbon dioxide

C Water vapor

D Nitrogen

4 Climatologists assembled this graph of the change in average global temperature from data collected over a 4-year-period. What can you conclude about average global temperatures?

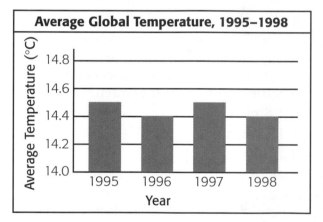

F Over time, average global temperatures are increasing.

G Over time, average global temperatures are fluctuating.

H Over time, average global temperatures are decreasing.

J Over time, average global temperatures are staying the same.

Chapter 19

Math

1 There are 12 girls and 10 boys in Sonya's science class. The name of each student is written on a piece of paper and placed in a hat. If 1 name is picked at random from the hat, what is the probability that Sonya's name will be picked?

A $\frac{1}{5}$

B $\frac{2}{3}$

C $\frac{1}{22}$

D $\frac{1}{12}$

2 Today's wind speed was measured at 18 km/h. At how many **meters per hour** was the wind speed measured?

F 1.8 m/h

G 180 m/h

H 1800 m/h

J 18,000 m/h

3 Rockport received 24.1 centimeters of rain on Monday, 12.5 centimeters of rain on Tuesday, and 5.8 centimeters of rain on Thursday. The rest of the week it did not rain. How much rain did Rockport receive?

A 36.6 cm

B 18.3 cm

C 42.4 cm

D 45.7 cm

4 Larone bought 6 CDs at the store. The prices of the CDs ranged from $12 to $16 each. What is a reasonable total cost for the CDs, not including tax?

F Less than $72

G More than $100

H Between $72 and $96

J Between $48 and $64

Reading

Read the passage. Then read each question that follows the passage. Decide which is the best answer to each question.

Automobile emissions are responsible for at least half of all city air pollution and a quarter of all carbon dioxide added to the air. So, to make a car that gives off no polluting gases is a big accomplishment. The only car that does not give off polluting gases is the electric car. Electric cars do not burn fuel. Some people believe that switching to electric cars will reduce air pollution in this country. But <u>skeptics</u> believe that taxpayers will pay an unfair share for this switch. And they believe that air pollution won't be reduced as much as promised.

1 In this passage, a <u>skeptic</u> is a person that is

A doubtful.

B enthusiastic.

C relieved.

D traditional.

2 Some people want to switch to electric cars because

F they believe taxes will go down.

G electric cars burn fuel.

H the switch will reduce air pollution.

J the switch will add carbon dioxide to the air.

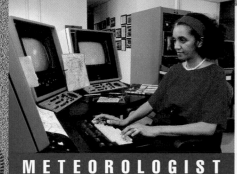

METEOROLOGIST

Observing a tornado develop inside a storm, watching the growth of a hurricane, and predicting floods are all in a day's work for **Cristy Mitchell**. As a meteorologist for the National Weather Service, Mitchell spends each working day watching the powerful forces of nature.

When asked what made her job interesting, Mitchell replied, "There's nothing like the adrenaline rush you get when you see a tornado coming! I would say that witnessing the powerful forces of nature is what really makes my job interesting."

Meteorology is the study of the Earth's atmosphere. Perhaps the most familiar field of meteorology is weather forecasting. However, meteorology is also used in air-pollution control, agricultural planning, and air and sea transportation. Meteorologists also study trends in Earth's climate, such as global warming and ozone loss.

Collecting the Data

Meteorologists collect data on air pressure, temperature, humidity, and wind speed. By applying what they know about the physical properties of the atmosphere and analyzing the mathematical relationships in the data, they are able to forecast the weather.

Meteorologists use many tools to collect the data they need to make weather forecasts. Mitchell explained, "The computer is an invaluable tool for me. Through it, I receive maps and detailed information, including temperature, wind speed, air pressure, lightning activity, and general sky conditions for a specific region." In addition to using computers, Mitchell uses radar and satellite imagery to show regional and national weather.

Find Out for Yourself

▶ Use the library or the Internet to find information about hurricanes, tornadoes, or thunderstorms. How do meteorologists define these storms? What trends in air pressure, temperature, and humidity do meteorologists use to forecast storms? ⭐TEKS

▼ *This photograph of Hurricane Elena was taken from the space shuttle* Discovery *in September 1985.*

SCIENCE

Beyond Our Planet

Place to Visit

★ Fort Davis

Near Fort Davis, high in the Davis Mountains of West Texas, one of the finest astronomical observatories in the entire world stares up into the night sky. Out in the middle of nowhere, between Marfa and Balmorhea, Texas, the McDonald Observatory sits atop the Davis Mountains. McDonald Observatory is home to six working optical telescopes, including the new Hobby-Eberly Telescope, the largest optical telescope in North America and the third largest in the world. If you visit the McDonald Observatory, you can go on a guided tour or even attend a star party!

The McDonald Observatory near Fort Davis, Texas

Scientific Research

Houston

NASA's Johnson Space Center and the Baylor College of Medicine teamed up to bring space technology down to Earth. The rocket engines in the space shuttle use specially designed turbopumps to boost their performance. The technology used in these turbopumps found its way into a medical device called a Ventricle Assist Device (VAD). The VAD is used in patients that are awaiting heart transplants to help their hearts pump blood. Currently, the VAD is a temporary device, but in the future, it could be implanted permanently.

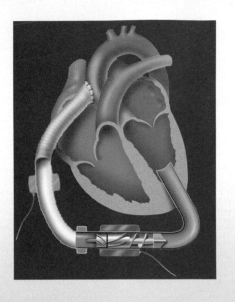

Science Career

Houston

Dr. Franklin Chang-Diaz is a NASA astronaut. Like all astronauts, he trained at the Johnson Space Center in Clear Lake, near Houston. Since becoming an astronaut in 1981, he has flown six missions on the space shuttle and has spent a total of 1,269 hours in space. Dr. Chang-Diaz has used his education in physics to conduct experiments aboard the space shuttle. He has studied lightning, ice crystal growth in space, and the effects of microgravity, or free fall, on plants.

internetconnect

go.hrw.com

go to: go.hrw.com
KEYWORD: HTXU67

Our Solar System

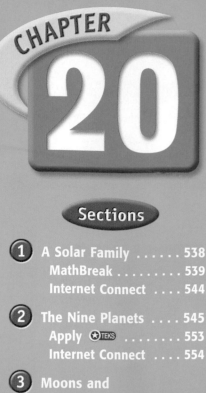

Callisto

Ganymede

Pre-Reading
Questions

1. What are the differences
   between planets, moons,
   comets, asteroids, and
   meteoroids? ⊛TEKS

2. How can surface features
   tell us about a planet's
   history?

A Place of Extremes

Here you see part of the giant planet Jupiter, with its Great
Red Spot—a storm system similar to a hurricane on Earth.
The only difference is that this storm is larger than Earth
and has lasted for several centuries! Next to Jupiter, you
see its four largest moons—Io (IE oh), Europa, Ganymede,
and Callisto. In this chapter, you will learn about all of
the bodies in our solar system—the sun, planets, moons,
comets, asteroids, and meteoroids.

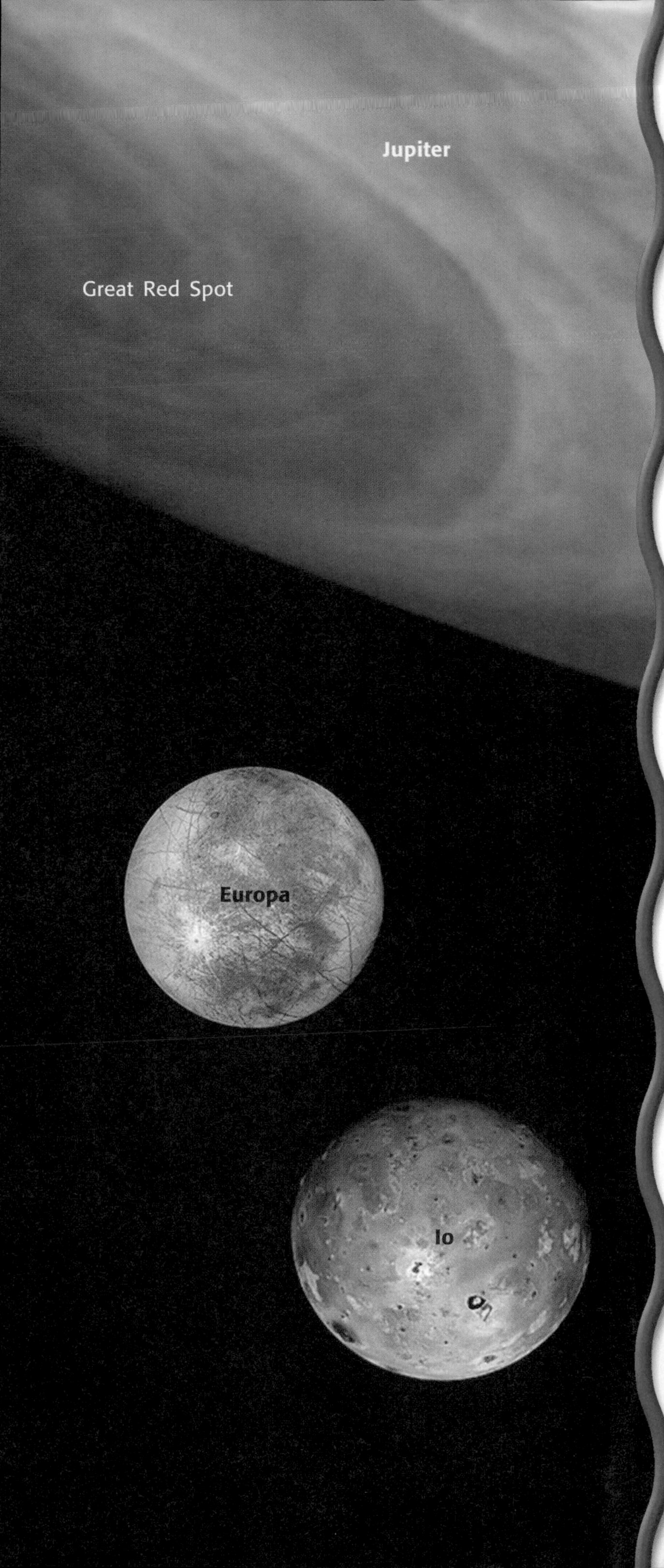

Jupiter

Great Red Spot

Europa

Io

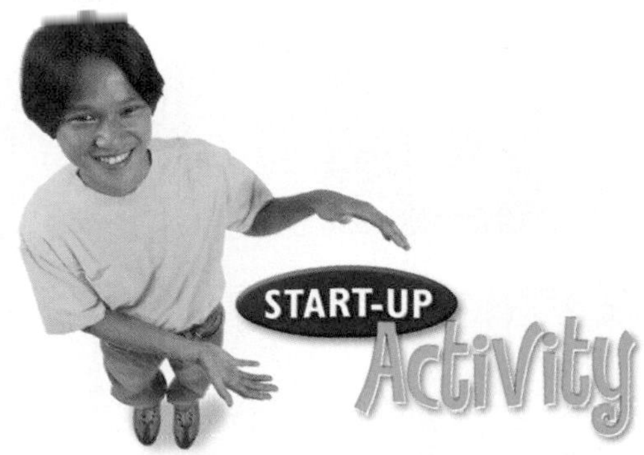

MEASURING SPACE ⭐TEKS

Mercury is nearly 58 million kilometers away from the sun, but Pluto is nearly 6 *billion* kilometers from the sun! It can be hard to visualize such huge distances. Do the following activity to get a better idea of your solar neighborhood.

Procedure

1. Use a **meterstick** and a piece of **chalk** to draw a line 2 m long on a **chalkboard.**

2. Draw a large dot at one end of th line. This dot will represent the s

3. Using the table below, draw smal dots on the line to represent the tive distances of each of the pla

Analysis

4. What do you notice about ho planets are spaced?

5. In what other way are mos outer planets different fro inner planets?

Planet (diameter in km)	Dist fro Million of km
Mercury (4,879)	57
Venus (12,104)	10
Earth (12,756)	14
Mars (6,794)	2
Jupiter (142,984)	
Saturn (120,536)	
Uranus (51,118)	
Neptune (49,528)	
Pluto (2,390)	

w the

of the

the

ance		
n sun		
s	Scaled to cm	
	2	
.9	4	
.2	5	
9.6	8	
27.9	26	
78.4	48	
,424	97	
2,872	151	
4,499	200	
5,943		

537

ar System

A Solar Family

Our solar system is an amazing place! Every year we make new and exciting discoveries about our cosmic neighborhood.

Our *solar system* includes the sun, planets, and many smaller objects. In some cases, these bodies may be organized into smaller *systems* of their own. For example, the Saturn system is made of the planet Saturn, its rings, and the moons in orbit around it. In this way, our solar system is really a combination of many smaller systems.

The Nine Planets: A Sense of Scale

What do you think of when you hear the phrase, "our solar system"? You probably think about the sun and the nine planets that make up our solar system. But how much do you know about the sun or the planets? Take a look at **Figure 1.** Notice how different these members of our solar system are from each other. Each planet has its own unique set of properties.

Figure 1 *These images show the relative sizes and diameters of the planets and the sun.*

arth
6 km

Mars
6,794 km

Jupiter
142,984 km

Sun

Earth

1 light-minute

1 astronomical unit

Figure 2 *One astronomical unit equals about 8.3 light-minutes.*

Measuring Interplanetary Distances

The distances between planets are mind boggling! Take a look at **Figure 2.** One way that we measure distances in space is by using astronomical units. One **astronomical unit** (AU) is the average distance between the Earth and the sun, or about 149,600,000 km. Another way to measure distance in space is by using the speed of light. Light travels at about 300,000 km/s in space. This means that in 1 second, light travels 300,000 km. This is the distance you would cover if you traveled around Earth 7.5 times!

In 1 minute, light travels nearly 18 million kilometers. This distance is also called 1 *light-minute*. It takes light from the sun 8.3 minutes to reach Earth, so the distance from Earth to the sun is 8.3 light-minutes. Distances in the solar system can be measured in light-minutes and light-hours, but the distances between stars are measured in light-*years*!

MathBreak

One astronomical unit (AU) is about 149,600,000 km. Saturn is about 1,424,000,000 km from the sun. In AU, how far is Saturn from the sun? Round your answer to the first decimal place.

Saturn
120,536 km

Uranus
51,118 km

Neptune
49,528 km

Our Solar

Planetary Motion

The solar system is not simply a collection of planets and other bodies. Every object in the solar system moves according to strict physical laws. The motions of Earth, for example, cause nighttime and daytime as well as the seasons.

Rotation and Revolution

How does Earth's motion cause nighttime and daytime? The answer has to do with the Earth's spinning on its axis. Take a look at **Figure 3.** The spin of an object in space is called **rotation.** The amount of time it takes for an object to rotate once is called its *period of rotation.* As Earth rotates, only one-half of the Earth faces the sun at any given time. The half facing the sun is light (daytime), and the half facing away from the sun is dark (nighttime).

In addition to its rotation, Earth also travels around the sun in a path called an *orbit.* The motion of a body as it travels around another body in space is called **revolution.** The other planets in our solar system also revolve around the sun. The amount of time it takes for a single trip around the sun is called a *period of revolution.* Earth's period of revolution is about 365 days, or 1 year. Saturn's period of revolution is 29 Earth years!

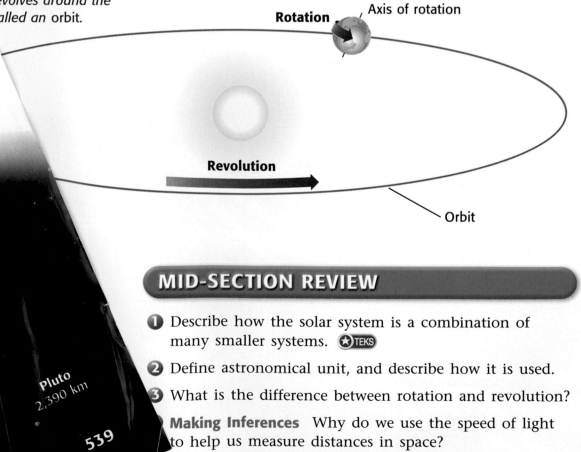

planet rotates on its d revolves around the called an orbit.

Rotation
Axis of rotation
Revolution
Orbit

Pluto
2,390 km

539

System

MID-SECTION REVIEW

❶ Describe how the solar system is a combination of many smaller systems. ⊛TEKS

❷ Define astronomical unit, and describe how it is used.

❸ What is the difference between rotation and revolution?

Making Inferences Why do we use the speed of light to help us measure distances in space?

The Sun: Head of the Family

Without the sun, life on Earth would be impossible. Energy from the sun lights and heats the Earth's surface. Energy from the sun even drives the weather. Making up over 99 percent of the solar system's mass, the sun is the dominant member of our solar system. Let's take a closer look.

The Structure of the Sun

Though it may look like the sun has a solid surface, it does not. When we see a picture of the sun, we are really seeing through the sun's outer atmosphere. The visible surface of the sun starts at the point where the gas becomes so thick we cannot see through it. As shown in **Figure 4,** the sun is made of several layers.

Figure 4 Structure of the Sun and Its Atmosphere

The **corona** forms the sun's outer atmosphere and can extend outward a distance equal to 10–12 times the diameter of the sun. The gases in the corona are so thin that the corona is visible only with special equipment.

The **chromosphere** is a thin region below the corona. It is only 3,000 km thick. Like the corona, the deep-red chromosphere is too faint to see without special equipment.

The **photosphere** is where the gases get thick enough to see. The photosphere is what we know as the visible surface of the sun. It is only about 600 km thick.

The **convective zone** is a region about 200,000 km thick where gases circulate in convection currents. Hot gases rise from the interior, while cooler gases sink toward the interior.

The **radiative zone** is a very dense region about 300,000 km thick. The atoms in this zone are so closely packed together that light can take millions of years to pass through.

The **core** is at the center of the sun. This is where the sun's energy is produced. The core has a radius of about 200,000 km and a temperature near 15,000,000°C.

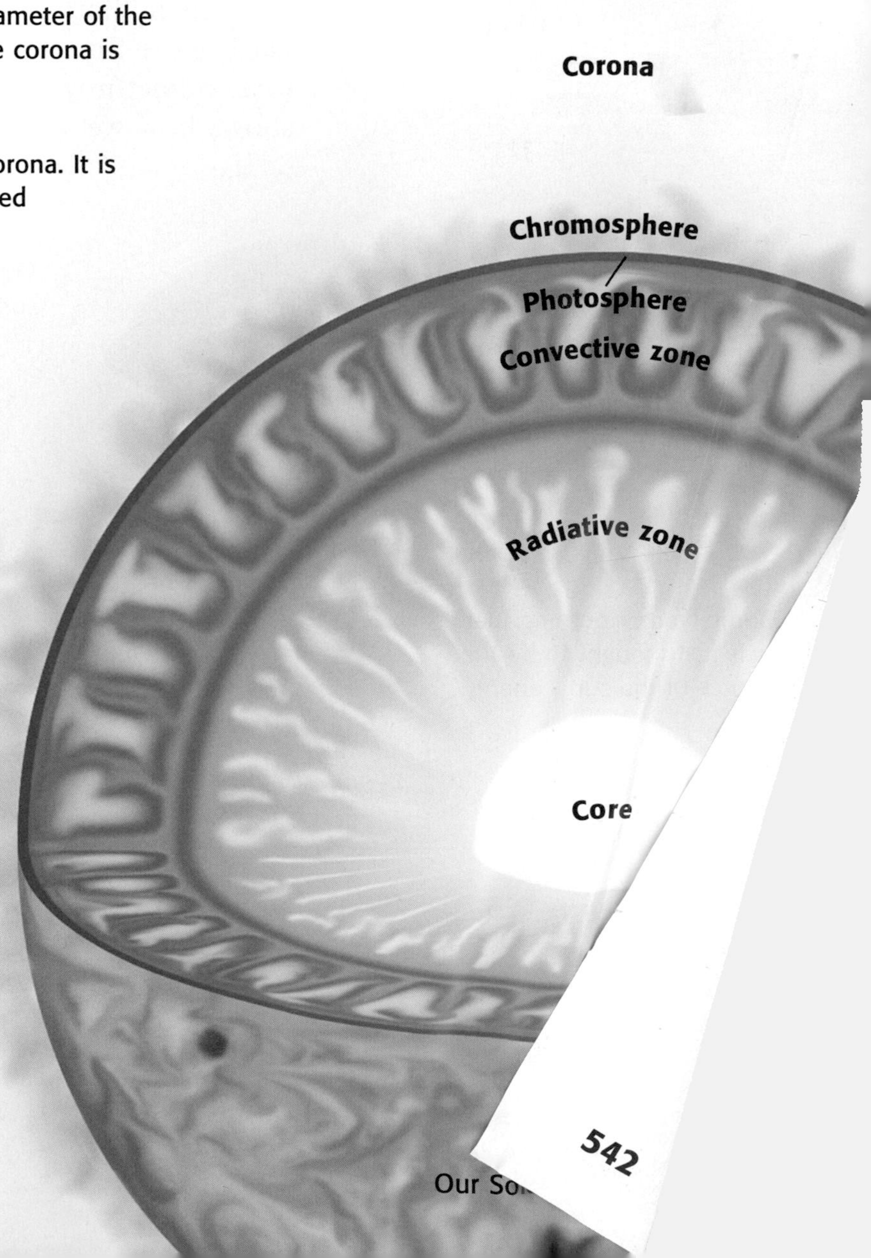

Corona

Chromosphere

Photosphere

Convective zone

Radiative zone

Core

Our So

Energy Production in the Sun

The sun has been shining on the Earth for about 4.6 billion years. How can the sun stay hot for so long? And what makes it shine? Over the years, several theories have been proposed to answer these questions. Because the sun is so bright and hot, many people thought that it was burning fuel to generate its energy. But the amount of energy released from burning would not be enough to power the sun. If the sun were simply burning, it would last only 10,000 years.

Burning or Shrinking?

It became clear that burning wouldn't last long enough to keep the sun shining. Scientists began to think that the sun was slowly shrinking because of gravity. They thought that perhaps this would release enough energy to heat the sun. While the release of gravitational energy is more powerful than burning, it is still not enough to power the sun. If all of the sun's gravitational energy were released, the sun would last for only 45 million years. We know that dinosaurs roamed the Earth more than 65 million years ago, so this couldn't be the case. Something even more powerful was needed. **Figure 5** shows how we arrived at our current theory.

Figure 5 *Ideas about the source of the sun's energy have changed over time.*

Some type of burning fuel was first thought to be the source of the sun's energy.

A shrinking sun was another explanation for solar energy.

Spotlight On . . .

Atoms

An atom consists of a *nucleus* surrounded by one or more *electrons*. Electrons have a negative charge. In most elements, the atom's nucleus is made up of two types of particles—*protons,* with a positive charge, and *neutrons,* with no charge. The positively charged protons in the nucleus are usually balanced by an equal number of negatively charged electrons. The helium atom shown here has two protons, two neutrons, and two electrons.

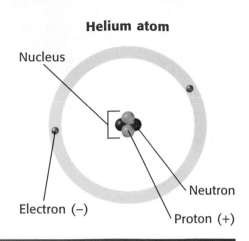

Helium atom

Nucleus

Electron (−)

Neutron

Proton (+)

Nuclear Fusion

At the beginning of the twentieth century, Albert Einstein showed that matter and energy are interchangeable. Matter can change into energy according to his famous formula: $E = mc^2$. (*E* is energy, *m* is mass, and *c* is the speed of light.) Because *c* is such a large number, tiny amounts of matter can produce a huge amount of energy. With this idea, we began to understand a very powerful source of energy. **Nuclear fusion** is the process by which two or more low-mass nuclei join together, or fuse, to form a more massive nucleus. In this way, two hydrogen nuclei can fuse to form a single nucleus of helium. During the process, energy is produced—a lot of it! We now know that the sun gets its energy from nuclear fusion.

The energy released during the nuclear fusion of 1 g of hydrogen is equal to about 100 metric tons of TNT! Each second, the sun changes more than 4 million tons of matter into pure energy.

Einstein's equation changed ideas about the sun's energy source by equating mass and energy.

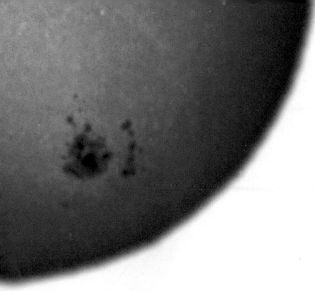

Figure 6 *Sunspots mark cooler areas on the sun's surface. They are related to changes in the magnetic properties of the sun.*

Solar Activity

The visible surface of the sun—the photosphere—is an ever-changing place. Thermal energy moves from the sun's interior by the circulation of gases in the convective zone. This causes the gas in the photosphere to boil and churn. This circulation, combined with the sun's rotation, creates magnetic fields that reach far out into space.

Sunspots

The sun's magnetic fields tend to slow down the activity in the convective zone. This causes areas of the photosphere to be cooler than surrounding areas. These cooler areas show up as sunspots. **Sunspots** are cooler, dark spots on the sun, as shown in **Figure 6.**

The number of sunspots changes in a regular cycle. Records of the number of sunspots have been kept ever since the invention of the telescope in the early 1600s. These records show that the sunspot cycle lasts about 11 years. Every 11 years, the amount of sunspot activity in the sun reaches a peak intensity and then decreases.

Solar Flares

The magnetic fields that cause sunspots also cause solar flares. **Solar flares** are giant storms on the sun's surface that send huge streams of electrically charged particles out into the solar system. When these particles hit Earth's upper atmosphere, they cause spectacular light shows called *auroras*. Solar flares can also interrupt radio communications on Earth and in orbit. Scientists are trying to find ways to give advanced warning of solar flares.

SECTION REVIEW

❶ What is the difference between revolution and orbit?

❷ Identify the characteristics of the sun. ⭐TEKS

❸ Explain both the strength and the weakness of the theory that the sun's energy comes from the force of gravity. ⭐TEKS

❹ **Analyzing Relationships** Describe how the properties of the solar system are different from the properties of the bodies that make up the solar system. ⭐TEKS

Terms to Learn

terrestrial planet
prograde rotation
retrograde rotation
gas giant

What You'll Do

- List the names of the planets in the order that they orbit the sun.
- Describe three ways in which gas giants and terrestrial planets are different from each other. ★ TEKS

The Nine Planets

In 1610, Galileo Galilei realized that planets are not just points of light—they are spherical bodies like Earth. We now know that some even have their own weather!

We've come a long way since the days of Galileo. Now we send space probes to learn about these alien worlds in much more detail. With the data from these space probes, we are always making new discoveries.

The Inner Planets

The solar system is divided into two main parts—the *inner solar system* and the *outer solar system*. The planets of the inner solar system are more closely spaced than the outer planets. The inner planets are called **terrestrial planets** because they are like Earth—small, dense, and rocky. The outer planets, except for icy Pluto, are much larger and are made mostly of gases. **Figure 7** shows the inner solar system.

Mercury—Closest to the Sun

Take a look at **Figure 8.** If you were to visit the planet Mercury, you would find a very strange world. For one thing, on Mercury you would weigh only 38 percent of what you weigh on Earth. Your weight on a planet is due to *surface gravity*, which depends on both the mass and the size of the planet. Also, because of Mercury's slow rotation, a day on Mercury is almost 59 Earth days long!

Another curious thing about Mercury is that its year is only 88 Earth days long. As you know, a *year* is the time it takes for a planet to go around the sun once. Every 88 Earth days, or 1.5 Mercurian days, Mercury revolves once around the sun.

Figure 7 *The lines show orbits of the inner planets. The arrows show the direction of motion and the location of each planet on January 1, 2005.*

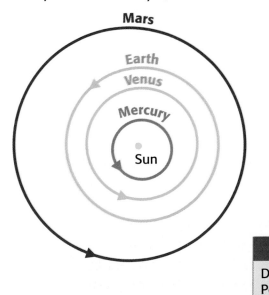

Figure 8 *This image of Mercury was taken by the* Mariner 10 *spacecraft on March 24, 1974, from a distance of 5,380,000 km.*

Mercury Statistics	
Distance from sun	3.2 light-minutes
Period of rotation	58 days, 16 hours
Period of revolution	88 days
Diameter	4,879 km
Density	5.43 g/cm^3
Surface temperature	−173°C to 427°C
Surface gravity	38% of Earth's

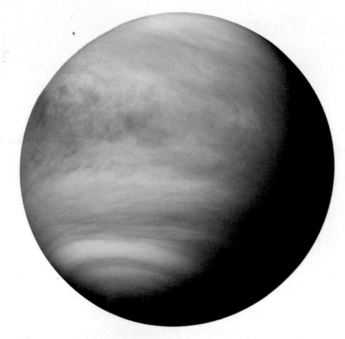

Figure 9 *This image of Venus was taken by* Mariner 10 *on February 5, 1974. The uppermost layer of clouds contains sulfuric acid.*

Venus Statistics	
Distance from sun	6.0 light-minutes
Period of rotation	243 days (R)
Period of revolution	224 days, 17 hours
Diameter	12,104 km
Density	5.24 g/cm³
Surface temperature	464°C
Surface gravity	91% of Earth's

R = retrograde rotation

Venus—Earth's Twin?

Take a look at **Figure 9.** In many ways, Venus is more like Earth than any other planet. Venus is only slightly smaller, less massive, and less dense than Earth is. But in other ways, Venus is very different from Earth. Unlike on Earth, on Venus the sun rises in the west and sets in the east. This is because Venus rotates in the opposite direction that Earth rotates. Earth is said to have **prograde rotation,** because when viewed from above its North Pole, Earth appears to spin in a *counterclockwise* direction. If a planet spins in a *clockwise* direction, it is said to have **retrograde rotation.**

The Atmosphere of Venus

Of all the terrestrial planets, Venus has the densest atmosphere. Venus's atmosphere has 90 times the pressure of Earth's atmosphere! The air on Venus is mostly carbon dioxide, but it is also made of some of the most destructive acids known. The carbon dioxide traps thermal energy from sunlight in a process called the *greenhouse effect.* This is why the surface temperature is so high. At 464°C, Venus has the hottest surface of any planet in the solar system.

Mapping Venus's Surface

Between 1990 and 1992, the *Magellan* spacecraft mapped the surface of Venus by using radar waves. The radar waves traveled through the clouds and bounced off of the planet's surface. The radar image in **Figure 10** shows that, like Earth, Venus has an active surface.

Figure 10 *This false-color image of a volcano on the surface of Venus was made with radar data gathered by the* Magellan *spacecraft. Bright areas are massive lava flows.*

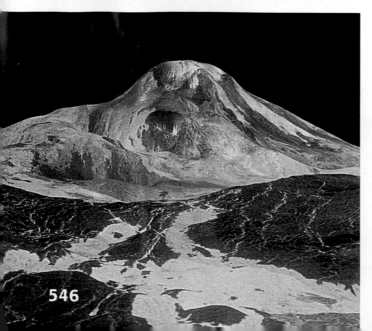

Earth—An Oasis in Space

As viewed from space, Earth is like a sparkling blue oasis in a black sea of stars. Constantly changing weather patterns create the swirls of clouds that blanket the blue and brown sphere we call home. Take a look at **Figure 11.** Why did Earth have such good fortune, while its two nearest neighbors, Venus and Mars, are unsuitable for life as we know it?

Water on Earth

Luckily for us, Earth formed at just the right distance from the sun. Our planet is warm enough to keep most of its water from freezing, as happens on Mars. But Earth is also cool enough to keep its water from boiling away, as happens on Venus. Liquid water is a vital part of the chemical processes that living things depend on for survival.

The Earth from Space

Take a look at **Figure 12.** You might think that the only goal of space exploration is to make discoveries beyond Earth. But NASA (National Aeronautics and Space Administration) has a program to study Earth using satellites—just as we study other planets. This program is called the Earth Science Enterprise. Its goal is to study the Earth as a global system that is made of smaller systems. These smaller systems include the atmosphere, the oceans, and the biosphere. The program will also help us understand the effects that humans have in changing the global environment. By studying Earth from space, we hope to understand how different parts of the global system interact.

Figure 11 *Earth is the only planet we know of that supports life.*

Figure 12 *This image of Earth was taken on December 7, 1972, by the crew of the* Apollo 17 *spacecraft while on their way to the moon.*

Earth Statistics	
Distance from sun	8.3 light-minutes
Period of rotation	23 hours, 56 minutes
Period of revolution	365 days, 6 hours
Diameter	12,756 km
Density	5.52 g/cm^3
Surface temperature	−13°C to 37°C
Surface gravity	100% of Earth's

Mars Statistics

Mars Statistics	
Distance from sun	12.7 light-minutes
Period of rotation	24 hours, 37 minutes
Period of revolution	1 year, 322 days
Diameter	6,794 km
Density	3.93 g/cm³
Surface temperature	−123°C to 37°C
Surface gravity	38% of Earth's

Mars—The Red Planet

Mars, shown in **Figure 13,** is perhaps the most studied planet in the solar system besides Earth. Much of our knowledge of Mars has come from data gathered by spacecraft. *Viking 1* and *Viking 2* landed on Mars in 1976, and *Mars Pathfinder* landed on Mars in 1997.

Figure 13 *This Viking orbiter image shows the eastern hemisphere of Mars. The large, circular feature in the center is the impact crater Schiaparelli, with a diameter of 450 km.*

The Atmosphere of Mars

Because of its thinner atmosphere and greater distance from the sun, Mars is a cold planet. Midsummer temperatures recorded by the *Mars Pathfinder* lander ranged from −13°C to −77°C. Martian air is so thin that on the planet's surface, the air pressure is about the same as it is 30 km above Earth's surface. This distance is about three times higher than most planes fly! The air pressure is so low that any liquid water would quickly boil away. The only water you'll find on Mars is in the form of ice.

Figure 14 *This Viking orbiter image shows a system of Martian valleys formed by running water.*

Water on Mars

We know that liquid water cannot exist on Mars's surface today. But there is strong evidence that it did exist there in the past. **Figure 14** shows an area on Mars with features that look like dry riverbeds on Earth. This means that in the past, Mars might have been a warmer place with a thicker atmosphere. Where is the water now?

The Martian landscape as seen from the *Mars Pathfinder* lander

Mars has two polar icecaps made of both frozen water and frozen carbon dioxide. But the polar icecaps do not have enough water to create a thick atmosphere or rivers. Looking closely at the walls of some Martian craters, scientists have found that the debris around the craters looks as if it were made by the flow of mud rather than dry soil. Where does this suggest some of the "lost" Martian water went? Many scientists think it is frozen beneath the Martian soil.

Martian Volcanoes

Unlike Earth, where volcanoes exist in many places, Mars has only two large volcanic systems. The largest, the Tharsis region, stretches 8,000 km across the planet. The largest mountain in the solar system, Olympus Mons, is an extinct shield volcano similar to Mauna Kea, on the island of Hawaii. Mars is not only smaller and cooler than Earth, but it also has a slightly different chemical makeup. This may have kept the Martian crust from moving around as Earth's crust has done. As a result, the volcanoes kept building up in the same spots. Images and data sent back by probes like the *Sojourner* rover, shown in **Figure 15,** are helping to explain Mars's mysterious past.

Physics
CONNECTION

At sea level on Earth's surface, water boils at 100°C. But if you try to boil water on top of a high mountain, you will find that the boiling point is lower than 100°C. This is because the air pressure is less at a higher altitude. The air pressure on the surface of Mars is so low that liquid water can't exist at all!

Figure 15 *The* Sojourner *rover, part of the Mars Pathfinder mission, is shown here creeping up to a rock named Yogi to measure its composition. The dark panel on top of the rover collected the solar energy used to power the rover's motor.*

MID-SECTION REVIEW

❶ Identify three characteristics that the inner planets have in common. ⭐TEKS

❷ Identify three differences and three similarities between Venus and Earth. ⭐TEKS

❸ **Analyzing Relationships** Mercury is closest to the sun, yet Venus has a higher surface temperature. Explain why.

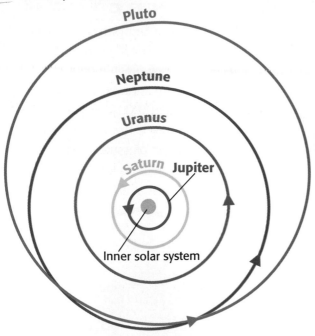

Pluto

Neptune

Uranus

Saturn   Jupiter

Inner solar system

The Outer Planets

The outer planets are different from the inner planets in composition and size. Except for Pluto, all of the outer planets are gas giants. **Gas giants** are very large planets that don't have any known solid surfaces. Their atmospheres blend smoothly into the denser layers of their interiors. **Figure 16** shows the outer solar system.

Jupiter—A Giant Among Giants

Like the sun, Jupiter is made mostly of hydrogen and helium. Clouds of water, methane, and ammonia make up the outer part of Jupiter's atmosphere. The beautiful colors in **Figure 17** are probably due to small amounts of organic materials.

At a depth of 10,000 km, the pressure is high enough to change hydrogen gas into a liquid. Deeper still, the pressure changes the liquid hydrogen into a metallic liquid state. Unlike most planets, Jupiter radiates much more energy into space than it receives from the sun. This is because thermal energy is always moving from Jupiter's interior to the outer layers, where it is radiated into space.

NASA Missions to Jupiter

NASA has sent five missions to Jupiter. These include two Pioneer missions, two Voyager missions, and the recent Galileo mission. The *Voyager 1* and *Voyager 2* spacecraft sent back images that showed a thin, faint ring around Jupiter. The Voyager missions also gave us the first detailed images of Jupiter's moons. The *Galileo* spacecraft reached Jupiter in 1995 and sent a probe into Jupiter's atmosphere. The probe sent back data on Jupiter's composition, temperature, and pressure.

Figure 17 *This* Voyager 2 *image of Jupiter was taken at a distance of 28.4 million kilometers. Io, one of Jupiter's largest moons, can also be seen in this image.*

Jupiter Statistics	
Distance from sun	43.3 light-minutes
Period of rotation	9 hours, 50 minutes
Period of revolution	11 years, 313 days
Diameter	142,984 km
Density	1.32 g/cm^3
Temperature	−153°C
Gravity	236% of Earth's

Saturn Statistics	
Distance from sun	1.3 light-hours
Period of rotation	10 hours, 30 minutes
Period of revolution	29 years, 155 days
Diameter	120,536 km
Density	0.69 g/cm³
Temperature	−185°C
Gravity	92% of Earth's

Saturn—Still Forming

Saturn, shown in **Figure 18,** is the second largest planet in the solar system. It has roughly 764 times the volume of Earth and is 95 times more massive. Saturn is made mostly of hydrogen and helium. Its upper atmosphere is also made of methane, ammonia, and ethane. Saturn's interior is probably much like Jupiter's. Also like Jupiter, Saturn gives off much more energy than it receives from the sun. Scientists think that Saturn's extra energy comes from helium falling out of the atmosphere and sinking to the core. In other words, Saturn is still forming!

Figure 18 *This* Voyager 2 *image of Saturn was taken from 21 million kilometers away. The dot you see below the rings is the shadow of Tethys, one of Saturn's moons.*

The Rings of Saturn

While all of the gas giants have rings, Saturn's are the largest. Saturn's rings have a total diameter of 272,000 km, which is as wide as 21 Earths placed side by side. Yet Saturn's rings are only a few hundred meters thick. The rings are made of icy particles. These particles range in size from a few centimeters to several meters across. **Figure 19** shows a close-up view of Saturn's rings.

Figure 19 *The false colors in this* Voyager 2 *image of Saturn's rings show differences in their chemical composition.*

NASA Goes to Saturn

Launched in 1997, the *Cassini* spacecraft will study Saturn's rings, its moons, and its atmosphere. Starting in 2004, *Cassini* will return more than 300,000 color images.

Figure 20 *This image of Uranus was taken by* Voyager 2 *at a distance of 9.1 million kilometers.*

Uranus Statistics	
Distance from sun	2.7 light-hours
Period of rotation	17 hours, 14 minutes (R)
Period of revolution	83 years, 274 days
Diameter	51,118 km
Density	1.32 g/cm^3
Temperature	−214°C
Gravity	89% of Earth's

R = retrograde rotation

Uranus—A Small Giant

Uranus (YOOR uh nuhs), shown in **Figure 20,** was discovered by the English amateur astronomer William Herschel in 1781. Through a telescope, Uranus looks like a featureless blue-green disk. The atmosphere is mostly hydrogen and methane. These gases absorb the red part of sunlight very strongly, giving Uranus its blue-green color. Uranus and Neptune have much less mass than Jupiter, but their densities are almost the same. This means their compositions are different from Jupiter's. They may have lower percentages of light elements and greater percentages of water.

A Tilted Planet

Unlike most other planets, Uranus is tipped over on its side. This means its *axis of rotation* lies almost in the *plane of its orbit*, as shown in **Figure 21.** For part of a Uranian year, one pole points toward the sun, while the other pole is in darkness. At the other end of Uranus's orbit, the poles are switched. Some scientists think that early in its history, a massive object hit Uranus, tipping it over.

Figure 21 *Uranus's axis of rotation is tilted, so it is nearly parallel to the plane of Uranus's orbit. The axes of most other planets are closer to being perpendicular to the plane of their orbits.*

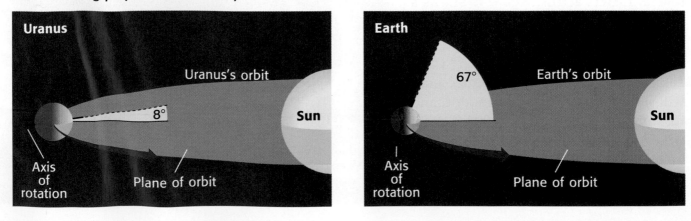

Through Galileo's Eyes ⭐TEKS

In 1610 CE, Galileo became the first person to observe the four largest moons revolving around Jupiter. He used what was a new piece of technology in his day—the telescope. You can relive Galileo's experience by visiting an observatory near you or by attending a star party. Star parties are gatherings in which amateur astronomers share views of the night sky through different telescopes. Look at Jupiter through a telescope, and try to see some of Jupiter's moons. In your ScienceLog, connect what you have learned about Jupiter with the contributions of Galileo.

TRY at HOME

Neptune—The Blue World

Irregularities in the orbit of Uranus suggested to early astronomers that there must be another planet beyond it. They thought that the gravity of this new planet pulled Uranus off its predicted path. By using the predictions of the new planet's orbit, astronomers discovered the planet Neptune in 1846. Neptune is shown in **Figure 22.**

The Atmosphere of Neptune

The *Voyager 2* spacecraft sent back images that gave us much new information about Neptune's atmosphere. Although the composition of Neptune's atmosphere is similar to that of Uranus, it has belts of clouds that are much more visible. At the time of *Voyager 2*'s visit, Neptune had a Great Dark Spot, similar to the Great Red Spot on Jupiter. And like the interiors of Jupiter and Saturn, Neptune's interior releases thermal energy to its outer layers. This helps the warm gases rise and the cool gases sink, setting up the wind patterns in the atmosphere that create the belts of clouds. *Voyager 2* images also revealed that Neptune has a set of very narrow rings.

Figure 22 *This* Voyager 2 *image of Neptune, taken at a distance of more than 7 million kilometers, shows the Great Dark Spot as well as some bright cloud bands.*

Neptune Statistics	
Distance from sun	4.2 light-hours
Period of rotation	16 hours, 7 minutes
Period of revolution	163 years, 263 days
Diameter	49,528 km
Density	1.64 g/cm^3
Temperature	−225°C
Gravity	112% of Earth's

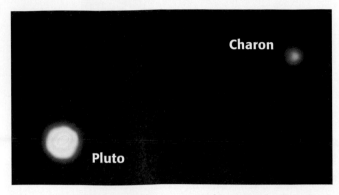

Pluto Statistics	
Distance from sun	5.5 light-hours
Period of rotation	6 days, 10 hours (R)
Period of revolution	248 years
Diameter	2,390 km
Density	2.05 g/cm³
Surface temperature	−236°C
Surface gravity	7% of Earth's

R = retrograde rotation

Figure 23 *This* Hubble Space Telescope *image is one of the clearest ever taken of Pluto and its moon, Charon.*

Figure 24 *An artist's view of the sun and Charon from Pluto shows just how little light and thermal energy Pluto receives from the sun.*

Pluto—A Double Planet?

Pluto is the farthest planet from the sun. It is also the smallest planet. It is less than half the size of Mercury. Another reason Pluto is unusual is that its moon, Charon (KER uhn), is more than half its size! In fact, Charon is the largest satellite relative to its planet in the solar system. **Figure 23** shows Pluto and Charon together.

From Earth, it is hard to separate the images of Pluto and Charon because they are so far away. **Figure 24** shows just how far away from the sun Pluto and Charon really are. From Pluto's surface the sun looks like a very distant, bright star.

From calculations of Pluto's density, we know that it must be made of rock and ice. A very thin atmosphere of methane has been detected. While Pluto is covered by frozen nitrogen, Charon is covered by frozen water. Pluto is the only planet that has not been visited by a NASA mission, but NASA is planning to visit this world and its moon in 2010.

SECTION REVIEW

1. How are the gas giants different from the terrestrial planets? ⓍTEKS

2. Explain what is so unusual about Uranus's axis of rotation. ⓍTEKS

3. What conclusion can you draw about a planet's properties just by knowing how far it is from the sun? ⓍTEKS

4. **Applying Concepts** Why is the word *surface* not used in the statistics for the gas giants? ⓍTEKS

Terms to Learn

satellite   meteoroid
comet   meteorite
asteroid   meteor
asteroid belt

What You'll Do

- Explain why the moon preserves a better record of cosmic impacts than the Earth does.
- Explain why comets, asteroids, and meteoroids are important to the study of the formation of the solar system.
- Compare the different types of asteroids with the different types of meteoroids. ★TEKS

Moons and Other Bodies

If you could, which moon would you want to visit? With volcanoes, craters, and possible underground oceans, the moons in our solar system would be interesting places to visit.

Studying moons, comets, asteroids, and meteoroids will help you learn about the history of our solar system. Unlike most of the planets, many of these smaller objects have changed very little since they first formed.

Moons

Satellites are natural or artificial bodies that revolve around more massive bodies such as planets. Except for Mercury and Venus, all of the planets have natural satellites called *moons*.

Luna: The Moon of Earth

We have learned a lot from studying Earth's moon—also called *Luna*. The lunar rocks brought back during the Apollo missions were found to be about 4.6 billion years old. Because these rocks have hardly changed since they formed, we know the solar system itself is about 4.6 billion years old.

As you can see in **Figure 25,** the moon's history is written on its face! The surfaces of bodies that have no atmospheres preserve a record of almost all of the impacts they have ever had. Because we now know the age of the moon, we can count the number of impact craters to find the rate of cratering since the birth of our solar system. By knowing the rate of cratering, scientists are able to use the number of craters on any body to estimate how old its surface is. That way they don't need to bring back rock samples!

Figure 25 *This image of the moon was taken by the* Galileo *spacecraft while on its way to Jupiter. The large, dark areas are lava plains called* maria.

Moon Statistics	
Period of rotation	27 days, 8 hours
Period of revolution	27 days, 8 hours
Diameter	3,476 km
Density	3.34 g/cm^3
Surface temperature	−170°C to 134°C
Surface gravity	17% of Earth's

Figure 26 *Above is Mars's largest moon, Phobos, which is 28 km long.*

The Moons of Mars

Mars's two moons, Phobos and Deimos, are both small, oddly shaped satellites. Both moons are very dark. Their surface materials are much like those of some asteroids—large, rocky bodies in space. Scientists think that these two moons are asteroids caught by Mars's gravity. Phobos is shown in **Figure 26.**

The Moons of Jupiter

Jupiter has dozens of moons, many of which have only recently been discovered. The four largest—Ganymede, Callisto, Io, and Europa—were discovered in 1610 by Galileo. They are known as the *Galilean satellites*. The largest moon, Ganymede, is even larger than the planet Mercury! Most of the smaller moons are probably captured asteroids.

Moving outward from Jupiter, the first Galilean satellite is Io, a truly bizarre world. Io is caught in a gravitational tug-of-war between Jupiter and Io's nearest neighbor, the moon Europa. This constant tugging stretches Io a little, causing it to heat up. Because of this, Io is the most volcanically active body in the solar system!

Recent pictures of Europa support the idea that liquid water may lie beneath the moon's icy surface. This idea has many scientists wondering if life could exist in underwater oceans on Europa. Both Io and Europa are shown in **Figure 27.**

Figure 27 *At left is a* Galileo *image of Jupiter's closest moon, Io. At right is a* Galileo *image of Jupiter's fourth-largest moon, Europa.*

The Moons of Saturn

Like Jupiter, Saturn has dozens of moons. Most of these moons are small bodies made mostly of frozen water with some rock. The largest moon, Titan, was discovered in 1655 by Christiaan Huygens. In 1980, the *Voyager 1* spacecraft flew past Titan and discovered a hazy orange atmosphere, as shown in **Figure 28.** Earth's early atmosphere may have been much like Titan's is now. But because Titan is so much farther from the sun, its surface is too cold to support life as we know it. In 1997, NASA launched the *Cassini* spacecraft to study Saturn and its moons, including Titan. By studying Titan, scientists hope to learn more about how life began on Earth.

Figure 28 *Titan is one of only two moons that have a thick atmosphere. Titan's hazy, orange atmosphere is made of nitrogen plus several other gases, including methane.*

Self-Check

What is one major difference between Titan and the early Earth that indicates there probably isn't life on Titan? *(See page 640 to check your answer.)* ⭐TEKS

The Moons of Uranus

Uranus has at least 21 moons, three of which were discovered by ground-based telescopes during the summer of 1999. Like the moons of Saturn, Uranus's largest moons are made of ice and rock and are heavily cratered. The small moon Miranda, shown in **Figure 29,** has some of the strangest features in the solar system. Miranda's surface has smooth, cratered plains as well as areas with grooves and cliffs up to 20 km high. Scientists think that Miranda may have been hit and broken apart in the past. Gravity pulled the pieces together again, leaving a patchwork surface.

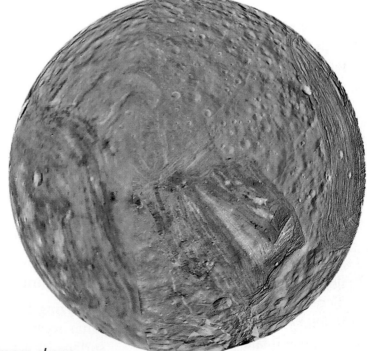

Figure 29 *This* Voyager 2 *image shows Miranda, Uranus's strangest moon. Its patchwork terrain shows that it has had a violent history.*

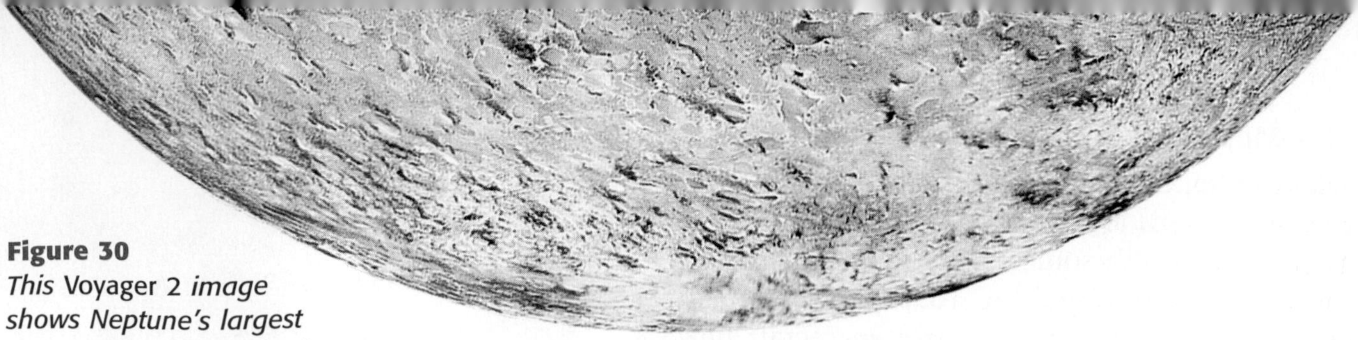

Figure 30
This Voyager 2 *image shows Neptune's largest moon, Triton. The polar icecap now facing the sun may have a slowly evaporating layer of nitrogen ice, adding to Triton's thin atmosphere.*

The Moons of Neptune

Neptune has at least eight moons, only one of which is large. This moon, Triton, shown in **Figure 30,** revolves around the planet in a *retrograde*, or "backward," orbit. This may mean that Triton was caught by Neptune's gravity. Triton has a very thin atmosphere made mostly of nitrogen. The surface of Triton is mostly frozen nitrogen and methane. *Voyager 2* images showed that it is geologically active. "Ice volcanoes," or geysers, were seen erupting nitrogen gas high into the atmosphere. The other seven moons of Neptune are small, rocky worlds much like the smaller moons of Saturn and Jupiter.

The Moon of Pluto

Pluto's only moon, Charon, was discovered in 1978. Charon's period of revolution is the same as Pluto's period of rotation— about 6.4 days. This means that one side of Pluto always faces Charon. In other words, if you stood on the surface of Pluto, Charon would always occupy the same place in the sky. Imagine Earth's moon staying in the same place every night! Charon's orbit around Pluto is tilted compared with Pluto's orbit around the sun. As a result, Pluto, as seen from Earth, is sometimes eclipsed by Charon. Astronomers first observed a series of these eclipses in 1985. But don't hold your breath; these eclipses will not happen again until more than 100 years from now.

Modeling Motion

1. Find **two spherical objects,** one of them smaller than the other. The larger one represents Pluto, and the other represents Charon.

2. Place a **piece of tape** on each sphere to mark a location on the surface.

3. Place the spheres on a **flat surface** so that the two pieces of tape are facing each other.

4. With one hand, slowly spin Pluto to simulate its rotation.

5. With the other hand, slide Charon around Pluto in a circle, simulating its revolution. Make sure that the two pieces of tape are always facing each other.

6. Is Charon rotating at the same time it is revolving around Pluto? Explain.

⊛TEKS   *TRY at HOME*

MID-SECTION REVIEW

1. Why does the moon have more impact craters than Earth? ⊛TEKS

2. Identify two properties of Neptune's moon Triton that make it unusual. ⊛TEKS

3. **Analyzing Methods** How does knowing the age of a lunar rock help astronomers estimate the age of the surface of a planet like Mercury?

Other Small Bodies

Some other small bodies include comets, asteroids, and meteoroids. These bodies can be some of the most spectacular objects in our solar system. Scientists are eager to study these objects not only for their beauty but also for what they can tell us about the composition of the early solar system.

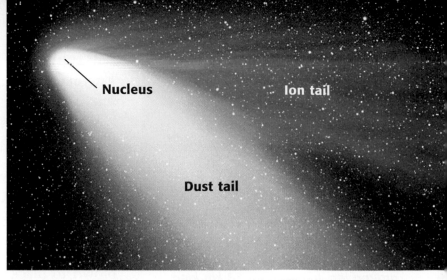

Comets

A **comet** is a small body of ice, rock, and cosmic dust loosely packed together. Because of their composition, comets are called "dirty snowballs" by some scientists. Comets formed in the cold, outer solar system. Nothing much has happened to them since the birth of our solar system, some 4.6 billion years ago. Comets are probably left over from the time when planets formed. As a result, each comet is a sample of the early solar system. Scientists want to learn more about comets in order to piece together the history of our solar system.

When a comet passes close enough to the sun, solar radiation heats the ice so that the comet gives off gas and dust in the form of a long tail, as shown in **Figure 31.** Sometimes a comet has two tails—an *ion tail* and a *dust tail*. The ion tail is made of electrically charged particles called *ions*. The solid center of a comet is called its *nucleus*. Comet nuclei can range in size from less than half a kilometer to more than 100 km in diameter.

Figure 31 *This image shows the physical features of a comet when it is close to the sun. The nucleus of a comet is hidden by brightly lit gases and dust.*

Comet Orbits

All orbits are *ellipses*—they have a circular shape. Though the orbits of most planets are close to perfect circles, comet orbits are very elongated.

Notice in **Figure 32** that a comet's ion tail always points away from the sun. This is because the ion tail is blown away from the sun by the *solar wind*, which is also made of ions. The dust tail tends to follow the comet's orbit around the sun. Dust tails do not always point away from the sun. When a comet is close to the sun, its dust tail can stretch millions of kilometers through space!

Figure 32 *Comets have very elongated orbits. When a comet gets close to the sun, the comet can develop one or two tails.*

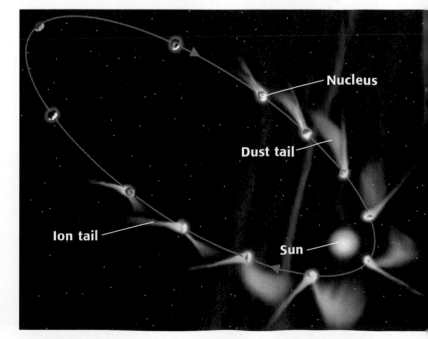

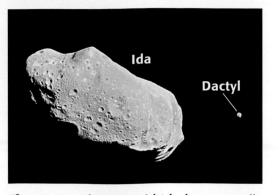

Figure 33 *The asteroid Ida has a small companion called Dactyl, which is in orbit around Ida. Ida is about 58 km long.*

Asteroids

Asteroids are small, rocky bodies that revolve around the sun. They range in size from a few meters to more than 900 km in diameter. As shown in **Figure 33,** asteroids can have odd shapes. Some of the larger ones, however, are spherical. Most asteroids revolve around the sun in a wide region between the orbits of Mars and Jupiter, called the **asteroid belt.**

Asteroids have different compositions, depending on which part of the asteroid belt they are in. In the outer region of the asteroid belt, asteroids have dark reddish brown to black surfaces. These asteroids may be rich in organic material. A little closer to the sun, asteroids have dark gray surfaces. These asteroids may be rich in iron. The inner part of the asteroid belt has light gray asteroids. These asteroids probably have either a stony or metallic composition. Like comets, asteroids are probably material left over after our solar system formed. Scientists are interested in studying these objects because they may tell us what the early solar system was like. **Figure 34** shows what some asteroids may look like.

Figure 34 The Asteroid Belt

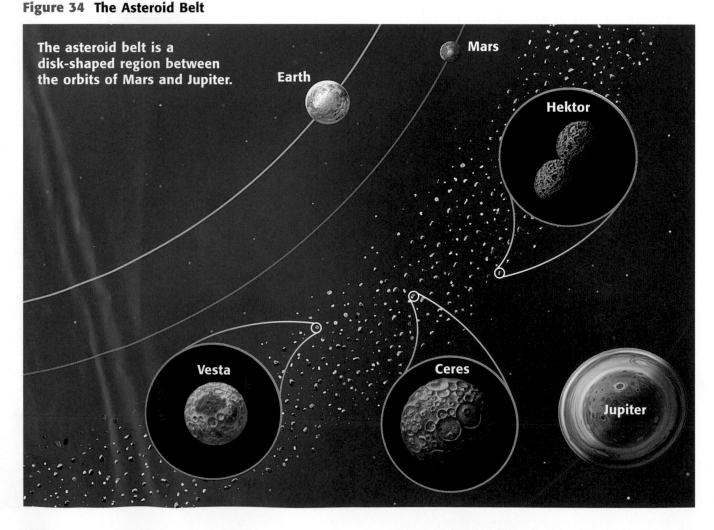

The asteroid belt is a disk-shaped region between the orbits of Mars and Jupiter.

Meteoroids

Meteoroids are small, rocky bodies that revolve around the sun. Meteoroids are like asteroids, but they are much smaller. In fact, most meteoroids are probably pieces of asteroids. When a meteoroid hits the ground, it is called a **meteorite.** As a meteoroid falls into Earth's atmosphere, it moves so fast that its surface melts. As it burns up, the meteoroid gives off a huge amount of light and thermal energy. From the ground, we see a shooting star, or meteor. **Meteors** are the bright streaks of light caused when a meteoroid or comet dust burns up in the atmosphere. *Meteor showers* happen at certain times of the year when Earth passes through the dusty debris that comets leave behind.

Like their cousins the asteroids, meteorites have different compositions. The three major types of meteorites—stony, metallic, and stony-iron—are shown in **Figure 35.** Many of the stony meteorites probably come from dark, carbon-rich asteroids. Stony meteorites may contain organic materials and water. Scientists use meteorites to study the early solar system. Like comets and asteroids, meteoroids are some of the building blocks of planets.

Figure 35   Three Major Types of Meteorites

Stony meteorite
rocky material

Metallic meteorite
iron and nickel

Stony-iron meteorite
rocky material, iron, and nickel

SECTION REVIEW

❶ Why is the study of comets, asteroids, and meteoroids important in understanding the formation of our solar system?

❷ Why do a comet's two tails often point in different directions? ⭐TEKS

❸ Identify and describe how the solar system is a combination of two or more other systems. ⭐TEKS

❹ **Identifying Relationships** There are three kinds of meteorites. Do you think that asteroids might also be divided into three different types? Explain. ⭐TEKS

Design Your Own Lab

Create a Calendar ⭐TEKS

Imagine that you live in the first colony on Mars. You have been trying to follow the Earth calendar, but it just isn't working anymore. Mars takes almost 2 Earth years to revolve around the sun—almost 687 Earth days! That means that there are only two Martian seasons for every Earth calendar year. One year, you get winter and spring, but the next year, you get only summer and fall. And Martian days are longer than Earth days. Mars takes 24.6 Earth hours to rotate on its axis. Even though they are similar, Earth days and Martian days just don't match.

MATERIALS

- calculator (optional)
- poster board
- metric ruler
- colored pencils
- marker

Ask a Question

1 How can I create a calendar based on the Martian cycles of rotation and revolution that includes months, weeks, and days?

Form a Hypothesis

2 In your ScienceLog, formulate a testable hypothesis that answers the question above.

Test the Hypothesis

3 Use a calculator and the following formulas to determine the number of Martian days there are in a Martian year:

$$\frac{687 \text{ Earth days}}{1 \text{ Martian year}} \times \frac{24 \text{ Earth hours}}{1 \text{ Earth day}} = \frac{\text{Earth hours}}{\text{per Martian year}}$$

$$\frac{\text{Earth hours}}{\text{Martian year}} \times \frac{1 \text{ Martian day}}{24.6 \text{ Earth hours}} = \frac{\text{Martian days}}{\text{per Martian year}}$$

4 Decide how to divide your calendar into a system of Martian months, weeks, and days. Will you have a leap day, a leap week, a leap month, or a leap year? How often will it happen?

5 Choose names for the months and days of your calendar. In your ScienceLog, explain why you chose each name. If you have time, explain how you would number the Martian years. For instance, would the first year correspond to a certain Earth year?

6 Follow your design to create your own calendar for Mars. Construct your calendar by using a computer to help organize your data. Draw the calendar on your piece of poster board. Make sure it is brightly colored and easy to follow.

7 Present your calendar to the class. Explain how you chose your months, weeks, and days.

Analyze the Results

8 What advantages does your calendar design have? Are there any disadvantages to your design?

9 Which student or group created the most original calendar? Which design was the most useful? Explain your answer.

10 What might you do to improve your calendar?

Draw Conclusions

11 Take a class vote to decide which design should be chosen as the new calendar for Mars. Why was this calendar chosen? How did it differ from other designs?

12 Why is it useful to have a calendar that matches the cycles of the planet on which you live?

Highlights

Section 1

Vocabulary

astronomical unit *(p. 539)*
rotation *(p. 540)*
revolution *(p. 540)*
nuclear fusion *(p. 543)*
sunspot *(p. 544)*
solar flare *(p. 544)*

Section Notes

- Our solar system is made of the sun, planets, and many smaller objects, which can be grouped into smaller systems. ⭐TEKS

- Distances within the solar system can be expressed in astronomical units (AU) or in light-minutes.

- Rotation is the spin of an object in space, while revolution is the motion of one object around another.

- The sun is a gaseous sphere made primarily of hydrogen and helium. ⭐TEKS

- The sun produces energy in its core by a process called nuclear fusion.

- Magnetic changes within the sun cause sunspots and solar flares, which can affect radio communications and cause auroras.

Section 2

Vocabulary

terrestrial planet *(p. 545)*
prograde rotation *(p. 546)*
retrograde rotation *(p. 546)*
gas giant *(p. 550)*

Section Notes

- The inner solar system is made of the terrestrial planets, which are small and rocky. ⭐TEKS

- The outer solar system is made of Pluto and the gas giants, which are large, gaseous planets. ⭐TEKS

- By learning about the properties of the planets, we gain a better understanding of global processes on Earth.

LabBook ⭐TEKS

Why Do They Wander? *(p. 636)*

Section 3

Vocabulary

satellite *(p. 555)*
comet *(p. 559)*
asteroid *(p. 560)*
asteroid belt *(p. 560)*
meteoroid *(p. 561)*
meteorite *(p. 561)*
meteor *(p. 561)*

Section Notes

- Satellites are bodies that revolve around more massive bodies. Moons are natural satellites.

- Planets and moons that do not have thick atmospheres preserve a better record of cosmic impacts.

- Comets are small bodies of frozen water and cosmic dust left over from the formation of the solar system. ⭐TEKS

- When a comet is heated by the sun, the ices convert to gases that leave the nucleus and form an ion tail. Dust also comes off of a comet to form a second kind of tail called a dust tail. ⭐TEKS

- All orbits are ellipses—they have a circular shape.

- Asteroids are small, rocky bodies that orbit the sun. Most are between the orbits of Mars and Jupiter. ⭐TEKS

- Meteoroids are small, rocky bodies that probably come from asteroids. ⭐TEKS

Review

USING VOCABULARY

For each pair of terms, explain how the meanings of the terms differ.

1. terrestrial planet/gas giant ⭐TEKS

2. asteroid/comet ⭐TEKS

3. meteor/meteorite ⭐TEKS

4. satellite/moon

5. sunspot/solar flare ⭐TEKS

Complete the following sentences by choosing the correct term from each pair of terms.

6. The average distance between the sun and Earth is 1 __?__. (*light-minute* or *AU*)

7. A small rock in space is called a __?__. (*meteorite* or *meteoroid*)

8. The time it takes for Earth to __?__ around the sun is 1 year. (*rotate* or *revolve*)

9. Most lunar craters are the result of __?__. (*volcanoes* or *impacts*) ⭐TEKS

UNDERSTANDING CONCEPTS

Multiple Choice

10. Which process releases the most energy?
    a. nuclear fusion
    b. burning
    c. shrinking due to gravity
    d. rotation

11. Of the following, which is the largest body? ⭐TEKS
    a. the moon   c. Mercury
    b. Pluto   d. Ganymede

12. Which planets have retrograde rotation? ⭐TEKS
    a. the terrestrial planets
    b. the gas giants
    c. Mercury, Venus, and Uranus
    d. Venus, Uranus, and Pluto

13. Which of these planets does NOT have any moons? ⭐TEKS
    a. Mercury   c. Uranus
    b. Mars   d. none of the above

14. The sun's energy is produced in its ⭐TEKS
    a. corona.
    b. convective zone.
    c. core.
    d. radiative zone.

15. Liquid water cannot exist on the surface of Mars because
    a. the temperature is too high.
    b. liquid water once existed there.
    c. the gravity of Mars is too weak.
    d. the atmospheric pressure is too low.

16. Which of the following planets is NOT a terrestrial planet? ⭐TEKS
    a. Mercury   c. Earth
    b. Mars   d. Pluto

17. A comet's ion tail is made of ⭐TEKS
    a. dust.
    b. electrically charged particles of gas.
    c. light rays.
    d. comet nuclei.

18. How did our understanding of the sun's energy change over time? ⭐TEKS

19. Identify characteristics of meteorites, comets, asteroids, and moons. ⭐TEKS

CONCEPT MAPPING

20. Use the following terms to create a concept map: *comets, terrestrial planets, gas giants, moons, the sun, asteroids, solar system,* and *meteoroids.*

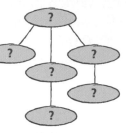

CRITICAL THINKING AND PROBLEM SOLVING

Write one or two sentences to answer the following questions:

21. Even though we haven't yet retrieved any rock samples from Mercury's surface for radiometric dating, we know that the surface of Mercury is much older than that of Earth. How do we know this?

22. Where in the solar system might we search for life? Explain. ⭐TEKS

23. Is the far side of Pluto's moon, Charon, always dark? Explain your answer. ⭐TEKS

24. If we could somehow bring Europa as close to the sun as Earth is, 1 AU, what do you think would happen?

MATH IN SCIENCE

25. Suppose you have an object that weighs 200 N (45 lb) on Earth. How much would that same object weigh on each of the other terrestrial planets?

INTERPRETING GRAPHICS

The graph below shows density versus mass for Earth, Uranus, and Neptune. Mass is given in Earth masses—the mass of Earth equals one. The relative volumes for the planets are shown by the size of each circle.

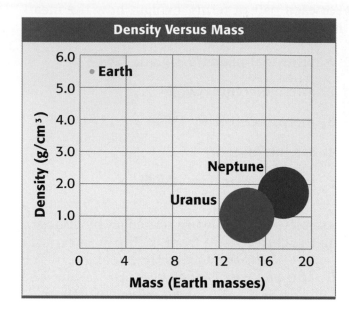

Density Versus Mass

26. Which planet is denser, Uranus or Neptune? How can you tell? ⭐TEKS

27. What is Earth's density? ⭐TEKS

28. You can see that although Earth has the smallest mass, it has the highest density. How can Earth be the densest of the three when Uranus and Neptune have so much more mass? ⭐TEKS

Reading Check-up

⭐TEKS

Take a minute to review your answers to the Pre-Reading Questions found at the bottom of page 536. Have your answers changed? If necessary, revise your answers based on what you have learned since you began this chapter.

Chapter 20

1 The visible surface of the sun is the
A chromosphere.
B corona.
C radiative zone.
D photosphere.

2 The difference between moons and planets is that
F moons do not revolve around the sun.
G moons are generally less massive and revolve around planets.
H moons have no atmospheres.
J moons do not rotate.

3 Which planet has the most mass?
A Earth
B Mars
C Venus
D Mercury

4 Comets and asteroids are different because
F only asteroids impact the Earth.
G only asteroids revolve around the sun.
H comets are made of only ice.
J comets are made mostly of ice.

5 The main difference between asteroids and meteoroids is
A size.
B composition.
C shape.
D speed.

6 According to the information below, which planet has the oldest surface?
F Planet A
G Planet B
H Planet C
J Planet D

Planet A
115 craters/km^2

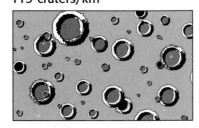

Planet B
75 craters/km^2

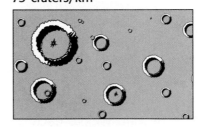

Planet C
121 craters/km^2

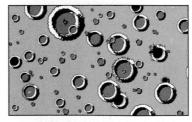

Planet D
97 craters/km^2

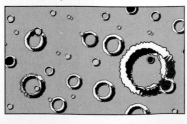

Chapter 20

Math

1 Venus's surface gravity is 91% of Earth's. If an object weighs 12 newtons on Earth, how much would it weigh on Venus?

A 53 N

B 11 N

C 13 N

D 8 N

2 Suppose you discovered a new planet that has a period of rotation 12 Earth hours long and a period of revolution 240 Earth days long. How many days are in a year on this new planet?

F 480

G 240

H 365

J 720

3 Earth has an overall density of 5.52 g/cm^3, while Saturn has a density of 0.69 g/cm^3. How many times denser is Earth?

A 9

B 11

C 12

D 8

Reading

Read the passage. Then read each question that follows the passage. Decide which is the best answer to each question.

Imagine that it is 200 BCE and you are an apprentice to a Greek astronomer. After years of observing the sky, he knows all of the constellations as well as you know the back of your hand. He shows you how the stars all move together—the whole sky spins slowly as the night goes on.

He also shows you that among the thousands of stars in the sky, some of the brighter ones slowly change their position relative to the other stars. He names these stars *planetai*, the Greek word for "wanderers." Building on the observations of the ancient Greeks, we now know that the *planetai* are actually planets, not wandering stars.

1 Which of the following did the ancient Greeks know to be true?

A All planets have at least one moon.

B The planets revolve around the sun.

C The planets are very small compared to the stars.

D The planets appear to move relative to the stars.

2 What can you infer about the ancient Greek astronomers?

F They were patient and observant.

G They knew much more about astronomy than we do.

H They spent all their time counting stars.

J They invented astrology.

SCIENTIFIC DEBATE

Is Pluto Really a Planet?

We have learned that Pluto is the planet farthest from the sun. Since it was discovered in 1930, astronomers have grouped it with the outer planets. However, Pluto is not a perfect fit for this group. Unlike the other outer planets, which are large and gaseous, Pluto is small and made of rock and ice. Pluto also has a very elliptical orbit that is unlike its neighboring planets. These and other factors once fueled a debate about whether Pluto should be classified as a planet.

Kuiper Belt

In the early 1990s, astronomers discovered a belt of comets outside the orbit of Neptune. The belt was named the *Kuiper* (KIE per) *belt* in honor of Gerard Kuiper, a Dutch-born American astronomer. So what does this belt have to do with Pluto? Given its proximity to Pluto, some astronomers thought Pluto might actually be a large comet that escaped the Kuiper belt.

Comet?

Comets are basically dirty snowballs made of ice and cosmic dust. Pluto is about 30 percent ice and 70 percent rock. This is much more rock than is in a normal comet.

A composite drawing of Triton, Pluto, Charon, and Halley's comet

Also, at 2,390 km in diameter, Pluto is much larger than a comet. For example, Halley's comet is only about 20 km in diameter. Even so, Pluto's orbit is very similar to that of a comet. Both have orbits that are very elliptical.

Escaped Moon?

Pluto and its moon, Charon, have much in common with Neptune's moon Triton. All three have atmospheres made of nitrogen and methane, which suggests that they share a similar origin. And because Triton has a "backward" orbit compared with Neptune's other moons, it may have been captured by Neptune's gravity. Some astronomers thought Pluto might also have been captured by Neptune but broke free by some cataclysmic event.

New Category of Planet?

Some astronomers suggested that perhaps we should create a new subclass of planets, such as the ice planets, to add to the gas giant and terrestrial classification we now use. Pluto would be the only planet in this class, but scientists think we are likely to find others. As there are more new discoveries, astronomers will likely continue to debate these issues. To date, however, Pluto is still officially considered a planet. This decision is firmly grounded by the fact that Pluto has been called a planet since its discovery.

You Decide

▶ Do some additional research about Pluto, the Kuiper belt, and comets. What do you think Pluto should be called?

Exploring Space

Pre-Reading Questions

1. What is the difference between an artificial satellite and a space probe?

2. How has the space program made our lives better? ⓍTEKS

3. What types of equipment and transportation are necessary for space travel? ⓍTEKS

A Shuttle to Outer Space

The space shuttle is the most recent vehicle that has been developed to take people into outer space. Because the shuttle can be reused, it lowers the cost of space launches by up to 90 percent. The lower cost of getting to outer space has opened a new era of space exploration in which space missions are more common. From these missions, scientists are able to gather important information that will eventually help humans adapt to living and working in space. In this chapter, you will see how technology and space exploration are connected and how they impact us on Earth.

START-UP Activity

ROCKET FUN ★TEKS

Rockets are used to send people into space. Rockets work by forcing hot gas out one end of a tube. As this gas escapes in one direction, the rocket moves in the opposite direction. While you may have let a full balloon loose many times before, here you will use a balloon to learn about the principles of rocket propulsion.

Procedure

1. Thread a **string** through a **drinking straw,** and tie each end of the string to something that won't move, like a chair. Make sure that the string is tight.

2. Blow into a **large balloon** until it is the size of a grapefruit. Pinch the neck of the balloon closed.

3. Use **tape** to attach the balloon to the straw so that the opening of the balloon points toward one end of the string.

4. Hold the balloon at one end of the string, and then release the balloon. Record what happens in your ScienceLog.

5. Fill the balloon until it is almost twice the size it was in step 2, and repeat steps 3 and 4. Again record your observations.

Analysis

6. What happened during the second test that was different from the first? Can you figure out why?

Figure 6 Sputnik 1 *was the first artificial satellite placed in Earth orbit.*

Artificial Satellites

Imagine being asked to take a photograph of the entire United States, including Alaska and Hawaii. How would you do it?

Using an artificial satellite would make this job easy. An **artificial satellite** is any human-made object placed in orbit around a body in space, such as the Earth. In the 1950s, the United States and the Soviet Union both began working to send the first artificial satellite into space. The Soviets launched their satellite first!

The Space Race Begins

On October 4, 1957, a Soviet satellite became the first human-made object to be placed in orbit around the Earth. *Sputnik 1,* shown in **Figure 6,** carried instruments to measure the properties of Earth's upper atmosphere. Less than a month later, the Soviets launched *Sputnik 2.* This satellite carried a dog named Laika.

Two months later, the U.S. Navy tried to launch its own satellite using a Vanguard rocket. To the embarrassment of the United States, the rocket rose only 1 m into the air and exploded.

The United States Takes a Close Second

At this time, the U.S. Army was also busy improving its military rockets to send a satellite into space. On January 31, 1958, *Explorer 1,* the first United States satellite, was successfully launched. The space race was on!

Explorer 1, shown in **Figure 7,** carried instruments to the upper atmosphere. There it measured cosmic rays and small dust particles, and it recorded temperatures. *Explorer 1* also discovered the Van Allen radiation belts around the Earth. These belts are part of the Earth's magnetic field where charged particles from the sun have been trapped.

Figure 7 *NASA scientists William Pickering, James Van Allen, and Wernher von Braun show off a model of the first American artificial satellite,* Explorer 1.

Into the Information Age

The first United States weather satellite, *Tiros 1,* was launched in April 1960. It gave meteorologists their first look at the Earth and its clouds from above. By helping scientists study wind patterns and ocean currents, weather satellites have given scientists an understanding of how storms grow and change. You can now see weather satellite images on your television or download them from the Internet at almost any time.

Just a few months after *Tiros 1* began returning signals to Earth, the United States launched its first communications satellite, *Echo 1.* This satellite reflected signals from the ground to other areas on Earth, as shown in **Figure 8.** Within 3 years, communications-satellite networks were able to send signals between continents.

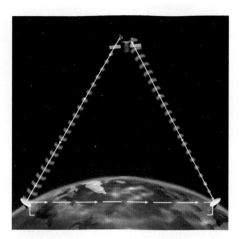

Figure 8 *Satellites can send signals around the curve of the Earth's surface, allowing communication around the world.*

Choose Your Orbit

All of the early satellites were placed in **low Earth orbit** (LEO), a few hundred kilometers above the Earth's surface. LEO, while considered space, is still in the outermost part of Earth's atmosphere. A satellite in LEO moves around the Earth very quickly. This motion can place the satellite out of contact much of the time.

Writer Arthur C. Clarke suggested a much higher orbit than LEO for weather and communications satellites. In this orbit, called a **geosynchronous** (JEE oh SING kruh nuhs) **orbit** (GEO), a satellite moves around the Earth at a speed that exactly matches the rotational speed of the Earth. This keeps the satellite above the same spot on Earth at all times. Today there are many satellites in GEO. Ground stations are in continuous contact with these satellites. Continuous contact keeps your television show or phone call from being interrupted.

 **Self-Check**

The space station being built by the United States and other countries is in LEO. What is good about this location? *(See page 640 to check your answer.)*

Anything GOES

The height above the Earth's surface for a geosynchronous orbit is 35,862 km. Today a network of Geostationary Operational Environment Satellites (GOES) gives us weather information from around the world. What would happen if a GOES satellite were placed in LEO rather than in GEO? How would that affect the information it was able to gather?

After more than 40 years of space launches, the space near Earth is getting crowded with "space junk." The United States Space Command—a new branch of the military—tracks nearly 10,000 objects larger than a few centimeters. Left uncontrolled, all this debris may become a problem for space vehicles!

Results of the Satellite Programs

Satellites gather information by *remote sensing*. Remote sensing is the gathering of information from high above the Earth's surface. The information helps us study the Earth's surface by measuring the light and other forms of energy that reflect off of the Earth. Some satellites use radar, which reflects radio waves off of the surface of objects and measures the returned signal.

Military Satellites

The United States military has a keen interest in satellites for defense and spying purposes. LEO was recognized to be a good place to put powerful telescopes. These telescopes could then be turned toward the Earth to photograph the surface anywhere in the world.

The period from the late 1940s to the late 1980s is known as the Cold War. During that time, the United States and the former Soviet Union built up their military forces in order to ensure that neither country became more powerful than the other. Both countries monitored each other using spy satellites. **Figure 9** shows a picture of part of the United States taken by a Soviet spy satellite during the Cold War.

The military also launches satellites into GEO to aid in navigation and to serve as early warning systems against missiles launched toward the United States. Even though the Cold War is over, spy satellites still play an important part in military defense.

Figure 9 *This picture was taken in 1989 by a Soviet spy satellite in LEO about 220 km above the city of San Francisco. Can you pick out any objects on the ground?*

BRAIN FOOD

Not all satellites look down on Earth. For example, the most important satellites to astronomers are the *Hubble Space Telescope* and the *Chandra X-ray Observatory*. Both of these satellites look out toward the stars.

Eyes on the Environment

Satellites have given us a new view of the Earth. By getting above the Earth's atmosphere and looking down, we have been able to study the Earth in ways that were never before possible.

One of the most successful remote-sensing projects is Landsat, which began in 1972 and continues today. It has given us the longest continuous record of Earth's surface as seen from space. The newest Landsat satellite (number 7) was launched in 1999. It will gather images in several frequencies—from visible light to infrared. The Landsat program has gathered millions of images. These are being used to find and track changes on Earth, as shown in **Figure 10.**

Remote sensing has allowed scientists to perform large-scale mapping, to look at changes in vegetation growth, to map the spread of cities, and to study the effect of humans on the global environment.

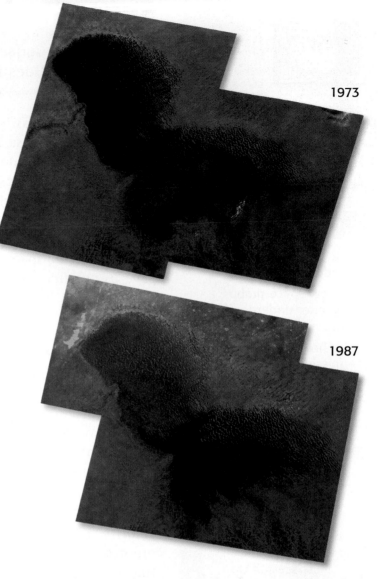

1973

1987

Figure 10 *These Landsat images of Lake Chad, Africa, show how environmental changes can be studied from orbit. These images were taken 14 years apart. Can you tell what changed?*

SECTION REVIEW

① What types of satellites did the United States first place in orbit? **⊙TEKS**

② Name two ways that the use of satellites has helped human society. **⊙TEKS**

③ Applying Concepts Would a satellite used to connect telephone calls be placed in LEO or GEO? Explain your answer.

The Moon

Luna 9 (USSR)
Launched: January 1966
Purpose: to land the first spacecraft on the moon

Clementine (US)
Launched: January 1994
Purpose: to map the composition of the moon's surface

Space Probes

What does the surface of Mars look like? Is there water on the moon? Does life exist anywhere else in the solar system?

To answer questions like these, scientists must send machines far into space. These machines visit planets, study asteroids, and gather data about many other things that are far away from Earth. These machines are called space probes. A **space probe** is a vehicle that carries scientific instruments to planets or other bodies in space. Unlike satellites, which stay in Earth orbit, space probes go away from Earth. The Soviets were the first to launch a space probe. This and other early space probes gave us our first close encounters with the other planets and their moons.

Visits to Our Planetary Neighborhood

The Earth's moon and the inner planets were the first bodies to be chosen for exploration. *Luna 1,* launched by the Soviets, was the first space probe. In January of 1959, it flew past the moon. Two months later, an American space probe—*Pioneer 4*—did the same thing. Follow along the next few pages to learn about space-probe missions since *Luna 1.*

The Luna 9 and Clementine Missions

Luna 9, a Soviet probe, made the first soft landing on the moon's surface. During the next 10 years, there were more than 30 lunar missions made by the Soviet Union and the United States. Thousands of pictures of the moon's surface were taken.

In 1994, the probe *Clementine* discovered possible evidence of water at the south pole of the moon. The image in **Figure 11** was taken by the *Clementine* space probe and shows the south pole of the moon. You can see that some of the craters at the pole are permanently in shadow. Elsewhere on the moon, sunlight would cause any ice to vaporize. Ice may have been left in the craters by comet impacts. If there is water at the pole, it will be very valuable to people seeking to colonize the moon.

Figure 11 *The dark craters at the moon's south pole are possible sites for water ice.*

The Venera 9 Mission

The Soviet Union landed the first probe on Venus. The probe, called *Venera 9,* parachuted into Venus's atmosphere and sent back the first images of the surface. *Venera 9* found that surface temperature and atmospheric pressure on Venus are much higher than on Earth. The probe also found that the rocks there are much like the rocks on Earth. Perhaps most importantly, *Venera 9* and other missions showed us a planet with an extreme greenhouse effect. Scientists study Venus's atmosphere to learn about how greenhouse gases trap thermal energy in the Earth's atmosphere.

The Magellan Mission

In 1989, the United States launched the *Magellan* probe. *Magellan* used radar to map 98 percent of the surface of Venus. The Magellan mission showed that, in many ways, the geology of Venus is similar to that of Earth. Venus has features that suggest plate tectonics happens there, as it does on Earth. Venus also has volcanoes. Some of them may have been active recently. The diagram in **Figure 12** below shows the *Magellan* probe using radar to get through the thick cloud layer. The radar data were sent back to Earth. Computers were then able to use the data to make maps like the one at below right.

Venus

Venera 9 (USSR)
Launched: June 1975
Purpose: to record the surface conditions of Venus

Magellan (US)
Launched: May 1989
Purpose: to make a global map of the surface of Venus

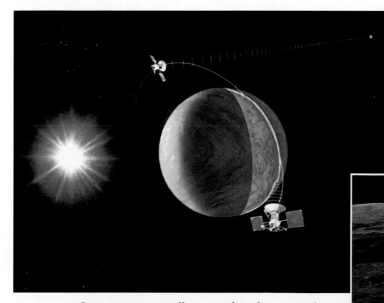

Figure 12 Magellan *used radar to gather information about the surface of Venus. This information was transmitted to Earth and was used to make maps of Venus like the one at right.*

Mars

Viking 2 (US)
Launched: September 1975
Purpose: to search for life on the surface of Mars

Mars Pathfinder (US)
Launched: December 1996
Purpose: to use less expensive technology to study the surface of Mars

The Viking Missions

In 1975, the United States sent a pair of probes—*Viking 1* and *Viking 2*—to Mars. The surface of Mars is more like the Earth's surface than that of any other planet. For this reason, one of the goals of the Viking missions was to look for signs of life. The probes carried instruments designed to gather soil and test it for signs of life. However, no hard evidence was found. The Viking missions did find signs that Mars was once much warmer and wetter than it is now. The probes sent back pictures of dry water channels on the planet's surface. This discovery led scientists to ask even more questions about Mars. Why and when did the Martian climate change?

The Mars Pathfinder Mission

More than 20 years later, in 1997, the surface of Mars was visited again by a NASA space probe. The goal of the Mars Pathfinder mission was to show that Martian exploration is possible at a lower cost than that of the larger Viking missions.

The *Mars Pathfinder* landed on Mars and released the *Sojourner* rover. *Sojourner* traveled across the surface for almost 3 months. During this time, it gathered data and recorded pictures of the Martian surface, as shown at left.

The Pioneer and Voyager Missions

The *Pioneer 10* and *Pioneer 11* space probes were the first to visit the outer planets. Among other things, these probes studied the *solar wind*—the flow of charged particles coming from the sun. The Pioneer probes also found that the dark belts on Jupiter are warmer than the light belts. These dark belts also allow deeper views into Jupiter's atmosphere. In June of 1983, *Pioneer 10* became the first space probe to go past the orbit of Pluto.

The Voyager space probes were the first to find Jupiter's faint rings. *Voyager 2*, launched in 1977, was the first space probe to fly by the four gas giant planets—Jupiter, Saturn, Uranus, and Neptune. The paths of the Pioneer and Voyager space probes are shown below in **Figure 13.** Today these probes are all near the edge of the solar system and are still sending back information.

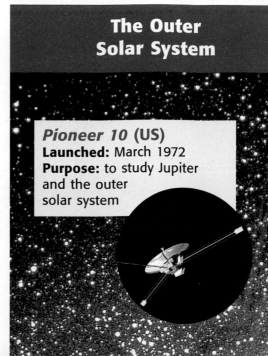

The Outer Solar System

Pioneer 10 (US)
Launched: March 1972
Purpose: to study Jupiter and the outer solar system

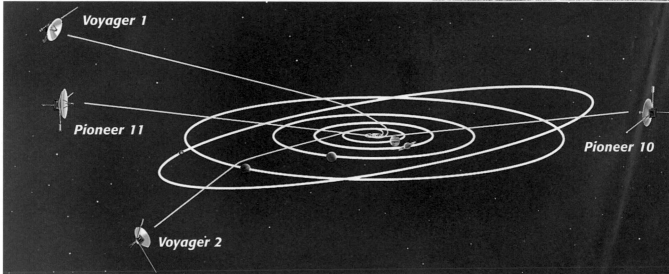

Figure 13 *The Pioneer and Voyager probes continue to send back information from the edges of the solar system.*

The Galileo Mission

The *Galileo* space probe reached Jupiter in 1995. *Galileo* itself began a long study of Jupiter's moons. A smaller probe was sent into Jupiter's atmosphere to take measurements. *Galileo* gathered data that allowed scientists to study the geology of Jupiter's major moons and Jupiter's magnetic properties more closely. The moons of Jupiter proved to be far more exciting than the Pioneer and Voyager images had suggested. The *Galileo* probe discovered that two of Jupiter's moons have magnetic fields. Also, one of its moons, Europa, may have an ocean of liquid water under its icy surface.

Galileo (US)
Launched: October 1989
Purpose: to study Jupiter and its moons

Space Probes—A New Approach

NASA is looking for missions that are "faster, cheaper, and better." The early space probes were very large and costly. Space probe missions such as *Voyager 2* and *Galileo* took years to develop and carry out. One new program, called Discovery, seeks ideas for smaller science programs. The missions are supposed to bring faster results at much lower costs. The first approved Discovery missions included sending small space probes to asteroids, studying the moon, and returning comet dust to Earth.

Stardust—Comet Detective

Launched in 1999, the *Stardust* space probe is a NASA Discovery mission and the first to focus only on a comet. As illustrated in **Figure 14,** the probe will arrive at the comet in 2004 and will gather samples of the comet's dust tail. It will return the dust to Earth in 2006. This mission will mark the first time that material from beyond the orbit of the moon has been brought back to Earth. The comet dust should help scientists better understand the evolution of the sun and the planets.

Figure 14 Stardust *will visit a comet and will gather samples of its dust tail.*

Deep Space 1—The New Kid in Town

Another NASA project is the New Millennium program. Its purpose is to test new technologies so that they can be used in the years to come. *Deep Space 1,* illustrated in **Figure 15,** is the first mission of this program. It is a space probe with an ion-propulsion system. Rather than burning chemical fuel, an *ion drive* uses charged particles, called *ions,* that exit the vehicle at high speeds. An ion drive still follows Newton's third law of motion, but it does so using a different kind of propulsion.

Figure 15 Deep Space 1 *uses a new type of propulsion—an ion drive.*

The Last of the Big Boys

On October 15, 1997, the *Cassini* space probe began a 7-year journey to Saturn. This is the last of the large old-style missions. The *Cassini* space probe will make a grand tour of Saturn's moons. As shown in **Figure 16,** a smaller probe called *Huygens* will detach itself from *Cassini*. *Huygens* will then descend into the atmosphere of Saturn's moon Titan.

Figure 16 *An artist's view of* Cassini *at Saturn, with* Huygens *falling toward Saturn's moon Titan.*

Future Missions

There are many ideas for future missions. These include a first-ever space-probe visit to Pluto and an orbiter for Jupiter's moon Europa that will use radar to determine whether Europa has a liquid ocean. An orbiter may also be sent to study Mercury, the planet closest to the sun. These are just a few of the many exciting missions planned for the future. These missions will open a new golden era of planetary exploration.

SECTION REVIEW

1. List three discoveries that have been made by space probes.

2. Which two planets best help us understand Earth's environment? Explain. ⭐TEKS

3. How is the new Discovery program different from the older space-probe missions?

4. **Inferring Conclusions** Why were space probes necessary to find water channels on Mars or ice on Europa?

Terms to Learn

space shuttle
space station

What You'll Do

- Summarize the benefits of the manned space program. ⭐TEKS
- Explain how large projects such as the Apollo program and the *International Space Station* developed. ⭐TEKS
- Study possibilities for human exploration of space.

Figure 17 *In 1962, John Glenn flew aboard* Friendship 7, *the first NASA spacecraft to orbit the Earth.*

Living and Working in Space

Is it safe to send people into space? Could a person stay in space for a long time?

In the beginning of the space program, nobody knew the answers to these questions. Sending humans into space was an early goal of the program, but it had to be done in small steps. The first step was to test the control of spacecraft with rocket-powered airplanes. Test flights in high-speed aircraft through the upper atmosphere were the beginnings of the Mercury program. The goal of the Mercury program was to put a man in orbit and to test how he functioned in space. Test flights began in 1959, but the dates for manned flight kept being delayed because of unreliable rockets.

Human Space Exploration

On April 12, 1961, a Soviet cosmonaut named Yuri Gagarin became the first human to orbit the Earth. The United States didn't make its first suborbital flight until May 5, 1961, when Alan B. Shepard reached space but not orbit. Because the Soviets were first once again, they appeared to be winning the Cold War. Many Americans began to see the advantages of a strong presence in space. On May 25, 1961, President John F. Kennedy made a speech that would set the tone for American space policy for the next 10 years.

> *"I believe that this nation should commit itself to achieving the goal, before this decade is out, of landing a man on the moon and returning him safely to the Earth. No single space project in this period will be more impressive to mankind, or more important for the long-range exploration of space."*
>
> — *John F. Kennedy, President of the United States*

Many people were expecting the simple announcement of an accelerated space program, but Kennedy's speech took everyone by surprise—even the leaders at NASA. Go to the moon? The United States had not even achieved Earth orbit yet! But the American people accepted the challenge. By February 1962, a new spaceport site in Florida and a manned space-center site were bought. John Glenn, shown in **Figure 17,** was launched into orbit around the Earth on February 20, 1962.

The Dream Comes True

On July 20, 1969, Kennedy's challenge was met. The *Apollo 11* landing module—the *Eagle,* shown in **Figure 18**—landed on the moon. Astronaut Neil Armstrong became the first person to set foot on a world other than Earth. This moment forever changed the way we view ourselves and our planet.

Although the main reason for the Apollo program was political (national pride), the program also helped advance science. *Apollo 11* returned nearly 22 kg of moon rocks to Earth for study. Its crew also put devices on the moon to study moonquake activity and the solar wind. The results from these studies helped shape our view of the solar system.

The Space Shuttle

The dream of human spaceflight and Kennedy's challenge were great for getting us into space. However, they could not be the motivation for the continued support of space exploration. The huge rockets that were needed to launch spacecraft were just too expensive.

Early in the manned spaceflight program, Wernher von Braun suggested that a reusable space transportation system would be needed. Proposals for reusable space vehicles were made in the 1950s and 1960s. However, the Kennedy challenge overshadowed other efforts, and these ideas were not given serious attention. Finally in 1972, President Richard Nixon proposed a space shuttle program to the American public as a cheaper way to get into space regularly. A **space shuttle** is a reusable vehicle that takes off like a rocket and lands like an airplane, as shown in **Figure 19.**

Figure 18 *Astronaut Neil Armstrong took this picture of Edwin "Buzz" Aldrin as he was about to become the second person to step onto the moon.*

Figure 19 Columbia, *shown below landing at Edwards Air Force Base in California, was one of NASA's first shuttles.*

The first shuttle was launched on April 12, 1981. This launch was followed by two dozen successful missions. In 1986, however, tragedy struck. On January 28, 1986, the booster rocket on the space shuttle *Challenger* exploded just after takeoff. All seven of the astronauts aboard were killed. One of these astronauts was Christa McAuliffe, who would have been the first teacher in space. All shuttle flights were grounded until this accident could be explained. Finally in 1988, the space shuttle program resumed with the return of shuttle *Discovery* to space.

Commuter Shuttle?

Efforts are now underway to make space travel easier and cheaper. NASA is working on a space plane called the *X33*. An illustration of the *X33* is shown in **Figure 20.** This craft will fly like a normal airplane, but it will have rocket engines for use in space. Once in operation, space planes may lower the cost of getting material to LEO by 90 percent. Research is now being done on the next generation of space vehicles. New kinds of rockets and rocket fuels, as well as other means of sending vehicles into space, are being studied.

Figure 20 *Future space planes may offer inexpensive transportation not only between Earth and space but also around the world.*

Biology
C O N N E C T I O N

When people stay in space for long periods of time without having to work against gravity, their bones lose mass and their muscles become weaker. Long space-station missions, which can last for months, are very important for studying whether people can survive trips to Mars and other planets. These trips will last for several years.

Space Stations—People Working in Space

On April 19, 1971, the Soviets became the first to place a manned space station in low Earth orbit. A **space station** is a long-term orbiting platform from which other vehicles can be launched or research can be carried out. In June of the same year, a crew of three Soviet cosmonauts entered the space station *Salyut 1* to conduct a 23-day mission. By 1982, the Soviets had put up a total of seven space stations. The Soviet Union became the world leader in space-station development and in the study of the effects of weightlessness on humans. The Soviet Union's studies will be important for future manned flights to other planets—journeys that will take years.

A Home Away from Home

Skylab, the United States's first space station, was a science and engineering lab. *Skylab* orbited the Earth at a height of 435 km. The lab, shown in **Figure 21,** was used for a wide variety of scientific studies, including astronomical, biological, and manufacturing experiments. Three different crews spent a total of 171 days on board *Skylab.*

Everything in LEO, including *Skylab,* eventually falls toward Earth. Even at several hundred kilometers above the Earth, there is still a small amount of atmosphere. The atmosphere slows down anything in orbit. Something must periodically push the object back to its proper orbit. *Skylab's* orbit began to decay in 1979. A space shuttle was supposed to return the lab to a higher orbit. However, delays in the shuttle program prevented the rescue of *Skylab,* and it fell into the Indian Ocean.

Figure 21 Skylab, *in orbit above Earth, was lifted into space by a Saturn V rocket.*

From Russia with Peace

In 1986, the Soviets began to launch the pieces for a much more ambitious space station called *Mir* (meaning "peace"). When finished, *Mir* had seven modules and measured 33 m long and 27 m wide. *Mir* was used to conduct astronomical studies, biological experiments, and manufacturing tests.

Astronauts from the United States and other countries eventually became visitors to *Mir,* as shown in **Figure 22.** *Mir* was almost continuously inhabited from 1987 to 1999. It also became the inspiration for the next generation of space station, the *International Space Station.*

Figure 22 Mir *allowed American astronauts and Russian cosmonauts to live and work together in space.*

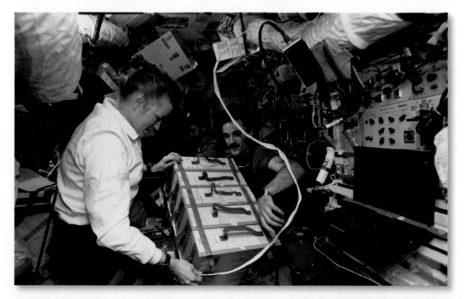

BRAIN FOOD

Space shuttle missions usually last only a few days. However, astronauts and cosmonauts spend much longer on space stations. Valeri Polyakov, a Russian doctor, was once aboard the space station *Mir* for 438 days!

The International Space Station

In 1993, a design for a new space station was proposed. It called for a collaboration between the newly formed Russian Republic and the United States, as well as many other countries. The new space station is called the *International Space Station* (*ISS*). A drawing of how the station will look when finished is shown in **Figure 23.**

The station is being built in LEO with parts brought up on the space shuttle or by Russian rockets. The United States is providing lab modules, the supporting truss, solar panels for energy, living quarters, and a biomedical laboratory. The Russians are contributing a service module, docking modules, life support and research modules, and transportation to and from the station. Other parts will come from Japan, Canada, and several European countries.

The *ISS* will present many benefits—some of which we cannot even predict. What we do know is that it will be a good place to perform experiments and perhaps to test new technologies. Hopefully, the *ISS* will also promote cooperation among countries and will continue the pioneering spirit of the first astronauts and cosmonauts.

BRAIN FOOD

More than 40 shuttle flights and 6 years will be needed to lift into space the 400 tons of materials needed for the construction of the *International Space Station*.

Figure 23 *This artist's view of the* International Space Station *shows what the station will look like once it is finished. The station is currently being assembled in orbit by astronauts like the one shown below.*

The Moon, Mars, and Beyond

We may one day need resources and living space beyond what Earth can offer. Space offers many resources. One interesting resource is a rare form of helium that can be found on the moon. Used as a fuel for nuclear reactors, this helium leaves no radioactive waste!

We have seen that there are also many scientific benefits to space exploration. For example, darkened craters on the moon could be ideal places from which to study the stars. The moon could also be a wonderful place to build factories that need a vacuum for manufacturing, as illustrated in **Figure 24.** A base in Earth orbit can make products that require low gravity. A colony or base on the moon or on Mars could help in bringing space resources to Earth. The key will be to make these missions economically worthwhile.

·····Activity·····

Inventions intended for space exploration have often led to new products that improve our lives here on Earth. NASA has a program that brings these new ideas and technologies to the public. Find out more about NASA's technology transfers on the Internet and about how many everyday technologies had their beginnings in the space program.

•• ⭐TEKS ••••••••••••••••

Figure 24 *Humans may one day colonize the moon for scientific, economic, and perhaps even recreational reasons.*

SECTION REVIEW

1. How was the race to explore our solar system influenced by the Cold War? ⭐TEKS

2. How did the missions to the moon benefit space science? ⭐TEKS

3. How will space stations help in the exploration of space? ⭐TEKS

4. **Making Inferences** Why did the United States quit sending people to the moon after the Apollo program ended?

internetconnect

SC*LINKS*
NSTA   GO TO: www.scilinks.org

TOPIC: Space Exploration and
        Space Stations
*sci*LINKS NUMBER: HSTE550

Making Models Lab

Reach for the Stars ⭐TEKS

Have you ever thought about living and working in space? Well, in order for you to do so, you would have to learn to deal with the new environment. Astronauts must adjust to the conditions of space. Meanwhile, they are also dealing with special tools used to repair and build space stations. In this activity, you will get the chance to model one tool that might help astronauts work in space.

MATERIALS

- cardboard box
- scissors
- metric ruler
- hole punch
- 2 brads
- metal wire
- 2 jumbo paper clips
- plastic-foam ball

Ask a Question

1 How can I build a piece of equipment that models how astronauts work in space?

Form a Hypothesis

2 Before you begin, write a hypothesis that answers the question in step 1. Explain your reasoning.

Test the Hypothesis

3 Cut three strips from the cardboard box. Each strip should be about 5 cm wide. The strips should be at least 20 cm long but not longer than 40 cm.

4 Punch holes near the center of each end of the three cardboard strips. The holes should be about 3 cm from the end of each strip.

5 Lay the strips end to end along your table. Slide the second strip toward the first strip so that a hole in the first strip lines up with a hole in the second strip. Slip a brad through the holes, and bend its ends out to attach the cardboard strips.

6 Use another brad to attach the third cardboard strip to the free end of the second strip. Now you have your mechanical arm. The brads form joints where the cardboard strips meet.

7 Straighten the wire, and slide it through the hole in one end of your mechanical arm. Bend about 3 cm of the wire in a 90° angle so that it will not slide back out of the hole.

8 Now try to move the arm by holding the free ends of the cardboard and wire. The arm should bend and straighten at the joints. If the arm is hard to move, adjust the design. Consider loosening the brads, for example.

9 Now your mechanical arm needs a hand. Otherwise it won't be able to pick things up! Straighten one paper clip, and slide it through the hole where you attached the wire in step 7. Bend one end of the paper clip to form a loop around the cardboard, and bend the other end to form a hook. You will use this hook to pick things up.

10 Bend a second paper clip into a U-shape. Stick the straight end of this paper clip into the foam ball. Leave the ball on your desk.

11 Move the arm so that you can lift the foam ball. The paper-clip hook on the arm will have to catch the paper clip on the ball.

Analyze the Results

12 Did you have any trouble moving the arm in step 8? What changes did you make?

13 Did you have trouble picking up the foam ball? What might have made this step easier?

Draw Conclusions

14 What changes could you make to your mechanical arm that might make it easier to use?

15 How would a tool like this one help people work in space?

Going Further

Adjust the design for your mechanical arm. Can you find a way to lift anything other than the foam ball? For example, can you lift heavier objects or ones that do not have a hook attached? Explain your answer.

Research the tools that astronauts use on space stations and on the space shuttle. How do their tools help them work in the conditions of space?

Highlights

Section 1

Vocabulary

rocket (*p. 572*)

NASA (*p. 573*)

thrust (*p. 574*)

orbital velocity (*p. 575*)

escape velocity (*p. 575*)

Section Notes

- Two pioneers of rocketry were Konstantin Tsiolkovsky and Robert Goddard. ⭐TEKS

- Rockets work according to Newton's third law of motion—for every action there is an equal and opposite reaction. ⭐TEKS

- NASA was formed in 1958, joining several rocket research programs. It was originally formed to compete with the Soviet Union's rocket program.

LabBook ⭐TEKS

Water Rockets Save the Day (*p. 638*)

Section 2

Vocabulary

artificial satellite (*p. 576*)

low Earth orbit (*p. 577*)

geosynchronous orbit (*p. 577*)

Section Notes

- The Soviet Union launched the first satellite in 1957. The first United States satellite went up in 1958.

- Low Earth orbits (LEOs) are a few hundred kilometers above the Earth's surface. Satellites in geosynchronous orbits (GEOs) have an orbit period of 24 hours and remain over one spot.

- Satellites are used for weather observations, communications, and mapping the Earth. Satellites also track ocean currents, crop growth, and city growth. ⭐TEKS

- One great legacy of the satellite program has been an increase in our awareness of the Earth's fragile environment. ⭐TEKS

Section 3

Vocabulary

space probe (*p. 580*)

Section Notes

- Exploration with space probes began with missions to the moon. The next targets of exploration were Mercury, Venus, and Mars.

- The United States has been the only country to explore the outer solar system, beginning with the Pioneer and Voyager missions.

- Space probes have given us information about how planets develop. This information has helped us better understand our own planet Earth. ⭐TEKS

Section 4

Vocabulary

space shuttle (*p. 587*)

space station (*p. 588*)

Section Notes

- The great race to start a manned spaceflight program and to reach the moon was politically motivated.

- The United States beat the Soviets to a manned moon landing with the Apollo moon flights in 1969. ⭐TEKS

- During the 1970s, the United States focused on developing the space shuttle. The Soviets focused on developing orbiting space stations. ⭐TEKS

- The United States, Russia, and 14 other countries are currently developing the *International Space Station*.

- For scientific, economic, and even recreational reasons, people may one day live and work on other planets and moons.

For each pair of terms, explain how the meanings of the terms differ.

1. geosynchronous orbit/low Earth orbit

2. space probe/space shuttle **★TEKS**

3. artificial satellite/moon

Complete the following sentences by choosing the correct term from each pair of terms.

4. The force that accelerates a rocket is called __?__. (*escape velocity* or *thrust*) **★TEKS**

5. Rockets need to have __?__ in order to burn their fuel. (*oxygen* or *nitrogen*)

Multiple Choice

6. Whose rocket research team surrendered to the Americans at the end of World War II? **★TEKS**
   a. K. Tsiolkovsky
   b. R. Goddard
   c. W. von Braun
   d. D. Eisenhower

7. Rockets work according to Newton's **★TEKS**
   a. first law of motion.
   b. second law of motion.
   c. third law of motion.
   d. law of universal gravitation.

8. The first artificial satellite to orbit the Earth was
   a. *Pioneer 4.*
   b. *Explorer 1.*
   c. *Voyager 2.*
   d. *Sputnik 1.*

9. Satellites are able to transfer TV signals across and between continents because satellites
   a. are located in LEOs.
   b. relay signals past the horizon.
   c. travel quickly around Earth.
   d. can be used during the day and night.

10. GEOs are better orbits for communications because satellites in GEO
    a. remain in position over one spot.
    b. are farther away from Earth's surface.
    c. do not revolve around the Earth.
    d. are only a few hundred kilometers high.

11. Which space probe discovered evidence of water at the moon's south pole?
    a. *Luna 9*
    b. *Viking 1*
    c. *Clementine*
    d. *Magellan*

12. When did humans first set foot on the moon?
    a. 1949
    b. 1959
    c. 1969
    d. 1979

13. Which one of these planets has not yet been visited by space probes?
    a. Mercury
    b. Neptune
    c. Mars
    d. Pluto

14. Of the following, which space probe is about to leave our solar system?
    a. *Galileo*
    b. *Magellan*
    c. *Mariner 10*
    d. *Pioneer 10*

15. Based on space-probe data, which of the following is the most likely place in our solar system to find liquid water?
    a. The moon
    b. Mars
    c. Europa
    d. Venus

Short Answer

16. Describe how Newton's third law of motion relates to the movement of rockets. ⭐TEKS

17. What is one disadvantage that objects in LEO have?

18. Why did the United States develop the space shuttle? ⭐TEKS

19. What impact has space research had on scientific thought, society, and the environment? ⭐TEKS

CONCEPT MAPPING

20. Use the following terms to create a concept map: *orbital velocity, thrust, LEO, artificial satellites, escape velocity, space probes, GEO,* and *rockets.*

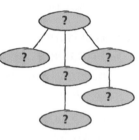

CRITICAL THINKING AND PROBLEM SOLVING

Write one or two sentences to answer the following questions:

21. What is the difference between speed and velocity?

22. Why must rockets that travel in outer space carry oxygen with them?

23. How will data from space probes help us understand the Earth's environment? ⭐TEKS

24. Why is it necessary for several nations to work together to create the *ISS*?

MATH IN SCIENCE

25. To escape Earth's gravity, a rocket must travel at least 11 km/s. About how many hours would it take to get to the moon at this speed? (The moon is about 384,000 km away from Earth.)

INTERPRETING GRAPHICS

The map below was made using satellite data. It indicates the different amounts of chlorophyll in the ocean. Chlorophyll, in turn, identifies the presence of marine plankton. In the ocean, the blues and purples show the smallest amount of chlorophyll, and red and yellow show the largest. Examine the map, and answer the questions that follow:

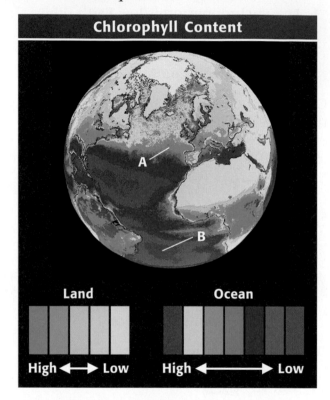

26. At which location, **A** or **B**, are more plankton concentrated?

27. What do you conclude about the conditions in which plankton live? ⭐TEKS

Reading Check-up

⭐TEKS Take a minute to review your answers to the Pre-Reading Questions found at the bottom of page 570. Have your answers changed? If necessary, revise your answers based on what you have learned since you began this chapter.

Chapter 21

1 Which of the following is a function of satellites?

   A To relay television signals

   B To carry space probes to other planets to study them

   C To carry astronauts into orbit

   D To return rock samples from the moon

2 The space shuttle was the first

   F rocket.

   G artificial satellite.

   H reusable space vehicle.

   J space plane.

3 The first human to orbit the Earth was

   A John Glenn.

   B Yuri Gagarin.

   C Neil Armstrong.

   D Alan B. Shepard.

4 Why might the discovery of liquid water on Europa be exciting to scientists searching for life in the solar system?

   F Liquid water is easier to study than ice.

   G Liquid water is required for life on Earth.

   H The presence of liquid water on Europa would mean that it has an atmosphere.

   J Liquid water would make a perfect landing spot for a space probe.

5 In the diagram below, the part of the rocket represented by Y is the

   A nozzle.

   B thrust shaft.

   C booster.

   D combustion chamber.

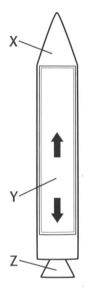

6 What is considered the ancestor of all space vehicles?

   F The booster rocket

   G The V-2

   H The *X33*

   J *Sputnik 1*

7 The *Mir* was a Russian

   A space station.

   B rocket.

   C weather satellite.

   D space plane.

Chapter 21

Math

The rocket equation states that the mass times the velocity of a rocket is equal to the mass times the velocity of the gas exiting the rocket. Use this equation to answer item 1.

$$m_r \times v_r = m_g \times v_g$$

(m_r = mass of the rocket; v_r = velocity of the rocket; m_g = mass of the exiting gas; v_g = velocity of the exiting gas)

1 Suppose that the mass of the gas exiting a rocket is 5 kilograms and that the velocity of the gas is 400 meters/second. If the rocket is moving at 10 meters/second, what is its mass?

A 8000 kg

B 20 kg

C 800 kg

D 200 kg

2 The speed required to reach Earth orbit is 8 kilometers/second. What does this equal in ***meters per hour***?

F 8000 m/h

G 28,800,000 m/h

H 88,000,000 m/h

J 288,000 m/h

Reading

Read the passage. Then read each question that follows the passage. Decide which is the best answer to each question.

One of the strange things about living in space is the reduced effect of gravity known as *free fall*. Everything inside the space station that is not fastened down will float! The designers of the *International Space Station* have come up with some intriguing solutions to this problem. For example, each astronaut will sleep in a sack similar to a sleeping bag that is fastened to the module. The sack will keep the astronauts from floating around while they sleep. Astronauts will shower with a hand-held nozzle. Afterward, the water droplets will be vacuumed up. Other problems being studied include how to prepare and serve food, how to design an effective toilet, and how to dispose of waste.

1 The main idea of the passage is

A that living in space is exciting.

B that astronauts will stay aboard the space station for long periods of time.

C that living in weightlessness presents interesting problems.

D that sleeping bags are needed to keep astronauts warm in space.

2 Which of the following is NOT a problem mentioned in the passage?

F How to serve and prepare food

G How to design an effective toilet

H How to drink water

J How to shower

Science Fiction

"Why I Left Harry's All-Night Hamburgers"

by Lawrence Watt-Evans

At 16, he needed a job. His dad was out of work and his family needed money. Right around the corner from his house was Harry's All-Night Hamburgers. With a little persistence, he talked Harry into giving him a job.

He worked from midnight to 7:30 A.M. so that he could still go to school. He was the counterman, waiter, busboy, and janitor, all in one. Harry's was pretty quiet most nights, especially because the interstate was 8 mi away and nobody wanted to drive to Harry's. Most of the time, the customers were pretty normal.

There were some, though, who were unusual. For instance, one guy came in dressed for Arctic winter, even though it was April and it was 60°F outside. Then there were the folks who parked a very strange vehicle right out in the parking lot for anyone to see.

Pretty soon, the captivated waiter starts asking questions. What he learns startles and fascinates him. Soon he's thinking about leaving Harry's. Find out why by reading "Why I Left Harry's All-Night Hamburgers," by Lawrence Watt-Evans, in the *Holt Anthology of Science Fiction*.

Contents

Graphing Data  ⊛TEKS

Performing an experiment usually requires the collection of data. To understand the data, it is often good to organize the data into a graph. Graphs can show trends and patterns that you might not notice in a table or list. In this exercise, you will practice collecting data and organizing the data into a graph.

Procedure

1. Pour 200 mL of water into a 400 mL beaker. Add ice to the beaker until the water line is at the 400 mL mark.

2. Place a Celsius thermometer into the beaker. Use a thermometer clip to prevent the thermometer from touching the bottom of the beaker. Record the temperature of the ice water in your ScienceLog.

3. Place the beaker and thermometer on a hot plate. Turn the hot plate on medium, and record the temperature every minute until the water temperature reaches 100°C.

4. Using heat-resistant gloves, remove the beaker from the hot plate. Continue to record the temperature of the water each minute for 10 more minutes.
   Caution: Don't forget to turn off the hot plate.

5. On a piece of graph paper or on a computer, create a graph similar to the one below. Label the horizontal axis (the *x*-axis) "Time (min)," and mark the axis in increments of 1 minute as shown. Label the vertical axis (the *y*-axis) "Temperature (°C)," and mark the axis in increments of 10° as shown.

6. Find the 1-minute mark on the *x*-axis, and move up the graph to the temperature you recorded at 1 minute. Place a dot on the graph at that point. Plot each temperature in the same way. When you have plotted all of your data, connect the dots with a smooth line.

Materials

- 200 mL of water
- 400 mL beaker
- ice
- Celsius thermometer with a clip
- hot plate
- clock or watch with a second hand
- heat-resistant gloves
- graph paper
- computer (optional)

Analysis

7. Examine your graph. Do you think the water heated faster than it cooled? Explain.

8. Estimate what the temperature of the water was 2.5 minutes after you placed the beaker on the hot plate. Explain how you can make a good estimate of temperature between any two measurements you recorded.

9. Explain how a graph may give more information than the same data in a chart.

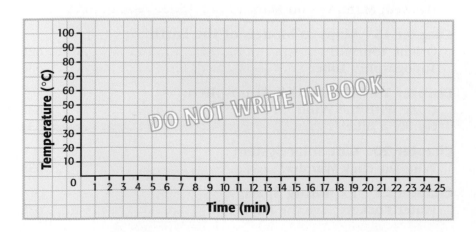

602 LabBook

DISCOVERY LAB

Layering Liquids ⭐TEKS

You have learned that liquids form layers according to the densities of the liquids. In this lab, you'll discover whether the order in which you add the liquids matters.

Materials

- liquid A
- liquid B
- liquid C
- beaker or other small, clear container
- 10 mL graduated cylinders (3)
- 3 funnels

Form a Hypothesis

1. Does the order in which you add liquids of different densities to a container affect the order of the layers formed by those liquids? Write your hypothesis in your ScienceLog.

Conduct an Experiment

2. Put on your safety goggles and an apron. Using separate graduated cylinders, add 10 mL of each liquid to the clear container. Remember to read the volume at the bottom of the meniscus. In your ScienceLog, record the order in which you added the liquids.

3. Observe the liquids in the container. In your ScienceLog, sketch what you see. Be sure to label the layers and the colors.

4. Add 10 mL more of liquid C. Observe what happens, and write your observations in your ScienceLog.

5. Add 20 mL more of liquid A. Observe what happens, and write your observations in your ScienceLog.

Analyze Your Results

6. Which of the liquids has the greatest density? Which has the least density? How can you tell?

7. Did the layers change position when you added more of liquid C? Explain your answer.

8. Did the layers change position when you added more of liquid A? Explain your answer.

9. Find out in what order your classmates added the liquids to the container. Compare your information with that of a classmate who added the liquids in a different order. Were your results different? In your ScienceLog, construct a reasonable explanation of why or why not.

Draw Conclusions

10. Based on your results, was your hypothesis supported? Communicate a valid conclusion.

Determining Density ⊛TEKS

How does the density of a small amount of a substance relate to the density of a larger amount of the same substance? In this lab, you will calculate the density of one marble and a group of marbles. Then you will confirm the relationship between the mass and volume of a substance.

Materials

- 100 mL graduated cylinder
- water
- paper towels
- 8 to 10 glass marbles
- metric balance
- graph paper

Collect Data

1. Copy the table below in your ScienceLog, or construct a similar table using a computer. Include one row for each marble.

Mass of marble, g	Total mass of marbles, g	Total volume, mL	Volume of marbles, mL (total volume minus 50.0 mL)	Density of marbles, g/mL (total mass of marbles divided by volume of marbles)
DO NOT WRITE IN BOOK			DO NOT WRITE IN BOOK	

2. Fill the graduated cylinder with 50.0 mL of water. If you put in too much water, twist one of the paper towels and use its end to absorb excess water.

3. Use the balance to measure the mass of a marble to at least one-tenth of a gram. Record the marble's mass in the table.

4. Carefully drop the marble in the tilted cylinder, and measure the total volume. Record the volume in the third column.

5. Measure and record the mass of another marble. Add the masses of the marbles together, and record this value in the second column of the table.

6. Carefully drop the second marble in the graduated cylinder. Complete the row of information in the table.

7. Repeat steps 5 and 6, adding one marble at a time. Stop when you run out of marbles, the water no longer completely covers the marbles, or the graduated cylinder is full.

Analyze the Results

8. Examine and evaluate the data in your table. As the number of marbles increases, what happens to the total mass and total volume of the marbles? What happens to the density of the marbles?

9. Using graph paper or a computer, graph the mass of the marbles (y-axis) versus the volume of the marbles (x-axis). Is the graph a straight line or a curved line?

Draw Conclusions

10. Does the density of a substance depend on the amount of substance present? (Interpret the information in your table, evaluate the data on your graph, and construct a reasonable explanation to answer this question.)

Going Further

Calculate the slope of the graph. How does the slope compare with the values in the column titled "Density of marbles"? Explain.

Using Scientific Methods

Full of Hot Air! ⭐TEKS

Why do hot-air balloons float gracefully above Earth, while balloons you blow up fall to the ground? The answer has to do with the density of the air inside the balloon. Density is mass per unit volume, and volume is affected by changes in temperature. In this experiment, you will investigate the relationship between the temperature and volume of a gas.

Materials

- 2 aluminum pans
- water
- metric ruler
- hot plate
- ice water
- balloon
- 250 mL beaker
- heat-resistant gloves

Ask a Question

1. In your ScienceLog, ask a question about how an increase or decrease in temperature affects the volume of a balloon.

Form a Hypothesis

2. Formulate a testable hypothesis that is a possible answer to your question in step 1.

Test the Hypothesis

3. Put on your safety goggles. Fill an aluminum pan with water about 4 to 5 cm deep. Put the pan on the hot plate, and turn the hot plate on. While the water is heating, fill the other pan 4 to 5 cm deep with ice water.

4. Blow up a balloon inside the beaker, as shown below. The balloon should fill the beaker but should not extend outside the beaker. Tie the balloon at its opening.

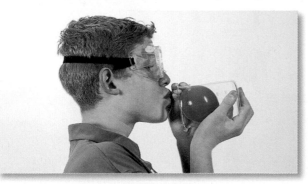

5. Place the beaker and balloon in the ice water. Observe what happens. Record your observations in your ScienceLog.

6. Remove the balloon and beaker from the ice water. Observe the balloon for several minutes. Record any changes.

7. Put on heat-resistant gloves. When the hot water begins to boil, put the beaker and balloon in the hot water. Observe the balloon for several minutes, and record your observations.

8. Turn off the hot plate. When the water has cooled, carefully dispose of it into a sink.

Analyze the Results

9. Summarize your observations of the balloon. Relate your observations to Charles's law.

10. Was your hypothesis for step 2 supported? If not, revise your hypothesis.

Draw Conclusions

11. Based on your observations, communicate a valid conclusion about how the density of a gas is affected by an increase or decrease in temperature.

12. Construct a reasonable explanation in terms of density and Charles's law for why heating the air allows a hot-air balloon to float.

Can Crusher

Condensation can occur when gas particles come near the surface of a liquid. The gas particles slow down because they are attracted to the liquid. This reduction in particle speed causes the gas to condense into a liquid. In this lab, you'll see that particles in a gas that has condensed into a liquid don't take up as much space and therefore don't exert as much pressure as they did in the gas.

Materials

- water
- 2 empty aluminum cans
- heat-resistant gloves
- hot plate
- tongs
- 1 L beaker

Conduct an Experiment

1. Place just enough water in an aluminum can to slightly cover the bottom. Fill the beaker with room-temperature water.

2. Put on heat-resistant gloves. Place the aluminum can on a hot plate turned to the highest temperature setting.

3. Heat the can until the water is boiling vigorously. Steam should be rising from the top of the can.

4. Using tongs, quickly pick up the can and place the top 2 cm of the can upside down in the beaker filled with water.

5. Describe your observations in your ScienceLog.

Analyze the Results

6. The can was crushed because the atmospheric pressure outside the can became greater than the pressure inside the can. Construct a reasonable explanation for what happened inside the can to cause this change in pressure.

Draw Conclusions

7. Inside every popcorn kernel is a small amount of water. When you make popcorn, the water inside the kernels is heated until it becomes steam. Explain how the popping of the kernels is the opposite of what you saw in this lab. Be sure to address the effects of pressure in your explanation.

Going Further

Try the experiment again, but use ice water instead of room-temperature water. Explain your results in terms of the effects of temperature.

Built for Speed ⭐TEKS

Imagine you and your classmates are engineers at GoCarCo, a toy-vehicle company. GoCarCo is trying to beat the competition by designing a new toy vehicle. Models of several new designs are being tested. Your boss (your teacher) has given you and your fellow engineers several designs to test. Your task is to determine which car is the fastest by measuring the speed of each car as accurately as possible with the tools you have. Your results could decide the fate of the company!

Materials

- toy vehicle
- meterstick
- masking tape
- stopwatch

Form a Hypothesis

1. Write a statement indicating whether you think the car you have been assigned to test is the fastest.

Test the Hypothesis

2. Plan an investigative procedure to test your hypothesis. Be sure to describe the equipment and technology you will use and to indicate that your procedure includes several trials.

3. Show your plan to your boss (teacher). Get his or her approval to carry out your procedure.

4. Perform your stated procedure. Observe, measure, and record all data in your ScienceLog. Be sure to express all data in the correct units.

Analyze the Results

5. What was the average speed of your vehicle? How does your result compare with the results of the other engineers?

6. Compare your technique for determining the speed of your vehicle with the techniques of the other engineers. Which technique do you think is the most effective?

Draw Conclusions

7. Was your toy vehicle the fastest? Explain why or why not.

Going Further

Think of several conditions that could affect your vehicle's speed. Plan an experiment to test your vehicle under one of those conditions. Write a paragraph in your ScienceLog to explain your procedure. Be sure to include an explanation of how that condition changes your vehicle's speed.

Science Friction ⓣTEKS

In this experiment, you will investigate three types of friction—static, sliding, and rolling—to determine which is the largest force and which is the smallest force.

Materials

- scissors
- string
- textbook (covered)
- spring scale (force meter)
- 3 or 4 wooden or metal rods

Ask a Question

1. Which type of friction is the largest force—static, sliding, or rolling? Which is the smallest?

Form a Hypothesis

2. In your ScienceLog, write a statement or statements that answer the questions above. Explain your reasoning.

Test the Hypothesis/Collect Data

3. Cut a piece of string, and tie it in a loop that fits in the textbook, as shown below. Hook the string to the spring scale.

4. Practice the next three steps several times before you collect data.

5. Put on your safety goggles. To measure the static friction between the book and the table, pull the spring scale very slowly. Record the largest force on the scale before the book starts to move.

6. After the book begins to move, you can measure the sliding friction. Record the force required to keep the book sliding at a slow, constant speed.

7. Place two or three rods under the book to act as rollers. Make sure the rollers are evenly spaced. Place another roller in front of the book so that the book will roll onto it. Pull the force meter slowly. Measure the force needed to keep the book rolling at a constant speed.

Analyze the Results

8. Which type of friction was the largest? Which was the smallest?

9. Do the results support your hypothesis? If not, how would you revise or retest your hypothesis?

Communicate Results

10. With another group, critique your explanation, including your hypothesis, according to its strengths and weaknesses. Working together, design a way to improve the experiment.

Relating Mass and Weight

Why do objects with more mass weigh more than objects with less mass? All objects have weight on Earth because their mass is affected by Earth's gravitational force. Because the mass of an object on Earth is constant, the relationship between the mass and weight of an object is also constant. You will measure the mass and weight of several objects to verify the relationship between mass and weight on the surface of Earth.

Materials

- metric balance
- small classroom objects
- spring scale (force meter)
- string
- scissors
- graph paper
- computer (optional)

Collect Data

1. Copy the table below into your ScienceLog, or construct a similar one using a computer.

Mass and Weight Measurements		
Object	Mass (g)	Weight (N)

DO NOT WRITE IN BOOK

2. Using the metric balance, find the mass of five or six small classroom objects designated by your teacher. Record the masses in your table.

3. Using the spring scale, find the weight of each object. Record the weights in your table. (You may need to use the string to create a hook with which to hang some objects from the spring scale, as shown at right.)

Analyze the Results

4. Using graph paper or a computer, construct a graph of weight (y-axis) versus mass (x-axis). Draw a line that best fits all your data points.

5. Interpret the information on your graph. Does your graph confirm the relationship between mass and weight on Earth? Explain your answer.

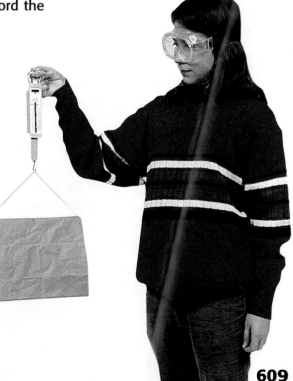

Energy of a Pendulum

A pendulum clock is a compound machine that uses stored energy to do work. A spring stores energy, and with each swing of the pendulum, some of that stored energy is used to move the hands of the clock. In this lab, you will take a close look at the energy conversions that occur as a pendulum swings.

Materials

- piece of string, 1 m long
- 100 g hooked mass
- marker
- meterstick

Collect Data

1. Make a pendulum by tying the string around the hook of the mass. Use the marker and the meterstick to mark points on the string that are 50 cm, 70 cm, and 90 cm away from the mass.

2. Put on your safety goggles. Hold the string at the 50 cm mark. Gently pull the mass to the side, and release it without pushing it. Observe at least 10 swings of the pendulum.

3. In your ScienceLog, record your observations. Be sure to note how fast and how high the pendulum swings.

4. Repeat steps 2 and 3 while holding the string at the 70 cm mark and again while holding the string at the 90 cm mark.

Analyze the Results

5. In your ScienceLog, list similarities and differences in the motion of the pendulum during all three trials.

6. At which point (or points) of the swing was the pendulum moving the slowest? the fastest?

Draw Conclusions

7. In each trial, at which point (or points) of the swing did the pendulum have the greatest potential energy? the smallest potential energy? (Hint: Interpret your answers to question 6.)

8. At which point (or points) of the swing did the pendulum have the greatest kinetic energy? the smallest kinetic energy? Use evidence from the trials to explain your answers.

9. Describe the relationship between the pendulum's potential energy and its kinetic energy on its way down.

DESIGN
YOUR OWN

Eggstremely Fragile ⭐TEKS

When a falling object hits the floor, the law of conservation of energy requires that its energy be transferred to another object or changed into another form of energy. When an unprotected egg hits the ground from a height of 1 m, most of the kinetic energy of the falling egg is transferred to the shell—with messy results. In this lab, you will design a protection system for an egg.

Materials

- raw egg
- empty half-pint milk carton
- assorted materials provided by your teacher

Ask a Question

1. What question are you trying to answer with this experiment?

Form a Hypothesis

2. Examine the materials provided by your teacher. Then formulate a testable hypothesis that is a possible solution to the question you asked in step 1.

Test the Hypothesis

3. Selecting from the materials provided, design a protection system that will prevent the egg from breaking when it is dropped from heights of 1, 2, and 3 m. Keep the following points in mind:

   a. The egg and its protection system must fit inside the closed milk carton. (Note: The milk carton will not be dropped with the egg.)

   b. The protective materials don't have to be soft.

   c. The protective materials can surround the egg or can be attached to the egg at various points.

4. In your ScienceLog, explain why you chose your materials.

5. Perform the three trials at a time and location specified by your teacher. Record your results for each trial in your ScienceLog.

Analyze the Results

6. Did your egg survive all three trials? If not, why did your egg-protection system fail? If your egg survived, what features of your egg-protection system transferred or absorbed the energy?

Draw Conclusions

7. How do egg cartons found in a grocery store protect eggs from mishandling?

DESIGN YOUR OWN

Battery Power ⭐TEKS

Suppose you're on your way to the beach. You've packed everything you need except batteries for your portable stereo. In the store you see a whole section full of different brands of batteries. Each brand claims to last the longest. But which brand will last the longest? In this lab, you'll design your own experiment to find out.

Materials

- 3 batteries or cells, each of a different brand
- watch
- battery-powered electronic device
- graph paper
- computer (optional)

Procedure

1. With your group members, choose three brands of batteries or cells to test. Make a list of the claims made about each brand. Write the list in your ScienceLog. What inferences can you draw based on this data?

2. Plan an investigative procedure to test which brand lasts the longest. Consider the following as you design your experiment:

   a. All brands should be the same voltage.

   b. All brands should be tested in the same electronic device or in identical electronic devices. You will need to choose an electronic device that can be left on safely for long periods of time, such as a flashlight or radio.

   c. It may be helpful to design your experiment so that you turn the device on at the beginning of class and turn it off at the end of class each day. Then, you could count the number of hours that each brand lasts.

3. Discuss your experimental design, including any equipment you need, with your teacher. Your teacher may have suggestions that will help you improve your design.

Conduct an Experiment

4. Once your design is approved, perform your experiment. Remember to record your data and observations in your ScienceLog.

Draw Conclusions

5. Which brand lasted the longest? Do your results back up the manufacturer's claims?

Communicate Your Results

6. Using graph paper or a computer, create a bar graph to evaluate your data, and communicate your conclusions to the class.

Going Further

Compare the cost of each battery with the length of time that it lasted. Is it better to buy more expensive or less expensive batteries? Explain.

DISCOVERY LAB

Stop the Static Electricity! ⭐TEKS

Sometimes your clothes cling together when they come out of the dryer. This annoying problem is caused by static electricity—the buildup of electric charges on an object. In this lab, you'll discover how this buildup occurs.

Materials

- piece of thread, 30 cm long
- plastic-foam packing peanut
- tape
- rubber rod
- wool cloth
- glass rod
- silk cloth

7. Now rub the rubber rod with the wool cloth, and bring the rod near the peanut again. Record your observations.

Ask a Question

1. How do electric charges build up on clothes in a dryer?

Form a Hypothesis

2. Write a statement that answers the question above. Explain your reasoning.

Test the Hypothesis

3. Tie a piece of thread approximately 30 cm in length to a packing peanut. Hang the peanut by the thread from the edge of a table. Tape the thread to the table.

4. Rub the rubber rod with the wool cloth for 10 to 15 seconds. Bring the rod near, but do not touch, the peanut. Observe the peanut, and record your observations. If nothing happens, repeat this step.

5. Touch the peanut with the rubber rod. Pull the rod away from the peanut, and then bring it near again. Record your observations.

6. Repeat steps 4 and 5 with the glass rod and silk cloth.

Analyze the Results

8. What caused the peanut to act different in steps 4 and 5?

9. Did the glass rod have the same effe on the peanut as the rubber rod did? E how the peanut reacted in each ca

10. Was the reaction of the peanut the e in steps 5 and 7? Explain.

Draw Conclusions

11. Based on your results, was your othesis correct? Explain your answer, an rite a new statement if necessary.

Communicate Results

12. Explain why the rubber rod a the glass rod affected the peanut.

Going Further

Do some research to find out ow a dryer sheet helps stop the buildup of electric charges in the dryer.

Potato Power

Have you ever wanted to look inside a D cell from a flashlight or an AA cell from a portable radio? All cells include the same basic components, as shown below. There is a metal "bucket," some electrolyte (a paste), and a rod of some other metal (or solid) in the middle. Even though the construction is simple, companies that manufacture cells are always trying to make a product with the highest voltage possible from the least expensive materials. Sometimes they try different pastes, and sometimes they try different combinations of metals. In this lab, you will make your own cell. Using inexpensive materials, including a potato, you will try to produce the highest voltage you can.

Materials

- labeled metal strips
- potato
- metric ruler
- voltmeter

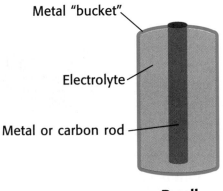

Metal "bucket"

Electrolyte

Metal or carbon rod

D cell

Procedure

1. Choose two metal strips. Carefully push one of the strips into the potato at least 2 cm deep. Insert the second strip the same way, and measure how far apart the two strips are. (If one of your metal strips is too soft to push into the potato, push a harder strip in first, remove it, and then push the soft strip into the slit.) In your ScienceLog, record the two metals you have used and the distance between the strips.
   Caution: The strips of metal may have sharp edges.

2. Connect the voltmeter to the two strips, and measure and record the voltage.

3. Move one of the strips closer to or farther from the other. Measure the new distance and voltage. Record your results.

4. Using different combinations of metal strips and distances, repeat steps 1 through 3 until you find the combination that produces the highest voltage.

Analysis

5. Which combination of metals and distance produced the highest voltage?

6. If you change only the distance but use the same metal strips, what is the effect on the voltage?

7. One of the metal strips tends to lose electrons, while the other metal strip tends to gain electrons. Construct a reasonable explanation for what would happen if you used two strips of the same metal.

Elephant-Sized Amoebas? ⭐TEKS

Why can't amoebas grow to be as large as elephants? An amoeba is a single-celled organism. Amoebas, like most cells, are microscopic. If an amoeba could grow to the size of a quarter, it would starve to death. To understand how this can be true, build a model of a cell and see for yourself.

Materials

- cubic cell patterns
- pieces of heavy paper or poster board
- scissors
- transparent tape
- fine sand
- scale or balance
- calculator (optional)

Procedure

1. Use heavy paper to make four cube-shaped cell models from the patterns supplied by your teacher. Cut out each cell model, fold the sides to make a cube, and tape the tabs on the sides. The smallest cell model has sides that are one unit long. The next-larger cell has sides of two units. The next cell has sides of three units, and the largest cell has sides of four units. These paper models represent the cell membrane, the part of a cell's exterior through which food and waste pass.

2. In your ScienceLog, copy the data table at right. Use each formula to calculate the data about your cell models. You may wish to use a calculator. A key to the formula symbols can be found on the next page. Record your calculations in the table. Calculations for the smallest cell have been done for you.

Two-unit cell model

Data Table for Measurements				
Length of side	Area of one side ($A = S \times S$)	Total surface area of cube cell ($TA = S \times S \times 6$)	Volume of cube cell ($V = S \times S \times S$)	Mass of cube cell
1	1 unit^2	6 unit^2	1 unit^3	
2				
3				
4				

DO NOT WRITE IN BOOK

3. Carefully fill each model with fine sand until the sand is level with the top edge. Use a scale or a balance to find the mass of the filled models. What does the sand in your model represent?

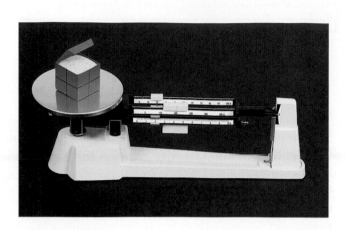

4. Record the mass of each cell model in the table. (Always remember to use the appropriate mass unit.)

5. In your ScienceLog, make a data table like the one below. You may decide to use a computer to construct your table.

Data Table for Ratios		
Length of side	Ratio of total surface area to volume	Ratio of total surface area to mass
1		
2		
3		
4		

DO NOT WRITE IN BOOK

6. Use the data from your data table for measurements to find the ratios for each of your cell models. Fill in the data table for ratios for each of the cell models.

Analysis

7. As a cell grows larger, does the ratio of total surface area to volume increase, decrease, or stay the same?

8. Which is better able to supply food to all the cytoplasm of the cell—the cell membrane of a small cell or the cell membrane of a large cell? Explain your answer.

9. As a cell grows larger, does the total surface area to mass ratio increase, decrease, or stay the same?

10. Is the cell membrane of a cell with high mass or the cell membrane of a cell with low mass better able to feed all the cytoplasm of the cell? You may explain your conclusions in a presentation to the class, or you may choose to write a report and illustrate it with drawings of your models.

Key to Formula Symbols

S = the length of one side
A = area
V = volume
TA = total area

Survival of the Chocolates ⭐TEKS

Imagine a world populated with candy, and hold that delicious thought for just a moment. Try to apply the idea of natural selection to a population of candy-coated chocolates. According to the theory of natural selection, individuals who have favorable adaptations are more likely to survive. In the "species" of candy that you will study in this experiment, shell strength is an adaptive advantage. Plan an experiment to find out which candy characteristics correspond to shell (candy coating) strength.

Materials

- small candy-coated chocolates in a variety of colors
- other materials as needed, according to the design of your experiment

Form a Hypothesis

1. Form a hypothesis and make a prediction. For example, if you chose to study candy color, your prediction might look like this: If the _____?_____ colored shell is the strongest, then fewer of the candies with this color of shell will _____?_____ when _____?_____.

Test Your Hypothesis

2. Design a procedure to determine which candy is best suited to survive by not "cracking under pressure." In your plan, be sure to include materials and tools you may need to complete this procedure. Check your experimental design with your teacher before you begin. Your teacher will supply the candy and will assist you in gathering materials and tools.

3. Record your results in a data table you have designed in your ScienceLog or on a computer. Be sure to organize your data in a clear and understandable way.

Analyze the Results

4. Write a report that describes your experiment. Explain how your data either support or do not support your hypothesis. Discuss your conclusions. Include possible errors and ways to improve your procedure.

Going Further

Can you think of another characteristic of these candies that can be tested to determine which candy is best adapted to survive? Explain your choice.

Weepy Weeds

You are trying to find a way to drain an area that is flooded with water polluted with fertilizer. You know that a plant releases water through the stomata in its leaves. As water evaporates from the leaves, more water is pulled up from the roots through the stem and into the leaves. By this process, called *transpiration,* water and nutrients are pulled into the plant from the soil. About 90 percent of the water a plant takes up through its roots is released into the atmosphere as water vapor through transpiration. Your idea is to add plants to the flooded area that will transpire the water and take up the fertilizer in their roots.

How much water can a plant take up and release in a certain period of time? In this activity, you will observe transpiration and determine one stem's rate of transpiration.

Materials

- 2 test tubes
- water
- test-tube rack
- *Coleus* or other plant stem cutting
- glass-marking pen
- metric ruler
- clock
- graph paper
- protective gloves

Procedure

1. In your ScienceLog or on a computer, make a data table similar to the one below for recording your measurements.

Height of Water in Test Tubes		
Time	Test tube with plant	Test tube without plant
Initial		
After 10 min		
After 20 min		
After 30 min		
After 40 min		
Overnight		

DO NOT WRITE IN BOOK

2. Put on your gloves and safety goggles. Fill each test tube approximately three-fourths full of water. Place both test tubes in a test-tube rack.

3. Place the plant stem so that it stands upright in one of the test tubes. Your test tubes should look like the ones in the photograph at right.

4. Use the glass-marking pen to mark the water level in each of the test tubes. Be sure you have the plant stem in place in its test tube before you mark the water level. Why is this necessary?

5. Measure the height of the water in each test tube. Be sure to hold the test tube level, and measure from the waterline to the bottom of the curve at the bottom of the test tube. Record these measurements on the row labeled "Initial."

6. Wait 10 minutes, and measure the height of the water in each test tube again. Record these measurements in your data table.

7. Repeat step 6 three more times. Record your measurements each time.

8. Wait 24 hours, and measure the height of the water in each test tube. Record these measurements in your data table.

9. In your ScienceLog or on a computer, construct a graph similar to the one at right. Plot the data from your data table. Draw a line for each test tube. Use a different color for each line, and make a key below your graph.

10. Calculate the rate of transpiration for your plant by using the following operations:

Test tube with plant:
   initial height
   — overnight height
   difference in height of water (**A**)

Test tube without plant:
   initial height
   — overnight height
   difference in height of water (**B**)

Water height difference due to transpiration:
   difference **A**
   — difference **B**
   water lost because of transpiration (in millimeters) in 24 hours

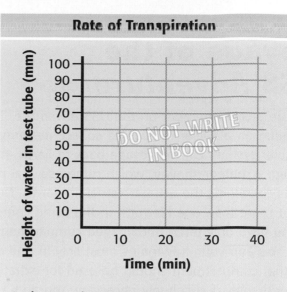

Rate of Transpiration

red—test tube without plant
blue—test tube with plant

Analysis

11. What was the purpose of the test tube that held only water?

12. What caused the water to go down in the test tube containing the plant stem? Did the same thing happen in the test tube with water only? Explain your answer.

13. What was the transpiration rate per day?

14. Using your graph to examine your data, compare the rate of transpiration with the rate of evaporation alone.

15. Prepare a presentation of your experiment for your class. Use your data tables, graphs, and calculations as visual aids.

Going Further

Does the surface area affect the evaporation rate? Design an experiment that compares the evaporation rate of water in a test tube with the evaporation rate of the same volume of water in a Petri dish. Based on your results, do you think that the size of a leaf affects the transpiration rate?

Voyage of the USS *Adventure* ★TEKS

You are a crew member on the USS *Adventure*. The *Adventure* has been on a 5-year mission to collect life-forms from outside the solar system. On the voyage back to Earth, your ship went through a meteor shower, which ruined several of the compartments containing the extraterrestrial life-forms. Now it is necessary to put more than one life-form in the same compartment.

You have only three undamaged compartments in your starship. You and your crewmates must stay in one compartment, and that compartment should be used for extraterrestrial life-forms only if absolutely necessary. You and your crewmates must decide which of the life-forms could be placed together. The crew thinks that similar life-forms will have similar needs. You can use only observable characteristics to group the life-forms.

Life-form 1

Life-form 2

Life-form 3

Life-form 4

Procedure — TRY at HOME

1. In your ScienceLog or on a computer, make a data table similar to the one below. Label each column with as many characteristics of the various life-forms as possible. Leave enough space in each square to write your observations. The life-forms are pictured on this page.

Life-form Characteristics				
	Color	Shape	Legs	Eyes
Life-form 1				
Life-form 2				
Life-form 3				
Life-form 4				

DO NOT WRITE IN BOOK

2. Describe each characteristic as completely as you can. Based on your observations, determine which of the life-forms are most alike.

Life-form 5

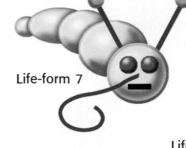

Life-form 7

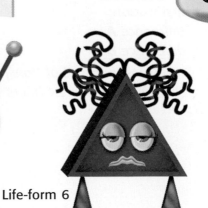

Life-form 6

3. In your ScienceLog or on a computer, make a data table like the one below. Fill in the table according to the decisions you made in step 2. State your reasons for the way you have grouped your life-forms.

Life-form Room Assignments		
Compartment	Life-forms	Reasons
1		
2		
3		

4. The USS *Adventure* has to make one more stop before returning home. On planet X437 you discover the most interesting life-form ever found outside of Earth—the CC9, shown at right. Make a decision, based on your previous grouping of life-forms, about whether you can safely include CC9 in one of the compartments for the trip to Earth.

Analysis

5. Describe the life-forms in compartment 1. How are they similar? How are they different?

6. Describe the life-forms in compartment 2. How are they similar? How do they differ from the life-forms in compartment 1?

7. Are there any life-forms in compartment 3? If so, describe their similarities. In which compartment will you and your crewmates remain for the journey home?

8. Are you able to safely transport life-form CC9 back to Earth? Why or why not? If you are able to include CC9, in which compartment will it be placed? How did you decide?

CC9

Going Further

In 1831, Charles Darwin sailed from England on a ship called the HMS *Beagle.* You have studied the finches that Darwin observed on the Galápagos Islands. What were some of the other unusual organisms he found there? For example, find out about the Galápagos tortoise.

The Cricket Caper ⭐TEKS

Insects are a special class of invertebrates that includes more than 750,000 known species. Insects may be the most successful group of animals on Earth. In this activity, you will observe a cricket's structure and the simple adaptive behaviors that help make it so successful. Remember, you will be handling a living animal that deserves to be treated with care.

Materials

- 2 crickets
- 600 mL beakers (2)
- plastic wrap
- apple
- magnifying lens (optional)
- masking tape
- aluminum foil
- lamp
- clock or watch with a second hand
- 2 sealable plastic bags
- crushed ice
- hot tap water

Procedure

1. Place a cricket in a clean 600 mL beaker, and quickly cover the beaker with plastic wrap. The supply of oxygen in the container is enough for the cricket to breathe while you complete your work.

2. While the cricket is getting used to the container, make a data table similar to the one below in your ScienceLog. Be sure to allow enough space to write your descriptions.

Cricket Body Structures	
Number	**Description**
Body segments	
Antennae	
Eyes	
Wings	

DO NOT WRITE IN BOOK

3. Without making much movement, begin to examine the cricket. Fill in your data table with your observations of the cricket's structure.

4. Place a small piece of apple in the beaker. Set the beaker on a table. Sit quietly for several minutes and observe the cricket. Any movement may cause the cricket to stop what it is doing. Record your observations in your ScienceLog.

5. Remove the plastic wrap from the beaker, remove the apple, and quickly attach a second beaker. Use masking tape to join the two beakers together at the mouths. Handle the beakers carefully. Remember, there is a living animal inside.

6. Wrap one of the joined beakers with aluminum foil.

7. If the cricket is hiding under the aluminum foil, gently tap the sides of the beaker until the cricket is exposed. Lay the joined beakers on their sides, and shine a lamp on the uncovered side. Record the cricket's location.

8. Record the cricket's location after 5 minutes. Without disturbing the cricket, carefully move the aluminum foil to the other beaker. After 5 minutes, record the cricket's location. Repeat this process one more time to see if you get the same result.

9. Fill a sealable plastic bag halfway with crushed ice. Fill another bag halfway with hot tap water. Seal both bags, and arrange them side by side on the table.

10. Remove the aluminum foil from the beakers. Gently rock the joined beakers from side to side until the cricket is in the center. Place the beakers on the plastic bags, as shown below.

11. Observe the cricket's behavior for 5 minutes. Record your observations in your ScienceLog.

12. Set the beakers on one end for several minutes to allow them to return to room temperature. Repeat steps 10–12 three times. (Why do you think it is necessary to allow the beakers to return to room temperature each time?)

13. Set the beakers on one end. Carefully remove the masking tape, and separate the beakers. Quickly replace the plastic wrap over the beaker containing the cricket. Allow your cricket to rest while you make two data tables similar to the tables at right in your ScienceLog or on a computer.

14. Observe the cricket's movement in the beaker every 15 seconds for 3 minutes. Fill in the "Cricket (alone)" data table using the following codes: 0 = no movement, 1 = slight movement, and 2 = rapid movement.

15. Obtain a second cricket from your teacher, and place this cricket in the container with the first cricket. Every 15 seconds, record the movement of each cricket in the "Cricket A and Cricket B" data table. Use the codes given in step 14.

Analysis

16. Describe the feeding behavior of crickets. Are they lappers, suckers, or chewers?

17. Do crickets prefer light or darkness? Explain.

18. From your observations, what can you infer about a cricket's temperature preferences?

19. Based on your observations of cricket A and cricket B, what general conclusions can you draw about the social behavior of crickets?

Going Further

Make a third data table titled "Cricket and Another Species of Insect." Introduce another insect, such as a grasshopper, into the beaker. Record your observations for 3 minutes. Write a short summary of the cricket's reaction to another species.

Cricket (alone)	
15 s	
30 s	
45 s	
60 s	
75 s	
90 s	DO NOT WRITE IN BOOK
105 s	
120 s	
135 s	
150 s	
165 s	
180 s	

Cricket A and Cricket B		
	A	B
15 s		
30 s		
45 s		
60 s		
75 s	DO NOT WRITE IN BOOK	
90 s		
105 s		
120 s		
135 s		
150 s		
165 s		
180 s		

A Prince of a Frog ⭐TEKS

Imagine that you are a scientist interested in amphibians. You have heard in the news about amphibians disappearing all over the world. What a great loss it will be to the environment if all amphibians become extinct! Your job is to learn as much as possible about how frogs normally behave so that you can act as a resource for other scientists who are studying the problem. In this activity, you will observe a normal frog in a dry container and in water.

Materials

- live frog in a dry container
- live crickets or other insects
- 600 mL beaker
- container half full of dechlorinated water
- large rock (optional)
- protective gloves

Procedure

1. Put on your safety goggles, gloves, and apron.

2. In your ScienceLog or on a computer, make a table, similar to the one below, in which to organize your observations of the frog in this investigation.

Observations of a Live Frog	
Characteristic	**Observation**
Breathing	
Eyes	
Legs	
Response to food	
Skin texture	
Swimming behavior	
Skin coloration	

DO NOT WRITE IN BOOK

3. Observe a live frog in a dry container. Draw the frog in your ScienceLog. Label the eyes, nostrils, front legs, and hind legs.

4. Watch the movements of the frog as it breathes air with its lungs. Write a description of the frog's breathing in your ScienceLog.

5. Look closely at the frog's eyes, and note their location. Examine the upper and lower eyelids as well as the transparent third eyelid. Which of these three eyelids actually moves over the eye?

6. Study the frog's legs. Note in your data table the difference between the front and hind legs.

7. Place a live insect, such as a cricket, in the container. Observe and record how the frog reacts.

8. Carefully pick up the frog, and examine its skin. How does it feel?
   Caution: Remember that a frog is a living thing and deserves to be handled gently and with respect.

9. Place a 600 mL beaker in the container. Place the frog in the beaker. Cover the beaker with your hand, and carry it to a container of dechlorinated water. Tilt the beaker, and gently submerge it in the water until the frog swims out of the beaker.

10. Watch the frog float and swim in the water. How does the frog use its legs to swim? Notice the position of the frog's head.

11. As the frog swims, bend down and look up into the water so that you can see the underside of the frog. Then look down on the frog from above. Compare the color on the top and underside of the frog. Record your observations in your data table.

Analysis

12. From the position of the frog's eyes, what can you infer about the frog's field of vision? How might the position of the frog's eyes benefit the frog while it is swimming?

13. How can a frog "breathe" while it is swimming in water?

14. How are the hind legs of a frog adapted for life on land and in water?

15. What differences did you notice in coloration on the frog's top side and underside? What advantage might these color differences provide?

16. How does the frog eat? What senses are involved in helping the frog catch its prey?

Going Further
Observe another type of amphibian, such as a salamander. How do the adaptations of other types of amphibians compare with those of the frog you observed in this investigation?

Wanted: Mammals on Mars ⭐TEKS

The year is 2256. There have been colonies on Mars for almost 50 years. Martian water is scarce but available, and temperatures are still extreme but livable. The Martian planet has slowly developed an atmosphere that humans can breathe because of the efforts of many scientists during the last 200 years. The Interplanetary Commission has announced that mammals from several different habitats on Earth should be sent to Mars. There the mammals will be housed in a zoo so that they can become accustomed to the climate before they are released in the wild.

Your job is to prepare for the Interplanetary Commission a presentation that describes at least three mammals that you think might be able to survive in a zoo on Mars. Select one mammal from a water environment, one mammal from a land environment, and one mammal that lives in the air part of the time.

Materials

- colored markers, crayons, pens, or similar drawing equipment
- poster paper, rolls of newsprint, or other drawing paper
- other materials as needed

TRY at HOME

Procedure

1. Research in the library or on the Internet to obtain information about the Martian environment as it is today. How might an atmosphere change the environment?

2. Research in the library or on the Internet to learn about different species of mammals and their environments on Earth. Use this information to select mammals that you think might be able to live on Mars.

3. Prepare your presentation for the Interplanetary Commission. Your presentation can be a poster, a mural, a diorama, a computer presentation, or any other format that you choose. Make sure your format is approved by your teacher.

Analysis

4. Name and describe the mammals you chose. Explain why you think your choice of mammals would be the right one for a zoo on Mars.

5. Describe what additions or changes should be made at the zoo to accommodate each of your mammals.

000783

CAUTION UNDER CONSTRUCTION

Orient Yourself! ⭐TEKS

In orienteering events, participants use maps and compasses to find their way along a course. Each participant must reach several control points. The object is to reach each control point and then the finish line. Orienteering events are often timed competitions. To find the fastest route through the course, the participants must read the map and use their compass correctly. Being the fastest runner does not necessarily guarantee finishing first. You also must choose the most direct route to follow. In this field activity, you will learn how to use a compass to orient yourself.

Materials

- magnetic compass
- course map
- ruler
- 2 colored pencils or markers

Procedure

1. Together as a class, go outside to the orienteering course your teacher has made.

2. Hold your compass flat in your hand. Turn the compass until the N is pointing straight in front of you. (The colored end of the needle in your compass will always point north.) Turn your body until the colored end of the needle lines up with the N on your compass. You are now facing north.

3. Regardless of which direction you want to face, you should always align the colored end of the needle with the N on your compass. If you are facing south, the colored end of the needle will be pointing directly toward your body. When the N is aligned with the colored end of the needle, the S will be directly in front of you, and you will be facing south.

4. Use your compass to face east. Align the colored end of the needle with the N. Where is the E? Turn to face that direction. When the colored end of the needle and the N are aligned and the E is directly in front of you, you are facing east.

5. In an orienteering competition, you will need to know how to determine which direction you are traveling. Now, face any direction you choose.

6. Do not move, but rotate the compass to align the colored end of the needle on your compass with the N. What direction are you facing? You are probably not facing directly north, south, east, or west. If you are facing between north and west, you are facing northwest. If you are facing between north and east, you are facing northeast.

7. Find a partner or partners to follow the course your teacher has made. Get a copy of the course map from your teacher. It will show several control points. You must stop at each one. You will need to follow this map to find your way through the course. Find and stand at the starting point.

8. Face the next control point on your map. Rotate your compass to align the colored end of the needle on your compass with the N. What direction are you facing?

9. Use the ruler to draw a line between the two control points on your map. Write the direction between the starting point and the next control point on your map.

10. Walk toward the control point. You might need to go around obstacles such as a fence or building. Use the map to find the easiest way around.
Caution: Keep your eyes on the horizon, not on your compass.

11. Record the color or code word you find at the control point next to the control point symbol on your map.

12. Repeat steps 8–11 for each control point. Follow the points in order as they are labeled. For example, determine the direction from control point 1 to control point 2. Be sure to include the direction between the final control point and the starting point.

Analysis

13. The object of an orienteering competition is to arrive at the finish line first. The maps provided at these events do not instruct the participants to follow a specific path. In one form of orienteering, called "score orienteering," competitors may find the control points in any order. Look at your map. If this course were used for a score-orienteering competition, would you change your route? Explain.

14. If there is time, follow the map again. This time, use your own path to find the control points. Draw this path and the directions on your map in a different color. Do you believe this route was faster? Why?

Going Further
Do some research to find out about orienteering events in your area. The Internet and local newspapers may be good sources for the information. Are there any events that you would like to attend?

Using Scientific Methods

Topographic Tuber ⊛TEKS

Imagine that you live on top of a tall mountain and often look down on the lake below. Every summer, an island appears. You call it Sometimes Island because it goes away again during heavy fall rains. This summer you begin to wonder if you could make a topographic map of Sometimes Island. You don't have fancy equipment to make the map, but you have an idea. What would happen if you placed a meterstick with the 0 m mark at the water level in the summer? Then as the expected fall rains come, you could draw the island from above as the water rises. Would this idea really work?

Materials

- clear plastic storage container with transparent lid
- transparency marker
- metric ruler
- potato, cut in half
- water
- tracing paper

Form a Hypothesis

1. Formulate a hypothesis based on the following question: How do I make a topographic map?

Conduct an Experiment

2. Place a mark at the storage container's base. Label this mark "0 cm" with a transparency marker.

3. Measure and mark 1 cm increments up the side of the container until you reach the top of the container. Label these marks "1 cm," "2 cm," "3 cm," and so on.

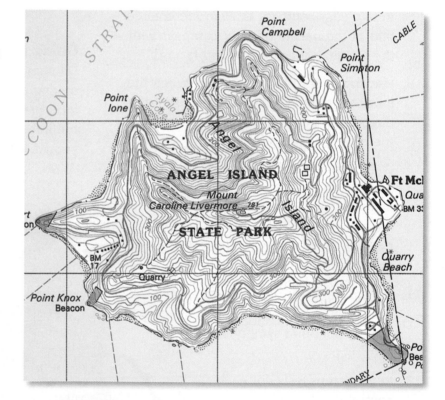

4. The scale for your map will be 1 cm = 10 m. Draw a line 2 cm long in the bottom right-hand corner of the lid. Place hash marks at 0 cm, 1 cm, and 2 cm. Label these marks "0 m," "10 m,"and "20 m."

5. Place the potato flat side down in the center of the container.

6. Place the lid on the container, and seal it.

7. Viewing the potato from above, use the transparency marker to trace the outline of the potato where it rests on the bottom of the container. The floor of the container corresponds to the summer water level in the lake.

8. Label this contour "0 m." (For this activity, assume that the water level in the lake during the summer is the same as sea level.)

9. Pour water into the container until it reaches the line labeled "1 cm."

10. Again place the lid on the container, and seal it. Part of the potato will be sticking out above the water. Viewing the potato from above, trace the part of the potato that touches the top of the water.

11. Label the elevation of the contour line you drew in step 10. According to the scale, the elevation is 10 m.

12. Remove the lid. Carefully pour water into the container until it reaches the line labeled "2 cm."

13. Place the lid on the container, and seal it. Viewing the potato from above, trace the part of the potato that touches the top of the water at this level.

14. Use the scale to calculate the elevation of this line. Label the elevation on your drawing.

15. Repeat steps 12–14, adding 1 cm to the depth of the water each time. Stop when the potato is completely covered.

16. Remove the lid, and set it on a tabletop. Place tracing paper on top of the lid. Trace the contours from the lid onto the paper. Label the elevation of each contour line. Congratulations! You have just made a topographic map!

Analyze the Results

17. What is the contour interval of this topographic map?

18. By looking at the contour lines, how can you tell which parts of the potato are steeper?

19. What is the elevation of the highest point on your map?

Draw Conclusions

20. Do all topographic maps have an elevation contour line of 0 m as a starting point? How would this affect a topographic map of Sometimes Island? Explain your answer.

21. Does this method of making a topographic map support your hypothesis? Would this method of measuring elevation be an effective way to make a topographic map of an actual area on Earth's surface? Why or why not?

Going Further

Place all of the potatoes on a table or desk at the front of the room. Your teacher will mix up the potatoes as you trade topographic maps with another group. By reading the topographic map you just received, can you pick out the matching potato?

MAKING MODELS

Gone with the Wind (★)TEKS

Pilots at the Fly Away Airport need your help—fast! Last night, lightning destroyed the orange windsock. This windsock helped pilots measure which direction the wind was blowing. But now the windsock is gone with the wind, and an incoming airplane needs to land. The pilot must know what direction the wind is blowing and is counting on you to make a device that can measure wind direction.

Materials

- paper plate
- drawing compass
- metric ruler
- protractor
- index card
- scissors
- stapler
- straight plastic straw
- sharpened pencil
- thumbtack or pushpin
- magnetic compass
- small rock

Form a Hypothesis

1. Formulate a hypothesis based on the following question: How can I measure wind direction?

Conduct an Experiment

2. Find the center of the plate by tracing around its edge with a drawing compass. The pointed end of the compass should poke a small hole in the center of the plate.

3. Use a ruler to draw a line across the center of the plate.

4. Use a protractor to help you draw a second line through the center of the plate. This new line should be at a 90° angle to the line you drew in step 3.

5. Moving clockwise, label each line "N," "E," "S," and "W".

6. Use a protractor to help you draw two more lines through the center of the plate. These lines should be at a 45° angle to the lines you drew in steps 3 and 4.

7. Moving clockwise from *N*, label these new lines "NE," "SE," "SW," and "NW". The plate now resembles the face of a magnetic compass. This plate will be the base of your wind-direction indicator. It will help you read the direction of the wind at a glance.

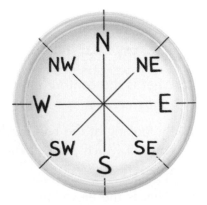

8. Measure and mark a 5 × 5 cm square on an index card. Cut the square out of the card. Fold the square in half to form a triangle.

9. Staple an open edge of the triangle to the straw so that one point of the triangle touches the end of the straw.

10. Hold the pencil at a 90° angle to the straw. The eraser should touch the balance point of the straw. Push a thumbtack or pushpin through the straw and into the eraser. The straw should spin without falling off.

11. Find a suitable area outside to measure the wind direction. The area should be clear of trees and buildings.

12. Press the sharpened end of the pencil through the center hole of the plate and into the ground. The labels on your paper plate should be facing the sky, as shown below.

13. Use a compass to find magnetic north. Rotate the plate so that the *N* on the plate points north. Place a small rock on top of the plate so that it does not turn.

14. You have just constructed a wind vane. Watch the straw as it rotates. The triangle will point in the direction the wind is blowing.

Analyze the Results

15. From what direction is the wind coming?

16. In what direction is the wind blowing?

Draw Conclusions

17. Would this wind vane be an effective way for pilots to measure wind direction? Why or why not?

18. What improvements would you suggest to Fly Away Airport to measure wind direction more accurately?

Going Further

Use your wind vane to measure and record wind direction for several days. What changes in wind direction occur as a front approaches? as a front passes?

Review magnetic declination in the chapter titled "Maps as Models of the Earth." How might magnetic declination affect your design for a tool to measure wind direction?

Go Fly a Bike! ⭐TEKS

Your friend Daniel just invented a bicycle that can fly! The trouble is, the bike can fly only when the wind speed is between 3 m/s and 10 m/s. If the wind is not blowing hard enough, the bike won't get enough lift to rise into the air, and if the wind is blowing too hard, the bike is difficult to control. Daniel needs to know if he can fly his bike today. Can you build a device that can estimate how fast the wind is blowing?

Form a Hypothesis

1. Formulate a hypothesis based on the following question: How can I construct a device to measure wind speed?

Construct an Anemometer

2. Cut off the rolled edges of all five paper cups. This will make them lighter and easier to spin.

3. Measure and place four equally spaced markings 1 cm below the rim of one of the paper cups.

4. Use the hole punch to punch a hole at each mark so that the cup has four equally spaced holes. Use the sharp pencil to carefully punch a hole in the center of the bottom of the cup.

5. Push a straw through two opposite holes in the side of the cup. This cup will be your center cup.

6. Repeat step 5 for the other two holes. The straws should form an X.

7. Measure 3 cm from the bottom of the remaining paper cups, and mark each spot with a dot.

8. At each dot, punch a hole in the paper cups with the hole punch.

9. Color the outside of one of the four cups.

10. Slide a cup on one of the straws attached to the center cup by pushing the straw through the punched hole. Rotate the cup so that the bottom faces to the right.

Materials

- scissors
- 5 small paper cups
- metric ruler
- hole punch
- 2 straight plastic straws
- colored marker
- small stapler
- thumbtack
- sharp pencil with an eraser
- modeling clay
- masking tape
- watch or clock that indicates seconds

11. Fold the end of the straw, and staple it to the inside of the cup directly across from the hole.

12. Repeat steps 10–11 for each of the remaining cups.

13. Push the tack through the intersection of the two straws.

14. Push the eraser end of a pencil through the bottom hole in the center cup. Push the tack as far as it will go into the end of the eraser.

15. Push the sharpened end of the pencil into some modeling clay to form a base. This base will allow the device to stand up without being knocked over, as shown at right.

16. Blow into the cups so that they spin. Adjust the tack so that the cups can freely spin without wobbling or falling apart. Congratulations! You have just constructed an anemometer.

Conduct an Experiment

17. Find a suitable area outside to place the anemometer vertically on a surface away from objects that would obstruct the wind, such as buildings and trees.

18. Use masking tape to mark the surface at the base of the anemometer. Label the tape "starting point."

19. Hold the colored cup over the starting point while your partner holds the watch.

20. Release the colored cup. At the same time, your partner should look at the watch or clock. As the cups spin, count the number of times the colored cup crosses the starting point in 10 seconds.

Analyze the Results

21. How many times did the colored cup cross the starting point in 10 seconds?

22. Divide your answer in step 21 by 10 to get the number of revolutions in 1 second.

23. Measure the diameter of your anemometer (the distance between the outside edges of two opposite cups) in centimeters. Multiply this number by 3.14 to get the circumference of the circle made by the cups of your anemometer.

24. Multiply your answer from step 23 by the number of revolutions per second (step 22). Divide that answer by 100 to get wind speed in meters per second.

25. Compare your results with those of your classmates. Did you get the same result? What could account for any slight differences in your results?

Draw Conclusions

26. Does this method of making a device to measure wind speed support your hypothesis?

27. Could Daniel fly his bicycle today? Why or why not? Communicate your conclusions to the class, and demonstrate their validity by showing your calculations.

MAKING MODELS

Why Do They Wander?

Before the discoveries of Nicholas Copernicus in the early 1500s, most people thought that the planets and the sun revolved around the Earth and that the Earth was the center of the solar system. But Copernicus observed that the sun is the center of the solar system and that all the planets, including Earth, revolve around the sun. He also explained a puzzling aspect of the movement of planets across the night sky.

If you watch a planet every night for several months, you'll notice that it appears to "wander" among the stars. While the stars remain in fixed positions relative to each other, the planets appear to move independently of the stars. First Mars travels to the left, then it goes back to the right a little, and finally it reverses direction and travels again to the left. No wonder the early Greeks called the planets wanderers!

In this lab, you will make your own model of part of the solar system to find out how Copernicus's model of the solar system explained this zigzag motion of the planets.

Materials

- drawing compass
- white paper
- metric ruler
- colored pencils

Form a Hypothesis

1. Formulate a hypothesis based on the following question: Why do the planets appear to move back and forth in the Earth's night sky?

Conduct an Experiment

2. Use the compass to draw on the paper a circle with a diameter of 9 cm. This circle will represent the orbit of the Earth around the sun. (Note: The orbits of the planets are actually slightly elliptical, but circles will work for this activity.)

3. Using the same center point, draw a circle with a diameter of 12 cm. This circle will represent the orbit of Mars.

4. Using a blue pencil, draw three parallel lines in a diagonal across one end of your paper, as shown at right. These lines will help you plot the path Mars appears to travel in Earth's night sky. Turn your paper so that the diagonal lines are at the top of the page.

5. Place 11 dots on your Earth orbit, as shown at right, and number them 1 through 11. These dots will represent Earth's position from month to month.

6. Now place 11 dots along the top of your Mars orbit, as shown at right. Number the dots as shown. These dots will represent the position of Mars at the same time intervals. Notice that Mars travels slower than Earth.

7. Use a green line to connect the first dot on Earth's orbit to the first dot on Mars's orbit, and extend the line all the way to the first diagonal line at the top of your paper. Place a green dot where this green line meets the first blue diagonal line, and label the green dot "1".

8. Now connect the second dot on Earth's orbit to the second dot on Mars's orbit, and extend the line all the way to the first diagonal at the top of your paper. Place a green dot where this line meets the first blue diagonal line, and label this dot "2".

9. Continue drawing green lines from Earth's orbit through Mars's orbit and finally to the blue diagonal lines. Pay attention to the pattern of dots you are adding to the diagonal lines. When the direction of the dots changes, extend the green line to the next diagonal and add the dots to that line instead.

10. When you are finished adding green lines, draw a red line to connect all the dots on the blue diagonal lines in the order you drew them.

Analyze the Results

11. What do the green lines connecting points along Earth's orbit and Mars's orbit represent?

12. What does the red line connecting the dots along the diagonal lines look like? How can you explain this?

Draw Conclusions

13. What does this demonstration show about the motion of Mars?

14. Why do planets appear to move back and forth across the sky?

15. Do your observations support your hypothesis? Explain your answer.

16. Were the Greeks justified in calling the planets wanderers? Explain your answer.

Water Rockets Save the Day! ⭐TEKS

Imagine that for the big Fourth of July celebration, you and your friends had planned a full day of swimming, volleyball, and fireworks at the lake. You've just learned, however, that the city passed a law that bans all fireworks within city limits. But you are not one to give up so easily on having fun. Last year at summer camp you learned how to build water rockets. And you kept the launcher in your garage all this time! With a little bit of creativity, you and your friends are going to celebrate with a splash!

Materials

- 2 L soda bottle with cap
- foam board
- modeling clay
- duct tape
- scissors
- water
- 5 gal bucket
- rocket launcher
- watch or clock that indicates seconds

Form a Hypothesis

1. Formulate a hypothesis based on the following question: How can I use water and a soda bottle to build a rocket?

Conduct an Experiment

2. Decide how you want your rocket to look. Draw a sketch in your ScienceLog.

3. Using only the materials listed, decide how to build your rocket. Describe your design in your ScienceLog. Keep in mind that you will need to leave the opening of your bottle clear. It will be placed over a rubber stopper on the rocket launcher.

4. Fins are often used to stabilize rockets. Do you want fins on your water rocket? Decide on the best shape for the fins, and then decide how many fins your rocket needs. Use the foam board to construct the fins.

5. Your rocket must be heavy enough to fly along a controlled pathway. Consider using clay in the body of your rocket to provide some additional weight and stability.

6. Pour water into your rocket until it is one-third to one-half full.

7. Your teacher will provide the launcher and will assist you during blastoff. Attach your rocket to the launcher by placing its opening on the rubber stopper.

8. When the rocket is in place, clear the immediate area and begin pumping air into your rocket. Watch the pump gauge, and take note of how much pressure is needed for liftoff.
Caution: Be sure to step back from the launch site. You should be several meters away from the bottle when you launch it.

9. Use the watch to time your rocket's flight. (How long was your rocket in the air?)

10. Make small changes in your rocket design that you think will improve the rocket's performance. Consider using different amounts of water and clay or experimenting with different fins. You may also want to compare your design with those of your classmates.

Analyze the Results

11. How did your rocket perform? If you used fins, do you think they helped your flight? Explain your answer.

12. What do you think propelled your rocket? Use Newton's third law of motion to justify your answer.

13. How did the amount of water in your rocket affect the launch?

Draw Conclusions

14. What modifications made your rocket fly for the longest time? How did the design help the rockets fly so far?

15. Which group's rockets were the most stable? How did the design help the rockets fly straight?

16. How can you improve your design to make your rocket perform even better?

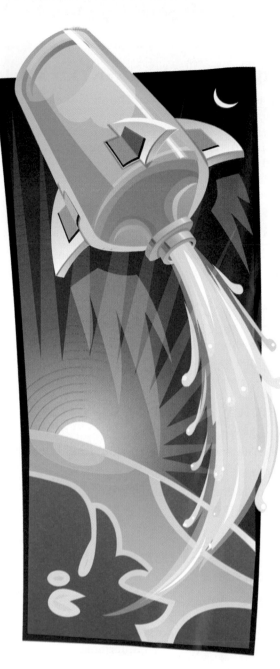

Newton's third law of motion: For every action, there is an equal and opposite reaction.

Self-Check Answers

Chapter 1—Science in Our World

Page 17: Sample answer: The model cannot take into account events such as natural disasters or war (which could slow population growth) or discoveries in medicine or agriculture (which could speed population growth).

Chapter 2—The Properties of Matter

Page 41: All matter has volume and mass.

Chapter 3—States of Matter

Page 72: Vaporization is an endothermic change because energy is absorbed by the liquid when it changes to a gas.

Chapter 4—Matter in Motion

Page 94: The net force on the object is 2 N north. Therefore, the object would move north.

Page 102: Gravity pulls the ball downward after the ball leaves your hand. So the ball travels along a curved path.

Chapter 5—Energy and Energy Resources

Page 125: A roller coaster has the greatest potential energy at the top of the highest hill (usually the first hill) and the greatest kinetic energy at the bottom of the highest hill.

Page 127: Electrical energy from the outlet is converted into thermal energy and light energy in the toaster. Thermal energy from the toaster causes a chemical change in the bread, and it turns brown while releasing chemical energy.

Page 132: The chemical energy of the fuel is converted into thermal energy when the fuel is burned. The thermal energy is then used to heat water or air.

Page 134: In a heating system, fuel is burned to convert chemical energy into thermal energy. The thermal energy is then moved throughout an area by using devices such as fans and radiators. In a cooling system, thermal energy is moved out of a warm area to an area outside by using devices such as compressors and condenser coils. These devices allow thermal energy to be transferred to and from the different parts of a cooling system.

Chapter 6—Introduction to Electricity

Page 154: Plastic wrap is charged by friction as it is pulled off of the roll.

Page 167: yes; A microwave oven is an example of a load because it uses electrical energy to do work.

Chapter 7—Cells: The Basic Units of Living Things

Page 187: DNA is the genetic material. It is contained in cells.

Page 190: Eukaryotes have nuclei and other membrane-bound organelles.

Page 192: Eubacteria, archaebacteria, and some eukaryotes—such as plants, algae, and some fungi—have cell walls.

Chapter 8—Population Changes and Heredity

Page 217: Organisms without bones or shells must be buried in very fine sediment with little or no oxygen.

Page 223: Selective breeding is the process through which humans choose which animals or plants should be allowed to breed based on traits that are desirable to people.

Page 228: Because the trees will lighten again, the light-colored trait will probably become more common, and the dark-colored trait will probably become less common.

Chapter 9—Senses and Responses of Living Things

Page 255: A low mineral level in the body is the stimulus. The elephant seeking out minerals in its environment is the response. The stimulus comes from inside the elephant, so the stimulus is internal.

Page 260: A tropism is the change in the growth of a plant due to a stimulus. Phototropism is a response to light, and gravitropism is a response to gravity.

Chapter 10—Connections in the Environment

Page 279: Humans are omnivores. An omnivore can eat both plants and animals. Humans can eat vegetables, grains, and fruits as well as meat, eggs, and milk.

Chapter 11—Classification of Living Things

Page 302: 1. The two kingdoms of bacteria are different from all other kingdoms because bacteria are prokaryotes—single-celled organisms that have no nuclei.

2. The organisms in the kingdom Protista are all eukaryotes because their cells have a nucleus and other organelles that are surrounded by a membrane.

Chapter 12—Invertebrates

Page 328: Segmented worms are annelid worms. Centipedes are arthropods. Centipedes have jointed legs, antennae, and mandibles. Segmented worms do not have any of these characteristics.

Chapter 13—Fishes, Amphibians, and Reptiles

Page 355: Amphibians use their skin to absorb oxygen from the air. Like a lung, their skin is thin, moist, and full of blood vessels.

Page 361: Thick, dry skin; lungs; and amniotic eggs help reptiles live on dry land.

Chapter 14—Birds and Mammals

Page 376: 1. A contour feather is composed of a central shaft that supports barbs, which are woven together by barbules. This structure creates a smooth surface. The function of contour feathers is to provide a bird's body with a streamlined surface, which helps a bird fly.

2. Birds need tremendous amounts of food for fuel because a lot of energy is needed to fly.

Page 389: Monotremes are mammals that lay eggs. Marsupials bear live young but carry them in pouches or skin folds before they are able to live independently. Placental mammals develop inside the mother's body, where they are nourished through a placenta.

Page 393: 1. Unlike birds, bats bear live young, have fur, and do not have feathers.

2. Both rodents and lagomorphs are small mammals that have sharp, gnawing teeth. Unlike rodents, lagomorphs have two sets of incisors and a short tail.

Chapter 15—Maps as Models of the Earth

Page 410: The Earth rotates around the geographic poles.

Page 421: If the lines are close together, then the mapped area is steep. If the lines are far apart, the mapped area has a gradual slope or is flat.

Chapter 17—The Restless Earth

Page 467: The type of stress that happens when an object is squeezed is called compression. The type of stress that happens when forces act to stretch an object is called tension. These two types of stress shape the features of the Earth.

Chapter 18—The Flow of Fresh Water

Page 485: Energy from the sun causes water to evaporate. Water vapor rises to form clouds. As water vapor condenses, it loses energy and liquid water falls as precipitation.

Page 488: If a river slowed down, the suspended load would be deposited.

Chapter 19—The Earth's Atmosphere

Page 511: The atmosphere is made of 78 percent nitrogen, 21 percent oxygen, and other gases, such as argon, carbon dioxide, and water vapor.

Page 521: Air moves from high pressure areas called anticyclones to low pressure areas called cyclones. The warm, rising air in a cyclone brings clouds and rain. The cool, sinking air in an anticyclone brings dry, clear weather.

Chapter 20—Our Solar System

Page 557: The surface of Titan is much colder than the surface of the Earth. (In fact, the temperature of Titan's surface is close to $-178°C$!)

Chapter 21—Exploring Space

Page 577: In LEO, the station can make observations of the entire world. If it was in GEO, the station would always be above the same spot.

CONTENTS

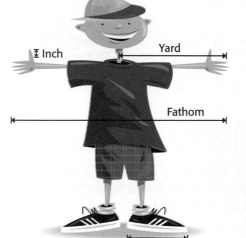

Inch   Yard

Fathom

Foot

Concept Mapping

What Is a Concept Map?

Have you ever tried to tell someone about a book or a chapter you've just read and found that you can remember only a few isolated words and ideas? Or maybe you've memorized facts for a test and then weeks later discovered you're not even sure what topics those facts covered.

In both cases, you may have understood the ideas or concepts by themselves but not in relation to one another. If you could somehow link the ideas together, you would probably understand them better and remember them longer. This is something a concept map can help you do. A concept map is a way to see how ideas or concepts fit together. It can help you see the "big picture."

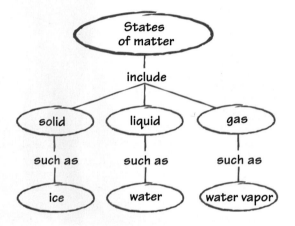

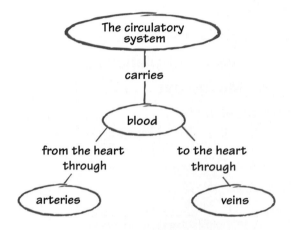

How to Make a Concept Map

❶ Make a list of the main ideas or concepts.

It might help to write each concept on its own slip of paper. This will make it easier to rearrange the concepts as many times as necessary to make sense of how the concepts are connected. After you've made a few concept maps this way, you can go directly from writing your list to actually making the map.

❷ Arrange the concepts in order from the most general to the most specific.

Put the most general concept at the top, and circle it. Ask yourself, How does this concept relate to the remaining concepts? As you see the relationships, arrange the concepts in order from general to specific.

❸ Connect the related concepts with lines.

❹ On each line, write an action word or short phrase that shows how the concepts are related.

Look at the concept maps on this page, and then see if you can make one for the following terms: *plants, water, photosynthesis, carbon dioxide,* and *sun's energy*.

One possible answer is provided at right, but don't look at it until you try the concept map yourself.

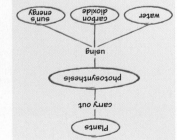

SI Measurement

The International System of Units, or SI, is the standard system of measurement used by many scientists. Using the same standards of measurement makes it easier for scientists to communicate with one another.

SI works by combining prefixes and base units. Each base unit can be used with different prefixes to define smaller and larger quantities. The table below lists common SI prefixes.

SI Prefixes			
Prefix	**Abbreviation**	**Factor**	**Example**
kilo-	k	1,000	kilogram, 1 kg = 1,000 g
hecto-	h	100	hectoliter, 1 hL = 100 L
deka-	da	10	dekameter, 1 dam = 10 m
		1	meter, liter
deci-	d	0.1	decigram, 1 dg = 0.1 g
centi-	c	0.01	centimeter, 1 cm = 0.01 m
milli-	m	0.001	milliliter, 1 mL = 0.001 L
micro-	μ	0.000 001	micrometer, 1 μm = 0.000 001 m

SI Conversion Table		
SI units	**From SI to English**	**From English to SI**
Length		
kilometer (km) = 1,000 m	1 km = 0.621 mi	1 mi = 1.609 km
meter (m) = 100 cm	1 m = 3.281 ft	1 ft = 0.305 m
centimeter (cm) = 0.01 m	1 cm = 0.394 in.	1 in. = 2.540 cm
millimeter (mm) = 0.001 m	1 mm = 0.039 in.	
micrometer (μm) = 0.000 001 m		
nanometer (nm) = 0.000 000 001 m		
Area		
square kilometer (km^2) = 100 hectares	1 km^2 = 0.386 mi^2	1 mi^2 = 2.590 km^2
hectare (ha) = 10,000 m^2	1 ha = 2.471 acres	1 acre = 0.405 ha
square meter (m^2) = 10,000 cm^2	1 m^2 = 10.765 ft^2	1 ft^2 = 0.093 m^2
square centimeter (cm^2) = 100 mm^2	1 cm^2 = 0.155 $in.^2$	1 $in.^2$ = 6.452 cm^2
Volume		
liter (L) = 1,000 mL = 1 dm^3	1 L = 1.057 fl qt	1 fl qt = 0.946 L
milliliter (mL) = 0.001 L = 1 cm^3	1 mL = 0.034 fl oz	1 fl oz = 29.575 mL
microliter (μL) = 0.000 001 L		
Mass		
kilogram (kg) = 1,000 g	1 kg = 2.205 lb	1 lb = 0.454 kg
gram (g) = 1,000 mg	1 g = 0.035 oz	1 oz = 28.349 g
milligram (mg) = 0.001 g		
microgram (μg) = 0.000 001 g		

Temperature Scales

Temperature can be expressed using three different scales: Fahrenheit, Celsius, and Kelvin. The SI unit for temperature is the kelvin (K).

Although 0 K is much colder than 0°C, a change of 1 K is equal to a change of 1°C.

Three Temperature Scales

	Fahrenheit	Celsius	Kelvin
Water boils	212°	100°	373
Body temperature	98.6°	37°	310
Room temperature	68°	20°	293
Water freezes	32°	0°	273

Temperature Conversions Table

To convert	Use this equation:	Example
Celsius to Fahrenheit °C ⟶ °F	$°F = \left(\dfrac{9}{5} \times °C\right) + 32$	Convert 45°C to °F. $°F = \left(\dfrac{9}{5} \times 45°C\right) + 32 = 113°F$
Fahrenheit to Celsius °F ⟶ °C	$°C = \dfrac{5}{9} \times (°F - 32)$	Convert 68°F to °C. $°C = \dfrac{5}{9} \times (68°F - 32) = 20°C$
Celsius to Kelvin °C ⟶ K	$K = °C + 273$	Convert 45°C to K. $K = 45°C + 273 = 318\ K$
Kelvin to Celsius K ⟶ °C	$°C = K - 273$	Convert 32 K to °C. $°C = 32\ K - 273 = -241°C$

Measuring Skills

Using a Graduated Cylinder

When using a graduated cylinder to measure volume, keep the following procedures in mind:

1 Make sure the cylinder is on a flat, level surface.

2 Move your head so that your eye is level with the surface of the liquid.

3 Read the mark closest to the liquid level. On glass graduated cylinders, read the mark closest to the center of the curve in the liquid's surface.

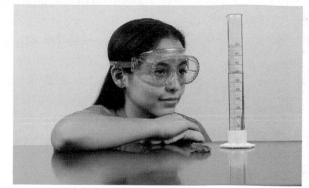

Using a Meterstick or Metric Ruler

When using a meterstick or metric ruler to measure length, keep the following procedures in mind:

1 Place the ruler firmly against the object you are measuring.

2 Align one edge of the object exactly with the zero end of the ruler.

3 Look at the other edge of the object to see which of the marks on the ruler is closest to that edge. (Note: Each small slash between the centimeters represents a millimeter, which is one-tenth of a centimeter.)

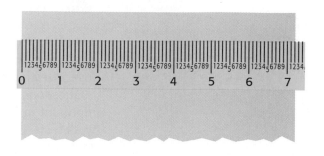

Using a Triple-Beam Balance

When using a triple-beam balance to measure mass, keep the following procedures in mind:

1 Make sure the balance is on a level surface.

2 Place all of the countermasses at zero. Adjust the balancing knob until the pointer rests at zero.

3 Place the object you wish to measure on the pan.
Caution: Do not place hot objects or chemicals directly on the balance pan.

4 Move the largest countermass along the beam to the right until it is at the last notch that does not tip the balance. Follow the same procedure with the next-largest countermass. Then move the smallest countermass until the pointer rests at zero.

5 Add the readings from the three beams together to determine the mass of the object.

6 When determining the mass of crystals or powders, use a piece of filter paper. First find the mass of the paper. Then add the crystals or powder to the paper and re-measure. The actual mass of the crystals or powder is the total mass minus the mass of the paper. When finding the mass of liquids, first find the mass of the empty container. Then find the mass of the liquid and container together. The mass of the liquid is the total mass minus the mass of the container.

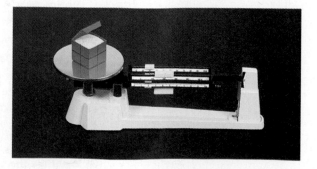

Scientific Methods

The ways in which scientists answer questions and solve problems are often called **scientific methods.** The same steps are often used by scientists as they look for answers. However, there is more than one way to use these steps. Scientists may use all of the steps or just some of the steps during an investigation. They may even repeat some of the steps. The goal of using scientific methods is to come up with reliable answers and solutions.

Six Steps of Scientific Methods

1 **Ask a Question** Good questions come from careful **observations.** You make observations by using your senses to gather information. Sometimes you may use instruments, such as microscopes and telescopes, to extend the range of your senses. As you observe the natural world, you will discover that you have many more questions than answers. These questions drive investigations.

Questions beginning with *what, why, how,* and *when* are very important in focusing an investigation, and they often lead to a hypothesis. (You will learn what a hypothesis is in the next step.) Here is an example of a question that could lead to further investigation.

Ask a Question

Question: How does acid rain affect plant growth?

2 **Form a Hypothesis** After you come up with a question, you need to turn the question into a **hypothesis.** A hypothesis is a clear statement of what you expect the answer to your question to be. Your hypothesis will represent your best "educated guess" based on what you have observed and what you already know. A good hypothesis is testable. If observations and information cannot be gathered or if an experiment cannot be designed to test your hypothesis, it is untestable, and the investigation can go no further.

Here is a hypothesis that could be formed from the question, How does acid rain affect plant growth?

Form a Hypothesis

Hypothesis: Acid rain causes plants to grow more slowly.

Notice that the hypothesis provides some specifics that lead to methods of testing. The hypothesis can also lead to predictions. A **prediction** is what you think the outcome of your experiment or data collection will be. Predictions are usually stated in an if-then format. For example, **if** meat is kept at room temperature, **then** it will spoil faster than meat kept in the refrigerator. More than one prediction can be made for a single hypothesis. Here is a sample prediction for the hypothesis that acid rain causes plants to grow more slowly.

Prediction: If a plant is watered with only acid rain (which has a pH of 4), then the plant will grow at half its normal rate.

3 **Test the Hypothesis** After you have formed a hypothesis and made a prediction, you should test your hypothesis. There are different ways to test it. Perhaps the most familiar way is to conduct a **controlled experiment.** A controlled experiment tests only one factor at a time. A controlled experiment has a **control group** and one or more **experimental groups.** All the factors for the control and experimental groups are the same except for one factor, which is called the **variable.** By changing only one factor, you can see the results of just that one change.

Sometimes, the nature of an investigation makes a controlled experiment impossible. For example, dinosaurs have been extinct for millions of years, and the Earth's core is surrounded by thousands of meters of rock. Conducting controlled experiments on such things would be difficult, if not impossible. Under such circumstances, a hypothesis may be tested by making detailed observations. Taking measurements is one way to make observations.

Test the Hypothesis

4 **Analyze the Results** After you have completed your experiments, made your observations, and collected your data, you must analyze all the information you have gathered. Tables and graphs are often used in this step to organize the data.

Analyze the Results

5 **Draw Conclusions** Based on the analysis of your data, you should conclude whether your results support your hypothesis. If your hypothesis is supported, you (or others) might want to repeat the observations or experiments to verify your results. If your hypothesis is not supported by the data, you may have to check your procedure for errors. You may even have to reject your hypothesis and make a new one. If you cannot draw a conclusion from your results, you may have to try the investigation again or carry out further observations or experiments.

Draw Conclusions

Do they support your hypothesis?

No

Yes

6 **Communicate Results** After any scientific investigation, you should report your results. By doing a written or oral report, you let others know what you have learned. They may want to repeat your investigation to see if they get the same results. Your report may even lead to another question, which in turn may lead to another investigation.

Communicate Results

Scientific Methods in Action

Scientific methods contain loops in which several steps may be repeated over and over again, while others may not be necessary. There is not a "straight line" of steps. For example, sometimes scientists will find that testing one hypothesis raises new questions and new hypotheses to be tested. And sometimes, testing the hypothesis leads directly to a conclusion. Furthermore, the steps of scientific methods are not always used in the same order. Follow the steps in the diagram below, and see how many different directions scientific methods can take you.

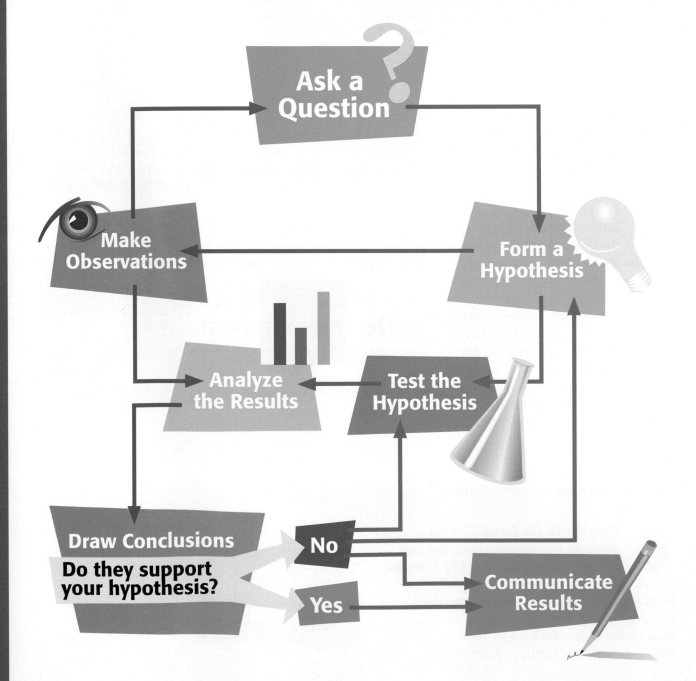

Making Charts and Graphs

Pie Charts

A pie chart shows how each group of data relates to all of the data. Each part of the circle forming the chart represents a category of the data. The entire circle represents all of the data. For example, a biologist studying a hardwood forest in Wisconsin found that there were five different types of trees. The data table at right summarizes the biologist's findings.

Wisconsin Hardwood Trees	
Type of tree	Number found
Oak	600
Maple	750
Beech	300
Birch	1,200
Hickory	150
Total	3,000

How to Make a Pie Chart

1 To make a pie chart of this data, first find the percentage of each type of tree. To do this, divide the number of individual trees by the total number of trees and multiply by 100.

$$\frac{600 \text{ oak}}{3,000 \text{ trees}} \times 100 = 20\%$$

$$\frac{750 \text{ maple}}{3,000 \text{ trees}} \times 100 = 25\%$$

$$\frac{300 \text{ beech}}{3,000 \text{ trees}} \times 100 = 10\%$$

$$\frac{1,200 \text{ birch}}{3,000 \text{ trees}} \times 100 = 40\%$$

$$\frac{150 \text{ hickory}}{3,000 \text{ trees}} \times 100 = 5\%$$

2 Now determine the size of the pie shapes that make up the chart. Do this by multiplying each percentage by 360°. Remember that a circle contains 360°.

20% × 360° = 72° 25% × 360° = 90°
10% × 360° = 36° 40% × 360° = 144°
5% × 360° = 18°

3 Then check that the sum of the percentages is 100 and the sum of the degrees is 360.

20% + 25% + 10% + 40% + 5% = 100%
72° + 90° + 36° + 144° + 18° = 360°

4 Use a compass to draw a circle and mark its center.

5 Then use a protractor to draw angles of 72°, 90°, 36°, 144°, and 18° in the circle.

6 Finally, label each part of the chart, and choose an appropriate title.

A Community of Wisconsin Hardwood Trees

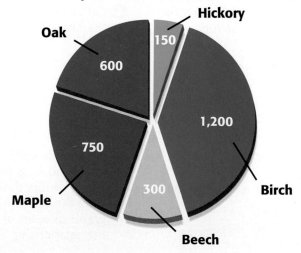

Line Graphs

Line graphs are most often used to demonstrate continuous change. For example, the students in Mr. Smith's science class analyzed the population records for their hometown, Appleton, between 1900 and 2000. Examine the data at left.

Because the year and the population change, they are the *variables*. The population is determined by, or dependent on, the year. Therefore, the population is called the **dependent variable**, and the year is called the **independent variable**. Each set of data is called a **data pair**. To prepare a line graph, you must first organize data pairs in a table like the one at left.

Population of Appleton, 1900–2000	
Year	Population
1900	1,800
1920	2,500
1940	3,200
1960	3,900
1980	4,600
2000	5,300

How to Make a Line Graph

❶ Place the independent variable along the horizontal (*x*) axis. Place the dependent variable along the vertical (*y*) axis.

❷ Label the *x*-axis "Year" and the *y*-axis "Population." Look at your largest and smallest values for the population. Determine a scale for the *y*-axis that will provide enough space to show these values. You must use the same scale for the entire length of the axis. Find an appropriate scale for the *x*-axis too.

❸ Choose reasonable starting points for each axis.

❹ Plot the data pairs as accurately as possible.

❺ Choose a title that accurately represents the data.

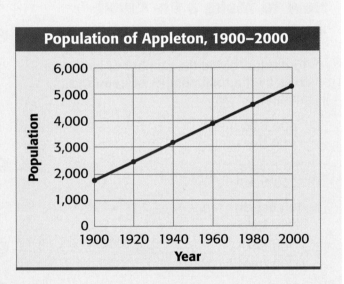

Population of Appleton, 1900–2000

How to Determine Slope

Slope is the ratio of the change in the *y*-axis to the change in the *x*-axis, or "rise over run."

❶ Choose two points on the line graph. For example, the population of Appleton in 2000 was 5,300 people. Therefore, you can define point A as (2000, 5,300). In 1900, the population was 1,800 people. Define point B as (1900, 1,800).

❷ Find the change in the *y*-axis.
(*y* at point A) − (*y* at point B)
5,300 people − 1,800 people = 3,500 people

❸ Find the change in the *x*-axis.
(*x* at point A) − (*x* at point B)
2000 − 1900 = 100 years

❹ Calculate the slope of the graph by dividing the change in *y* by the change in *x*.

$$slope = \frac{change\ in\ y}{change\ in\ x}$$

$$slope = \frac{3,500\ people}{100\ years}$$

$$slope = 35\ people\ per\ year$$

In this example, the population in Appleton increased by a fixed amount each year. The graph of this data is a straight line. Therefore, the relationship is **linear.** When the graph of a set of data is not a straight line, the relationship is **nonlinear.**

Using Algebra to Determine Slope

The equation in step 4 may also be arranged to be:

$$y = kx$$

where y represents the change in the y-axis, k represents the slope, and x represents the change in the x-axis.

$$slope = \frac{change\ in\ y}{change\ in\ x}$$

$$k = \frac{y}{x}$$

$$k \times x = \frac{y \times x}{x}$$

$$kx = y$$

Bar Graphs

Bar graphs are used to demonstrate change that is not continuous. These graphs can be used to indicate trends when the data are taken over a long period of time. A meteorologist gathered the precipitation records at right for Hartford, Connecticut, for April 1–15, 1996, and used a bar graph to represent the data.

Precipitation in Hartford, Connecticut April 1–15, 1996

Date	Precipitation (cm)	Date	Precipitation (cm)
April 1	0.5	April 9	0.25
April 2	1.25	April 10	0.0
April 3	0.0	April 11	1.0
April 4	0.0	April 12	0.0
April 5	0.0	April 13	0.25
April 6	0.0	April 14	0.0
April 7	0.0	April 15	6.50
April 8	1.75		

How to Make a Bar Graph

1 Use an appropriate scale and a reasonable starting point for each axis.

2 Label the axes, and plot the data.

3 Choose a title that accurately represents the data.

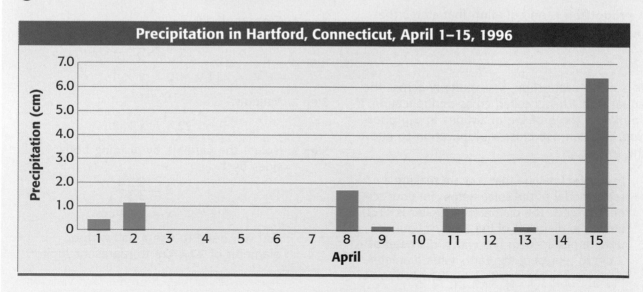

Precipitation in Hartford, Connecticut, April 1–15, 1996

Math Refresher

Science requires an understanding of many math concepts. The following pages will help you review some important math skills.

Averages

An **average**, or **mean,** simplifies a list of numbers into a single number that *approximates* the value of all of the numbers.

Example: Find the average of the following set of numbers: 5, 4, 7, and 8.

Step 1: Find the sum.

$$5 + 4 + 7 + 8 = 24$$

Step 2: Divide the sum by the number of numbers in your set. Because there are four numbers in this example, divide the sum by 4.

$$\frac{24}{4} = 6$$

The average, or mean, is **6.**

Ratios

A **ratio** is a comparison between numbers, and it is usually written as a fraction.

Example: Find the ratio of thermometers to students if you have 36 thermometers and 48 students in your class.

Step 1: Make the ratio.

$$\frac{36 \text{ thermometers}}{48 \text{ students}}$$

Step 2: Reduce the fraction to its simplest form.

$$\frac{36}{48} = \frac{36 \div 12}{48 \div 12} = \frac{3}{4}$$

The ratio of thermometers to students is **3 to 4,** or $\frac{3}{4}$. The ratio may also be written in the form 3:4.

Proportions

A **proportion** is an equation that states that two ratios are equal.

$$\frac{3}{1} = \frac{12}{4}$$

To solve a proportion, first multiply across the equal sign. This is called cross-multiplication. If you know three of the quantities in a proportion, you can use cross-multiplication to find the fourth.

Example: Imagine that you are making a scale model of the solar system for your science project. The diameter of Jupiter is 11.2 times the diameter of the Earth. If you are using a plastic-foam ball with a diameter of 2 cm to represent the Earth, what diameter does the ball representing Jupiter need to be?

$$\frac{11.2}{1} = \frac{x}{2 \text{ cm}}$$

Step 1: Cross-multiply.

$$\frac{11.2}{1} \diagdown\!\!\!\!\diagup \frac{x}{2}$$

$$11.2 \times 2 = x \times 1$$

Step 2: Multiply.

$$22.4 = x \times 1$$

Step 3: Isolate the variable by dividing both sides by 1.

$$x = \frac{22.4}{1}$$

$$x = 22.4 \text{ cm}$$

You will need to use a ball with a diameter of **22.4 cm** to represent Jupiter.

Percentages

A **percentage** is a ratio of a given number to 100.

Example: What is 85 percent of 40?

Step 1: Rewrite the percentage by moving the decimal point two places to the left.

$$_{\sim}85$$

Step 2: Multiply the decimal by the number you are calculating the percentage of.

$$0.85 \times 40 = 34$$

85 percent of 40 is **34.**

Decimals

To **add** or **subtract decimals,** line up the digits vertically so that the decimal points line up. Then add or subtract the columns from right to left. Carry or borrow numbers as necessary.

Example: Add the following numbers: 3.1415 and 2.96.

Step 1: Line up the digits vertically so that the decimal points line up.

$$
\begin{array}{r}
3.1415 \\
+\ 2.96 \\
\hline
\end{array}
$$

Step 2: Add the columns from right to left, and carry numbers when necessary.

$$
\begin{array}{r}
1\ 1 \\
3.1415 \\
+\ 2.96 \\
\hline
6.1015
\end{array}
$$

The sum is **6.1015.**

Fractions

Numbers tell you how many; **fractions** tell you *how much of a whole.*

Example: Your class has 24 plants. Your teacher instructs you to put 5 in a shady spot. What fraction do these 5 plants represent?

Step 1: Write a fraction with the total number of parts in the whole as the denominator.

$$\frac{?}{24}$$

Step 2: Write the number of parts of the whole being represented as the numerator.

$$\frac{5}{24}$$

$\frac{5}{24}$ of the plants will be in the shade.

Reducing Fractions

It is usually best to express a fraction in simplest form. This is called *reducing* a fraction.

Example: Reduce the fraction $\frac{30}{45}$ to its simplest form.

Step 1: Find the largest whole number that will divide evenly into both the numerator and denominator. This number is called the greatest common factor (GCF).

factors of the numerator 30: 1, 2, 3, 5, 6, 10, **15,** 30

factors of the denominator 45: 1, 3, 5, 9, **15,** 45

Step 2: Divide both the numerator and the denominator by the GCF, which in this case is 15.

$$\frac{30}{45} = \frac{30 \div 15}{45 \div 15} = \frac{2}{3}$$

$\frac{30}{45}$ reduced to its simplest form is $\frac{2}{3}$.

Adding and Subtracting Fractions

To **add** or **subtract fractions** that have the **same denominator,** simply add or subtract the numerators.

Examples:

$$\frac{3}{5} + \frac{1}{5} = ? \text{ and } \frac{3}{4} - \frac{1}{4} = ?$$

Step 1: Add or subtract the numerators.

$$\frac{3}{5} + \frac{1}{5} = \frac{4}{} \text{ and } \frac{3}{4} - \frac{1}{4} = \frac{2}{}$$

Step 2: Write the sum or difference over the denominator.

$$\frac{3}{5} + \frac{1}{5} = \frac{4}{5} \text{ and } \frac{3}{4} - \frac{1}{4} = \frac{2}{4}$$

Step 3: If necessary, reduce the fraction to its simplest form.

$\frac{4}{5}$ cannot be reduced, and $\frac{2}{4} = \frac{1}{2}$.

To **add** or **subtract fractions** that have **different denominators,** first find the least common denominator (LCD).

Examples:

$$\frac{1}{2} + \frac{1}{6} = ? \text{ and } \frac{3}{4} - \frac{2}{3} = ?$$

Step 1: Write the equivalent fractions with a common denominator.

$$\frac{3}{6} + \frac{1}{6} = ? \text{ and } \frac{9}{12} - \frac{8}{12} = ?$$

Step 2: Add or subtract.

$$\frac{3}{6} + \frac{1}{6} = \frac{4}{6} \text{ and } \frac{9}{12} - \frac{8}{12} = \frac{1}{12}$$

Step 3: If necessary, reduce the fraction to its simplest form.

$\frac{4}{6} = \frac{2}{3}$, and $\frac{1}{12}$ cannot be reduced.

Multiplying Fractions

To **multiply fractions,** multiply the numerators and the denominators together, and then reduce the fraction to its simplest form.

Example:

$$\frac{5}{9} \times \frac{7}{10} = ?$$

Step 1: Multiply the numerators and denominators.

$$\frac{5}{9} \times \frac{7}{10} = \frac{5 \times 7}{9 \times 10} = \frac{35}{90}$$

Step 2: Reduce.

$$\frac{35}{90} = \frac{35 \div 5}{90 \div 5} = \frac{7}{18}$$

Dividing Fractions

To **divide fractions,** first rewrite the divisor (the number you divide *by*) upside down. This is called the reciprocal of the divisor. Then you can multiply and reduce if necessary.

Example:

$$\frac{5}{8} \div \frac{3}{2} = ?$$

Step 1: Rewrite the divisor as its reciprocal.

$$\frac{3}{2} \rightarrow \frac{2}{3}$$

Step 2: Multiply.

$$\frac{5}{8} \times \frac{2}{3} = \frac{5 \times 2}{8 \times 3} = \frac{10}{24}$$

Step 3: Reduce.

$$\frac{10}{24} = \frac{10 \div 2}{24 \div 2} = \frac{5}{12}$$

Scientific Notation

Scientific notation is a short way of representing very large and very small numbers without writing all of the place-holding zeros.

Example: Write 653,000,000 in scientific notation.

Step 1: Write the number without the place-holding zeros.

653

Step 2: Place the decimal point after the first digit.

6.53

Step 3: Find the exponent by counting the number of places that you moved the decimal point.

6.53000000

The decimal point was moved eight places to the left. Therefore, the exponent of 10 is positive 8. Remember, if the decimal point had moved to the right, the exponent would be negative.

Step 4: Write the number in scientific notation.

$$6.53 \times 10^8$$

Area

Area is the number of square units needed to cover the surface of an object.

Formulas:
$area\ of\ a\ square = side \times side$
$area\ of\ a\ rectangle = length \times width$
$area\ of\ a\ triangle = \frac{1}{2} \times base \times height$

Examples: Find the areas.

Triangle
$area = \frac{1}{2} \times base \times height$
$area = \frac{1}{2} \times 3\ cm \times 4\ cm$
$area = \textbf{6 cm}^2$

4 cm
3 cm

Rectangle
$area = length \times width$
$area = 6\ cm \times 3\ cm$
$area = \textbf{18 cm}^2$

3 cm
6 cm

Square
$area = side \times side$
$area = 3\ cm \times 3\ cm$
$area = \textbf{9 cm}^2$

3 cm
3 cm

Volume

Volume is the amount of space something occupies.

Formulas:
$volume\ of\ a\ cube = side \times side \times side$

$volume\ of\ a\ prism = area\ of\ base \times height$

Examples: Find the volume of the solids.

Cube
$volume = side \times side \times side$
$volume = 4\ cm \times 4\ cm \times 4\ cm$
$volume = \textbf{64 cm}^3$

4 cm
4 cm
4 cm

4 cm
3 cm
5 cm

Prism
$volume = area\ of\ base \times height$
$volume = area\ of\ triangle \times height$
$volume = \left(\frac{1}{2} \times 3\ cm \times 4\ cm \right) \times 5\ cm$
$volume = 6\ cm^2 \times 5\ cm$
$volume = \textbf{30 cm}^3$

Periodic Table of the Elements

Each square on the table includes an element's name, chemical symbol, atomic number, and atomic mass.

Atomic number —— 6

Chemical symbol —— **C**

Element name —— Carbon

Atomic mass —— 12.0

The color of the **chemical symbol** indicates the physical state at room temperature. Carbon is a solid.

The **background** color indicates the type of element. Carbon is a nonmetal.

Background

Metals	
Metalloids	
Nonmetals	

Chemical symbol

Solid	
Liquid	
Gas	

Period 1

| 1 |
| **H** |
| Hydrogen |
| 1.0 |

	Group 1	Group 2
Period 2	3 **Li** Lithium 6.9	4 **Be** Beryllium 9.0
Period 3	11 **Na** Sodium 23.0	12 **Mg** Magnesium 24.3

	Group 1	Group 2	Group 3	Group 4	Group 5	Group 6	Group 7	Group 8	Group 9
Period 4	19 **K** Potassium 39.1	20 **Ca** Calcium 40.1	21 **Sc** Scandium 45.0	22 **Ti** Titanium 47.9	23 **V** Vanadium 50.9	24 **Cr** Chromium 52.0	25 **Mn** Manganese 54.9	26 **Fe** Iron 55.8	27 **Co** Cobalt 58.9
Period 5	37 **Rb** Rubidium 85.5	38 **Sr** Strontium 87.6	39 **Y** Yttrium 88.9	40 **Zr** Zirconium 91.2	41 **Nb** Niobium 92.9	42 **Mo** Molybdenum 95.9	43 **Tc** Technetium (97.9)	44 **Ru** Ruthenium 101.1	45 **Rh** Rhodium 102.9
Period 6	55 **Cs** Cesium 132.9	56 **Ba** Barium 137.3	57 **La** Lanthanum 138.9	72 **Hf** Hafnium 178.5	73 **Ta** Tantalum 180.9	74 **W** Tungsten 183.8	75 **Re** Rhenium 186.2	76 **Os** Osmium 190.2	77 **Ir** Iridium 192.2
Period 7	87 **Fr** Francium (223.0)	88 **Ra** Radium (226.0)	89 **Ac** Actinium (227.0)	104 **Rf** Rutherfordium (261.1)	105 **Db** Dubnium (262.1)	106 **Sg** Seaborgium (263.1)	107 **Bh** Bohrium (262.1)	108 **Hs** Hassium (265)	109 **Mt** Meitnerium (266)

A row of elements is called a period.

A column of elements is called a group or family.

Lanthanides	58 **Ce** Cerium 140.1	59 **Pr** Praseodymium 140.9	60 **Nd** Neodymium 144.2	61 **Pm** Promethium (144.9)	62 **Sm** Samarium 150.4
Actinides	90 **Th** Thorium 232.0	91 **Pa** Protactinium 231.0	92 **U** Uranium 238.0	93 **Np** Neptunium (237.0)	94 **Pu** Plutonium 244.1

These elements are placed below the table to allow the table to be narrower.

Group 18

| 2 **He** Helium 4.0 |

Group 13 **Group 14** **Group 15** **Group 16** **Group 17**

This zigzag line reminds you where the metals, nonmetals, and metalloids are.

| 5 **B** Boron 10.8 | 6 **C** Carbon 12.0 | 7 **N** Nitrogen 14.0 | 8 **O** Oxygen 16.0 | 9 **F** Fluorine 19.0 | 10 **Ne** Neon 20.2 |

| 13 **Al** Aluminum 27.0 | 14 **Si** Silicon 28.1 | 15 **P** Phosphorus 31.0 | 16 **S** Sulfur 32.1 | 17 **Cl** Chlorine 35.5 | 18 **Ar** Argon 39.9 |

Group 10 **Group 11** **Group 12**

| 28 **Ni** Nickel 58.7 | 29 **Cu** Copper 63.5 | 30 **Zn** Zinc 65.4 | 31 **Ga** Gallium 69.7 | 32 **Ge** Germanium 72.6 | 33 **As** Arsenic 74.9 | 34 **Se** Selenium 79.0 | 35 **Br** Bromine 79.9 | 36 **Kr** Krypton 83.8 |

| 46 **Pd** Palladium 106.4 | 47 **Ag** Silver 107.9 | 48 **Cd** Cadmium 112.4 | 49 **In** Indium 114.8 | 50 **Sn** Tin 118.7 | 51 **Sb** Antimony 121.8 | 52 **Te** Tellurium 127.6 | 53 **I** Iodine 126.9 | 54 **Xe** Xenon 131.3 |

| 78 **Pt** Platinum 195.1 | 79 **Au** Gold 197.0 | 80 **Hg** Mercury 200.6 | 81 **Tl** Thallium 204.4 | 82 **Pb** Lead 207.2 | 83 **Bi** Bismuth 209.0 | 84 **Po** Polonium (209.0) | 85 **At** Astatine (210.0) | 86 **Rn** Radon (222.0) |

| 110 **Uun*** Ununnilium (271) | 111 **Uuu*** Unununium (272) | 112 **Uub*** Ununbium (277) | | 114 **Uuq*** Ununquadium (285) | | 116 **Uuh*** Ununhexium (289) | | 118 **Uuo*** Ununoctium (293) |

A number in parentheses is the mass number of the most stable form of that element.

| 63 **Eu** Europium 152.0 | 64 **Gd** Gadolinium 157.3 | 65 **Tb** Terbium 158.9 | 66 **Dy** Dysprosium 162.5 | 67 **Ho** Holmium 164.9 | 68 **Er** Erbium 167.3 | 69 **Tm** Thulium 168.9 | 70 **Yb** Ytterbium 173.0 | 71 **Lu** Lutetium 175.0 |

| 95 **Am** Americium (243.1) | 96 **Cm** Curium (247.1) | 97 **Bk** Berkelium (247.1) | 98 **Cf** Californium (251.1) | 99 **Es** Einsteinium (252.1) | 100 **Fm** Fermium (257.1) | 101 **Md** Mendelevium (258.1) | 102 **No** Nobelium (259.1) | 103 **Lr** Lawrencium (262.1) |

The official names and symbols for the elements greater than 109 will eventually be approved by a committee of scientists.

Physical Laws and Equations

Law of Conservation of Energy

The law of conservation of energy states that energy can be neither created nor destroyed.

The total amount of energy in a closed system is always the same. Energy can be changed from one form to another, but all the different forms of energy in a system always add up to the same total amount of energy, no matter how many energy conversions occur.

Law of Universal Gravitation

The law of universal gravitation states that all objects in the universe attract each other by a force called gravity. The size of the force depends on the masses of the objects and the distance between them.

The first part of the law explains that a bowling ball is much harder to lift than a table-tennis ball. Because the bowling ball has a much larger mass than the table-tennis ball, the amount of gravity between the Earth and the bowling ball is greater than the amount of gravity between the Earth and the table-tennis ball.

The second part of the law explains that a satellite can remain in orbit around the Earth. The satellite is carefully placed at a distance great enough to prevent the Earth's gravity from immediately pulling it down but small enough to prevent it from completely escaping the Earth's gravity and wandering off into space.

Newton's Laws of Motion

Newton's first law of motion states that an object at rest remains at rest and an object in motion remains in motion at constant speed and in a straight line unless acted on by an unbalanced force.

The first part of the law explains that a football will remain on a tee until it is kicked off or until a gust of wind blows it off.

The second part of the law explains that a bike's rider will continue moving forward after the bike tire runs into a crack in the sidewalk and the bike comes to an abrupt stop until gravity and the sidewalk stop the rider.

Newton's second law of motion states that the acceleration of an object depends on the mass of the object and the amount of force applied.

The first part of the law explains that the acceleration of a 4 kg bowling ball will be greater than the acceleration of a 6 kg bowling ball if the same force is applied to both.

The second part of the law explains that the acceleration of a bowling ball will be larger if a larger force is applied to it.

The relationship of acceleration (a) to mass (m) and force (F) can be expressed mathematically by the following equation:

$$acceleration = \frac{force}{mass} \quad \text{or} \quad a = \frac{F}{m}$$

This equation is often rearranged to the form:

$$force = mass \times acceleration$$
$$\text{or}$$
$$F = m \times a$$

Newton's third law of motion states that whenever one object exerts a force on a second object, the second object exerts an equal and opposite force on the first.

This law explains that a runner is able to move forward because of the equal and opposite force the ground exerts on the runner's foot after each step.

Useful Equations

Average speed

$$\text{average speed} = \frac{\text{total distance}}{\text{total time}}$$

Example: A bicycle messenger traveled a distance of 136 km in 8 hours. What was the messenger's average speed?

$$\frac{136 \text{ km}}{8 \text{ h}} = 17 \text{ km/h}$$

The messenger's average speed was **17 km/h.**

Average acceleration

$$\frac{\text{average}}{\text{acceleration}} = \frac{\text{final velocity} - \text{starting velocity}}{\text{time it takes to change velocity}}$$

Example: Calculate the average acceleration of an Olympic 100 m dash sprinter who reaches a velocity of 20 m/s south at the finish line. The race was in a straight line and lasted 10 seconds.

$$\frac{20 \text{ m/s} - 0 \text{ m/s}}{10 \text{ s}} = 2 \text{ m/s}^2$$

The sprinter's average acceleration is **2 m/s² south.**

Net force

Forces in the Same Direction
When forces are in the same direction, add the forces together to determine the net force.

Example: Calculate the net force on a stalled car that is being pushed by two people. One person is pushing with a force of 13 N northwest, and the other person is pushing with a force of 8 N in the same direction.

$$13 \text{ N} + 8 \text{ N} = 21 \text{ N}$$

The net force is **21 N northwest.**

Forces in Opposite Directions
When forces are in opposite directions, subtract the smaller force from the larger force to determine the net force.

Net force (cont'd)

Example: Calculate the net force on a rope that is being pulled on each end. One person is pulling on one end of the rope with a force of 12 N south. Another person is pulling on the opposite end of the rope with a force of 7 N north.

$$12 \text{ N} - 7 \text{ N} = 5 \text{ N}$$

The net force is **5 N south.**

Density

$$\text{density} = \frac{\text{mass}}{\text{volume}}$$

Example: Calculate the density of a sponge with a mass of 10 g and a volume of 40 mL.

$$\frac{10 \text{ g}}{40 \text{ mL}} = 0.25 \text{ g/mL}$$

The density of the sponge is **0.25 g/mL.**

Pressure

Pressure is the force exerted over a given area. The SI unit for pressure is the pascal, which is abbreviated Pa.

$$\text{pressure} = \frac{\text{force}}{\text{area}}$$

Example: Calculate the pressure of the air in a soccer ball if the air exerts a force of 10 N over an area of 0.5 m².

$$\text{Pressure} = \frac{10 \text{ N}}{0.5 \text{ m}^2} = 20 \text{ N/m}^2 = 20 \text{ Pa}$$

The pressure of the air inside of the soccer ball is **20 Pa.**

Concentration

$$\text{concentration} = \frac{\text{mass of solute}}{\text{volume of solvent}}$$

Example: Calculate the concentration of a solution in which 10 g of sugar is dissolved in 125 mL of water.

$$\frac{10 \text{ g of sugar}}{125 \text{ mL of water}} = 0.08 \text{ g/mL}$$

The concentration of this solution is **0.08 g/mL.**

Using the Microscope

Parts of the Compound Light Microscope

- The **ocular lens** magnifies the image 10×.
- The **low-power objective** magnifies the image 10×.
- The **high-power objective** magnifies the image either 40× or 43×.
- The **revolving nosepiece** holds the objectives and can be turned to change from one magnification to another.
- The **body tube** maintains the correct distance between the ocular lens and objectives.
- The **coarse-adjustment knob** moves the body tube up and down to allow focusing of the image.

- The **fine-adjustment knob** moves the body tube slightly to bring the image into sharper focus.
- The **stage** supports a slide.
- **Stage clips** hold the slide in place for viewing.
- The **diaphragm** controls the amount of light coming through the stage.
- The light source provides a **light** for viewing the slide.
- The **arm** supports the body tube.
- The **base** supports the microscope.

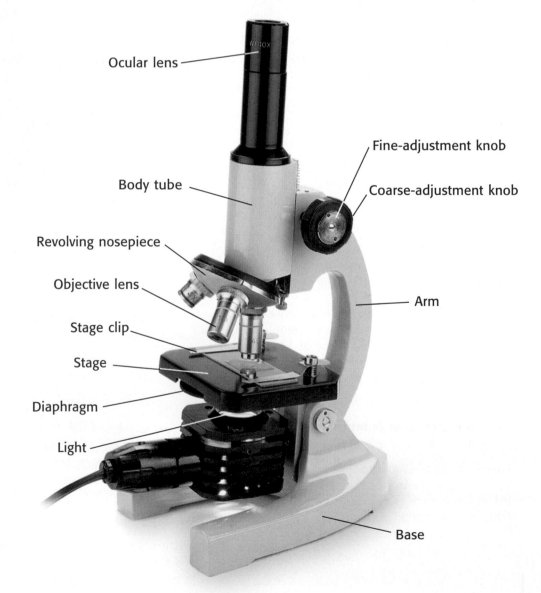

Ocular lens

Fine-adjustment knob

Body tube

Coarse-adjustment knob

Revolving nosepiece

Objective lens

Arm

Stage clip

Stage

Diaphragm

Light

Base

Proper Use of the Compound Light Microscope

❶ Carry the microscope to your lab table using both hands. Place one hand beneath the base, and use the other hand to hold the arm of the microscope. Hold the microscope close to your body while moving it to your lab table.

❷ Place the microscope on the lab table at least 5 cm from the edge of the table.

❸ Check to see what type of light source is used by your microscope. If the microscope has a lamp, plug it in and make sure that the cord is out of the way. If the microscope has a mirror, adjust it to reflect light through the hole in the stage.
Caution: If your microscope has a mirror, do not use direct sunlight as a light source. Direct sunlight can damage your eyes.

❹ Always begin work with the low-power objective in line with the body tube. Adjust the revolving nosepiece.

❺ Place a prepared slide over the hole in the stage. Secure the slide with the stage clips.

❻ Look through the ocular lens. Move the diaphragm to adjust the amount of light coming through the stage.

❼ Look at the stage from eye level. Slowly turn the coarse adjustment to lower the objective until it almost touches the slide. Do not allow the objective to touch the slide.

❽ Look through the ocular lens. Turn the coarse adjustment to raise the low-power objective until the image is in focus. Always focus by raising the objective away from the slide. *Never focus the objective downward.* Use the fine adjustment to sharpen the focus. Keep both eyes open while viewing a slide.

❾ Make sure that the image is exactly in the center of your field of vision. Then switch to the high-power objective. Focus the image by using only the fine adjustment. *Never use the coarse adjustment at high power.*

❿ When you are finished using the microscope, remove the slide. Clean the ocular lens and objective lenses with lens paper. Return the microscope to its storage area. Remember, you should use both hands to carry the microscope.

Making a Wet Mount

❶ Use lens paper to clean a glass slide and a coverslip.

❷ Place the specimen you wish to observe in the center of the slide.

❸ Using a medicine dropper, place one drop of water on the specimen.

❹ Hold the coverslip at the edge of the water and at a 45° angle to the slide. Make sure that the water runs along the edge of the coverslip.

❺ Lower the coverslip slowly to avoid trapping air bubbles.

❻ Water might evaporate from the slide as you work. Add more water to keep the specimen fresh. Place the tip of the medicine dropper next to the edge of the coverslip. Add a drop of water. (You can also use this method to add stain or solutions to a wet mount.) Remove excess water from the slide by using the corner of a paper towel as a blotter. Do not lift the coverslip to add or remove water.

Astronomical Data

Planetary Data

Planet	Distance from sun (AU)	Orbital period (Earth years)	Mean orbital speed (km/s)	Inclination of orbit to ecliptic (°)
Mercury	0.39	0.24	47.9	7.0
Venus	0.72	0.62	35.0	3.4
Earth	1.00	1.00	29.8	0.0
Mars	1.52	1.88	24.1	1.8
Jupiter	5.20	11.86	13.1	1.3
Saturn	9.5	29.46	9.6	2.5
Uranus	19.2	84.0	6.8	0.8
Neptune	30.1	164.8	5.4	1.8
Pluto	39.7	248.6	4.7	17.2

Planetary Data in Relation to the Earth

Planet	Diameter	Mass	Surface gravity
Mercury	0.38	0.06	0.38
Venus	0.95	0.82	0.91
Earth	1.00	1.00	1.00
Mars	0.53	0.11	0.38
Jupiter	11.21	317.8	2.36
Saturn	9.45	94.3	0.92
Uranus	4.01	14.6	0.89
Neptune	3.88	17.2	1.12
Pluto	0.19	0.003	0.07

Solar Eclipses from Present Through the Year 2017

Date	Duration of totality (min)	Location
December 4, 2002	2.1	South Africa, Australia
November 23, 2003	2.0	Antarctica
April 8, 2005	0.7	South Pacific Ocean
March 29, 2006	4.1	Africa, Asia Minor, Russia
August 1, 2008	2.4	Arctic Ocean, Siberia, China
July 22, 2009	6.6	India, China, South Pacific
July 11, 2010	5.3	South Pacific Ocean, Southern South America
November 13, 2012	4.0	Northern Australia, South Pacific
November 3, 2013	1.7	Atlantic Ocean, Central Africa
March 20, 2015	4.1	North Atlantic, Arctic Ocean
March 9, 2016	4.5	Indonesia, Pacific Ocean
August 21, 2017	2.7	Pacific Ocean, United States, Atlantic Ocean

Glossary

A

acceleration   the rate at which velocity changes; an object accelerates if its speed, direction, or both change (89)

active solar heating   a solar-heating system consisting of solar collectors and a network of pipes that distributes energy from the sun throughout a building (133)

adaptation   a characteristic that helps an organism survive and reproduce in its environment (219)

aerial photograph   a photograph taken from the air (417)

air pressure   the measure of the force with which air particles push on a surface (509)

air sacs   special organs attached to a bird's lungs that store air (376)

alluvial fan   a fan-shaped river deposit that forms on dry land (493)

altitude   the height of an object above the Earth's surface (509)

amniotic (AM nee AHT ik) **egg**   an egg containing amniotic fluid that protects the developing embryo; usually surrounded by a hard shell (360)

amorphous (uh MAWR fuhs) the term that describes the type of solid that is made of particles that are in no special order (63)

ampere (A) the unit for expressing electric current; often shortened to amp (162)

Animalia   a classification kingdom made up of complex, many-celled organisms that have no cell walls, are usually able to move about, and have nervous systems that help them sense and react to their surroundings (305)

antenna   a feeler on an arthropod's head that senses touch, taste, or smell (328)

anticline   a type of fold made when horizontal stress acts on rock (466)

anticyclone   an area that has higher pressure than the surrounding areas (521)

aquifer   a rock layer that stores ground water and allows it to flow (494)

Archaebacteria (AHR kee bak TIR ee uh) a classification kingdom made up of bacteria that live in extreme environments (301)

area   a measure of how much surface an object has (23)

arthropod   a member of the largest group of animals on Earth; an arthropod has a segmented body with specialized parts, jointed limbs, an exoskeleton, and a well-developed nervous system (326)

artificial satellite   any human-made object placed in orbit around a body in space (576)

asteroid   a small, rocky body that revolves around the sun (560)

asteroid belt   the region of the solar system that most asteroids occupy; roughly between the orbits of Mars and Jupiter (560)

asthenosphere (as THEN uh SFIR) the soft layer of the mantle on which pieces of the lithosphere move (459)

astronomical unit (AU) the average distance between the Earth and the sun; approximately 149,600,000 km (539)

asymmetry (ay SIM uh tree) a body plan in which there is no symmetry (318)

atmosphere   a mixture of gases that surrounds a planet, such as Earth (508)

atom   the smallest particle into which an element can be divided and still be the same substance (123, 543)

auroras   colorful regions of light in the sky caused when electrically charged particles from the sun interact with the atmosphere (544)

axis   an imaginary line that runs through the north and south poles of a celestial body that rotates (409)

axis of rotation   the imaginary straight line that runs through the north and south poles of a celestial body that rotates (552)

azimuthal (AZ uh MYOOTH uhl) **projection**   a map projection that is made by moving the contents of the globe onto a plane (416)

B

battery   a device that is made of one or more cells and converts chemical energy into electrical energy (159)

bilateral symmetry (bie LAT uhr uhl SIM uh tree) a body plan in which two equal halves of an organism's body mirror each other (318)

biomass   organic matter that can be burned to release energy (140)

biosphere   all of the ecosystems on Earth; the part of Earth where life exists (273)

bird of prey   a bird that hunts and eats other vertebrates (381)

blubber   a thick layer of fat under the skin of whales and other mammals that live in cold oceans (385)

boiling vaporization that occurs throughout a liquid (72)

boiling point the temperature at which a liquid boils and becomes a gas (72)

Boyle's law the law that states that for a fixed amount of gas at a constant temperature, the volume of the gas increases as its pressure decreases and the volume of the gas decreases as its pressure increases (67)

brooding a bird's use of its body heat to keep its eggs warm until they hatch (379)

C

canine one of four large, stabbing teeth that some mammals use to grab food and hold onto it (386)

cardinal directions north, south, east, and west (409)

carnivore a meat-eating mammal that has large canines and special teeth for slicing meat (392)

cell (biological) the basic unit of living things; cells carry out many functions that serve to sustain life (184)

cell (electric) a device that produces an electric current by converting chemical energy into electrical energy (159)

cell membrane a lipid bilayer that encloses a cell (187)

cell wall a rigid structure that surrounds the cell membrane and provides support (191)

cephalothorax (SEF uh loh THAWR aks) a body part of an arachnid, which is made of the head and the thorax (329)

cetacean a fishlike mammal that lives in the water and uses echolocation to find food; a whale, dolphin, or porpoise (394)

change of state the change of a substance from one physical form to another (70)

channel the path that a stream follows (487)

characteristic property a property of a substance that is always the same whether the sample observed is large or small (71)

Charles's law the law that states that for a fixed amount of gas at a constant pressure, the volume of the gas increases as its temperature increases, and the volume of the gas decreases as its temperature decreases (68)

chemical change a change that occurs when one or more substances are changed into entirely new substances with different properties; chemical changes cannot be reversed using physical means (49)

chemical energy the energy stored in a substance that can be released when the substance reacts (121)

chemical property a property of matter that describes a substance based on its ability to change into a new substance or substances with different properties (47)

chlorophyll the green pigment that plants use to make food in photosynthesis (261)

chloroplast (KLAWR uh PLAST) an organelle found in plant and algal cells; the organelle in which photosynthesis occurs (195)

chromosphere a thin layer of the sun's atmosphere between the corona and the photosphere; too faint to see except during a total solar eclipse (541)

circuit a complete, closed path through which electric charges flow (166)

class the third most general level of classification; the largest group into which organisms in a phylum are divided (296)

classification the arranging of things in groups based on their similarities (294)

clockwise in the direction in which the hands of a clock rotate (546)

closed circulatory system a system in which a heart circulates blood through a network of blood vessels that form a closed loop (323)

closed system a well-defined group of objects that transfer energy between one another (128)

cnidarian (ni DER ee uhn) a member of a group of simple invertebrates that have radial symmetry, tissues, a gut, a nervous system, and tentacles covered in stinging cells (320)

collar cell a type of cell found inside a sponge's body; a collar cell removes food from the water and digests food (319)

comet a small body of ice, rock, and cosmic dust loosely packed together that gives off gas and dust in the form of a tail as it passes close to the sun (559)

community all of the populations of different species that live in the same area (273)

compass a tool that uses the natural magnetism of the Earth to show direction (410)

composition the chemical makeup of a rock; describes either the minerals or elements present in it (435, 456)

compound eye an eye that is made of many light-sensitive units that are alike and work together (327)

compression the type of stress that occurs when an object is squeezed (465)

condensation the change of state from a gas to a liquid (73)

condensation point the temperature at which a gas becomes a liquid (73)

conduction (electrical) a method of charging an object that happens when electrons move from one object to another by direct contact (154)

conduction (thermal) the transfer of thermal energy from one substance to another through direct contact; conduction can also occur within a substance (515)

conductor (electrical) a material in which charges can move easily (156)

conic projection a map projection that is made by moving the contents of the globe onto a cone (416)

consumer an organism that eats other organisms (279)

continental crust the thinnest, outermost layer of the Earth that has a make up similar to granite; it has an average thickness of 30 km (456)

contour feather a stiff feather on the body or wing of a bird (375)

contour interval the difference in elevation between one contour line and the next (421)

contour line a line that connects points of equal elevation (420)

convection the transfer of energy by the movement of a liquid or a gas (515)

convection cell a circular pattern of air made by the rising of warm air and the sinking of cool air (519)

convection current the circular motion of liquids or gases due to density differences that result from temperature differences (515)

convective zone the layer of the sun where gases circulate in convection currents, bringing the sun's energy to the surface (541)

convergent boundary the area where two tectonic plates with continental crusts bump into each other or pull apart (469)

core the central, spherical part of the Earth below the mantle (457); *also* the spherical center of the sun where the sun's energy is produced (541)

Coriolis effect the curving of moving objects from a straight path as a result of the Earth's rotation (520)

corona the sun's outer atmosphere, which extends outward a distance equal to 10 to 12 times the diameter of the sun; it is too faint to see except during a total solar eclipse (541)

counterclockwise in the opposite direction from which the hands of a clock rotate (546)

crop the part of a bird's digestive system where food is stored (375)

crust the thin, outermost layer of the Earth (456); *also* the uppermost part of the lithosphere (459)

crystalline (KRIS tuhl in) the type of solid that has a very orderly, three-dimensional arrangement of particles (63)

current a continuous flow of charge caused by the motion of electrons; the rate at which charge passes a given point; expressed in amperes (A) (159, 162)

cyclone an area in the atmosphere that has lower pressure than the surrounding areas (521)

cytoplasm (SIET oh PLAZ uhm) the fluid, membranes, and organelles inside a cell, excluding the nucleus (187)

cytoskeleton (SIET oh SKEL uh tuhn) a web of proteins that helps with cell support and movement (193)

D

data any pieces of information gathered through experimentation (13)

decomposer an organism that gets energy by breaking down the remains of dead organisms (279)

deformation the change in the shape of rock in response to stress (465)

delta a fan-shaped pattern formed as rivers deposit their load in a body of water (492)

density the amount of matter in a given space or volume; the mass per unit volume of a substance (44, 511)

deposition the process in which water, ice, wind, and gravity drop newly formed sediments (442, 491)

diaphragm (DIE uh FRAM) a large muscle at the bottom of the rib cage that helps bring air into a mammal's lungs (385)

dichotomous (die KAHT uh muhs) **key** a guide made up of pairs of descriptive statements that help to identify an organism (298)

discharge the amount of water that a stream or river carries in a given amount of time (487)

distortion on a map, a change in the shapes and sizes of landmasses and oceans—and in distance between and location of landmasses—that happens when information is moved from a curved surface onto a flat surface (414)

divide an area of higher ground that separates watersheds (486)

DNA deoxyribonucleic (dee AHKS ee RIE boh noo KLEE ik) acid; the hereditary material that controls all the activities of a cell, contains the information to make new cells, and provides instructions for making proteins (187, 234)

doldrums an area of low pressure around the equator (523)

down feather a fluffy, insulating feather that lies next to a bird's body (375)

dust tail the tail of a comet that consists of dust particles; tends to follow behind a comet along its orbit (559)

E

echolocation (EK oh loh KAY shuhn) the act of navigating or finding food or prey using high-pitched sound waves and echoes (254, 391)

ecology the study of the relationships between organisms and their environment (272)

ecosystem a community of organisms and their nonliving environment (273)

ectotherm an animal whose body temperature fluctuates with the temperature of its environment (348)

electrical energy the energy of moving electrons (122)

electric current a continuous flow of electric charges; the rate at which charges pass a given point (159, 162)

electric discharge the loss of static electricity as charges move off an object (157)

electric field the region around a charged object in which an electric force is exerted on another charged object (153)

electric force the force between charged objects (153)

electric power the rate at which electrical energy is used to do work; expressed in watts (W) (164)

electrode the part of a cell through which charges enter or exit (159)

electrolyte in a cell, a mixture of chemicals that carries an electric current; chemical changes between the electrolyte and the electrodes convert chemical energy into electrical energy (159)

electron the lightweight, negatively charged subatomic particle that surrounds the nucleus of an atom (543)

elevation the height of an object above sea level (420)

ellipse a circular path; either a perfect circle or an elongated circle (559)

endoplasmic reticulum (EN doh PLAZ mik ri TIK yuh luhm) an organelle composed of membranes that produces lipids, breaks down substances, and packages proteins for delivery out of the cell (194)

endoskeleton (EN doh SKEL uh tuhn) the skeleton inside an animal's body (332)

endotherm an animal that maintains a constant body temperature despite temperature changes in its environment (348)

endothermic the term used to describe a physical or chemical change in which energy is absorbed (71)

energy the ability to do work (118)

energy conversion a change from one form of energy into another; any form of energy can be converted into any other form of energy (124)

energy efficiency (e FISH uhn see) a comparison of the amount of energy before a conversion and the amount of useful energy after a conversion (129)

energy pyramid a triangular diagram that shows the loss of energy at each level of a food chain (282)

energy resource a natural resource that can be converted by humans into other forms of energy in order to do useful work (136)

environment everything that affects an organism (272)

equator an imaginary circle halfway between the poles that divides the Earth into the Northern and Southern Hemispheres (411)

erosion the process by which particles of rock are removed from their source; the removal and transport of rock and soil by the flow of water and by the actions of gravity, wind, and ice (442, 484)

escape velocity the speed and direction a rocket must travel to completely break away from a planet's gravitational pull (575)

Eubacteria (YOO bak TIR ee uh) a classification kingdom made up of all modern bacteria except archaebacteria (301)

eukaryotes (yoo KAR ee OHTZ) single-celled or many-celled organisms whose cells have a nucleus and organelles surrounded by a membrane (188, 302)

evaporation (ee VAP uh RAY shuhn) vaporization that occurs at the surface of a liquid below the liquid's boiling point (72)

evolution the process by which populations accumulate inherited changes over time (214)

exoskeleton a hard skeleton that is made of protein and chitin and covers the outside of an arthropod's body (327)

exothermic the term used to describe a physical or chemical change in which energy is given off (71)

external stimulus a stimulus that comes from outside the body (254)

F

family the fifth most general level of classification; the largest group into which organisms in an order are divided (296)

fault a break in the Earth's crust along which blocks of the crust slide relative to one another (467)

fault-block mountain a mountain that forms when faulting causes large blocks of the Earth's crust to drop down relative to other blocks (472)

fin a fanlike structure that helps fish move, turn, stop, and balance (350)

flood plain the land that is flooded when a river overflows its banks (493)

fluid friction the type of friction that exists between the surfaces of two fluids or between the surface of a fluid and the surface of an object moving through the fluid (99)

folded mountain a mountain that forms when rock layers are squeezed together and pushed upward (470)

folding the bending of rock layers due to stress in the Earth's crust (466)

foliated metamorphic rock that has obvious layering or banding of minerals (438)

food chain the path of energy from one feeding level to another (280)

food web all of the food chains in a community linked together; represents the many paths by which energy can flow through an ecosystem (281)

force a push or a pull; all forces have both size and direction (92)

fossil the physical evidence of an organism, such as remains or imprints, preserved by geologic processes; commonly preserved in sedimentary rock (215)

fossil fuels nonrenewable energy resources that form in the Earth's crust over millions of years from the buried remains of once-living organisms (136)

freezing the change of state from a liquid to a solid (71)

freezing point the temperature at which a liquid changes into a solid (71)

friction a force that opposes motion between two surfaces that are touching (96, 128)

function the job a part of an organism does (203)

Fungi a classification kingdom made up of complex organisms that get food by breaking down dead matter in their surroundings and taking in the nutrients (304)

fur a thick coat of hair (385)

G

Galilean satellites the four largest moons of Jupiter: Io, Europa, Ganymede, and Callisto; discovered by Galileo in 1610 (556)

gas the state in which matter changes in both shape and volume (65)

gas giant a large, gaseous planet of the outer solar system with no known solid surface (550)

gene a segment of DNA that carries hereditary instructions and is passed from parent to offspring (234)

genus the level of classification above species; the largest group into which organisms in a family are divided (296)

geosynchronous orbit (GEO) the orbit in which a satellite travels around the Earth at a speed that exactly matches the rotational speed of the Earth, which keeps the satellite positioned above the same spot on Earth at all times (577)

geothermal energy the energy resulting from the heating of the Earth's crust (140)

gestation the time during which an embryo develops within the mother (389)

gills organs that remove oxygen from the water and carbon dioxide from the blood (350)

gizzard the part of a bird's digestive system where food is ground into small particles that can be digested (375)

Global Positioning System (GPS) a network of satellites that orbits the Earth to measure positions on the Earth's surface (461)

global warming a rise in average global temperatures (516)

global winds the winds that are part of a pattern of air flow that moves across the Earth (522)

Golgi (GAWL jee) **complex** the organelle that modifies, packages, and transports materials out of the cell (196)

gradient the measure of the change in elevation over a certain distance (487)

gravitational potential energy the energy due to an object's position above the Earth's surface (120)

gravitropism (grav i TROH PIZ uhm) a plant's growth response to gravity (259)

gravity a force of attraction between objects that is due to their masses (101)

greenhouse effect the natural heating process of a planet, such as Earth, by which gases in the atmosphere trap thermal energy, which heats the atmosphere (516, 546)

greenhouse gases the gases in the a planet's atmosphere that trap reradiated energy, which heats the atmosphere (516)

ground water the water beneath the Earth's surface (494)

H

heat the transfer of energy between objects at different temperatures (512)

heredity the passing of traits from parent to offspring (231)

hibernation (HIE buhr NAY shuhn) a period of inactivity and lowered body temperature that some animals undergo in winter (257)

hoof a thick pad like a fingernail that covers a mammal's toe (392)

hormone a chemical made in one part of the body that is carried in the blood and can cause a change in another part of the body (253)

horse latitudes areas of high pressure at about 30° north and 30° south latitude (523)

host a living thing upon which another living thing feeds (321)

hydraulic (hie DRAW lik) the term that describes devices that use liquids to transmit pressure from one point to another (64)

hypothesis a possible explanation or answer to a question (12)

I

igneous rock the type of rock that forms when hot, liquid rock, or magma, cools and hardens (436)

incisors the cutting teeth in the front of a mammal's mouth (386)

index contour a darker, heavier contour line on a map that is usually every fifth line and is labeled by elevation (421)

induction a method of charging an object that occurs when charges in an uncharged object are rearranged without direct contact with a charged object (154)

inertia the tendency of all objects to resist any change in motion (42)

inexhaustible resource a resource that exists in such large supply that it is considered almost limitless (139)

inner core the solid, dense center of the Earth (459)

inner solar system the small, inner part of the solar system; encompasses the terrestrial planets Mercury, Venus, Earth, and Mars (545)

insectivore an insect-eating mammal (390)

insulator (electrical) a material in which charges cannot easily move (156)

internal stimulus a stimulus that comes from inside the body (252)

invertebrate (in VUHR tuh brit) an animal that does not have a backbone (318)

ion an electrically charged particle; an atom that has become electrically charged because of a loss or gain of electrons (513, 559)

ionosphere the upper part of the mesosphere and the lower part of the thermosphere that is made up of ions (513)

ion tail the tail of a comet that consists of electrically charged particles called ions; always points directly away from the sun (559)

J

jet stream a narrow belt of high-speed wind that blows in the upper troposphere and the lower stratosphere (524)

joey a young kangaroo (388)

joule (J) the unit used to express energy; equivalent to the newton-meter (N•m) (118)

K

keel a large breastbone that anchors the flight muscles of birds (377)

kinetic (ki NET ik) **energy** the energy of motion that depends on speed and mass (119)

kingdom the most general of the seven levels of classification of organisms (296)

L

lagomorph a placental mammal that has two sets of sharp, gnawing teeth in the front of its upper jaw and a short tail (391)

lateral line system a row or rows of tiny sense organs along the sides of a fish's body that sense water vibrations (350)

latitude the distance north or south from the equator; expressed in degrees (411)

law a summary of many experimental results and observations; a law tells how things work (19)

law of conservation of energy the law that states that energy is neither created nor destroyed (128)

law of electric charges the law that states that like charges repel and opposite charges attract (152)

lift the upward pressure on a bird's wing that helps keep the bird in the air; caused by a difference in air pressure above and below the wing (378)

light energy the energy produced by the vibrations of electrically charged particles (123)

light-minute a unit of length equal to the distance light travels in space in 1 minute; approximately 18 million kilometers (539)

light-year a unit of length equal to the distance light travels in space in 1 year; approximately 9.5 trillion kilometers or 63,000 AU (539)

liquid the state in which matter takes the shape of its container and has a definite volume (64)

lithosphere (LITH oh SFIR) the outermost, rigid layer of the Earth that consists of the crust and the rigid, upper part of the mantle (458)

load a device that uses electrical energy to do work (166); *also* the materials carried by a stream (488)

local winds the winds that move short distances and can move from any direction (522)

longitude the distance east and west from the prime meridian; expressed in degrees (412)

low Earth orbit (LEO) an orbit that is located a few hundred kilometers above the Earth's surface (577)

Luna Earth's moon; Roman goddess of the moon (555)

lung a saclike organ that delivers oxygen from the air to the blood (354)

lysosome (LIE suh SOHM) a vesicle found in animal and fungal cells; lysosomes digest food particles, wastes, and foreign invaders (197)

M

machine a device that helps make work easier by changing the size or direction (or both) of a force; machines can transfer energy and convert energy from one form into another (130)

magma the hot liquid that forms when rock partially or completely melts (457)

magnetic declination the angle of correction for the difference between geographic north and magnetic north (410)

mammary gland a gland, found only in mammals, that makes milk (384)

mantle the layer of the Earth between the crust and the core (457)

map a model of the Earth's surface (408)

maria dark, lava-covered regions of Earth's moon (555)

marsupial (mahr SOO pee UHL) a mammal that has a pouch and gives birth to live, partially developed young (388)

mass the amount of matter that something is made of; its value does not change with the object's location in the universe (24, 41, 105)

matter anything that has volume and mass (38)

mechanical energy the sum of an object's kinetic and potential energy (125)

melting the change of state from a solid to a liquid (71)

melting point the temperature at which a substance changes from a solid to a liquid (71)

meniscus the curve at a liquid's surface by which you measure the volume of the liquid (39)

Mercator (muhr KAYT uhr) **projection** a map projection that is made when the contents of the globe are moved onto a cylinder (415)

mesosphere literally, the "middle sphere"—the strong, lower part of the mantle between the asthenosphere and the outer core (459); *also* the coldest layer of the atmosphere (512)

metamorphic rock the type of rock that forms when existing rocks are heated or squeezed (435)

metamorphosis (MET uh MAWR fuh sis) the process by which an insect or other animal develops from an embryo or larva into an adult (330, 356)

meteor a bright streak of light caused when a meteoroid or comet dust burns up in the atmosphere; a shooting star (561)

meteorite a meteoroid that reaches the Earth's surface without burning up completely (561)

meteoroid a very small, rocky body that revolves around the sun (512, 561)

meteor shower an event in which a large number of meteors occur when the Earth passes through the debris left behind by a comet (561)

meter (m) the basic SI unit of length (23)

mid-ocean ridge a long mountain chain that forms on the ocean floor where tectonic plates pull apart (462)

migrate to move from one place to another when the seasons change (256)

milk teeth the first set of teeth to grow into a mammal's mouth; baby teeth (386)

mineral any naturally forming solid matter with a crystal structure (434)

mitochondria (MIET oh KAHN dree uh) organelles surrounded by two membranes; mitochondria break down food molecules to make ATP (195)

model a representation of an object or system (16)

molars flat teeth in the back of a mammal's mouth; used for grinding (386)

molting in birds, the process of shedding feathers (374)

monocline a type of fold made when vertical stress acts upon rocks (466)

monotreme a mammal that lays eggs (387)

moon a natural satellite of a planet (555)

motion an object's change in position relative to a reference point over a period of time (86)

mutation a change in an organism's hereditary information (233)

N

NASA National Aeronautics and Space Administration; founded to combine all of the separate rocket-development teams in the United States (547, 573)

natural selection the process by which organisms with certain traits survive and reproduce at a higher rate than organisms without these traits (225)

nerve a group of cells that carries impulses from one part of the body to another (246)

net force the force that results from combining all the forces exerted on an object (93)

neutron a heavy subatomic particle with no charge in the nucleus of an atom (543)

newton (N) the SI unit of force (92)

nonfoliated the term describing metamorphic rock that does not have obvious layering or banding of minerals (438)

nonrenewable resources natural resources that cannot be replaced or that can be replaced only over thousands or millions of years (136)

normal fault a fault in which the hanging wall moves down relative to the footwall (467)

nuclear (NOO klee uhr) **energy** the form of energy associated with changes in the nucleus of an atom (123)

nuclear fusion the process by which two or more low-mass atomic nuclei join together, or *fuse,* to form a larger, more massive nucleus, releasing energy in the process (543)

nucleus (NOO klee uhs) (*pl.* nuclei) the tiny, extremely dense, positively charged region in the center of an atom; made up of protons and neutrons (123); *also* a double membrane-covered organelle found in eukaryotic cells; the nucleus contains a cell's DNA (187); *also* the solid center of a comet as it passes close to the sun (543, 559)

O

observation any use of the senses to gather information (11)

oceanic crust the thinnest, outermost layer of the Earth that has a make up similar to basalt; it is between 5 and 8 km thick (456)

ohm (Ω) the unit that expresses electrical resistance (163)

olfactory cells the receptor cells that detect smells (249)

open circulatory system a system in which a heart pumps fluid through vessels that empty into spaces in an animal's body called sinuses (323)

orbit the elliptical path an object takes in space while revolving around another object (540)

orbital velocity the speed and direction a rocket must travel in order to orbit the Earth (575)

order the fourth most general level of classification; the largest group into which organisms in a class are divided (296)

organ a combination of two or more tissues that work together to perform a specific function in the body (201)

organelle a structure within a cell, sometimes surrounded by one or more membranes (187)

organism anything that can independently carry out life processes (203)

organ system a group of organs that work together to perform body functions (202)

osculum (AHS kyoo luhm) a hole at the top of a sponge's body from which water exits (319)

outer core the liquid layer of the Earth's core that lies beneath the mantle and surrounds the inner core (456)

outer solar system the large, outer part of the solar system; encompasses the gas giant planets Jupiter, Saturn, Uranus, and Neptune, as well as Pluto (545)

ozone a substance that is made up of three oxygen atoms and that absorbs ultraviolet radiation from the sun (511)

ozone layer a layer of ozone located in the stratosphere that absorbs ultraviolet radiation from the sun (511)

P

parallel circuit a circuit in which each load is placed on a separate branch (169)

parasite a living thing that feeds upon another living thing (321)

passive solar heating a solar heating system that relies on thick walls and large windows to use energy from the sun as a means of heating (133)

period a definite amount of time (540)

period of revolution the amount of time it takes one body to make one complete orbit, or *revolution,* around another body in space (540)

period of rotation the amount of time it takes for an object to rotate once (540)

permeability a rock's ability to let water pass through it (494)

perpetual (puhr PECH oo uhl) **motion machine** a machine that runs forever without any additional energy input; perpetual motion machines are impossible to create (129)

photocell the part of a solar panel that converts light energy into electrical energy (161)

photosphere the thin layer of the sun where the gases are thick enough to see; the visible surface of the sun (541)

photosynthesis (FOHT oh SIN thuh sis) a process by which plants use the sun's energy to make food (303)

phototropism (foh TAH troh PIZ uhm) a plant's growth response to the direction of light (259)

phylum the second most general level of classification; the largest group into which organisms in a family are divided (296)

physical change a change that affects one or more physical properties of a substance; some physical changes can be undone (48)

physical property a property of matter that can be observed or measured without changing the identity of the matter (43, 456)

pinniped a group of carnivorous ocean mammals that eat fish (392)

placenta a special attachment to a mother's uterus that brings food and oxygen to a growing embryo (389)

placental mammal a mammal that nourishes unborn offspring with a placenta inside the uterus (389)

placer deposit sediment that is deposited at places where a river's current slows down (492)

plane of orbit the imaginary, two-dimensional surface that contains the orbit of a particular planet (552)

planet a body that revolves around a star and has enough mass that gravity forces it to assume a spherical shape; not a satellite of another planet (538)

Plantae a classification kingdom made up of plants—complex, many-celled organisms that are usually green and use the sun's energy to make sugar by photosynthesis (303)

plasma the state of matter that does not have a definite shape or volume and whose particles have broken apart (69)

polar easterlies wind systems that are found between the poles and 60° latitude in both hemispheres (523)

population a group of individuals of the same species that live together in the same area (273)

porosity the amount of space between the particles that make up a rock (494)

potential difference the energy per unit charge; specifically, the difference in energy per unit charge as a charge moves between two points in the path of a current (same as voltage); expressed in volts (V) (160)

potential energy the energy of position or shape (120)

predator an animal that eats another animal (254)

preening the activity in which a bird uses its beak to spread oil on its feathers (375)

pressure the amount of force exerted on a given area (66)

prey an animal that gets eaten by another animal (254)

primate a mammal that has forward-facing eyes, opposable thumbs, and a large brain for an animal of its size; a human, monkey, prosimian, or ape (395)

prime meridian the line that represents 0° longitude (412)

producer an organism that uses sunlight directly to make food (278)

prograde revolution the counterclockwise motion of one body around another body as seen from above the north pole of the more massive body (558)

prograde rotation the counterclockwise spin of a planet or moon as seen from above the planet's north pole (546)

prokaryote (proh KAR ee OHT) an organism that consists of only one cell that does not have a nucleus or any other membrane-covered organelles, also called a bacterium (188, 301)

Protista a classification kingdom of one-celled or many-celled, simple organisms; made up of all eukaryotes that are not plants, animals, or fungi (302)

proton a heavy, positively charged subatomic particle in the nucleus of an atom (543)

R

radial symmetry (RAY dee uhl SIM uh tree) a body plan in which the parts of an animal's body are organized around a center point, like the spokes of a wheel (318)

radiation the transfer of energy through matter or space as waves (514)

radiation balance the balance between energy coming into the Earth's atmosphere and energy leaving the Earth's atmosphere (517)

radiative zone the very dense layer of the sun in which the atoms are so closely packed that light can take millions of years to pass through (541)

recharge zone the ground surface where water enters an aquifer (495)

reference point a fixed place on the Earth's surface from which direction and location can be described (409)

relief the difference in elevation between the highest and lowest points of an area being mapped (421)

remote sensing the gathering of information about something without being there (417)

renewable resources natural resources that can be used and replaced over a relatively short time (139)

resistance the opposition to the flow of electric charge; expressed in ohms (Ω) (163)

retrograde revolution the clockwise motion of one body around another body as seen from above the north pole of the more massive body (558)

retrograde rotation the clockwise spin of a planet or moon as seen from above the planet's north pole (546)

reverse fault a fault in which the hanging wall moves up relative to the footwall (467)

revolution the elliptical motion of a body as it travels around another, more massive body in space (540)

ribosome the organelle that makes proteins (194)

river system a network of streams and rivers that drain an area of its runoff (486)

rock a solid mixture of crystals of one or more minerals (434)

rock cycle the continual process by which new rock is formed from old rock material (439)

rocket a vehicle or device that contains all the substances needed to burn fuel and that uses escaping gas from the burning of fuel to move (572)

rolling friction the type of friction that exists between the surface of a rolling object and the surface of the object it is rolling over (98)

rotation the spin of an object in space (520, 540)

S

satellite a natural or artificial body that revolves around a more massive body like a planet (555)

scales bony structures that protect a fish's body (350)

scavenger an animal that feeds on the dead bodies of other animals (279)

science a process of gathering knowledge about the natural world (4)

scientific methods the ways in which scientists answer questions and solve problems (10)

sediment particles of rock that are eroded and deposited to form sedimentary rock (437)

sedimentary rock the type of rock that forms when particles of rock, or sediment, collect and harden into new rock (437)

segment one of many identical, or almost identical, repeating body parts (324)

seismic waves the type of waves of energy that travel through the Earth (457)

seismograph an instrument located at or near the surface of the Earth that records seismic waves (457)

selective breeding the controlled breeding of organisms that have a certain trait (223)

sensory receptor a cell that detects stimuli in an organism's body or surroundings (246)

series circuit a circuit in which all parts are connected in a single loop (168)

sex cell an egg or sperm; a sex cell carries half the number of chromosomes found in other body cells (235)

sirenia a small group of water mammals that live along coasts or in large rivers; sea cows (394)

sliding friction the type of friction that exists between the surfaces of two objects that are sliding across each other (98)

solar flare a giant storm on the surface of the sun in which huge streams of electrically charged particles are flung out into the solar system (544)

solar system the system composed of the sun (a star) and the planets and other bodies that travel around the sun (538)

solar wind the constant stream of charged particles, or ions, that flows outward from the sun (559)

solid the state in which matter has a definite shape and volume (63)

sound energy the energy caused by an object's vibrations (122)

space probe a vehicle that carries scientific instruments to planets or other bodies in space (580)

space shuttle a reusable vehicle that takes off like a rocket and lands like an airplane (587)

space station a long-term orbiting platform from which other vehicles can be launched or scientific research can be carried out (588)

species the most specific of the seven levels of classification; in sexually reproducing organisms, characterized by a group of organisms that can breed with one another to produce fertile offspring (229, 296)

speed the rate at which an object moves; speed depends on the distance traveled and the time taken to travel that distance (87)

spring an area where the water table reaches the Earth's surface and water flows out from the ground (496)

stalactite (stuh LAK tiet) an icicle-shaped depositional feature that forms on cave ceilings (497)

stalagmite (stuh LAG MIET) a cone-shaped depositional feature that forms on cave floors (497)

states of matter the physical forms in which a substance can exist; states include solid, liquid, gas, and plasma (62)

static electricity the buildup of electric charges on an object (156)

static friction the amount of frictional force between two surfaces that must be overcome to move one of the objects (99)

stimulus anything that causes a reaction in an organism (246)

stratosphere the atmospheric layer above the troposphere (511)

stress the amount of force per unit area that is put on a given material (465)

strike-slip fault a fault in which the two fault blocks move past each other horizontally (468)

structure the shape of part of an organism and the material that part is made of (203)

sublimation (SUHB luh MAY shuhn) the change of state from a solid to a gas (74)

sunspot a cooler region in the sun's photosphere; a cooler, dark spot on the sun's surface (544)

supercontinent the name used to describe all the continents on the Earth when they are joined together into one continent (464)

supercontinent cycle the idea that supercontinents form and break apart over time (464)

surface gravity the percentage of your Earth weight you would have on another planet; the weight an object has at a planet's surface (545)

surface tension a force that acts on the particles at the surface of a liquid and causes the liquid to form spherical drops (65)

swim bladder a balloonlike organ that is filled with oxygen and other gases; gives bony fishes their buoyancy (353)

syncline a type of fold made when horizontal stress acts on rock (466)

system a group of objects that, taken together, form a larger object (538)

T

tadpole an immature amphibian that must live in water (356)

taxonomy (taks AHN uh mee) the science of identifying, classifying, and naming living things (295)

tectonic plate a piece of the lithosphere that moves around on top of the asthenosphere (461)

temperature a measure of how hot (or cold) something is (25); *also* a measure of the average kinetic energy of moving particles in a substance (512)

tension the type of stress that occurs when forces act to stretch an object (465)

terrestrial planet a small, dense, rocky planet similar to Earth (545)

texture the sizes, shapes, and positions of the minerals in a rock (435)

theory a unifying explanation for a broad range of hypotheses and observations that have been supported by testing (18)

therapsids the early reptile ancestors of mammals (383)

thermal energy the total energy of the particles that make up an object (121)

thermocouple a device that converts thermal energy into electrical energy (161)

thermosphere the uppermost layer of the Earth's atmosphere (512)

thigmotropism (thig MAH truh PIZ uhm) a plant's growth response to touch (258)

thrust the force that accelerates a rocket (574)

tissue a group of similar cells that work together to perform a specific job in the body (210)

topographic (TAHP uh GRAF ik) **map** a map that shows the surface features, or topography, of Earth (420)

trade winds the winds that blow from 30° latitude to the equator (522)

trait a distinguishing quality that can be passed from one generation to another (223)

tributary a smaller stream or river that flows into a larger one (486)

tropism (TROH PIZ uhm) a plant's growth response to an external stimulus (258)

troposphere the lowest layer of the Earth's atmosphere (511)

true north the geographic North Pole (410)

U

uplift the process by which regions of the Earth's crust are raised to a higher elevation (469)

uterus an organ inside a female mammal's body where an embryo grows and develops (389)

V

vacuole (VAK yoo OHL) a vesicle found in plants and some protists; vacuoles hold water (197)

vaporization the change of state from a liquid to a gas; includes boiling and evaporation (72)

velocity the speed of an object in a particular direction (88)

vertebrae (VUHR tuh BREE) segments of bone or cartilage that interlock to form a backbone (347)

vertebrate (VUHR tuh brit) an animal with a skull and a backbone (346)

vesicle (VES i kuhl) a membrane-covered compartment (196)

viscosity (vis KAHS uh tee) a liquid's resistance to flow (63)

volcanic mountain a mountain that forms when molten rock erupts onto the Earth's surface (473)

voltage the difference in energy per unit charge as a charge moves between two points in the path of a current (same as potential difference); expressed in volts (V) (163)

volume the amount of space that something occupies or the amount of space that something contains (24, 38)

W

water cycle the continuous movement of water between the Earth and its atmosphere (485)

waterfowl a water bird; includes ducks, cranes, and geese (381)

watershed the region of land drained by a river system (486)

water table an underground boundary where the zone of aeration and the zone of saturation meet (494)

water vascular system a system in which the movement of water helps an animal move, eat, and breathe; echinoderms use this system (333)

weathering the process by which water, ice, heat, and wind act to break down rocks (442)

weight a measure of the gravitational force exerted on an object; its value can change with the location of the object in the universe (41, 104)

well a human-made hole that is deeper than the level of the water table (496)

westerlies wind systems found in both the Northern and Southern Hemispheres between 30° and 60° latitude (523)

wind the movement of air as a result of differences in air pressure (518)

work the action that results when a force causes an object to move in the direction of the force (118)

Z

zone of aeration an underground area above the water table (494)

zone of saturation an underground area below the water table (494)

Spanish Glossary

A

acceleration/aceleración la tasa de cambio de la velocidad; ocurre cuando un objeto cambia su velocidad, dirección o ambas (89)

active solar heating/sistema activo de calefacción por energía solar un sistema de calefacción solar que consta de colectores y tubos que distribuyen energía tomada del Sol a través de un edificio (133)

adaptation/adaptación una característica que ayuda a un organismo a sobrevivir y reproducirse en su medio ambiente (219)

aerial photograph/fotografía aérea una fotografía tomada desde el aire (417)

air pressure/presión del aire la medida de la fuerza con la que las moléculas de aire empujan una superficie (509)

air sacs/bolsas de aire órganos especiales que se encuentran unidos a los pulmones de un ave y almacenan aire (376)

alluvial fan/abanico aluvial el depósito en forma de abanico de la carga de un río que se forma en la tierra seca (493)

altitude/altitud la altura de un objeto sobre la superficie terrestre (509)

amniotic egg/huevo amniótico huevo que contiene líquido amniótico para proteger al embrión en desarrollo; por lo general está rodeado de una cáscara dura (360)

amorphous/amorfo el término que se usa para describir el tipo de sólido que está formado por partículas que no se encuentran en ningún orden particular (63)

ampere/ampere (o amperio) (A) la unidad para expresar una corriente eléctrica; a veces, se abrevia como amp (162)

Animalia/Animalia un reino de clasificación formado por organismos complejos, multicelulares, cuyas células no tienen pared celular; estos organismos pueden desplazarse de un lado a otro y poseen un sistema nervioso que les permite percibir y reaccionar a su medio ambiente (305)

antenna/antena apéndice que se encuentra en la cabeza de un artrópodo y responde al tacto, olor o gusto (328)

anticline/anticlinal un pliegue en forma de taza que se forma en las capas de roca sedimentaria (466)

anticyclone/anticiclón un área de presión más alta que las áreas circundantes (521)

aquifer/acuífero una capa rocosa que almacena agua subterránea y le permite fluir (494)

Archaebacteria/Archaebacteria un reino de clasificación formado por bacterias que viven en ambientes extremos (301)

area/área una medida de la superficie de un objeto (23)

arthropod/artrópodo un miembro del grupo más grande de animales en la Tierra; los artrópodos tienen cuerpos segmentados con partes especializadas, extremidades articuladas, exoesqueleto y un sistema nervioso bien desarrollado (326)

artificial satellite/satélite artificial cualquier objeto hecho por los seres humanos y colocado en órbita alrededor de un cuerpo celeste (576)

asteroid/asteroide un cuerpo pequeño, rocoso, que gira alrededor del Sol (560)

asteroid belt/cinturón de asteroides la región del Sistema Solar ocupada por la mayor parte de los asteroides; se encuentra entre las órbitas de Marte y Júpiter (560)

asthenosphere/astenosfera la capa suave del manto en la que se mueven partes de la litosfera (459)

astronomical unit/unidad astronómica (UA) la distancia promedio entre la Tierra y el Sol; aproximadamente 149,600,000 km (539)

asymmetry/asimetría el plano de un cuerpo en el que no hay simetría (318)

atmosphere/atmósfera una mezcla de gases que rodea un planeta, como la Tierra (508)

atom/átomo la partícula más pequeña en la que se puede dividir un elemento y seguir siendo la misma substancia (123, 543)

auroras/auroras regiones coloridas de luz en el cielo, producidas cuando partículas del Sol cargadas eléctricamente interactúan con la atmósfera (544)

axis/eje una línea imaginaria que va del polo norte al polo sur de un cuerpo celeste en rotación (409)

axis of rotation/eje de rotación la línea recta imaginaria que va del polo norte al polo sur de un cuerpo celeste en rotación (552)

azimuthal projection/proyección azimutal una proyección cartográfica que se hace al transferir el contenido del globo a un plano (416)

B

battery/pila un aparato formado por una o varias celdas que convierte la energía química en energía eléctrica (159)

bilateral symmetry/simetría bilateral condición del cuerpo de un organismo en el que las dos mitades son iguales entre sí con respecto a un plano (318)

biomass/biomasa materia orgánica que libera energía al quemarse (140)

biosphere/biosfera todos los ecosistemas de la Tierra; la parte de la Tierra donde hay vida (273)

bird of prey/ave de rapiña un ave que caza y se alimenta de otros vertebrados (381)

blubber/grasa de ballena una capa gruesa de grasa que mantiene calientes a los animales que viven en aguas frías del océano (385)

boiling/ebullición vaporización que ocurre en todo el líquido (72)

boiling point/punto de ebullición la temperatura a la que un líquido hierve y se convierte en gas (72)

Boyle's law/ley de Boyle la ley que establece que a una temperatura constante, el volumen de un gas aumenta a medida que su presión disminuye y el volumen de un gas disminuye a medida que su presión aumenta (67)

brooding/empollar sentarse un ave sobre sus huevos para mantenerlos calientes hasta que nacen los pichones (379)

C

canine/colmillo uno de los cuatro dientes largos y punzantes con los que algunos mamíferos toman su comida (386)

cardinal directions/puntos cardinales Norte, Sur, Este y Oeste (409)

carnivore/carnívoro un mamífero que come carne y tiene colmillos largos y dientes especiales para cortar la carne (392)

cell (biological)/célula la unidad fundamental de todos los seres vivos; las células desempeñan muchas funciones esenciales para mantener la vida (184)

cell (electric)/celda un aparato que genera una corriente eléctrica al transformar la energía química en energía eléctrica (159)

cell membrane/membrana celular una bicapa de lípidos que envuelve a la célula (187)

cell wall/pared celular una estructura rígida que rodea a la membrana celular y le da soporte a la célula (191)

cephalothorax/cefalotórax una parte del cuerpo de un arácnido, constituida por la cabeza y el tórax (329)

cetacean/cetáceo un mamífero parecido a un pez que vive en el agua y utiliza la ecolocación para encontrar su alimento; una ballena, delfín o marsopa (394)

change of state/cambio de estado el paso de una substancia de un estado físico a otro (70)

channel/cauce el trayecto que sigue una corriente de agua (487)

characteristic property/propiedad característica la propiedad de una substancia que es siempre igual, sin importar si la muestra observada es grande o pequeña (71)

Charles's law/ley de Charles la ley que establece que a una presión constante, el volumen de un gas aumenta a medida que su temperatura aumenta, y el volumen de un gas disminuye a medida que su temperatura disminuye (68)

chemical change/cambio químico un cambio que ocurre cuando una o más substancias se transforman en substancias nuevas con propiedades distintas; los cambios químicos no pueden revertirse por medios físicos (49)

chemical energy/energía química la energía almacenada en una substancia que se libera cuando la substancia reacciona (121)

chemical property/propiedad química una propiedad de la materia que describe a una substancia en función de su capacidad para transformarse en una substancia o substancias nueva con propiedades distintas (47)

chlorophyll/clorofila el pigmento verde que las plantas utilizan para elaborar su alimento durante la fotosíntesis (261)

chloroplast/cloroplasto un organelo que se encuentra en las células vegetales y en las células de las algas; el organelo en que ocurre la fotosíntesis (195)

chromosphere/cromosfera una capa delgada de la atmósfera del Sol que se encuentra entre la corona y la fotosfera; es demasiado tenue como para verse a simple vista, excepto durante un eclipse total de Sol (541)

circuit/circuito un trayecto completo y cerrado, por el cual circulan las cargas eléctricas (166)

class/clase el tercer nivel general de clasificación; el grupo más grande en que se dividen los organismos que pertenecen a un mismo phylum (296)

classification/clasificación el arreglo de las cosas en grupos en función de sus semejanzas (294)

clockwise/en sentido de las manecillas del reloj en la dirección en que rotan las manecillas del reloj (546)

closed circulatory system/sistema cerrado de circulación un sistema en el que el corazón hace circular la sangre a través de una red de vasos sanguíneos que forman un sistema cerrado (323)

closed system/sistema cerrado un grupo bien definido de objetos que intercambian energía entre ellos (128)

cnidarian/cnidario un miembro del grupo de invertebrados simples que tienen simetría radial, tejidos, intestino, sistema nervioso y tentáculos cubiertos de células urticantes (320)

collar cell/coanocito un tipo de célula que se encuentra en el interior del cuerpo de una esponja; un coanocito toma alimento del agua y lo digiere (319)

comet/cometa un cuerpo pequeño formado por hielo, roca y polvo cósmico unidos de forma poco rígida, cuyos gases y polvo forman una cola cuando pasa cerca del Sol (559)

community/comunidad todas las poblaciones de especies diferentes que viven en una misma área (273)

compass/brújula una herramienta que utiliza el magnetismo natural de la Tierra para indicar la dirección (410)

composition/composición la composición química de una roca; describe los minerales o los elementos presentes en ella (435, 456)

compound eye/ojo compuesto ojo formado por muchas unidades idénticas que trabajan en conjunto (327)

compression/compresión el tipo de presión que ocurre cuando se aprieta un objeto (465)

condensation/condensación el cambio de estado de gas a líquido (73)

condensation point/punto de condensación la temperatura a la que un gas se convierte en líquido (73)

conduction (electrical)/conducción (eléctrica) un método para cargar eléctricamente un objeto que ocurre cuando los electrones pasan de un objeto al otro por contacto directo (154)

conduction (thermal)/conducción (térmica) el paso de energía térmica de una substancia a otra por contacto directo; también puede ocurrir dentro de una misma substancia (515)

conductor (electrical)/conductor (eléctrico) un material por el cual las cargas eléctricas se mueven libremente (156)

conic projection/proyección cónica una proyección cartográfica que se hace al transferir el contenido del globo a un cono (416)

consumer/consumidor un organismo que se alimenta de otros organismos (279)

continental crust/corteza continental la capa externa y más delgada de la Tierra, cuya constitución es similar a la del granito; su grosor promedio es de 30 km (456)

contour feather/pluma de contorno una pluma rígida en el cuerpo o ala de un ave (375)

contour interval/equidistancia de las curvas de nivel la diferencia en elevación entre una curva de nivel y la siguiente (421)

contour line/curva de nivel una línea que conecta puntos que tienen la misma elevación (420)

convection/convección la transferencia de energía debida al movimiento de un líquido o un gas (515)

convection cell/celda de convección un patrón circular del aire producido por aire caliente que sube y aire frío que baja (519)

convection current/corriente de convección el movimiento circular de los líquidos y gases que se da debido a diferencias en la densidad que son causadas por diferencias en la temperatura (515)

convection zone/zona de convección la capa del Sol donde los gases circulan en corrientes de convección y, así, llevan la energía del Sol a su superficie (541)

convergent boundary/límite convergente el área donde dos placas tectónicas con cortezas continentales chocan una con otra o se separan (469)

core/núcleo la parte central y esférica de la Tierra que se encuentra debajo del manto (457); *también* el centro esférico del Sol, donde se produce su energía (541)

Coriolis effect/efecto Coriolis el movimiento o desviación de los objetos de una línea recta como resultado de la rotación de la Tierra (520)

corona/corona la atmósfera exterior del Sol, que se extiende hacia afuera una distancia de 10 a 12 veces el diámetro del Sol; es demasiado tenue como para verse a simple vista, excepto durante un eclipse total de Sol (541)

counterclockwise/en sentido contrario al de las manecillas del reloj en dirección opuesta a la que rotan las manecillas del reloj (546)

crop/buche parte del sistema digestivo de un ave en el cual se almacena alimento (375)

crust/corteza la delgada capa externa de la Tierra (456); *también* la parte superior de la litosfera (459)

crystalline/cristalino el tipo de sólido cuyas partículas están distribuidas en un arreglo tridimensional muy ordenado (63)

current/corriente el flujo continuo de una carga generado por el movimiento de los electrones; la velocidad a la que una carga pasa por un punto dado; se expresa en amperes (A) (159, 162)

cyclone/ciclón un área de la atmósfera cuya presión es más baja que la de las áreas circundantes (521)

cytoplasm/citoplasma el fluido que se encuentra dentro de una célula (187)

cytoskeleton/citoesqueleto una red de proteínas que le da soporte y movimiento a la célula (193)

D

data/datos cualquier información recopilada a partir de experimentos (13)

decomposer/descomponedor un organismo que obtiene su energía a partir de los desechos de organismos muertos (279)

deformation/deformación el cambio en la forma de una roca en respuesta a la presión (465)

delta/delta un patrón en forma de abanico que se forma a medida que los ríos depositan su carga en una masa de agua (492)

density/densidad la cantidad de materia presente en un determinado espacio o volumen; la masa de una substancia por unidad de volumen (44, 511)

deposition/sedimentación el proceso en el que el agua, el hielo, el viento y la gravedad depositan sedimentos recién formados (442, 491)

diaphragm/diafragma un músculo grande que se encuentra al fondo de la caja torácica, el cual ayuda a llevar el aire adentro de los pulmones de los mamíferos (385)

dichotomous key/clave dicotómica una guía formada por pares de oraciones descriptivas que permite identificar a un organismo (298)

discharge/descarga la cantidad de agua que lleva un arroyo o río en un momento dado (487)

distortion/distorsión un cambio en el tamaño y forma de las masas de tierra y los océanos, y en la distancia y dirección entre las masas de tierra, que ocurre cuando se transfiere información de una superficie curva a una plana (414)

divide/cresta divisoria un área de tierra más alta que separa cuencas de drenaje (486)

DNA/ADN ácido desoxirribonucleico; el material hereditario que controla todas las actividades de la célula, contiene la información para hacer células nuevas y da instrucciones para hacer proteínas (187, 234)

doldrums/calmas ecuatoriales un área de baja presión que se encuentra alrededor del ecuador (523)

down feather/plumón una pluma esponjosa y aislante que está en contacto directo con el cuerpo de un ave (375)

dust tail/cola de polvo la cola de un cometa, formada por partículas de polvo; tiende a seguir al cometa alrededor de su órbita (559)

E

echolocation/ecolocación el uso de ondas sonoras de alta frecuencia y ecos para encontrar alimento o una presa (254, 391)

ecology/ecología el estudio de las relaciones entre los organismos y su medio ambiente (272)

ecosystem/ecosistema una comunidad de organismos y su medio ambiente inerte, o sin vida (273)

ectotherm/heterotermo un animal cuya temperatura fluctúa con la temperatura del ambiente (348)

electrical energy/energía eléctrica la energía producida por el movimiento de los electrones (122)

electric current/corriente eléctrica flujo continuo de cargas eléctricas; la tasa a la que las cargas pasan por un punto dado (159, 162)

electric discharge/descarga eléctrica la pérdida de electricidad estática que ocurre cuando las cargas salen de un objeto (157)

electric field/campo eléctrico la región alrededor de un objeto cargado eléctricamente en la cual se puede aplicar una fuerza eléctrica en otro objeto cargado (153)

electric force/fuerza eléctrica la fuerza que existe entre objetos con carga eléctrica (153)

electric power/potencia eléctrica la tasa a la que se utiliza la electricidad para hacer un trabajo; se expresa en watts, o vatios (W) (164)

electrode/electrodo la parte de una celda por la que entran o salen las descargas (159)

electrolyte/electrolito mezcla de substancias químicas que transporta una corriente eléctrica en una celda; cambios químicos entre el electrolito y los electrodos transforman la energía química en energía eléctrica (159)

electron/electrón la partícula subatómica de muy poco peso que está cargada negativamente y se mueve alrededor del núcleo del átomo (543)

elevation/elevación la altura de un objeto sobre el nivel del mar (420)

ellipse/elipse un trayecto circular; un círculo perfecto o un círculo alargado (559)

endoplasmic reticulum/retículo endoplásmico un organelo formado por membranas, el cual produce lípidos, descompone substancias y empaca proteínas para su distribución al exterior de la célula (194)

endoskeleton/endoesqueleto el esqueleto que se encuentra adentro del cuerpo de un animal (332)

endotherm/homotermo un animal que mantiene la temperatura de su cuerpo constante a pesar de los cambios de temperatura de su medio ambiente (348)

endothermic/endotérmico el término que se usa para describir un cambio físico o químico en el que se absorbe energía (71)

energy/energía la capacidad de hacer un trabajo (118)

energy conversión/transformación de la energía el paso de una forma de energía a otra; cualquier forma de energía puede transformarse en otra (124)

energy efficiency/eficiencia energética una comparación de la cantidad de energía presente antes de una conversión y la cantidad de energía útil después de la conversión (129)

energy pyramid/pirámide de energía   un dia-grama triangular que muestra la pérdida de energía en cada nivel de la cadena alimenticia (282)

energy resource/recurso energético   un recurso natural que los seres humanos pueden transformar en otras formas de energía para hacer un trabajo útil (136)

environment/medio ambiente   todo lo que afecta a un organismo (272)

equator/ecuador   un círculo imaginario que se encuentra en un punto medio entre los polos y que divide a la Tierra en los hemisferios norte y sur (411)

erosion/erosión   el proceso por el cual partículas de roca se desprenden de su fuente; el desprendimiento y traslado de rocas y suelo debido al paso del agua, la gravedad, el viento y el hielo (442, 484)

escape velocity/velocidad de escape   es la rapi-dez y dirección en la que un cohete debe viajar para liberarse completamente de la atracción gra-vitacional de un planeta (575)

Eubacteria/Eubacteria   un reino de clasificación formado por todas las bacterias actuales, excepto las arqueobacterias (301)

eukaryotes/eucariotas   organismos unicelulares o pluricelulares cuyas células tienen un núcleo y organelos envueltos por una membrana (188, 302)

evaporation/evaporación   vaporización que ocurre en la superficie de un líquido antes de llegar a su punto de ebullición (72)

evolution/evolución   el proceso por el cual las poblaciones acumulan cambios heredados a través del tiempo (214)

exoskeleton/exoesqueleto   un esqueleto duro formado por proteína y quitina, que cubre la parte exterior del cuerpo de un artrópodo (327)

exothermic/exotérmico   el término que se usa para describir un cambio físico o químico en el cual se libera energía (71)

external stimulus/estímulo externo   un estímulo que proviene del exterior del cuerpo (254)

F

family/familia   el quinto nivel general de clasifi-cación; el grupo más grande en que se dividen los organismos de un mismo orden (296)

fault/falla   una grieta en la corteza terrestre a lo largo de la cual se deslizan los bloques de la corteza (467)

fault-block mountain/montaña de bloque de falla   una montaña que se forma cuando las fallas hacen que grandes bloques de la corteza terrestre se hundan con respecto a otros bloques (472)

fin/aleta   una estructura en forma de abanico que les permite a los peces moverse, volverse, dete-nerse y balancearse (350)

flood plain/planicie aluvial   el terreno que se inunda cuando un río se desborda (493)

fluid friction/fricción de fluidos   el tipo de fric-ción que se da entre las superficies de dos líquidos o entre la superficie de un fluido y la superficie de un objeto que se mueve a través de un fluido (99)

folded mountain/montaña de plegamiento   una montaña que se forma cuando capas de roca se comprimen y son empujadas hacia arriba (470)

folding/plegamiento   doblez de las capas de roca debido a los movimientos de la corteza terrestre (466)

foliated/esquistosa   roca metamórfica en la que los minerales están alineados o en bandas (438)

food chain/cadena alimenticia   el paso de la energía de un nivel de alimentación al siguiente (280)

food web/red alimenticia   enlace de todas las cadenas alimenticias de una comunidad; representa los distintos caminos que la energía puede tomar para moverse en un ecosistema (281)

force/fuerza   un empuje o tirón; todas las fuerzas tienen magnitud y sentido (92)

fossil/fósil   la prueba física (por ejemplo, restos o huellas) de la existencia de un organismo conser-vado por procesos geológicos; normalmente se conservan en rocas sedimentarias (215)

fossil fuels/combustibles fósiles   recursos no renovables de energía que se forman en la corteza terrestre a través de millones de años, a partir de los restos de organismos vivos (136)

freezing/congelación   el cambio de estado de líquido a sólido (71)

freezing point/punto de congelación   la tempe-ratura a la que un líquido se convierte en sólido (71)

friction/fricción   una fuerza que se opone al movimiento entre dos superficies que están en contacto (96, 128)

function/función   el trabajo que hace una parte de un organismo (203)

Fungi/Fungi   un reino de clasificación formado por organismos complejos que obtienen alimento a partir de los nutrientes de la materia muerta de su medio ambiente (304)

fur/pelaje   una capa gruesa de pelo (385)

G

Galilean satellites/satélites galileanos   las cuatro lunas más grandes de Júpiter: Io, Europa, Ganimedes y Calisto; fueron descubiertas por Galileo en 1610 (556)

gas/gas   el estado en que la materia cambia de forma y de volumen (65)

gas giant/gigante gaseoso   un planeta grande y gaseoso que se encuentra en la parte externa del Sistema Solar y que no tiene superficie sólida (550)

gene/gene   un segmento de ADN que contiene las instrucciones de la herencia y es transmitido de los padres a las crías (234)

genus/género   el nivel de clasificación que se encuentra sobre la especie; el grupo más grande en que se dividen los organismos de una misma familia (296)

geosynchronous orbit/órbita geosincrónica   la órbita en que se mueve un satélite alrededor de la Tierra, a una velocidad exactamente igual a la velocidad de rotación de la Tierra, de forma tal que el satélite queda ubicado sobre el mismo punto todo el tiempo (577)

geothermal energy/energía geotérmica   energía producida por el calentamiento de la corteza terrestre (140)

gestation/gestación   el tiempo que le toma a un embrión desarrollarse dentro de su madre (389)

gills/branquias   órganos que extraen oxígeno del agua y dióxido de carbono de la sangre (350)

gizzard/molleja   la parte del sistema digestivo de un ave donde la carne se muele en partículas pequeñas digeribles (375)

Global Positioning System/sistema global de posición   una red de satélites que se encuentran en órbita alrededor de la Tierra para medir posiciones en la superficie terrestre (461)

global warming/calentamiento global   aumento en las temperaturas globales promedio (516)

global winds/vientos globales   los vientos que son parte de un patrón de flujo de aire que se mueve por toda la Tierra (522)

Golgi complex/aparato de Golgi   el organelo que transforma, empaca y transporta materiales al exterior de la célula (196)

gradient/gradiente   la medida del cambio en la elevación en una distancia dada (487)

gravitational potential energy/energía potencial gravitatoria   la energía generada por la posición de un objeto sobre la superficie terrestre (120)

gravitropism/gravitropismo   el crecimiento de una planta en respuesta a la gravedad (259)

gravity/gravedad   una fuerza de atracción entre objetos debida a su masa (101)

greenhouse effect/efecto invernadero   el proceso de calentamiento natural de un planeta, como la Tierra, por medio del cual los gases de la atmósfera atrapan la energía térmica, y ésta calienta la atmósfera (516, 546)

greenhouse gases/gases invernadero   los gases que se encuentran en la atmósfera del planeta que atrapan la energía irradiada que calienta la atmósfera (516)

ground water/agua subterránea   agua que se encuentra bajo la superficie terrestre (494)

H

heat/calor   la transferencia de energía entre objetos que están a distintas temperaturas (512)

heredity/herencia   la transmisión de rasgos de los padres a sus crías (231)

hibernation/hibernación   un período de inactividad que algunos animales experimentan en el invierno, en el que la temperatura del cuerpo disminuye (257)

hoof/pezuña   almohadilla en forma de uña que cubre el dedo del pie de algunos mamíferos (392)

hormone/hormona   una substancia química elaborada en una parte del cuerpo que es transportada en la sangre y puede ocasionar un cambio en otra parte del cuerpo (253)

horse latitudes/calmas tropicales   áreas de alta presión que se encuentran alrededor de los 30° de latitud norte y 30° de latitud sur (523)

host/huésped   un ser vivo del que se alimenta otro organismo (321)

hydraulic/hidráulico   el término que describe aparatos que transmiten presión de un punto a otro mediante el movimiento de líquidos (64)

hypotesis/hipótesis   una explicación o respuesta posible a una pregunta (12)

I

igneous rock/roca ígnea   el tipo de roca que se forma cuando la roca caliente y líquida, o magma, se enfría y endurece (436)

incisors/incisivos   los dientes cortantes que se encuentran en la parte frontal de la boca de un mamífero (386)

index contour/curva de nivel indicador   una curva de nivel más gruesa y obscura, marcada por la elevación y que normalmente se encuentra cada quinta curva en un mapa (421)

induction/inducción   un método para cargar eléctricamente un objeto, que ocurre cuando las cargas de un cuerpo que no está cargado se reacomodan sin entrar en contacto directo con un cuerpo cargado (154)

inertia/inercia   la resistencia que presentan todos los objetos a los cambios de movimiento (42)

inner core/núcelo interno   el centro sólido y denso de la Tierra (459)

inner solar system/Sistema Solar interno   la parte pequeña e interna del Sistema Solar; abarca los planetas terrestres, como Mercurio, Venus, la Tierra y Marte (545)

insectivore/insectívoro   un mamífero que se alimenta de insectos (390)

insulator (electrical)/aislante (eléctrico) un material que no deja pasar las cargas eléctricas fácilmente (156)

internal stimulus/estímulo interno un estímulo que proviene del interior del cuerpo (252)

invertebrate/invertebrado un animal que no tiene columna vertebral (318)

ion/ion una partícula con carga eléctrica; un átomo que se ha cargado eléctricamente debido a que ganó o perdió electrones (513, 559)

ionosphere/ionosfera la parte superior de la mesosfera y la parte inferior de la termosfera, que está formada por iones (513)

ion tail/cola iónica la cola de un cometa formada por partículas cargadas eléctricamente, llamadas iones; siempre apunta hacia fuera del Sol (559)

J

jet stream/chorro de viento una banda estrecha de vientos de alta velocidad que sopla en la parte superior de la troposfera y en la parte inferior de la estratosfera (524)

joule/joule (o julio) (J) la unidad que se utiliza para expresar energía; equivale al newton-metro (N•m) (118)

K

keel/quilla un hueso grande del pecho de las aves que les permite volar (377)

kinetic energy/energía cinética la energía del movimiento, que depende de la velocidad y la masa (119)

kingdom/reino el más general de los siete niveles de clasificación de los organismos (296)

L

lagomorph/lagomorfo un mamífero placentario que tiene dos hileras de dientes filosos y punzantes en la parte frontal de la mandíbula superior y una cola corta (391)

lateral line system/sistema de líneas laterales una hilera o hileras de pequeños órganos de los sentidos que perciben vibraciones del agua y están localizadas en los costados del cuerpo de un pez (350)

latitude/latitud la distancia hacia el Norte o hacia el Sur del ecuador; se expresa en grados (411)

law/ley un resumen de muchas observaciones y resultados experimentales; una ley dice cómo funcionan las cosas (19)

law of conservation of energy/ley de la conservación de la energía la ley que establece que la energía ni se crea ni se destruye (128)

law of electric charges/ley de las cargas eléctricas la ley que establece que las cargas iguales se repelen y las cargas opuestas se atraen (152)

lift/sustentación la presión ascendente en el ala de un ave que permite que el ave se mantenga en el aire; es causada por una diferencia en la presión del aire entre la parte superior e inferior del ala (378)

light energy/energía luminosa la energía producida por la vibración de las partículas con carga eléctrica (123)

light-minute/minuto luz una unidad de longitud equivalente a la distancia que la luz recorre en el espacio en un minuto; aproximadamente 18,000,000 km (539)

light-year/año luz una unidad de longitud equivalente a la distancia que la luz recorre en el espacio en un año; aproximadamente 9,500,000,000,000 km o 63,000 UA (539)

liquid/líquido el estado en que la materia adopta la forma del recipiente que la contiene y tiene un volumen definido (64)

lithosphere/litosfera la capa externa y rígida de la Tierra formada por la corteza y la parte superior y rígida del manto (458)

load/carga un aparato que consume energía eléctrica para producir un trabajo (166); *también* los materiales arrastrados por una corriente de agua (488)

local winds/vientos locales los vientos que se mueven distancias cortas en cualquier dirección (522)

longitude/longitud la distancia hacia el Este y Oeste del primer meridiano; se expresa en grados (412)

low Earth orbit/órbita cercana a la Tierra una órbita que se encuentra a unos cuantos kilómetros de la superficie terrestre (577)

Luna/Luna la luna de la Tierra; la diosa romana de la Luna (555)

lung/pulmón un órgano en forma de bolsa que suministra oxígeno del aire a la sangre (354)

lysosome/lisosoma una vesícula que se encuentra en las células animales y en las células de los hongos; los lisosomas digieren partículas de alimento, desechos e invasores (197)

M

machine/máquina un aparato que facilita el trabajo al cambiar la magnitud o la dirección de una fuerza (o ambas); las máquinas pueden transferir energía y transformarla de una forma a otra (130)

magma/magma el líquido caliente que se forma cuando una roca se derrite parcial o totalmente (457)

magma/magma   el líquido caliente que se forma cuando una roca se derrite parcial o totalmente (457)

magnetic declination/declinación magnética   el ángulo de corrección de la diferencia entre el Norte geográfico y el norte magnético (410)

mammary gland/glándula mamaria   una glándula, que se encuentra sólo en los mamíferos, que elabora leche (384)

mantle/manto   la capa de la Tierra que se encuentra entre la superficie y el núcleo (457)

map/mapa   una representación de la superficie terrestre (408)

maria/mares (de la Luna)   regiones obscuras y cubiertas de lava de la superficie de la Luna (555)

marsupial/marsupial   un mamífero que tiene una bolsa y que da a luz crías vivas, parcialmente desarrolladas (388)

mass/masa   cantidad de materia de que está hecho un objeto; su valor no cambia en función de la ubicación del objeto en el universo (24, 41, 105)

matter/materia   todo lo que tiene volumen y masa (38)

mechanical energy/energía mecánica   suma de las energías cinética y potencial de un objeto (125)

melting/fusión   el cambio de estado de sólido a líquido (71)

melting point/punto de fusión   la temperatura a la que una substancia pasa del estado sólido al líquido (71)

meniscus/menisco   curvatura que se forma en la superficie de un líquido mediante la cual se mide su volumen (39)

Mercator projection/proyección de Mercator   una proyección cartográfica que se hace al transferir el contenido del globo a un cilindro (415)

mesosphere/mesosfera   literalmente, la "esfera intermedia"—la parte inferior y fuerte del manto que se encuentra entre la astenosfera y el núcleo externo (459); *también* la capa más fría de la atmósfera (512)

metamorphic rock/roca metamórfica   el tipo de roca que se forma cuando las rocas existentes se calientan o comprimen (435)

metamorphosis/metamorfosis   el proceso por el cual un insecto u otro animal se desarrolla a partir de un embrión o larva y se convierte en un adulto (330, 356)

meteor/meteoro   un rayo de luz brillante producido cuando un meteoroide o polvo de cometa se quema en la atmósfera; una estrella fugaz (561)

meteorite/meteorito   un meteoroide que llega a la superficie terrestre sin haberse quemado completamente (561)

meteoroid/meteoroide   un cuerpo rocoso, muy pequeño, que gira alrededor del Sol (512, 561)

meteor shower/lluvia de meteoros   un acontecimiento en el que caen muchos meteoros cuando la Tierra pasa a través de los restos de un cometa (561)

meter/metro   (m) la unidad fundamental SI de longitud (23)

mid-ocean ridge/dorsal oceánica   cadena larga de montañas que se forma en el fondo del océano donde las placas tectónicas se separan (462)

migrate/migrar   trasladarse de un lugar a otro cuando las estaciones cambian (256)

milk teeth/dientes de leche   el primer juego de dientes que crecen en la boca de un mamífero; dientes de bebé o niño (386)

mineral/mineral   cualquier material sólido que se forma naturalmente con una estructura cristalina (434)

mitochondria/mitocondrias   organelos rodeados de dos membranas; las mitocondrias descomponen las moléculas de alimento para hacer ATP (195)

model/modelo   una representación de un objeto o sistema (16)

molars/muelas   dientes planos que se encuentran en la parte posterior de la boca de un mamífero; se usan para moler (386)

molting/muda   en las aves, el proceso de cambiar las plumas (374)

monocline/monoclinal   un tipo de pliegue que se forma cuando se ejerce presión vertical sobre las rocas (466)

monotreme/monotrema   un mamífero que pone huevos (387)

moon/luna   un satélite natural de un planeta (555)

motion/movimiento   el cambio de posición de un objeto respecto a un punto de referencia en un período de tiempo (86)

mutation/mutación   un cambio en la información hereditaria de un organismo (233)

N

NASA/NASA   Administración Nacional de Aeronáutica y del Espacio; establecida para unificar a todos los equipos dedicados al desarrollo de cohetes en los Estados Unidos (547, 573)

natural selection/selección natural   el proceso por el cual los organismos que tienen ciertos rasgos sobreviven y se reproducen a una tasa mayor que los organismos que no tienen esos rasgos (225)

nerve/nervio   un grupo de células que transporta impulsos de una parte del cuerpo a otra (246)

net force/fuerza neta   la fuerza que resulta de la suma de todas las fuerzas que actúan sobre un objeto (93)

neutron/neutron   una partícula subatómica sin carga y pesada que se encuentra en el núcleo del átomo (543)

newton/newton   (N) la unidad SI de fuerza (92)

nonfoliated/no esquistosa   el término que describe a una roca metamórfica en que los minerales no están ni alineados ni en bandas (438)

nonrenewable resources/recursos no renovables recursos naturales que no son reemplazables o que sólo se pueden reemplazar a través de miles o millones de años (136)

normal fault/falla normal   falla en la que la pared colgante se mueve hacia abajo en relación con la pared baja (467)

nuclear energy/energía nuclear   la forma de energía asociada con cambios que ocurren en el núcleo del átomo (123)

nuclear fusion/fusión nuclear   el proceso mediante el cual dos o más núcleos de masa atómica baja se unen, o *fusionan,* para formar un núcleo más grande y masivo, liberando energía en el proceso (543)

nucleus/núcleo   la región pequeñísima y extremadamente densa, cargada positivamente, que se encuentra en el centro del átomo; está formado por neutrones y protones (123); *también* un organelo cubierto por una membrana doble que se encuentra en las células eucariotas; el núcleo contiene el ADN de la célula (187); *también* el centro sólido de un cometa al pasar cerca del Sol (543, 559)

O

observation/observación   recopilación de información por medio de los sentidos (11)

oceanic crust/corteza oceánica   la capa externa y más delgada de la Tierra, cuya constitución es similar a la del basalto; tiene de 5 a 8 km de espesor (456)

ohm/ohm (u ohmio)   (Ω) la unidad que expresa resistencia eléctrica (163)

olfactory cells/células olfatorias   células receptoras que detectan olores (249)

open circulatory system/sistema abierto de circulación   un sistema en el que el corazón hace circular la sangre a través de una red de vasos sanguíneos que se vacían en espacios del cuerpo de un animal llamados senos (323)

orbit/órbita   la trayectoria elíptica que un objeto sigue en el espacio al girar alrededor de otro objeto (540)

orbital velocity/velocidad orbital   la rapidez y dirección que un cohete debe tener para moverse en órbita alrededor de la Tierra (575)

order/orden   el cuarto nivel general de clasificación; el grupo más grande en que se dividen los organismos que pertenecen a una misma clase (296)

organ/órgano   una combinación de dos o más tejidos que trabajan en conjunto para realizar una función específica del cuerpo (201)

organelle/organelo   una estructura que se encuentra en el interior de la célula y que a veces está rodeada de una o más membranas (187)

organism/organismo   cualquier cosa que puede llevar a cabo los procesos de la vida independientemente (203)

organ system/sistema de órganos   un grupo de órganos que trabajan en conjunto para realizar funciones del cuerpo (202)

osculum/ósculo   un agujero en la parte superior del cuerpo de una esponja por el que sale agua (319)

outer core/núcleo externo   la capa líquida del núcleo de la Tierra que se encuentra debajo del manto y rodea al núcleo interno (456)

outer solar system/Sistema Solar externo   la parte grande y externa del Sistema Solar; abarca a los gigantes gaseosos: Júpiter, Saturno, Urano y Neptuno, y también a Plutón (545)

ozone/ozono   una substancia que está formada por tres átomos de oxígeno y que absorbe la radiación ultravioleta del Sol (511)

ozone layer/capa de ozono   una capa de ozono que se encuentra en la estratosfera y absorbe la radiación ultravioleta del Sol (511)

P

parallel circuit/circuito en paralelo   un circuito en que cada carga está colocada en un trayecto separado (169)

parasite/parásito   un ser vivo que se alimenta de otro organismo vivo (321)

passive solar heating/sistema pasivo de calefacción por energía solar   un sistema de calefacción solar que cuenta con paredes gruesas y ventanas grandes para utilizar la energía del Sol como fuente de calefacción (133)

period/período   una cantidad específica de tiempo (540)

period of revolution/período de revolución   la cantidad de tiempo que le toma a un cuerpo completar una órbita, o *revolución,* alrededor de otro cuerpo en el espacio (540)

period of rotation/período de rotación   la cantidad de tiempo que le toma a un objeto completar una rotación (540)

permeability/permeabilidad   la capacidad de una roca de permitir que el agua fluya a través de ella (494)

perpetual motion machine/máquina de movimiento perpetuo   una máquina que funciona para siempre, sin necesidad de aplicarle energía adicional; es imposible fabricar máquinas de movimiento perpetuo (129)

photocell/fotocelda la parte de un panel solar que transforma la energía luminosa en energía eléctrica (161)

photosphere/fotosfera la capa delgada del Sol donde los gases son suficientemente espesos como para verse a simple vista; la superficie visible del Sol (541)

photosynthesis/fotosíntesis un proceso por medio del cual las plantas utilizan la energía del Sol para elaborar su alimento (303)

phototropism/fototropismo el crecimiento de una planta en dirección a la luz (259)

phylum/phylum el segundo nivel general de clasificación; el grupo más grande en que se dividen los organismos de una misma familia (296)

physical change/cambio físico un cambio que afecta a una o más propiedades físicas de la substancia; algunos cambios físicos se pueden revertir (48)

physical property/propiedad física una propiedad de la materia que se puede observar y medir sin cambiar la identidad de la materia (43, 456)

pinniped/pinnípedo un grupo de mamíferos carnívoros del océano que comen peces (392)

placenta/placenta órgano adjunto al útero de la madre que le lleva alimento y oxígeno al embrión en crecimiento (389)

placental mammal/mamífero placentario un mamífero que nutre a las crías que todavía no han nacido por medio de una placenta dentro de su útero (389)

placer deposit/yacimiento de aluvión sedimento que se ha depositado en lugares donde la corriente de un río disminuye su velocidad (492)

plane of orbit/plano de órbita la superficial imaginaria, bidimensional, que contiene la órbita de un determinado planeta (552)

planet/planeta un cuerpo que gira alrededor de una estrella y que tiene suficiente masa como para que la gravedad lo fuerce a tener una forma esférica; no se trata de un satélite de otro planeta (538)

Plantae/Plantae un reino de clasificación formado por plantas: organismos complejos y pluricelulares que generalmente son verdes y utilizan la energía del Sol para elaborar azúcares a través de la fotosíntesis (303)

plasma/plasma el estado de la materia que no tiene forma o volumen definido y cuyas partículas se han separado (69)

polar easterlies/vientos polares del levante sistemas de viento que se encuentran entre los polos y los 60° de latitud en ambos hemisferios (523)

population/población un grupo de individuos de la misma especie que viven juntos en una misma área (273)

porosity/porosidad la cantidad de espacio entre las partículas que forman una roca (494)

potential difference/diferencia de potencial la energía por unidad de carga; específicamente, la diferencia en energía por unidad de carga a medida que la carga se mueve de un punto a otro en un circuito (es lo mismo que el voltaje); se expresa en volts, o voltios (V) (160)

potential energy/energía potencial la energía generada por la forma o posición (120)

predator/depredador un animal que se come a otro animal (254)

preening/arreglo de las plumas actividad en la que un ave utiliza el pico para esparcir aceite en sus plumas (375)

pressure/presión la cantidad de fuerza que se aplica en un área determinada (66)

prey/presa un animal que es comido por otro animal (254)

primate/primate un mamífero que tiene visión binocular, pulgares oponibles y un cerebro grande para un animal de su tamaño; un ser humano, mono, prosimio o chimpancé (395)

prime meridian/primer meridiano la línea que representa la longitud 0° (412)

producer/productor un organismo que utiliza la luz del Sol directamente para elaborar alimento (278)

prograde revolution/revolución avanzada el movimiento de un cuerpo alrededor de otro en sentido contrario al de las manecillas del reloj, visto desde el polo norte del cuerpo más grande (558)

prograde rotation/rotación avanzada el giro de un planeta o luna en sentido contrario al de las manecillas del reloj, visto desde su polo norte (546)

prokaryote/procariota una célula que no tiene núcleo ni otros organelos cubierto por membranas, también llamada un bacterium (188, 301)

Protista/Protista un reino de clasificación de organismos simples, unicelulares o pluricelulares; constituido por todos los eucariotas que no son plantas, animales u hongos (302)

proton/protón una partícula subatómica pesada y cargada positivamente que se encuentra en el núcleo del átomo (543)

R

radial symmetry/simetría radial condición del cuerpo de un organismo en que las partes están organizadas alrededor de un punto central, como los rayos de una rueda (318)

radiation/radiación la transferencia de energía a través de la materia o el espacio en forma de ondas (514) radiation balance/balance de radiación el balance entre la energía que llega a la atmósfera de la Tierra y la energía que la abandona (517)

radiative zone/zona radioactiva una capa muy densa del Sol en la que los átomos se encuentran tan apretados que la luz tarda millones de años en atravesarla (541)

recharge zone/zona de recarga la superficie del suelo donde el agua entra a un acuífero (495)

reference point/punto de referencia un lugar fijo en la superficie terrestre a partir del cual se determinan la dirección y ubicación (409)

relief/relieve la diferencia de elevación entre el punto más alto y el más bajo de un área (421)

remote sensing/teledetección la recopilación de información acerca de algo sin estar ahí (417)

renewable resources/recursos renovables recursos naturales que se usan y reemplazan en períodos de tiempo relativamente cortos (139)

resistance/resistencia la oposición al flujo de cargas eléctricas; se expresa en ohms, u ohmios (Ω) (163)

retrograde revolution/revolución retrógada el movimiento de un cuerpo alrededor de otro, en el sentido de las manecillas del reloj, visto desde el polo norte del cuerpo más grande (558)

retrograde rotation/rotación retrógada el giro de un planeta o luna en el sentido de las manecillas del reloj, visto desde su polo norte (546)

reverse fault/falla inversa falla en que la pared colgante se mueve hacia arriba con respecto al muro de falla (467)

revolution/revolución el movimiento elíptico de un cuerpo a medida que se desplaza alrededor de otro cuerpo más grande en el espacio (540)

ribosome/ribosoma el organelo que elabora las proteínas (194)

river system/sistema fluvial una red de ríos y corrientes de agua que drenan un área (486)

rock/roca una mezcla sólida de cristales de uno o más minerales (434)

rock cycle/ciclo de las rocas el proceso continuo por el cual se forman nuevas rocas a partir de material rocoso viejo (439)

rocket/cohete un vehículo o aparato que contiene todas las substancias necesarias para quemar combustible y utiliza gas de escape del combustible para moverse (572)

rolling friction/fricción de rodamiento el tipo de fricción que se da entre la superficie de un objeto rodante y el objeto sobre el cual está rodando (98)

rotation/rotación el giro de un objeto alrededor de su eje en el espacio (520, 540)

S

satellite/satélite un cuerpo natural o artificial que gira alrededor de un cuerpo más masivo como, por ejemplo, un planeta (555)

scales/escamas estructuras óseas que protegen el cuerpo de un pez (350)

scavenger/carroñero un animal que se alimenta de los cuerpos muertos de otros animales (279)

science/ciencia un proceso de recopilación de conocimientos acerca del mundo natural (4)

scientific methods/métodos científicos las formas en que los científicos responden preguntas y resuelven problemas (10)

sediment/sedimento partículas de roca que se erosionan y depositan para formar rocas sedimentarias (437)

sedimentary rock/roca sedimentaria el tipo de roca que se forma cuando partículas de roca, o sedimento, se juntan y endurecen, y forman una roca nueva (437)

segment/segmento uno o más partes repetidas e idénticas o casi idénticas del cuerpo (324)

seismic waves/ondas sísimcas el tipo de ondas de energía que viajan a través de la Tierra (457)

seismograph/sismógrafo un instrumento localizado en la superficie terrestre, o cerca de ella, que registra las ondas sísmicas (457)

selective breeding/reproducción selectiva la reproducción controlada de organismos que tienen un cierto rasgo (223)

sensory receptor/receptor sensorial una célula que detecta estímulos en el cuerpo del organismo o en el medio ambiente (246)

series circuit/circuito en serie un circuito en el que las partes están conectadas en un mismo trayecto (168)

sex cell/gameto un óvulo o un espermatozoide; un gameto lleva la mitad de los cromosomas que se encuentran en otras células del cuerpo (235)

sirenia/sirénidos un grupo pequeño de mamíferos acuáticos que viven en las costas o en ríos grandes; vacas marinas (394)

sliding friction/fricción de deslizamiento el tipo de fricción que se da entre la superficies de dos objetos que se deslizan uno sobre el otro (98)

solar flare/erupción solar una tormenta gigantesca que ocurre en la superficie del Sol, en la cual un torrente de partículas cargadas eléctricamente son despedidas hacia el Sistema Solar (544)

solar system/Sistema Solar el sistema formado por el Sol (una estrella), los planetas y otros cuerpos que giran alrededor del Sol (538)

solar wind/viento solar el flujo constante de partículas cargadas eléctricamente, o iones, hacia el exterior del Sol (559)

solid/sólido   el estado en que la materia tiene forma y volumen definidos (63)

sound energy/energía sonora   la energía producida por las vibraciones de un objeto (122)

space probe/sonda espacial   un vehículo que lleva instrumentos científicos a otros planetas o cuerpos en el espacio (580)

space shuttle/transbordador espacial   un vehículo reutilizable que despega como un cohete y aterriza como un avión (587)

space station/estación espacial   una plataforma de largo plazo que se encuentra en órbita, a partir de la cual pueden despegar otros vehículos y en la que se pueden llevar a cabo investigaciones científicas (588)

species/especie   el más específico de los niveles de clasificación; en los organismos que se reproducen sexualmente, se caracteriza por un grupo de organismos que pueden cruzarse y producir descendencia fértil (229, 296)

speed/rapidez   la tasa a la que un objeto se mueve; depende de la distancia recorrida y del tiempo que toma recorrerla (87)

spring/manantial   un área donde el nivel freático llega a la superficie terrestre y el agua fluye hacia el exterior (496)

stalactite/estalactita   una característica de sedimentación en forma de carámbano que se forma en el techo de las cavernas (497)

stalagmite/estalagmita   una característica de sedimentación que se forma en el suelo de las cavernas (497)

states of matter/estados de la materia   las formas físicas en que se puede encontrar una substancia (62)

static electricity/electricidad estática   la acumulación de cargas eléctricas en un objeto (156)

static friction/fricción estática   la fuerza de fricción entre dos superficies que hay que vencer para poder mover uno de los objetos (99)

stimulus/estímulo   cualquier cosa que causa una reacción en un organismo (246)

stratosphere/estratosfera   la capa atmosférica que se encuentra sobre la troposfera (511)

stress/presión   la cantidad de fuerza por unidad de área que se aplica en un material (465)

strike-slip fault/falla de deslizamiento longitudinal   falla en la que uno de los bloques de falla se mueve más allá del otro en forma horizontal (468)

structure/estructura   la forma de una parte de un organismo y el material del que está hecho la parte (203)

sublimation/sublimación   el cambio de estado de sólido a gas (74)

sunspot/mancha solar   una región más fría de la fotosfera del Sol; una mancha obscura y más fría en la superficie del Sol (544)

supercontinent/supercontinente   el nombre con que se describen todos los continentes de la Tierra cuando estaban unidos en un sólo continente (464)

supercontinent cycle/ciclo del supercontinente   la idea de que se forman y desintegran supercontinentes a través del tiempo (464)

surface gravity/gravedad superficial   el porcentaje de tu peso en la Tierra que tendrías en otro planeta; el peso de un objeto en la superficie de un planeta (545)

surface tensión/tensión superficial   una fuerza que actúa en las partículas que se encuentran en la superficie de un líquido, que hace que el líquido forme gotas esféricas (65)

swim bladder/vejiga natatoria   órgano similar a un globo, lleno de oxígeno y otros gases, que les da a los peces óseos la capacidad de flotar (353)

syncline/sinclinal   un tipo de pliegue que se forma cuando se ejerce presión horizontal sobre las rocas (466)

system/sistema   un grupo de objetos que, si se considera en su conjunto, forma un objeto más grande (538)

T

tadpole/renacuajo   un anfibio joven que debe vivir en el agua (356)

taxonomy/taxonomía   la ciencia que identifica, clasifica y nombra a los seres vivos (295)

tectonic plate/placa tectónica   una pieza de la litosfera que se mueve en la superficie de la astenosfera (461)

temperature/temperatura   una medida de qué tan caliente (o frío) está algo (25); *también* una medida de la energía cinética promedio de las partículas en movimiento de una substancia (512)

tension/tensión   el tipo de presión que ocurre cuando ciertas fuerzas actúan para estirar un objeto (465)

terrestrial planet/planetas terrestres   planetas pequeños, densos y rocosos, parecidos a la Tierra (545)

texture/textura   los tamaños, formas y posiciones de los minerales en una roca (435)

theory/teoría   una explicación que resume diversas hipótesis y observaciones apoyadas por experimentación (18)

therapsids/terápsidos   los antiguos ancestros de los mamíferos (383)

thermal energy/energía térmica   la energía cinética total de las partículas que forman un objeto (121)

thermocouple/termopar aparato que transforma la energía térmica en energía eléctrica (161)

thermosphere/termosfera la capa superior de la atmósfera de la Tierra (512)

thigmotropism/tigmotropismo el crecimiento de una planta en respuesta al tacto (258)

thrust/empuje la fuerza que acelera a un cohete (574)

tissue/tejido un grupo de células similares que trabajan en conjunto para realizar una función específica del cuerpo (210)

topographic map/mapa topográfico un mapa que muestra las características de la superficie, o topografía, de la Tierra (420)

trade winds/vientos alisios los vientos que soplan entre los 30° de latitud y el ecuador (522)

trait/rasgo una cualidad distintiva que puede transmitirse de generación en generación (223)

tributary/afluente corriente o río más pequeño que desemboca en uno más grande (486)

tropism/tropismo el crecimiento de una planta en respuesta a un estímulo (258)

troposphere/troposfera la capa inferior de la atmósfera de la Tierra (511)

true north/norte verdadero el Polo Norte geográfico (410)

U

uplift/levantamiento el proceso por el cual ciertas regiones de la Tierra se elevan a mayor altitud (469)

uterus/útero un órgano dentro del cuerpo de un mamífero hembra, donde el embrión crece y se desarrolla (389)

V

vacuole/vacuola una vesícula que se encuentra en las plantas y en algunos protistas; las vacuolas almacenan agua (197)

vaporization/vaporización el cambio de estado de líquido a gas; incluye la ebullición y la evaporación (72)

velocity/velocidad la rapidez de un objeto en una dirección determinada (88)

vertebrae/vértebras segmentos de hueso o cartílago que se entrelazan para forman la columna vertebral (347)

vertebrate/vertebrado un animal con cráneo y columna vertebral (346)

vesicle/vesícula un compartimiento cubierto por una membrana (196)

viscosity/viscosidad resistencia que un líquido opone al flujo (63)

volcanic mountain/montaña volcánica una montaña que se forma cuando roca derretida hace erupción a la corteza terrestre (473)

voltage/voltaje la diferencia en energía por unidad de carga a medida que la carga se mueve de un punto a otro en un circuito (es lo mismo que la diferencia de potencial); se expresa en volts, o voltios (V) (163)

volume/volumen la cantidad de espacio que algo ocupa, o la cantidad de espacio que algo contiene (24, 38)

W

water cycle/ciclo del agua el movimiento continuo del agua entre la Tierra y la atmósfera (485)

waterfowl/ave acuática aves como los patos, grullas y gansos (381)

watershed/cuenca de drenaje la región del terreno drenada por un sistema fluvial (486)

water table/nivel freático un límite subterráneo donde se unen la zona de aeración y la zona de saturación (494)

water vascular system/sistema vascular de agua un sistema en el cual el movimiento del agua permite al animal moverse, comer y respirar; los equinodermos utilizan este sistema (333)

weathering/meteorización el proceso por el cual el agua, hielo, calor y viento rompen las rocas (442)

weight/peso una medida de la fuerza gravitacional ejercida sobre un objeto; su valor puede cambiar en función de la ubicación del objeto en el universo (41, 104)

well/pozo un agujero hecho por los seres humanos que es más profundo que el nivel freático (496)

westerlies/céfiros sistemas de vientos que se encuentran tanto en el hemisferio norte como en el sur, entre los 30° y 60° de latitud (523)

wind/viento el movimiento del aire que resulta de diferencias en la presión del aire (518)

work/trabajo la acción que resulta cuando una fuerza hace que un objeto se mueva en la dirección de la fuerza (118)

Z

zone of aeration/zona de aeración un área subterránea que se encuentra sobre el nivel freático (494)

zone of saturation/zona de saturación un área subterránea que se encuentra debajo del nivel freático (494)

Index

Credits

Abbreviations used: (t) top, (c) center, (b) bottom, (l) left, (r) right, (bkgd) background

ILLUSTRATIONS

All work, unless otherwise noted, contributed by Holt, Rinehart & Winston.

Chapter One: Page 9 (b), Barbara Hoopes-Ambler; 13 (cr), Carlyn Iverson; 14 (b), Christy Krames; 22, 25 (tr), Stephen Durke/Washington Artists; 28 (br), Barbara Hoopes-Ambler; 30 (tr), Annie Bissett; 31 (cr), Thomas Gagliano.

Chapter Two: Page 57, Thomas Gagliano; 59 (tc), Daniels and Daniels.

Chapter Three: Page 62 (b), 63 (b), 64 (tl), 65 (c), 66 (cl,cr), 67, 68 (b), Stephen Durke/Washington Artists; 68 (cl), Preface, Inc.; 70, David Schleinkofer; 72, Mark Heine; 75, David Schleinkofer; 78, Stephen Durke/Washington Artists; 80 (cr), Preface, Inc.; 81, Thomas Gagliano.

Chapter Four: Page 89, Marty Roper/Planet Rep; 90 (stopwatches), Mike Carroll; 97, 99, Gary Ferster; 102, Doug Henry; 103 (c,b), Stephen Durke/Washington Artists; 104, Craig Attebery/Jeff Lavaty Artist Agent; 105, Terry Guyer; 110, Preface, Inc.; 111 (tl) Thomas Gagliano.

Chapter Five: Page 121, Stephen Durke/Washington Artists; 122 (tl), Stephen Durke/Washington Artists; 122 (cl), Gary Ferster; 126 (c), Will Nelson/Sweet Reps; 127 (c), Uhl Studios Inc.; 128 (c), Dan McGeehan/Koralick Associates; 131,132,133,134,135,136, Uhl Studios Inc.; 137, Preface, Inc.; 138, Patrick Gnan; 140 (cl), Uhl Studios Inc.; 146 (cr), Dave Joly; 147 (cl), Thomas Gagliano.

Chapter Six: Page 152, Stephen Durke/Washington Artists; 153, John White/The Neis Group; 154 (br), Stephen Durke/Washington Artists; 157, Uhl Studios Inc.; 159,161, Mark Heine; 162,163, Geoffrey P. Smith; 164 (t), Will Nelson/Sweet Reps; 170 (b), Dan McGeehan/Koralick Associates; 176 (cr), 177, Thomas Gagliano.

Chapter Seven: Page 186 (c), Morgan-Cain & Associates; 188 (b), Morgan-Cain & Associates; 190 (tl), Morgan-Cain & Associates; 191 (bl), Morgan-Cain & Associates; 191 (bc), Morgan-Cain & Associates; 192 (b), Morgan-Cain & Associates; 192 (c), Morgan-Cain & Associates; 193 (bl), Morgan-Cain & Associates; 194 (br), Morgan-Cain & Associates; 194 (bl), Morgan-Cain & Associates; 195 (tr), Morgan-Cain & Associates; 195 (b), Morgan-Cain & Associates; 196 (bl), Morgan-Cain & Associates; 196 (br), Morgan-Cain & Associates; 197 (bl), Morgan-Cain & Associates; 198, Morgan-Cain & Associates; 199, Morgan-Cain & Associates; 202 (cl), Morgan-Cain & Associates; 202 (cl), Morgan-Cain & Associates; 202 (cr), Christy Krames; 202 (c), Morgan-Cain & Associates; 203 (cr), Christy Krames; 205 (br), Morgan-Cain & Associates; 205 (bl), Morgan-Cain & Associates; 208 (tr), Morgan-Cain & Associates; 208 (cr), Morgan-Cain & Associates; 209 (bl), Morgan-Cain & Associates; 209 (cl), Morgan-Cain & Associates.

Chapter Eight: Page 214 (b), Barbara Hoopes-Ambler; 217 (bl), Ross, Culbert and Lavery; 222 (bl), John White/The Neis Group; 222 (bc), John White/The Neis Group; 222 (br), John White/The Neis Group; 222 (tl), Tony Morse/Ivy Glick; 222 (cl), Tony Morse/Ivy Glick; 225 (tr), Ross, Culbert and Lavery; 226 (tr), Will Nelson/Sweet Reps; 226 (tr), Will Nelson/Sweet Reps; 226 (cr), Will Nelson/Sweet Reps; 227 (bl), Carlyn Iverson; 227 (bc), Carlyn Iverson; 227 (bl), Carlyn Iverson; 227 (br), Carlyn Iverson; 230, Carlyn Iverson; 232 (t), John White/The Neis Group; 232 (b), John White/The Neis Group; 232 (b), John White/The Neis Group; 232 (br), John White/The Neis Group; 232 (br), John White/The Neis Group; 237 (br), John White/The Neis Group; 240 (tr), Ross, Culbert and Lavery; 241 (tl), Leslie Kell.

Chapter Nine: Page 247 (bl), Keith Kasnot; 248 (tl), Keith Kasnot; 249 (tr), Christy Krames; 250 (tl), Keith Kasnot; 254 (b), Robert Hynes/Mendola Artists; 259 (r), Carlyn Iverson; 265 (tr), Keith Kasnot; 266 (cr), Leslie Kell; 267 (tr), Robert Hynes/Mendola Artists; 268 (tl), Leslie Kell.

Chapter Ten: Page 272 (b), Barbara Hoopes-Ambler; 273 (b), Barbara Hoopes-Ambler; 278 & 279 (b), Will Nelson/Sweet Reps; 280 (bc), Robert Hynes/Mendola Artists; 281 (b), Robert Hynes/Mendola Artists; 282 (b), Will Nelson/Sweet Reps; 286 (bc), Will Nelson/Sweet Reps; 288 (cr), Will Nelson/Sweet Reps; 290 (tr), Leslie Kell.

Chapter Eleven: Page 295 (brown bear), Michael Woods/Morgan-Cain & Associates; 295 (lion), Will Nelson/Sweet Reps; 295 (platypus), Michael Woods/Morgan-Cain & Associates; 295 (br), The Mazer Corporation; 295 (cat), Will Nelson/Sweet Reps; 296 (cat), Will Nelson/Sweet Reps; 296 (bird), Michael Woods/Morgan-Cain & Associates; 296 (bear), Michael Woods/Morgan-Cain & Associates; 296 (human), Frank Ordaz/Dimension; 296 (lion), Will Nelson/Sweet Reps; 296 (lynx), David Ashby; 296 (bug), Bridgette James; 297 (cr), John White/The Neis Group; 298 (t), Marty Roper/Planet Rep; 299 (tr), John White/The Neis Group; 299 (tl), John White/The Neis Group; 299 (cladogram), The Mazer Corporation; 299 (plants), Cy Baker/WAA; 299 (br), Cy Baker/WAA; 306 (b), Rob Schuster/Hankins and Tegenborg; 307 (tr), The Mazer Corporation; 308 (br), John White/The Neis Group; 310 (cladogram), The Mazer Corporation; 310 (lemur), Will Nelson/Sweet Reps; 310 (baboon), Graham Allen; 310 (chimpanzee), Michael Woods/Morgan-Cain & Associates; 310 (human), Frank Ordaz; 311 (b), HRW; 313 (cl), John White/The Neis Group; 313 (tr), Barbara Hoopes-Ambler.

Chapter Twelve: Page 318 (bl), Barbara Hoopes-Ambler; 318 (bc), Barbara Hoopes-Ambler; 318 (br), Barbara Hoopes-Ambler; 319 (b), Alexander & Turner ; 319 (c), Alexander & Turner ; 319 (br), Alexander & Turner ; 323 (br), Alexander & Turner; 329 (tr), Will Nelson/Sweet Reps; 330 (tl), Bridgette James; 330 (tl), Bridgette James; 330 (bl), Steve Roberts; 331 (br), Bridgette James; 333 (tl), Alexander & Turner ; 333 (b), Alexander & Turner ; 341 (tl), Leslie Kell; 341 (br), Leslie Kell.

Chapter Thirteen: Page 347 (t), Alexander & Turner ; 350 (c), Will Nelson/Sweet Reps; 356 (t), Will Nelson/Sweet Reps; 361 (tc), Kip Carter; 365 (cl), John Huxtable/Black Creative; 367 (bl), Will Nelson/Sweet Reps; 368 (cr), Rob Schuster/Hankins and Tegenborg; 370 (tl), Leslie Kell; 370 (cr), Leslie Kell; 371 (b), Ron Kimball.

Chapter Fourteen: Page 375 (tr), Will Nelson/Sweet Reps; 375 (tc), Kip Carter; 375 (br), Will Nelson/Sweet Reps; 375 (br), Kip Carter; 376 (c), Will Nelson/Sweet Reps; 377 (bc), Will Nelson/Sweet Reps; 377 (c), Will Nelson/Sweet Reps; 378 (c), Will Nelson/Sweet Reps; 383 (bl), Howard Freidman; 396 (br), Will Nelson/Sweet Reps; 396 (cr), Kip Carter; 438 & 439 (b), Will Nelson/Sweet Reps.

Chapter Fifteen: Page 409 (bl), John White/The Neis Group; 411 (tl), MapQuest.com; 411 (br), MapQuest.com; 412 (tl), MapQuest.com; 413 (cl), MapQuest.com; 415 (bl), MapQuest.com; 415 (br), MapQuest.com; 416 (cl), MapQuest.com; 416 (cr), MapQuest.com; 416 (bl), MapQuest.com; 416 (br), MapQuest.com; 422 (b), USGS.

Chapter Sixteen: Page 435 (cr), Sidney Jablonski; 440 - 441 Uhl Studios, Inc.

Chapter Seventeen: Page 456 (bc), Uhl Studios, Inc.; 457 (br), Uhl Studios, Inc.; 458 (c), Uhl Studios, Inc.; 459 (b), Uhl Studios, Inc.; 460 (cl), Uhl Studios, Inc.; 463 (bc), Uhl Studios, Inc.; 466 (tl), Uhl Studios, Inc.; 466 (tc), Uhl Studios, Inc.; 466 (tr), Uhl Studios, Inc.; 467 (tr), Marty Roper/Planet Rep; 467 (cr), Uhl Studios, Inc.; 467 (br), Uhl Studios, Inc.; 469 (bc), Uhl Studios, Inc.; 470 (cl), Uhl Studios, Inc.; 471 (c), Tony Morse/Ivy Glick; 471 (bc), Tony Morse/Ivy Glick; 472 (c), Uhl Studios, Inc.; 476 (bl), Uhl Studios, Inc.; 477 (cr), Uhl Studios, Inc.

Chapter Eighteen: Page 485 (b), Mike Wepplo/Das Group; 488 (bkgd), Uhl Studios, Inc.; 488 (cl), Uhl Studios, Inc.; 488 (cr), Uhl Studios, Inc.; 488 (bl), Uhl Studios, Inc.; 494 (bl), Stephen Durke/Washington Artists; 495 (tr), MapQuest.com; 496 (cl), Stephen Durke/Washington Artists; 499 (tr), Mark Heine; 502 (cr), Sidney Jablonski.

Chapter Nineteen: Page 508 (bl), Sidney Jablonski; 509 (br), Stephen Durke/Washington Artists; 510 (b), Stephen Durke/Washington Artists; 510 (bl), Stephen Durke/Washington Artists; 511 (cl), Stephen Durke/Washington Artists; 512 (bc), Stephen Durke/Washington Artists; 514 - 515 (b), Uhl Studios, Inc.; 515 (b), Uhl Studios, Inc.; 516 (c), John Huxtable/Black Creative; 519 (c), Stephen Durke/Washington Artists; 521 (br), MapQuest.com; 522 (b), Stephen Durke/Washington Artists; 523 (br), MapQuest.com; 524 (c), Stephen Durke/Washington Artists; 524 (b), Stephen Durke/Washington Artists; 525 (cl), Stephen Durke/Washington Artists; 527 (bl), Mark Heine; 528 (bc), John Huxtable/Black Creative.

Unit Seven: Page 534, Christy Krames.

Chapter Twenty: Page 538 (b), Uhl Studios, Inc.; 539 (t), Sidney Jablonski; 540 (c), Sidney Jablonski; 541 (br), Uhl Studios, Inc.; 542 (cl), Marty Roper/Planet Rep; 542 (br), Marty Roper/Planet Rep; 543 (bc), Marty Roper/Planet Rep; 543 (tr), Stephen Durke/Washington Artists; 545 (bl), Sidney Jablonski; 550 (tl), Sidney Jablonski; 552 (bl), Sidney Jablonski; 552 (br), Sidney Jablonski; 554 (cl), Paul DiMare; 559 (br), Stephen Durke/Washington Artists; 560 (b), Craig Attebery/Jeff Lavaty Artist Agent; 562 (br), Paul DiMare; 569 (tr), Paul DiMare.

Chapter Twenty-One: Page 573 (b), Stephen Durke/Washington Artists; 574 (cl), John Huxtable/Black Creative; 577 (tr), Stephen Durke/Washington Artists; 580 (cl), Stephen Durke/Washington Artists; 580 (bl), Stephen Durke/Washington Artists; 581 (tr), Stephen Durke/Washington Artists; 581 (cr), Stephen Durke/Washington Artists; 582 (cl), Stephen Durke/Washington Artists; 582 (b), Stephen Durke/Washington Artists; 583 (tr), Stephen Durke/Washington Artists; 583 (br), Stephen Durke/Washington Artists; 583 (c), Craig Attebery/Jeff Lavaty Artist Agent; 585 (cl), Paul DiMare; 591 (b), Paul DiMare.

LabBook: Page 600 (l), Stephen Durke/Washington Artists; 602 (br), The Mazer Corporation; 611 (r), Marty Roper/Planet Rep; 614 (cr), Gary Ferster; 614 (br), Dave Joly; 615 (cr), Rob Schuster/Hankins and Tegenborg; 615 (tl), David Merrell/Suzanne Craig Represents Inc.; 617 (br), Keith Locke/Suzanne Craig Represents Inc.; 620 (tr), Rob Schuster/Hankins and Tegenborg; 620 (c), Rob Schuster/Hankins and Tegenborg; 620 (cr), Rob Schuster/Hankins and Tegenborg; 620 (c), Rob Schuster/Hankins and Tegenborg; 620 (bl), Rob Schuster/Hankins and Tegenborg; 620 (br), Rob Schuster/Hankins and Tegenborg; 621 (cr), Rob Schuster/Hankins and Tegenborg; 622 (br), Marty Roper/Planet Rep; 624 (b), Keith Locke/Suzanne Craig Represents Inc.; 627 (b), Blake Thornton/Rita Marie; 632 (tl), Dan McGeehan/Koralick Associates; 632 (br), Mark Heine; 635 (tr), Mark Heine; 639 (tr), Geoff Smith/Scott Hull.

Appendix: Page 643 (cl), Blake Thornton/Rita Marie; 646 (t), Terry Guyer; 653 (b), Mazer.

PHOTOGRAPHY

Cover Images: (tl), CORBIS; (tc), Philip James Corwin/CORBIS; (tr), ©1998 Artville, LLC; (br), Chase Swift/CORBIS; (bl), SuperStock; (bkgd), Corbis Images.

Title Page: (c), Chase Swift/CORBIS.

Table of Contents: v (tr), Sam Dudgeon/HRW Photo; v (br), NASA; vi (tl), Peter Van Steen/HRW Photo; vi (bl), Sam Dudgeon/HRW Photo; vii (tr), Scott Van Osdol/HRW photo; vii (bl), Sergio Putrell/Foca/HRW Photo; viii (tl), John Langford/HRW photo; viii (bl), Sam Dudgeon/HRW photo; ix (bl), Visuals Unlimited/James Beveridge; x (tl), ©2002/Philip & Karen Smith/Adventure Photo & Film; x (bl), Merlin D. Tuttle/Bat Conservation International; xi (bl), CNRI/Science Photo Library/Photo Researchers; xii (tl), Visuals Unlimited/Rob & Ann Simpson; xii (bl), Edwin & Peggy Bauer/Bruce Coleman; xiii (bl), Victoria Smith/HRW Photo; xiv (tl), G.R. Roberts Photo Library; xvi (tl), NASA/Science Photo Library/Photo Researchers, Inc.; xvi (bl), NASA; xvii (bc), Sam Dudgeon/HRW Photo; xviii (tl, tr, br), Sam Dudgeon/HRW Photo; xix (tl), Sam Dudgeon/HRW Photo; xix (tc), Peter Van Steen/HRW Photo; xix (b), Sam Dudgeon/HRW Photo; xxi (br), Sam Dudgeon/HRW Photo; xxiv (bl), Sam Dudgeon/HRW Photo; xxv (tr), John Langford/HRW Photo; xxv (cl), Michelle Bridwell/HRW Photo; xxv (bl), Sam Dudgeon/HRW Photo; xxv (br), Image Copyright ©2001 Photodisc, Inc. ; xxvi (cl), Victoria Smith/HRW Photo; xxvi (tr), Sam Dudgeon/HRW Photo; xxvi (bl), Stephanie Morris/HRW Photo; xxvi (br), Sam Dudgeon/HRW Photo; xxvii (tl), Sam Dudgeon/HRW Photo; xxvii (tr), Jana Birchum/HRW Photo; xxvii (b), Peter Van Steen/HRW Photo.

Chapter One: 2-3 (c), John Dawson/National Geographic Society Image Collection; 3 (inset), O. Louis Mazzatenta/National Geographic Society Image Collection; 4 (bl), Peter Van Steen/HRW Photo; 5 (tr), Peter Van Steen/HRW Photo; 5 (br), Victoria Smith/HRW Photo; 5 (computer screen), International Colored Gemstone Association (ICA); 6 (tl), Warren Morgan/CORBIS; 6 (bl), Carr Clifton/Minden Pictures; 7 (br), Mark Howard/Westfall Eco Images; 7 (tr), ©2000 Ron Kimball Studios; 8 (c), Annie Griffiths/Westlight/Corbis; 11 (b), Peter Van Steen/HRW Photo; 12 (c), Dr. David Gillette; 13 (tr), Thomas R. Hester, The University of Texas at Austin; 15 (tl), Paul Fraughton/HRW Photo; 16 (bl), Sam Dudgeon/HRW Photo; 16 (br), Jim Sugar Photography/CORBIS; 18 (tl), Victoria Smith/HRW Photo; 18 (bl), AKG Photo, London; 18 (br), Image Copyright ©2001 PhotoDisc, Inc.; 19 (tr), Victoria Smith/HRW Photo; 20 (bl), CENCO; 20 (br), Robert Brons/Tony Stone Images; 21 (tl), Sam Dudgeon/HRW Photo; 21 (tcl, tcr, tr, c, cl), Victoria Smith/HRW Photo; 23 (tr), Peter Van Steen/HRW Photo; 24 (bl, br), Peter Van Steen/HRW Photo; 24 (tl), Scott Van Osdol/HRW Photo; 26 (bl), Victoria Smith/HRW Photo; 29 (br), Victoria Smith/HRW Photo; 29 (tr), Sam Dudgeon/HRW Photo.

Unit One: 34 (c), Peter Van Steen; 35 (tr), Courtesy Don Harrington Discovery Center and Museum; 35 (bl), Peter Yang/HRW Photo.

Chapter Two: 36 (c), Ken Reid/FPG International; 38 (b), Sam Dudgeon/HRW Photo; 39 (br, cr), Sam Dudgeon/HRW Photo; 40 (cl), Sam Dudgeon/HRW Photo; 41 (bl, r), Sam Dudgeon/HRW Photo; 42 (tr), Sam Dudgeon/HRW Photo; 42 (cl), Victoria Smith/HRW Photo; 43 (br), Sam Dudgeon/HRW Photo; 44 (bl), Victoria Smith/HRW Photo; 44 (bc), Sam Dudgeon/HRW Photo; 44 (br), Peter Van Steen/HRW Photo; 44 (cl), John Morrison/Morrison Photography; 45 (br), John Morrison/Morrison Photography; 45 (bl), Sam Dudgeon/HRW Photo; 45 (tr), Richard Megna/Fundamental Photographs; 45 (bc), Sam Dudgeon/HRW Photo; 46 (bl), Victoria Smith/HRW Photo; 47 (br), Sam Dudgeon/HRW Photo; 47 (bl), Rob Boudreau/Tony Stone; 48 (tl), ©W. Cody/CORBIS; 48 (cl), ©Doug Wilson/CORBIS; 48 (tr, tc, c, cl), Sam Dudgeon/HRW Photo; 49 (tr), Lance Schriner/HRW photo; 50 (tl, cr), Sam Dudgeon/HRW Photo; 50 (c), Morrison Photography; 50 (bl), Joseph Drivas/Image Bank; 50 (br), SuperStock; 51 (cr), Sam Dudgeon/HRW Photo; 53 (b), Sam Dudgeon/HRW Photo; 54 (br), Richard Megna/Fundamental Photographs; 55 (b, tr), John Langford/HRW photo; 56 (cl), Sam Dudgeon/HRW Photo; 56 (cr), Lance Schriner/HRW photo.

Chapter Three: 60 (c), Phil Degginger/Tony Stone; 63 (br), Scott Van Osdol/HRW photo; 63 (bl), Sam Dudgeon/HRW Photo; 64 (tl, b), Scott Van Osdol/HRW photo; 65 (br), Scott Van Osdol/HRW photo; 65 (tr), Dr. Harold E. Edgerton/© The Harold E. Edgerton 1992 Trust/Courtesy Palm Press, Inc.; 66 (cl), John Langford/HRW Photo ; 66 (cr), Sam Dudgeon/HRW photo; 69 (tr), Scott Van Osdol/HRW photo; 69 (cr), Pekka Parviainen/Science Photo Library/Photo Researchers, Inc.; 71 (tr), Richard Megna/Fundamental Photographs; 71 (br), Scott Van Osdol/HRW photo; 73 (b), Victoria Smith/ HRW Photo; 74 (tl), Scott Van Osdol/HRW photo; 76 (b), Victoria Smith/ HRW Photo; 77 (tr), Victoria Smith/ HRW Photo; 79 (tr), Myrleen Ferguson/PhotoEdit; 80 (cl), Charles D. Winters/Photo Researchers; 83 (cl), Union Pacific Museum Collection.

Chapter Four: 84 (c), ©Bettman/CORBIS; 86 (bl), SuperStock; 86 (bc), SuperStock; 88 (cl), Tom Tietz/Tony Stone Images; 90 (t), Sergio Putrell/Foca/HRW Photo; 91 (tr), Gene Peach/The Picture Cube; 92 (b), Michelle Bridwell/HRW Photo; 93 (tr, bc), Michelle Bridwell/HRW Photo; 94 (c), Daniel Schaefer/HRW Photo; 95 (br), Arthur C. Smith/Grant Heilman Photography; 95 (cr), Sam Dudgeon/HRW Photo; 96 (bl), Biological Photo Service; 98 (bl, br), Michelle Bridwell/HRW Photo; 99 (tr), Tony Freedman/PhotoEdit; 100 (cl), Sam Dudgeon/HRW photo; 101 (br), NASA; 106 (br), Sam Dudgeon/HRW Photo; 107 (b), Sam Dudgeon/HRW Photo; 108 (bl), SuperStock; 109 (tc), John Langford/ HRW Photo; 110 (cl), Mavournea Hay/HRW Photo; 113 (bl), Bruce Hands/Tony Stone Images.

Unit Two: 114 (c), Courtesy of Texas Highways Magazine; 115 (bl), Peter Yang/HRW Photo; 115 (tr), Courtesy of Texas Highways Magazine.

Chapter Five: 116-117 (c), Kaku Kurita/Liaison Agency; 118 Al Bello/Allsport; 119 Peter Weimann/Animals Animals; 120 Peter Van Steen/HRW Photo; 121 (cl), John Langford/HRW photo; 121 (c), Paul A. Souders/Corbis; 121 (cr), Tony Freeman/Photo Edit; 121 (br), Peter Van Steen/HRW Photo; 122 (cl), Sam Dudgeon/HRW Photo; 123 (tr), Richard Megna/Fundamental Photographs; 123 (cr), NASA; 124 (all), Peter Van Steen/ HRW photo; 125 (tr), Richard Megna/Fundamental Photographs; 125 (bl, c, br), John Langford/HRW photo; 126 (br), John Langford/HRW photo; 129 (cr, br), Courtesy of Honda; 130 John Langford/HRW photo; 136 (cl), Ted Clutter/Photo Researchers, Inc.; 137 (tl), Tom Carroll/Phototake; 137 (bl), John Langford/HRW photo; 137 (cl), Sam Dudgeon/HRW Photo; 139 (tr), D.O.E./Science Source/Photo Researchers, Inc.; 139 (cr), John Langford/HRW photo; 139 (br), John D. Cunningham/Visuals Unlimited; 140 (b), Coronado Rodney Jones/HRW photo; 140 (tl), LCRA; 143 (tr), Richard Hutchings/Photo Researchers, Inc.; 144 NASA; 145 Peter Weimann/Animals Animals; 146 (bl), Mike Powell/Allsport; 149 (tl, br), Robert Wolf/HRW photo.

Chapter Six: 150-151 (c), Peter Van Steen/HRW Photo; 154 (bc), John Langford/HRW photo; 154 (bl), Sam Dudgeon/HRW photo; 155 (tr), John Langford/HRW photo; 156 (bl), Peter Van Steen/HRW photo; 156 (tl), Sam Dudgeon/HRW Photo; 158 (cl), Paul Katz/Index Stock Imagery/Picture Quest; 160 (tl), John Langford/HRW photo; 160 (bl), Sam Dudgeon/HRW photo; 161 (tr), Victoria Smith/HRW Photo; 164 (bl), Sam Dudgeon/HRW Photo; 165 (tr), Visuals Unlimited/Science Visuals Unlimited; 166 (bl, inset), Sam Dudgeon/HRW photo; 166 (br), John Langford/HRW photo; 166 (bl), Richard T. Nowitz/Photo Researchers, Inc.; 166 (bc), Sam Dudgeon/HRW photo; 167 (cl, cr), John Langford/HRW photo; 168 (c), John Langford/HRW photo; 169 (t), Sam Dudgeon/HRW photo; 170 (tl), John Langford/HRW photo; 171 (tr), Paul Silverman/Fundamental Photographs; 171 (cr), Sam Dudgeon/HRW Photo; 173 (b), Sam Dudgeon/HRW Photo; 174 (br), Sam Dudgeon/HRW photo; 175 (bc), John Langford/HRW photo; 176 (bl), Sam Dudgeon/HRW photo ; 179 (cl), Daniel Osborne, University of Alaska/Detlev Ban Ravenswaay/Science Photo Library/Photo Researchers Inc; 179 (inset), STARLab, Stanford University.

Unit Three: 180 (c), Courtesy of Texas Highways Magazine; 181 (bl), C. Allan Morgan; 181 (tr), Greg Grant.

Chapter Seven: 182-183 (c), Dennis Kunkel/Phototake; 184 (bl), Visuals Unlimited/Kevin Collins; 184 (bc), Leonard Lessin/Peter Arnold; 184 (br), John D. Cunningham/Visuals Unlimited; 185 (spirogyra), T.E. Adams/Visuals Unlimited; 185 (stentor), Roland Birke/Peter Arnold, Inc.; 185 (cl), Jerome Wexler/Photo Researchers, Inc.; 185 (microcystis), Biophoto Associates/Photo Researchers, Inc.; 185 (euglena), M.I. Walker/Photo Researchers, Inc.; 186 (cl), copyright ©2001 PhotoDisc, Inc.; 187 (tr), William Dentler/BPS/Stone; 187 (br), Dr. Gopal Murti/Science Photo Library/Photo Researchers, Inc.; 189 (tc), Visuals Unlimited/David M. Phillips; 189 (cl), Fran Heyl Associates; 189 (tr), CNRI/Science Photo Library/Photo Researchers; 189 (bl), Jerry Mason/Science Photo Library/Photo Researchers, Inc.; 189 (br), Alfred Pasieka/Science Photo Library/Photo Researchers, Inc.; 190 (cl), Biophoto Associates/Photo Researchers, Inc.; 193 (bc), Don Fawcett/Visuals Unlimited; 193 (tr), Dr. Peter Dawson/ Science Photo Library/Photo Researchers, Inc.; 194 (cl), R. Bolender-D. Fawcett/Visuals Unlimited; 195 (tr), Don Fawcett/Visuals Unlimited; 195 (br), Newcomb & Wergin/BPS/Tony Stone Images; 196 (cl), Garry T Cole/BPS/Stone; 197 (tr), Dr. Gopal Murti/Science Photo Library/Photo Researchers, Inc.; 197 (br), Dr. Jeremy Burgess/Science PhotoLibrary/Science Source/Photo Researchers; 200 (b), Quest/Science Photo Library/Photo Researchers, Inc.; 201 (tr), Michael Abbey/Photo Researchers; 201 (cr), Manfred Kage/Peter Arnold, Inc. ; 201 (br), A. & F. Michler/Peter Arnold, Inc.; 203 (tr), Manfred Kage/Peter Arnold; 204 (bl), Runk/Schoenberger/Grant Heilman; 206 (br), Manfred Kage/Peter Arnold; 207 (tr), Fran Heyl Associates; 207 (tc), Visuals Unlimited/David M. Phillips; 211 (cl), Hans Reinhard/Bruce Coleman; 211 (r), Andrew Syred/Tony Stone Images.

Chapter Eight: 212-213 (c), Jeff Rotman/Tony Stone; 215 (tc), Ken Lucas; 215 (tr), John Cancalosi/Tom Stack & Associates; 215 (b), SuperStock; 216 (b), Paleontological Research Institution; 218 (br), Dennis Flaherty/Photo Researchers, Inc.; 218 (bl), Robert & Linda Mitchell; 219 (tr), Doug Wechsler/Animals Animals; 219 (cr), Gail Shumway/FPG International; 219 (cl), Visuals Unlimited/James Beveridge; 220 (bl), Visuals Unlimited/H.W. Robison; 220 (tc), Leonard Lee Rue III/Animals Animals; 221 (inset), © William E. Ferguson; 221 (b), Christopher Ralling; 223 (b), Carolyn A. McKeone/Photo Researchers, Inc. ; 224 (cl), Joanna McCarthy/The Image Bank; 224 (cr), Jonelle Weaver/FPG International; 228 (cl, cr), M.W. Tweedie/Photo Researchers; 229 (tl), Carr Clifton/Minden Pictures; 229 (bc), Mickey Gibson/Animals Animals; 229 (cr), Pat & Tom Leeson/Photo Researchers, Inc.; 231 (bl), Corbis; 233 (tr), Gerard Lacz/Animals Animals; 233 (br), Clyde H. Smith/Peter Arnold, Inc.; 234 (all), Sam Dudgeon/HRW Photo; 235 (tr), C. Milkins/Animals Animals; 235 (cr), Stewart Cohen/Tony Stone; 238 (bc), Gail Shumway/FPG International; 239 (tr), Mickey Gibson/Animals Animals; 239 (bl), Pat & Tom Leeson/Photo Researchers, Inc.; 243 (c), Thomas W. Martin, APSA/Photo Researchers; 243 (tr), Doug Wilson/Westlight.

Chapter Nine: 244-245 Bianca Lavies/National Geographic Society Image Collection; 246 M.I. Walker/Science Source/Photo Researchers, Inc.; 247 (cr), NHMPL/Tony Stone; 247 (tr), Paul Johnson/BPS/Tony Stone; 248 (br), Brian Kenney; 248 (bc), Jerome Wexler/Photo Researchers, Inc.; 249 (bl), Brian Kenney; 249 (cl), Serraillie/Rapho/Photo Researchers, Inc.; 250 (br), Robert Maier/Animals Animals; 251 (tr), Terry Vine/Tony Stone; 251 (cl), Gary Meszaros/Visuals Unlimited; 252 (bl), ©2002/Philip & Karen Smith/Adventure Photo & Film; 253 (tr), Bob Krist/CORBIS; 253 (br), Brian Kenney; 255 (tl), David J. Wrobel/Visuals Unlimited; 256 (bc), Joel Sartore/Grant Heilman Photography; 257 (c), Leonard Lee Rue III/Visuals Unlimited; 257 (cr), Joe McDonald/Visuals Unlimited; 258 (bc), R. Catherine/Visuals Unlimited; 259 (cl), Cathlyn Melloan/Tony Stone; 259 (br), R. F. Evert; 260 (bc), Dick Keen/Unicorn; 260 (br), Visuals Unlimited/E. Webber; 261 (all), Rich Iwasaki/Tony Stone; 262 (br), John Langford/HRW Photo; 263 (tr, cr), Victoria Smith/HRW Photo; 264 (tr), Gary Meszaros/Visuals Unlimited; 265 (br), NHMPL/Tony Stone; 269 (cr), John Elk/Tony Stone.

Chapter Ten: 270 (c), Merlin D. Tuttle/Bat Conservation International; 274 (bl), George Ranalli/Photo Researchers, Inc.; 274 (bc), George O. Miller/TexaStock; 274 (br), Anthony Bannister/NHPA; 275 (bl), David T. Roberts/Nature's Images, Inc. ; 275 (bc), Shane Moore/Animals Animals; 275 (br), David Muench/CORBIS; 276 (tl), Joe McDonald/Animals Animals; 276 (tr), Lynn Stone/Earth Scenes; 277 (tl), Dr. Tony Brian & David Parker/Science Photo Library/ Photo Researchers; 277 (tr), Patti Murray/Animals Animals; 283 (tr), Laguna Photo/Liaison International; 283 (cr), Tom & Pat Leeson/Photo Researchers, Inc.; 285 (bc), Victoria Smith/HRW Photo; 287 (tr), David Muench/CORBIS; 291 (cl), Dr. Verena Tunnicliffe.

Chapter Eleven: 292 (c), Frans Lanting/Minden Pictures; 294 (bc), Gerry Ellis/ENP Images; 295 (cr), Library of Congress/Corbis; 300 (tc), Biophoto Associates/Photo Researchers; 301 (tr), Sherrie Jones/Photo Researchers; 301 (bl, br), Dr. Tony Brian & David Parker/Science Photo Library/ Photo Researchers; 302 (cl), Visuals Unlimited/M.Abbey; 302 (c), Visuals Unlimited/Stanley Flegler; 302 (br), Chuck Davis/Tony Stone Images; 303 (cl), Corbis Images; 303 (bl), David R. Frazier/Photo Researchers, Inc.; 304 (cl), Robert Maier; 304 (cr), Visuals Unlimited/Sherman Thomson; 304 (br), Visuals Unlimited/Richard Thom; 305 (cl), G. Randall/FPG; 305 (bl), SuperStock; 305 (tr), Arthur Morris/The Stock Market; 305 (bl), Hal Beral/Visuals Unlimited; 308 (tc), SuperStock; 309 (br), Dr. Tony Brian & David Parker/Science Photo Library/Photo Researchers; 310 (bl), Visuals Unlimited/M.Abbey.

Unit Four: 314 (c), D. Robert Franz/CORBIS; 315 (bl), Roy Toft; 315 (tr), Brian Keeley/Bat Conservation International.

Chapter Twelve: 316-317 (c), W. Gregory Brown/Animals Animals; 320 (br), Randy Morse/Tom Stack & Associates; 320 (bc), Biophoto Associates/Science Source/Photo Researchers; 320 (cl), Lee Foster/FPG; 320 (cr), David B. Fleetham/Visuals Unlimited; 321 (tr), Visuals Unlimited/T. E. Adams; 321 (cr), Visuals Unlimited/A. M. Siegelman; 322 (bl), Nigel Cattlin/Holt Studios International/Photo Researchers; 322 (bc), Visuals Unlimited/David M. Phillips; 324 (l), Milton Rand/Tom Stack & Associates; 324 (br), Daniel Schaefer/HRW Photo; 325 (cr), St. Bartholomew's Hospital/Science Photo Library/Photo Researchers; 325 (tr), Mary Beth Angelo/Photo Researchers; 326 (b), Leroy Simon/Visuals Unlimited; 327 (br), Sergio Purcell/FOCA; 327 (bc), CNRI/Science Photo Library/Photo Researchers; 327 (tr), John Beatty/Stone; 328 (tl), Visuals Unlimited/A. Kerstitch; 328 (tc), Larry Stepanowicz/Visuals Unlimited; 328 (b), Daniel Gotshall/Visuals Unlimited; 329 (bl), Visuals Unlimited/R. Calentine; 330 (cl), Leroy Simon/Visuals Unlimited; 332 (bl), Visuals Unlimited/Cabisco; 332 (br), Scott Johnson/Animals Animals/Earth Scenes; 334 (tl), Darryl Torckler/Tony Stone Images; 334 (cr), Visuals Unlimited/Marty Snyderman; 334 (b), Daniel Gotshall/Visuals Unlimited; 334 (cl), Flip Nicklin/Minden Pictures; 335 (cl), Andrew J. Martinez/Photo Researchers; 335 (tr), Robert Dunne/Photo Researchers; 335 (cr), Chesher/Photo Researchers; 337 Victoria Smith/HRW Photo; 338 (tc), SuperStock; 339 (tr), Carl Roessler/FPG; 340 (bl), Sergio Purcell/FOCA; 340 (tr), Leroy Simon/Visuals Unlimited; 343 (b), Visuals Unlimited/Diane R. Nelson.

Chapter Thirteen: 344-345 (c), J. Schauer/Aquatech; 345 (bl), Visuals Unlimited; 346 (bl), Randy Morse/Tom Stack; 346 (br), G.I. Bernard OSF/Animals Animals; 347 (br, bc), Grant Heilman; 348 (c), Uniphoto; 349 (br), Doug Perrine/DRK Photo; 349 (cr), Animals Animals; 349 (cl), Bruce Coleman; 349 (bl), Tom McHugh/Photo Researchers, Inc.; 349 (bc), ©2000 Norbert Wu/www.norbertwu.com; 351 (bl), Steinhart Aquarium/Photo Researchers, Inc.; 351 (br), Hans Reinhard/Bruce Coleman; 352 (b), Index Stock; 352 (cr), Martin Barraud/Tony Stone; 352 (cl), ©2000 Norbert Wu/www.norbertwu.com; 353 (tr), Bruce Coleman; 353 (tl), Steinhart Aquarium/Tom McHugh/Photo Researchers; 353 (tc), Ron & Valerie Taylor/Bruce Coleman, Inc.; 354 (bc), Michael Fogden/DRK Photo; 354 (bl), Visuals Unlimited/Nathan W. Cohen; 354 (cr), Billy Moore/LCRA; 355 (tr), David M. Dennis/Tom Stack & Associates; 355 (br), C. K. Lorenz/Photo Researchers; 356 (bl), Michael and Patricia Fogden; 357 (tr), M.P.L. Fogden/Bruce Coleman; 357 (br), Stephen Dalotn/NHPA; 357 (bl), Richard Thom/Visuals Unlimited; 358 (tl), Leonard Lee Rue/Photo Researchers; 358 (tr), Breck P. Kent; 359 (cr), Visuals Unlimited/Rob & Ann Simpson; 359 (br), Visuals Unlimited; 359 (bl), Kenneth Fink/Bruce Coleman, Inc.; 359 (cl), Danilo B. Donadoni/Bruce Coleman, Inc.; 360 (tl), Gail Shumway/FPG; 360 (bl), Stanley Breeden/DRK Photo; 360 (br), Visuals Unlimited/Joe McDonald; 362 (tl), Mike Severns/Tony Stone Images; 362 (bl), Kevin Schafer/Peter Arnold; 362 (br), Wayne Lynch/DRK Photo; 362 (tr), Carl Ernst; 363 (tr), C. E. Schmida/F.P./Bruce Coleman, Inc.; 363 (cr), C.K. Lorenz/Photo Researchers, Inc.; 363 (tc), E. R. Degginger/Bruce Coleman, Inc.; 364 (b), Peter Van Steen/HRW Photo; 366 (tr), Stephen Dalotn/NHPA; 367 (tr), Animals Animals.

Chapter Fourteen: 372 (c), Nigel J. Dennis/Photo Researchers, Inc.; 374 (cl), G.C. Kelley/Photo Researchers; 374 (cr), Gail Shumway/FPG; 374 (br), Runk/Schoenberger/Grant Heilman; 374 (br), Peggy Heard/Frank Lane Picture Agency/CORBIS; 378 (bc), Ben Osborne/Tony Stone; 379 (c), D. Cavagnaro/DRK Photo; 379 (tr), Frans Lanting/Minden Pictures; 380 (br), Gavriel Jecan/Tony Stone; 380 (bc), APL/J. Carnemolla/Westlight; 380 (bl), Kevin Schafer/Tony Stone; 381 (tl), Tui De Roy/Minden Pictures; 381 (tr), Wayne Lankinen/Bruce Coleman; 381 (tc), S. Nielsen/DRK Photo; 381 (br), Greg Vaughn/Tony Stone; 381 (bl), Fritz Polking/Bruce Coleman; 382 (c), Stephen J. Krasemann/DRK Photo; 382 (cr), Visuals Unlimited/S. Maslowski; 382 (cl), Frans Lanting/Minden Pictures; 383 (cr), Gerard Lacz/Animals Animals; 383 (cl), Tim Davis/Photo Researchers; 383 (c), Nigel Dennis/Photo Researchers; 384 (bl), Hans Reinhard/Bruce Coleman; 384 (c), Kathy Bushue/Tony Stone; 385 (tr), Peter Van Steen/HRW Photo; 385 (br), David E. Myers/Tony Stone; 386 (tl), Tom Tietz/Tony Stone; 386 (cl), Sylvain Cordier/Photo Researchers; 387 (bl), Edwin & Peggy Bauer/Bruce Coleman; 387 (br), Dave Watts/Tom Stack; 388 (bc), Jean-Paul Ferrero/AUSCAPE; 388 (cr), Hans Reinhard/Bruce Coleman; 388 (bl), Art Wolfe/Tony Stone; 389 (bl), Wayne Lynch/DRK Photo; 389 (br), John D. Cunningham/Visuals Unlimited; 390 (tr), Gail Shumway/FPG; 390 (tl), D. R. Kuhn/Bruce Coleman; 390 (br), Frans Lanting/Minden Pictures; 390 (br), Gerry Ellis/Minden Pictures; 391 (tr), David Cavagnaro/Peter Arnold; 391 (tl), John Cancalosi; 391 (bl), Art Wolfe/Stone; 391 (br), Merlin D. Tuttle/Bat Conservation International; 392 (tr), Gail Shumway/FPG; 392 (tl), Arthur C. Smith III/Grant Heilman; 392 (bl), Scott Daniel Peterson/Liaison; 392 (br), Gail Shumway/FPG; 393 (bl), Art Wolfe/Tony Stone; 393 (br), Manoi Shah/Stone; 394 (tl), Flip Nicklin/Minden Pictures; 394 (bl), Tom & Therisa Stack; 394 (tr), Flip Nicklin/Minden Pictures; 395 (cl), J. & P. Wegner/Animals Animals; 395 (cr), Inga Spence/Tom Stack; 397 (bc), Sam Dudgeon/HRW Photo; 398 (tc), Gail Shumway/FPG International; 399 (tr), Edwin and Peggy Bauer/Bruce Coleman; 403 (br), Raymond A. Mendez/Animals Animals.

Unit Five: 404 (c), Courtesy of Texas Highways Magazine; 405 (tr), Glenn Hayes/KAC Productions; 405 (bl), Peter Van Steen/HRW Photo.

Chapter Fifteen: 406-407 (c), Sean Ellis/Tony Stone; 408 (b), Royal Geographical Society, London , UK/The Bridgeman Art Library; 409 (tr), Sam Dudgeon/HRW Photo; 410 (c), Tom Van Sant/The Stock Market; 412 (br), Sam Dudgeon/HRW Photo; 414 (bl, bc), Andy Christiansen/HRW Photo; 417 (bl), Space Imaging; 418-419 (c), © Texas Department of Transportation; 419 (cr), © Texas Department of Transportation; 420 (bl), USGS; 421 (cl), USGS; 421 (cr), USGS; 422 (c), USGS; 425 Sam Dudgeon/HRW Photo; 426 (b), Tom Van Sant/The Stock Market; 427 (br), Andy Christiansen/HRW Photo; 428 (cr), USGS; 431 (br), JPL/NASA.

Chapter Sixteen: 432-433 (c), Tom Till; 434 (cl, bc), Sam Dudgeon/HRW Photo; 434 (bl, br, cr), Victoria Smith/HRW Photo; 435 (granite), Pat Lanza/Bruce Coleman Inc.; 435 (siltstone), Sam Dudgeon/HRW Photo; 435 (sandstone), Dorling Kindersley; 435 (conglomerate), Breck Kent; 435 (feldspar), Victoria Smith/HRW Photo; 435 (quartz), Sam Dugeon/HRW Photo; 435 (biotite mica), Sam Dudgeon/HRW Photo; 436 (rhyolite), Breck P. Kent; 436 (basalt), Victoria Smith/HRW Photo; 436 (granite), Breck P. Kent; 436 (gabbro), Breck P. Kent; 436 (bl), Victoria Smith/HRW Photo; 437 (inset), Breck P. Kent; 437 (tc), Sam Dudgeon/HRW Photo; 437 (tr), E. R. Degginger/Animals Animals/Earth Scenes; 437 (b), John Lemker/Animals Animals/Earth Scenes; 438 (l, r), Breck P. Kent; 439 (c), Joyce Photographics/Photo Researchers, Inc.; 439 (bl), Pat Lanza/Bruce Coleman Inc.; 439 (br), Sam Dudgeon/HRW Photo; 439 (bc), James Watt/Animals Animals/Earth Scenes; 442 (tl), Ed Reschke/Peter Arnold, Inc.; 442 (b), Jim Brandenburg/Minden Pictures; 443 (c), John S. Shelton; 444 (bl), Peter Van Steen/HRW Photo; 445 (b), Peter Van Steen/HRW Photo; 446 (tr), Ed Reschke/Peter Arnold, Inc.; 447 (tr), James Watt/Animals Animals/Earth Scenes; 448 (br), Salaber/Liaison International; 448 (tl), Michael Lyon; 451 (tc), Wolfgang Kaehler/Liason International.

Unit Six: 452 (c), Laurence Parent; 453 (tr), © Reuters NewMedia Inc./CORBIS; 453 (bl), Peter Yang/HRW Photo.

Chapter Seventeen: 454-455 (c), Robert A. Eplett/OES; 457 (bl), World Perspective/Tony Stone Images; 461 (cl), ESA/CE/Eurocontrol/Science Photo Library/Photo Researchers, Inc.; 461 (bl), NASA; 462 (b), Bruce C. Heezen and Marie Tharp; 464 (all), Paleogeographic Maps by Christopher R. Scotese, PALEOMAP Project, University of Texas at Arlington, www.scotese.com; 465 (cl, bc), Peter Van Steen/HRW Photo; 466 (bl), Visuals Unlimited/SylvesterAllred; 466 (inset), The G.R. "Dick" Roberts Photo Library; 468 (tl), Tom Bean; 468 (tr), Landform Slides; 470 (b), William Manning/The Stock Market; 470 (inset), M. Colbeck/Animals Animals/Earth Scenes; 472 (b), Michelle & Tom Grimm/Tony Stone Images; 473 (tr), The G.R. "Dick"Roberts Photo Library; 473 (cr), G.R. Roberts Photo Library; 474 (b), Sam Dudgeon/HRW Photo; 475 (bl), Sam Dudgeon/HRW Photo; 481 (bl), NASA/Science Photo Library/Photo Researchers, Inc.

Chapter Eighteen: 482-483 (c), Frans Lanting/Minden Pictures; 484 David Muench Photography; 486 (tl), Victoria Smith/HRW Photo; 486 (br), E.R.I.M./Stone; 487 (bl), Ed Reschke/Peter Arnold, Inc.; 487 (br), Jim Work/Peter Arnold, Inc.; 489 (tr), Laurence Parent; 489 (b), Frans Lanting/Minden Pictures; 490 (tl), The G.R. "Dick" Roberts Photo Library; 490 (cl), Galen Rowell/Peter Arnold, Inc.; 491 (b), Glenn M. Oliver/Visuals Unlimited; 492 (tl), The Huntington Library/SuperStock; 492 (b), Earth Satellite Corporation/Science Photo Library/Photo Researchers, Inc.; 493 (tr), Visuals Unlimited/Martin G. Miller; 493 (cr), Earth Satellite Corporation; 495 Victoria Smith/HRW Photo; 497 (t), Peter Gridley/FPG International; 498 Victoria Smith/HRW Photo; 500 Donald Nausbaum/Tony Stone Images; 501 Jim Work/Peter Arnold, Inc.; 505 Jeff and Alexa Henry.

Chapter Nineteen: 506-507 (c), Joseph McBride/Tony Stone; 509 (bc), Peter Van Steen/HRW Photo; 511 (br), Sam Dudgeon/HRW Photo; 512 (br), Image Copyright ©2001 PhotoDisc, Inc.; 513 (cl), Johnny Johnson/DRK Photo; 517 (bl), Renee Lynn/Photo Researchers, Inc.; 518 (bc), Jaime Puebla/AP/Wide World Photos; 520 (br), David R. Frazier/Photo Researchers, Inc.; 523 (bl), Luc Marescot/Liaison International; 524 (tl), NASA/Science Photo Library/Photo Researchers, Inc.; 526 (bc), Sam Dudgeon/HRW Photo; 529 (tr), Telegraph Colour Library/FPG International; 530 (bl), NASA/Science Photo Library/Photo Researchers, Inc.

Unit Seven: 534 (c), Laurence Parent; 535 (bl), NASA.

Chapter Twenty: 536-537 (c), NASA; 538 (Mercury), NASA; 538 (Venus), NASA/Peter Arnold, Inc; 538 (Earth), Paul Morrell/Tony Stone Images; 538 (Mars), USGS/TSADO/Tom Stack & Associates; 538 (Jupiter), Reta Beebe (New Mexico State University)/NASA; 539 (Saturn), NASA; 539 (Uranus), NASA; 539 (Neptune), NASA; 539 (Pluto), NASA; 544 (tl), NASA/Mark Marten/Photo Researchers, Inc. ; 545 (br), NASA/Mark S. Robinson; 546 (tl), NASA; 546 (bl), Mark Marten/NASA/Science Source/Photo Researchers, Inc.; 547 (br), NASA; 547 (tr), Frans Lanting/Minden Pictures; 548-549 (b), NASA; 548 (c), NASA; 548 (tl), World Perspective/Tony Stone Images; 549 (cr), NASA; 550 (bl), NASA/Peter Arnold, Inc.; 551 (tr, br, tl), NASA; 553 (tr), Hulton Getty/Liaison Agency; 553 (br), NASA; 554 (tl), NASA; 555 (br), NASA; 556 (tl, bl, br), NASA; 557 (tr), NASA; 557 (br), USGS/Science Photo Library/Photo Researchers, Inc.; 558 (t), World Perspectives/Tony Stone Images; 559 (tr), Bob Yen/Liaison Agency; 560 (tl), NASA/Science Photo Library/Photo Researchers, Inc.; 561 (c), Breck P. Kent/Animals Animals/Earth Scenes; 561 (cl), E.R. Degginger/Bruce Coleman Inc.; 561 (cr), Ken Nichols/Institute of Meteorites; 563 (b), Sam Dudgeon/HRW Photo; 564 (b), NASA/Science Photo Library/Photo Researchers, Inc.; 565 (tr), Ken Nichols/Institute of Meteorites.

Chapter Twenty-One: 570 (c), Smithsonian Institution/Lockhead Corporation,/Courtesy of U.S. National Museum of Science and History/,SI (br), NASA;/ 572 (tr), Bettman/CORBIS; 573 (tr), Hulton Getty Images/Gamma Liaison; 576 (bl), Brian Parker/Tom Stack & Associates; 576 (br), NASA; 578 (br), Hesler, Chester, Jentoff-Nilsen/ NASA Goddard Lab of Atmospheres & Nielsen, U. of Hawaii ; 578 (bc), Aerial Images, Inc. and SOVINFORMSPUTNIK; 579 (tr, cr), EROS Data Center/USGS; 580 (br), NASA; 580 (bl), Jim Ballard/Tony Stone Images; 581 (bl), NASA/Liaison Agency; 581 (br), JPL/TSADO/Tom Stack & Associates; 581 (cr), Jim Ballard/Tony Stone Images; 582 (cr), NASA; 582 (cl), Jim Ballard/Tony Stone Images; 582 (bl), NASA/Science Photo Library/Photo Researchers, Inc.; 583 (cr), Jim Ballard/Tony Stone Images; 584 (cl), NASA/JPL; 584 (bl), JPL/NASA; 586 (bl), SuperStock; 587 (tr), NASA; 587 (bc), NASA; 588 (cl), NASA; 589 (tr), NASA/Science Photo Library/Photo Researchers, Inc.; 589 (bl), NASA; 590 (bc, br), NASA; 592 (bc), NASA/Tony Stone Images; 593 (c), Sam Dudgeon/HRW Photo; 594 (br), NASA; 595 (bl), NASA; 596 (cr), Dr. Gene Feldman, NASA GSFC/Photo Researchers, Inc.

LabBook/Appendix: 600 (l, tr), Sam Dudgeon/HRW Photo; 600 (tc), Scott Van Osdol/HRW Photo; 600 (br), Sam Dudgeon/HRW Photo; 603 Sam Dudgeon/HRW Photo; 604 Sam Dudgeon/HRW Photo; 605 Sam Dudgeon/HRW photo; 606 Sam Dudgeon/HRW Photo; 607 Sam Dudgeon/HRW Photo; 608 Sam Dudgeon/HRW Photo; 609 Sam Dudgeon/HRW Photo; 610 Victoria Smith/HRW Photo; 612 Peter Van Steen/HRW Photo; 613 Sam Dudgeon/HRW Photo; 616 Sam Dudgeon/HRW Photo; 618 Sam Dudgeon/HRW Photo; 623 (t), Sam Dudgeon/HRW Photo; 623 (b), Sam Dudgeon/HRW Photo; 625 Rod Planck/Photo Researchers; 626 Peter Van Steen/HRW Photo; 628 Sam Dudgeon/HRW Photo; 629 Sam Dudgeon/HRW Photo; 630 USGS; 631 Sam Dudgeon/HRW Photo; 633 Sam Dudgeon/HRW Photo; 634 Sam Dudgeon/HRW Photo; 636 Sam Dudgeon/HRW Photo; 638 Jeff Hunter/The Image Bank; 643 (b), Sam Dudgeon/HRW Photo; 643 (tr), Sam Dudgeon/HRW Photo; 647 (tr), Peter Van Steen/HRW Photo; 647 (br), Sam Dudgeon/HRW Photo; 662 (c), CENCO.

Feature Borders:

Unless otherwise noted below, all images copyright ©2001 PhotoDisc/HRW.

Across the Sciences, all images by HRW; Careers, (sand bkgd and Saturn), Corbis Images; (DNA), Morgan Cain & Associates; (scuba gear), ©1997 Radlund & Associates for Artville; Eureka:, copyright ©2001 PhotoDisc/HRW; Eye on the Environment:, (clouds and sea in bkgd), HRW; (bkgd grass, red eyed frog), Corbis Images; (pelican), Animals Animals/Earth Scenes; (rat), Visuals Unlimited/John Grelach; Health Watch:, (dumbell), Sam Dudgeon/HRW Photo; (aloe vera, EKG), Victoria Smith/HRW Photo; (basketball), ©1997 Radlund & Associates for Artville; (shoes, bubbles), Greg Geisler; Science Across Texas; (alamo), © Digital Vision; (flowers), Darrell Gulin/CORBIS; (skyline), Corbis Images; (gecko), David A. Northcott/CORBIS; (astronaut), Roger Ressmeyer/CORBIS; (capitol), Danny Lehman/CORBIS;Scientific Debate:, Sam Dudgeon/HRW Photo; Science Fiction:, (saucers), Ian Christopher/Greg Geisler; (book), HRW; (bkgd), Dave Cutler Studio, Inc./SIS; Science Technology and Society, (robot), Greg Geisler;Weird Science:, (mite), David Burder/Tony Stone; (atom balls), J/B Woolsey Associates; (walking stick, turtle), EclectiCollection.

Lab Book Header:

"L", Corbis Images, "a", Letraset Phototone, "b" and "B", HRW, "o" and "k",images copyright ©2001 PhotoDisc/HRW

Start-up activity kids: Sam Dudgeon/HRW Photo.